The Law Governing Lawyers

The Law Governing Lawyers

National Rules, Standards, Statutes, and State Lawyer Codes

2005 Edition

Susan R. Martyn
Stoepler Professor of Law and Values
University of Toledo College of Law

Lawrence J. Fox
Partner, Drinker Biddle & Reath
Adjunct Professor, University of Pennsylvania Law School

W. Bradley Wendel
Associate Professor of Law
Cornell Law School

ASPEN
PUBLISHERS

111 Eighth Avenue, New York, NY 10011
www.aspenpublishers.com

Printed in the United States of America.

1 2 3 4 5 6 7 8 9 0

ISBN 0-07355-5671-7

ISSN 1555-4244

About Aspen Publishers

Aspen Publishers, headquartered in New York City, is a leading information provider for attorneys, business professionals, and law students. Written by preeminent authorities, our products consist of analytical and practical information covering both U.S. and international topics. We publish in the full range of formats, including updated manuals, books, periodicals, CDs, and online products.

Our proprietary content is complemented by 2,500 legal databases, containing over 11 million documents, available through our Loislaw division. Aspen Publishers also offers a wide range of topical legal and business databases linked to Loislaw's primary material. Our mission is to provide accurate, timely, and authoritative content in easily accessible formats, supported by unmatched customer care.

To order any Aspen Publishers title, go to *www.aspenpublishers.com* or call 1-800-638-8437.

To reinstate your manual update service, call 1-800-638-8437.

For more information on Loislaw products, go to *www.loislaw.com* or call 1-800-364-2512.

For Customer Care issues, e-mail CustomerCare@aspenpublishers.com; call 1-800-234-1660; or fax 1-800-901-9075.

Aspen Publishers
A Wolters Kluwer Company

Contents

To the Reader

This volume introduces you to national standards (the American Bar Association's Model Rules of Professional Conduct, the American Law Institute's Restatement of the Law Governing Lawyers, and selected federal statutes and rules) to illustrate the growing body of law that governs lawyer conduct. We focus on these national standards because they provide the template for most state law.

Most of these documents appear in full, but others have been edited for clarity or for length. We offer here a guide to our editorial style.

1. We include the full text of the **ABA Model Rules of Professional Conduct** at pp. 6-101, along with the ABA Correlation Tables at pp. 102-108.
2. We prepared the **charts** that compare state lawyer code provisions at pp. 109-123. The rules cited in these charts are current through September 1, 2005.
3. We include the full text of the Ethical Considerations (ECs) and Disciplinary Rules (DRs) of the **ABA Model Code of Professional Conduct** at pp. 124-162. We have, however, deleted all of the Model Code's voluminous footnotes.
4. We offer the full text of the black letter sections of the American Law Institute's **Restatement of the Law (Third), The Law Governing Lawyers** as well as a large number of selected comments and illustrations at pp. 163-287 We include comments and illustrations that either expand on coverage in the lawyer codes or address issues not covered by the lawyer codes at all, such as the evidentiary privileges. Comments and illustrations retain their original numbers or letters. We use ellipses to indicate edits within a comment or illustration but do not include them to designate completely omitted comments or illustrations.
5. We reproduce a few relevant **federal statutes, regulations and rules** at pp. 288-315 and use ellipses to indicate edits within a statute or rule provision.
6. We include the entire **ABA Model Code of Judicial Conduct** at pp. 316-339. We have deleted only a few footnotes, and the rest retain their original numbers.
7. The CD in the back of this volume includes the text of the print volume as well as the full text of **each jurisdiction's lawyer code**, current through September 1, 2005. We have tried to ensure that the most up-to-date versions of the rules are included, but in some cases it was difficult to obtain this information. If you notice a discrepancy between the version of the rules on the CD and the rules in a particular jurisdiction, please inform the publisher or send an e-mail to *bradley-wendel@lawschool.cornell.edu*.

We thank the copyright holders of these documents for their permission to reprint them: The American Bar Association for permission to reproduce the ABA Model Rules of Professional Conduct, the ABA Model Code of Professional Responsibility, Correlation Tables between these two codes, and the ABA Model Code of Judicial Conduct. We thank the American Law Institute for permission to reproduce the Restatement of the Law (Third), The Law Governing Lawyers. Thanks are also due to the Legal Information Institute at Cornell Law School for providing the text of many state rules. We hope you find these sources of the law governing lawyers the basis for an interesting and enlightening law study.

Susan Martyn, Larry Fox, Brad Wendel   May 2005

The Law Governing Lawyers

INTRODUCTION: UNDERSTANDING AND FINDING THE LAW GOVERNING LAWYERS

Understanding the Sources and Structure of the Law Governing Lawyers

The title of this volume mirrors the title of the Restatement, and, like the Restatement, refers to two intricate bodies of law: lawyer codes that are tied to professional licensure and general law that has been applied to lawyer conduct, such as agency, tort, contract, and trust law. Each body of law is linked to distinct legal consequences (professional discipline for violation of lawyer codes and malpractice, disqualification, fee forfeiture, and other judicial remedies for other breaches of professional duty). The lawyer codes and other law have developed in parallel and have cross-fertilized each other over the past century.

For example, the professional obligations of communication and competence were first articulated in malpractice cases, but are now restated in several lawyer code provisions. Confidentiality, which first appeared in the attorney-client privilege in evidence law, now exists as an independent professional obligation in every lawyer code. Similarly, the lawyer code loyalty obligation that requires lawyers to avoid and resolve conflicts of interest originated in agency law, which provided distinctive remedies, such as constructive trust, breach of fiduciary duty, and disqualification.

Today, courts look to the historical roots of the lawyer codes in general law to understand the application of lawyer code provisions in lawyer disciplinary cases. At the same time, they refer to and rely on lawyer code provisions to understand lawyer obligations that arise in contexts beyond professional discipline, such as malpractice or ineffective assistance of counsel, because lawyer codes provide a modern articulation of a common law rule applied to lawyer conduct. To further understand this interrelationship, we untangle and explain the basic sources of the law governing lawyers and then provide you with a step-by-step guide to finding jurisdiction-specific law.

Lawyer Professional Codes

Lawyer professional codes govern the conduct of all lawyers admitted to practice law. Violation of any provision of an applicable code subjects a lawyer to professional discipline, with sanctions ranging from disbarment, suspension from practice, and fines, to public and private reprimands. A lawyer charged with a disciplinary violation has access to a hearing (most often before an administrative body designated by the highest state court), and a right to appeal, which usually results in a written court opinion.

Over the past twenty years, most jurisdictions have patterned their lawyer codes on the American Bar Association's original 1983 Model Rules of Professional Conduct. In 2002 and 2003, the ABA enacted extensive amendments to the Model Rules in response to the Ethics 2000 Commission's recommendations. The ABA's recent amendments have stimulated individual jurisdictions to consider similar changes. A good number already have enacted revised rules and others are somewhere in the process.

Before the 1983 Model Rules, nearly all jurisdictions adopted a version of the previous Model Code of Professional Responsibility, first recommended in 1969. Tables that correlate related sections of the Model Rules and Model Code can be found at page 102 of this volume. Before 1969, each jurisdiction followed the ABA Canons of Professional Ethics, first promulgated in 1908. For judges, the ABA has recommended a Model Code of Judicial Conduct, which most jurisdictions have used to develop their own Judicial Codes. Proposed revisions to the

1990 Code of Judicial Conduct are currently under consideration and should be presented to the ABA House of Delegates in 2006.

The Restatement

Published in 2000 after thirteen years of development, the Restatement of the Law (Third), The Law Governing Lawyers addresses nearly all the law governing lawyer conduct, including lawyer codes, common law, and statutes. It is organized by topic and covers most issues addressed by lawyer professional codes, with the exception of advertising and solicitation. It also includes in-depth coverage of some issues not specifically governed by lawyer codes, such as civil liability, the attorney-client privilege and work-product doctrine. Extensive comments and illustrations as well as Reporter's Notes, which include citations to relevant primary and secondary authority, follow each Restatement section.

While the Restatement was being developed between 1988-1999, many court opinions, articles, and books cited to section numbers of tentative drafts. The final text renumbered the section numbers consecutively, changing some of the earlier cited section numbers. Page 287 of this volume includes a chart that enables you to move between section numbers in the Restatement drafts and the final Restatement. You can search the full text of the Restatement on Westlaw under the topic headings of "Restatements" or "Legal Ethics and Professional Responsibility." Be careful to select the final version, not the archive database, which contains the numerous tentative drafts.

Treatises

Treatises can help you understand the history, development and current status of the law governing lawyers. We list some of these resources below in alphabetical order. Be careful to note the date of any volume you consult, because recent changes in lawyer code provisions or common law may create a different result or issue. Hornbooks or treatises about the law governing lawyers in a specific jurisdiction or related to a practice specialty also may assist you. Increasing numbers of law review articles and ALR annotations also address a wide variety of issues about lawyer conduct. You may find one or several directly on point.

A.   ABA, *Annotated Model Rules of Professional Conduct* (5th ed. 2003). 1003 pages.

Organized by Model Rule number, this series of case annotations provides representative examples of court and ethics opinions as well as selected citations to secondary authorities. A new edition is published every few years. Two tables at the end of the volume provide parallel tables between the ABA Model Rules and the ABA Model Code.

B.   *ABA/BNA Lawyer's Manual on Professional Responsibility* (2001).
3 loose-leaf volumes, monthly updates.

This resource is divided into three volumes. The first, called the "Manual," is organized by topics that generally follow the order of the Model Rules. Each topic begins with a short "practice guide," followed by "background" and "application" sections. Bibliographies follow each topic. Although the manual covers the scope of the entire law governing lawyers, special sections also focus on specialized types of practice and malpractice. It also includes a topical and case index and is available on Westlaw, under the topic heading "Legal Ethics and Professional Responsibility." The second volume includes the full text of ABA ethics opinions and some state ethics opinions. Other state opinions are described in annotations. The third volume contains "Current Reports" and an index to these reports; both are published every two weeks. The current reports are the most complete updates to case law, rules changes and ethics opinions.

C.   Lawrence J. Fox and Susan R. Martyn,
        Red Flags: A Lawyer's Handbook on Legal Ethics (ALI-ABA 2005). 225 pages.

Shorter than other resources, this book offers easy access to basic information. Topics are presented in the order a practicing lawyer might encounter them, from identifying client-lawyer relationships and fees, to fiduciary obligations, the limits of the law, and remedies. Brief questions and answers introduce each topic, followed by short footnoted essays about relevant law. The book includes several charts that compare state lawyer codes provisions. The last chapter, "When You Need to Seek Additional Advice and Perspective" warns about the "ultimate red flags" that can ensnare unsuspecting lawyers.

D.   Geoffrey C. Hazard, Jr. & W. William Hodes,
        The Law of Lawyering (Aspen 3d ed. 2001). 2 loose-leaf volumes, yearly updates.

This resource is organized topically, following the order of the Model Rules of Professional Conduct. The treatise covers recent developments in the law of lawyering, including citations to the Restatement, ethics opinions and case law. The authors discuss multiple remedies, including malpractice, disqualification, discipline and fee forfeiture. Each section includes illustrations that apply the law governing lawyers to concrete situations.

E.   Ronald D. Rotunda & John S. Dzienkowski, *Legal Ethics: The Lawyer's Deskbook on Professional Responsibility* (ABA 2005). 1973 pages

This treatise follows the organization and logic of the Model Rules. It includes footnotes with citations to some cases and Restatement sections. Footnotes include citations to relevant portions of the predecessor Model Code of Professional Responsibility and to ABA Ethics Opinions. Appendices include 12 ABA Model Rules or Standards for Regulating Lawyers, such as Trust Account Overdraft Notification, Fee Arbitration, Lawyer Disciplinary Enforcement and Aspirational Goals for Lawyer Advertising.

F.   Charles W. Wolfram, *Modern Legal Ethics* (West 1987). 1003 pages.

This comprehensive hornbook is organized by topic. Though dated, it is especially helpful for understanding the historical development of the law governing lawyers, as well as comparisons between the Model Code and Model Rules provisions. Appendices include parallel tables between the ABA Canons, ABA Model Code and ABA Model Rules.

Finding the Law Governing Lawyers

Once you understand the various sources of the law governing lawyers, you can find and apply relevant law. Researching a legal ethics issue is comparable to any legal research, but requires that you understand the importance of finding both jurisdiction-specific lawyer code provisions and general law applied to lawyers. We list below the specific steps you can follow to find and understand this law, and emphasize some additional specialized resources and helpful research techniques.

Step One: Spotting All of the Issues

When a problem involving the conduct of lawyers arises, you must first identify all of the relevant issues. Your legal ethics or professional responsibility course should help you do this by familiarizing you with sections of the lawyer codes that speak to lawyers' obligations, such as competence, confidentiality, and conflicts of interest, and by exposing you to various legal consequences, such as professional discipline, malpractice, and disqualification. Consulting a treatise or the Restatement also can help you spot issues. When you identify an issue, stay open to the possibility that additional professional rules or other legal remedies also may be relevant to your inquiry.

Step Two: Finding Lawyer Code Provisions

Once you spot legal ethics issues, you should recall that both lawyer code provisions and general law might apply. Even if you are not directly concerned with professional discipline, a lawyer code provision may speak to the underlying issue, and courts often cite code provisions in decisions involving other judicial remedies, such as disqualification, malpractice, or ineffective assistance of counsel. For this reason, you should always begin your search by finding any applicable lawyer code provisions.

You can find the full text of each jurisdiction's lawyer code on the CD included with this volume, or search state or federal court rules in most jurisdictions (because the judicial branch of government regulates lawyers, lawyer codes are found in state court rules). These court rules may often be found in a separate volume of a set of annotated statutes, as well as online at the website of the highest state court. On LEXIS or Westlaw, go to your state's court rules file ("XXRule" on LEXIS, "XXRules" on Westlaw, with "XX" being your jurisdiction's two-letter postal code). Most federal courts have adopted some version of the state court rules of the jurisdictions in which they sit. To find these lawyer codes, check each federal district court's local trial rules.

You may be surprised to find that your jurisdiction's code contains distinctive language or provisions not found in the ABA Model Rules. This occurs frequently, so never rely on the Model Rules (or Model Code) provisions alone. Further, nearly every jurisdiction has just completed or is in the process of reviewing its lawyer code. Be careful to identify the version of your jurisdiction's rules that applies to the conduct in question. To find the most recent version of a particular jurisdiction's lawyer code, go to http://www.abanet.org/cpr/links.html or http://www.law.cornell.edu/ethics/. If you are not sure when a particular code applies, check on your state bar or state supreme court website.

Step Three: Identifying Judicial Remedies

When you have found relevant lawyer code provisions, you should turn your attention to the other part of the law governing lawyers: general common law and statutes that provide for additional obligations and remedies beyond professional discipline. Sections 6, 51, and 56-57 of the Restatement catalogue judicial remedies available to both clients and non-clients. These consequences beyond professional discipline may crop up in your initial research, but often will require a specific search by topic, such as "disqualification," "fee forfeiture," "constructive trust," "malpractice," "fraud" or "attorney-client privilege."

Reference to cases or treatises may assist you in understanding your jurisdiction's view of these and other remedies. For some topics, a hornbook in a related area of law may come in handy. For example, a text on criminal procedure would help in understanding ineffective assistance of counsel, just as a treatise on evidence can assist you in understanding the finer points of the attorney-client privilege or work product doctrine.

Step Four: Uncovering Case Law

After you have identified the relevant lawyer code provisions and common law rules and remedies, you can begin to search for cases that apply and construe these rules. Most instances of professional discipline result in written court opinions, which you can find in annotated volumes of court rules or by using other standard research techniques. You can easily start an online search by using the number or text of a relevant lawyer code provision. Once you have found some cases construing a lawyer code provision, be sure to search for cases construing parallel provisions from earlier or later lawyer codes. You also can check Shepard's Professional and Judicial Conduct Citations, which collects citations to the ABA Model Code and Model Rules, Code of Judicial Conduct, and ethics opinions.

You also might begin your search with cases you have discovered in a secondary source. Professional responsibility treatises and the Restatement also can help you find cases, and are especially helpful in finding remedies and obligations in general law applied to lawyers. They also help when no prior authority exists in a given jurisdiction, or in identifying majority and minority rules. Before you decide to cite a treatise, the Restatement, or a case from another jurisdiction, be sure that the authority construes a lawyer code or common law or statutory rule similar to the one in your jurisdiction. If it addresses a judicial remedy, such as breach of fiduciary duty or disqualification, check what your jurisdiction has to say about the substantive and procedural requirements for that remedy.

Step Five: Discovering Additional Guidance in Ethics Opinions

If you find no authority in your jurisdiction, or want to inquire about how the authority you have found may be construed or applied in the situation you face, ethics opinions can help. These opinions respond to lawyers' inquiries about the application of state rules to a proposed course of conduct. The American Bar Association has a rich tradition of addressing the application of its Model Rules to current issues in its ethics opinions. Most state and local bars have ethics committees that answer individual questions as well, often before they ever reach a court. Bar associations and disciplinary counsel in many states also offer ethics hotlines to answer questions or to get lawyers started on finding an answer. Although these opinions are not binding, courts are very reluctant to discipline a lawyer who complies with an ethics committee's advice. If you find an ethics opinion on point, be sure to search your jurisdiction's cases to see whether it has been addressed, approved, or disapproved by a court.

Ethics opinions are most easily accessed online. Most state bar associations have websites for their members, which often include the full text of recent ethics opinions. Many states also publish these opinions in state or local bar journals. Both LEXIS and Westlaw include ethics opinions, but neither service covers all jurisdictions. ABA ethics opinions can be found in both places, however. Here, the topical approach works well. For LEXIS, click on "Ethics," for Westlaw, "Legal Ethics and Professional Responsibility." The menus that follow list the jurisdictions included in that service. Because ethics opinions construe and apply a given jurisdiction's lawyer code, search by using the text or number of a relevant rule. Remember that ethics committees usually do not address the rest of the law governing lawyers, so you will have to research other remedies, such as disqualification or malpractice, and other issues, such as the attorney-client privilege, on your own.

Step Six: Putting Your Research in Perspective

To put your findings in perspective, you may need to compare the result in your jurisdiction to results in other jurisdictions. If your jurisdiction lacks authority, other states may have addressed the issue in lawyer code provisions, cases, or ethics opinions. If the result in your jurisdiction strikes you as odd or even wrong, other jurisdictions may agree and offer you the opportunity to clarify or change local law. Many courts find the Restatement especially helpful in addressing a new issue or application of the law.

Overall, courts increasingly view the law governing lawyers the way they view contract and tort law: as a generally agreed-upon set of legal rules, with distinctive nuances in each jurisdiction. Judges also understand the interrelationship between the lawyer codes and the general law applied to lawyers, so they often will refer to one body of law in addressing a remedy available in another. We hope the materials in this volume help you discover both.

2004 AMERICAN BAR ASSOCIATION
MODEL RULES OF PROFESSIONAL CONDUCT

Contents

[Handwritten annotations in margin:]

new
- scope
- C check
- fee
- other
- termination letter

Client Crime/Fraud

1.2 (d)
1.6 (b)
1.16 (b)(2) + (3)
1.13 (c)
Crime Fraud Exception

Attny Fraud
3.1
3.3
3.4
4.1
5.1
5.2
8.1
8.3
8.4 (c)

LAW FIRMS AND ASSOCIATIONS

Rules

Handwritten margin notes:

Share/Referral
1.5(e)
7.2(b)
non - 7.2(b)(a)
5.4
7.2(b)

CC / Fraud
1.7   1.13(org)
1.4   a
1.10   b
1.6   c d f
        3.3
ACP
5.2
5.1
8.4
8.3
4.2
4.3
Conflict ✓

Handwritten notes lower portion:

Adversary Sys :: AT, 1Just.
                PA, DIg.
· win/lose
· neutral 3rd
· present mm z sent (dispute)
· initiated by party
· oppor. for review

8.4 ,177
289
213 AC
88 WP 235, 233
229 CF excer.

- don't: need to show relationship (A/c)
- bill-J Exchange
- meet c
- formal acceptable

- A/C Relation. Based
atty-client relationship
pg. 177

PREAMBLE: A LAWYER'S RESPONSIBILITIES

Policy- what you've observed / system about

[1] A lawyer, as a member of the legal profession, is a representative of clients, an officer of the legal system and a public citizen having special responsibility for the quality of justice.

[2] As a representative of clients, a lawyer performs various functions. As advisor, a lawyer provides a client with an informed understanding of the client's legal rights and obligations and explains their practical implications. As advocate, a lawyer zealously asserts the client's position under the rules of the adversary system. As negotiator, a lawyer seeks a result advantageous to the client but consistent with requirements of honest dealings with others. As an evaluator, a lawyer acts by examining a client's legal affairs and reporting about them to the client or to others.

[3] In addition to these representational functions, a lawyer may serve as a third-party neutral, a nonrepresentational role helping the parties to resolve a dispute or other matter. Some of these Rules apply directly to lawyers who are or have served as third-party neutrals. See, e.g., Rules 1.12 and 2.4. In addition, there are Rules that apply to lawyers who are not active in the practice of law or to practicing lawyers even when they are acting in a nonprofessional capacity.

For example, a lawyer who commits fraud in the conduct of a business is subject to discipline for engaging in conduct involving dishonesty, fraud, deceit or misrepresentation. See Rule 8.4.

[4] In all professional functions a lawyer should be competent, prompt and diligent. A lawyer should maintain communication with a client concerning the representation. A lawyer should keep in confidence information relating to representation of a client except so far as disclosure is required or permitted by the Rules of Professional Conduct or other law.

[5] A lawyer's conduct should conform to the requirements of the law, both in professional service to clients and in the lawyer's business and personal affairs. A lawyer should use the law's procedures only for legitimate purposes and not to harass or intimidate others. A lawyer should demonstrate respect for the legal system and for those who serve it, including judges, other lawyers and public officials. While it is a lawyer's duty, when necessary, to challenge the rectitude of official action, it is also a lawyer's duty to uphold legal process.

[6] As a public citizen, a lawyer should seek improvement of the law, access to the legal system, the administration of justice and the quality of service rendered by the legal profession. As a member of a learned profession, a lawyer should cultivate knowledge of the law beyond its use for clients, employ that knowledge in reform of the law and work to strengthen legal education. In addition, a lawyer should further the public's understanding of and confidence in the rule of law and the justice system because legal institutions in a constitutional democracy depend on popular participation and support to maintain their authority. A lawyer should be mindful of deficiencies in the administration of justice and of the fact that the poor, and sometimes persons who are not poor, cannot afford adequate legal assistance. Therefore, all lawyers should devote professional time and resources and use civic influence to ensure equal access to our system of justice for all those who because of economic or social barriers cannot afford or secure adequate legal counsel. A lawyer should aid the legal profession in pursuing these objectives and should help the bar regulate itself in the public interest.

[7] Many of a lawyer's professional responsibilities are prescribed in the Rules of Professional Conduct, as well as substantive and procedural law. However, a lawyer is also guided by personal conscience and the approbation of professional peers. A lawyer should strive to attain the highest level of skill, to improve the law and the legal profession and to exemplify the legal profession's ideals of public service.

[8] A lawyer's responsibilities as a representative of clients, an officer of the legal system and a public citizen are usually harmonious. Thus, when an opposing party is well represented, a lawyer can be a zealous advocate on behalf of a client and at the same time assume that justice is being done. So also, a lawyer can be sure that preserving client confidences ordinarily serves the public interest because people are more likely to seek legal advice, and thereby heed their legal obligations, when they know their communications will be private.

[9] In the nature of law practice, however, conflicting responsibilities are encountered. Virtually all difficult ethical problems arise from conflict between a lawyer's responsibilities to clients, to the legal system and to the lawyer's own interest in remaining an ethical person while earning a satisfactory living. The Rules of Professional Conduct often prescribe terms for resolving such conflicts. Within the framework of these Rules, however, many difficult issues of professional discretion can arise. Such issues must be resolved through the exercise of sensitive professional and moral judgment guided by the basic principles underlying the Rules. These principles include the lawyer's obligation zealously to protect and pursue a client's legitimate interests, within the bounds of the law, while maintaining a professional, courteous and civil attitude toward all persons involved in the legal system.

[10] The legal profession is largely self-governing. Although other professions also have been granted powers of self-government, the legal profession is unique in this respect because of the close relationship between the profession and the processes of government and law enforcement. This connection is manifested in the fact that ultimate authority over the legal profession is vested largely in the courts.

[11] To the extent that lawyers meet the obligations of their professional calling, the occasion for government regulation is obviated. Self-regulation also helps maintain the legal profession's independence from government domination. An independent legal profession is an important force in preserving government under law, for abuse of legal authority is more readily challenged by a profession whose members are not dependent on government for the right to practice.

[12] The legal profession's relative autonomy carries with it special responsibilities of self-government. The profession has a responsibility to assure that its regulations are conceived in the public interest and not in furtherance of parochial or self-interested concerns of the bar. Every lawyer is responsible for observance of the Rules of Professional Conduct. A lawyer should also aid in securing their observance by other lawyers. Neglect of these responsibilities compromises the independence of the profession and the public interest which it serves.

[13] Lawyers play a vital role in the preservation of society. The fulfillment of this role requires an understanding by lawyers of their relationship to our legal system. The Rules of Professional Conduct, when properly applied, serve to define that relationship.

SCOPE

[14] The Rules of Professional Conduct are rules of reason. They should be interpreted with reference to the purposes of legal representation and of the law itself. Some of the Rules are imperatives, cast in the terms "shall" or "shall not." These define proper conduct for purposes of professional discipline. Others, generally cast in the term "may," are permissive and define areas under the Rules in which the lawyer has discretion to exercise professional judgment. No disciplinary action should be taken when the lawyer chooses not to act or acts within the bounds of such discretion. Other Rules define the nature of relationships between the lawyer and others. The Rules are thus partly obligatory and disciplinary and partly constitutive and descriptive in that they define a lawyer's professional role. Many of the Comments use the term "should." Comments do not add obligations to the Rules but provide guidance for practicing in compliance with the Rules.

[15] The Rules presuppose a larger legal context shaping the lawyer's role. That context includes court rules and statutes relating to matters of licensure, laws defining specific obligations of lawyers and substantive and procedural law in general. The Comments are sometimes used to alert lawyers to their responsibilities under such other law.

[16] Compliance with the Rules, as with all law in an open society, depends primarily upon understanding and voluntary compliance, secondarily upon reinforcement by peer and public opinion and finally, when necessary, upon enforcement through disciplinary proceedings. The Rules do not, however, exhaust the moral and ethical considerations that should inform a lawyer, for no worthwhile human activity can be completely defined by legal rules. The Rules simply provide a framework for the ethical practice of law.

[17] Furthermore, for purposes of determining the lawyer's authority and responsibility, principles of substantive law external to these Rules determine whether a client-lawyer relationship exists. Most of the duties flowing from the client-lawyer relationship attach only after the client has requested the lawyer to render legal services and the lawyer has agreed to do so. But there are some duties, such as that of confidentiality under Rule 1.6, that attach when the lawyer agrees to consider whether a client-lawyer relationship shall be established. See Rule 1.18. Whether a client-lawyer relationship exists for any specific purpose can depend on the circumstances and may be a question of fact.

[18] Under various legal provisions, including constitutional, statutory and common law, the responsibilities of government lawyers may include authority concerning legal matters that ordinarily reposes in the client in private client-lawyer relationships. For example, a lawyer for a government agency may have authority on behalf of the government to decide upon settlement or

whether to appeal from an adverse judgment. Such authority in various respects is generally vested in the attorney general and the state's attorney in state government, and their federal counterparts, and the same may be true of other government law officers. Also, lawyers under the supervision of these officers may be authorized to represent several government agencies in intragovernmental legal controversies in circumstances where a private lawyer could not represent multiple private clients. These Rules do not abrogate any such authority.

[19] Failure to comply with an obligation or prohibition imposed by a Rule is a basis for invoking the disciplinary process. The Rules presuppose that disciplinary assessment of a lawyer's conduct will be made on the basis of the facts and circumstances as they existed at the time of the conduct in question and in recognition of the fact that a lawyer often has to act upon uncertain or incomplete evidence of the situation. Moreover, the Rules presuppose that whether or not discipline should be imposed for a violation, and the severity of a sanction, depend on all the circumstances, such as the willfulness and seriousness of the violation, extenuating factors and whether there have been previous violations.

[20] Violation of a Rule should not itself give rise to a cause of action against a lawyer nor should it create any presumption in such a case that a legal duty has been breached. In addition, violation of a Rule does not necessarily warrant any other nondisciplinary remedy, such as disqualification of a lawyer in pending litigation. The Rules are designed to provide guidance to lawyers and to provide a structure for regulating conduct through disciplinary agencies. They are not designed to be a basis for civil liability. Furthermore, the purpose of the Rules can be subverted when they are invoked by opposing parties as procedural weapons. The fact that a Rule is a just basis for a lawyer's self-assessment, or for sanctioning a lawyer under the administration of a disciplinary authority, does not imply that an antagonist in a collateral proceeding or transaction has standing to seek enforcement of the Rule. Nevertheless, since the Rules do establish standards of conduct by lawyers, a lawyer's violation of a Rule may be evidence of breach of the applicable standard of conduct.

[21] The Comment accompanying each Rule explains and illustrates the meaning and purpose of the Rule. The Preamble and this note on Scope provide general orientation. The Comments are intended as guides to interpretation, but the text of each Rule is authoritative.

RULE 1.0: TERMINOLOGY

(a) **"Belief" or "believes" denotes that the person involved actually supposed the fact in question to be true. A person's belief may be inferred from circumstances.**

(b) **"Confirmed in writing," when used in reference to the informed consent of a person, denotes informed consent that is given in writing by the person or a writing that a lawyer promptly transmits to the person confirming an oral informed consent. See paragraph (e) for the definition of "informed consent." If it is not feasible to obtain or transmit the writing at the time the person gives informed consent, then the lawyer must obtain or transmit it within a reasonable time thereafter.**

(c) **"Firm" or "law firm" denotes a lawyer or lawyers in a law partnership, professional corporation, sole proprietorship or other association authorized to practice law; or lawyers employed in a legal services organization or the legal department of a corporation or other organization.**

(d) **"Fraud" or "fraudulent" denotes conduct that is fraudulent under the substantive or procedural law of the applicable jurisdiction and has a purpose to deceive.**

(e) **"Informed consent" denotes the agreement by a person to a proposed course of conduct after the lawyer has communicated adequate information and explanation about the material risks of and reasonably available alternatives to the proposed course of conduct.**

(f) "Knowingly," "known," or "knows" denotes actual knowledge of the fact in question. A person's knowledge may be inferred from circumstances.

(g) "Partner" denotes a member of a partnership, a shareholder in a law firm organized as a professional corporation, or a member of an association authorized to practice law.

(h) "Reasonable" or "reasonably" when used in relation to conduct by a lawyer denotes the conduct of a reasonably prudent and competent lawyer.

(i) "Reasonable belief" or "reasonably believes" when used in reference to a lawyer denotes that the lawyer believes the matter in question and that the circumstances are such that the belief is reasonable.

(j) "Reasonably should know" when used in reference to a lawyer denotes that a lawyer of reasonable prudence and competence would ascertain the matter in question.

C8-10 **(k)** "Screened" denotes the isolation of a lawyer from any participation in a matter through the timely imposition of procedures within a firm that are reasonably adequate under the circumstances to protect information that the isolated lawyer is obligated to protect under these Rules or other law.

(l) "Substantial" when used in reference to degree or extent denotes a material matter of clear and weighty importance.

(m) "Tribunal" denotes a court, an arbitrator in a binding arbitration proceeding or a legislative body, administrative agency or other body acting in an adjudicative capacity. A legislative body, administrative agency or other body acts in an adjudicative capacity when a neutral official, after the presentation of evidence or legal argument by a party or parties, will render a binding legal judgment directly affecting a party's interests in a particular matter.

(n) "Writing" or "written" denotes a tangible or electronic record of a communication or representation, including handwriting, typewriting, printing, photostating, photography, audio or videorecording and e-mail. A "signed" writing includes an electronic sound, symbol or process attached to or logically associated with a writing and executed or adopted by a person with the intent to sign the writing.

COMMENT

Confirmed in Writing

[1] If it is not feasible to obtain or transmit a written confirmation at the time the client gives informed consent, then the lawyer must obtain or transmit it within a reasonable time thereafter. If a lawyer has obtained a client's informed consent, the lawyer may act in reliance on that consent so long as it is confirmed in writing within a reasonable time thereafter.

Firm

[2] Whether two or more lawyers constitute a firm within paragraph (c) can depend on the specific facts. For example, two practitioners who share office space and occasionally consult or assist each other ordinarily would not be regarded as constituting a firm. However, if they present themselves to the public in a way that suggests that they are a firm or conduct themselves as a firm, they should be regarded as a firm for purposes of the Rules. The terms of any formal agreement between associated lawyers are relevant in determining whether they are a firm, as is the fact that they have mutual access to information concerning the clients they serve. Furthermore, it is relevant in doubtful cases to consider the underlying purpose of the Rule that is involved. A group of lawyers could be regarded as a firm for purposes of the Rule that the same lawyer should not represent opposing parties in litigation, while it might not be so regarded for purposes of the Rule that information acquired by one lawyer is attributed to another.

[3] With respect to the law department of an organization, including the government, there is ordinarily no question that the members of the department constitute a firm within the meaning of the Rules of Professional Conduct. There can be uncertainty, however, as to the identity of the client. For example, it may not be clear whether the law department of a corporation represents a subsidiary or an affiliated corporation, as well as the corporation by which the members of the department are directly employed. A similar question can arise concerning an unincorporated association and its local affiliates.

[4] Similar questions can also arise with respect to lawyers in legal aid and legal services organizations. Depending upon the structure of the organization, the entire organization or different components of it may constitute a firm or firms for purposes of these Rules.

Fraud

[5] When used in these Rules, the terms "fraud" or "fraudulent" refer to conduct that is characterized as such under the substantive or procedural law of the applicable jurisdiction and has a purpose to deceive. This does not include merely negligent misrepresentation or negligent failure to apprise another of relevant information. For purposes of these Rules, it is not necessary that anyone has suffered damages or relied on the misrepresentation or failure to inform.

Informed Consent

[6] Many of the Rules of Professional Conduct require the lawyer to obtain the informed consent of a client or other person (e.g., a former client or, under certain circumstances, a prospective client) before accepting or continuing representation or pursuing a course of conduct. See, e.g., Rules 1.2(c), 1.6(a) and 1.7(b). The communication necessary to obtain such consent will vary according to the Rule involved and the circumstances giving rise to the need to obtain informed consent. The lawyer must make reasonable efforts to ensure that the client or other person possesses information reasonably adequate to make an informed decision. Ordinarily, this will require communication that includes a disclosure of the facts and circumstances giving rise to the situation, any explanation reasonably necessary to inform the client or other person of the material advantages and disadvantages of the proposed course of conduct and a discussion of the client's or other person's options and alternatives. In some circumstances it may be appropriate for a lawyer to advise a client or other person to seek the advice of other counsel. A lawyer need not inform a client or other person of facts or implications already known to the client or other person; nevertheless, a lawyer who does not personally inform the client or other person assumes the risk that the client or other person is inadequately informed and the consent is invalid. In determining whether the information and explanation provided are reasonably adequate, relevant factors include whether the client or other person is experienced in legal matters generally and in making decisions of the type involved, and whether the client or other person is independently represented by other counsel in giving the consent. Normally, such persons need less information and explanation than others, and generally a client or other person who is independently represented by other counsel in giving the consent should be assumed to have given informed consent.

[7] Obtaining informed consent will usually require an affirmative response by the client or other person. In general, a lawyer may not assume consent from a client's or other person's silence. Consent may be inferred, however, from the conduct of a client or other person who has reasonably adequate information about the matter. A number of Rules require that a person's consent be confirmed in writing. See Rules 1.7(b) and 1.9(a). For a definition of "writing" and "confirmed in writing," see paragraphs (n) and (b). Other Rules require that a client's consent be obtained in a writing signed by the client. See, e.g., Rules 1.8(a) and (g). For a definition of "signed," see paragraph (n).

Screened

[8] This definition applies to situations where screening of a personally disqualified lawyer is permitted to remove imputation of a conflict of interest under Rules 1.11, 1.12 or 1.18.

[9] The purpose of screening is to assure the affected parties that confidential information known by the personally disqualified lawyer remains protected. The personally disqualified lawyer should acknowledge the obligation not to communicate with any of the other lawyers in the firm with respect to the matter. Similarly, other lawyers in the firm who are working on the matter should be informed that the screening is in place and that they may not communicate with the personally disqualified lawyer with respect to the matter. Additional screening measures that are appropriate for the particular matter will depend on the circumstances. To implement, reinforce and remind all affected lawyers of the presence of the screening, it may be appropriate for the firm to undertake such procedures as a written undertaking by the screened lawyer to avoid any communication with other firm personnel and any contact with any firm files or other materials relating to the matter, written notice and instructions to all other firm personnel forbidding any communication with the screened lawyer relating to the matter, denial of access by the screened lawyer to firm files or other materials relating to the matter and periodic reminders of the screen to the screened lawyer and all other firm personnel.

[10] In order to be effective, screening measures must be implemented as soon as practical after a lawyer or law firm knows or reasonably should know that there is a need for screening.

CLIENT-LAWYER RELATIONSHIP

RULE 1.1: COMPETENCE

A lawyer shall provide competent representation to a client. Competent representation requires the legal knowledge, skill, thoroughness and preparation reasonably necessary for the representation.

COMMENT

Legal Knowledge and Skill

[1] In determining whether a lawyer employs the requisite knowledge and skill in a particular matter, relevant factors include the relative complexity and specialized nature of the matter, the lawyer's general experience, the lawyer's training and experience in the field in question, the preparation and study the lawyer is able to give the matter and whether it is feasible to refer the matter to, or associate or consult with, a lawyer of established competence in the field in question. In many instances, the required proficiency is that of a general practitioner. Expertise in a particular field of law may be required in some circumstances.

[2] A lawyer need not necessarily have special training or prior experience to handle legal problems of a type with which the lawyer is unfamiliar. A newly admitted lawyer can be as competent as a practitioner with long experience. Some important legal skills, such as the analysis of precedent, the evaluation of evidence and legal drafting, are required in all legal problems. Perhaps the most fundamental legal skill consists of determining what kind of legal problems a situation may involve, a skill that necessarily transcends any particular specialized knowledge. A lawyer can provide adequate representation in a wholly novel field through necessary study. Competent representation can also be provided through the association of a lawyer of established competence in the field in question.

[3] In an emergency a lawyer may give advice or assistance in a matter in which the lawyer does not have the skill ordinarily required where referral to or consultation or association with another lawyer would be impractical. Even in an emergency, however, assistance should be

13

limited to that reasonably necessary in the circumstances, for ill-considered action under emergency conditions can jeopardize the client's interest.

[4] A lawyer may accept representation where the requisite level of competence can be achieved by reasonable preparation. This applies as well to a lawyer who is appointed as counsel for an unrepresented person. See also Rule 6.2.

Thoroughness and Preparation

[5] Competent handling of a particular matter includes inquiry into and analysis of the factual and legal elements of the problem, and use of methods and procedures meeting the standards of competent practitioners. It also includes adequate preparation. The required attention and preparation are determined in part by what is at stake; major litigation and complex transactions ordinarily require more extensive treatment than matters of lesser complexity and consequence. An agreement between the lawyer and the client regarding the scope of the representation may limit the matters for which the lawyer is responsible. See Rule 1.2(c).

Maintaining Competence

[6] To maintain the requisite knowledge and skill, a lawyer should keep abreast of changes in the law and its practice, engage in continuing study and education and comply with all continuing legal education requirements to which the lawyer is subject.

RULE 1.2: SCOPE OF REPRESENTATION AND ALLOCATION OF AUTHORITY BETWEEN CLIENT AND LAWYER

(a) Subject to paragraphs (c) and (d), a lawyer shall abide by a client's decisions concerning the objectives of representation and, as required by Rule 1.4, shall consult with the client as to the means by which they are to be pursued. A lawyer may take such action on behalf of the client as is impliedly authorized to carry out the representation. A lawyer shall abide by a client's decision whether to settle a matter. In a criminal case, the lawyer shall abide by the client's decision, after consultation with the lawyer, as to a plea to be entered, whether to waive jury trial and whether the client will testify.

(b) A lawyer's representation of a client, including representation by appointment, does not constitute an endorsement of the client's political, economic, social or moral views or activities.

(c) A lawyer may limit the scope of the representation if the limitation is reasonable under the circumstances and the client gives informed consent.

(d) A lawyer shall not counsel a client to engage, or assist a client, in conduct that the lawyer knows is criminal or fraudulent, but a lawyer may discuss the legal consequences of any proposed course of conduct with a client and may counsel or assist a client to make a good faith effort to determine the validity, scope, meaning or application of the law.

COMMENT

Allocation of Authority between Client and Lawyer

[1] Paragraph (a) confers upon the client the ultimate authority to determine the purposes to be served by legal representation, within the limits imposed by law and the lawyer's professional obligations. The decisions specified in paragraph (a), such as whether to settle a civil matter, must also be made by the client. See Rule 1.4(a)(1) for the lawyer's duty to communicate with the client about such decisions. With respect to the means by which the client's objectives are to be pursued, the lawyer shall consult with the client as required by Rule 1.4(a)(2) and may take such action as is impliedly authorized to carry out the representation.

[2] On occasion, however, a lawyer and a client may disagree about the means to be used to accomplish the client's objectives. Clients normally defer to the special knowledge and skill of their lawyer with respect to the means to be used to accomplish their objectives, particularly with respect to technical, legal and tactical matters. Conversely, lawyers usually defer to the client regarding such questions as the expense to be incurred and concern for third persons who might be adversely affected. Because of the varied nature of the matters about which a lawyer and client might disagree and because the actions in question may implicate the interests of a tribunal or other persons, this Rule does not prescribe how such disagreements are to be resolved. Other law, however, may be applicable and should be consulted by the lawyer. The lawyer should also consult with the client and seek a mutually acceptable resolution of the disagreement. If such efforts are unavailing and the lawyer has a fundamental disagreement with the client, the lawyer may withdraw from the representation. See Rule 1.16(b)(4). Conversely, the client may resolve the disagreement by discharging the lawyer. See Rule 1.16(a)(3).ᴐⁱᶠ w/ drew

[3] At the outset of a representation, the client may authorize the lawyer to take specific action on the client's behalf without further consultation. Absent a material change in circumstances and subject to Rule 1.4, a lawyer may rely on such an advance authorization. The client may, however, revoke such authority at any time.

[4] In a case in which the client appears to be suffering diminished capacity, the lawyer's duty to abide by the client's decisions is to be guided by reference to Rule 1.14.

Independence from Client's Views or Activities

[5] Legal representation should not be denied to people who are unable to afford legal services, or whose cause is controversial or the subject of popular disapproval. By the same token, representing a client does not constitute approval of the client's views or activities.

Agreements Limiting Scope of Representation

[6] The scope of services to be provided by a lawyer may be limited by agreement with the client or by the terms under which the lawyer's services are made available to the client. When a lawyer has been retained by an insurer to represent an insured, for example, the representation may be limited to matters related to the insurance coverage. A limited representation may be appropriate because the client has limited objectives for the representation. In addition, the terms upon which representation is undertaken may exclude specific means that might otherwise be used to accomplish the client's objectives. Such limitations may exclude actions that the client thinks are too costly or that the lawyer regards as repugnant or imprudent.

[7] Although this Rule affords the lawyer and client substantial latitude to limit the representation, the limitation must be reasonable under the circumstances. If, for example, a client's objective is limited to securing general information about the law the client needs in order to handle a common and typically uncomplicated legal problem, the lawyer and client may agree that the lawyer's services will be limited to a brief telephone consultation. Such a limitation, however, would not be reasonable if the time allotted was not sufficient to yield advice upon which the client could rely. Although an agreement for a limited representation does not exempt a lawyer from the duty to provide competent representation, the limitation is a factor to be considered when determining the legal knowledge, skill, thoroughness and preparation reasonably necessary for the representation. See Rule 1.1.

[8] All agreements concerning a lawyer's representation of a client must accord with the Rules of Professional Conduct and other law. See, e.g., Rules 1.1, 1.8 and 5.6.

Criminal, Fraudulent and Prohibited Transactions

[9] Paragraph (d) prohibits a lawyer from knowingly counseling or assisting a client to commit a crime or fraud. This prohibition, however, does not preclude the lawyer from giving an honest opinion about the actual consequences that appear likely to result from a client's conduct. Nor does the fact that a client uses advice in a course of action that is criminal or fraudulent of itself make a lawyer a party to the course of action. There is a critical distinction between

presenting an analysis of legal aspects of questionable conduct and recommending the means by which a crime or fraud might be committed with impunity.

[10] When the client's course of action has already begun and is continuing, the lawyer's responsibility is especially delicate. The lawyer is required to avoid assisting the client, for example, by drafting or delivering documents that the lawyer knows are fraudulent or by suggesting how the wrongdoing might be concealed. A lawyer may not continue assisting a client in conduct that the lawyer originally supposed was legally proper but then discovers is criminal or fraudulent. The lawyer must, therefore, withdraw from the representation of the client in the matter. See Rule 1.16(a). In some cases, withdrawal alone might be insufficient. It may be necessary for the lawyer to give notice of the fact of withdrawal and to disaffirm any opinion, document, affirmation or the like. See Rule 4.1.

[11] Where the client is a fiduciary, the lawyer may be charged with special obligations in dealings with a beneficiary.

[12] Paragraph (d) applies whether or not the defrauded party is a party to the transaction. Hence, a lawyer must not participate in a transaction to effectuate criminal or fraudulent avoidance of tax liability. Paragraph (d) does not preclude undertaking a criminal defense incident to a general retainer for legal services to a lawful enterprise. The last clause of paragraph (d) recognizes that determining the validity or interpretation of a statute or regulation may require a course of action involving disobedience of the statute or regulation or of the interpretation placed upon it by governmental authorities.

[13] If a lawyer comes to know or reasonably should know that a client expects assistance not permitted by the Rules of Professional Conduct or other law or if the lawyer intends to act contrary to the client's instructions, the lawyer must consult with the client regarding the limitations on the lawyer's conduct. See Rule 1.4(a)(5).

RULE 1.3: DILIGENCE

A lawyer shall act with reasonable diligence and promptness in representing a client.

COMMENT

[1] A lawyer should pursue a matter on behalf of a client despite opposition, obstruction or personal inconvenience to the lawyer, and take whatever lawful and ethical measures are required to vindicate a client's cause or endeavor. A lawyer must also act with commitment and dedication to the interests of the client and with zeal in advocacy upon the client's behalf. A lawyer is not bound, however, to press for every advantage that might be realized for a client. For example, a lawyer may have authority to exercise professional discretion in determining the means by which a matter should be pursued. See Rule 1.2. The lawyer's duty to act with reasonable diligence does not require the use of offensive tactics or preclude the treating of all persons involved in the legal process with courtesy and respect.

[2] A lawyer's work load must be controlled so that each matter can be handled competently.

[3] Perhaps no professional shortcoming is more widely resented than procrastination. A client's interests often can be adversely affected by the passage of time or the change of conditions; in extreme instances, as when a lawyer overlooks a statute of limitations, the client's legal position may be destroyed. Even when the client's interests are not affected in substance, however, unreasonable delay can cause a client needless anxiety and undermine confidence in the lawyer's trustworthiness. A lawyer's duty to act with reasonable promptness, however, does not preclude the lawyer from agreeing to a reasonable request for a postponement that will not prejudice the lawyer's client.

[4] Unless the relationship is terminated as provided in Rule 1.16, a lawyer should carry through to conclusion all matters undertaken for a client. If a lawyer's employment is limited to a specific matter, the relationship terminates when the matter has been resolved. If a lawyer has served a client over a substantial period in a variety of matters, the client sometimes may assume that the lawyer will continue to serve on a continuing basis unless the lawyer gives notice of withdrawal. Doubt about whether a client-lawyer relationship still exists should be clarified by the lawyer, preferably in writing, so that the client will not mistakenly suppose the lawyer is looking after the client's affairs when the lawyer has ceased to do so. For example, if a lawyer has handled a judicial or administrative proceeding that produced a result adverse to the client and the lawyer and the client have not agreed that the lawyer will handle the matter on appeal, the lawyer must consult with the client about the possibility of appeal before relinquishing responsibility for the matter. See Rule 1.4(a)(2). Whether the lawyer is obligated to prosecute the appeal for the client depends on the scope of the representation the lawyer has agreed to provide to the client. See Rule 1.2.

[5] To prevent neglect of client matters in the event of a sole practitioner's death or disability, the duty of diligence may require that each sole practitioner prepare a plan, in conformity with applicable rules, that designates another competent lawyer to review client files, notify each client of the lawyer's death or disability, and determine whether there is a need for immediate protective action. Cf. Rule 28 of the American Bar Association Model Rules for Lawyer Disciplinary Enforcement (providing for court appointment of a lawyer to inventory files and take other protective action in absence of a plan providing for another lawyer to protect the interests of the clients of a deceased or disabled lawyer).

RULE 1.4: COMMUNICATION

(a) A lawyer shall:

    (1) promptly inform the client of any decision or circumstance with respect to which the client's informed consent, as defined in Rule 1.0(e), is required by these Rules;

    (2) reasonably consult with the client about the means by which the client's objectives are to be accomplished;

    (3) keep the client reasonably informed about the status of the matter;

    (4) promptly comply with reasonable requests for information; and

    (5) consult with the client about any relevant limitation on the lawyer's conduct when the lawyer knows that the client expects assistance not permitted by the Rules of Professional Conduct or other law.

(b) A lawyer shall explain a matter to the extent reasonably necessary to permit the client to make informed decisions regarding the representation.

COMMENT

[1] Reasonable communication between the lawyer and the client is necessary for the client effectively to participate in the representation.

Communicating with Client

[2] If these Rules require that a particular decision about the representation be made by the client, paragraph (a)(1) requires that the lawyer promptly consult with and secure the client's consent prior to taking action unless prior discussions with the client have resolved what action the client wants the lawyer to take. For example, a lawyer who receives from opposing counsel an offer of settlement in a civil controversy or a proffered plea bargain in a criminal case must

promptly inform the client of its substance unless the client has previously indicated that the proposal will be acceptable or unacceptable or has authorized the lawyer to accept or to reject the offer. See Rule 1.2(a).

[3] Paragraph (a)(2) requires the lawyer to reasonably consult with the client about the means to be used to accomplish the client's objectives. In some situations—depending on both the importance of the action under consideration and the feasibility of consulting with the client— this duty will require consultation prior to taking action. In other circumstances, such as during a trial when an immediate decision must be made, the exigency of the situation may require the lawyer to act without prior consultation. In such cases the lawyer must nonetheless act reasonably to inform the client of actions the lawyer has taken on the client's behalf. Additionally, paragraph (a)(3) requires that the lawyer keep the client reasonably informed about the status of the matter, such as significant developments affecting the timing or the substance of the representation.

[4] A lawyer's regular communication with clients will minimize the occasions on which a client will need to request information concerning the representation. When a client makes a reasonable request for information, however, paragraph (a)(4) requires prompt compliance with the request, or if a prompt response is not feasible, that the lawyer, or a member of the lawyer's staff, acknowledge receipt of the request and advise the client when a response may be expected. Client telephone calls should be promptly returned or acknowledged.

Explaining Matters

[5] The client should have sufficient information to participate intelligently in decisions concerning the objectives of the representation and the means by which they are to be pursued, to the extent the client is willing and able to do so. Adequacy of communication depends in part on the kind of advice or assistance that is involved. For example, when there is time to explain a proposal made in a negotiation, the lawyer should review all important provisions with the client before proceeding to an agreement. In litigation a lawyer should explain the general strategy and prospects of success and ordinarily should consult the client on tactics that are likely to result in significant expense or to injure or coerce others. On the other hand, a lawyer ordinarily will not be expected to describe trial or negotiation strategy in detail. The guiding principle is that the lawyer should fulfill reasonable client expectations for information consistent with the duty to act in the client's best interests, and the client's overall requirements as to the character of representation. In certain circumstances, such as when a lawyer asks a client to consent to a representation affected by a conflict of interest, the client must give informed consent, as defined in Rule 1.0(e).

[6] Ordinarily, the information to be provided is that appropriate for a client who is a comprehending and responsible adult. However, fully informing the client according to this standard may be impracticable, for example, where the client is a child or suffers from diminished capacity. See Rule 1.14. When the client is an organization or group, it is often impossible or inappropriate to inform every one of its members about its legal affairs; ordinarily, the lawyer should address communications to the appropriate officials of the organization. See Rule 1.13. Where many routine matters are involved, a system of limited or occasional reporting may be arranged with the client.

Withholding Information

[7] In some circumstances, a lawyer may be justified in delaying transmission of information when the client would be likely to react imprudently to an immediate communication. Thus, a lawyer might withhold a psychiatric diagnosis of a client when the examining psychiatrist indicates that disclosure would harm the client. A lawyer may not withhold information to serve the lawyer's own interest or convenience or the interests or convenience of another person. Rules or court orders governing litigation may provide that information supplied to a lawyer may not be disclosed to the client. Rule 3.4(c) directs compliance with such rules or orders.

RULE 1.5: FEES w/ Nonlawyers
5.4 + 5.4 (2)(3)

(a) A lawyer shall not make an agreement for, charge, or collect an <u>unreasonable</u> fee or an unreasonable amount for expenses. The factors to be considered in determining the reasonableness of a fee include the following:

    (1) the time and labor required, the novelty and difficulty of the questions involved, and the skill requisite to perform the legal service properly;

    (2) the likelihood, if apparent to the client, that the acceptance of the particular employment will preclude other employment by the lawyer;

    (3) the fee customarily charged in the locality for similar legal services;

    (4) the amount involved and the results obtained;

    (5) the time limitations imposed by the client or by the circumstances;

    (6) the nature and length of the professional relationship with the client;

    (7) the experience, reputation, and ability of the lawyer or lawyers performing the services; and

    (8) whether the fee is fixed or contingent.

(b) The scope of the representation and the basis or rate of the fee and expenses fo which the client will be responsible shall be communicated to the client, preferably i writing, before or within a reasonable time after commencing the representation, except when the lawyer will charge a regularly represented client on the same basis or rate. Any changes in the basis or rate of the fee or expenses shall also be communicated to the client.

(c) A fee may be contingent on the outcome of the matter for which the service is rendered, except in a matter in which a contingent fee is prohibited by paragraph (d) or other law. A contingent fee agreement shall be in a writing signed by the client and shall state the method by which the fee is to be determined, including the percentage or percentages that shall accrue to the lawyer in the event of settlement, trial or appeal; litigation and other expenses to be deducted from the recovery; and whether such expenses are to be deducted before or after the contingent fee is calculated. The agreement must clearly notify the client of any expenses for which the client will be liable whether or not the client is the prevailing party. Upon conclusion of a contingent fee matter, the lawyer shall provide the client with a written statement stating the outcome of the matter and, if there is a recovery, showing the remittance to the client and the method of its determination.

(d) A lawyer shall not enter into an arrangement for, charge, or collect:

    (1) any fee in a domestic relations matter, the payment or amount of which is contingent upon the securing of a divorce or upon the amount of alimony or support, or property settlement in lieu thereof; or

    (2) a contingent fee for representing a defendant in a criminal case.

(e) A division of a fee between lawyers who are not in the same firm may be made only if:

    (1) the division is in proportion to the services performed by each lawyer or each lawyer assumes joint responsibility for the representation;

    (2) the client agrees to the arrangement, including the share each lawyer will receive, and the agreement is confirmed in writing; and

    (3) the total fee is reasonable.

19, open

ABA Model Rules of Professional Conduct (2004)

COMMENT

Reasonableness of Fee and Expenses

[1] Paragraph (a) requires that lawyers charge fees that are reasonable under the circumstances. The factors specified in (1) through (8) are not exclusive. Nor will each factor be relevant in each instance. Paragraph (a) also requires that expenses for which the client will be charged must be reasonable. A lawyer may seek reimbursement for the cost of services performed in-house, such as copying, or for other expenses incurred in-house, such as telephone charges, either by charging a reasonable amount to which the client has agreed in advance or by charging an amount that reasonably reflects the cost incurred by the lawyer.

Basis or Rate of Fee

[2] When the lawyer has regularly represented a client, they ordinarily will have evolved an understanding concerning the basis or rate of the fee and the expenses for which the client will be responsible. In a new client-lawyer relationship, however, an understanding as to fees and expenses must be promptly established. Generally, it is desirable to furnish the client with at least a simple memorandum or copy of the lawyer's customary fee arrangements that states the general nature of the legal services to be provided, the basis, rate or total amount of the fee and whether and to what extent the client will be responsible for any costs, expenses or disbursements in the course of the representation. A written statement concerning the terms of the engagement reduces the possibility of misunderstanding.

[3] Contingent fees, like any other fees, are subject to the reasonableness standard of paragraph (a) of this Rule. In determining whether a particular contingent fee is reasonable, or whether it is reasonable to charge any form of contingent fee, a lawyer must consider the factors that are relevant under the circumstances. Applicable law may impose limitations on contingent fees, such as a ceiling on the percentage allowable, or may require a lawyer to offer clients an alternative basis for the fee. Applicable law also may apply to situations other than a contingent fee, for example, government regulations regarding fees in certain tax matters.

Terms of Payment

[4] A lawyer may require advance payment of a fee, but is obliged to return any unearned portion. See Rule 1.16(d). A lawyer may accept property in payment for services, such as an ownership interest in an enterprise, providing this does not involve acquisition of a proprietary interest in the cause of action or subject matter of the litigation contrary to Rule 1.8(i). However, a fee paid in property instead of money may be subject to the requirements of Rule 1.8(a) because such fees often have the essential qualities of a business transaction with the client.

[5] An agreement may not be made whose terms might induce the lawyer improperly to curtail services for the client or perform them in a way contrary to the client's interest. For example, a lawyer should not enter into an agreement whereby services are to be provided only up to a stated amount when it is foreseeable that more extensive services probably will be required, unless the situation is adequately explained to the client. Otherwise, the client might have to bargain for further assistance in the midst of a proceeding or transaction. However, it is proper to define the extent of services in light of the client's ability to pay. A lawyer should not exploit a fee arrangement based primarily on hourly charges by using wasteful procedures.

Prohibited Contingent Fees

[6] Paragraph (d) prohibits a lawyer from charging a contingent fee in a domestic relations matter when payment is contingent upon the securing of a divorce or upon the amount of alimony or support or property settlement to be obtained. This provision does not preclude a contract for a contingent fee for legal representation in connection with the recovery of post-judgment balances due under support, alimony or other financial orders because such contracts do not implicate the same policy concerns.

20

Division of Fee

[7] A division of fee is a single billing to a client covering the fee of two or more lawyers who are not in the same firm. A division of fee facilitates association of more than one lawyer in a matter in which neither alone could serve the client as well, and most often is used when the fee is contingent and the division is between a referring lawyer and a trial specialist. Paragraph (e) permits the lawyers to divide a fee either on the basis of the proportion of services they render or if each lawyer assumes responsibility for the representation as a whole. In addition, the client must agree to the arrangement, including the share that each lawyer is to receive, and the agreement must be confirmed in writing. Contingent fee agreements must be in a writing signed by the client and must otherwise comply with paragraph (c) of this Rule. Joint responsibility for the representation entails financial and ethical responsibility for the representation as if the lawyers were associated in a partnership. A lawyer should only refer a matter to a lawyer whom the referring lawyer reasonably believes is competent to handle the matter. See Rule 1.1.

[8] Paragraph (e) does not prohibit or regulate division of fees to be received in the future for work done when lawyers were previously associated in a law firm.

Disputes over Fees

[9] If a procedure has been established for resolution of fee disputes, such as an arbitration or mediation procedure established by the bar, the lawyer must comply with the procedure when it is mandatory, and, even when it is voluntary, the lawyer should conscientiously consider submitting to it. Law may prescribe a procedure for determining a lawyer's fee, for example, in representation of an executor or administrator, a class or a person entitled to a reasonable fee as part of the measure of damages. The lawyer entitled to such a fee and a lawyer representing another party concerned with the fee should comply with the prescribed procedure.

RULE 1.6: CONFIDENTIALITY OF INFORMATION

(a) A lawyer shall not reveal information relating to the representation of a client unless the client gives informed consent, the disclosure is impliedly authorized in order to carry out the representation or the disclosure is permitted by paragraph (b).

(b) A lawyer may reveal information relating to the representation of a client to the extent the lawyer reasonably believes necessary:

(1) to prevent reasonably certain death or substantial bodily harm;

(2) to prevent the client from committing a crime or fraud that is reasonably certain to result in substantial injury to the financial interests or property of another and in furtherance of which the client has used or is using the lawyer's services;

(3) to prevent, mitigate or rectify substantial injury to the financial interests or property of another that is reasonably certain to result or has resulted from the client's commission of a crime or fraud in furtherance of which the client has used the lawyer's services;

(4) to secure legal advice about the lawyer's compliance with these Rules;

(5) to establish a claim or defense on behalf of the lawyer in a controversy between the lawyer and the client, to establish a defense to a criminal charge or civil claim against the lawyer based upon conduct in which the client was involved, or to respond to allegations in any proceeding concerning the lawyer's representation of the client; or

(6) to comply with other law or a court order.

21

COMMENT

[1] This Rule governs the disclosure by a lawyer of information relating to the representation of a client during the lawyer's representation of the client. See Rule 1.18 for the lawyer's duties with respect to information provided to the lawyer by a prospective client, Rule 1.9(c)(2) for the lawyer's duty not to reveal information relating to the lawyer's prior representation of a former client and Rules 1.8(b) and 1.9(c)(1) for the lawyer's duties with respect to the use of such information to the disadvantage of clients and former clients.

[2] A fundamental principle in the client-lawyer relationship is that, in the absence of the client's informed consent, the lawyer must not reveal information relating to the representation. See Rule 1.0(e) for the definition of informed consent. This contributes to the trust that is the hallmark of the client-lawyer relationship. The client is thereby encouraged to seek legal assistance and to communicate fully and frankly with the lawyer even as to embarrassing or legally damaging subject matter. The lawyer needs this information to represent the client effectively and, if necessary, to advise the client to refrain from wrongful conduct. Almost without exception, clients come to lawyers in order to determine their rights and what is, in the complex of laws and regulations, deemed to be legal and correct. Based upon experience, lawyers know that almost all clients follow the advice given, and the law is upheld. *- listen to 2 things*

[3] The principle of client-lawyer confidentiality is given effect by related bodies of law: the attorney-client privilege, the work product doctrine and the rule of confidentiality established in professional ethics. The attorney-client privilege and work product doctrine apply in judicial and other proceedings in which a lawyer may be called as a witness or otherwise required to produce evidence concerning a client. The rule of client-lawyer confidentiality applies in situations other than those where evidence is sought from the lawyer through compulsion of law. The confidentiality rule, for example, applies not only to matters communicated in confidence by the client but also to all information relating to the representation, whatever its source. A lawyer may not disclose such information except as authorized or required by the Rules of Professional Conduct or other law. See also Scope. *↳ all matters - not just communicated.*

[4] Paragraph (a) prohibits a lawyer from revealing information relating to the representation of a client. This prohibition also applies to disclosures by a lawyer that do not in themselves reveal protected information but could reasonably lead to the discovery of such information by a third person. A lawyer's use of a hypothetical to discuss issues relating to the representation is permissible so long as there is no reasonable likelihood that the listener will be able to ascertain the identity of the client or the situation involved. *Hypos*

Authorized Disclosure

[5] Except to the extent that the client's instructions or special circumstances limit that authority, a lawyer is impliedly authorized to make disclosures about a client when appropriate in carrying out the representation. In some situations, for example, a lawyer may be impliedly authorized to admit a fact that cannot properly be disputed or to make a disclosure that facilitates a satisfactory conclusion to a matter. Lawyers in a firm may, in the course of the firm's practice, disclose to each other information relating to a client of the firm, unless the client has instructed that particular information be confined to specified lawyers.

Disclosure Adverse to Client

[6] Although the public interest is usually best served by a strict rule requiring lawyers to preserve the confidentiality of information relating to the representation of their clients, the confidentiality rule is subject to limited exceptions. Paragraph (b)(1) recognizes the overriding value of life and physical integrity and permits disclosure reasonably necessary to prevent reasonably certain death or substantial bodily harm. Such harm is reasonably certain to occur if it will be suffered imminently or if there is a present and substantial threat that a person will suffer such harm at a later date if the lawyer fails to take action necessary to eliminate the threat. Thus, a

lawyer who knows that a client has accidentally discharged toxic waste into a town's water supply may reveal this information to the authorities if there is a present and substantial risk that a person who drinks the water will contract a life-threatening or debilitating disease and the lawyer's disclosure is necessary to eliminate the threat or reduce the number of victims.

[7] Paragraph (b)(2) is a limited exception to the rule of confidentiality that permits the lawyer to reveal information to the extent necessary to enable affected persons or appropriate authorities to prevent the client from committing a crime or fraud, as defined in Rule 1.0(d), that is reasonably certain to result in substantial injury to the financial or property interests of another and in furtherance of which the client has used or is using the lawyer's services. Such a serious abuse of the client-lawyer relationship by the client forfeits the protection of this Rule. The client can, of course, prevent such disclosure by refraining from the wrongful conduct. Although paragraph (b)(2) does not require the lawyer to reveal the client's misconduct, the lawyer may not counsel or assist the client in conduct the lawyer knows is criminal or fraudulent. See Rule 1.2(d). See also Rule 1.16 with respect to the lawyer's obligation or right to withdraw from the representation of the client in such circumstances, and Rule 1.13(c), which permits the lawyer, where the client is an organization, to reveal information relating to the representation in limited circumstances.

[8] Paragraph (b)(3) addresses the situation in which the lawyer does not learn of the client's crime or fraud until after it has been consummated. Although the client no longer has the option of preventing disclosure by refraining from the wrongful conduct, there will be situations in which the loss suffered by the affected person can be prevented, rectified or mitigated. In such situations, the lawyer may disclose information relating to the representation to the extent necessary to enable the affected persons to prevent or mitigate reasonably certain losses or to attempt to recoup their losses. Paragraph (b)(3) does not apply when a person who has committed a crime or fraud thereafter employs a lawyer for representation concerning that offense.

[9] A lawyer's confidentiality obligations do not preclude a lawyer from securing confidential legal advice about the lawyer's personal responsibility to comply with these Rules. In most situations, disclosing information to secure such advice will be impliedly authorized for the lawyer to carry out the representation. Even when the disclosure is not impliedly authorized, paragraph (b)(4) permits such disclosure because of the importance of a lawyer's compliance with the Rules of Professional Conduct.

[10] Where a legal claim or disciplinary charge alleges complicity of the lawyer in a client's conduct or other misconduct of the lawyer involving representation of the client, the lawyer may respond to the extent the lawyer reasonably believes necessary to establish a defense. The same is true with respect to a claim involving the conduct or representation of a former client. Such a charge can arise in a civil, criminal, disciplinary or other proceeding and can be based on a wrong allegedly committed by the lawyer against the client or on a wrong alleged by a third person, for example, a person claiming to have been defrauded by the lawyer and client acting together. The lawyer's right to respond arises when an assertion of such complicity has been made. Paragraph (b)(5) does not require the lawyer to await the commencement of an action or proceeding that charges such complicity, so that the defense may be established by responding directly to a third party who has made such an assertion. The right to defend also applies, of course, where a proceeding has been commenced.

[11] A lawyer entitled to a fee is permitted by paragraph (b)(5) to prove the services rendered in an action to collect it. This aspect of the rule expresses the principle that the beneficiary of a fiduciary relationship may not exploit it to the detriment of the fiduciary.

[12] Other law may require that a lawyer disclose information about a client. Whether such a law supersedes Rule 1.6 is a question of law beyond the scope of these Rules. When disclosure of information relating to the representation appears to be required by other law, the lawyer must discuss the matter with the client to the extent required by Rule 1.4. If, however, the

other law supersedes this Rule and requires disclosure, paragraph (b)(6) permits the lawyer to make such disclosures as are necessary to comply with the law.

[13] A lawyer may be ordered to reveal information relating to the representation of a client by a court or by another tribunal or governmental entity claiming authority pursuant to other law to compel the disclosure. Absent informed consent of the client to do otherwise, the lawyer should assert on behalf of the client all nonfrivolous claims that the order is not authorized by other law or that the information sought is protected against disclosure by the attorney-client privilege or other applicable law. In the event of an adverse ruling, the lawyer must consult with the client about the possibility of appeal to the extent required by Rule 1.4. Unless review is sought, however, paragraph (b)(6) permits the lawyer to comply with the court's order.

[14] Paragraph (b) permits disclosure only to the extent the lawyer reasonably believes the disclosure is necessary to accomplish one of the purposes specified. Where practicable, the lawyer should first seek to persuade the client to take suitable action to obviate the need for disclosure. In any case, a disclosure adverse to the client's interest should be no greater than the lawyer reasonably believes necessary to accomplish the purpose. If the disclosure will be made in connection with a judicial proceeding, the disclosure should be made in a manner that limits access to the information to the tribunal or other persons having a need to know it and appropriate protective orders or other arrangements should be sought by the lawyer to the fullest extent practicable.

[15] Paragraph (b) permits but does not require the disclosure of information relating to a client's representation to accomplish the purposes specified in paragraphs (b)(1) through (b)(6). In exercising the discretion conferred by this Rule, the lawyer may consider such factors as the nature of the lawyer's relationship with the client and with those who might be injured by the client, the lawyer's own involvement in the transaction and factors that may extenuate the conduct in question. A lawyer's decision not to disclose as permitted by paragraph (b) does not violate this Rule. Disclosure may be required, however, by other Rules. Some Rules require disclosure only if such disclosure would be permitted by paragraph (b). See Rules 1.2(d), 4.1(b), 8.1 and 8.3. Rule 3.3, on the other hand, requires disclosure in some circumstances regardless of whether such disclosure is permitted by this Rule. See Rule 3.3(c).

Acting Competently to Preserve Confidentiality

[16] A lawyer must act competently to safeguard information relating to the representation of a client against inadvertent or unauthorized disclosure by the lawyer or other persons who are participating in the representation of the client or who are subject to the lawyer's supervision. See Rules 1.1, 5.1 and 5.3.

[17] When transmitting a communication that includes information relating to the representation of a client, the lawyer must take reasonable precautions to prevent the information from coming into the hands of unintended recipients. This duty, however, does not require that the lawyer use special security measures if the method of communication affords a reasonable expectation of privacy. Special circumstances, however, may warrant special precautions. Factors to be considered in determining the reasonableness of the lawyer's expectation of confidentiality include the sensitivity of the information and the extent to which the privacy of the communication is protected by law or by a confidentiality agreement. A client may require the lawyer to implement special security measures not required by this Rule or may give informed consent to the use of a means of communication that would otherwise be prohibited by this Rule.

Former Client

[18] The duty of confidentiality continues after the client-lawyer relationship has terminated. See Rule 1.9(c)(2). See Rule 1.9(c)(1) for the prohibition against using such information to the disadvantage of the former client.

RULE 1.7: CONFLICT OF INTEREST: CURRENT CLIENTS

(a) Except as provided in paragraph (b), a lawyer shall not represent a client if the representation involves a concurrent conflict of interest. A concurrent conflict of interest exists if:

(1) the representation of one client will be directly adverse to another client;

(2) there is a significant risk that the representation of one or more clients will be materially limited by the lawyer's responsibilities to another client, a former client or a third person or by a personal interest of the lawyer.

(b) Notwithstanding the existence of a concurrent conflict of interest under paragraph (a), a lawyer may represent a client if:

(1) the lawyer reasonably believes that the lawyer will be able to provide competent and diligent representation to each affected client;

(2) the representation is not prohibited by law;

(3) the representation does not involve the assertion of a claim by one client against another client represented by the lawyer in the same litigation or other proceeding before a tribunal; and

(4) each affected client gives informed consent, confirmed in writing.

COMMENT

General Principles

[1] Loyalty and independent judgment are essential elements in the lawyer's relationship to a client. Concurrent conflicts of interest can arise from the lawyer's responsibilities to another client, a former client or a third person or from the lawyer's own interests. For specific Rules regarding certain concurrent conflicts of interest, see Rule 1.8. For former client conflicts of interest, see Rule 1.9. For conflicts of interest involving prospective clients, see Rule 1.18. For definitions of "informed consent" and "confirmed in writing," see Rule 1.0(e) and (b).

[2] Resolution of a conflict of interest problem under this Rule requires the lawyer to: 1) clearly identify the client or clients; 2) determine whether a conflict of interest exists; 3) decide whether the representation may be undertaken despite the existence of a conflict, i.e., whether the conflict is consentable; and 4) if so, consult with the clients affected under paragraph (a) and obtain their informed consent, confirmed in writing. The clients affected under paragraph (a) include both of the clients referred to in paragraph (a)(1) and the one or more clients whose representation might be materially limited under paragraph (a)(2).

[3] A conflict of interest may exist before representation is undertaken, in which event the representation must be declined, unless the lawyer obtains the informed consent of each client under the conditions of paragraph (b). To determine whether a conflict of interest exists, a lawyer should adopt reasonable procedures, appropriate for the size and type of firm and practice, to determine in both litigation and non-litigation matters the persons and issues involved. See also Comment to Rule 5.1. Ignorance caused by a failure to institute such procedures will not excuse a lawyer's violation of this Rule. As to whether a client-lawyer relationship exists or, having once been established, is continuing, see Comment to Rule 1.3 and Scope.

[4] If a conflict arises after representation has been undertaken, the lawyer ordinarily must withdraw from the representation, unless the lawyer has obtained the informed consent of the client under the conditions of paragraph (b). See Rule 1.16. Where more than one client is involved, whether the lawyer may continue to represent any of the clients is determined both by the lawyer's ability to comply with duties owed to the former client and by the lawyer's ability to

25

represent adequately the remaining client or clients, given the lawyer's duties to the former client. See Rule 1.9. See also Comments [5] and [29].

[5] Unforeseeable developments, such as changes in corporate and other organizational affiliations or the addition or realignment of parties in litigation, might create conflicts in the midst of a representation, as when a company sued by the lawyer on behalf of one client is bought by another client represented by the lawyer in an unrelated matter. Depending on the circumstances, the lawyer may have the option to withdraw from one of the representations in order to avoid the conflict. The lawyer must seek court approval where necessary and take steps to minimize harm to the clients. See Rule 1.16. The lawyer must continue to protect the confidences of the client from whose representation the lawyer has withdrawn. See Rule 1.9(c).

Identifying Conflicts of Interest: Directly Adverse

[6] Loyalty to a current client prohibits undertaking representation directly adverse to that client without that client's informed consent. Thus, absent consent, a lawyer may not act as an advocate in one matter against a person the lawyer represents in some other matter, even when the matters are wholly unrelated. The client as to whom the representation is directly adverse is likely to feel betrayed, and the resulting damage to the client-lawyer relationship is likely to impair the lawyer's ability to represent the client effectively. In addition, the client on whose behalf the adverse representation is undertaken reasonably may fear that the lawyer will pursue that client's case less effectively out of deference to the other client, i.e., that the representation may be materially limited by the lawyer's interest in retaining the current client. Similarly, a directly adverse conflict may arise when a lawyer is required to cross-examine a client who appears as a witness in a lawsuit involving another client, as when the testimony will be damaging to the client who is represented in the lawsuit. On the other hand, simultaneous representation in unrelated matters of clients whose interests are only economically adverse, such as representation of competing economic enterprises in unrelated litigation, does not ordinarily constitute a conflict of interest and thus may not require consent of the respective clients.

[7] Directly adverse conflicts can also arise in transactional matters. For example, if a lawyer is asked to represent the seller of a business in negotiations with a buyer represented by the lawyer, not in the same transaction but in another, unrelated matter, the lawyer could not undertake the representation without the informed consent of each client.

Identifying Conflicts of Interest: Material Limitation

[8] Even where there is no direct adverseness, a conflict of interest exists if there is a significant risk that a lawyer's ability to consider, recommend or carry out an appropriate course of action for the client will be materially limited as a result of the lawyer's other responsibilities or interests. For example, a lawyer asked to represent several individuals seeking to form a joint venture is likely to be materially limited in the lawyer's ability to recommend or advocate all possible positions that each might take because of the lawyer's duty of loyalty to the others. The conflict in effect forecloses alternatives that would otherwise be available to the client. The mere possibility of subsequent harm does not itself require disclosure and consent. The critical questions are the likelihood that a difference in interests will eventuate and, if it does, whether it will materially interfere with the lawyer's independent professional judgment in considering alternatives or foreclose courses of action that reasonably should be pursued on behalf of the client.

Lawyer's Responsibilities to Former Clients and Other Third Persons

[9] In addition to conflicts with other current clients, a lawyer's duties of loyalty and independence may be materially limited by responsibilities to former clients under Rule 1.9 or by the lawyer's responsibilities to other persons, such as fiduciary duties arising from a lawyer's service as a trustee, executor or corporate director.

1) Is there potential conflict
2) what kind
3) what rules apply
4) what legal test
5) Analyze facts using rules
- what could happen b/c of conflict
- what more do want to know
- how can find out such facts

ABA Model Rules of Professional Conduct (2004)

Personal Interest Conflicts *concludes even?*

[10] The lawyer's own interests should not be permitted to have an adverse effect on representation of a client. For example, if the probity of a lawyer's own conduct in a transaction is in serious question, it may be difficult or impossible for the lawyer to give a client detached advice. Similarly, when a lawyer has discussions concerning possible employment with an opponent of the lawyer's client, or with a law firm representing the opponent, such discussions could materially limit the lawyer's representation of the client. In addition, a lawyer may not allow related business interests to affect representation, for example, by referring clients to an enterprise in which the lawyer has an undisclosed financial interest. See Rule 1.8 for specific Rules pertaining to a number of personal interest conflicts, including business transactions with clients. See also Rule 1.10 (personal interest conflicts under Rule 1.7 ordinarily are not imputed to other lawyers in a law firm).

[11] When lawyers representing different clients in the same matter or in substantially related matters are closely related by blood or marriage, there may be a significant risk that client confidences will be revealed and that the lawyer's family relationship will interfere with both loyalty and independent professional judgment. As a result, each client is entitled to know of the existence and implications of the relationship between the lawyers before the lawyer agrees to undertake the representation. Thus, a lawyer related to another lawyer, e.g., as parent, child, sibling or spouse, ordinarily may not represent a client in a matter where that lawyer is representing another party, unless each client gives informed consent. The disqualification arising from a close family relationship is personal and ordinarily is not imputed to members of firms with whom the lawyers are associated. See Rule 1.10.

[12] A lawyer is prohibited from engaging in sexual relationships with a client unless the sexual relationship predates the formation of the client-lawyer relationship. See Rule 1.8(j).

Interest of Person Paying for a Lawyer's Service

[13] A lawyer may be paid from a source other than the client, including a co-client, if the client is informed of that fact and consents and the arrangement does not compromise the lawyer's duty of loyalty or independent judgment to the client. See Rule 1.8(f). If acceptance of the payment from any other source presents a significant risk that the lawyer's representation of the client will be materially limited by the lawyer's own interest in accommodating the person paying the lawyer's fee or by the lawyer's responsibilities to a payer who is also a co-client, then the lawyer must comply with the requirements of paragraph (b) before accepting the representation, including determining whether the conflict is consentable and, if so, that the client has adequate information about the material risks of the representation.

Prohibited Representations

[14] Ordinarily, clients may consent to representation notwithstanding a conflict. However, as indicated in paragraph (b), some conflicts are nonconsentable, meaning that the lawyer involved cannot properly ask for such agreement or provide representation on the basis of the client's consent. When the lawyer is representing more than one client, the question of consentability must be resolved as to each client.

[15] Consentability is typically determined by considering whether the interests of the clients will be adequately protected if the clients are permitted to give their informed consent to representation burdened by a conflict of interest. Thus, under paragraph (b)(1), representation is prohibited if in the circumstances the lawyer cannot reasonably conclude that the lawyer will be able to provide competent and diligent representation. See Rule 1.1 (competence) and Rule 1.3 (diligence).

[16] Paragraph (b)(2) describes conflicts that are nonconsentable because the representation is prohibited by applicable law. For example, in some states substantive law provides that the same lawyer may not represent more than one defendant in a capital case, even with the consent of the clients, and under federal criminal statutes certain representations by a

27

former government lawyer are prohibited, despite the informed consent of the former client. In addition, decisional law in some states limits the ability of a governmental client, such as a municipality, to consent to a conflict of interest.

[17] Paragraph (b)(3) describes conflicts that are nonconsentable because of the institutional interest in vigorous development of each client's position when the clients are aligned directly against each other in the same litigation or other proceeding before a tribunal. Whether clients are aligned directly against each other within the meaning of this paragraph requires examination of the context of the proceeding. Although this paragraph does not preclude a lawyer's multiple representation of adverse parties to a mediation (because mediation is not a proceeding before a "tribunal" under Rule 1.0(m)), such representation may be precluded by paragraph (b)(1).

Informed Consent

[18] Informed consent requires that each affected client be aware of the relevant circumstances and of the material and reasonably foreseeable ways that the conflict could have adverse effects on the interests of that client. See Rule 1.0(e) (informed consent). The information required depends on the nature of the conflict and the nature of the risks involved. When representation of multiple clients in a single matter is undertaken, the information must include the implications of the common representation, including possible effects on loyalty, confidentiality and the attorney-client privilege and the advantages and risks involved. See Comments [30] and [31] (effect of common representation on confidentiality).

[19] Under some circumstances it may be impossible to make the disclosure necessary to obtain consent. For example, when the lawyer represents different clients in related matters and one of the clients refuses to consent to the disclosure necessary to permit the other client to make an informed decision, the lawyer cannot properly ask the latter to consent. In some cases the alternative to common representation can be that each party may have to obtain separate representation with the possibility of incurring additional costs. These costs, along with the benefits of securing separate representation, are factors that may be considered by the affected client in determining whether common representation is in the client's interests.

Consent Confirmed in Writing

[20] Paragraph (b) requires the lawyer to obtain the informed consent of the client, confirmed in writing. Such a writing may consist of a document executed by the client or one that the lawyer promptly records and transmits to the client following an oral consent. See Rule 1.0(b). See also Rule 1.0(n) (writing includes electronic transmission). If it is not feasible to obtain or transmit the writing at the time the client gives informed consent, then the lawyer must obtain or transmit it within a reasonable time thereafter. See Rule 1.0(b). The requirement of a writing does not supplant the need in most cases for the lawyer to talk with the client, to explain the risks and advantages, if any, of representation burdened with a conflict of interest, as well as reasonably available alternatives, and to afford the client a reasonable opportunity to consider the risks and alternatives and to raise questions and concerns. Rather, the writing is required in order to impress upon clients the seriousness of the decision the client is being asked to make and to avoid disputes or ambiguities that might later occur in the absence of a writing.

Revoking Consent

[21] A client who has given consent to a conflict may revoke the consent and, like any other client, may terminate the lawyer's representation at any time. Whether revoking consent to the client's own representation precludes the lawyer from continuing to represent other clients depends on the circumstances, including the nature of the conflict, whether the client revoked consent because of a material change in circumstances, the reasonable expectations of the other clients and whether material detriment to the other clients or the lawyer would result.

Consent to Future Conflict

[22] Whether a lawyer may properly request a client to waive conflicts that might arise in the future is subject to the test of paragraph (b). The effectiveness of such waivers is generally determined by the extent to which the client reasonably understands the material risks that the waiver entails. The more comprehensive the explanation of the types of future representations that might arise and the actual and reasonably foreseeable adverse consequences of those representations, the greater the likelihood that the client will have the requisite understanding. Thus, if the client agrees to consent to a particular type of conflict with which the client is already familiar, then the consent ordinarily will be effective with regard to that type of conflict. If the consent is general and open-ended, then the consent ordinarily will be ineffective, because it is not reasonably likely that the client will have understood the material risks involved. On the other hand, if the client is an experienced user of the legal services involved and is reasonably informed regarding the risk that a conflict may arise, such consent is more likely to be effective, particularly if, e.g., the client is independently represented by other counsel in giving consent and the consent is limited to future conflicts unrelated to the subject of the representation. In any case, advance consent cannot be effective if the circumstances that materialize in the future are such as would make the conflict nonconsentable under paragraph (b).

Conflicts in Litigation

[23] Paragraph (b)(3) prohibits representation of opposing parties in the same litigation, regardless of the clients' consent. On the other hand, simultaneous representation of parties whose interests in litigation may conflict, such as coplaintiffs or codefendants, is governed by paragraph (a)(2). A conflict may exist by reason of substantial discrepancy in the parties' testimony, incompatibility in positions in relation to an opposing party or the fact that there are substantially different possibilities of settlement of the claims or liabilities in question. Such conflicts can arise in criminal cases as well as civil. The potential for conflict of interest in representing multiple defendants in a criminal case is so grave that ordinarily a lawyer should decline to represent more than one codefendant. On the other hand, common representation of persons having similar interests in civil litigation is proper if the requirements of paragraph (b) are met.

[24] Ordinarily a lawyer may take inconsistent legal positions in different tribunals at different times on behalf of different clients. The mere fact that advocating a legal position on behalf of one client might create precedent adverse to the interests of a client represented by the lawyer in an unrelated matter does not create a conflict of interest. A conflict of interest exists, however, if there is a significant risk that a lawyer's action on behalf of one client will materially limit the lawyer's effectiveness in representing another client in a different case; for example, when a decision favoring one client will create a precedent likely to seriously weaken the position taken on behalf of the other client. Factors relevant in determining whether the clients need to be advised of the risk include: where the cases are pending, whether the issue is substantive or procedural, the temporal relationship between the matters, the significance of the issue to the immediate and long-term interests of the clients involved and the clients' reasonable expectations in retaining the lawyer. If there is significant risk of material limitation, then absent informed consent of the affected clients, the lawyer must refuse one of the representations or withdraw from one or both matters.

[25] When a lawyer represents or seeks to represent a class of plaintiffs or defendants in a class-action lawsuit, unnamed members of the class are ordinarily not considered to be clients of the lawyer for purposes of applying paragraph (a)(1) of this Rule. Thus, the lawyer does not typically need to get the consent of such a person before representing a client suing the person in an unrelated matter. Similarly, a lawyer seeking to represent an opponent in a class action does not typically need the consent of an unnamed member of the class whom the lawyer represents in an unrelated matter.

Nonlitigation Conflicts

[26] Conflicts of interest under paragraphs (a)(1) and (a)(2) arise in contexts other than litigation. For a discussion of directly adverse conflicts in transactional matters, see Comment [7]. Relevant factors in determining whether there is significant potential for material limitation include the duration and intimacy of the lawyer's relationship with the client or clients involved, the functions being performed by the lawyer, the likelihood that disagreements will arise and the likely prejudice to the client from the conflict. The question is often one of proximity and degree. See Comment [8].

[27] For example, conflict questions may arise in estate planning and estate administration. A lawyer may be called upon to prepare wills for several family members, such as husband and wife, and, depending upon the circumstances, a conflict of interest may be present. In estate administration the identity of the client may be unclear under the law of a particular jurisdiction. Under one view, the client is the fiduciary; under another view the client is the estate or trust, including its beneficiaries. In order to comply with conflict of interest rules, the lawyer should make clear the lawyer's relationship to the parties involved.

[28] Whether a conflict is consentable depends on the circumstances. For example, a lawyer may not represent multiple parties to a negotiation whose interests are fundamentally antagonistic to each other, but common representation is permissible where the clients are generally aligned in interest even though there is some difference in interest among them. Thus, a lawyer may seek to establish or adjust a relationship between clients on an amicable and mutually advantageous basis; for example, in helping to organize a business in which two or more clients are entrepreneurs, working out the financial reorganization of an enterprise in which two or more clients have an interest or arranging a property distribution in settlement of an estate. The lawyer seeks to resolve potentially adverse interests by developing the parties' mutual interests. Otherwise, each party might have to obtain separate representation, with the possibility of incurring additional cost, complication or even litigation. Given these and other relevant factors, the clients may prefer that the lawyer act for all of them.

Special Considerations in Common Representation

[29] In considering whether to represent multiple clients in the same matter, a lawyer should be mindful that if the common representation fails because the potentially adverse interests cannot be reconciled, the result can be additional cost, embarrassment and recrimination. Ordinarily, the lawyer will be forced to withdraw from representing all of the clients if the common representation fails. In some situations, the risk of failure is so great that multiple representation is plainly impossible. For example, a lawyer cannot undertake common representation of clients where contentious litigation or negotiations between them are imminent or contemplated. Moreover, because the lawyer is required to be impartial between commonly represented clients, representation of multiple clients is improper when it is unlikely that impartiality can be maintained. Generally, if the relationship between the parties has already assumed antagonism, the possibility that the clients' interests can be adequately served by common representation is not very good. Other relevant factors are whether the lawyer subsequently will represent both parties on a continuing basis and whether the situation involves creating or terminating a relationship between the parties.

[30] A particularly important factor in determining the appropriateness of common representation is the effect on client-lawyer confidentiality and the attorney-client privilege. With regard to the attorney-client privilege, the prevailing rule is that, as between commonly represented clients, the privilege does not attach. Hence, it must be assumed that if litigation eventuates between the clients, the privilege will not protect any such communications, and the clients should be so advised.

[31] As to the duty of confidentiality, continued common representation will almost certainly be inadequate if one client asks the lawyer not to disclose to the other client information relevant to the common representation. This is so because the lawyer has an equal duty of loyalty

30

to each client, and each client has the right to be informed of anything bearing on the representation that might affect that client's interests and the right to expect that the lawyer will use that information to that client's benefit. See Rule 1.4. The lawyer should, at the outset of the common representation and as part of the process of obtaining each client's informed consent, advise each client that information will be shared and that the lawyer will have to withdraw if one client decides that some matter material to the representation should be kept from the other. In limited circumstances, it may be appropriate for the lawyer to proceed with the representation when the clients have agreed, after being properly informed, that the lawyer will keep certain information confidential. For example, the lawyer may reasonably conclude that failure to disclose one client's trade secrets to another client will not adversely affect representation involving a joint venture between the clients and agree to keep that information confidential with the informed consent of both clients.

[32] When seeking to establish or adjust a relationship between clients, the lawyer should make clear that the lawyer's role is not that of partisanship normally expected in other circumstances and, thus, that the clients may be required to assume greater responsibility for decisions than when each client is separately represented. Any limitations on the scope of the representation made necessary as a result of the common representation should be fully explained to the clients at the outset of the representation. See Rule 1.2(c).

[33] Subject to the above limitations, each client in the common representation has the right to loyal and diligent representation and the protection of Rule 1.9 concerning the obligations to a former client. The client also has the right to discharge the lawyer as stated in Rule 1.16.

Organizational Clients

[34] A lawyer who represents a corporation or other organization does not, by virtue of that representation, necessarily represent any constituent or affiliated organization, such as a parent or subsidiary. See Rule 1.13(a). Thus, the lawyer for an organization is not barred from accepting representation adverse to an affiliate in an unrelated matter, unless the circumstances are such that the affiliate should also be considered a client of the lawyer, there is an understanding between the lawyer and the organizational client that the lawyer will avoid representation adverse to the client's affiliates, or the lawyer's obligations to either the organizational client or the new client are likely to limit materially the lawyer's representation of the other client.

[35] A lawyer for a corporation or other organization who is also a member of its board of directors should determine whether the responsibilities of the two roles may conflict. The lawyer may be called on to advise the corporation in matters involving actions of the directors. Consideration should be given to the frequency with which such situations may arise, the potential intensity of the conflict, the effect of the lawyer's resignation from the board and the possibility of the corporation's obtaining legal advice from another lawyer in such situations. If there is material risk that the dual role will compromise the lawyer's independence of professional judgment, the lawyer should not serve as a director or should cease to act as the corporation's lawyer when conflicts of interest arise. The lawyer should advise the other members of the board that in some circumstances matters discussed at board meetings while the lawyer is present in the capacity of director might not be protected by the attorney-client privilege and that conflict of interest considerations might require the lawyer's recusal as a director or might require the lawyer and the lawyer's firm to decline representation of the corporation in a matter.

RULE 1.8: CONFLICT OF INTEREST: CURRENT CLIENTS: SPECIFIC RULES

(a) A lawyer **shall not enter into a** business transaction **with a client or knowingly acquire an ownership, possessory, security or other pecuniary interest adverse to a client unless:**

(1) the transaction and terms on which the lawyer acquires the interest are fair and reasonable to the client and are fully disclosed and transmitted in writing in a manner that can be reasonably understood by the client;

(2) the client is advised in writing of the desirability of seeking and is given a reasonable opportunity to seek the advice of independent legal counsel on the transaction; and

(3) the client gives informed consent, in a writing signed by the client, to the essential terms of the transaction and the lawyer's role in the transaction, including whether the lawyer is representing the client in the transaction.

(b) A lawyer shall not use information relating to representation of a client to the disadvantage of the client unless the client gives informed consent, except as permitted or required by these Rules.

(c) A lawyer shall not solicit any substantial gift from a client, including a testamentary gift, or prepare on behalf of a client an instrument giving the lawyer or a person related to the lawyer any substantial gift unless the lawyer or other recipient of the gift is related to the client. For purposes of this paragraph, related persons include a spouse, child, grandchild, parent, grandparent or other relative or individual with whom the lawyer or the client maintains a close, familial relationship.

(d) Prior to the conclusion of representation of a client, a lawyer shall not make or negotiate an agreement giving the lawyer literary or media rights to a portrayal or account based in substantial part on information relating to the representation.

(e) A lawyer shall not provide financial assistance to a client in connection with pending or contemplated litigation, except that: Do not give/take loans

(1) a lawyer may advance court costs and expenses of litigation, the repayment of which may be contingent on the outcome of the matter; and

(2) a lawyer representing an indigent client may pay court costs and expenses of litigation on behalf of the client.

(f) A lawyer shall not accept compensation for representing a client from one other than the client unless:

(1) the client gives informed consent;

(2) there is no interference with the lawyer's independence of professional judgment or with the client-lawyer relationship; and

(3) information relating to representation of a client is protected as required by Rule 1.6.

(g) A lawyer who represents two or more clients shall not participate in making an aggregate settlement of the claims of or against the clients, or in a criminal case an aggregated agreement as to guilty or nolo contendere pleas, unless each client gives informed consent, in a writing signed by the client. The lawyer's disclosure shall include the existence and nature of all the claims or pleas involved and of the participation of each person in the settlement.

(h) A lawyer shall not: K14 +15

(1) make an agreement prospectively limiting the lawyer's liability to a client for malpractice unless the client is independently represented in making the agreement; or

(2) settle a claim or potential claim for such liability with an unrepresented client or former client unless that person is advised in writing of the desirability of seeking and is given a reasonable opportunity to seek the advice of independent legal counsel in connection therewith.

(i) A lawyer shall not acquire a proprietary interest in the cause of action or subject matter of litigation the lawyer is conducting for a client, except that the lawyer may:

    (1) acquire a lien authorized by law to secure the lawyer's fee or expenses; and

    (2) contract with a client for a reasonable contingent fee in a civil case.

(j) A lawyer shall not have sexual relations with a client unless a consensual sexual relationship existed between them when the client-lawyer relationship commenced.

(k) While lawyers are associated in a firm, a prohibition in the foregoing paragraphs (a) through (i) that applies to any one of them shall apply to all of them.

[handwritten marginalia: C18/9; Sexual; Still see 1.7(a)(2) to see if concurrent in continuing relation; ORG C19]

COMMENT

Business Transactions Between Client and Lawyer

[1] A lawyer's legal skill and training, together with the relationship of trust and confidence between lawyer and client, create the possibility of overreaching when the lawyer participates in a business, property or financial transaction with a client, for example, a loan or sales transaction or a lawyer investment on behalf of a client. The requirements of paragraph (a) must be met even when the transaction is not closely related to the subject matter of the representation, as when a lawyer drafting a will for a client learns that the client needs money for unrelated expenses and offers to make a loan to the client. The Rule applies to lawyers engaged in the sale of goods or services related to the practice of law, for example, the sale of title insurance or investment services to existing clients of the lawyer's legal practice. See Rule 5.7. It also applies to lawyers purchasing property from estates they represent. It does not apply to ordinary fee arrangements between client and lawyer, which are governed by Rule 1.5, although its requirements must be met when the lawyer accepts an interest in the client's business or other nonmonetary property as payment of all or part of a fee. In addition, the Rule does not apply to standard commercial transactions between the lawyer and the client for products or services that the client generally markets to others, for example, banking or brokerage services, medical services, products manufactured or distributed by the client, and utilities' services. In such transactions, the lawyer has no advantage in dealing with the client, and the restrictions in paragraph (a) are unnecessary and impracticable.

[2] Paragraph (a)(1) requires that the transaction itself be fair to the client and that its essential terms be communicated to the client, in writing, in a manner that can be reasonably understood. Paragraph (a)(2) requires that the client also be advised, in writing, of the desirability of seeking the advice of independent legal counsel. It also requires that the client be given a reasonable opportunity to obtain such advice. Paragraph (a)(3) requires that the lawyer obtain the client's informed consent, in a writing signed by the client, both to the essential terms of the transaction and to the lawyer's role. When necessary, the lawyer should discuss both the material risks of the proposed transaction, including any risk presented by the lawyer's involvement, and the existence of reasonably available alternatives and should explain why the advice of independent legal counsel is desirable. See Rule 1.0(e) (definition of informed consent).

[3] The risk to a client is greatest when the client expects the lawyer to represent the client in the transaction itself or when the lawyer's financial interest otherwise poses a significant risk that the lawyer's representation of the client will be materially limited by the lawyer's financial interest in the transaction. Here the lawyer's role requires that the lawyer must comply, not only with the requirements of paragraph (a), but also with the requirements of Rule 1.7. Under that Rule, the lawyer must disclose the risks associated with the lawyer's dual role as both legal adviser and participant in the transaction, such as the risk that the lawyer will structure the transaction or give legal advice in a way that favors the lawyer's interests at the expense of the client. Moreover, the lawyer must obtain the client's informed consent. In some cases, the

lawyer's interest may be such that Rule 1.7 will preclude the lawyer from seeking the client's consent to the transaction.

[4] If the client is independently represented in the transaction, paragraph (a)(2) of this Rule is inapplicable, and the paragraph (a)(1) requirement for full disclosure is satisfied either by a written disclosure by the lawyer involved in the transaction or by the client's independent counsel. The fact that the client was independently represented in the transaction is relevant in determining whether the agreement was fair and reasonable to the client as paragraph (a)(1) further requires.

Use of Information Related to Representation

[5] Use of information relating to the representation to the disadvantage of the client violates the lawyer's duty of loyalty. Paragraph (b) applies when the information is used to benefit either the lawyer or a third person, such as another client or business associate of the lawyer. For example, if a lawyer learns that a client intends to purchase and develop several parcels of land, the lawyer may not use that information to purchase one of the parcels in competition with the client or to recommend that another client make such a purchase. The Rule does not prohibit uses that do not disadvantage the client. For example, a lawyer who learns a government agency's interpretation of trade legislation during the representation of one client may properly use that information to benefit other clients. Paragraph (b) prohibits disadvantageous use of client information unless the client gives informed consent, except as permitted or required by these Rules. See Rules 1.2(d), 1.6, 1.9(c), 3.3, 4.1(b), 8.1 and 8.3.

Gifts to Lawyers

[6] A lawyer may accept a gift from a client, if the transaction meets general standards of fairness. For example, a simple gift such as a present given at a holiday or as a token of appreciation is permitted. If a client offers the lawyer a more substantial gift, paragraph (c) does not prohibit the lawyer from accepting it, although such a gift may be voidable by the client under the doctrine of undue influence, which treats client gifts as presumptively fraudulent. In any event, due to concerns about overreaching and imposition on clients, a lawyer may not suggest that a substantial gift be made to the lawyer or for the lawyer's benefit, except where the lawyer is related to the client as set forth in paragraph (c).

[7] If effectuation of a substantial gift requires preparing a legal instrument such as a will or conveyance the client should have the detached advice that another lawyer can provide. The sole exception to this Rule is where the client is a relative of the donee.

[8] This Rule does not prohibit a lawyer from seeking to have the lawyer or a partner or associate of the lawyer named as executor of the client's estate or to another potentially lucrative fiduciary position. Nevertheless, such appointments will be subject to the general conflict of interest provision in Rule 1.7 when there is a significant risk that the lawyer's interest in obtaining the appointment will materially limit the lawyer's independent professional judgment in advising the client concerning the choice of an executor or other fiduciary. In obtaining the client's informed consent to the conflict, the lawyer should advise the client concerning the nature and extent of the lawyer's financial interest in the appointment, as well as the availability of alternative candidates for the position.

Literary Rights

[9] An agreement by which a lawyer acquires literary or media rights concerning the conduct of the representation creates a conflict between the interests of the client and the personal interests of the lawyer. Measures suitable in the representation of the client may detract from the publication value of an account of the representation. Paragraph (d) does not prohibit a lawyer representing a client in a transaction concerning literary property from agreeing that the lawyer's fee shall consist of a share in ownership in the property, if the arrangement conforms to Rule 1.5 and paragraphs (a) and (i).

Financial Assistance

[10] Lawyers may not subsidize lawsuits or administrative proceedings brought on behalf of their clients, including making or guaranteeing loans to their clients for living expenses, because to do so would encourage clients to pursue lawsuits that might not otherwise be brought and because such assistance gives lawyers too great a financial stake in the litigation. These dangers do not warrant a prohibition on a lawyer lending a client court costs and litigation expenses, including the expenses of medical examination and the costs of obtaining and presenting evidence, because these advances are virtually indistinguishable from contingent fees and help ensure access to the courts. Similarly, an exception allowing lawyers representing indigent clients to pay court costs and litigation expenses regardless of whether these funds will be repaid is warranted.

Person Paying for a Lawyer's Services

[11] Lawyers are frequently asked to represent a client under circumstances in which a third person will compensate the lawyer, in whole or in part. The third person might be a relative or friend, an indemnitor (such as a liability insurance company) or a co-client (such as a corporation sued along with one or more of its employees). Because third-party payers frequently have interests that differ from those of the client, including interests in minimizing the amount spent on the representation and in learning how the representation is progressing, lawyers are prohibited from accepting or continuing such representations unless the lawyer determines that there will be no interference with the lawyer's independent professional judgment and there is informed consent from the client. See also Rule 5.4(c) (prohibiting interference with a lawyer's professional judgment by one who recommends, employs or pays the lawyer to render legal services for another).

[12] Sometimes, it will be sufficient for the lawyer to obtain the client's informed consent regarding the fact of the payment and the identity of the third-party payer. If, however, the fee arrangement creates a conflict of interest for the lawyer, then the lawyer must comply with Rule 1.7. The lawyer must also conform to the requirements of Rule 1.6 concerning confidentiality. Under Rule 1.7(a), a conflict of interest exists if there is significant risk that the lawyer's representation of the client will be materially limited by the lawyer's own interest in the fee arrangement or by the lawyer's responsibilities to the third-party payer (for example, when the third-party payer is a co-client). Under Rule 1.7(b), the lawyer may accept or continue the representation with the informed consent of each affected client, unless the conflict is nonconsentable under that paragraph. Under Rule 1.7(b), the informed consent must be confirmed in writing.

Aggregate Settlements

[13] Differences in willingness to make or accept an offer of settlement are among the risks of common representation of multiple clients by a single lawyer. Under Rule 1.7, this is one of the risks that should be discussed before undertaking the representation, as part of the process of obtaining the clients' informed consent. In addition, Rule 1.2(a) protects each client's right to have the final say in deciding whether to accept or reject an offer of settlement and in deciding whether to enter a guilty or nolo contendere plea in a criminal case. The rule stated in this paragraph is a corollary of both these Rules and provides that, before any settlement offer or plea bargain is made or accepted on behalf of multiple clients, the lawyer must inform each of them about all the material terms of the settlement, including what the other clients will receive or pay if the settlement or plea offer is accepted. See also Rule 1.0(e) (definition of informed consent). Lawyers representing a class of plaintiffs or defendants, or those proceeding derivatively, may not have a full client-lawyer relationship with each member of the class; nevertheless, such lawyers must comply with applicable rules regulating notification of class members and other procedural requirements designed to ensure adequate protection of the entire class.

Limiting Liability and Settling Malpractice Claims

[14] Agreements prospectively limiting a lawyer's liability for malpractice are prohibited unless the client is independently represented in making the agreement because they are likely to undermine competent and diligent representation. Also, many clients are unable to evaluate the desirability of making such an agreement before a dispute has arisen, particularly if they are then represented by the lawyer seeking the agreement. This paragraph does not, however, prohibit a lawyer from entering into an agreement with the client to arbitrate legal malpractice claims, provided such agreements are enforceable and the client is fully informed of the scope and effect of the agreement. Nor does this paragraph limit the ability of lawyers to practice in the form of a limited-liability entity, where permitted by law, provided that each lawyer remains personally liable to the client for his or her own conduct and the firm complies with any conditions required by law, such as provisions requiring client notification or maintenance of adequate liability insurance. Nor does it prohibit an agreement in accordance with Rule 1.2 that defines the scope of the representation, although a definition of scope that makes the obligations of representation illusory will amount to an attempt to limit liability.

[15] Agreements settling a claim or a potential claim for malpractice are not prohibited by this Rule. Nevertheless, in view of the danger that a lawyer will take unfair advantage of an unrepresented client or former client, the lawyer must first advise such a person in writing of the appropriateness of independent representation in connection with such a settlement. In addition, the lawyer must give the client or former client a reasonable opportunity to find and consult independent counsel.

Acquiring Proprietary Interest in Litigation

[16] Paragraph (i) states the traditional general rule that lawyers are prohibited from acquiring a proprietary interest in litigation. Like paragraph (e), the general rule has its basis in common law champerty and maintenance and is designed to avoid giving the lawyer too great an interest in the representation. In addition, when the lawyer acquires an ownership interest in the subject of the representation, it will be more difficult for a client to discharge the lawyer if the client so desires. The Rule is subject to specific exceptions developed in decisional law and continued in these Rules. The exception for certain advances of the costs of litigation is set forth in paragraph (e). In addition, paragraph (i) sets forth exceptions for liens authorized by law to secure the lawyer's fees or expenses and contracts for reasonable contingent fees. The law of each jurisdiction determines which liens are authorized by law. These may include liens granted by statute, liens originating in common law and liens acquired by contract with the client. When a lawyer acquires by contract a security interest in property other than that recovered through the lawyer's efforts in the litigation, such an acquisition is a business or financial transaction with a client and is governed by the requirements of paragraph (a). Contracts for contingent fees in civil cases are governed by Rule 1.5.

Client-Lawyer Sexual Relationships

[17] The relationship between lawyer and client is a fiduciary one in which the lawyer occupies the highest position of trust and confidence. The relationship is almost always unequal; thus, a sexual relationship between lawyer and client can involve unfair exploitation of the lawyer's fiduciary role, in violation of the lawyer's basic ethical obligation not to use the trust of the client to the client's disadvantage. In addition, such a relationship presents a significant danger that, because of the lawyer's emotional involvement, the lawyer will be unable to represent the client without impairment of the exercise of independent professional judgment. Moreover, a blurred line between the professional and personal relationships may make it difficult to predict to what extent client confidences will be protected by the attorney-client evidentiary privilege, since client confidences are protected by privilege only when they are imparted in the context of the client-lawyer relationship. Because of the significant danger of harm to client interests and because the client's own emotional involvement renders it unlikely

that the client could give adequate informed consent, this Rule prohibits the lawyer from having sexual relations with a client regardless of whether the relationship is consensual and regardless of the absence of prejudice to the client.

[18] Sexual relationships that predate the client-lawyer relationship are not prohibited. Issues relating to the exploitation of the fiduciary relationship and client dependency are diminished when the sexual relationship existed prior to the commencement of the client-lawyer relationship. However, before proceeding with the representation in these circumstances, the lawyer should consider whether the lawyer's ability to represent the client will be materially limited by the relationship. See Rule 1.7(a)(2).

[19] When the client is an organization, paragraph (j) of this Rule prohibits a lawyer for the organization (whether inside counsel or outside counsel) from having a sexual relationship with a constituent of the organization who supervises, directs or regularly consults with that lawyer concerning the organization's legal matters.

Imputation of Prohibitions

[20] Under paragraph (k), a prohibition on conduct by an individual lawyer in paragraphs (a) through (i) also applies to all lawyers associated in a firm with the personally prohibited lawyer. For example, one lawyer in a firm may not enter into a business transaction with a client of another member of the firm without complying with paragraph (a), even if the first lawyer is not personally involved in the representation of the client. The prohibition set forth in paragraph (j) is personal and is not applied to associated lawyers.

RULE 1.9: DUTIES TO FORMER CLIENTS

(a) A lawyer who has formerly represented a client in a matter shall not thereafter represent another person in the same or a substantially related matter in which that person's interests are materially adverse to the interests of the former client unless the former client gives informed consent, confirmed in writing.

(b) A lawyer shall not knowingly represent a person in the same or a substantially related matter in which a firm with which the lawyer formerly was associated had previously represented a client

> **(1) whose interests are materially adverse to that person; and**

> **(2) about whom the lawyer had acquired information protected by Rules 1.6 and 1.9(c) that is material to the matter;**

unless the former client gives informed consent, confirmed in writing.

(c) A lawyer who has formerly represented a client in a matter or whose present or former firm has formerly represented a client in a matter shall not thereafter:

> **(1) use information relating to the representation to the disadvantage of the former client except as these Rules would permit or require with respect to a client, or when the information has become generally known; or**

> **(2) reveal information relating to the representation except as these Rules would permit or require with respect to a client.**

COMMENT

[1] After termination of a client-lawyer relationship, a lawyer has certain continuing duties with respect to confidentiality and conflicts of interest and thus may not represent another client except in conformity with this Rule. Under this Rule, for example, a lawyer could not properly seek to rescind on behalf of a new client a contract drafted on behalf of the former client. So also a lawyer who has prosecuted an accused person could not properly represent the accused

successive   v.   *Non (current)*

· work took 1 day   · maintain contact (big issue)
· firm called, client declined service   · It's what client reas. believes
· send lett r to all clients
· rep. By rs 2 go

ABA Model Rules of Professional Conduct (2004)

in a subsequent civil action against the government concerning the same transaction. Nor could a lawyer who has represented multiple clients in a matter represent one of the clients against the others in the same or a substantially related matter after a dispute arose among the clients in that matter, unless all affected clients give informed consent. See Comment [9]. Current and former government lawyers must comply with this Rule to the extent required by Rule 1.11.

[2] The scope of a "matter" for purposes of this Rule depends on the facts of a particular situation or transaction. The lawyer's involvement in a matter can also be a question of degree. When a lawyer has been directly involved in a specific transaction, subsequent representation of other clients with materially adverse interests in that transaction clearly is prohibited. On the other hand, a lawyer who recurrently handled a type of problem for a former client is not precluded from later representing another client in a factually distinct problem of that type even though the subsequent representation involves a position adverse to the prior client. Similar considerations can apply to the reassignment of military lawyers between defense and prosecution functions within the same military jurisdictions. The underlying question is whether the lawyer was so involved in the matter that the subsequent representation can be justly regarded as a changing of sides in the matter in question.

[3] Matters are "substantially related" for purposes of this Rule if they involve the same transaction or legal dispute or if there otherwise is a substantial risk that confidential factual information as would normally have been obtained in the prior representation would materially advance the client's position in the subsequent matter. For example, a lawyer who has represented a businessperson and learned extensive private financial information about that person may not then represent that person's spouse in seeking a divorce. Similarly, a lawyer who has previously represented a client in securing environmental permits to build a shopping center would be precluded from representing neighbors seeking to oppose rezoning of the property on the basis of environmental considerations; however, the lawyer would not be precluded, on the grounds of substantial relationship, from defending a tenant of the completed shopping center in resisting eviction for nonpayment of rent. Information that has been disclosed to the public or to other parties adverse to the former client ordinarily will not be disqualifying. Information acquired in a prior representation may have been rendered obsolete by the passage of time, a circumstance that may be relevant in determining whether two representations are substantially related. In the case of an organizational client, general knowledge of the client's policies and practices ordinarily will not preclude a subsequent representation; on the other hand, knowledge of specific facts gained in a prior representation that are relevant to the matter in question ordinarily will preclude such a representation. A former client is not required to reveal the confidential information learned by the lawyer in order to establish a substantial risk that the lawyer has confidential information to use in the subsequent matter. A conclusion about the possession of such information may be based on the nature of the services the lawyer provided the former client and information that would in ordinary practice be learned by a lawyer providing such services.

Lawyers Moving Between Firms

[4] When lawyers have been associated within a firm but then end their association, the question of whether a lawyer should undertake representation is more complicated. There are several competing considerations. First, the client previously represented by the former firm must be reasonably assured that the principle of loyalty to the client is not compromised. Second, the rule should not be so broadly cast as to preclude other persons from having reasonable choice of legal counsel. Third, the rule should not unreasonably hamper lawyers from forming new associations and taking on new clients after having left a previous association. In this connection, it should be recognized that today many lawyers practice in firms, that many lawyers to some degree limit their practice to one field or another, and that many move from one association to another several times in their careers. If the concept of imputation were applied with unqualified rigor, the result would be radical curtailment of the opportunity of lawyers to move from one practice setting to another and of the opportunity of clients to change counsel.

[5] Paragraph (b) operates to disqualify the lawyer only when the lawyer involved has actual knowledge of information protected by Rules 1.6 and 1.9(c). Thus, if a lawyer while with one firm acquired no knowledge or information relating to a particular client of the firm, and that lawyer later joined another firm, neither the lawyer individually nor the second firm is disqualified from representing another client in the same or a related matter even though the interests of the two clients conflict. See Rule 1.10(b) for the restrictions on a firm once a lawyer has terminated association with the firm.

[6] Application of paragraph (b) depends on a situation's particular facts, aided by inferences, deductions or working presumptions that reasonably may be made about the way in which lawyers work together. A lawyer may have general access to files of all clients of a law firm and may regularly participate in discussions of their affairs; it should be inferred that such a lawyer in fact is privy to all information about all the firm's clients. In contrast, another lawyer may have access to the files of only a limited number of clients and participate in discussions of the affairs of no other clients; in the absence of information to the contrary, it should be inferred that such a lawyer in fact is privy to information about the clients actually served but not those of other clients. In such an inquiry, the burden of proof should rest upon the firm whose disqualification is sought.

[7] Independent of the question of disqualification of a firm, a lawyer changing professional association has a continuing duty to preserve confidentiality of information about a client formerly represented. See Rules 1.6 and 1.9(c).

[8] Paragraph (c) provides that information acquired by the lawyer in the course of representing a client may not subsequently be used or revealed by the lawyer to the disadvantage of the client. However, the fact that a lawyer has once served a client does not preclude the lawyer from using generally known information about that client when later representing another client.

[9] The provisions of this Rule are for the protection of former clients and can be waived if the client gives informed consent, which consent must be confirmed in writing under paragraphs (a) and (b). See Rule 1.0(e). With regard to the effectiveness of an advance waiver, see Comment [22] to Rule 1.7. With regard to disqualification of a firm with which a lawyer is or was formerly associated, see Rule 1.10.

RULE 1.10: IMPUTATION OF CONFLICTS OF INTEREST: GENERAL RULE

(a) While lawyers are associated in a firm, none of them shall knowingly represent a client when any one of them practicing alone would be prohibited from doing so by Rules 1.7 or 1.9, unless the prohibition is based on a personal interest of the prohibited lawyer and does not present a significant risk of materially limiting the representation of the client by the remaining lawyers in the firm.

(b) When a lawyer has terminated an association with a firm, the firm is not prohibited from thereafter representing a person with interests materially adverse to those of a client represented by the formerly associated lawyer and not currently represented by the firm, unless:

(1) the matter is the same or substantially related to that in which the formerly associated lawyer represented the client; and

(2) any lawyer remaining in the firm has information protected by Rules 1.6 and 1.9(c) that is material to the matter.

(c) A disqualification prescribed by this rule may be waived by the affected client under the conditions stated in Rule 1.7.

(d) The disqualification of lawyers associated in a firm with former or current government lawyers is governed by Rule 1.11.

COMMENT

Definition of "Firm"

[1] For purposes of the Rules of Professional Conduct, the term "firm" denotes lawyers in a law partnership, professional corporation, sole proprietorship or other association authorized to practice law; or lawyers employed in a legal services organization or the legal department of a corporation or other organization. See Rule 1.0(c). Whether two or more lawyers constitute a firm within this definition can depend on the specific facts. See Rule 1.0, Comments [2] - [4].

Principles of Imputed Disqualification

[2] The rule of imputed disqualification stated in paragraph (a) gives effect to the principle of loyalty to the client as it applies to lawyers who practice in a law firm. Such situations can be considered from the premise that a firm of lawyers is essentially one lawyer for purposes of the rules governing loyalty to the client, or from the premise that each lawyer is vicariously bound by the obligation of loyalty owed by each lawyer with whom the lawyer is associated. Paragraph (a) operates only among the lawyers currently associated in a firm. When a lawyer moves from one firm to another, the situation is governed by Rules 1.9(b) and 1.10(b).

[3] The rule in paragraph (a) does not prohibit representation where neither questions of client loyalty nor protection of confidential information are presented. Where one lawyer in a firm could not effectively represent a given client because of strong political beliefs, for example, but that lawyer will do no work on the case and the personal beliefs of the lawyer will not materially limit the representation by others in the firm, the firm should not be disqualified. On the other hand, if an opposing party in a case were owned by a lawyer in the law firm, and others in the firm would be materially limited in pursuing the matter because of loyalty to that lawyer, the personal disqualification of the lawyer would be imputed to all others in the firm.

[4] The rule in paragraph (a) also does not prohibit representation by others in the law firm where the person prohibited from involvement in a matter is a nonlawyer, such as a paralegal or legal secretary. Nor does paragraph (a) prohibit representation if the lawyer is prohibited from acting because of events before the person became a lawyer, for example, work that the person did while a law student. Such persons, however, ordinarily must be screened from any personal participation in the matter to avoid communication to others in the firm of confidential information that both the nonlawyers and the firm have a legal duty to protect. See Rules 1.0(k) and 5.3.

[5] Rule 1.10(b) operates to permit a law firm, under certain circumstances, to represent a person with interests directly adverse to those of a client represented by a lawyer who formerly was associated with the firm. The Rule applies regardless of when the formerly associated lawyer represented the client. However, the law firm may not represent a person with interests adverse to those of a present client of the firm, which would violate Rule 1.7. Moreover, the firm may not represent the person where the matter is the same or substantially related to that in which the formerly associated lawyer represented the client and any other lawyer currently in the firm has material information protected by Rules 1.6 and 1.9(c).

[6] Rule 1.10(c) removes imputation with the informed consent of the affected client or former client under the conditions stated in Rule 1.7. The conditions stated in Rule 1.7 require the lawyer to determine that the representation is not prohibited by Rule 1.7(b) and that each affected client or former client has given informed consent to the representation, confirmed in writing. In some cases, the risk may be so severe that the conflict may not be cured by client consent. For a discussion of the effectiveness of client waivers of conflicts that might arise in the future, see Rule 1.7, Comment [22]. For a definition of informed consent, see Rule 1.0(e).

[7] Where a lawyer has joined a private firm after having represented the government, imputation is governed by Rule 1.11(b) and (c), not this Rule. Under Rule 1.11(d), where a lawyer represents the government after having served clients in private practice, nongovernmental

employment or in another government agency, former-client conflicts are not imputed to government lawyers associated with the individually disqualified lawyer.

[8] Where a lawyer is prohibited from engaging in certain transactions under Rule 1.8, paragraph (k) of that Rule, and not this Rule, determines whether that prohibition also applies to other lawyers associated in a firm with the personally prohibited lawyer.

RULE 1.11: SPECIAL CONFLICTS OF INTEREST FOR FORMER AND CURRENT GOVERNMENT OFFICERS AND EMPLOYEES

(a) Except as law may otherwise expressly permit, a lawyer who has formerly served as a public officer or employee of the government:

(1) is subject to Rule 1.9(c); and

(2) shall not otherwise represent a client in connection with a matter in which the lawyer participated personally and substantially as a public officer or employee, unless the appropriate government agency gives its informed consent, confirmed in writing, to the representation.

(b) When a lawyer is disqualified from representation under paragraph (a), no lawyer in a firm with which that lawyer is associated may knowingly undertake or continue representation in such a matter unless:

(1) the disqualified lawyer is timely screened from any participation in the matter and is apportioned no part of the fee therefrom; and

(2) written notice is promptly given to the appropriate government agency to enable it to ascertain compliance with the provisions of this rule.

(c) Except as law may otherwise expressly permit, a lawyer having information that the lawyer knows is confidential government information about a person acquired when the lawyer was a public officer or employee, may not represent a private client whose interests are adverse to that person in a matter in which the information could be used to the material disadvantage of that person. As used in this Rule, the term "confidential government information" means information that has been obtained under governmental authority and which, at the time this Rule is applied, the government is prohibited by law from disclosing to the public or has a legal privilege not to disclose and which is not otherwise available to the public. A firm with which that lawyer is associated may undertake or continue representation in the matter only if the disqualified lawyer is timely screened from any participation in the matter and is apportioned no part of the fee therefrom.

(d) Except as law may otherwise expressly permit, a lawyer currently serving as a public officer or employee:

(1) is subject to Rules 1.7 and 1.9; and

(2) shall not:

(i) participate in a matter in which the lawyer participated personally and substantially while in private practice or nongovernmental employment, unless the appropriate government agency gives its informed consent, confirmed in writing; or

(ii) negotiate for private employment with any person who is involved as a party or as lawyer for a party in a matter in which the lawyer is participating personally and substantially, except that a lawyer serving as a law clerk to a judge, other adjudicative officer or arbitrator may negotiate

for private employment as permitted by Rule 1.12(b) and subject to the conditions stated in Rule 1.12(b).

(e) As used in this Rule, the term "matter" includes:

(1) any judicial or other proceeding, application, request for a ruling or other determination, contract, claim, controversy, investigation, charge, accusation, arrest or other particular matter involving a specific party or parties, and

(2) any other matter covered by the conflict of interest rules of the appropriate government agency.

COMMENT

[1] A lawyer who has served or is currently serving as a public officer or employee is personally subject to the Rules of Professional Conduct, including the prohibition against concurrent conflicts of interest stated in Rule 1.7. In addition, such a lawyer may be subject to statutes and government regulations regarding conflict of interest. Such statutes and regulations may circumscribe the extent to which the government agency may give consent under this Rule. See Rule 1.0(e) for the definition of informed consent.

[2] Paragraphs (a)(1), (a)(2) and (d)(1) restate the obligations of an individual lawyer who has served or is currently serving as an officer or employee of the government toward a former government or private client. Rule 1.10 is not applicable to the conflicts of interest addressed by this Rule. Rather, paragraph (b) sets forth a special imputation rule for former government lawyers that provides for screening and notice. Because of the special problems raised by imputation within a government agency, paragraph (d) does not impute the conflicts of a lawyer currently serving as an officer or employee of the government to other associated government officers or employees, although ordinarily it will be prudent to screen such lawyers.

[3] Paragraphs (a)(2) and (d)(2) apply regardless of whether a lawyer is adverse to a former client and are thus designed not only to protect the former client, but also to prevent a lawyer from exploiting public office for the advantage of another client. For example, a lawyer who has pursued a claim on behalf of the government may not pursue the same claim on behalf of a later private client after the lawyer has left government service, except when authorized to do so by the government agency under paragraph (a). Similarly, a lawyer who has pursued a claim on behalf of a private client may not pursue the claim on behalf of the government, except when authorized to do so by paragraph (d). As with paragraphs (a)(1) and (d)(1), Rule 1.10 is not applicable to the conflicts of interest addressed by these paragraphs.

[4] This Rule represents a balancing of interests. On the one hand, where the successive clients are a government agency and another client, public or private, the risk exists that power or discretion vested in that agency might be used for the special benefit of the other client. A lawyer should not be in a position where benefit to the other client might affect performance of the lawyer's professional functions on behalf of the government. Also, unfair advantage could accrue to the other client by reason of access to confidential government information about the client's adversary obtainable only through the lawyer's government service. On the other hand, the rules governing lawyers presently or formerly employed by a government agency should not be so restrictive as to inhibit transfer of employment to and from the government. The government has a legitimate need to attract qualified lawyers as well as to maintain high ethical standards. Thus a former government lawyer is disqualified only from particular matters in which the lawyer participated personally and substantially. The provisions for screening and waiver in paragraph (b) are necessary to prevent the disqualification rule from imposing too severe a deterrent against entering public service. The limitation of disqualification in paragraphs (a)(2) and (d)(2) to matters involving a specific party or parties, rather than extending disqualification to all substantive issues on which the lawyer worked, serves a similar function.

[5] When a lawyer has been employed by one government agency and then moves to a second government agency, it may be appropriate to treat that second agency as another client for purposes of this Rule, as when a lawyer is employed by a city and subsequently is employed by a federal agency. However, because the conflict of interest is governed by paragraph (d), the latter agency is not required to screen the lawyer as paragraph (b) requires a law firm to do. The question of whether two government agencies should be regarded as the same or different clients for conflict of interest purposes is beyond the scope of these Rules. See Rule 1.13 Comment [9].

[6] Paragraphs (b) and (c) contemplate a screening arrangement. See Rule 1.0(k) (requirements for screening procedures). These paragraphs do not prohibit a lawyer from receiving a salary or partnership share established by prior independent agreement, but that lawyer may not receive compensation directly relating the lawyer's compensation to the fee in the matter in which the lawyer is disqualified.

[7] Notice, including a description of the screened lawyer's prior representation and of the screening procedures employed, generally should be given as soon as practicable after the need for screening becomes apparent.

[8] Paragraph (c) operates only when the lawyer in question has knowledge of the information, which means actual knowledge; it does not operate with respect to information that merely could be imputed to the lawyer.

[9] Paragraphs (a) and (d) do not prohibit a lawyer from jointly representing a private party and a government agency when doing so is permitted by Rule 1.7 and is not otherwise prohibited by law.

[10] For purposes of paragraph (e) of this Rule, a "matter" may continue in another form. In determining whether two particular matters are the same, the lawyer should consider the extent to which the matters involve the same basic facts, the same or related parties, and the time elapsed.

RULE 1.12: FORMER JUDGE, ARBITRATOR, MEDIATOR OR OTHER THIRD-PARTY NEUTRAL

(a) Except as stated in paragraph (d), a lawyer shall not represent anyone in connection with a matter in which the lawyer participated personally and substantially as a judge or other adjudicative officer or law clerk to such a person or as an arbitrator, mediator or other third-party neutral, unless all parties to the proceeding give informed consent, confirmed in writing.

(b) A lawyer shall not negotiate for employment with any person who is involved as a party or as lawyer for a party in a matter in which the lawyer is participating personally and substantially as a judge or other adjudicative officer or as an arbitrator, mediator or other third-party neutral. A lawyer serving as a law clerk to a judge or other adjudicative officer may negotiate for employment with a party or lawyer involved in a matter in which the clerk is participating personally and substantially, but only after the lawyer has notified the judge or other adjudicative officer.

(c) If a lawyer is disqualified by paragraph (a), no lawyer in a firm with which that lawyer is associated may knowingly undertake or continue representation in the matter unless:

(1) the disqualified lawyer is timely screened from any participation in the matter and is apportioned no part of the fee therefrom; and

(2) written notice is promptly given to the parties and any appropriate tribunal to enable them to ascertain compliance with the provisions of this rule.

(d) An arbitrator selected as a partisan of a party in a multimember arbitration panel is not prohibited from subsequently representing that party.

COMMENT

[1] This Rule generally parallels Rule 1.11. The term "personally and substantially" signifies that a judge who was a member of a multimember court, and thereafter left judicial office to practice law, is not prohibited from representing a client in a matter pending in the court, but in which the former judge did not participate. So also the fact that a former judge exercised administrative responsibility in a court does not prevent the former judge from acting as a lawyer in a matter where the judge had previously exercised remote or incidental administrative responsibility that did not affect the merits. Compare the Comment to Rule 1.11. The term "adjudicative officer" includes such officials as judges pro tempore, referees, special masters, hearing officers and other parajudicial officers, and also lawyers who serve as part-time judges. Paragraphs C(2), D(2) and E(2) of the Application Section of the Model Code of Judicial Conduct provide that a part-time judge, judge pro tempore or retired judge recalled to active service, shall not "act as a lawyer in a proceeding in which the judge has served as a judge or in any other proceeding related thereto." Although phrased differently from this Rule, those Rules correspond in meaning.

[2] Like former judges, lawyers who have served as arbitrators, mediators or other third-party neutrals may be asked to represent a client in a matter in which the lawyer participated personally and substantially. This Rule forbids such representation unless all of the parties to the proceedings give their informed consent, confirmed in writing. See Rule 1.0(e) and (b). Other law or codes of ethics governing third-party neutrals may impose more stringent standards of personal or imputed disqualification. See Rule 2.4.

[3]Although lawyers who serve as third-party neutrals do not have information concerning the parties that is protected under Rule 1.6, they typically owe the parties an obligation of confidentiality under law or codes of ethics governing third-party neutrals. Thus, paragraph (c) provides that conflicts of the personally disqualified lawyer will be imputed to other lawyers in a law firm unless the conditions of this paragraph are met.

[4] Requirements for screening procedures are stated in Rule 1.0(k). Paragraph (c)(1) does not prohibit the screened lawyer from receiving a salary or partnership share established by prior independent agreement, but that lawyer may not receive compensation directly related to the matter in which the lawyer is disqualified.

[5] Notice, including a description of the screened lawyer's prior representation and of the screening procedures employed, generally should be given as soon as practicable after the need for screening becomes apparent.

RULE 1.13: ORGANIZATION AS CLIENT

(a) A lawyer employed or retained by an organization represents the organization acting through its duly authorized constituents. rep. org = client

(b) If a lawyer for an organization knows that an officer, employee or other person associated with the organization is engaged in action, intends to act or refuses to act in a matter related to the representation that is a violation of a legal obligation to the organization, or a violation of law that reasonably might be imputed to the organization, and that is likely to result in substantial injury to the organization, then the lawyer shall proceed as is reasonably necessary in the best interest of the organization. Unless the lawyer reasonably believes that it is not necessary in the best interest of the organization to do so, the lawyer shall refer the matter to higher authority in the organization, including, if warranted by the circumstances, to the highest authority that can act on behalf of the organization as determined by applicable law. 1.6 preserves up corp. ladder

(c) Except as provided in paragraph (d), if

(1) despite the lawyer's efforts in accordance with paragraph (b) the highest authority that can act on behalf of the organization insists upon or fails to address in a timely and appropriate manner an action or a refusal to act, that is clearly a violation of law, and

(2) the lawyer reasonably believes that the violation is reasonably certain to result in substantial injury to the organization,

then the lawyer may reveal information relating to the representation whether or not Rule 1.6 permits such disclosure, but only if and to the extent the lawyer reasonably believes necessary to prevent substantial injury to the organization.

(d) Paragraph (c) shall not apply with respect to information relating to a lawyer's representation of an organization to investigate an alleged violation of law, or to defend the organization or an officer, employee or other constituent associated with the organization against a claim arising out of an alleged violation of law.

(e) A lawyer who reasonably believes that he or she has been discharged because of the lawyer's actions taken pursuant to paragraphs (b) or (c), or who withdraws under circumstances that require or permit the lawyer to take action under either of those paragraphs, shall proceed as the lawyer reasonably believes necessary to assure that the organization's highest authority is informed of the lawyer's discharge or withdrawal.

(f) In dealing with an organization's directors, officers, employees, members, shareholders or other constituents, a lawyer shall explain the identity of the client when the lawyer knows or reasonably should know that the organization's interests are adverse to those of the constituents with whom the lawyer is dealing.

(g) A lawyer representing an organization may also represent any of its directors, officers, employees, members, shareholders or other constituents, subject to the provisions of Rule 1.7. If the organization's consent to the dual representation is required by Rule 1.7, the consent shall be given by an appropriate official of the organization other than the individual who is to be represented, or by the shareholders.

COMMENT

The Entity as the Client

[1] An organizational client is a legal entity, but it cannot act except through its officers, directors, employees, shareholders and other constituents. Officers, directors, employees and shareholders are the constituents of the corporate organizational client. The duties defined in this Comment apply equally to unincorporated associations. "Other constituents" as used in this Comment means the positions equivalent to officers, directors, employees and shareholders held by persons acting for organizational clients that are not corporations.

[2] When one of the constituents of an organizational client communicates with the organization's lawyer in that person's organizational capacity, the communication is protected by Rule 1.6. Thus, by way of example, if an organizational client requests its lawyer to investigate allegations of wrongdoing, interviews made in the course of that investigation between the lawyer and the client's employees or other constituents are covered by Rule 1.6. This does not mean, however, that constituents of an organizational client are the clients of the lawyer. The lawyer may not disclose to such constituents information relating to the representation except for disclosures explicitly or impliedly authorized by the organizational client in order to carry out the representation or as otherwise permitted by Rule 1.6.

[3] When constituents of the organization make decisions for it, the decisions ordinarily must be accepted by the lawyer even if their utility or prudence is doubtful. Decisions concerning policy and operations, including ones entailing serious risk, are not as such in the lawyer's province. Paragraph (b) makes clear, however, that when the lawyer knows that the organization

is likely to be substantially injured by action of an officer or other constituent that violates a legal obligation to the organization or is in violation of law that might be imputed to the organization, the lawyer must proceed as is reasonably necessary in the best interest of the organization. As defined in Rule 1.0(f), knowledge can be inferred from circumstances, and a lawyer cannot ignore the obvious.

[4] In determining how to proceed under paragraph (b), the lawyer should give due consideration to the seriousness of the violation and its consequences, the responsibility in the organization and the apparent motivation of the person involved, the policies of the organization concerning such matters, and any other relevant considerations. Ordinarily, referral to a higher authority would be necessary. In some circumstances, however, it may be appropriate for the lawyer to ask the constituent to reconsider the matter; for example, if the circumstances involve a constituent's innocent misunderstanding of law and subsequent acceptance of the lawyer's advice, the lawyer may reasonably conclude that the best interest of the organization does not require that the matter be referred to higher authority. If a constituent persists in conduct contrary to the lawyer's advice, it will be necessary for the lawyer to take steps to have the matter reviewed by a higher authority in the organization. If the matter is of sufficient seriousness and importance or urgency to the organization, referral to higher authority in the organization may be necessary even if the lawyer has not communicated with the constituent. Any measures taken should, to the extent practicable, minimize the risk of revealing information relating to the representation to persons outside the organization. Even in circumstances where a lawyer is not obligated by Rule 1.13 to proceed, a lawyer may bring to the attention of an organizational client, including its highest authority, matters that the lawyer reasonably believes to be of sufficient importance to warrant doing so in the best interest of the organization.

[5] Paragraph (b) also makes clear that when it is reasonably necessary to enable the organization to address the matter in a timely and appropriate manner, the lawyer must refer the matter to higher authority, including, if warranted by the circumstances, the highest authority that can act on behalf of the organization under applicable law. The organization's highest authority to whom a matter may be referred ordinarily will be the board of directors or similar governing body. However, applicable law may prescribe that under certain conditions the highest authority reposes elsewhere, for example, in the independent directors of a corporation.

Relation to Other Rules

[6] The authority and responsibility provided in this Rule are concurrent with the authority and responsibility provided in other Rules. In particular, this Rule does not limit or expand the lawyer's responsibility under Rules 1.8, 1.16, 3.3 or 4.1. Paragraph (c) of this Rule supplements Rule 1.6(b) by providing an additional basis upon which the lawyer may reveal information relating to the representation, but does not modify, restrict, or limit the provisions of Rule 1.6(b)(1)-(6). Under paragraph (c) the lawyer may reveal such information only when the organization's highest authority insists upon or fails to address threatened or ongoing action that is clearly a violation of law, and then only to the extent the lawyer reasonably believes necessary to prevent reasonably certain substantial injury to the organization. It is not necessary that the lawyer's services be used in furtherance of the violation, but it is required that the matter be related to the lawyer's representation of the organization. If the lawyer's services are being used by an organization to further a crime or fraud by the organization, Rules 1.6(b)(2) and 1.6(b)(3) may permit the lawyer to disclose confidential information. In such circumstances Rule 1.2(d) may also be applicable, in which event, withdrawal from the representation under Rule 1.16(a)(1) may be required.

[7] Paragraph (d) makes clear that the authority of a lawyer to disclose information relating to a representation in circumstances described in paragraph (c) does not apply with respect to information relating to a lawyer's engagement by an organization to investigate an alleged violation of law or to defend the organization or an officer, employee or other person associated with the organization against a claim arising out of an alleged violation of law. This is

necessary in order to enable organizational clients to enjoy the full benefits of legal counsel in conducting an investigation or defending against a claim.

[8] A lawyer who reasonably believes that he or she has been discharged because of the lawyer's actions taken pursuant to paragraph (b) or (c), or who withdraws in circumstances that require or permit the lawyer to take action under either of these paragraphs, must proceed as the lawyer reasonably believes necessary to assure that the organization's highest authority is informed of the lawyer's discharge or withdrawal.

Government Agency

[9] The duty defined in this Rule applies to governmental organizations. Defining precisely the identity of the client and prescribing the resulting obligations of such lawyers may be more difficult in the government context and is a matter beyond the scope of these Rules. See Scope [18]. Although in some circumstances the client may be a specific agency, it may also be a branch of government, such as the executive branch, or the government as a whole. For example, if the action or failure to act involves the head of a bureau, either the department of which the bureau is a part or the relevant branch of government may be the client for purposes of this Rule. Moreover, in a matter involving the conduct of government officials, a government lawyer may have authority under applicable law to question such conduct more extensively than that of a lawyer for a private organization in similar circumstances. Thus, when the client is a governmental organization, a different balance may be appropriate between maintaining confidentiality and assuring that the wrongful act is prevented or rectified, for public business is involved. In addition, duties of lawyers employed by the government or lawyers in military service may be defined by statutes and regulation. This Rule does not limit that authority. See Scope.

Clarifying the Lawyer's Role

[10] There are times when the organization's interest may be or become adverse to those of one or more of its constituents. In such circumstances the lawyer should advise any constituent, whose interest the lawyer finds adverse to that of the organization of the conflict or potential conflict of interest, that the lawyer cannot represent such constituent, and that such person may wish to obtain independent representation. Care must be taken to assure that the individual understands that, when there is such adversity of interest, the lawyer for the organization cannot provide legal representation for that constituent individual, and that discussions between the lawyer for the organization and the individual may not be privileged.

[11] Whether such a warning should be given by the lawyer for the organization to any constituent individual may turn on the facts of each case.

Dual Representation

[12] Paragraph (g) recognizes that a lawyer for an organization may also represent a principal officer or major shareholder.   — can rep. shareholder

Derivative Actions

[13] Under generally prevailing law, the shareholders or members of a corporation may bring suit to compel the directors to perform their legal obligations in the supervision of the organization. Members of unincorporated associations have essentially the same right. Such an action may be brought nominally by the organization, but usually is, in fact, a legal controversy over management of the organization.

[14] The question can arise whether counsel for the organization may defend such an action. The proposition that the organization is the lawyer's client does not alone resolve the issue. Most derivative actions are a normal incident of an organization's affairs, to be defended by the organization's lawyer like any other suit. However, if the claim involves serious charges of wrongdoing by those in control of the organization, a conflict may arise between the lawyer's

duty to the organization and the lawyer's relationship with the board. In those circumstances, Rule 1.7 governs who should represent the directors and the organization.

RULE 1.14: CLIENT WITH DIMINISHED CAPACITY

(a) When a client's capacity to make adequately considered decisions in connection with a representation is diminished, whether because of minority, mental impairment or for some other reason, the lawyer shall, as far as reasonably possible, maintain a normal client-lawyer relationship with the client.

(b) When the lawyer reasonably believes that the client has diminished capacity, is at risk of substantial physical, financial or other harm unless action is taken and cannot adequately act in the client's own interest, the lawyer may take reasonably necessary protective action, including consulting with individuals or entities that have the ability to take action to protect the client and, in appropriate cases, seeking the appointment of a guardian ad litem, conservator or guardian.

(c) Information relating to the representation of a client with diminished capacity is protected by Rule 1.6. When taking protective action pursuant to paragraph (b), the lawyer is impliedly authorized under Rule 1.6(a) to reveal information about the client, but only to the extent reasonably necessary to protect the client's interests.

COMMENT

[1] The normal client-lawyer relationship is based on the assumption that the client, when properly advised and assisted, is capable of making decisions about important matters. When the client is a minor or suffers from a diminished mental capacity, however, maintaining the ordinary client-lawyer relationship may not be possible in all respects. In particular, a severely incapacitated person may have no power to make legally binding decisions. Nevertheless, a client with diminished capacity often has the ability to understand, deliberate upon, and reach conclusions about matters affecting the client's own well-being. For example, children as young as five or six years of age, and certainly those of ten or twelve, are regarded as having opinions that are entitled to weight in legal proceedings concerning their custody. So also, it is recognized that some persons of advanced age can be quite capable of handling routine financial matters while needing special legal protection concerning major transactions.

[2] The fact that a client suffers a disability does not diminish the lawyer's obligation to treat the client with attention and respect. Even if the person has a legal representative, the lawyer should as far as possible accord the represented person the status of client, particularly in maintaining communication.

[3] The client may wish to have family members or other persons participate in discussions with the lawyer. When necessary to assist in the representation, the presence of such persons generally does not affect the applicability of the attorney-client evidentiary privilege. Nevertheless, the lawyer must keep the client's interests foremost and, except for protective action authorized under paragraph (b), must to look to the client, and not family members, to make decisions on the client's behalf.

[4] If a legal representative has already been appointed for the client, the lawyer should ordinarily look to the representative for decisions on behalf of the client. In matters involving a minor, whether the lawyer should look to the parents as natural guardians may depend on the type of proceeding or matter in which the lawyer is representing the minor. If the lawyer represents the guardian as distinct from the ward, and is aware that the guardian is acting adversely to the ward's interest, the lawyer may have an obligation to prevent or rectify the guardian's misconduct. See Rule 1.2(d).

Taking Protective Action

[5] If a lawyer reasonably believes that a client is at risk of substantial physical, financial or other harm unless action is taken, and that a normal client-lawyer relationship cannot be maintained as provided in paragraph (a) because the client lacks sufficient capacity to communicate or to make adequately considered decisions in connection with the representation, then paragraph (b) permits the lawyer to take protective measures deemed necessary. Such measures could include: consulting with family members, using a reconsideration period to permit clarification or improvement of circumstances, using voluntary surrogate decisionmaking tools such as durable powers of attorney or consulting with support groups, professional services, adult-protective agencies or other individuals or entities that have the ability to protect the client. In taking any protective action, the lawyer should be guided by such factors as the wishes and values of the client to the extent known, the client's best interests and the goals of intruding into the client's decisionmaking autonomy to the least extent feasible, maximizing client capacities and respecting the client's family and social connections.

[6] In determining the extent of the client's diminished capacity, the lawyer should consider and balance such factors as: the client's ability to articulate reasoning leading to a decision, variability of state of mind and ability to appreciate consequences of a decision; the substantive fairness of a decision; and the consistency of a decision with the known long-term commitments and values of the client. In appropriate circumstances, the lawyer may seek guidance from an appropriate diagnostician.

[7] If a legal representative has not been appointed, the lawyer should consider whether appointment of a guardian ad litem, conservator or guardian is necessary to protect the client's interests. Thus, if a client with diminished capacity has substantial property that should be sold for the client's benefit, effective completion of the transaction may require appointment of a legal representative. In addition, rules of procedure in litigation sometimes provide that minors or persons with diminished capacity must be represented by a guardian or next friend if they do not have a general guardian. In many circumstances, however, appointment of a legal representative may be more expensive or traumatic for the client than circumstances in fact require. Evaluation of such circumstances is a matter entrusted to the professional judgment of the lawyer. In considering alternatives, however, the lawyer should be aware of any law that requires the lawyer to advocate the least restrictive action on behalf of the client.

Disclosure of the Client's Condition

[8] Disclosure of the client's diminished capacity could adversely affect the client's interests. For example, raising the question of diminished capacity could, in some circumstances, lead to proceedings for involuntary commitment. Information relating to the representation is protected by Rule 1.6. Therefore, unless authorized to do so, the lawyer may not disclose such information. When taking protective action pursuant to paragraph (b), the lawyer is impliedly authorized to make the necessary disclosures, even when the client directs the lawyer to the contrary. Nevertheless, given the risks of disclosure, paragraph (c) limits what the lawyer may disclose in consulting with other individuals or entities or seeking the appointment of a legal representative. At the very least, the lawyer should determine whether it is likely that the person or entity consulted with will act adversely to the client's interests before discussing matters related to the client. The lawyer's position in such cases is an unavoidably difficult one.

Emergency Legal Assistance

[9] In an emergency where the health, safety or a financial interest of a person with seriously diminished capacity is threatened with imminent and irreparable harm, a lawyer may take legal action on behalf of such a person even though the person is unable to establish a client-lawyer relationship or to make or express considered judgments about the matter, when the person or another acting in good faith on that person's behalf has consulted with the lawyer. Even in such an emergency, however, the lawyer should not act unless the lawyer reasonably believes

that the person has no other lawyer, agent or other representative available. The lawyer should take legal action on behalf of the person only to the extent reasonably necessary to maintain the status quo or otherwise avoid imminent and irreparable harm. A lawyer who undertakes to represent a person in such an exigent situation has the same duties under these Rules as the lawyer would with respect to a client.

[10] A lawyer who acts on behalf of a person with seriously diminished capacity in an emergency should keep the confidences of the person as if dealing with a client, disclosing them only to the extent necessary to accomplish the intended protective action. The lawyer should disclose to any tribunal involved and to any other counsel involved the nature of his or her relationship with the person. The lawyer should take steps to regularize the relationship or implement other protective solutions as soon as possible. Normally, a lawyer would not seek compensation for such emergency actions taken.

RULE 1.15: SAFEKEEPING PROPERTY

(a) A lawyer shall hold property of clients or third persons that is in a lawyer's possession in connection with a representation separate from the lawyer's own property. Funds shall be kept in a separate account maintained in the state where the lawyer's office is situated, or elsewhere with the consent of the client or third person. Other property shall be identified as such and appropriately safeguarded. Complete records of such account funds and other property shall be kept by the lawyer and shall be preserved for a period of [five years] after termination of the representation.

(b) A lawyer may deposit the lawyer's own funds in a client trust account for the sole purpose of paying bank service charges on that account, but only in an amount necessary for that purpose.

(c) A lawyer shall deposit into a client trust account legal fees and expenses that have been paid in advance, to be withdrawn by the lawyer only as fees are earned or expenses incurred.

(d) Upon receiving funds or other property in which a client or third person has an interest, a lawyer shall promptly notify the client or third person. Except as stated in this rule or otherwise permitted by law or by agreement with the client, a lawyer shall promptly deliver to the client or third person any funds or other property that the client or third person is entitled to receive and, upon request by the client or third person, shall promptly render a full accounting regarding such property.

(e) When in the course of representation a lawyer is in possession of property in which two or more persons (one of whom may be the lawyer) claim interests, the property shall be kept separate by the lawyer until the dispute is resolved. The lawyer shall promptly distribute all portions of the property as to which the interests are not in dispute.

COMMENT

[1] A lawyer should hold property of others with the care required of a professional fiduciary. Securities should be kept in a safe deposit box, except when some other form of safekeeping is warranted by special circumstances. All property that is the property of clients or third persons, including prospective clients, must be kept separate from the lawyer's business and personal property and, if monies, in one or more trust accounts. Separate trust accounts may be warranted when administering estate monies or acting in similar fiduciary capacities. A lawyer should maintain on a current basis books and records in accordance with generally accepted accounting practice and comply with any recordkeeping rules established by law or court order. See, e.g., ABA Model Financial Recordkeeping Rule.

[2] While normally it is impermissible to commingle the lawyer's own funds with client funds, paragraph (b) provides that it is permissible when necessary to pay bank service charges on that account. Accurate records must be kept regarding which part of the funds are the lawyer's.

[3] Lawyers often receive funds from which the lawyer's fee will be paid. The lawyer is not required to remit to the client funds that the lawyer reasonably believes represent fees owed. However, a lawyer may not hold funds to coerce a client into accepting the lawyer's contention. The disputed portion of the funds must be kept in a trust account and the lawyer should suggest means for prompt resolution of the dispute, such as arbitration. The undisputed portion of the funds shall be promptly distributed.

[4] Paragraph (e) also recognizes that third parties may have lawful claims against specific funds or other property in a lawyer's custody, such as a client's creditor who has a lien on funds recovered in a personal injury action. A lawyer may have a duty under applicable law to protect such third-party claims against wrongful interference by the client. In such cases, when the third-party claim is not frivolous under applicable law, the lawyer must refuse to surrender the property to the client until the claims are resolved. A lawyer should not unilaterally assume to arbitrate a dispute between the client and the third party, but, when there are substantial grounds for dispute as to the person entitled to the funds, the lawyer may file an action to have a court resolve the dispute.

[5] The obligations of a lawyer under this Rule are independent of those arising from activity other than rendering legal services. For example, a lawyer who serves only as an escrow agent is governed by the applicable law relating to fiduciaries even though the lawyer does not render legal services in the transaction and is not governed by this Rule.

[6] A lawyers' fund for client protection provides a means through the collective efforts of the bar to reimburse persons who have lost money or property as a result of dishonest conduct of a lawyer. Where such a fund has been established, a lawyer must participate where it is mandatory, and, even when it is voluntary, the lawyer should participate.

RULE 1.16: DECLINING OR TERMINATING REPRESENTATION

(a) Except as stated in paragraph (c), a lawyer shall not represent a client or, where representation has commenced, shall withdraw from the representation of a client if:

    (1) the representation will result in violation of the rules of professional conduct or other law;

    (2) the lawyer's physical or mental condition materially impairs the lawyer's ability to represent the client; or

    (3) the lawyer is discharged.

(b) Except as stated in paragraph (c), a lawyer may withdraw from representing a client if:

    (1) withdrawal can be accomplished without material adverse effect on the interests of the client;

    (2) the client persists in a course of action involving the lawyer's services that the lawyer reasonably believes is criminal or fraudulent;

    (3) the client has used the lawyer's services to perpetrate a crime or fraud;

    (4) the client insists upon taking action that the lawyer considers repugnant or with which the lawyer has a fundamental disagreement;

    (5) the client fails substantially to fulfill an obligation to the lawye regarding the lawyer's services and has been given reasonable warning that th lawyer will withdraw unless the obligation is fulfilled;

(6) the representation will result in an unreasonable financial burden on the lawyer or has been rendered unreasonably difficult by the client; or

(7) other good cause for withdrawal exists.

(c) A lawyer must comply with applicable law requiring notice to or permission of a tribunal when terminating a representation. When ordered to do so by a tribunal, a lawyer shall continue representation notwithstanding good cause for terminating the representation.

(d) Upon termination of representation, a lawyer shall take steps to the extent reasonably practicable to protect a client's interests, such as giving reasonable notice to the client, allowing time for employment of other counsel, surrendering papers and property to which the client is entitled and refunding any advance payment of fee or expense that has not been earned or incurred. The lawyer may retain papers relating to the client to the extent permitted by other law.

COMMENT

[1] A lawyer should not accept representation in a matter unless it can be performed competently, promptly, without improper conflict of interest and to completion. Ordinarily, a representation in a matter is completed when the agreed-upon assistance has been concluded. See Rules 1.2(c) and 6.5. See also Rule 1.3, Comment [4].

Mandatory Withdrawal

[2] A lawyer ordinarily must decline or withdraw from representation if the client demands that the lawyer engage in conduct that is illegal or violates the Rules of Professional Conduct or other law. The lawyer is not obliged to decline or withdraw simply because the client suggests such a course of conduct; a client may make such a suggestion in the hope that a lawyer will not be constrained by a professional obligation.

[3] When a lawyer has been appointed to represent a client, withdrawal ordinarily requires approval of the appointing authority. See also Rule 6.2. Similarly, court approval or notice to the court is often required by applicable law before a lawyer withdraws from pending litigation. Difficulty may be encountered if withdrawal is based on the client's demand that the lawyer engage in unprofessional conduct. The court may request an explanation for the withdrawal, while the lawyer may be bound to keep confidential the facts that would constitute such an explanation. The lawyer's statement that professional considerations require termination of the representation ordinarily should be accepted as sufficient. Lawyers should be mindful of their obligations to both clients and the court under Rules 1.6 and 3.3.

Discharge

[4] A client has a right to discharge a lawyer at any time, with or without cause, subject to liability for payment for the lawyer's services. Where future dispute about the withdrawal may be anticipated, it may be advisable to prepare a written statement reciting the circumstances.

[5] Whether a client can discharge appointed counsel may depend on applicable law. A client seeking to do so should be given a full explanation of the consequences. These consequences may include a decision by the appointing authority that appointment of successor counsel is unjustified, thus requiring self-representation by the client.

[6] If the client has severely diminished capacity, the client may lack the legal capacity to discharge the lawyer, and in any event the discharge may be seriously adverse to the client's interests. The lawyer should make special effort to help the client consider the consequences and may take reasonably necessary protective action as provided in Rule 1.14.

- refer to another attorney in writing
- set out SOL- you assume they know more
- written notice-
it's over!   ABA Model Rules of Professional Conduct (2004)

Optional Withdrawal

[7] A lawyer may withdraw from representation in some circumstances. The lawyer has the option to withdraw if it can be accomplished without material adverse effect on the client's interests. Withdrawal is also justified if the client persists in a course of action that the lawyer reasonably believes is criminal or fraudulent, for a lawyer is not required to be associated with such conduct even if the lawyer does not further it. Withdrawal is also permitted if the lawyer's services were misused in the past even if that would materially prejudice the client. The lawyer may also withdraw where the client insists on taking action that the lawyer considers repugnant or with which the lawyer has a fundamental disagreement.

[8] A lawyer may withdraw if the client refuses to abide by the terms of an agreement relating to the representation, such as an agreement concerning fees or court costs or an agreement limiting the objectives of the representation.

Assisting the Client upon Withdrawal

[9] Even if the lawyer has been unfairly discharged by the client, a lawyer must take all reasonable steps to mitigate the consequences to the client. The lawyer may retain papers as security for a fee only to the extent permitted by law. See Rule 1.15.

RULE 1.17: SALE OF LAW PRACTICE

A lawyer or a law firm may sell or purchase a law practice, or an area of law practice, including good will, if the following conditions are satisfied:

(a) The seller ceases to engage in the private practice of law, or in the area of practice that has been sold, [in the geographic area] [in the jurisdiction] (a jurisdiction may elect either version) in which the practice has been conducted;

(b) The entire practice, or the entire area of practice, is sold to one or more lawyers or law firms;

(c) The seller gives written notice to each of the seller's clients regarding:

(1) the proposed sale;

(2) the client's right to retain other counsel or to take possession of the file; and

(3) the fact that the client's consent to the transfer of the client's files will be presumed if the client does not take any action or does not otherwise object within ninety (90) days of receipt of the notice.

If a client cannot be given notice, the representation of that client may be transferred to the purchaser only upon entry of an order so authorizing by a court having jurisdiction. The seller may disclose to the court in camera information relating to the representation only to the extent necessary to obtain an order authorizing the transfer of a file.

(d) The fees charged clients shall not be increased by reason of the sale.

COMMENT

[1] The practice of law is a profession, not merely a business. Clients are not commodities that can be purchased and sold at will. Pursuant to this Rule, when a lawyer or an entire firm ceases to practice, or ceases to practice in an area of law, and other lawyers or firms take over the representation, the selling lawyer or firm may obtain compensation for the reasonable value of the practice as may withdrawing partners of law firms. See Rules 5.4 and 5.6.

Termination of Practice by the Seller

[2] The requirement that all of the private practice, or all of an area of practice, be sold is satisfied if the seller in good faith makes the entire practice, or the area of practice, available for sale to the purchasers. The fact that a number of the seller's clients decide not to be represented by the purchasers but take their matters elsewhere, therefore, does not result in a violation. Return to private practice as a result of an unanticipated change in circumstances does not necessarily result in a violation. For example, a lawyer who has sold the practice to accept an appointment to judicial office does not violate the requirement that the sale be attendant to cessation of practice if the lawyer later resumes private practice upon being defeated in a contested or a retention election for the office or resigns from a judiciary position.

[3] The requirement that the seller cease to engage in the private practice of law does not prohibit employment as a lawyer on the staff of a public agency or a legal services entity that provides legal services to the poor, or as in-house counsel to a business.

[4] The Rule permits a sale of an entire practice attendant upon retirement from the private practice of law within the jurisdiction. Its provisions, therefore, accommodate the lawyer who sells the practice on the occasion of moving to another state. Some states are so large that a move from one locale therein to another is tantamount to leaving the jurisdiction in which the lawyer has engaged in the practice of law. To also accommodate lawyers so situated, states may permit the sale of the practice when the lawyer leaves the geographical area rather than the jurisdiction. The alternative desired should be indicated by selecting one of the two provided for in Rule 1.17(a).

[5] This Rule also permits a lawyer or law firm to sell an area of practice. If an area of practice is sold and the lawyer remains in the active practice of law, the lawyer must cease accepting any matters in the area of practice that has been sold, either as counsel or co-counsel or by assuming joint responsibility for a matter in connection with the division of a fee with another lawyer as would otherwise be permitted by Rule 1.5(e). For example, a lawyer with a substantial number of estate planning matters and a substantial number of probate administration cases may sell the estate planning portion of the practice but remain in the practice of law by concentrating on probate administration; however, that practitioner may not thereafter accept any estate planning matters. Although a lawyer who leaves a jurisdiction or geographical area typically would sell the entire practice, this Rule permits the lawyer to limit the sale to one or more areas of the practice, thereby preserving the lawyer's right to continue practice in the areas of the practice that were not sold.

Sale of Entire Practice or Entire Area of Practice

[6] The Rule requires that the seller's entire practice, or an entire area of practice, be sold. The prohibition against sale of less than an entire practice area protects those clients whose matters are less lucrative and who might find it difficult to secure other counsel if a sale could be limited to substantial fee-generating matters. The purchasers are required to undertake all client matters in the practice or practice area, subject to client consent. This requirement is satisfied, however, even if a purchaser is unable to undertake a particular client matter because of a conflict of interest.

Client Confidences, Consent and Notice

[7] Negotiations between seller and prospective purchaser prior to disclosure of information relating to a specific representation of an identifiable client no more violate the confidentiality provisions of Model Rule 1.6 than do preliminary discussions concerning the possible association of another lawyer or mergers between firms, with respect to which client consent is not required. Providing the purchaser access to client-specific information relating to the representation and to the file, however, requires client consent. The Rule provides that before such information can be disclosed by the seller to the purchaser the client must be given actual written notice of the contemplated sale, including the identity of the purchaser, and must be told

that the decision to consent or make other arrangements must be made within 90 days. If nothing is heard from the client within that time, consent to the sale is presumed.

[8] A lawyer or law firm ceasing to practice cannot be required to remain in practice because some clients cannot be given actual notice of the proposed purchase. Since these clients cannot themselves consent to the purchase or direct any other disposition of their files, the Rule requires an order from a court having jurisdiction authorizing their transfer or other disposition. The Court can be expected to determine whether reasonable efforts to locate the client have been exhausted, and whether the absent client's legitimate interests will be served by authorizing the transfer of the file so that the purchaser may continue the representation. Preservation of client confidences requires that the petition for a court order be considered in camera. (A procedure by which such an order can be obtained needs to be established in jurisdictions in which it presently does not exist.)

[9] All elements of client autonomy, including the client's absolute right to discharge a lawyer and transfer the representation to another, survive the sale of the practice or area of practice.

Fee Arrangements Between Client and Purchaser

[10] The sale may not be financed by increases in fees charged the clients of the practice. Existing arrangements between the seller and the client as to fees and the scope of the work must be honored by the purchaser.

Other Applicable Ethical Standards

[11] Lawyers participating in the sale of a law practice or a practice area are subject to the ethical standards applicable to involving another lawyer in the representation of a client. These include, for example, the seller's obligation to exercise competence in identifying a purchaser qualified to assume the practice and the purchaser's obligation to undertake the representation competently (see Rule 1.1); the obligation to avoid disqualifying conflicts, and to secure the client's informed consent for those conflicts that can be agreed to (see Rule 1.7 regarding conflicts and Rule 1.0(e) for the definition of informed consent); and the obligation to protect information relating to the representation (see Rules 1.6 and 1.9).

[12] If approval of the substitution of the purchasing lawyer for the selling lawyer is required by the rules of any tribunal in which a matter is pending, such approval must be obtained before the matter can be included in the sale (see Rule 1.16).

Applicability of the Rule

[13] This Rule applies to the sale of a law practice of a deceased, disabled or disappeared lawyer. Thus, the seller may be represented by a non-lawyer representative not subject to these Rules. Since, however, no lawyer may participate in a sale of a law practice which does not conform to the requirements of this Rule, the representatives of the seller as well as the purchasing lawyer can be expected to see to it that they are met.

[14] Admission to or retirement from a law partnership or professional association, retirement plans and similar arrangements, and a sale of tangible assets of a law practice, do not constitute a sale or purchase governed by this Rule.

[15] This Rule does not apply to the transfers of legal representation between lawyers when such transfers are unrelated to the sale of a practice or an area of practice.

RULE 1.18: DUTIES TO PROSPECTIVE CLIENT

(a) A person who discusses with a lawyer the possibility of forming a client-lawyer relationship with respect to a matter is a prospective client.

(b) Even when no client-lawyer relationship ensues, a lawyer who has had discussions with a prospective client shall not use or reveal information learned in the consultation, except as Rule 1.9 would permit with respect to information of a former client.

(c) A lawyer subject to paragraph (b) shall not represent a client with interests materially adverse to those of a prospective client in the same or a substantially related matter if the lawyer received information from the prospective client that could be significantly harmful to that person in the matter, except as provided in paragraph (d). If a lawyer is disqualified from representation under this paragraph, no lawyer in a firm with which that lawyer is associated may knowingly undertake or continue representation in such a matter, except as provided in paragraph (d).

(d) When the lawyer has received disqualifying information as defined in paragraph (c), representation is permissible if:

(1) both the affected client and the prospective client have given informed consent, confirmed in writing, or:

(2) the lawyer who received the information took reasonable measures to avoid exposure to more disqualifying information than was reasonably necessary to determine whether to represent the prospective client; and

(i) the disqualified lawyer is timely screened from any participation in the matter and is apportioned no part of the fee therefrom; and

(ii) written notice is promptly given to the prospective client.

COMMENT

[1] Prospective clients, like clients, may disclose information to a lawyer, place documents or other property in the lawyer's custody, or rely on the lawyer's advice. A lawyer's discussions with a prospective client usually are limited in time and depth and leave both the prospective client and the lawyer free (and sometimes required) to proceed no further. Hence, prospective clients should receive some but not all of the protection afforded clients.

[2] Not all persons who communicate information to a lawyer are entitled to protection under this Rule. A person who communicates information unilaterally to a lawyer, without any reasonable expectation that the lawyer is willing to discuss the possibility of forming a client-lawyer relationship, is not a "prospective client" within the meaning of paragraph (a).

[3] It is often necessary for a prospective client to reveal information to the lawyer during an initial consultation prior to the decision about formation of a client-lawyer relationship. The lawyer often must learn such information to determine whether there is a conflict of interest with an existing client and whether the matter is one that the lawyer is willing to undertake. Paragraph (b) prohibits the lawyer from using or revealing that information, except as permitted by Rule 1.9, even if the client or lawyer decides not to proceed with the representation. The duty exists regardless of how brief the initial conference may be.

[4] In order to avoid acquiring disqualifying information from a prospective client, a lawyer considering whether or not to undertake a new matter should limit the initial interview to only such information as reasonably appears necessary for that purpose. Where the information indicates that a conflict of interest or other reason for non-representation exists, the lawyer should so inform the prospective client or decline the representation. If the prospective client wishes to retain the lawyer, and if consent is possible under Rule 1.7, then consent from all affected present or former clients must be obtained before accepting the representation.

[5] A lawyer may condition conversations with a prospective client on the person's informed consent that no information disclosed during the consultation will prohibit the lawyer from representing a different client in the matter. See Rule 1.0(e) for the definition of informed

consent. If the agreement expressly so provides, the prospective client may also consent to the lawyer's subsequent use of information received from the prospective client.

[6] Even in the absence of an agreement, under paragraph (c), the lawyer is not prohibited from representing a client with interests adverse to those of the prospective client in the same or a substantially related matter unless the lawyer has received from the prospective client information that could be significantly harmful if used in the matter.

[7] Under paragraph (c), the prohibition in this Rule is imputed to other lawyers as provided in Rule 1.10, but, under paragraph (d)(1), imputation may be avoided if the lawyer obtains the informed consent, confirmed in writing, of both the prospective and affected clients. In the alternative, imputation may be avoided if the conditions of paragraph (d)(2) are met and all disqualified lawyers are timely screened and written notice is promptly given to the prospective client. See Rule 1.0(k) (requirements for screening procedures). Paragraph (d)(2)(i) does not prohibit the screened lawyer from receiving a salary or partnership share established by prior independent agreement, but that lawyer may not receive compensation directly related to the matter in which the lawyer is disqualified.

[8] Notice, including a general description of the subject matter about which the lawyer was consulted, and of the screening procedures employed, generally should be given as soon as practicable after the need for screening becomes apparent.

[9] For the duty of competence of a lawyer who gives assistance on the merits of a matter to a prospective client, see Rule 1.1. For a lawyer's duties when a prospective client entrusts valuables or papers to the lawyer's care, see Rule 1.15.

COUNSELOR

RULE 2.1: ADVISOR

In representing a client, a lawyer **shall** exercise independent professional judgment and render candid advice. In rendering advice, a lawyer **may** refer not only to law but to other considerations such as moral, economic, social and political factors, that may be relevant to the client's situation. *optional to consider*

Δ dr found tumor, not disclose, should tell Δ → Δ "consents" to telling Π

COMMENT

Scope of Advice

[1] A client is entitled to straightforward advice expressing the lawyer's honest assessment. Legal advice often involves unpleasant facts and alternatives that a client may be disinclined to confront. In presenting advice, a lawyer endeavors to sustain the client's morale and may put advice in as acceptable a form as honesty permits. However, a lawyer should not be deterred from giving candid advice by the prospect that the advice will be unpalatable to the client.

[2] Advice couched in narrow legal terms may be of little value to a client, especially where practical considerations, such as cost or effects on other people, are predominant. Purely technical legal advice, therefore, can sometimes be inadequate. It is proper for a lawyer to refer to relevant moral and ethical considerations in giving advice. Although a lawyer is not a moral advisor as such, moral and ethical considerations impinge upon most legal questions and may decisively influence how the law will be applied.

[3] A client may expressly or impliedly ask the lawyer for purely technical advice. When such a request is made by a client experienced in legal matters, the lawyer may accept it at face value. When such a request is made by a client inexperienced in legal matters, however, the lawyer's responsibility as advisor may include indicating that more may be involved than strictly legal considerations.

[4] Matters that go beyond strictly legal questions may also be in the domain of another profession. Family matters can involve problems within the professional competence of psychiatry, clinical psychology or social work; business matters can involve problems within the competence of the accounting profession or of financial specialists. Where consultation with a professional in another field is itself something a competent lawyer would recommend, the lawyer should make such a recommendation. At the same time, a lawyer's advice at its best often consists of recommending a course of action in the face of conflicting recommendations of experts.

Offering Advice

[5] In general, a lawyer is not expected to give advice until asked by the client. However, when a lawyer knows that a client proposes a course of action that is likely to result in substantial adverse legal consequences to the client, the lawyer's duty to the client under Rule 1.4 may require that the lawyer offer advice if the client's course of action is related to the representation. Similarly, when a matter is likely to involve litigation, it may be necessary under Rule 1.4 to inform the client of forms of dispute resolution that might constitute reasonable alternatives to litigation. A lawyer ordinarily has no duty to initiate investigation of a client's affairs or to give advice that the client has indicated is unwanted, but a lawyer may initiate advice to a client when doing so appears to be in the client's interest.

RULE 2.2 (Deleted)*

RULE 2.3: EVALUATION FOR USE BY THIRD PERSONS

(a) A lawyer may provide an evaluation of a matter affecting a client for the use of someone other than the client if the lawyer reasonably believes that making the evaluation is compatible with other aspects of the lawyer's relationship with the client.

(b) When the lawyer knows or reasonably should know that the evaluation is likely to affect the client's interests materially and adversely, the lawyer shall not provide the evaluation unless the client gives informed consent.

(c) Except as disclosure is authorized in connection with a report of an evaluation, information relating to the evaluation is otherwise protected by Rule 1.6.

COMMENT

Definition

[1] An evaluation may be performed at the client's direction or when impliedly authorized in order to carry out the representation. See Rule 1.2. Such an evaluation may be for the primary purpose of establishing information for the benefit of third parties; for example, an opinion concerning the title of property rendered at the behest of a vendor for the information of a prospective purchaser, or at the behest of a borrower for the information of a prospective lender. In some situations, the evaluation may be required by a government agency; for example, an opinion concerning the legality of the securities registered for sale under the securities laws. In other instances, the evaluation may be required by a third person, such as a purchaser of a business.

[2] A legal evaluation should be distinguished from an investigation of a person with whom the lawyer does not have a client-lawyer relationship. For example, a lawyer retained by a purchaser to analyze a vendor's title to property does not have a client-lawyer relationship with

---

* Author's Note: Rule 2.2, Lawyer as Intermediary, was deleted in 2002. Special issues of common representation are dealt with in Rule 1.7, Comments 29-33.

the vendor. So also, an investigation into a person's affairs by a government lawyer, or by special counsel by a government lawyer, or by special counsel employed by the government, is not an evaluation as that term is used in this Rule. The question is whether the lawyer is retained by the person whose affairs are being examined. When the lawyer is retained by that person, the general rules concerning loyalty to client and preservation of confidences apply, which is not the case if the lawyer is retained by someone else. For this reason, it is essential to identify the person by whom the lawyer is retained. This should be made clear not only to the person under examination, but also to others to whom the results are to be made available.

Duties Owed to Third Person and Client

[3] When the evaluation is intended for the information or use of a third person, a legal duty to that person may or may not arise. That legal question is beyond the scope of this Rule. However, since such an evaluation involves a departure from the normal client-lawyer relationship, careful analysis of the situation is required. The lawyer must be satisfied as a matter of professional judgment that making the evaluation is compatible with other functions undertaken in behalf of the client. For example, if the lawyer is acting as advocate in defending the client against charges of fraud, it would normally be incompatible with that responsibility for the lawyer to perform an evaluation for others concerning the same or a related transaction. Assuming no such impediment is apparent, however, the lawyer should advise the client of the implications of the evaluation, particularly the lawyer's responsibilities to third persons and the duty to disseminate the findings.

Access to and Disclosure of Information

[4] The quality of an evaluation depends on the freedom and extent of the investigation upon which it is based. Ordinarily a lawyer should have whatever latitude of investigation seems necessary as a matter of professional judgment. Under some circumstances, however, the terms of the evaluation may be limited. For example, certain issues or sources may be categorically excluded, or the scope of search may be limited by time constraints or the noncooperation of persons having relevant information. Any such limitations that are material to the evaluation should be described in the report. If after a lawyer has commenced an evaluation, the client refuses to comply with the terms upon which it was understood the evaluation was to have been made, the lawyer's obligations are determined by law, having reference to the terms of the client's agreement and the surrounding circumstances. In no circumstances is the lawyer permitted to knowingly make a false statement of material fact or law in providing an evaluation under this Rule. See Rule 4.1.

Obtaining Client's Informed Consent

[5] Information relating to an evaluation is protected by Rule 1.6. In many situations, providing an evaluation to a third party poses no significant risk to the client; thus, the lawyer may be impliedly authorized to disclose information to carry out the representation. See Rule 1.6(a). Where, however, it is reasonably likely that providing the evaluation will affect the client's interests materially and adversely, the lawyer must first obtain the client's consent after the client has been adequately informed concerning the important possible effects on the client's interests. See Rules 1.6(a) and 1.0(e).

Financial Auditors' Requests for Information

[6] When a question concerning the legal situation of a client arises at the instance of the client's financial auditor and the question is referred to the lawyer, the lawyer's response may be made in accordance with procedures recognized in the legal profession. Such a procedure is set forth in the American Bar Association Statement of Policy Regarding Lawyers' Responses to Auditors' Requests for Information, adopted in 1975.

RULE 2.4: LAWYER SERVING AS THIRD-PARTY NEUTRAL

(mediator)/Arbitration

(a) A lawyer serves as a third-party neutral when the lawyer assists two or more persons who are not clients of the lawyer to reach a resolution of a dispute or other matter that has arisen between them. Service as a third-party neutral may include service as an arbitrator, a mediator or in such other capacity as will enable the lawyer to assist the parties to resolve the matter.

(b) A lawyer serving as a third-party neutral shall inform unrepresented parties that the lawyer is not representing them. When the lawyer knows or reasonably should know that a party does not understand the lawyer's role in the matter, the lawyer shall explain the difference between the lawyer's role as a third-party neutral and a lawyer's role as one who represents a client.

COMMENT

[1] Alternative dispute resolution has become a substantial part of the civil justice system. Aside from representing clients in dispute-resolution processes, lawyers often serve as third-party neutrals. A third-party neutral is a person, such as a mediator, arbitrator, conciliator or evaluator, who assists the parties, represented or unrepresented, in the resolution of a dispute or in the arrangement of a transaction. Whether a third-party neutral serves primarily as a facilitator, evaluator or decisionmaker depends on the particular process that is either selected by the parties or mandated by a court.

[2] The role of a third-party neutral is not unique to lawyers, although, in some court-connected contexts, only lawyers are allowed to serve in this role or to handle certain types of cases. In performing this role, the lawyer may be subject to court rules or other law that apply either to third-party neutrals generally or to lawyers serving as third-party neutrals. Lawyer-neutrals may also be subject to various codes of ethics, such as the Code of Ethics for Arbitration in Commercial Disputes prepared by a joint committee of the American Bar Association and the American Arbitration Association or the Model Standards of Conduct for Mediators jointly prepared by the American Bar Association, the American Arbitration Association and the Society of Professionals in Dispute Resolution.

[3] Unlike nonlawyers who serve as third-party neutrals, lawyers serving in this role may experience unique problems as a result of differences between the role of a third-party neutral and a lawyer's service as a client representative. The potential for confusion is significant when the parties are unrepresented in the process. Thus, paragraph (b) requires a lawyer-neutral to inform unrepresented parties that the lawyer is not representing them. For some parties, particularly parties who frequently use dispute-resolution processes, this information will be sufficient. For others, particularly those who are using the process for the first time, more information will be required. Where appropriate, the lawyer should inform unrepresented parties of the important differences between the lawyer's role as third-party neutral and a lawyer's role as a client representative, including the inapplicability of the attorney-client evidentiary privilege. The extent of disclosure required under this paragraph will depend on the particular parties involved and the subject matter of the proceeding, as well as the particular features of the dispute-resolution process selected.

[4] A lawyer who serves as a third-party neutral subsequently may be asked to serve as a lawyer representing a client in the same matter. The conflicts of interest that arise for both the individual lawyer and the lawyer's law firm are addressed in Rule 1.12.

[5] Lawyers who represent clients in alternative dispute-resolution processes are governed by the Rules of Professional Conduct. When the dispute-resolution process takes place before a tribunal, as in binding arbitration (see Rule 1.0(m)), the lawyer's duty of candor is

governed by Rule 3.3. Otherwise, the lawyer's duty of candor toward both the third-party neutral and other parties is governed by Rule 4.1.

ADVOCATE

RULE 3.1: MERITORIOUS CLAIMS AND CONTENTIONS

A lawyer shall not bring or defend a proceeding, or assert or controvert an issue therein, unless there is a basis in law and fact for doing so that is not frivolous, which includes a good faith argument for an extension, modification or reversal of existing law. A lawyer for the defendant in a criminal proceeding, or the respondent in a proceeding that could result in incarceration, may nevertheless so defend the proceeding as to require that every element of the case be established.

COMMENT

[1] The advocate has a duty to use legal procedure for the fullest benefit of the client's cause, but also a duty not to abuse legal procedure. The law, both procedural and substantive, establishes the limits within which an advocate may proceed. However, the law is not always clear and never is static. Accordingly, in determining the proper scope of advocacy, account must be taken of the law's ambiguities and potential for change.

[2] The filing of an action or defense or similar action taken for a client is not frivolous merely because the facts have not first been fully substantiated or because the lawyer expects to develop vital evidence only by discovery. What is required of lawyers, however, is that they inform themselves about the facts of their clients' cases and the applicable law and determine that they can make good faith arguments in support of their clients' positions. Such action is not frivolous even though the lawyer believes that the client's position ultimately will not prevail. The action is frivolous, however, if the lawyer is unable either to make a good faith argument on the merits of the action taken or to support the action taken by a good faith argument for an extension, modification or reversal of existing law.

[3] The lawyer's obligations under this Rule are subordinate to federal or state constitutional law that entitles a defendant in a criminal matter to the assistance of counsel in presenting a claim or contention that otherwise would be prohibited by this Rule.

RULE 3.2: EXPEDITING LITIGATION

A lawyer shall make reasonable efforts to expedite litigation consistent with the interests of the client.

COMMENT

[1] Dilatory practices bring the administration of justice into disrepute. Although there will be occasions when a lawyer may properly seek a postponement for personal reasons, it is not proper for a lawyer to routinely fail to expedite litigation solely for the convenience of the advocates. Nor will a failure to expedite be reasonable if done for the purpose of frustrating an opposing party's attempt to obtain rightful redress or repose. It is not a justification that similar conduct is often tolerated by the bench and bar. The question is whether a competent lawyer acting in good faith would regard the course of action as having some substantial purpose other than delay. Realizing financial or other benefit from otherwise improper delay in litigation is not a legitimate interest of the client.

also look @ 8.4

Client Perjury (b)(3)

RULE 3.3: CANDOR TOWARD THE TRIBUNAL

C7 **(a) A lawyer shall not knowingly:**

(1) make a false statement of fact or law to a tribunal or fail to correct a false statement of material fact or law previously made to the tribunal by the lawyer;

(2) fail to disclose to the tribunal legal authority in the controlling jurisdiction known to the lawyer to be directly adverse to the position of the client and not disclosed by opposing counsel; or

(3) offer evidence that the lawyer knows to be false. If a lawyer, the lawyer's client, or a witness called by the lawyer, has offered material evidence and the lawyer comes to know of its falsity, the lawyer shall take reasonable remedial measures, including, if necessary, disclosure to the tribunal. A lawyer may refuse to offer evidence, other than the testimony of a defendant in a criminal matter, that the lawyer reasonably believes is false. *) can omit except crim.△*

(b) A lawyer who represents a client in an adjudicative proceeding and who knows that a person intends to engage, is engaging or has engaged in criminal or fraudulent conduct related to the proceeding shall take reasonable remedial measures, including, if necessary, disclosure to the tribunal.

(c) The duties stated in paragraphs (a) and (b) continue to the conclusion of the proceeding, and apply even if compliance requires disclosure of information otherwise protected by Rule 1.6. *3.3 trumps 1.6.*

(d) In an ex parte proceeding *the side presents* **, a lawyer shall inform the tribunal of all material facts known to the lawyer that will enable the tribunal to make an informed decision, whether or not the facts are adverse.**

COMMENT

Know v. reas believe / may act except. crim. case / C10

[1] This Rule governs the conduct of a lawyer who is representing a client in the proceedings of a tribunal. See Rule 1.0(m) for the definition of "tribunal." It also applies when the lawyer is representing a client in an ancillary proceeding conducted pursuant to the tribunal's adjudicative authority, such as a deposition. Thus, for example, paragraph (a)(3) requires a lawyer to take reasonable remedial measures if the lawyer comes to know that a client who is testifying in a deposition has offered evidence that is false.

[2] This Rule sets forth the special duties of lawyers as officers of the court to avoid conduct that undermines the integrity of the adjudicative process. A lawyer acting as an advocate in an adjudicative proceeding has an obligation to present the client's case with persuasive force. Performance of that duty while maintaining confidences of the client, however, is qualified by the advocate's duty of candor to the tribunal. Consequently, although a lawyer in an adversary proceeding is not required to present an impartial exposition of the law or to vouch for the evidence submitted in a cause, the lawyer must not allow the tribunal to be misled by false statements of law or fact or evidence that the lawyer knows to be false.

Representations by a Lawyer

[3] An advocate is responsible for pleadings and other documents prepared for litigation, but is usually not required to have personal knowledge of matters asserted therein, for litigation documents ordinarily present assertions by the client, or by someone on the client's behalf, and not assertions by the lawyer. Compare Rule 3.1. However, an assertion purporting to be on the lawyer's own knowledge, as in an affidavit by the lawyer or in a statement in open court, may properly be made only when the lawyer knows the assertion is true or believes it to be true on the

basis of a reasonably diligent inquiry. There are circumstances where failure to make a disclosure is the equivalent of an affirmative misrepresentation. The obligation prescribed in Rule 1.2(d) not to counsel a client to commit or assist the client in committing a fraud applies in litigation. Regarding compliance with Rule 1.2(d), see the Comment to that Rule. See also the Comment to Rule 8.4(b).

Legal Argument

[4] Legal argument based on a knowingly false representation of law constitutes dishonesty toward the tribunal. A lawyer is not required to make a disinterested exposition of the law, but must recognize the existence of pertinent legal authorities. Furthermore, as stated in paragraph (a)(2), an advocate has a duty to disclose directly adverse authority in the controlling jurisdiction that has not been disclosed by the opposing party. The underlying concept is that legal argument is a discussion seeking to determine the legal premises properly applicable to the case.

Offering Evidence

[5] Paragraph (a)(3) requires that the lawyer refuse to offer evidence that the lawyer knows to be false, regardless of the client's wishes. This duty is premised on the lawyer's obligation as an officer of the court to prevent the trier of fact from being misled by false evidence. A lawyer does not violate this Rule if the lawyer offers the evidence for the purpose of establishing its falsity.

[6] If a lawyer knows that the client intends to testify falsely or wants the lawyer to introduce false evidence, the lawyer should seek to persuade the client that the evidence should not be offered. If the persuasion is ineffective and the lawyer continues to represent the client, the lawyer must refuse to offer the false evidence. If only a portion of a witness's testimony will be false, the lawyer may call the witness to testify but may not elicit or otherwise permit the witness to present the testimony that the lawyer knows is false.

[7] The duties stated in paragraphs (a) and (b) apply to all lawyers, including defense counsel in criminal cases. In some jurisdictions, however, courts have required counsel to present the accused as a witness or to give a narrative statement if the accused so desires, even if counsel knows that the testimony or statement will be false. The obligation of the advocate under the Rules of Professional Conduct is subordinate to such requirements. See also Comment [9].

[8] The prohibition against offering false evidence only applies if the lawyer knows that the evidence is false. A lawyer's reasonable belief that evidence is false does not preclude its presentation to the trier of fact. A lawyer's knowledge that evidence is false, however, can be inferred from the circumstances. See Rule 1.0(f). Thus, although a lawyer should resolve doubts about the veracity of testimony or other evidence in favor of the client, the lawyer cannot ignore an obvious falsehood. *resolve doubt in client's favor*

[9] Although paragraph (a)(3) only prohibits a lawyer from offering evidence the lawyer knows to be false, it permits the lawyer to refuse to offer testimony or other proof that the lawyer reasonably believes is false. Offering such proof may reflect adversely on the lawyer's ability to discriminate in the quality of evidence and thus impair the lawyer's effectiveness as an advocate. Because of the special protections historically provided criminal defendants, however, this Rule does not permit a lawyer to refuse to offer the testimony of such a client where the lawyer reasonably believes but does not know that the testimony will be false. Unless the lawyer knows the testimony will be false, the lawyer must honor the client's decision to testify. See also Comment [7].

Remedial Measures

[10] Having offered material evidence in the belief that it was true, a lawyer may subsequently come to know that the evidence is false. Or, a lawyer may be surprised when the lawyer's client, or another witness called by the lawyer, offers testimony the lawyer knows to be false, either during the lawyer's direct examination or in response to cross-examination by the

opposing lawyer. In such situations or if the lawyer knows of the falsity of testimony elicited from the client during a deposition, the lawyer must take reasonable remedial measures. In such situations, the advocate's proper course is to remonstrate with the client confidentially, advise the client of the lawyer's duty of candor to the tribunal and seek the client's cooperation with respect to the withdrawal or correction of the false statements or evidence. If that fails, the advocate must take further remedial action. If withdrawal from the representation is not permitted or will not undo the effect of the false evidence, the advocate must make such disclosure to the tribunal as is reasonably necessary to remedy the situation, even if doing so requires the lawyer to reveal information that otherwise would be protected by Rule 1.6. It is for the tribunal then to determine what should be done—making a statement about the matter to the trier of fact, ordering a mistrial or perhaps nothing.

[11] The disclosure of a client's false testimony can result in grave consequences to the client, including not only a sense of betrayal but also loss of the case and perhaps a prosecution for perjury. But the alternative is that the lawyer cooperate in deceiving the court, thereby subverting the truth-finding process which the adversary system is designed to implement. See Rule 1.2(d). Furthermore, unless it is clearly understood that the lawyer will act upon the duty to disclose the existence of false evidence, the client can simply reject the lawyer's advice to reveal the false evidence and insist that the lawyer keep silent. Thus the client could in effect coerce the lawyer into being a party to fraud on the court.

Preserving Integrity of Adjudicative Process

[12] Lawyers have a special obligation to protect a tribunal against criminal or fraudulent conduct that undermines the integrity of the adjudicative process, such as bribing, intimidating or otherwise unlawfully communicating with a witness, juror, court official or other participant in the proceeding, unlawfully destroying or concealing documents or other evidence or failing to disclose information to the tribunal when required by law to do so. Thus, paragraph (b) requires a lawyer to take reasonable remedial measures, including disclosure if necessary, whenever the lawyer knows that a person, including the lawyer's client, intends to engage, is engaging or has engaged in criminal or fraudulent conduct related to the proceeding.

Duration of Obligation

[13] A practical time limit on the obligation to rectify false evidence or false statements of law and fact has to be established. The conclusion of the proceeding is a reasonably definite point for the termination of the obligation. A proceeding has concluded within the meaning of this Rule when a final judgment in the proceeding has been affirmed on appeal or the time for review has passed.

Ex Parte Proceedings

[14] Ordinarily, an advocate has the limited responsibility of presenting one side of the matters that a tribunal should consider in reaching a decision; the conflicting position is expected to be presented by the opposing party. However, in any ex parte proceeding, such as an application for a temporary restraining order, there is no balance of presentation by opposing advocates. The object of an ex parte proceeding is nevertheless to yield a substantially just result. The judge has an affirmative responsibility to accord the absent party just consideration. The lawyer for the represented party has the correlative duty to make disclosures of material facts known to the lawyer and that the lawyer reasonably believes are necessary to an informed decision.

Withdrawal

[15] Normally, a lawyer's compliance with the duty of candor imposed by this Rule does not require that the lawyer withdraw from the representation of a client whose interests will be or have been adversely affected by the lawyer's disclosure. The lawyer may, however, be required by Rule 1.16(a) to seek permission of the tribunal to withdraw if the lawyer's compliance with

this Rule's duty of candor results in such an extreme deterioration of the client-lawyer relationship that the lawyer can no longer competently represent the client. Also see Rule 1.16(b) for the circumstances in which a lawyer will be permitted to seek a tribunal's permission to withdraw. In connection with a request for permission to withdraw that is premised on a client's misconduct, a lawyer may reveal information relating to the representation only to the extent reasonably necessary to comply with this Rule or as otherwise permitted by Rule 1.6.

RULE 3.4: FAIRNESS TO OPPOSING PARTY AND COUNSEL

A lawyer shall not:

(a) unlawfully obstruct another party's access to evidence or unlawfully alter, destroy or conceal a document or other material having potential evidentiary value. A lawyer shall not counsel or assist another person to do any such act;

(b) falsify evidence, counsel or assist a witness to testify falsely, or offer an inducement to a witness that is prohibited by law;

(c) knowingly disobey an obligation under the rules of a tribunal, except for an open refusal based on an assertion that no valid obligation exists;

(d) in pretrial procedure, make a frivolous discovery request or fail to make reasonably diligent effort to comply with a legally proper discovery request by an opposing party;

(e) in trial, allude to any matter that the lawyer does not reasonably believe is relevant or that will not be supported by admissible evidence, assert personal knowledge of facts in issue except when testifying as a witness, or state a personal opinion as to the justness of a cause, the credibility of a witness, the culpability of a civil litigant or the guilt or innocence of an accused; or

(f) request a person other than a client to refrain from voluntarily giving relevant information to another party unless:

(1) the person is a relative or an employee or other agent of a client; and

(2) the lawyer reasonably believes that the person's interests will not be adversely affected by refraining from giving such information.

COMMENT

[1] The procedure of the adversary system contemplates that the evidence in a case is to be marshalled competitively by the contending parties. Fair competition in the adversary system is secured by prohibitions against destruction or concealment of evidence, improperly influencing witnesses, obstructive tactics in discovery procedure, and the like.

[2] Documents and other items of evidence are often essential to establish a claim or defense. Subject to evidentiary privileges, the right of an opposing party, including the government, to obtain evidence through discovery or subpoena is an important procedural right. The exercise of that right can be frustrated if relevant material is altered, concealed or destroyed. Applicable law in many jurisdictions makes it an offense to destroy material for purpose of impairing its availability in a pending proceeding or one whose commencement can be foreseen. Falsifying evidence is also generally a criminal offense. Paragraph (a) applies to evidentiary material generally, including computerized information. Applicable law may permit a lawyer to take temporary possession of physical evidence of client crimes for the purpose of conducting a limited examination that will not alter or destroy material characteristics of the evidence. In such a case, applicable law may require the lawyer to turn the evidence over to the police or other prosecuting authority, depending on the circumstances.

[3] With regard to paragraph (b), it is not improper to pay a witness's expenses or to compensate an expert witness on terms permitted by law. The common law rule in most jurisdictions is that it is improper to pay an occurrence witness any fee for testifying and that it is improper to pay an expert witness a contingent fee.

[4] Paragraph (f) permits a lawyer to advise employees of a client to refrain from giving information to another party, for the employees may identify their interests with those of the client. See also Rule 4.2.

RULE 3.5: IMPARTIALITY AND DECORUM OF THE TRIBUNAL

A lawyer shall not:

(a) seek to influence a judge, juror, prospective juror or other official by means prohibited by law;

(b) communicate ex parte with such a person during the proceeding unless authorized to do so by law or court order;

(c) communicate with a juror or prospective juror after discharge of the jury if:

(1) the communication is prohibited by law or court order;

(2) the juror has made known to the lawyer a desire not to communicate; or

(3) the communication involves misrepresentation, coercion, duress or harassment; or

(d) engage in conduct intended to disrupt a tribunal.

COMMENT

[1] Many forms of improper influence upon a tribunal are proscribed by criminal law. Others are specified in the ABA Model Code of Judicial Conduct, with which an advocate should be familiar. A lawyer is required to avoid contributing to a violation of such provisions.

[2] During a proceeding a lawyer may not communicate ex parte with persons serving in an official capacity in the proceeding, such as judges, masters or jurors, unless authorized to do so by law or court order.

[3] A lawyer may on occasion want to communicate with a juror or prospective juror after the jury has been discharged. The lawyer may do so unless the communication is prohibited by law or a court order but must respect the desire of the juror not to talk with the lawyer. The lawyer may not engage in improper conduct during the communication.

[4] The advocate's function is to present evidence and argument so that the cause may be decided according to law. Refraining from abusive or obstreperous conduct is a corollary of the advocate's right to speak on behalf of litigants. A lawyer may stand firm against abuse by a judge but should avoid reciprocation; the judge's default is no justification for similar dereliction by an advocate. An advocate can present the cause, protect the record for subsequent review and preserve professional integrity by patient firmness no less effectively than by belligerence or theatrics.

[5] The duty to refrain from disruptive conduct applies to any proceeding of a tribunal, including a deposition. See Rule 1.0(m).

RULE 3.6: TRIAL PUBLICITY

(a) A lawyer who is participating or has participated in the investigation or litigation of a matter shall not make an extrajudicial statement that the lawyer knows or reasonably should know will be disseminated by means of public communication and will

have a substantial likelihood of materially prejudicing an adjudicative proceeding in the matter.

(b) Notwithstanding paragraph (a), a lawyer may state:

(1) the claim, offense or defense involved and, except when prohibited by law, the identity of the persons involved;

(2) information contained in a public record;

(3) that an investigation of a matter is in progress;

(4) the scheduling or result of any step in litigation;

(5) a request for assistance in obtaining evidence and information necessary thereto;

(6) a warning of danger concerning the behavior of a person involved, when there is reason to believe that there exists the likelihood of substantial harm to an individual or to the public interest; and

(7) in a criminal case, in addition to subparagraphs (1) through (6):

(i) the identity, residence, occupation and family status of the accused;

(ii) if the accused has not been apprehended, information necessary to aid in apprehension of that person;

(iii) the fact, time and place of arrest; and

(iv) the identity of investigating and arresting officers or agencies and the length of the investigation.

(c) Notwithstanding paragraph (a), a lawyer may make a statement that a reasonable lawyer would believe is required to protect a client from the substantial undue prejudicial effect of recent publicity not initiated by the lawyer or the lawyer's client. A statement made pursuant to this paragraph shall be limited to such information as is necessary to mitigate the recent adverse publicity.

(d) No lawyer associated in a firm or government agency with a lawyer subject to paragraph (a) shall make a statement prohibited by paragraph (a).

COMMENT

[1] It is difficult to strike a balance between protecting the right to a fair trial and safeguarding the right of free expression. Preserving the right to a fair trial necessarily entails some curtailment of the information that may be disseminated about a party prior to trial, particularly where trial by jury is involved. If there were no such limits, the result would be the practical nullification of the protective effect of the rules of forensic decorum and the exclusionary rules of evidence. On the other hand, there are vital social interests served by the free dissemination of information about events having legal consequences and about legal proceedings themselves. The public has a right to know about threats to its safety and measures aimed at assuring its security. It also has a legitimate interest in the conduct of judicial proceedings, particularly in matters of general public concern. Furthermore, the subject matter of legal proceedings is often of direct significance in debate and deliberation over questions of public policy.

[2] Special rules of confidentiality may validly govern proceedings in juvenile, domestic relations and mental disability proceedings, and perhaps other types of litigation. Rule 3.4(c) requires compliance with such rules.

[3] The Rule sets forth a basic general prohibition against a lawyer's making statements that the lawyer knows or should know will have a substantial likelihood of materially prejudicing

an adjudicative proceeding. Recognizing that the public value of informed commentary is great and the likelihood of prejudice to a proceeding by the commentary of a lawyer who is not involved in the proceeding is small, the rule applies only to lawyers who are, or who have been involved in the investigation or litigation of a case, and their associates.

[4] Paragraph (b) identifies specific matters about which a lawyer's statements would not ordinarily be considered to present a substantial likelihood of material prejudice, and should not in any event be considered prohibited by the general prohibition of paragraph (a). Paragraph (b) is not intended to be an exhaustive listing of the subjects upon which a lawyer may make a statement, but statements on other matters may be subject to paragraph (a).

[5] There are, on the other hand, certain subjects that are more likely than not to have a material prejudicial effect on a proceeding, particularly when they refer to a civil matter triable to a jury, a criminal matter, or any other proceeding that could result in incarceration. These subjects relate to:

(1) the character, credibility, reputation or criminal record of a party, suspect in a criminal investigation or witness, or the identity of a witness, or the expected testimony of a party or witness;

(2) in a criminal case or proceeding that could result in incarceration, the possibility of a plea of guilty to the offense or the existence or contents of any confession, admission, or statement given by a defendant or suspect or that person's refusal or failure to make a statement;

(3) the performance or results of any examination or test or the refusal or failure of a person to submit to an examination or test, or the identity or nature of physical evidence expected to be presented;

(4) any opinion as to the guilt or innocence of a defendant or suspect in a criminal case or proceeding that could result in incarceration;

(5) information that the lawyer knows or reasonably should know is likely to be inadmissible as evidence in a trial and that would, if disclosed, create a substantial risk of prejudicing an impartial trial; or

(6) the fact that a defendant has been charged with a crime, unless there is included therein a statement explaining that the charge is merely an accusation and that the defendant is presumed innocent until and unless proven guilty.

[6] Another relevant factor in determining prejudice is the nature of the proceeding involved. Criminal jury trials will be most sensitive to extrajudicial speech. Civil trials may be less sensitive. Non-jury hearings and arbitration proceedings may be even less affected. The Rule will still place limitations on prejudicial comments in these cases, but the likelihood of prejudice may be different depending on the type of proceeding.

[7] Finally, extrajudicial statements that might otherwise raise a question under this Rule may be permissible when they are made in response to statements made publicly by another party, another party's lawyer, or third persons, where a reasonable lawyer would believe a public response is required in order to avoid prejudice to the lawyer's client. When prejudicial statements have been publicly made by others, responsive statements may have the salutary effect of lessening any resulting adverse impact on the adjudicative proceeding. Such responsive statements should be limited to contain only such information as is necessary to mitigate undue prejudice created by the statements made by others.

[8] See Rule 3.8(f) for additional duties of prosecutors in connection with extrajudicial statements about criminal proceedings.

RULE 3.7: LAWYER AS WITNESS

(a) A lawyer shall not act as advocate at a trial in which the lawyer is likely to be a necessary witness unless:

(1) the testimony relates to an uncontested issue;

(2) the testimony relates to the nature and value of legal services rendered in the case; or

(3) disqualification of the lawyer would work substantial hardship on the client.

(b) A lawyer may act as advocate in a trial in which another lawyer in the lawyer's firm is likely to be called as a witness unless precluded from doing so by Rule 1.7 or Rule 1.9.

COMMENT

[1] Combining the roles of advocate and witness can prejudice the tribunal and the opposing party and can also involve a conflict of interest between the lawyer and client.

Advocate-Witness Rule

[2] The tribunal has proper objection when the trier of fact may be confused or misled by a lawyer serving as both advocate and witness. The opposing party has proper objection where the combination of roles may prejudice that party's rights in the litigation. A witness is required to testify on the basis of personal knowledge, while an advocate is expected to explain and comment on evidence given by others. It may not be clear whether a statement by an advocate-witness should be taken as proof or as an analysis of the proof.

[3] To protect the tribunal, paragraph (a) prohibits a lawyer from simultaneously serving as advocate and necessary witness except in those circumstances specified in paragraphs (a)(1) through (a)(3). Paragraph (a)(1) recognizes that if the testimony will be uncontested, the ambiguities in the dual role are purely theoretical. Paragraph (a)(2) recognizes that where the testimony concerns the extent and value of legal services rendered in the action in which the testimony is offered, permitting the lawyers to testify avoids the need for a second trial with new counsel to resolve that issue. Moreover, in such a situation the judge has firsthand knowledge of the matter in issue; hence, there is less dependence on the adversary process to test the credibility of the testimony.

[4] Apart from these two exceptions, paragraph (a)(3) recognizes that a balancing is required between the interests of the client and those of the tribunal and the opposing party. Whether the tribunal is likely to be misled or the opposing party is likely to suffer prejudice depends on the nature of the case, the importance and probable tenor of the lawyer's testimony, and the probability that the lawyer's testimony will conflict with that of other witnesses. Even if there is risk of such prejudice, in determining whether the lawyer should be disqualified, due regard must be given to the effect of disqualification on the lawyer's client. It is relevant that one or both parties could reasonably foresee that the lawyer would probably be a witness. The conflict of interest principles stated in Rules 1.7, 1.9 and 1.10 have no application to this aspect of the problem.

[5] Because the tribunal is not likely to be misled when a lawyer acts as advocate in a trial in which another lawyer in the lawyer's firm will testify as a necessary witness, paragraph (b) permits the lawyer to do so except in situations involving a conflict of interest.

Conflict of Interest

[6] In determining if it is permissible to act as advocate in a trial in which the lawyer will be a necessary witness, the lawyer must also consider that the dual role may give rise to a conflict of interest that will require compliance with Rules 1.7 or 1.9. For example, if there is likely to be substantial conflict between the testimony of the client and that of the lawyer the representation involves a conflict of interest that requires compliance with Rule 1.7. This would be true even though the lawyer might not be prohibited by paragraph (a) from simultaneously serving as advocate and witness because the lawyer's disqualification would work a substantial hardship on

the client. Similarly, a lawyer who might be permitted to simultaneously serve as an advocate and a witness by paragraph (a)(3) might be precluded from doing so by Rule 1.9. The problem can arise whether the lawyer is called as a witness on behalf of the client or is called by the opposing party. Determining whether or not such a conflict exists is primarily the responsibility of the lawyer involved. If there is a conflict of interest, the lawyer must secure the client's informed consent, confirmed in writing. In some cases, the lawyer will be precluded from seeking the client's consent. See Rule 1.7. See Rule 1.0(b) for the definition of "confirmed in writing" and Rule 1.0(e) for the definition of "informed consent."

[7] Paragraph (b) provides that a lawyer is not disqualified from serving as an advocate because a lawyer with whom the lawyer is associated in a firm is precluded from doing so by paragraph (a). If, however, the testifying lawyer would also be disqualified by Rule 1.7 or Rule 1.9 from representing the client in the matter, other lawyers in the firm will be precluded from representing the client by Rule 1.10 unless the client gives informed consent under the conditions stated in Rule 1.7.

RULE 3.8: SPECIAL RESPONSIBILITIES OF A PROSECUTOR

The prosecutor in a criminal case shall:

(a) refrain from prosecuting a charge that the prosecutor knows is not supported by probable cause;

(b) make reasonable efforts to assure that the accused has been advised of the right to, and the procedure for obtaining, counsel and has been given reasonable opportunity to obtain counsel;

(c) not seek to obtain from an unrepresented accused a waiver of important pretrial rights, such as the right to a preliminary hearing;

(d) make timely disclosure to the defense of all evidence or information known to the prosecutor that tends to negate the guilt of the accused or mitigates the offense, and, in connection with sentencing, disclose to the defense and to the tribunal all unprivileged mitigating information known to the prosecutor, except when the prosecutor is relieved of this responsibility by a protective order of the tribunal;

(e) not subpoena a lawyer in a grand jury or other criminal proceeding to present evidence about a past or present client unless the prosecutor reasonably believes:

(1) the information sought is not protected from disclosure by any applicable privilege;

(2) the evidence sought is essential to the successful completion of an ongoing investigation or prosecution; and

(3) there is no other feasible alternative to obtain the information;

(f) except for statements that are necessary to inform the public of the nature and extent of the prosecutor's action and that serve a legitimate law enforcement purpose, refrain from making extrajudicial comments that have a substantial likelihood of heightening public condemnation of the accused and exercise reasonable care to prevent investigators, law enforcement personnel, employees or other persons assisting or associated with the prosecutor in a criminal case from making an extrajudicial statement that the prosecutor would be prohibited from making under Rule 3.6 or this Rule.

COMMENT

[1] A prosecutor has the responsibility of a minister of justice and not simply that of an advocate. This responsibility carries with it specific obligations to see that the defendant is

accorded procedural justice and that guilt is decided upon the basis of sufficient evidence. Precisely how far the prosecutor is required to go in this direction is a matter of debate and varies in different jurisdictions. Many jurisdictions have adopted the ABA Standards of Criminal Justice Relating to the Prosecution Function, which in turn are the product of prolonged and careful deliberation by lawyers experienced in both criminal prosecution and defense. Applicable law may require other measures by the prosecutor and knowing disregard of those obligations or a systematic abuse of prosecutorial discretion could constitute a violation of Rule 8.4.

[2] In some jurisdictions, a defendant may waive a preliminary hearing and thereby lose a valuable opportunity to challenge probable cause. Accordingly, prosecutors should not seek to obtain waivers of preliminary hearings or other important pretrial rights from unrepresented accused persons. Paragraph (c) does not apply, however, to an accused appearing *pro se* with the approval of the tribunal. Nor does it forbid the lawful questioning of an uncharged suspect who has knowingly waived the rights to counsel and silence.

[3] The exception in paragraph (d) recognizes that a prosecutor may seek an appropriate protective order from the tribunal if disclosure of information to the defense could result in substantial harm to an individual or to the public interest.

[4] Paragraph (e) is intended to limit the issuance of lawyer subpoenas in grand jury and other criminal proceedings to those situations in which there is a genuine need to intrude into the client-lawyer relationship.

[5] Paragraph (f) supplements Rule 3.6, which prohibits extrajudicial statements that have a substantial likelihood of prejudicing an adjudicatory proceeding. In the context of a criminal prosecution, a prosecutor's extrajudicial statement can create the additional problem of increasing public condemnation of the accused. Although the announcement of an indictment, for example, will necessarily have severe consequences for the accused, a prosecutor can, and should, avoid comments which have no legitimate law enforcement purpose and have a substantial likelihood of increasing public opprobrium of the accused. Nothing in this Comment is intended to restrict the statements which a prosecutor may make which comply with Rule 3.6(b) or 3.6(c).

[6] Like other lawyers, prosecutors are subject to Rules 5.1 and 5.3, which relate to responsibilities regarding lawyers and nonlawyers who work for or are associated with the lawyer's office. Paragraph (f) reminds the prosecutor of the importance of these obligations in connection with the unique dangers of improper extrajudicial statements in a criminal case. In addition, paragraph (f) requires a prosecutor to exercise reasonable care to prevent persons assisting or associated with the prosecutor from making improper extrajudicial statements, even when such persons are not under the direct supervision of the prosecutor. Ordinarily, the reasonable care standard will be satisfied if the prosecutor issues the appropriate cautions to law-enforcement personnel and other relevant individuals.

RULE 3.9: ADVOCATE IN NONADJUDICATIVE PROCEEDINGS

A lawyer representing a client before a legislative body or administrative agency in a nonadjudicative proceeding shall disclose that the appearance is in a representative capacity and shall conform to the provisions of Rules 3.3(a) through (c), 3.4(a) through (c), and 3.5.

COMMENT

[1] In representation before bodies such as legislatures, municipal councils, and executive and administrative agencies acting in a rule-making or policy-making capacity, lawyers present facts, formulate issues and advance argument in the matters under consideration. The decision-making body, like a court, should be able to rely on the integrity of the submissions made to it. A

lawyer appearing before such a body must deal with it honestly and in conformity with applicable rules of procedure. See Rules 3.3(a) through (c), 3.4(a) through (c) and 3.5.

[2] Lawyers have no exclusive right to appear before nonadjudicative bodies, as they do before a court. The requirements of this Rule therefore may subject lawyers to regulations inapplicable to advocates who are not lawyers. However, legislatures and administrative agencies have a right to expect lawyers to deal with them as they deal with courts.

[3] This Rule only applies when a lawyer represents a client in connection with an official hearing or meeting of a governmental agency or a legislative body to which the lawyer or the lawyer's client is presenting evidence or argument. It does not apply to representation of a client in a negotiation or other bilateral transaction with a governmental agency or in connection with an application for a license or other privilege or the client's compliance with generally applicable reporting requirements, such as the filing of income-tax returns. Nor does it apply to the representation of a client in connection with an investigation or examination of the client's affairs conducted by government investigators or examiners. Representation in such matters is governed by Rules 4.1 through 4.4.

TRANSACTIONS WITH PERSONS OTHER THAN CLIENTS

RULE 4.1: TRUTHFULNESS IN STATEMENTS TO OTHERS

3rd parties

In the course of representing a client a lawyer shall not knowingly:

(a) make a false statement of material fact or law to a third person; or

(b) fail to disclose a material fact when disclosure is necessary to avoid assisting a criminal or fraudulent act by a client, unless disclosure is prohibited by Rule 1.6.

1.6 trumps 4.1(b) oppo is 3.3

misstatement by omission

COMMENT

Misrepresentation
no duty to tell opposing party facts

[1] A lawyer is required to be truthful when dealing with others on a client's behalf, but generally has no affirmative duty to inform an opposing party of relevant facts. A misrepresentation can occur if the lawyer incorporates or affirms a statement of another person that the lawyer knows is false. Misrepresentations can also occur by partially true but misleading statements or omissions that are the equivalent of affirmative false statements. For dishonest conduct that does not amount to a false statement or for misrepresentations by a lawyer other than in the course of representing a client, see Rule 8.4.

Statements of Fact
ok to misrep. value for settlement

[2] This Rule refers to statements of fact. Whether a particular statement should be regarded as one of fact can depend on the circumstances. Under generally accepted conventions in negotiation, certain types of statements ordinarily are not taken as statements of material fact. Estimates of price or value placed on the subject of a transaction and a party's intentions as to an acceptable settlement of a claim are ordinarily in this category, and so is the existence of an undisclosed principal except where nondisclosure of the principal would constitute fraud. Lawyers should be mindful of their obligations under applicable law to avoid criminal and tortious misrepresentation.

Crime or Fraud by Client

[3] Under Rule 1.2(d), a lawyer is prohibited from counseling or assisting a client in conduct that the lawyer knows is criminal or fraudulent. Paragraph (b) states a specific application of the principle set forth in Rule 1.2(d) and addresses the situation where a client's crime or fraud takes the form of a lie or misrepresentation. Ordinarily, a lawyer can avoid

assisting a client's crime or fraud by withdrawing from the representation. Sometimes it may be necessary for the lawyer to give notice of the fact of withdrawal and to disaffirm an opinion, document, affirmation or the like. In extreme cases, substantive law may require a lawyer to disclose information relating to the representation to avoid being deemed to have assisted the client's crime or fraud. If the lawyer can avoid assisting a client's crime or fraud only by disclosing this information, then under paragraph (b) the lawyer is required to do so, unless the disclosure is prohibited by Rule 1.6.

RULE 4.2: COMMUNICATION WITH PERSON REPRESENTED BY COUNSEL

In representing a client, a lawyer shall not communicate about the subject of the representation with a person the lawyer knows to be represented by another lawyer in the matter, unless the lawyer has the consent of the other lawyer or is authorized to do so by law or a court order.

COMMENT

[1] This Rule contributes to the proper functioning of the legal system by protecting a person who has chosen to be represented by a lawyer in a matter against possible overreaching by other lawyers who are participating in the matter, interference by those lawyers with the client-lawyer relationship and the uncounselled disclosure of information relating to the representation.

[2] This Rule applies to communications with any person who is represented by counsel concerning the matter to which the communication relates.

[3] The Rule applies even though the represented person initiates or consents to the communication. A lawyer must immediately terminate communication with a person if, after commencing communication, the lawyer learns that the person is one with whom communication is not permitted by this Rule.

[4] This Rule does not prohibit communication with a represented person, or an employee or agent of such a person, concerning matters outside the representation. For example, the existence of a controversy between a government agency and a private party, or between two organizations, does not prohibit a lawyer for either from communicating with nonlawyer representatives of the other regarding a separate matter. Nor does this Rule preclude communication with a represented person who is seeking advice from a lawyer who is not otherwise representing a client in the matter. A lawyer may not make a communication prohibited by this Rule through the acts of another. See Rule 8.4(a). Parties to a matter may communicate directly with each other, and a lawyer is not prohibited from advising a client concerning a communication that the client is legally entitled to make. Also, a lawyer having independent justification or legal authorization for communicating with a represented person is permitted to do so.

[5] Communications authorized by law may include communications by a lawyer on behalf of a client who is exercising a constitutional or other legal right to communicate with the government. Communications authorized by law may also include investigative activities of lawyers representing governmental entities, directly or through investigative agents, prior to the commencement of criminal or civil enforcement proceedings. When communicating with the accused in a criminal matter, a government lawyer must comply with this Rule in addition to honoring the constitutional rights of the accused. The fact that a communication does not violate a state or federal constitutional right is insufficient to establish that the communication is permissible under this Rule.

[6] A lawyer who is uncertain whether a communication with a represented person is permissible may seek a court order. A lawyer may also seek a court order in exceptional circumstances to authorize a communication that would otherwise be prohibited by this Rule, for

example, where communication with a person represented by counsel is necessary to avoid reasonably certain injury.

[7] In the case of a represented organization, this Rule prohibits communications with a constituent of the organization who supervises, directs or regularly consults with the organization's lawyer concerning the matter or has authority to obligate the organization with respect to the matter or whose act or omission in connection with the matter may be imputed to the organization for purposes of civil or criminal liability. Consent of the organization's lawyer is not required for communication with a former constituent. If a constituent of the organization is represented in the matter by his or her own counsel, the consent by that counsel to a communication will be sufficient for purposes of this Rule. Compare Rule 3.4(f). In communicating with a current or former constituent of an organization, a lawyer must not use methods of obtaining evidence that violate the legal rights of the organization. See Rule 4.4.

[8] The prohibition on communications with a represented person only applies in circumstances where the lawyer knows that the person is in fact represented in the matter to be discussed. This means that the lawyer has actual knowledge of the fact of the representation; but such actual knowledge may be inferred from the circumstances. See Rule 1.0(f). Thus, the lawyer cannot evade the requirement of obtaining the consent of counsel by closing eyes to the obvious.

[9] In the event the person with whom the lawyer communicates is not known to be represented by counsel in the matter, the lawyer's communications are subject to Rule 4.3.

RULE 4.3: DEALING WITH UNREPRESENTED PERSON

In dealing on behalf of a client with a person who is not represented by counsel, a lawyer shall not state or imply that the lawyer is disinterested. When the lawyer knows or reasonably should know that the unrepresented person misunderstands the lawyer's role in the matter, the lawyer shall make reasonable efforts to correct the misunderstanding. The lawyer shall not give legal advice to an unrepresented person, other than the advice to secure counsel, if the lawyer knows or reasonably should know that the interests of such a person are or have a reasonable possibility of being in conflict with the interests of the client.

COMMENT

[1] An unrepresented person, particularly one not experienced in dealing with legal matters, might assume that a lawyer is disinterested in loyalties or is a disinterested authority on the law even when the lawyer represents a client. In order to avoid a misunderstanding, a lawyer will typically need to identify the lawyer's client and, where necessary, explain that the client has interests opposed to those of the unrepresented person. For misunderstandings that sometimes arise when a lawyer for an organization deals with an unrepresented constituent, see Rule 1.13(f).

[2] The Rule distinguishes between situations involving unrepresented persons whose interests may be adverse to those of the lawyer's client and those in which the person's interests are not in conflict with the client's. In the former situation, the possibility that the lawyer will compromise the unrepresented person's interests is so great that the Rule prohibits the giving of any advice, apart from the advice to obtain counsel. Whether a lawyer is giving impermissible advice may depend on the experience and sophistication of the unrepresented person, as well as the setting in which the behavior and comments occur. This Rule does not prohibit a lawyer from negotiating the terms of a transaction or settling a dispute with an unrepresented person. So long as the lawyer has explained that the lawyer represents an adverse party and is not representing the person, the lawyer may inform the person of the terms on which the lawyer's client will enter into an agreement or settle a matter, prepare documents that require the person's signature and explain

the lawyer's own view of the meaning of the document or the lawyer's view of the underlying legal obligations.

RULE 4.4: RESPECT FOR RIGHTS OF THIRD PERSONS

(a) In representing a client, a lawyer shall not use means that have no substantial purpose other than to embarrass, delay, or burden a third person, or use methods of obtaining evidence that violate the legal rights of such a person.

(b) A lawyer who receives a document relating to the representation of the lawyer's client and knows or reasonably should know that the document was inadvertently sent shall promptly notify the sender.

COMMENT

[1] Responsibility to a client requires a lawyer to subordinate the interests of others to those of the client, but that responsibility does not imply that a lawyer may disregard the rights of third persons. It is impractical to catalogue all such rights, but they include legal restrictions on methods of obtaining evidence from third persons and unwarranted intrusions into privileged relationships, such as the client-lawyer relationship.

[2] Paragraph (b) recognizes that lawyers sometimes receive documents that were mistakenly sent or produced by opposing parties or their lawyers. If a lawyer knows or reasonably should know that such a document was sent inadvertently, then this Rule requires the lawyer to promptly notify the sender in order to permit that person to take protective measures. Whether the lawyer is required to take additional steps, such as returning the original document, is a matter of law beyond the scope of these Rules, as is the question of whether the privileged status of a document has been waived. Similarly, this Rule does not address the legal duties of a lawyer who receives a document that the lawyer knows or reasonably should know may have been wrongfully obtained by the sending person. For purposes of this Rule, "document" includes e-mail or other electronic modes of transmission subject to being read or put into readable form.

[3] Some lawyers may choose to return a document unread, for example, when the lawyer learns before receiving the document that it was inadvertently sent to the wrong address. Where a lawyer is not required by applicable law to do so, the decision to voluntarily return such a document is a matter of professional judgment ordinarily reserved to the lawyer. See Rules 1.2 and 1.4.

LAW FIRMS AND ASSOCIATIONS

RULE 5.1: RESPONSIBILITIES OF PARTNERS, MANAGERS, AND SUPERVISORY LAWYERS

C1-3 **(a) A partner in a law firm, and a lawyer who individually or together with other lawyers possesses comparable managerial authority in a law firm, shall make reasonable efforts to ensure that the firm has in effect measures giving reasonable assurance that all lawyers in the firm conform to the Rules of Professional Conduct.**

C1,6 1.0 **(b) A lawyer having <u>direct supervisory authority</u> over another lawyer shall make reasonable efforts to ensure that the other lawyer conforms to the Rules of Professional Conduct.**

C4-6 **(c) A lawyer shall be responsible for another lawyer's violation of the Rules of Professional Conduct if:**

See 8.4(a)↗

(1) the lawyer orders or, with knowledge of the specific conduct, ratifies the conduct involved; or

(2) the lawyer is a partner or has comparable managerial authority in the law firm in which the other lawyer practices, or has direct supervisory authority over the other lawyer, and knows of the conduct at a time when its consequences can be avoided or mitigated but fails to take reasonable remedial action.

COMMENT

[1] Paragraph (a) applies to lawyers who have managerial authority over the professional work of a firm. See Rule 1.0(c). This includes members of a partnership, the shareholders in a law firm organized as a professional corporation, and members of other associations authorized to practice law; lawyers having comparable managerial authority in a legal services organization or a law department of an enterprise or government agency; and lawyers who have intermediate managerial responsibilities in a firm. Paragraph (b) applies to lawyers who have supervisory authority over the work of other lawyers in a firm.

[2] Paragraph (a) requires lawyers with managerial authority within a firm to make reasonable efforts to establish internal policies and procedures designed to provide reasonable assurance that all lawyers in the firm will conform to the Rules of Professional Conduct. Such policies and procedures include those designed to detect and resolve conflicts of interest, identify dates by which actions must be taken in pending matters, account for client funds and property and ensure that inexperienced lawyers are properly supervised.

[3] Other measures that may be required to fulfill the responsibility prescribed in paragraph (a) can depend on the firm's structure and the nature of its practice. In a small firm of experienced lawyers, informal supervision and periodic review of compliance with the required systems ordinarily will suffice. In a large firm, or in practice situations in which difficult ethical problems frequently arise, more elaborate measures may be necessary. Some firms, for example, have a procedure whereby junior lawyers can make confidential referral of ethical problems directly to a designated senior partner or special committee. See Rule 5.2. Firms, whether large or small, may also rely on continuing legal education in professional ethics. In any event, the ethical atmosphere of a firm can influence the conduct of all its members, and the partners may not assume that all lawyers associated with the firm will inevitably conform to the Rules.

[4] Paragraph (c) expresses a general principle of personal responsibility for acts of another. See also Rule 8.4(a).

[5] Paragraph (c)(2) defines the duty of a partner or other lawyer having comparable managerial authority in a law firm, as well as a lawyer who has direct supervisory authority over performance of specific legal work by another lawyer. Whether a lawyer has supervisory authority in particular circumstances is a question of fact. Partners and lawyers with comparable authority have at least indirect responsibility for all work being done by the firm, while a partner or manager in charge of a particular matter ordinarily also has supervisory responsibility for the work of other firm lawyers engaged in the matter. Appropriate remedial action by a partner or managing lawyer would depend on the immediacy of that lawyer's involvement and the seriousness of the misconduct. A supervisor is required to intervene to prevent avoidable consequences of misconduct if the supervisor knows that the misconduct occurred. Thus, if a supervising lawyer knows that a subordinate misrepresented a matter to an opposing party in negotiation, the supervisor as well as the subordinate has a duty to correct the resulting misapprehension.

[6] Professional misconduct by a lawyer under supervision could reveal a violation of paragraph (b) on the part of the supervisory lawyer even though it does not entail a violation of paragraph (c) because there was no direction, ratification or knowledge of the violation.

[7] Apart from this Rule and Rule 8.4(a), a lawyer does not have disciplinary liability for the conduct of a partner, associate or subordinate. Whether a lawyer may be liable civilly or criminally for another lawyer's conduct is a question of law beyond the scope of these Rules.

[8] The duties imposed by this Rule on managing and supervising lawyers do not alter the personal duty of each lawyer in a firm to abide by the Rules of Professional Conduct. See Rule 5.2(a).

RULE 5.2: RESPONSIBILITIES OF A SUBORDINATE LAWYER

(a) A lawyer is bound by the Rules of Professional Conduct notwithstanding that the lawyer acted at the direction of another person.

(b) A subordinate lawyer does not violate the Rules of Professional Conduct if that lawyer acts in accordance with a supervisory lawyer's reasonable resolution of an arguable question of professional duty.

COMMENT

[1] Although a lawyer is not relieved of responsibility for a violation by the fact that the lawyer acted at the direction of a supervisor, that fact may be relevant in determining whether a lawyer had the knowledge required to render conduct a violation of the Rules. For example, if a subordinate filed a frivolous pleading at the direction of a supervisor, the subordinate would not be guilty of a professional violation unless the subordinate knew of the document's frivolous character.

[2] When lawyers in a supervisor-subordinate relationship encounter a matter involving professional judgment as to ethical duty, the supervisor may assume responsibility for making the judgment. Otherwise a consistent course of action or position could not be taken. If the question can reasonably be answered only one way, the duty of both lawyers is clear and they are equally responsible for fulfilling it. However, if the question is reasonably arguable, someone has to decide upon the course of action. That authority ordinarily reposes in the supervisor, and a subordinate may be guided accordingly. For example, if a question arises whether the interests of two clients conflict under Rule 1.7, the supervisor's reasonable resolution of the question should protect the subordinate professionally if the resolution is subsequently challenged.

RULE 5.3: RESPONSIBILITIES REGARDING NONLAWYER ASSISTANTS

With respect to a nonlawyer employed or retained by or associated with a lawyer:

(a) a partner, and a lawyer who individually or together with other lawyers possesses comparable managerial authority in a law firm shall make reasonable efforts to ensure that the firm has in effect measures giving reasonable assurance that the person's conduct is compatible with the professional obligations of the lawyer;

(b) a lawyer having direct supervisory authority over the nonlawyer shall make reasonable efforts to ensure that the person's conduct is compatible with the professional obligations of the lawyer; and

(c) a lawyer shall be responsible for conduct of such a person that would be a violation of the Rules of Professional Conduct if engaged in by a lawyer if:

(1) the lawyer orders or, with the knowledge of the specific conduct, ratifies the conduct involved; or

(2) the lawyer is a partner or has comparable managerial authority in the law firm in which the person is employed, or has direct supervisory authority over

the person, and knows of the conduct at a time when its consequences can be avoided or mitigated but fails to take reasonable remedial action.

COMMENT

[1] Lawyers generally employ assistants in their practice, including secretaries, investigators, law student interns, and paraprofessionals. Such assistants, whether employees or independent contractors, act for the lawyer in rendition of the lawyer's professional services. A lawyer must give such assistants appropriate instruction and supervision concerning the ethical aspects of their employment, particularly regarding the obligation not to disclose information relating to representation of the client, and should be responsible for their work product. The measures employed in supervising nonlawyers should take account of the fact that they do not have legal training and are not subject to professional discipline.

[2] Paragraph (a) requires lawyers with managerial authority within a law firm to make reasonable efforts to establish internal policies and procedures designed to provide reasonable assurance that nonlawyers in the firm will act in a way compatible with the Rules of Professional Conduct. See Comment [1] to Rule 5.1. Paragraph (b) applies to lawyers who have supervisory authority over the work of a nonlawyer. Paragraph (c) specifies the circumstances in which a lawyer is responsible for conduct of a nonlawyer that would be a violation of the Rules of Professional Conduct if engaged in by a lawyer.

RULE 5.4: PROFESSIONAL INDEPENDENCE OF A LAWYER

(a) A lawyer or law firm shall not share legal fees with a nonlawyer, except that:

(1) an agreement by a lawyer with the lawyer's firm, partner, or associate may provide for the payment of money, over a reasonable period of time after the lawyer's death, to the lawyer's estate or to one or more specified persons;

(2) a lawyer who purchases the practice of a deceased, disabled, or disappeared lawyer may, pursuant to the provisions of Rule 1.17, pay to the estate or other representative of that lawyer the agreed-upon purchase price;

(3) a lawyer or law firm may include nonlawyer employees in a compensation or retirement plan, even though the plan is based in whole or in part on a profit-sharing arrangement; and

(4) a lawyer may share court-awarded legal fees with a nonprofit organization that employed, retained or recommended employment of the lawyer in the matter.

(b) A lawyer shall not form a partnership with a nonlawyer if any of the activities of the partnership consist of the practice of law.

(c) A lawyer shall not permit a person who recommends, employs, or pays the lawyer to render legal services for another to direct or regulate the lawyer's professional judgment in rendering such legal services.

(d) A lawyer shall not practice with or in the form of a professional corporation or association authorized to practice law for a profit, if:

(1) a nonlawyer owns any interest therein, except that a fiduciary representative of the estate of a lawyer may hold the stock or interest of the lawyer for a reasonable time during administration;

(2) a nonlawyer is a corporate director or officer thereof or occupies the position of similar responsibility in any form of association other than a corporation; or

(3) a nonlawyer has the right to direct or control the professional judgment of a lawyer.

COMMENT

[1] The provisions of this Rule express traditional limitations on sharing fees. These limitations are to protect the lawyer's professional independence of judgment. Where someone other than the client pays the lawyer's fee or salary, or recommends employment of the lawyer, that arrangement does not modify the lawyer's obligation to the client. As stated in paragraph (c), such arrangements should not interfere with the lawyer's professional judgment.

[2] This Rule also expresses traditional limitations on permitting a third party to direct or regulate the lawyer's professional judgment in rendering legal services to another. See also Rule 1.8(f) (lawyer may accept compensation from a third party as long as there is no interference with the lawyer's independent professional judgment and the client gives informed consent).

RULE 5.5: UNAUTHORIZED PRACTICE OF LAW; MULTIJURISDICTIONAL PRACTICE OF LAW

(a) A lawyer shall not practice law in a jurisdiction in violation of the regulation of the legal profession in that jurisdiction, or assist another in doing so.

(b) A lawyer who is not admitted to practice in this jurisdiction shall not:

(1) except as authorized by these Rules or other law, establish an office or other systematic and continuous presence in this jurisdiction for the practice of law; or

(2) hold out to the public or otherwise represent that the lawyer is admitted to practice law in this jurisdiction.

(c) A lawyer admitted in another United States jurisdiction, and not disbarred or suspended from practice in any jurisdiction, may provide legal services on a temporary basis in this jurisdiction that:

(1) are undertaken in association with a lawyer who is admitted to practice in this jurisdiction and who actively participates in the matter;

(2) are in or reasonably related to a pending or potential proceeding before a tribunal in this or another jurisdiction, if the lawyer, or a person the lawyer is assisting, is authorized by law or order to appear in such proceeding or reasonably expects to be so authorized;

(3) are in or reasonably related to a pending or potential arbitration, mediation, or other alternative dispute resolution proceeding in this or another jurisdiction, if the services arise out of or are reasonably related to the lawyer's practice in a jurisdiction in which the lawyer is admitted to practice and are not services for which the forum requires pro hac vice admission; or

(4) are not within paragraphs (c)(2) or (c)(3) and arise out of or are reasonably related to the lawyer's practice in a jurisdiction in which the lawyer is admitted to practice.

(d) A lawyer admitted in another United States jurisdiction, and not disbarred or suspended from practice in any jurisdiction, may provide legal services in this jurisdiction that:

(1) are provided to the lawyer's employer or its organizational affiliates and are not services for which the forum requires pro hac vice admission; or

(2) are services that the lawyer is authorized by federal or other law to provide in this jurisdiction.

COMMENT

[1] A lawyer may practice law only in a jurisdiction in which the lawyer is authorized to practice. A lawyer may be admitted to practice law in a jurisdiction on a regular basis or may be authorized by court rule or order or by law to practice for a limited purpose or on a restricted basis. Paragraph (a) applies to unauthorized practice of law by a lawyer, whether through the lawyer's direct action or by the lawyer assisting another person.

[2] The definition of the practice of law is established by law and varies from one jurisdiction to another. Whatever the definition, limiting the practice of law to members of the bar protects the public against rendition of legal services by unqualified persons. This Rule does not prohibit a lawyer from employing the services of paraprofessionals and delegating functions to them, so long as the lawyer supervises the delegated work and retains responsibility for their work. See Rule 5.3. *—what annys do— circular definition*

[3] A lawyer may provide professional advice and instruction to nonlawyers whose employment requires knowledge of the law; for example, claims adjusters, employees of financial or commercial institutions, social workers, accountants and persons employed in government agencies. Lawyers also may assist independent nonlawyers, such as paraprofessionals, who are authorized by the law of a jurisdiction to provide particular law-related services. In addition, a lawyer may counsel nonlawyers who wish to proceed pro se. *defend self*

[4] Other than as authorized by law or this Rule, a lawyer who is not admitted to practice generally in this jurisdiction violates paragraph (b) if the lawyer establishes an office or other systematic and continuous presence in this jurisdiction for the practice of law. Presence may be systematic and continuous even if the lawyer is not physically present here. Such a lawyer must not hold out to the public or otherwise represent that the lawyer is admitted to practice law in this jurisdiction. See also Rules 7.1(a) and 7.5(b).

[5] There are occasions in which a lawyer admitted to practice in another United States jurisdiction, and not disbarred or suspended from practice in any jurisdiction, may provide legal services on a temporary basis in this jurisdiction under circumstances that do not create an unreasonable risk to the interests of their clients, the public or the courts. Paragraph (c) identifies four such circumstances. The fact that conduct is not so identified does not imply that the conduct is or is not authorized. With the exception of paragraphs (d)(1) and (d)(2), this Rule does not authorize a lawyer to establish an office or other systematic and continuous presence in this jurisdiction without being admitted to practice generally here.

[6] There is no single test to determine whether a lawyer's services are provided on a "temporary basis" in this jurisdiction, and may therefore be permissible under paragraph (c). Services may be "temporary" even though the lawyer provides services in this jurisdiction on a recurring basis, or for an extended period of time, as when the lawyer is representing a client in a single lengthy negotiation or litigation.

[7] Paragraphs (c) and (d) apply to lawyers who are admitted to practice law in any United States jurisdiction, which includes the District of Columbia and any state, territory or commonwealth of the United States. The word "admitted" in paragraph (c) contemplates that the lawyer is authorized to practice in the jurisdiction in which the lawyer is admitted and excludes a lawyer who while technically admitted is not authorized to practice, because, for example, the lawyer is on inactive status.

[8] Paragraph (c)(1) recognizes that the interests of clients and the public are protected if a lawyer admitted only in another jurisdiction associates with a lawyer licensed to practice in this jurisdiction. For this paragraph to apply, however, the lawyer admitted to practice in this jurisdiction must actively participate in and share responsibility for the representation of the client.

[9] Lawyers not admitted to practice generally in a jurisdiction may be authorized by law or order of a tribunal or an administrative agency to appear before the tribunal or agency. This

authority may be granted pursuant to formal rules governing admission pro hac vice or pursuant to informal practice of the tribunal or agency. Under paragraph (c)(2), a lawyer does not violate this Rule when the lawyer appears before a tribunal or agency pursuant to such authority. To the extent that a court rule or other law of this jurisdiction requires a lawyer who is not admitted to practice in this jurisdiction to obtain admission pro hac vice before appearing before a tribunal or administrative agency, this Rule requires the lawyer to obtain that authority.

[10] Paragraph (c)(2) also provides that a lawyer rendering services in this jurisdiction on a temporary basis does not violate this Rule when the lawyer engages in conduct in anticipation of a proceeding or hearing in a jurisdiction in which the lawyer is authorized to practice law or in which the lawyer reasonably expects to be admitted pro hac vice. Examples of such conduct include meetings with the client, interviews of potential witnesses, and the review of documents. Similarly, a lawyer admitted only in another jurisdiction may engage in conduct temporarily in this jurisdiction in connection with pending litigation in another jurisdiction in which the lawyer is or reasonably expects to be authorized to appear, including taking depositions in this jurisdiction.

[11] When a lawyer has been or reasonably expects to be admitted to appear before a court or administrative agency, paragraph (c)(2) also permits conduct by lawyers who are associated with that lawyer in the matter, but who do not expect to appear before the court or administrative agency. For example, subordinate lawyers may conduct research, review documents, and attend meetings with witnesses in support of the lawyer responsible for the litigation.

[12] Paragraph (c)(3) permits a lawyer admitted to practice law in another jurisdiction to perform services on a temporary basis in this jurisdiction if those services are in or reasonably related to a pending or potential arbitration, mediation, or other alternative dispute resolution proceeding in this or another jurisdiction, if the services arise out of or are reasonably related to the lawyer's practice in a jurisdiction in which the lawyer is admitted to practice. The lawyer, however, must obtain admission pro hac vice in the case of a court-annexed arbitration or mediation or otherwise if court rules or law so require.

[13] Paragraph (c)(4) permits a lawyer admitted in another jurisdiction to provide certain legal services on a temporary basis in this jurisdiction that arise out of or are reasonably related to the lawyer's practice in a jurisdiction in which the lawyer is admitted but are not within paragraphs (c)(2) or (c)(3). These services include both legal services and services that nonlawyers may perform but that are considered the practice of law when performed by lawyers.

[14] Paragraphs (c)(3) and (c)(4) require that the services arise out of or be reasonably related to the lawyer's practice in a jurisdiction in which the lawyer is admitted. A variety of factors evidence such a relationship. The lawyer's client may have been previously represented by the lawyer, or may be resident in or have substantial contacts with the jurisdiction in which the lawyer is admitted. The matter, although involving other jurisdictions, may have a significant connection with that jurisdiction. In other cases, significant aspects of the lawyer's work might be conducted in that jurisdiction or a significant aspect of the matter may involve the law of that jurisdiction. The necessary relationship might arise when the client's activities or the legal issues involve multiple jurisdictions, such as when the officers of a multinational corporation survey potential business sites and seek the services of their lawyer in assessing the relative merits of each. In addition, the services may draw on the lawyer's recognized expertise developed through the regular practice of law on behalf of clients in matters involving a particular body of federal, nationally-uniform, foreign, or international law.

[15] Paragraph (d) identifies two circumstances in which a lawyer who is admitted to practice in another United States jurisdiction, and is not disbarred or suspended from practice in any jurisdiction, may establish an office or other systematic and continuous presence in this jurisdiction for the practice of law as well as provide legal services on a temporary basis. Except as provided in paragraphs (d)(1) and (d)(2), a lawyer who is admitted to practice law in another

jurisdiction and who establishes an office or other systematic or continuous presence in this jurisdiction must become admitted to practice law generally in this jurisdiction.

[16] Paragraph (d)(1) applies to a lawyer who is employed by a client to provide legal services to the client or its organizational affiliates, i.e., entities that control, are controlled by, or are under common control with the employer. This paragraph does not authorize the provision of personal legal services to the employer's officers or employees. The paragraph applies to in-house corporate lawyers, government lawyers and others who are employed to render legal services to the employer. The lawyer's ability to represent the employer outside the jurisdiction in which the lawyer is licensed generally serves the interests of the employer and does not create an unreasonable risk to the client and others because the employer is well situated to assess the lawyer's qualifications and the quality of the lawyer's work.

[17] If an employed lawyer establishes an office or other systematic presence in this jurisdiction for the purpose of rendering legal services to the employer, the lawyer may be subject to registration or other requirements, including assessments for client protection funds and mandatory continuing legal education.

[18] Paragraph (d)(2) recognizes that a lawyer may provide legal services in a jurisdiction in which the lawyer is not licensed when authorized to do so by federal or other law, which includes statute, court rule, executive regulation or judicial precedent.

[19] A lawyer who practices law in this jurisdiction pursuant to paragraphs (c) or (d) or otherwise is subject to the disciplinary authority of this jurisdiction. See Rule 8.5(a).

[20] In some circumstances, a lawyer who practices law in this jurisdiction pursuant to paragraphs (c) or (d) may have to inform the client that the lawyer is not licensed to practice law in this jurisdiction. For example, that may be required when the representation occurs primarily in this jurisdiction and requires knowledge of the law of this jurisdiction. See Rule 1.4(b).

[21] Paragraphs (c) and (d) do not authorize communications advertising legal services to prospective clients in this jurisdiction by lawyers who are admitted to practice in other jurisdictions. Whether and how lawyers may communicate the availability of their services to prospective clients in this jurisdiction is governed by Rules 7.1 to 7.5.

RULE 5.6: RESTRICTIONS ON RIGHT TO PRACTICE

A lawyer shall not participate in offering or making:

(a) a partnership, shareholders, operating, employment, or other similar type of agreement that restricts the right of a lawyer to practice after termination of the relationship, except an agreement concerning benefits upon retirement; or

(b) an agreement in which a restriction on the lawyer's right to practice is part of the settlement of a client controversy.

COMMENT

[1] An agreement restricting the right of lawyers to practice after leaving a firm not only limits their professional autonomy but also limits the freedom of clients to choose a lawyer. Paragraph (a) prohibits such agreements except for restrictions incident to provisions concerning retirement benefits for service with the firm.

[2] Paragraph (b) prohibits a lawyer from agreeing not to represent other persons in connection with settling a claim on behalf of a client.

[3] This Rule does not apply to prohibit restrictions that may be included in the terms of the sale of a law practice pursuant to Rule 1.17.

RULE 5.7: RESPONSIBILITIES REGARDING LAW-RELATED SERVICES

(a) A lawyer shall be subject to the Rules of Professional Conduct with respect to the provision of law-related services, as defined in paragraph (b), if the law-related services are provided:

(1) by the lawyer in circumstances that are not distinct from the lawyer's provision of legal services to clients; or

(2) in other circumstances by an entity controlled by the lawyer individually or with others if the lawyer fails to take reasonable measures to assure that a person obtaining the law-related services knows that the services are not legal services and that the protections of the client-lawyer relationship do not exist.

(b) The term "law-related services" denotes services that might reasonably be performed in conjunction with and in substance are related to the provision of legal services, and that are not prohibited as unauthorized practice of law when provided by a nonlawyer.

COMMENT

[1] When a lawyer performs law-related services or controls an organization that does so, there exists the potential for ethical problems. Principal among these is the possibility that the person for whom the law-related services are performed fails to understand that the services may not carry with them the protections normally afforded as part of the client-lawyer relationship. The recipient of the law-related services may expect, for example, that the protection of client confidences, prohibitions against representation of persons with conflicting interests, and obligations of a lawyer to maintain professional independence apply to the provision of law-related services when that may not be the case.

[2] Rule 5.7 applies to the provision of law-related services by a lawyer even when the lawyer does not provide any legal services to the person for whom the law-related services are performed and whether the law-related services are performed through a law firm or a separate entity. The Rule identifies the circumstances in which all of the Rules of Professional Conduct apply to the provision of law-related services. Even when those circumstances do not exist, however, the conduct of a lawyer involved in the provision of law-related services is subject to those Rules that apply generally to lawyer conduct, regardless of whether the conduct involves the provision of legal services. See, e.g., Rule 8.4.

[3] When law-related services are provided by a lawyer under circumstances that are not distinct from the lawyer's provision of legal services to clients, the lawyer in providing the law-related services must adhere to the requirements of the Rules of Professional Conduct as provided in paragraph (a)(1). Even when the law-related and legal services are provided in circumstances that are distinct from each other, for example through separate entities or different support staff within the law firm, the Rules of Professional Conduct apply to the lawyer as provided in paragraph (a)(2) unless the lawyer takes reasonable measures to assure that the recipient of the law-related services knows that the services are not legal services and that the protections of the client-lawyer relationship do not apply.

[4] Law-related services also may be provided through an entity that is distinct from that through which the lawyer provides legal services. If the lawyer individually or with others has control of such an entity's operations, the Rule requires the lawyer to take reasonable measures to assure that each person using the services of the entity knows that the services provided by the entity are not legal services and that the Rules of Professional Conduct that relate to the client-lawyer relationship do not apply. A lawyer's control of an entity extends to the ability to direct its operation. Whether a lawyer has such control will depend upon the circumstances of the particular case.

[5] When a client-lawyer relationship exists with a person who is referred by a lawyer to a separate law-related service entity controlled by the lawyer, individually or with others, the lawyer must comply with Rule 1.8(a).

[6] In taking the reasonable measures referred to in paragraph (a)(2) to assure that a person using law-related services understands the practical effect or significance of the inapplicability of the Rules of Professional Conduct, the lawyer should communicate to the person receiving the law-related services, in a manner sufficient to assure that the person understands the significance of the fact, that the relationship of the person to the business entity will not be a client-lawyer relationship. The communication should be made before entering into an agreement for provision of or providing law-related services, and preferably should be in writing.

[7] The burden is upon the lawyer to show that the lawyer has taken reasonable measures under the circumstances to communicate the desired understanding. For instance, a sophisticated user of law-related services, such as a publicly held corporation, may require a lesser explanation than someone unaccustomed to making distinctions between legal services and law-related services, such as an individual seeking tax advice from a lawyer-accountant or investigative services in connection with a lawsuit.

[8] Regardless of the sophistication of potential recipients of law-related services, a lawyer should take special care to keep separate the provision of law-related and legal services in order to minimize the risk that the recipient will assume that the law-related services are legal services. The risk of such confusion is especially acute when the lawyer renders both types of services with respect to the same matter. Under some circumstances the legal and law-related services may be so closely entwined that they cannot be distinguished from each other, and the requirement of disclosure and consultation imposed by paragraph (a)(2) of the Rule cannot be met. In such a case a lawyer will be responsible for assuring that both the lawyer's conduct and, to the extent required by Rule 5.3, that of nonlawyer employees in the distinct entity that the lawyer controls complies in all respects with the Rules of Professional Conduct.

[9] A broad range of economic and other interests of clients may be served by lawyers' engaging in the delivery of law-related services. Examples of law-related services include providing title insurance, financial planning, accounting, trust services, real estate counseling, legislative lobbying, economic analysis, social work, psychological counseling, tax preparation, and patent, medical or environmental consulting.

[10] When a lawyer is obliged to accord the recipients of such services the protections of those Rules that apply to the client-lawyer relationship, the lawyer must take special care to heed the proscriptions of the Rules addressing conflict of interest (Rules 1.7 through 1.11, especially Rules 1.7(a)(2) and 1.8(a), (b) and (f)), and to scrupulously adhere to the requirements of Rule 1.6 relating to disclosure of confidential information. The promotion of the law-related services must also in all respects comply with Rules 7.1 through 7.3, dealing with advertising and solicitation. In that regard, lawyers should take special care to identify the obligations that may be imposed as a result of a jurisdiction's decisional law.

[11] When the full protections of all of the Rules of Professional Conduct do not apply to the provision of law-related services, principles of law external to the Rules, for example, the law of principal and agent, govern the legal duties owed to those receiving the services. Those other legal principles may establish a different degree of protection for the recipient with respect to confidentiality of information, conflicts of interest and permissible business relationships with clients. See also Rule 8.4 (Misconduct).

PUBLIC SERVICE

RULE 6.1: VOLUNTARY PRO BONO PUBLICO SERVICE

not mandatory

Every lawyer **has a** professional responsibility to provide legal services to those unable to pay. A lawyer **should** aspire to render at least (50) **hours** of pro bono publico legal services per year. In fulfilling this responsibility, the lawyer **should:**

(a) provide a substantial majority of the (50) hours of legal services <u>without fee or</u> expectation of fee to:

C 2-5 (1) persons of limited means or

(2) charitable, religious, civic, community, governmental and educational *2* organizations in matters that are designed primarily to address the needs of persons of limited means; and

c5 (b) provide any additional services through:

c6 (1) delivery of legal services at no fee or substantially reduced fee to individuals, groups or organizations seeking to secure or protect civil rights, civil liberties or public rights, or charitable, religious, civic, community, governmental and educational organizations in matters in furtherance of their organizational purposes, where the payment of standard legal fees would significantly deplete the organization's economic resources or would be otherwise inappropriate;

c7 (2) delivery of legal services at a substantially reduced fee to persons of limited means; or

c8 (3) participation in activities for improving the law, the legal system or the legal profession.

In addition, a lawyer should voluntarily contribute financial support to organizations that provide legal services to persons of limited means.

COMMENT

[1] Every lawyer, regardless of professional prominence or professional work load, has a responsibility to provide legal services to those unable to pay, and personal involvement in the problems of the disadvantaged can be one of the most rewarding experiences in the life of a lawyer. The American Bar Association urges all lawyers to provide a minimum of 50 hours of pro bono services annually. States, however, may decide to choose a higher or lower number of hours of annual service (which may be expressed as a percentage of a lawyer's professional time) depending upon local needs and local conditions. It is recognized that in some years a lawyer may render greater or fewer hours than the annual standard specified, but during the course of his or her legal career, each lawyer should render on average per year, the number of hours set forth in this Rule. Services can be performed in civil matters or in criminal or quasi-criminal matters for which there is no government obligation to provide funds for legal representation, such as post-conviction death penalty appeal cases.

[2] Paragraphs (a)(1) and (2) <u>recognize the critical need for legal services that exists</u> among persons of limited means by providing that a substantial majority of the legal services rendered annually to the disadvantaged be furnished without fee or expectation of fee. Legal services under these paragraphs consist of a full range of activities, including individual and class representation, the provision of legal advice, legislative lobbying, administrative rule making and the provision of free training or mentoring to those who represent persons of limited means. The variety of these activities should facilitate participation by government lawyers, even when restrictions exist on their engaging in the outside practice of law.

[3] Persons eligible for legal services under paragraphs (a)(1) and (2) are those who qualify for participation in programs funded by the Legal Services Corporation and those whose incomes and financial resources are slightly above the guidelines utilized by such programs but nevertheless, cannot afford counsel. Legal services can be rendered to individuals or to organizations such as homeless shelters, battered women's centers and food pantries that serve those of limited means. The term "governmental organizations" includes, but is not limited to, public protection programs and sections of governmental or public sector agencies.

[4] Because service must be provided without fee or expectation of fee, the intent of the lawyer to render free legal services is essential for the work performed to fall within the meaning of paragraphs (a)(1) and (2). Accordingly, services rendered cannot be considered pro bono if an anticipated fee is uncollected, but the award of statutory attorneys' fees in a case originally accepted as pro bono would not disqualify such services from inclusion under this section. Lawyers who do receive fees in such cases are encouraged to contribute an appropriate portion of such fees to organizations or projects that benefit persons of limited means.

[5] While it is possible for a lawyer to fulfill the annual responsibility to perform pro bono services exclusively through activities described in paragraphs (a)(1) and (2), to the extent that any hours of service remained unfulfilled, the remaining commitment can be met in a variety of ways as set forth in paragraph (b). Constitutional, statutory or regulatory restrictions may prohibit or impede government and public sector lawyers and judges from performing the pro bono services outlined in paragraphs (a)(1) and (2). Accordingly, where those restrictions apply, government and public sector lawyers and judges may fulfill their pro bono responsibility by performing services outlined in paragraph (b).

[6] Paragraph (b)(1) includes the provision of certain types of legal services to those whose incomes and financial resources place them above limited means. It also permits the pro bono lawyer to accept a substantially reduced fee for services. Examples of the types of issues that may be addressed under this paragraph include First Amendment claims, Title VII claims and environmental protection claims. Additionally, a wide range of organizations may be represented, including social service, medical research, cultural and religious groups.

[7] Paragraph (b)(2) covers instances in which lawyers agree to and receive a modest fee for furnishing legal services to persons of limited means. Participation in judicare programs and acceptance of court appointments in which the fee is substantially below a lawyer's usual rate are encouraged under this section.

[8] Paragraph (b)(3) recognizes the value of lawyers engaging in activities that improve the law, the legal system or the legal profession. Serving on bar association committees, serving on boards of pro bono or legal services programs, taking part in Law Day activities, acting as a continuing legal education instructor, a mediator or an arbitrator and engaging in legislative lobbying to improve the law, the legal system or the profession are a few examples of the many activities that fall within this paragraph.

[9] Because the provision of pro bono services is a professional responsibility, it is the individual ethical commitment of each lawyer. Nevertheless, there may be times when it is not feasible for a lawyer to engage in pro bono services. At such times a lawyer may discharge the pro bono responsibility by providing financial support to organizations providing free legal services to persons of limited means. Such financial support should be reasonably equivalent to the value of the hours of service that would have otherwise been provided. In addition, at times it may be more feasible to satisfy the pro bono responsibility collectively, as by a firm's aggregate pro bono activities.

[10] Because the efforts of individual lawyers are not enough to meet the need for free legal services that exists among persons of limited means, the government and the profession have instituted additional programs to provide those services. Every lawyer should financially support such programs, in addition to either providing direct pro bono services or making financial contributions when pro bono service is not feasible.

[11] Law firms should act reasonably to enable and encourage all lawyers in the firm to provide the pro bono legal services called for by this Rule.

[12] The responsibility set forth in this Rule is not intended to be enforced through disciplinary process.

RULE 6.2: ACCEPTING APPOINTMENTS

A lawyer shall not seek to avoid appointment by a tribunal to represent a person except for good cause, such as:

(a) representing the client is likely to result in violation of the Rules of Professional Conduct or other law;

(b) representing the client is likely to result in an unreasonable financial burden on the lawyer; or

(c) the client or the cause is so repugnant to the lawyer as to be likely to impair the client-lawyer relationship or the lawyer's ability to represent the client.

COMMENT

[1] A lawyer ordinarily is not obliged to accept a client whose character or cause the lawyer regards as repugnant. The lawyer's freedom to select clients is, however, qualified. All lawyers have a responsibility to assist in providing pro bono publico service. See Rule 6.1. An individual lawyer fulfills this responsibility by accepting a fair share of unpopular matters or indigent or unpopular clients. A lawyer may also be subject to appointment by a court to serve unpopular clients or persons unable to afford legal services.

Appointed Counsel

[2] For good cause a lawyer may seek to decline an appointment to represent a person who cannot afford to retain counsel or whose cause is unpopular. Good cause exists if the lawyer could not handle the matter competently, see Rule 1.1, or if undertaking the representation would result in an improper conflict of interest, for example, when the client or the cause is so repugnant to the lawyer as to be likely to impair the client-lawyer relationship or the lawyer's ability to represent the client. A lawyer may also seek to decline an appointment if acceptance would be unreasonably burdensome, for example, when it would impose a financial sacrifice so great as to be unjust.

[3] An appointed lawyer has the same obligations to the client as retained counsel, including the obligations of loyalty and confidentiality, and is subject to the same limitations on the client-lawyer relationship, such as the obligation to refrain from assisting the client in violation of the Rules.

RULE 6.3: MEMBERSHIP IN LEGAL SERVICES ORGANIZATION

A lawyer may serve as a director, officer or member of a legal services organization, apart from the law firm in which the lawyer practices, notwithstanding that the organization serves persons having interests adverse to a client of the lawyer. The lawyer shall not knowingly participate in a decision or action of the organization:

(a) if participating in the decision or action would be incompatible with the lawyer's obligations to a client under Rule 1.7; or

(b) where the decision or action could have a material adverse effect on the representation of a client of the organization whose interests are adverse to a client of the lawyer.

COMMENT

[1] Lawyers should be encouraged to support and participate in legal service organizations. A lawyer who is an officer or a member of such an organization does not thereby have a client-lawyer relationship with persons served by the organization. However, there is potential conflict between the interests of such persons and the interests of the lawyer's clients. If the possibility of such conflict disqualified a lawyer from serving on the board of a legal services organization, the profession's involvement in such organizations would be severely curtailed.

[2] It may be necessary in appropriate cases to reassure a client of the organization that the representation will not be affected by conflicting loyalties of a member of the board. Established, written policies in this respect can enhance the credibility of such assurances.

RULE 6.4: LAW REFORM ACTIVITIES AFFECTING CLIENT INTERESTS

A lawyer may serve as a director, officer or member of an organization involved in reform of the law or its administration notwithstanding that the reform may affect the interests of a client of the lawyer. When the lawyer knows that the interests of a client may be materially benefitted by a decision in which the lawyer participates, the lawyer shall disclose that fact but need not identify the client.

COMMENT

[1] Lawyers involved in organizations seeking law reform generally do not have a client-lawyer relationship with the organization. Otherwise, it might follow that a lawyer could not be involved in a bar association law reform program that might indirectly affect a client. See also Rule 1.2(b). For example, a lawyer specializing in antitrust litigation might be regarded as disqualified from participating in drafting revisions of rules governing that subject. In determining the nature and scope of participation in such activities, a lawyer should be mindful of obligations to clients under other Rules, particularly Rule 1.7. A lawyer is professionally obligated to protect the integrity of the program by making an appropriate disclosure within the organization when the lawyer knows a private client might be materially benefitted.

RULE 6.5: NONPROFIT AND COURT-ANNEXED LIMITED LEGAL SERVICES PROGRAMS

(a) A lawyer who, under the auspices of a program sponsored by a nonprofit organization or court, provides short-term limited legal services to a client without expectation by either the lawyer or the client that the lawyer will provide continuing representation in the matter:

(1) is subject to Rules 1.7 and 1.9(a) only if the lawyer knows that the representation of the client involves a conflict of interest; and

(2) is subject to Rule 1.10 only if the lawyer knows that another lawyer associated with the lawyer in a law firm is disqualified by Rule 1.7 or 1.9(a) with respect to the matter.

(b) Except as provided in paragraph (a)(2), Rule 1.10 is inapplicable to a representation governed by this Rule.

COMMENT

[1] Legal services organizations, courts and various nonprofit organizations have established programs through which lawyers provide short-term limited legal services—such as

advice or the completion of legal forms—that will assist persons to address their legal problems without further representation by a lawyer. In these programs, such as legal-advice hotlines, advice-only clinics or pro se counseling programs, a client-lawyer relationship is established, but there is no expectation that the lawyer's representation of the client will continue beyond the limited consultation. Such programs are normally operated under circumstances in which it is not feasible for a lawyer to systematically screen for conflicts of interest as is generally required before undertaking a representation. See, e.g., Rules 1.7, 1.9 and 1.10.

[2] A lawyer who provides short-term limited legal services pursuant to this Rule must secure the client's informed consent to the limited scope of the representation. See Rule 1.2(c). If a short-term limited representation would not be reasonable under the circumstances, the lawyer may offer advice to the client but must also advise the client of the need for further assistance of counsel. Except as provided in this Rule, the Rules of Professional Conduct, including Rules 1.6 and 1.9(c), are applicable to the limited representation.

[3] Because a lawyer who is representing a client in the circumstances addressed by this Rule ordinarily is not able to check systematically for conflicts of interest, paragraph (a) requires compliance with Rules 1.7 or 1.9(a) only if the lawyer knows that the representation presents a conflict of interest for the lawyer, and with Rule 1.10 only if the lawyer knows that another lawyer in the lawyer's firm is disqualified by Rules 1.7 or 1.9(a) in the matter.

[4] Because the limited nature of the services significantly reduces the risk of conflicts of interest with other matters being handled by the lawyer's firm, paragraph (b) provides that Rule 1.10 is inapplicable to a representation governed by this Rule except as provided by paragraph (a)(2). Paragraph (a)(2) requires the participating lawyer to comply with Rule 1.10 when the lawyer knows that the lawyer's firm is disqualified by Rules 1.7 or 1.9(a). By virtue of paragraph (b), however, a lawyer's participation in a short-term limited legal services program will not preclude the lawyer's firm from undertaking or continuing the representation of a client with interests adverse to a client being represented under the program's auspices. Nor will the personal disqualification of a lawyer participating in the program be imputed to other lawyers participating in the program.

[5] If, after commencing a short-term limited representation in accordance with this Rule, a lawyer undertakes to represent the client in the matter on an ongoing basis, Rules 1.7, 1.9(a) and 1.10 become applicable.

INFORMATION ABOUT LEGAL SERVICES

RULE 7.1: COMMUNICATIONS CONCERNING A LAWYER'S SERVICES

A lawyer shall not make a false or misleading communication about the lawyer or the lawyer's services. A communication is false or misleading if it contains a material misrepresentation of fact or law, or omits a fact necessary to make the statement considered as a whole not materially misleading.

COMMENT

[1] This Rule governs all communications about a lawyer's services, including advertising permitted by Rule 7.2. Whatever means are used to make known a lawyer's services, statements about them must be truthful.

[2] Truthful statements that are misleading are also prohibited by this Rule. A truthful statement is misleading if it omits a fact necessary to make the lawyer's communication considered as a whole not materially misleading. A truthful statement is also misleading if there is a substantial likelihood that it will lead a reasonable person to formulate a specific conclusion about the lawyer or the lawyer's services for which there is no reasonable factual foundation.

[3] An advertisement that truthfully reports a lawyer's achievements on behalf of clients or former clients may be misleading if presented so as to lead a reasonable person to form an unjustified expectation that the same results could be obtained for other clients in similar matters without reference to the specific factual and legal circumstances of each client's case. Similarly, an unsubstantiated comparison of the lawyer's services or fees with the services or fees of other lawyers may be misleading if presented with such specificity as would lead a reasonable person to conclude that the comparison can be substantiated. The inclusion of an appropriate disclaimer or qualifying language may preclude a finding that a statement is likely to create unjustified expectations or otherwise mislead a prospective client.

[4] See also Rule 8.4(e) for the prohibition against stating or implying an ability to influence improperly a government agency or official or to achieve results by means that violate the Rules of Professional Conduct or other law.

RULE 7.2: ADVERTISING

(a) Subject to the requirements of Rules 7.1 and 7.3, a lawyer may advertise services through written, recorded or electronic communication, including public media.

(b) A lawyer shall not give anything of value to a person for recommending the lawyer's services except that a lawyer may

(1) pay the reasonable costs of advertisements or communications permitted by this Rule;

(2) pay the usual charges of a legal service plan or a not-for-profit or qualified lawyer referral service. A qualified lawyer referral service is a lawyer referral service that has been approved by an appropriate regulatory authority;

(3) pay for a law practice in accordance with Rule 1.17; and

(4) refer clients to another lawyer or a nonlawyer professional pursuant to an agreement not otherwise prohibited under these Rules that provides for the other person to refer clients or customers to the lawyer, if

(i) the reciprocal referral agreement is not exclusive, and

(ii) the client is informed of the existence and nature of the agreement.

(c) Any communication made pursuant to this rule shall include the name and office address of at least one lawyer or law firm responsible for its content.

COMMENT

[1] To assist the public in obtaining legal services, lawyers should be allowed to make known their services not only through reputation but also through organized information campaigns in the form of advertising. Advertising involves an active quest for clients, contrary to the tradition that a lawyer should not seek clientele. However, the public's need to know about legal services can be fulfilled in part through advertising. This need is particularly acute in the case of persons of moderate means who have not made extensive use of legal services. The interest in expanding public information about legal services ought to prevail over considerations of tradition. Nevertheless, advertising by lawyers entails the risk of practices that are misleading or overreaching.

[2] This Rule permits public dissemination of information concerning a lawyer's name or firm name, address and telephone number; the kinds of services the lawyer will undertake; the basis on which the lawyer's fees are determined, including prices for specific services and payment and credit arrangements; a lawyer's foreign language ability; names of references and,

with their consent, names of clients regularly represented; and other information that might invite the attention of those seeking legal assistance.

[3] Questions of effectiveness and taste in advertising are matters of speculation and subjective judgment. Some jurisdictions have had extensive prohibitions against television advertising, against advertising going beyond specified facts about a lawyer, or against "undignified" advertising. Television is now one of the most powerful media for getting information to the public, particularly persons of low and moderate income; prohibiting television advertising, therefore, would impede the flow of information about legal services to many sectors of the public. Limiting the information that may be advertised has a similar effect and assumes that the bar can accurately forecast the kind of information that the public would regard as relevant. Similarly, electronic media, such as the Internet, can be an important source of information about legal services, and lawful communication by electronic mail is permitted by this Rule. But see Rule 7.3(a) for the prohibition against the solicitation of a prospective client through a real-time electronic exchange that is not initiated by the prospective client.

[4] Neither this Rule nor Rule 7.3 prohibits communications authorized by law, such as notice to members of a class in class action litigation.

Paying Others to Recommend a Lawyer

[5] Lawyers are not permitted to pay others for channeling professional work. Paragraph (b)(1), however, allows a lawyer to pay for advertising and communications permitted by this Rule, including the costs of print directory listings, on-line directory listings, newspaper ads, television and radio airtime, domain-name registrations, sponsorship fees, banner ads, and group advertising. A lawyer may compensate employees, agents and vendors who are engaged to provide marketing or client-development services, such as publicists, public-relations personnel, business-development staff and website designers. See Rule 5.3 for the duties of lawyers and law firms with respect to the conduct of nonlawyers who prepare marketing materials for them.

[6] A lawyer may pay the usual charges of a legal service plan or a not-for-profit or qualified lawyer referral service. A legal service plan is a prepaid or group legal service plan or a similar delivery system that assists prospective clients to secure legal representation. A lawyer referral service, on the other hand, is any organization that holds itself out to the public as a lawyer referral service. Such referral services are understood by laypersons to be consumer-oriented organizations that provide unbiased referrals to lawyers with appropriate experience in the subject matter of the representation and afford other client protections, such as complaint procedures or malpractice insurance requirements. Consequently, this Rule only permits a lawyer to pay the usual charges of a not-for-profit or qualified lawyer referral service. A qualified lawyer referral service is one that is approved by an appropriate regulatory authority as affording adequate protections for prospective clients. See, e.g., the American Bar Association's Model Supreme Court Rules Governing Lawyer Referral Services and Model Lawyer Referral and Information Service Quality Assurance Act (requiring that organizations that are identified as lawyer referral services (i) permit the participation of all lawyers who are licensed and eligible to practice in the jurisdiction and who meet reasonable objective eligibility requirements as may be established by the referral service for the protection of prospective clients; (ii) require each participating lawyer to carry reasonably adequate malpractice insurance; (iii) act reasonably to assess client satisfaction and address client complaints; and (iv) do not refer prospective clients to lawyers who own, operate or are employed by the referral service).

[7] A lawyer who accepts assignments or referrals from a legal service plan or referrals from a lawyer referral service must act reasonably to assure that the activities of the plan or service are compatible with the lawyer's professional obligations. See Rule 5.3. Legal service plans and lawyer referral services may communicate with prospective clients, but such communication must be in conformity with these Rules. Thus, advertising must not be false or misleading, as would be the case if the communications of a group advertising program or a group legal services plan would mislead prospective clients to think that it was a lawyer referral

service sponsored by a state agency or bar association. Nor could the lawyer allow in-person, telephonic, or real-time contacts that would violate Rule 7.3.

[8] A lawyer also may agree to refer clients to another lawyer or a nonlawyer professional, in return for the undertaking of that person to refer clients or customers to the lawyer. Such reciprocal referral arrangements must not interfere with the lawyer's professional judgment as to making referrals or as to providing substantive legal services. See Rules 2.1 and 5.4(c). Except as provided in Rule 1.5(e), a lawyer who receives referrals from a lawyer or nonlawyer professional must not pay anything solely for the referral, but the lawyer does not violate paragraph (b) of this Rule by agreeing to refer clients to the other lawyer or nonlawyer professional, so long as the reciprocal referral agreement is not exclusive and the client is informed of the referral agreement. Conflicts of interest created by such arrangements are governed by Rule 1.7. Reciprocal referral agreements should not be of indefinite duration and should be reviewed periodically to determine whether they comply with these Rules. This Rule does not restrict referrals or divisions of revenues or net income among lawyers within firms comprised of multiple entities.

RULE 7.3: DIRECT CONTACT WITH PROSPECTIVE CLIENTS

(a) A lawyer shall not by in-person, live telephone or real-time electronic contact solicit professional employment from a prospective client when a significant motive for the lawyer's doing so is the lawyer's pecuniary gain, unless the person contacted:

    (1) is a lawyer; or

    (2) has a family, close personal, or prior professional relationship with the lawyer.

(b) A lawyer shall not solicit professional employment from a prospective client by written, recorded or electronic communication or by in-person, telephone or real-time electronic contact even when not otherwise prohibited by paragraph (a), if:

    (1) the prospective client has made known to the lawyer a desire not to be solicited by the lawyer; or

    (2) the solicitation involves coercion, duress or harassment.

(c) Every written, recorded or electronic communication from a lawyer soliciting professional employment from a prospective client known to be in need of legal services in a particular matter shall include the words "Advertising Material" on the outside envelope, if any, and at the beginning and ending of any recorded or electronic communication, unless the recipient of the communication is a person specified in paragraphs (a)(1) or (a)(2).

(d) Notwithstanding the prohibitions in paragraph (a), a lawyer may participate with a prepaid or group legal service plan operated by an organization not owned or directed by the lawyer that uses in-person or telephone contact to solicit memberships or subscriptions for the plan from persons who are not known to need legal services in a particular matter covered by the plan.

COMMENT

[1] There is a potential for abuse inherent in direct in-person, live telephone or real-time electronic contact by a lawyer with a prospective client known to need legal services. These forms of contact between a lawyer and a prospective client subject the layperson to the private importuning of the trained advocate in a direct interpersonal encounter. The prospective client, who may already feel overwhelmed by the circumstances giving rise to the need for legal services, may find it difficult fully to evaluate all available alternatives with reasoned judgment and appropriate self-interest in the face of the lawyer's presence and insistence upon being

retained immediately. The situation is fraught with the possibility of undue influence, intimidation, and over-reaching.

[2] This potential for abuse inherent in direct in-person, live telephone or real-time electronic solicitation of prospective clients justifies its prohibition, particularly since lawyer advertising and written and recorded communication permitted under Rule 7.2 offer alternative means of conveying necessary information to those who may be in need of legal services. Advertising and written and recorded communications which may be mailed or autodialed make it possible for a prospective client to be informed about the need for legal services, and about the qualifications of available lawyers and law firms, without subjecting the prospective client to direct in-person, telephone or real-time electronic persuasion that may overwhelm the client's judgment.

[3] The use of general advertising and written, recorded or electronic communications to transmit information from lawyer to prospective client, rather than direct in-person, live telephone or real-time electronic contact, will help to assure that the information flows cleanly as well as freely. The contents of advertisements and communications permitted under Rule 7.2 can be permanently recorded so that they cannot be disputed and may be shared with others who know the lawyer. This potential for informal review is itself likely to help guard against statements and claims that might constitute false and misleading communications, in violation of Rule 7.1. The contents of direct in-person, live telephone or real-time electronic conversations between a lawyer and a prospective client can be disputed and may not be subject to third-party scrutiny. Consequently, they are much more likely to approach (and occasionally cross) the dividing line between accurate representations and those that are false and misleading.

[4] There is far less likelihood that a lawyer would engage in abusive practices against an individual who is a former client, or with whom the lawyer has a close personal or family relationship, or in situations in which the lawyer is motivated by considerations other than the lawyer's pecuniary gain. Nor is there a serious potential for abuse when the person contacted is a lawyer. Consequently, the general prohibition in Rule 7.3(a) and the requirements of Rule 7.3(c) are not applicable in those situations. Also, paragraph (a) is not intended to prohibit a lawyer from participating in constitutionally protected activities of public or charitable legal-service organizations or bona fide political, social, civic, fraternal, employee or trade organizations whose purposes include providing or recommending legal services to its members or beneficiaries.

[5] But even permitted forms of solicitation can be abused. Thus, any solicitation which contains information which is false or misleading within the meaning of Rule 7.1, which involves coercion, duress or harassment within the meaning of Rule 7.3(b)(2), or which involves contact with a prospective client who has made known to the lawyer a desire not to be solicited by the lawyer within the meaning of Rule 7.3(b)(1) is prohibited. Moreover, if after sending a letter or other communication to a client as permitted by Rule 7.2 the lawyer receives no response, any further effort to communicate with the prospective client may violate the provisions of Rule 7.3(b).

[6] This Rule is not intended to prohibit a lawyer from contacting representatives of organizations or groups that may be interested in establishing a group or prepaid legal plan for their members, insureds, beneficiaries or other third parties for the purpose of informing such entities of the availability of and details concerning the plan or arrangement which the lawyer or lawyer's firm is willing to offer. This form of communication is not directed to a prospective client. Rather, it is usually addressed to an individual acting in a fiduciary capacity seeking a supplier of legal services for others who may, if they choose, become prospective clients of the lawyer. Under these circumstances, the activity which the lawyer undertakes in communicating with such representatives and the type of information transmitted to the individual are functionally similar to and serve the same purpose as advertising permitted under Rule 7.2.

[7] The requirement in Rule 7.3(c) that certain communications be marked "Advertising Material" does not apply to communications sent in response to requests of potential clients or their spokespersons or sponsors. General announcements by lawyers, including changes in personnel or office location, do not constitute communications soliciting professional employment from a client known to be in need of legal services within the meaning of this Rule.

[8] Paragraph (d) of this Rule permits a lawyer to participate with an organization which uses personal contact to solicit members for its group or prepaid legal service plan, provided that the personal contact is not undertaken by any lawyer who would be a provider of legal services through the plan. The organization must not be owned by or directed (whether as manager or otherwise) by any lawyer or law firm that participates in the plan. For example, paragraph (d) would not permit a lawyer to create an organization controlled directly or indirectly by the lawyer and use the organization for the in-person or telephone solicitation of legal employment of the lawyer through memberships in the plan or otherwise. The communication permitted by these organizations also must not be directed to a person known to need legal services in a particular matter, but is to be designed to inform potential plan members generally of another means of affordable legal services. Lawyers who participate in a legal service plan must reasonably assure that the plan sponsors are in compliance with Rules 7.1, 7.2 and 7.3(b). See 8.4(a).

RULE 7.4: COMMUNICATION OF FIELDS OF PRACTICE AND SPECIALIZATION

(a) A lawyer may communicate the fact that the lawyer does or does not practice in particular fields of law.

(b) A lawyer admitted to engage in patent practice before the United States Patent and Trademark Office may use the designation "Patent Attorney" or a substantially similar designation.

(c) A lawyer engaged in Admiralty practice may use the designation "Admiralty," "Proctor in Admiralty" or a substantially similar designation.

(d) A lawyer shall not state or imply that a lawyer is certified as a specialist in a particular field of law, unless:

(1) the lawyer has been certified as a specialist by an organization that has been approved by an appropriate state authority or that has been accredited by the American Bar Association; and

(2) the name of the certifying organization is clearly identified in the communication.

COMMENT

[1] Paragraph (a) of this Rule permits a lawyer to indicate areas of practice in communications about the lawyer's services. If a lawyer practices only in certain fields, or will not accept matters except in a specified field or fields, the lawyer is permitted to so indicate. A lawyer is generally permitted to state that the lawyer is a "specialist," practices a "specialty," or "specializes in" particular fields, but such communications are subject to the "false and misleading" standard applied in Rule 7.1 to communications concerning a lawyer's services.

[2] Paragraph (b) recognizes the long-established policy of the Patent and Trademark Office for the designation of lawyers practicing before the Office. Paragraph (c) recognizes that designation of Admiralty practice has a long historical tradition associated with maritime commerce and the federal courts.

[3] Paragraph (d) permits a lawyer to state that the lawyer is certified as a specialist in a field of law if such certification is granted by an organization approved by an appropriate state

authority or accredited by the American Bar Association or another organization, such as a state bar association, that has been approved by the state authority to accredit organizations that certify lawyers as specialists. Certification signifies that an objective entity has recognized an advanced degree of knowledge and experience in the specialty area greater than is suggested by general licensure to practice law. Certifying organizations may be expected to apply standards of experience, knowledge and proficiency to insure that a lawyer's recognition as a specialist is meaningful and reliable. In order to insure that consumers can obtain access to useful information about an organization granting certification, the name of the certifying organization must be included in any communication regarding the certification.

RULE 7.5: FIRM NAMES AND LETTERHEADS

(a) A lawyer shall not use a firm name, letterhead or other professional designation that violates Rule 7.1. A trade name may be used by a lawyer in private practice if it does not imply a connection with a government agency or with a public or charitable legal services organization and is not otherwise in violation of Rule 7.1.

(b) A law firm with offices in more than one jurisdiction may use the same name or other professional designation in each jurisdiction, but identification of the lawyers in an office of the firm shall indicate the jurisdictional limitations on those not licensed to practice in the jurisdiction where the office is located.

(c) The name of a lawyer holding a public office shall not be used in the name of a law firm, or in communications on its behalf, during any substantial period in which the lawyer is not actively and regularly practicing with the firm.

(d) Lawyers may state or imply that they practice in a partnership or other organization only when that is the fact.

COMMENT

[1] A firm may be designated by the names of all or some of its members, by the names of deceased members where there has been a continuing succession in the firm's identity or by a trade name such as the "ABC Legal Clinic." A lawyer or law firm may also be designated by a distinctive website address or comparable professional designation. Although the United States Supreme Court has held that legislation may prohibit the use of trade names in professional practice, use of such names in law practice is acceptable so long as it is not misleading. If a private firm uses a trade name that includes a geographical name such as "Springfield Legal Clinic," an express disclaimer that it is a public legal aid agency may be required to avoid a misleading implication. It may be observed that any firm name including the name of a deceased partner is, strictly speaking, a trade name. The use of such names to designate law firms has proven a useful means of identification. However, it is misleading to use the name of a lawyer not associated with the firm or a predecessor of the firm, or the name of a nonlawyer.

[2] With regard to paragraph (d), lawyers sharing office facilities, but who are not in fact associated with each other in a law firm, may not denominate themselves as, for example, "Smith and Jones," for that title suggests that they are practicing law together in a firm.

RULE 7.6: POLITICAL CONTRIBUTIONS TO OBTAIN GOVERNMENT LEGAL ENGAGEMENTS OR APPOINTMENTS BY JUDGES

A lawyer or law firm shall not accept a government legal engagement or an appointment by a judge if the lawyer or law firm makes a political contribution or solicits political contributions for the purpose of obtaining or being considered for that type of legal engagement or appointment.

COMMENT

[1] Lawyers have a right to participate fully in the political process, which includes making and soliciting political contributions to candidates for judicial and other public office. Nevertheless, when lawyers make or solicit political contributions in order to obtain an engagement for legal work awarded by a government agency, or to obtain appointment by a judge, the public may legitimately question whether the lawyers engaged to perform the work are selected on the basis of competence and merit. In such a circumstance, the integrity of the profession is undermined.

[2] The term "political contribution" denotes any gift, subscription, loan, advance or deposit of anything of value made directly or indirectly to a candidate, incumbent, political party or campaign committee to influence or provide financial support for election to or retention in judicial or other government office. Political contributions in initiative and referendum elections are not included. For purposes of this Rule, the term "political contribution" does not include uncompensated services.

[3] Subject to the exceptions below, (i) the term "government legal engagement" denotes any engagement to provide legal services that a public official has the direct or indirect power to award; and (ii) the term "appointment by a judge" denotes an appointment to a position such as referee, commissioner, special master, receiver, guardian or other similar position that is made by a judge. Those terms do not, however, include (a) substantially uncompensated services; (b) engagements or appointments made on the basis of experience, expertise, professional qualifications and cost following a request for proposal or other process that is free from influence based upon political contributions; and (c) engagements or appointments made on a rotational basis from a list compiled without regard to political contributions.

[4] The term "lawyer or law firm" includes a political action committee or other entity owned or controlled by a lawyer or law firm.

[5] Political contributions are for the purpose of obtaining or being considered for a government legal engagement or appointment by a judge if, but for the desire to be considered for the legal engagement or appointment, the lawyer or law firm would not have made or solicited the contributions. The purpose may be determined by an examination of the circumstances in which the contributions occur. For example, one or more contributions that in the aggregate are substantial in relation to other contributions by lawyers or law firms, made for the benefit of an official in a position to influence award of a government legal engagement, and followed by an award of the legal engagement to the contributing or soliciting lawyer or the lawyer's firm would support an inference that the purpose of the contributions was to obtain the engagement, absent other factors that weigh against existence of the proscribed purpose. Those factors may include among others that the contribution or solicitation was made to further a political, social, or economic interest or because of an existing personal, family, or professional relationship with a candidate.

[6] If a lawyer makes or solicits a political contribution under circumstances that constitute bribery or another crime, Rule 8.4(b) is implicated.

MAINTAINING THE INTEGRITY OF THE PROFESSION

RULE 8.1: BAR ADMISSION AND DISCIPLINARY MATTERS

An applicant for admission to the bar, or a lawyer in connection with a bar admission application or in connection with a disciplinary matter, shall not:

(a) knowingly make a false statement of material fact; or

(b) fail to disclose a fact necessary to correct a misapprehension known by the person to have arisen in the matter, or knowingly fail to respond to a lawful demand for

*pro hac
vice*

information from an admissions or disciplinary authority, **except that this rule does not require disclosure of information otherwise protected by Rule 1.6.**

COMMENT

[1] The duty imposed by this Rule extends to persons seeking admission to the bar as well as to lawyers. Hence, if a person makes a material false statement in connection with an application for admission, it may be the basis for subsequent disciplinary action if the person is admitted, and in any event may be relevant in a subsequent admission application. The duty imposed by this Rule applies to a lawyer's own admission or discipline as well as that of others. Thus, it is a separate professional offense for a lawyer to knowingly make a misrepresentation or omission in connection with a disciplinary investigation of the lawyer's own conduct. Paragraph (b) of this Rule also requires correction of any prior misstatement in the matter that the applicant or lawyer may have made and affirmative clarification of any misunderstanding on the part of the admissions or disciplinary authority of which the person involved becomes aware.

[2] This Rule is subject to the provisions of the fifth amendment of the United States Constitution and corresponding provisions of state constitutions. A person relying on such a provision in response to a question, however, should do so openly and not use the right of nondisclosure as a justification for failure to comply with this Rule.

[3] A lawyer representing an applicant for admission to the bar, or representing a lawyer who is the subject of a disciplinary inquiry or proceeding, is governed by the rules applicable to the client-lawyer relationship, including Rule 1.6 and, in some cases, Rule 3.3.

RULE 8.2: JUDICIAL AND LEGAL OFFICIALS

(a) A lawyer shall not make a statement that the lawyer knows to be false or with reckless disregard as to its truth or falsity concerning the qualifications or integrity of a judge, adjudicatory officer or public legal officer, or of a candidate for election or appointment to judicial or legal office.

(b) A lawyer who is a candidate for judicial office shall comply with the applicable provisions of the Code of Judicial Conduct.

COMMENT

[1] Assessments by lawyers are relied on in evaluating the professional or personal fitness of persons being considered for election or appointment to judicial office and to public legal offices, such as attorney general, prosecuting attorney and public defender. Expressing honest and candid opinions on such matters contributes to improving the administration of justice. Conversely, false statements by a lawyer can unfairly undermine public confidence in the administration of justice.

[2] When a lawyer seeks judicial office, the lawyer should be bound by applicable limitations on political activity.

[3] To maintain the fair and independent administration of justice, lawyers are encouraged to continue traditional efforts to defend judges and courts unjustly criticized.

Attny trier of fact — look also @ 5.1, 5.2, 5.3

RULE 8.3: REPORTING PROFESSIONAL MISCONDUCT

Rat on your friends

(a) A lawyer who **knows** that another lawyer has committed a violation of the Rules of Professional Conduct that raises a **substantial** question as to that lawyer's honesty, trustworthiness or fitness as a lawyer in other respects, **shall** inform the appropriate professional authority.

Md, Attny grievance commission

(b) A lawyer who knows that a judge has committed a violation of applicable rules of judicial conduct that raises a substantial question as to the judge's fitness for office shall inform the appropriate authority.

(c) This Rule does not require disclosure of information otherwise protected by Rule 1.6 or information gained by a lawyer or judge while participating in an approved lawyers assistance program.

[handwritten: —no incentive to report wants —who wants enemies?]

COMMENT

[1] Self-regulation of the legal profession requires that members of the profession initiate disciplinary investigation when they know of a violation of the Rules of Professional Conduct. Lawyers have a similar obligation with respect to judicial misconduct. An apparently isolated violation may indicate a pattern of misconduct that only a disciplinary investigation can uncover. Reporting a violation is especially important where the victim is unlikely to discover the offense.

[2] A report about misconduct is not required where it would involve violation of Rule 1.6. However, a lawyer should encourage a client to consent to disclosure where prosecution would not substantially prejudice the client's interests.

[3] If a lawyer were obliged to report every violation of the Rules, the failure to report any violation would itself be a professional offense. Such a requirement existed in many jurisdictions but proved to be unenforceable. This Rule limits the reporting obligation to those offenses that a self-regulating profession must vigorously endeavor to prevent. A measure of judgment is, therefore, required in complying with the provisions of this Rule. The term "substantial" refers to the seriousness of the possible offense and not the quantum of evidence of which the lawyer is aware. A report should be made to the bar disciplinary agency unless some other agency, such as a peer review agency, is more appropriate in the circumstances. Similar considerations apply to the reporting of judicial misconduct.

[4] The duty to report professional misconduct does not apply to a lawyer retained to represent a lawyer whose professional conduct is in question. Such a situation is governed by the Rules applicable to the client-lawyer relationship. *[handwritten: N/A if rep. 2tnry for violation]*

[5] Information about a lawyer's or judge's misconduct or fitness may be received by a lawyer in the course of that lawyer's participation in an approved lawyers or judges assistance program. In that circumstance, providing for an exception to the reporting requirements of paragraphs (a) and (b) of this Rule encourages lawyers and judges to seek treatment through such a program. Conversely, without such an exception, lawyers and judges may hesitate to seek assistance from these programs, which may then result in additional harm to their professional careers and additional injury to the welfare of clients and the public. These Rules do not otherwise address the confidentiality of information received by a lawyer or judge participating in an approved lawyers assistance program; such an obligation, however, may be imposed by the rules of the program or other law.

RULE 8.4: MISCONDUCT

It is professional misconduct for a lawyer to:

(a) violate or attempt to violate the Rules of Professional Conduct, knowingly assist or induce another to do so, or do so through the acts of another; *[handwritten: no runners if you can't do it, can't order another to]*

(b) commit a criminal act that reflects adversely on the lawyer's honesty, trustworthiness or fitness as a lawyer in other respects;

(c) engage in conduct involving dishonesty, fraud, deceit or misrepresentation;

(d) engage in conduct that is prejudicial to the administration of justice;

(e) state or imply an ability to influence improperly a government agency or official or to achieve results by means that violate the Rules of Professional Conduct or other law; or

(f) knowingly assist a judge or judicial officer in conduct that is a violation of applicable rules of judicial conduct or other law.

COMMENT

[1] Lawyers are subject to discipline when they violate or attempt to violate the Rules of Professional Conduct, knowingly assist or induce another to do so or do so through the acts of another, as when they request or instruct an agent to do so on the lawyer's behalf. Paragraph (a), however, does not prohibit a lawyer from advising a client concerning action the client is legally entitled to take.

[2] Many kinds of illegal conduct reflect adversely on fitness to practice law, such as offenses involving fraud and the offense of willful failure to file an income tax return. However, some kinds of offenses carry no such implication. Traditionally, the distinction was drawn in terms of offenses involving "moral turpitude." That concept can be construed to include offenses concerning some matters of personal morality, such as adultery and comparable offenses, that have no specific connection to fitness for the practice of law. Although a lawyer is personally answerable to the entire criminal law, a lawyer should be professionally answerable only for offenses that indicate lack of those characteristics relevant to law practice. Offenses involving violence, dishonesty, breach of trust, or serious interference with the administration of justice are in that category. A pattern of repeated offenses, even ones of minor significance when considered separately, can indicate indifference to legal obligation.

[3] A lawyer who, in the course of representing a client, knowingly manifests by words or conduct, bias or prejudice based upon race, sex, religion, national origin, disability, age, sexual orientation or socioeconomic status, violates paragraph (d) when such actions are prejudicial to the administration of justice. Legitimate advocacy respecting the foregoing factors does not violate paragraph (d). A trial judge's finding that peremptory challenges were exercised on a discriminatory basis does not alone establish a violation of this rule.

[4] A lawyer may refuse to comply with an obligation imposed by law upon a good faith belief that no valid obligation exists. The provisions of Rule 1.2(d) concerning a good faith challenge to the validity, scope, meaning or application of the law apply to challenges of legal regulation of the practice of law.

[5] Lawyers holding public office assume legal responsibilities going beyond those of other citizens. A lawyer's abuse of public office can suggest an inability to fulfill the professional role of lawyers. The same is true of abuse of positions of private trust such as trustee, executor, administrator, guardian, agent and officer, director or manager of a corporation or other organization.

RULE 8.5: DISCIPLINARY AUTHORITY; CHOICE OF LAW

(a) Disciplinary Authority. A lawyer admitted to practice in this jurisdiction is subject to the disciplinary authority of this jurisdiction, regardless of where the lawyer's conduct occurs. A lawyer not admitted in this jurisdiction is also subject to the disciplinary authority of this jurisdiction if the lawyer provides or offers to provide any legal services in this jurisdiction. A lawyer may be subject to the disciplinary authority of both this jurisdiction and another jurisdiction for the same conduct.

(b) Choice of Law. In any exercise of the disciplinary authority of this jurisdiction, the rules of professional conduct to be applied shall be as follows:

(1) for conduct in connection with a matter pending before a tribunal, the rules of the jurisdiction in which the tribunal sits, unless the rules of the tribunal provide otherwise; and

(2) for any other conduct, the rules of the jurisdiction in which the lawyer's conduct occurred, or, if the predominant effect of the conduct is in a different jurisdiction, the rules of that jurisdiction shall be applied to the conduct. A lawyer shall not be subject to discipline if the lawyer's conduct conforms to the rules of a jurisdiction in which the lawyer reasonably believes the predominant effect of the lawyer's conduct will occur.

COMMENT

Disciplinary Authority

[1] It is longstanding law that the conduct of a lawyer admitted to practice in this jurisdiction is subject to the disciplinary authority of this jurisdiction. Extension of the disciplinary authority of this jurisdiction to other lawyers who provide or offer to provide legal services in this jurisdiction is for the protection of the citizens of this jurisdiction. Reciprocal enforcement of a jurisdiction's disciplinary findings and sanctions will further advance the purposes of this Rule. See, Rules 6 and 22, ABA *Model Rules for Lawyer Disciplinary Enforcement*. A lawyer who is subject to the disciplinary authority of this jurisdiction under Rule 8.5(a) appoints an official to be designated by this Court to receive service of process in this jurisdiction. The fact that the lawyer is subject to the disciplinary authority of this jurisdiction may be a factor in determining whether personal jurisdiction may be asserted over the lawyer for civil matters.

Choice of Law

[2] A lawyer may be potentially subject to more than one set of rules of professional conduct which impose different obligations. The lawyer may be licensed to practice in more than one jurisdiction with differing rules, or may be admitted to practice before a particular court with rules that differ from those of the jurisdiction or jurisdictions in which the lawyer is licensed to practice. Additionally, the lawyer's conduct may involve significant contacts with more than one jurisdiction.

[3] Paragraph (b) seeks to resolve such potential conflicts. Its premise is that minimizing conflicts between rules, as well as uncertainty about which rules are applicable, is in the best interest of both clients and the profession (as well as the bodies having authority to regulate the profession). Accordingly, it takes the approach of (i) providing that any particular conduct of a lawyer shall be subject to only one set of rules of professional conduct, (ii) making the determination of which set of rules applies to particular conduct as straightforward as possible, consistent with recognition of appropriate regulatory interests of relevant jurisdictions, and (iii) providing protection from discipline for lawyers who act reasonably in the face of uncertainty.

[4] Paragraph (b)(1) provides that as to a lawyer's conduct relating to a proceeding pending before a tribunal, the lawyer shall be subject only to the rules of professional conduct of that tribunal. As to all other conduct, including conduct in anticipation of a proceeding not yet pending before a tribunal, paragraph (b)(2) provides that a lawyer shall be subject to the rules of the jurisdiction in which the lawyer's conduct occurred, or, if the predominant effect of the conduct is in another jurisdiction, the rules of that jurisdiction shall be applied to the conduct. In the case of conduct in anticipation of a proceeding that is likely to be before a tribunal, the predominant effect of such conduct could be where the conduct occurred, where the tribunal sits or in another jurisdiction.

[5] When a lawyer's conduct involves significant contacts with more than one jurisdiction, it may not be clear whether the predominant effect of the lawyer's conduct will occur

in a jurisdiction other than the one in which the conduct occurred. So long as the lawyer's conduct conforms to the rules of a jurisdiction in which the lawyer reasonably believes the predominant effect will occur, the lawyer shall not be subject to discipline under this Rule.

[6] If two admitting jurisdictions were to proceed against a lawyer for the same conduct, they should, applying this rule, identify the same governing ethics rules. They should take all appropriate steps to see that they do apply the same rule to the same conduct, and in all events should avoid proceeding against a lawyer on the basis of two inconsistent rules.

[7] The choice of law provision applies to lawyers engaged in transnational practice, unless international law, treaties or other agreements between competent regulatory authorities in the affected jurisdictions provide otherwise.

ABA CORRELATION TABLES BETWEEN MODEL RULES AND MODEL CODE RELATED PROVISIONS

TABLE A: ABA Model Rules Cross-Referenced to Related Provisions of ABA Model Code

ABA MODEL RULES	ABA MODEL CODE	ABA MODEL RULES	ABA MODEL CODE
Competence		Rule 1.8(b)	EC 4-5; DC 4-101(B)
Rule 1.1	EC 1-1, 1-2, 6-1, 6-2, 6-3, 6-4, 6-5; DR 6-101(A)	Rule 1.8(c)	EC 5-1, 5-2, 5-5, 5-6
		Rule 1.8(d)	EC 5-1, 5-3, 5-4; DR 5-104(B)
Scope of Representation and Allocation of Authority between Client and Lawyer		Rule 1.8(e)	EC 5-1, 5-3, 5-7, 5-8; DR 5-103(B)
Rule 1.2(a)	EC 5-12, 7-7, 7-8; DR 7-101(A)(1)	Rule 1.8(f)	EC 2-21, 5-1, 5-22, 5-23; DR 5-107(A) & (B)
Rule 1.2(b)	EC 7-17	Rule 1.8(g)	EC 5-1; DR 5-106(A)
Rule 1.2(c)	EC 7-8, 7-9; DR 7-101(B)(1)	Rule 1.8(h)	EC 6-6; DR 6-102(A)
Rule 1.2(d)	EC 7-1, 7-2, 7-5, 7-22; DR 7-102(A)(6)-(8), 7-106	Rule 1.8(i)	EC 5-1, 5-7; DR 5-101(A), 5-103(A)
Diligence		Rule 1.8(j)	None
Rule 1.3	EC 2-31, 6-4, 7-1, 7-38; DR 6-101(A)(3), 7-101(A)(1) & (3)	Rule 1.8(k)	None
		Duties to Former Clients	
Communication		Rule 1.9(a)	DR 5-105(C)
Rule 1.4(a)	EC 7-8, 9-2; DR 2-110(C)(1) (c), 6-101(A)(3), 9-102(B)(1)	Rule 1.9(b)	EC 4-5, 4-6
		Rule 1.9(c)	None
Rule 1.4(b)	EC 7-8	*Imputation of Conflicts of Interest: General Rule*	
Fees			
Rule 1.5(a)	EC 2-16, 2-17, 2-18; DR 2-106(A) & (B)	Rule 1.10(a)	EC 4-5; DR 5-105(D)
		Rule 1.10(b)	EC 4-5; DR 5-105(D)
Rule 1.5(b)	EC 2-19	Rule 1.10(c)	DR 5-105(A)
Rule 1.5(c)	EC 2-20, 5-7	Rule 1.10(d)	None
Rule 1.5(d)	EC 2-20; DR 2-106(C)	*Special Conflicts of Interest for Former and Current Government Officers and Employees*	
Rule 1.5(e)	EC 2-22; DR 2-107(A)		
Confidentiality of Information		Rule 1.11(a)	EC 9-3; DR 9-101(B)
Rule 1.6(a)	EC 4-1, 4-2, 4-3, 4-4; DR 4-101(A), (B) & (C)	Rule 1.11(b)	None
		Rule 1.11(c)	None
Rule 1.6(b)(1)	EC 4-2; DR 4-101(C)(3), 7-102(B)	Rule 1.11(d)	EC 8-8
		Rule 1.11(e)	None
Rule 1.6(b)(2)	None	*Former Judge, Arbitrator, Mediator or Other Third-Party Neutral*	
Rule 1.6(b)(3)	DR 4-101(C)(4)		
Rule 1.6(b)(4)	DR 4-101(C)(2)	Rule 1.12(a) & (b)	EC 5-20, 9-3; DR 9-101(A) & (B)
Conflict of Interest: Current Clients			
Rule 1.7(a)	EC 2-21, 5-1, 5-2, 5-3, 5-9, 5-11, 5-13, 5-14, 5-15, 5-17, 5-21, 5-22, 5-23; DR 5-101(A) & (B), 5-102, 5-104(A), 5-105(A) & (B), 5-107(A) & (B)	Rule 1.12(c)	DR 5-105(D)
		Rule 1.12(d)	None
		Organization as Client	
		Rule 1.13(a)	EC 5-18, 5-24
		Rule 1.13(b)	EC 5-18, 5-24; DR 5-107(B)
		Rule 1.13(c)	EC 5-18, 5-24; DR 5-105(D), 5-107(B)
Rule 1.7(b)	EC 2-21, 5-15, 5-16, 5-17, 5-19, 5-23; DC 5-101(A) & (B), 5-102, 5-104(A), 5-105(C), 5-107(A)	Rule 1.13(d)	EC 5-16
		Rule 1.13(e)	EC 4-4, 5-16; DR 5-105(B) & (C)
Conflict of Interest: Current Clients: Specific Rules		*Client with Diminished Capacity*	
		Rule 1.14(a)	EC 7-11, 7-12
Rule 1.8(a)	EC 5-3, 5-5, 5-104(A)	Rule 1.14(b)	EC 7-12

ABA MODEL RULES	ABA MODEL CODE	ABA MODEL RULES	ABA MODEL CODE
Rule 1.14(c)	None	Rule 3.3(a)(2)	EC 7-23; DR 1-102(A)(5), 7-106(B)(1)
Safekeeping Property		Rule 3.3(a)(3)	EC 7-5, 7-6, 7-26, 8-5;
Rule 1.15	EC 5-7, 9-5, 9-7; DR 5-103(A)(1), 9-102		DR 1-102(A)(4) & (5), 7-102(A)(4), (6) & (7), 7-102(B)(1) & (2)
Declining or Terminating Representation		Rule 3.3(b)	EC 7-5, 7-26, 7-27, 7-32, 8-5;
Rule 1.16(a)(1)	EC 2-30, 2-31, 2-32; DR 2-103(E), 2-104(A), 2-109(A), 2-110(B)(1) & (2)		DR 1-102(A)(4) & (5), 7-102(A)(4), (6) & (7), 7-102(B)(1) & (2), 7-108(G), 7-109(A) & (B)
Rule 1.16(a)(2)	EC 1-6, 2-30, 2-31, 2-32; DR 2-110(B)(3), & (C)(4)	Rule 3.3(c)	EC 8-5; DR 7-102(B)
Rule 1.16(a)(3)	EC 2-31, 2-32; DR 2-110(B)(4)	Rule 3.3(d)	EC 7-24, 7-27
Rule 1.16(b)(1)	EC 2-32; DR 2-110(A)(2), 2-110(C)(5)	*Fairness to Opposing Party and Counsel*	
		Rule 3.4(a)	EC 7-6, 7-27; DR 1-102(A)(4) & (5), 7-106(C)(7), 7-109(A) & (B)
Rule 1.16(b)(2)	EC 2-31, 2-32; DR 2-110(C)(1)(b) & (c), 2-110(C)(2)	Rule 3.4(b)	EC 7-6, 7-28; DR 1-102(A)(4), (5) & (6), 7-102(A)(6), 7-109(C)
Rule 1.16(b)(3)	EC 2-31, 2-32; DR 2-110(C)(2)	Rule 3.4(c)	EC 7-22, 7-25, 7-38; DR 1-102(A)(5), 7-106(A), 7-106(C)(5) & (7)
Rule 1.16(b)(4)	EC 2-30, 2-31, 2-32; DR 2-110(C)(1)(d)	Rule 3.4(d)	DR 1-102(A)(5), 7-106(A), 7-106(C)(7)
Rule 1.16(b)(5)	EC 2-31, 2-32; DR 2-110(C)(1)(f)(i)(j)	Rule 3.4(e)	EC 7-24, 7-25; DR 1-102(A)(5), 7-106(C)(1), (2), (3) & (4)
Rule 1.16(b)(6)	EC 2-32; DR 2-110(C)(1)(d) & (e)	Rule 3.4(f)	EC 7-27; DR 1-102(A)(5), 7-104(A)(2), 7-109(B)
Rule 1.16(b)(7)	EC 2-32; DR 2-110(C)(6)	*Impartiality and Decorum of the Tribunal*	
Rule 1.16(c)	EC 2-32; DR 2-110(A)(1)	Rule 3.5(a)	EC 7-20, 7-29, 7-31, 7-32, 7-34; DR 7-106, 7-108, 7-109, 7-110, 8-101(A)
Rule 1.16(d)	EC 2-32; DR 2-110(A)(2) & (3)		
Sale of Law Practice		Rule 3.5(b)	EC 7-35; DR 7-108, 7-110(A) & (B)
Rule 1.17	None	Rule 3.5(c)	EC 7-29, 7-30, 7-31, 7-32; DR 7-108
Duties to Prospective Client		Rule 3.5(d)	EC 7-20, 7-25, 7-36, 7-37; DR 7-101(A)(1), 7-106(C)(6)
Rule 1.18	EC 4-1		
Advisor		*Trial Publicity*	
Rule 2.1	EC 5-11, 7-3, 7-8; DR 5-107(B)	Rule 3.6	EC 7-25, 7-33; DR 7-107
Evaluation for Use by Third Persons		*Lawyer as Witness*	
Rule 2.3	None	Rule 3.7(a)	EC 5-9, 5-10; DR 5-101(B)(1) & (2), 5-102
Lawyer Serving As Third-Party Neutral		Rule 3.7(b)	EC 5-9; DR 5-101(B), 5-102
Rule 2.4	EC 5-20	*Special Responsibilities of a Prosecutor*	
Meritorious Claims and Contentions		Rule 3.8(a)	EC 7-11, 7-13, 7-14; DR 7-103(A)
Rule 3.1	EC 7-1, 7-4, 7-5, 7-14, 7-25; DR 2-109(A)(B)(1), 5-102(A)(5), 7-102(A)(1) & (2)	Rule 3.8(b)	EC 7-11, 7-13
		Rule 3.8(c)	EC 7-11, 7-13, 7-18
Expediting Litigation		Rule 3.8(d)	EC 7-11, 7-13; DR 7-103(B)
Rule 3.2	EC 7-20; DR 1-102(A)(5), 7-101(A)(1) & (2)	Rule 3.8(e)	None
Candor toward the Tribunal		Rule 3.8(f)	EC 7-14
Rule 3.3(a)(1)	EC 7-4, 7-26, 7-32, 8-5; DR 1-102(A)(4) & (5), DR 7-102(A)(4) & (5)		

Table A: ABA Model Rules Cross-Referenced to Related Provisions of ABA Model Code

ABA MODEL RULES	ABA MODEL CODE	ABA MODEL RULES	ABA MODEL CODE
Advocate in Nonadjudicative Proceedings		*Voluntary Pro Bono Publico Service*	
Rule 3.9	EC 7-11, 7-15, 7-16, 8-4, 8-5; DR 7-106(B)(2), 9-101(C)	Rule 6.1	EC 1-2, 1-4, 2-1, 2-2, 2-16, 2-24, 2-25, 6-2, 8-1, 8-2, 8-3, 8-7, 8-9
Truthfulness in Statements to Others		*Accepting Appointments*	
Rule 4.1	EC 7-5; DR 7-102(A)(3), (4), (5) & (7), 7-102(B)	Rule 6.2 (a)	EC 2-1, 2-25, 2-27, 2-28, 2-29, 8-3
Communication with Person Represented by Counsel		Rule 6.2(b)	EC 2-16, 2-25, 2-29, 2-30
Rule 4.2	EC 2-30, 7-18; DR 7-104(A)(1)	Rule 6.2(c)	EC 2-25, 2-27, 2-29, 2-30
Dealing with Unrepresented Person		*Membership in Legal Services Organization*	
		Rule 6.3	EC 2-33; DR 5-101(A)
Rule 4.3	EC 2-3, 7-18; DR 7-104(A)(2)	*Law Reform Activities Affecting Client Interests*	
Respect for Rights of Third Person		Rule 6.4	EC 2-33; DR 5-101(A), 8-101
Rule 4.4(a)	EC 7-10, 7-14, 7-21, 7-25, 7-29, 7-30, 7-37; DR 2-110(B)(1), 7-101(A)(1), 7-102(A)(1), 7-106(C)(2), 7-107(D), (E) & (F), 7-108(D), (E), & (F)	*Nonprofit and Court-Annexed Limited Legal Services Programs*	
		Rule 6.5	None
		Communications Concerning a Lawyer's Services	
		Rule 7.1	EC 2-8, 2-9, 2-10; DR 2-101(A), (B), (C), (E), (F) & (G), 2-102(E)
Rule 4.4(b)	None	*Advertising*	
Responsibilities of Partners, Managers, and Supervisory Lawyers		Rule 7.2(a)	EC 2-1, 2-2, 2-6, 2-7, 2-8, 2-15; DR 2-101(B) & (H), 2-102(A) & (B), 2-103(B), 2-104(A)(4) & (5)
Rule 5.1(a) & (b)	EC 4-5; DR 4-101(D), 7-107(J)		
Rule 5.1(c)	DR 1-102(A)(2), 1-103(A), 7-108(E)	Rule 7.2(b)	EC 2-8, 2-15; DR 2-101(I), 2-103(B), (C) & (D)
Responsibilities of a Subordinate Lawyer		Rule 7.2(c)	None
Rule 5.2	None	*Direct Contact with Prospective Clients*	
Responsibilities Regarding Nonlawyer Assistants		Rule 7.3	EC 2-3, 2-4, 5-6; DR 2-103(A), 2-103(C)(1), 2-103(D)(4)(b) & (c), 2-104(A)(1), (2), (3), & (5)
Rule 5.3(a)	EC 3-6, 4-2, 4-5, 7-28; DR 4-101(D), 7-107(J)		
Rule 5.3(b)	DR 1-102(A)(2), 7-107(J), 7-108(B), 7-108(E)	*Communication of Fields of Practice and Specialization*	
Rule 5.3(c)	None	Rule 7.4(a)	EC 2-1, 2-7, 2-8, 2-14; DR 2-101(B)(2), 2-102(A)(3), 2-102(E), 2-105(A)
Professional Independence of a Lawyer			
Rule 5.4(a)	EC 2-33, 3-8, 5-24; DR 2-103(D)(1), 2-103(D)(2), 2-103(D)(4)(a), (d), (e) & (f), 3-102(A), 5-107(C)(3)	Rule 7.4(b)	DR 2-105(A)(1)
		Rule 7.4(c)	EC 2-14
		Rule 7.4(d)	EC 2-8, 2-14; DR 2-105(A)(2) & (3)
Rule 5.4(b)	EC 2-33, 3-8; DR 3-103(A)	*Firm Names and Letterheads*	
Rule 5.4(c)	EC 2-33, 5-22, 5-23; DR 2-103(C), 5-107(B)	Rule 7.5(a)	EC 2-11, 2-13; DR 2-102(A)(4), 2-102(B), (D) & (E), 2-105
Rule 5.4(d)	EC 2-33, 3-8; DR 5-107(C)		
Unauthorized Practice of Law		Rule 7.5(b)	EC 2-11; DR 2-102(D)
Rule 5.5(a)	DR 3-101(A) & (B)	Rule 7.5(c)	EC 2-11, 2-12; DR 2-102(B)
Restrictions on Right to Practice		Rule 7.5(d)	EC 2-11, 2-13; DR 2-102(C)
Rule 5.6	DR 2-108		
Responsibilities Regarding Law-Related Services			
Rule 5.7	None		

ABA MODEL RULES	**ABA MODEL CODE**
Political Contributions to Obtain Government Legal Engagements or Appointments by Judges	
Rule 7.6	None
Bar Admission and Disciplinary Matters	
Rule 8.1(a)	EC 1-1, 1-2, 1-3; DR 1-101(A) & (B)
Rule 8.1(b)	DR 1-102(A)(5), 1-103(B)
Judicial and Legal Officials	
Rule 8.2(a)	EC 8-6; DR 8-102
Rule 8.2(b)	DR 8-103
Reporting Professional Misconduct	
Rule 8.3	EC 1-3; DR 1-103(A)
Misconduct	
Rule 8.4(a)	EC 1-5, 1-6, 9-6; DR 1-102(A)(1) & (2), 2-103(E), 7-102(A) & (B)
Rule 8.4(b)	EC 1-5; DR 1-102(A)(3) & (6), 7-102(A)(8), 8-101(A)(3)
Rule 8.4(c)	EC 1-5, 9-4; DR 1-102(A)(4), 8-101(A)(3)
Rule 8.4(d)	EC 3-9, 8-3; DR 1-102(A)(5), 3-101(B)
Rule 8.4(e)	EC 1-5, 9-2, 9-4, 9-6; DR 9-101(C)
Rule 8.4(f)	EC 1-5, 7-34, 9-1; DR 1-102(A)(3), (4), (5) & (6), 7-110(A), 8-101(A)(2)
Disciplinary Authority; Choice of Law	
Rule 8.5	None

TABLE B: ABA Model Code Cross-Referenced to Related Provisions of ABA Model Rules

ABA MODEL CODE	ABA MODEL RULES
Canon 1: Integrity of Profession	
EC 1-1	Rule 1.1, 8.1(a)
EC 1-2	Rules 1.1, 6.1, 8.1(a)
EC 1-3	Rules 8.1(a), 8.3
EC 1-4	Rule 6.1
EC 1-5	Rule 8.4(a), (b), (c), (e) & (f)
EC 1-6	Rules 1.16(a)(2), 8.4(a)
DR 1-101	Rule 8.1(a)
DR 1-102(A)(1)	Rule 8.4(a)
DR 1-102(A)(2)	Rules 5.1(c), 5.3(b), 8.4(a)
DR 1-102(A)(3)	Rules 8.4(b) & (f)
DR 1-102(A)(4)	Rules 3.3(a)(1), (3) & (b), 3.4(a) & (b), 8.4(c) & (f)
DR 1-102(A)(5)	Rules 3.1, 3.2, 3.3(a) & (b), 3.4, 8.4(d) & (f)
DR 1-102(A)(6)	Rules 3.4(b), 8.4(b) & (f)
DR 1-103(A)	Rules 5.1(c), 8.3
DR 1-103(B)	Rules 8.1(b)
Canon 2: Making Counsel Available	
EC 2-1	Rules 6.1, 6.2(a), 7.2(a), 7.4
EC 2-2	Rules 6.1, 7.2(a)
EC 2-3	Rules 4.3, 7.3
EC 2-4	Rule 7.3
EC 2-5	None
EC 2-6	Rule 7.2(a)
EC 2-7	Rules 7.2(a), 7.4
EC 2-8	Rules 7.1, 7.2(a) & (b), 7.4
EC 2-9	Rule 7.1
EC 2-10	Rule 7.1
EC 2-11	Rule 7.5
EC 2-12	Rule 7.5(c)
EC 2-13	Rule 7.5(a) & (d)
EC 2-14	Rule 7.4
EC 2-15	Rule 7.2(a) & (b)
EC 2-16	Rules 1.5(a), 6.1, 6.2(b)
EC 2-17	Rule 1.5(a)
EC 2-18	Rule 1.5(a)
EC 2-19	Rule 1.5(b)
EC 2-20	Rule 1.5(c) & (d)
EC 2-21	Rules 1.7(a), 1.8(f)
EC 2-22	Rule 1.5(e)
EC 2-23	None
EC 2-24	Rule 6.1
EC 2-25	Rules 6.1, 6.2
EC 2-26	None
EC 2-27	Rule 6.2(a) & (c)
EC 2-28	Rule 6.2(a)
EC 2-29	Rule 6.2
EC 2-30	Rules 1.16(a)(1) & (2), 1.16(b)(4), 4.2, 6.2(b) & (c)
EC 2-31	Rules 1.3, 1.16(a) & (b)

ABA MODEL CODE	ABA MODEL RULES
EC 2-32	Rule 1.16
EC 2-33	Rules 5.4, 6.3, 6.4
DR 2-101(A)	Rule 7.1
DR 2-101(B)	Rules 7.1, 7.2(a)
DR 2-101(C)	Rule 7.1
DR 2-101(D)	None
DR 2-101(E)	Rule 7.1
DR 2-101(F)	Rule 7.1
DR 2-101(G)	Rule 7.1
DR 2-101(H)	Rule 7.2
DR 2-101(I)	Rule 7.2(b)
DR 2-102(A)	Rule 7.2(a), 7.4
DR 2-102(B)	Rules 7.2(a), 7.5(a) & (c)
DR 2-102(C)	Rule 7.5(d)
DR 2-102(D)	Rule 7.5(a) & (b)
DR 2-102(E)	Rules 7.1, 7.4, 7.5(a)
DR 2-103(A)	Rule 7.3
DR 2-103(B)	Rule 7.2(a) & (b)
DR 2-103(C)	Rules 5.4(a), 7.2(b), 7.3
DR 2-103(D)	Rules 1.16(a)(1), 5.4(a), 7.2(b), 7.3
DR 2-103(E)	Rules 1.16(a), 7.2(a), 7.3
DR 2-104	Rules 1.16(a), 7.3
DR 2-105	Rule 7.4
DR 2-106(A)	Rule 1.5(a)
DR 2-106(B)	Rule 1.5(a)
DR 2-106(C)	Rule 1.5(d)
DR 2-107(A)	Rule 1.5(e)
DR 2-107(B)	Rule 5.4(a)(1)
DR 2-108(A)	Rule 5.6
DR 2-108(B)	Rule 5.6
DR 2-109(A)	Rules 1.16(a)(1), 3.1
DR 2-110(A)	Rule 1.16(b)(1), (c) & (d)
DR 2-110(B)	Rules 1.16(a), 3.1, 4.4(a)
DR 2-110(C)	Rules 1.4(a)(5), 1.16(a) & (b)
Canon 3: Unauthorized Practice	
EC 3-1	None
EC 3-2	None
EC 3-3	Rule 8.4(e)
EC 3-4	None
EC 3-5	None
EC 3-6	Rule 5.3(a)
EC 3-7	None
EC 3-8	Rule 5.4(a), (b) & (d)
EC 3-9	Rule 8.4(d)
DR 3-101(A)	Rule 5.5(a)
DR 3-101(B)	Rules 5.5(a), 8.4(d)
DR 3-102	Rule 5.4(a)
DR 3-103	Rule 5.4(b)
Canon 4: Confidences and Secrets	
EC 4-1	Rules 1.6(a), 1.18

ABA MODEL CODE	ABA MODEL RULES	ABA MODEL CODE	ABA MODEL RULES
EC 4-2	Rules 1.6(a) & (b)(1), 5.3(a)	DR 5-107(B)	Rules 1.7(a), 1.8(f),
EC 4-3	Rule 1.6(a)		1.13(b) & (c), 2.1, 5.4(c)
EC 4-4	Rules 1.6(a), 1.13(e)	DR 5-107(C)	Rule 5.4(a) & (d)
EC 4-5	Rules 1.8(b), 1.9(b),	*Canon 6: Competence*	
	1.10(a) & (b), 5.1(a) & (c),	EC 6-1	Rule 1.1
	5.3(a)	EC 6-2	Rules 1.1, 5.1(a) & (b), 6.1
EC 4-6	Rule 1.9(b)	EC 6-3	Rule 1.1
DR 4-101(A)	Rule 1.6(a)	EC 6-4	Rules 1.1, 1.3
DR 4-101(B)	Rules 1.6(a), 1.8(b), 1.9(b)	EC 6-5	Rule 1.1
DR 4-101(C)	Rules 1.6(a) & (b)	EC 6-6	Rule 1.8(h)
DR 4-101(D)	Rules 5.1(a) & (b),	DR 6-101	Rules 1.1, 1.3, 1.4(a)
	5.3(a) & (b)	DR 6-102	Rule 1.8(h)
Canon 5: Independent Judgment		*Canon 7: Zeal Within the Law*	
EC 5-1	Rules 1.7(a), 1.8(c)-(g) & (i)	EC 7-1	Rules 1.2(d), 1.3, 3.1
EC 5-2	Rules 1.7(a), 1.8(c)	EC 7-2	Rules 1.2(d)
EC 5-3	Rules 1.7, 1.8(a), (d) & (e)	EC 7-3	Rule 2.1
EC 5-4	Rule 1.8(d)	EC 7-4	Rules 3.1, 3.3(a)(1)
EC 5-5	Rule 1.8(a) & (c)	EC 7-5	Rules 1.2(d), 3.1,
EC 5-6	Rules 1.8(c), 7.3		3.3(a)(3) & (b), 4.1
EC 5-7	Rules 1.5(c), 1.8(e) & (i),	EC 7-6	Rule 3.4(a) & (b)
	1.15	EC 7-7	Rule 1.2(a)
EC 5-8	Rule 1.8(e)	EC 7-8	Rules 1.2(a) & (c), 1.4, 2.1
EC 5-9	Rules 1.7(a), 3.7	EC 7-9	Rule 1.2(c)
EC 5-10	Rule 3.7(a)	EC 7-10	Rule 4.4(a)
EC 5-11	Rules 1.7(a), 2.1	EC 7-11	Rules 1.14(a), 3.8(a)-(d), 3.9
EC 5-12	Rule 1.2(a)	EC 7-12	Rule 1.14
EC 5-13	Rule 1.7(a)	EC 7-13	Rule 3.8
EC 5-14	Rule 1.7(a)	EC 7-14	Rules 3.1, 3.8(a) & (f),
EC 5-15	Rule 1.7		4.4(a)
EC 5-16	Rules 1.7(b), 1.13(d) & (e)	EC 7-15	Rule 3.9
EC 5-17	Rule 1.7	EC 7-16	Rule 3.9
EC 5-18	Rule 1.13(a), (b) & (c)	EC 7-17	Rule 1.2(b)
EC 5-19	Rule 1.7(b)	EC 7-18	Rule 3.8(c), 4.2, 4.3
EC 5-20	Rules 1.12(a) & (b), 2.4	EC 7-19	None
EC 5-21	Rule 1.7	EC 7-20	Rules 3.2, 3.5(a) & (d)
EC 5-22	Rule 1.7	EC 7-21	Rule 4.4(a)
EC 5-23	Rules 1.7(a), 1.8(f), 5.4(c)	EC 7-22	Rules 1.2(d), 3.4(c)
EC 5-24	Rules 1.13(a), (b) & (c),	EC 7-23	Rule 3.3(a)(2)
	5.4(a)	EC 7-24	Rules 3.3(d), 3.4(e)
DR 5-101(A)	Rule 1.7, 1.8(i), 6.3, 6.4	EC 7-25	Rules 3.1, 3.4(c) & (e),
DR 5-101(B)	Rules 1.7, 3.7		3.5(d), 3.6, 4.4(a)
DR 5-102(A)	Rules 1.7, 3.7	EC 7-26	Rule 3.3(a)(3) & (b)
DR 5-102(B)	Rules 1.7(b), 3.7	EC 7-27	Rules 3.3(b) & (d),
DR 5-103(A)	Rules 1.8(i), 1.15		3.4(a) & (f)
DR 5-103(B)	Rule 1.8(e)	EC 7-28	Rules 3.4(b), 5.3(a)
DR 5-104(A)	Rules 1.7, 1.8(a)	EC 7-29	Rules 3.5(a) & (c), 4.4(a)
DR 5-104(B)	Rule 1.8(d)	EC 7-30	Rules 3.5(c), 4.4(a)
DR 5-105(A)	Rules 1.7, 1.10(c)	EC 7-31	Rule 3.5(a) & (c)
DR 5-105(B)	Rules 1.7, 1.13(e)	EC 7-32	Rules 3.3(a)(1) & (b),
DR 5-105(C)	Rules 1.7(b), 1.13(e), 1.9(a)		3.5(a) & (c)
DR 5-105(D)	Rules 1.10(a), 1.12(c),	EC 7-33	Rule 3.6
	1.13(c)	EC 7-34	Rules 3.5(a), 8.4(f)
DR 5-106	Rule 1.8(g)	EC 7-35	Rule 3.5(b)
DR 5-107(A)	Rules 1.7(b), 1.8(f)	EC 7-36	Rule 3.5(d)

Table B: ABA Model Code Cross-Referenced to Related Provisions of ABA Model Rules

ABA MODEL CODE	ABA MODEL RULES	ABA MODEL CODE	ABA MODEL RULES
EC 7-37	Rules 3.5(d), 4.4(a)	DR 7-108(E)	Rules 3.5(a), (b) & (c), 4.4(a), 5.1(c), 5.3(b)
EC 7-38	Rules 1.3, 3.4(c)		
EC 7-39	None	DR 7-108(F)	Rules 3.5(a), (b) & (c), 4.4(a)
DR 7-101(A)	Rules 1.2(a), 1.3, 3.2, 3.5(d), 4.4(a)		
		DR 7-108(G)	Rules 3.3(b), 3.5(c)
DR 7-101(B)	Rules 1.2(b), 1.16(b)	DR 7-109(A)	Rules 3.3(a)(1), (a)(3), & (b), 3.4(a)
DR 7-102(A)(1)	Rules 3.1, 4.4(a)		
DR 7-102(A)(2)	Rule 3.1	DR 7-109(B)	Rules 3.3(b), 3.4(a) & (f)
DR 7-102(A)(3)	Rules 3.3(a)(1), (a)(3) & (b), 4.1	DR 7-109(C)	Rule 3.4(b)
		DR 7-110(A)	Rules 3.5(a), 8.4(f)
DR 7-102(A)(4)	Rules 3.3(a) & (b), 4.1	DR 7-110(B)	Rule 3.5(a) & (b)
DR 7-102(A)(5)	Rules 3.3(a)(1), 4.1	*Canon 8: Improving Legal System*	
DR 7-102(A)(6)	Rules 1.2(d), 3.3(b), 3.4(b)	EC 8-1	Rule 6.1
DR 7-102(A)(7)	Rules 1.2(d), 3.3(a)(3) & (b), 4.1	EC 8-2	Rule 6.1
		EC 8-3	Rules 6.1, 6.2(a), 8.4(d)
DR 7-102(A)(8)	Rules 1.2(d), 8.4(a) & (b)	EC 8-4	Rule 3.9
DR 7-102(B)	Rules 1.6(b)(1), 3.3(b) & (c), 4.1	EC 8-5	Rules 3.3(a)(1), (a)(3) & (b), 3.9
DR 7-103(A)	Rule 3.8(a)	EC 8-6	Rule 8.2(a)
DR 7-103(B)	Rule 3.8(d)	EC 8-7	Rule 6.1
DR 7-104	Rules 3.4(f), 4.2, 4.3	EC 8-8	Rule 1.11(d)
DR 7-105	None	EC 8-9	Rule 6.1
DR 7-106(A)	Rules 1.2(d), 3.4(c) & (d), 3.5(a)	DR 8-101	Rules 3.5, 8.4(b), (c) & (f)
		DR 8-102	Rule 8.2(a)
DR 7-106(B)	Rules 3.3(a)(2), 3.9	DR 8-103	Rule 8.2(b)
DR 7-106(C)	Rules 3.4(a), (c), (d) & (e), 3.5(d), 4.4(a)	*Canon 9: Appearance of Impropriety*	
		EC 9-1	Rule 8.4(f)
DR 7-107(A)-(I)	Rule 3.6	EC 9-2	Rules 1.4(a), 8.4(e)
		EC 9-3	Rules 1.11(a), 1.12(a) & (b)
DR 7-107(D)-(F)	Rule 4.4(a)	EC 9-4	Rule 8.4(c) & (e)
		EC 9-5	Rule 1.15
DR 7-107(J)	Rules 5.1(a) & (b), 5.3(a) & (b)	EC 9-6	Preamble, Rule 8.4(e)
		EC 9-7	Rule 1.15
DR 7-108(A)	Rules 3.5(a), (b) & (c)	DR 9-101(A)	Rule 1.12(a) & (b)
DR 7-108(B)	Rules 3.5(a), (b) & (c), 5.3(b)	DR 9-101(B)	Rules 1.11(a), 1.12(a) & (b)
		DR 9-101(C)	Rules 1.4(a)(5), 3.9, 8.4(e)
DR 7-108(C)	Rules 3.5(a), (b) & (c)	DR 9-102	Rules 1.4(a), 1.15
DR 7-108(D)	Rules 3.5(c)(3), 4.4(a)		

STATE LAWYER CODE PROVISIONS
THAT REQUIRE WRITTEN FEE AGREEMENTS

	Contingent Fees	Other Fees
ABA Model Rules	1.5(c): Writing Required	1.5(b): The scope of representation and the basis or rate of the fee and expenses for which the client will be responsible shall be communicated to the client, preferably in writing, before or within a reasonable time after commencing the representation, except when the lawyer will charge a regularly represented client on the same basis or rate. Any changes in the basis or rate of the fee or expenses shall be communicated to the client.
Alabama	1.5(c): Writing Required	1.5(b): Writing Preferred
Alaska	1.5(c): Writing Required	1.5(b): Writing Required if fee >$500; writing must be consistent with Rule 1.4(c).
Arizona	1.5(c): Writing Required	1.5(b): Writing Required
Arkansas	1.5(c): Writing Required	1.5(b): Writing Preferred
California	Bus. & Prof. Code §6147: Writing Required	Bus. & Prof. Code §6148: Writing Required if fee > $1,000 and client not a corporation.
Colorado	1.5(c): Writing Required	1.5(b): Writing Required
Connecticut	1.5(c): Writing Required	1.5(b): Writing Required, except public defenders or when the lawyer will be paid by the court or a state agency.
Delaware	1.5(c): Writing Required	1.5(b): Writing Preferred
District of Columbia	1.5(c): Writing Required	1.5(b): Writing Required
Florida	4-1.5(b): Writing Required	4-1.5(e): Writing Preferred
Georgia	1.5(c): Writing Required	1.5(b): Writing Preferred
Hawaii	1.5(c): Writing Required	1.5(b): Writing Preferred
Idaho	1.5(c): Writing Required	1.5(b): Writing Preferred
Illinois	1.5(c): Writing Required	1.5(b): Writing Required
Indiana	1.5(c): Writing Required	1.5(b): Writing Preferred
Iowa	32:1.5(c): Writing Required	32:1.5(b): Writing Preferred
Kansas	1.5(d): Writing Required	1.5(b): Writing Preferred
Kentucky	1.5(c): Writing Required	1.5(b): Writing Preferred

	Contingent Fees	**Other Fees**
Louisiana	1.5(c): Writing Required	1.5(b): Writing Preferred
Maine	Maine Bar Rule 8(d): Writing Required	3.3(a): Factors to be considered as guides in determining the reasonableness of a fee include: (9) the informed written consent of the client.
Maryland	1.5(c): Writing Required	1.5(b): Writing Preferred
Massachusetts	1.5(c): Writing Required	1.5(b): Writing Preferred
Michigan	1.5(c): Writing Required	1.5(b): Writing Preferred
Minnesota	1.5(c): Writing Required	1.5(b): Writing Preferred
Mississippi	1.5(c): Writing Required	1.5(b): Writing Preferred
Missouri	R. 4-1.5(c),(d): Writing Required	R. 4-1.5(b): Writing Preferred
Montana	1.5(c): Writing Required	1.5(b): Writing Required if >$500.
Nebraska	EC 2-19: Writing Preferred	EC 2-19: Writing Preferred
Nevada	SCR 155(3): Writing Required	SCR 155(2): Writing Preferred
New Hampshire	1.5(c): Writing Required	1.5(b): Writing Preferred
New Jersey	RPC 1.5(c): Writing Required	RPC 1.5(b): Writing Required
New Mexico	R 16-105(C): Writing Required	R 16-105(B): Writing Preferred
New York	DR 2-106(d): Writing Required	DR 2-106(c)(2)(ii): Writing Required in domestic relations matters, and 22 N.Y.C. R.R. Part 1215: all other fees >$3,000.
North Carolina	1.5(c): Writing Required	1.5(b): Writing Preferred
North Dakota	1.5(c): Writing Required	1.5(b): Writing Required
Ohio	ORC §4705.15(B): Writing Required for tort claims	EC 2-18: Writing Preferred
Oklahoma	1.5(c): Writing Required	1.5(b) Writing Preferred
Oregon	ORS §20.340: Writing Required for personal injury and property damage claims.	1.5 No writing required
Pennsylvania	1.5(c): Writing Required	1.5(b): Writing Required
Rhode Island	1.5(c): Writing Required	1.5(b): Writing Required for billings regarding the fees, costs, and on a quarterly basis or as otherwise provided in the agreement.

	Contingent Fees	Other Fees
South Carolina	1.5(c): Writing Required	1.5(b): Writing Preferred
South Dakota	1.5(c): Writing Required	1.5(b): Writing Preferred
Tennessee	1.5(c): Writing Required	**1.5(b):** Writing Preferred
Texas	1.04(d): Writing Required	1.04(c): Writing Preferred
Utah	1.5(c): Writing Required	1.5(b): Writing Required if fee > $750.
Vermont	1.5(c): Writing Required	1.5(b): Writing Preferred
Virginia	1.5(c): Writing Required	1.5(b): Writing Preferred
Washington	1.5(c)(1): Writing Required	1.5(b): Writing Preferred. Upon the request of the client in any matter, the lawyer shall communicate to the client in writing the basis or rate of the fee.
West Virginia	1.5(c): Writing Required	1.5(b): Writing Preferred
Wisconsin	20:1-5(c): Writing Required	20:1.5(b): Writing Preferred
Wyoming	1.5(c): Writing Required	1.5(b): Writing Required

STATE LAWYER CODE EXCEPTIONS TO CLIENT CONFIDENTIALITY THAT PERMIT (MAY) OR REQUIRE (MUST) DISCLOSURE

Jurisdiction	Express Authority	Implied Authority / Entities (E) / Clients with Diminished Capacity (DC)	To Prevent Future Crime (CR), Fraud (FR), Death /Subs. Bodily Harm (D/SBH), or Subs. Financial Harm (SFH)	To Secure Legal Advice	Lawyer Self-Defense	To Comply with Law or Court Order / Fraud on Tribunal / Assisting Client Fraud
ABA Model Rules	1.6(a) May	1.6(a) May / 1.13(c)(2),(d) May (E) / 1.14(c) May (DC)	1.6(b)(1)May (D/SBH) / 1.6(b)(2) May (CR or FR & SFH)	1.6(b)(4) May	1.6(b)(5) May	1.6(b)(6) May / 3.3 Must / 4.1(b), Must if 1.6(b)(3)
Alabama	1.6(a) May	1.6(a) May	1.6(b)(1) May (CR & D/SBH)	None	1.6(b)(2) May	1.6 Comment / 3.3 Must / 4.1(b), Must not
Alaska	1.6(a) May	1.6(a) May	1.6(b)(1) May (CR/FR & D/SBH/SFH)	None	1.6(b)(2) May	1.6 Comment / 3.3 Must / 4.1(b), Must if 1.6(b)(1)
Arizona	1.6(a) May	1.6(a) May / 1.14(c) May (DC)	1.6(b) Must (CR & D/SBH) / 1.6(c) May (CR) / 1.6(d)(1) May (CR/FR & SFH)	1.6(d)(3) May	1.6(d)(4) May	1.6(d)(5) May / 3.3 Must / 4.1(b), Must if 1.6(d)(2)
Arkansas	1.6(a) May	1.6(a) May	1.6(b)(1) May (CR)	None	1.6(b)(2) May	None / 3.3 Must / 4.1(b), Must if 1.6(c)
California	None	None	§6068(e)(2) May (CR & D/SBH)	None	None	None / None / None

Jurisdiction	Express Authority	Implied Authority Entities (E) Clients with Diminished Capacity (DC)	To Prevent Future Crime (CR), Fraud (FR), Death /Subs. Bodily Harm (D/SBH), or Subs. Financial Harm (SFH)	To Secure Legal Advice	Lawyer Self-Defense	To Comply with Law or Court Order Fraud on Tribunal Assisting Client Fraud
Colorado	1.6(a) May	1.6(a) May	1.6(b) May (CR)	None	1.6(c) May	1.6 Comment 3.3 Must 4.1(b) Must not
Connecticut	1.6(a) May	1.6(a) May	1.6(b) Must (CR & D/SBH) 1.6(c)(1) May (CR & SFH)	None	1.6(d) May	1.6 Comment 3.3 Must 4.1(b), Must if 1.6(c)(2)
Delaware	1.6(a) May	1.6(a) May 1.14(c) May (DC)	1.6(b)(1) May (D/SBH) 1.6(b)(2) May (CR/FR & SFH)	1.6(b)(4) May	1.6(b)(5) May	1.6(b)(6) May 3.3 Must 4.1(b), Must if 1.6(b)(3)
District of Columbia	1.6(d)(1) May	1.6(d)(4) May	1.6(c)(1) May (CR & D/SBH)	None	1.6(d)(3)(5) May	1.6(d)(2)(A) May 3.3 Must if 1.6 4.1(b) Must if 1.6.
Florida	4-1.6(a) May	4-1.6 comment	4-1.6(b)(1) Must (CR) 4-1.6(b)(2) Must (D/SBH)	None	4-1.6(c)(2) May 4-1.6(c)(3) May 4-1.6(c)(4) May	4-1.6 Comment 4-3.3 Must 4.1(b), Must if 1.6(c)(5)
Georgia	1.6(a) May	1.6(a) May	1.6(b)(1)(i) May (CR & SFH) 1.6(b)(1)(ii) May (D/SBH)	None	1.6(b)(1)(iii) May	1.6(a) May 3.3 Must 4.1(b), must if 1.6(b)
Hawaii	1.6(a) May	1.6(a) May	1.6(c)(1) May (CR/FR & D/SBH/SFH)	None	1.6(c)(3) May	1.6(c)(6) May 3.3 Must 4.1 (b), 1.6(b) Must

State Lawyer Code Exceptions to Client Confidentiality That Permit (May) or Require (Must) Disclosure

Jurisdiction	Express Authority	Implied Authority Entities (E) Clients with Diminished Capacity (DC)	To Prevent Future Crime (CR), Fraud (FR), Death /Subs. Bodily Harm (D/SBH), or Subs. Financial Harm (SFH)	To Secure Legal Advice	Lawyer Self-Defense	To Comply with Law or Court Order Fraud on Tribunal Assisting Client Fraud
Idaho	1.6(a) May	1.6(a) May 1.13(c), (d) May (E) 1.14(c) May (DC)	1.6(b)(1) May (CR) 1.6(b)(2) May (D/SBH)	1.6(b)(4) May	1.6(b)(5) May	1.6(b)(6) May 3.3 Must 4.1(b), Must if 1.6(b)(3)
Illinois	1.6(a) May	None	1.6(b) Must (D/SBH) 1.6(c)(2) May (CR)	None	1.6(c)(3) May	1.6(c)(1) May 3.3 Must 4.1(b), Must if 1.6(c)
Indiana	1.6(a) May	1.6(a) May 1.13(c) (d) May (E) 1.14(c) May (DC)	1.6(b)(1) May (D/SBH) 1.6(b)(2) May (CR/FR & SFH)	1.6(b)(4) May	1.6(b)(5) May	1.6(b)(6) May 3.3 Must 4.1(b), Must if 1.6(b)(3)
Iowa	4-101 (C)(1) May	None	4-101(C)(3) May (CR)	None	4-101(C)(4) May	4-101(C)(2) May 7-102(B) (all fraud) Must unless Iowa Code §622.10 (client) Must (non-clients)
Kansas	1.6(a) May	1.6(a) May	1.6(b)(1) May (CR)	None	1.6(b)(3) May	1.6(b)(2) May 3.3 Must 4.1 Must not

Jurisdiction	Express Authority	Implied Authority **Entities (E)** **Clients with Diminished Capacity (DC)**	To Prevent Future Crime (CR), Fraud (FR), Death /Subs. Bodily Harm (D/SBH), or Subs. Financial Harm (SFH)	To Secure Legal Advice	Lawyer Self-Defense	To Comply with Law or Court Order **Fraud on Tribunal** **Assisting Client Fraud**
Kentucky	1.6(a) May	1.6(a) May	1.6(b)(1) May (CR& D/SBH)	None	1.6(b)(2) May	1.6(b)(3) May 3.3 Must Must not
Louisiana	1.6(a) May	1.6(a) May 1.13(c), (d) May (E) 1.14(c) May (DC)	1.6(b)(1) May (D/SBH) 1.6(b)(2) May (CR/FR & SFH)	1.6(b)(4) May	1.6(b)(5) May	1.6(b)(6) May 3.3 Must 4.1, Must if 1.6(b)
Maine	3.6(h)(1) May	3.6(j) May (DC)	3.6(h)(4) May (CR)	None	3.6(h)(3) May	3.6(b) (all fraud): Must if client and not privileged Must if non-client
Maryland	1.6(a) May	1.6(a) May 1.13(c) May (E) 1.14(c) May (DC)	1.6(b)(1) May (D/SBH) 1.6(b)(2) May (CR/FR & SFH)	1.6(b)(4)	1.6(b)(5) May	1.6(b)(6) May 3.3 Must 4.1 Must
Massachusetts	1.6(a) May	1.6(a) May 1.14(b) May (DC)	1.6(b)(1) May (CR/FR & D/SBH/SFH)	None	1.6(b)(2) May	1.6(b)(4) May 3.3, 1.6(b) Must, 3.3 (e) (criminal defense) 4.1(b) Must if 1.6(2)(2)
Michigan	1.6(c)(1) May	1.6 comment 1.13(c) May (E)	1.6(c)(4) May (CR)	None	1.6(c)(5) May	1.6(c)(2) May 3.3 Must 1.6(c)(3) May
Minnesota	1.6(b)(1) May	1.6 comment	1.6(b)(3) May (CR)	None	1.6(b)(5) May	1.6(b)(2) May 3.3 Must 1.6(b)(4) May

State Lawyer Code Exceptions to Client Confidentiality That Permit (May) or Require (Must) Disclosure

Jurisdiction	Express Authority	Implied Authority **Entities (E)** **Clients with Diminished Capacity (DC)**	To Prevent Future Crime (CR), Fraud (FR), Death /Subs. Bodily Harm (D/SBH), or Subs. Financial Harm (SFH)	To Secure Legal Advice	Lawyer Self-Defense	To Comply with Law or Court Order **Fraud on Tribunal** **Assisting Client Fraud**
Mississippi	1.6(a) May	1.6 comment	1.6(b)(1) May (CR)	None	1.6(b)(2) May	1.6(e) May 3.3 Must 4.1 Must
Missouri	1.6(a) May	1.6(a) May	1.6(b)(1) May (CR & D/SBH)	None	1.6(b)(2) May	1.6 comment 3.3 Must 4.1 Must not
Montana	1.6(a) May	1.6(a) May 1.14(c) May (DC)	1.6(b)(1) May (D/SBH)	1.6(b)(2) May	1.6(b)(3) May	1.6(b)(4) May 3.3 Must 4.1 Must
Nebraska	4-101 (C)(1) May	None	4-101(C)(3) May (CR)	None	4-101(C)(4) May	4-101(C) (2) May 7-102(B) (all fraud): Must not (client); Must (non-client)
Nevada	156(1) May	156(1) May	156(2) Must (CR & D/SBH)	None	156(3)(b) May	None 172 Must 156(3)(a) May
New Hampshire	1.6(a) May	1.6(a) May 1.13(c) May (E)	1.6(b)(1) May (CR & D/SBH/SFH)	None	1.6(b)(2) May	None 3.3 Must 4.1, Must if 1.6(b)(1)
New Jersey	1.6(a) May	1.6(a) May 1.13(c) May (E) 1.14(c) May (DC)	1.6(b)(1) Must (CR/FR & D/SBH/SFH)	None	1.6(d)(2) May	1.6(d)(3) May 3.3 Must 4.1(b) Must
New Mexico	16-106(A) May	16-106(A) May	16-106(B) Should (CR & D/SBH) 16-106(C) May (CR & SFH)	None	16-106(D) May	16-106 comment 16-303 Must 16-401, Must if 16-106(C)

Jurisdiction	Express Authority	Implied Authority Entities (E) Clients with Diminished Capacity (DC)	To Prevent Future Crime (CR), Fraud (FR), Death /Subs. Bodily Harm (D/SBH), or Subs. Financial Harm (SFH)	To Secure Legal Advice	Lawyer Self-Defense	To Comply with Law or Court Order Fraud on Tribunal Assisting Client Fraud
New York	4-101(c)(1) May	None	4-101(c)(3) May (CR)	None	4-101(c)(4) May	4-101(c)(2) May 7-102(b) (all fraud): Must not (client); Must (non-client); 4-101(c)(5) may if reliance on opinion
North Carolina	1.6(a) May	1.6(a) May 1.14(c) May (DC)	1.6(b)(2) May (CR) 1.6(b)(3) May (D/SBH)	1.6(b)(5) May	1.6(b)(6) May	1.6(b)(1) May 3.3 Must 1.6(b)(4) May
North Dakota	1.6(b) May	1.6(c) May	1.6(a) Must (Imminent D/SBH) 1.6(d) May (CR/FR & Non-imminent D/SBH/SFH)	None	1.6(e) May	1.6(g) May 3.3 must not (client) Must (non-client) 1.6(f) May
Ohio	4-101 (C)(1) May	None	4-101(C)(2) May (CR)	None	4-101(C)(4) May	4-101(C)(2) May 7-102(B) (all fraud): Must
Oklahoma	1.6(a) May	1.6(a) May	1.6(b)(1) May (CR)	None	1.6(b)(3) May	1.6(c) May 3.3 Must 4.1(b), Must if 1.6(b)(2)

State Lawyer Code Exceptions to Client Confidentiality That Permit (May) or Require (Must) Disclosure

Jurisdiction	Express Authority	Implied Authority Entities (E) Clients with Diminished Capacity (DC)	To Prevent Future Crime (CR), Fraud (FR), Death /Subs. Bodily Harm (D/SBH), or Subs. Financial Harm (SFH)	To Secure Legal Advice	Lawyer Self-Defense	To Comply with Law or Court Order Fraud on Tribunal Assisting Client Fraud
Oregon	1.6(a) May	1.6(a) May 1.13(c), (d) May (E) 1.14(c) May (DC)	1.6(b)(1) May (CR) 1.6(b)(2) May (D/SBH)	1.6(b)(3) May	1.6(b)(4) May	1.6(b)(5) May 3.3 Must 4.1(b), Must if 1.6(b)(5)
Pennsylvania	1.6(a) May	1.6(a) May 1.14(c) May (DC)	1.6(c)(1) May (D/SBH) 1.6(c)(2) May (CR & SFH)	1.6(c)(5) May	1.6(c)(4) May	1.6 Comments [18], [19] 3.3 Must 4.1(b), Must if 1.6(c)(3)
Rhode Island	1.6(a) May	1.6(a) May	1.6(b)(1) May (CR & D/SBH)	None	1.6(b)(2) May	None 3.3 May 4.1(b) Must not
South Carolina	1.6(a) May	1.6(a) May	1.6(b)(1) May (CR)	None	1.6(b)(2) May	1.6 Comment 3.3 Must 4.1(b) Must not
South Dakota	1.6(a) May	1.6(a) May 1.14(c) May (DC)	1.6(b)(1) May (CR & D/SBH)	1.6(b)(2) May	1.6(b)(3) May	1.6(b)(5) May 3.3 Must 4.1(b), Must if 1.6(b)(4)
Tennessee	1.6(a) May	1.6(a) May	1.6(b)(1) May (CR) 1.6(c)(1) Must (D/SBH)	1.6(b)(2) May	1.6(b)(3) May	1.6(c) Must 3.3 Must 4.1(b) Must
Texas	1.05(c)(1) May 1.05(c)(2) May	1.05(d)(1) May	1.05(c)(7) May (CR/FR) 1.05(e) Must (CR & D/SBH)	None	1.05(c)(5) May 1.06(c)(6) May 1.05(d)(2) May	1.05(c)(4) May 3.03 Must 4.01(b) Must

State Lawyer Code Exceptions to Client Confidentiality That Permit (May) or Require (Must) Disclosure

Jurisdiction	Express Authority	Implied Authority Entities (E) Clients with Diminished Capacity (DC)	To Prevent Future Crime (CR), Fraud (FR), Death /Subs. Bodily Harm (D/SBH), or Subs. Financial Harm (SFH)	To Secure Legal Advice	Lawyer Self-Defense	To Comply with Law or Court Order Fraud on Tribunal Assisting Client Fraud
Utah	1.6(a) May	1.6 comment	1.6(b)(1) May (CR/FR & D/SBH/SFH)	None	1.6(b)(3) May	1.6(b)(4) May 1.6 and 3.3 Must 4.1(b), Must if 1.6(b)(2)
Vermont	1.6(a) May	1.6(a) May	1.6(b)(1) Must (CR & D/SBH) 1.6(c)(1) May (CR)	None	1.6(c)(2) May	1.6 Comment 3.3 Must 1.6(b)(2) Must
Virginia	1.6(a) May	1.6(a) May 1.14(c) May (DC)	1.6(c)(1) Must (CR)	None	1.6(b)(2) May	1.6(b)(1) May 1.6(c)(2) 3.3 Must 4.1(b) Must
Washington	1.6(a) May	1.6(a) May	1.6(b)(1) May (CR)	None	1.6(b)(2) May	1.6(b)(2) May 3.3 Must 4.1(b), Must if 1.6(b)(3)
West Virginia	1.6(a) May	1.6(a) May	1.6(b)(1) May (CR)	None	1.6(b)(2) May	None 3.3 Must 4.1 Must not
Wisconsin	20:1.6(a) May	20:1.6(a) May	20:1.6(b) Must (CR/FR & D/SBH/SFH)	None	20:1.6(c)(2) May	20:1.6 Comment 20:3.3 Must 20:4.1 Must if 20:1.6(c)(1); 20:1.6(b) Must
Wyoming	1.6(a) May	1.6(a) May 1.6(b)(3) May (DC)	1.6(b)(1) May (CR)	None	1.6(b)(2) May	1.6 Comment 3.3 Must 4.1 Must not

STATE LAWYER CODE SCREENING RULES THAT PREVENT IMPUTED DISQUALIFICATION[1]

	Former Clients	Former Government Officers and Employees	Former Judge, (J), Arbitrator (A), Mediator, (M), or Other Third Party Neutral	Prospective Clients Other
ABA Model Rules	Only with former client consent, 1.9(a), 1.10(a)	1.11(b), (c); yes	1.12(c) J, A and M, yes	1.18(d); yes
Alabama	Only with former client consent, 1.9(a), 1.10(a)	1.11(a), (b); yes	1.12(c) J, A; yes	None
Alaska	Only with former client consent, 1.9(a), 1.10(a)	1.11(a), (b); yes	1.12(c) J, A; yes	None
Arizona	Only with former client consent, 1.9(a), 1.10(a)	1.11(a), (b); yes	1.12(c) J, A and M; yes	1.18(d); yes
Arkansas	Only with former client consent, 1.9(a), 1.10(a)	1.11(a), (b); yes	1.12(c) J, A; yes	None
California	Only with former client consent, 3-310(E)	None	None	None
Colorado	Only with former client consent, 1.9(a), 1.10(a)	1.11(a), (b)	1.12(c) J, A; yes	None
Connecticut	Only with former client consent, 1.9(a), 1.10(a)	1.11(a), (b)	1.12(c) J, A; yes	None
Delaware	1.9(a), 1.10(a); yes	1.11(b), (c)	1.12 (c) J, A and M; yes	1.18(d); yes
District of Columbia	Only with former client consent, 1.9(a), 1.10(a)	1.11(d); yes	1.11(c) J, yes	1.10(a)[2]
Florida	Only with former client consent, 4-1.9(a), 4-1.10(a)	4-1.11(a), (b); yes	4-1.12(c) J, A; yes	None
Georgia	Only with former client consent, 1.9(a), 1.10(a)	1.11(a), (b); yes	1.12(c), J, A; yes	None
Hawaii	Only with former client consent, 1.9(a), 1.10(a)	1.11(a), (b); yes	1.12(c) J, A; yes	None

---

[1] This chart compiles the lawyer code provisions but it does <u>not</u> include judicial decisions, which may allow screens in some circumstances.

[2] No imputed disqualification if lawyer consults with a potential client.

	Former Clients	Former Government Officers and Employees	Former Judge, (J), Arbitrator (A), Mediator, (M), or Other Third Party Neutral	Prospective Clients Other
Idaho	Only with former client consent, 1.9(a), 1.10(a)	1.11(b), (c); yes	1.12(c), J, A, and M; yes	1.18(d); yes
Illinois	1.9(a)(1), 1.10(a); yes	1.11(a), (b); yes	1.12(c), J, A; yes	None
Indiana	1.10(c); yes	1.11(b), (c); yes	1.12(c), J, A, and M; yes	1.18(d); yes
Iowa	Only with former client consent, 32:1.9(a), 32:1.10(a)	32:1.11(b), (c); yes	32:1.12(c), J, A, and M; yes	32:1.18(d); yes
Kansas	Only with former client consent, 1.9(a), 1.10(a)	1.11(a), (b); yes	1.12(c), J, A; yes	None
Kentucky	Only with former client consent, 1.9(a), 1.10(a)	1.11(a), (b); yes	1.12(c), J, A; yes	None
Louisiana	Only with former client consent, 1.9(a), 1.10(a)	1.11(b), (c); yes	1.12(c), J, A, and M; yes	None
Maine	Only with former client consent, 3.4(d)(1)	3.4(d)(2); yes	3.4(g)(2) J, A; yes 3.4(h)(7) M; yes	None 3.4(b)(3)(ii); yes (Law School Clinics)
Maryland	(c); yes (a), 1.10(a)	1.11(b), (c); yes	1.12(c), J, As, and M; yes	1.18(d); yes
Massachusetts	1.9(a), 1.10(a), 1.10(d); yes	1.11(a), (b); yes	1.12(c), J, A; yes	None
Michigan	1.9(a), 1.10(a); yes	1.11(a), (b); yes	1.12(c), J, A; yes	None
Minnesota	1.9(a), 1.10(a), 1.10(b); yes	1.11(a), (b); yes	1.12(c), J, A; yes	None
Mississippi	Only with former client consent, 1.9(a), 1.10(a)	1.11(a), (b); yes	1.12(c), J, A; yes	None
Missouri	Only with former client consent, 1.9(a); 1.10(a); 1.10(c)	1.11(a), (b); yes	1.12(c), J, A; yes	None
Montana	Only with former client consent, 1.9(a), 1.10(c), 1.10(d)	1.11(b), 1.11(c); yes	1.12(c) J, A, and M; yes	1.20(d); yes

	Former Clients	Former Government Officers and Employees	Former Judge, (J), Arbitrator (A), Mediator, (M), or Other Third Party Neutral	Prospective Clients Other
Nebraska	Only with former client consent, DR 5-108	None	None	None Support Personnel: Only with former client consent, DR 5-109
Nevada	SCR 160; yes	SCR 161(1), (2); yes	SCR 162(3) J, A; yes	SCR 156.1(4), 156.1(6); yes
New Hampshire	Only with former client consent, 1.9(a), 1.10(a), 1.10(b), 1.10(c)	1.11(a), (b); yes	1.12(c) J, A; yes	None
New Jersey	1.9(a), 1.10(c); yes	1.11(c); yes	1.12(b), J, A, and M; yes	1.18(c); yes
New Mexico	Only with former client consent, R 16-109.A, R 16-110.D	R 16-111.A, B; yes	R 16-112.C; J, A; yes	None
New York	Only with former client consent, DR 5-108 [1200.27]	DR 9-101(b) [1200.45], yes	None	None
North Carolina	1.9(a), 1.10(c); yes	1.11(b), 1.11(c); yes	1.12(b) J, A, and M; yes	1.18(d); yes
North Dakota	Only with former client consent 1.9(a), 1.10(d)	1.11(a), (b); yes	1.12(c), J, A; yes	None
Ohio	Only with former client consent, DR 5-105; DR 4-101(D)	None	None	None
Oklahoma	Only with former client consent, 1.9, 1.10	1.11(a), 1.11(b)	1.12(c), J, A	None
Oregon	1.9(a), 1.10(c); yes	1.11(b), (c); yes	1.12(c) J, A, and M; yes	1.18(d); yes
Pennsylvania	1.9(a), 1.10 (b); yes	1.11(b), (c); yes	1.12(c) J, A, and M; yes	None
Rhode Island	Only with former client consent, 1.9(a), 1.10(a)	1.11(a); yes	1.12(c) J, A; yes	None
South Carolina	Only with former client consent, 1.9(a), 1.10(a)	1.11(a), (b); yes	1.12(c) J, A; yes	None
South Dakota	Only with former client consent, 1.9(a), 1.10(a)	1.11(b), (c); yes	1.12(c) J, A; yes	1.18(d); yes

	Former Clients	Former Government Officers and Employees	Former Judge, (J), Arbitrator (A), Mediator, (M), or Other Third Party Neutral	Prospective Clients Other
Tennessee	Only with former client consent, 1.9(a),1.10(a)	1.11(a), (b);yes	1.12(b),(c) J, A, yes; 2.4 (e)(2) M, no	None
Texas	Only with former client consent, 1.9(a), (b)	1.10(b), (d); yes	1.11(c) J; yes	None
Utah	Only with former client consent, 1.9(a), 1.10(a), (b)	1.11(a), (b); yes	1.12(c) J, A; yes	None
Vermont	Only with former client consent, 1.9(a), 1.10(c)	1.11(a), (b); yes	1.12(c) J, A; yes	None
Virginia	Only with former client consent, 1.9(a), 1.10(a)	1.11(b), (c); yes	1.12(c) J, A; yes 1.10(a), 2.10(e) M; no	None
Washington	1.9(a), 1.10(e); yes	1.11(b), (c); yes	1.12(c) J, A and M; yes	None
West Virginia	Only with former client consent, 1.9(a), 1.10(a)	1.11(a), (b); yes	1.12 (c) J, A; yes	None
Wisconsin	Only with former client consent, 20:1.9(a), 20:1.10(a)	20:1.11(a), (b); yes	20:1.12(d) J, A; yes	None
Wyoming	Only with former client consent, 1.9(a), 1.10 (c)	1.11(a), (b); yes	1.12(c) J, A; yes	None

ABA MODEL CODE OF PROFESSIONAL RESPONSIBILITY

© 1983 American Bar Association. All rights reserved. Reprinted with permission.
(Footnotes omitted)

Contents

PREFACE

On August 14, 1964, at the request of President Lewis F. Powell, Jr., the House of Delegates of the American Bar Association created a Special Committee on Evaluation of Ethical Standards to examine the then current Canons of Professional Ethics and to make recommendations for changes. That committee produced the Model Code of Professional Responsibility which was adopted by the House of Delegates in 1969 and became effective January 1, 1970. The new Model Code revised the previous Canons in four principal particulars: (1) there were important areas involving the conduct of lawyers that were either only partially covered in or totally omitted from the Canons; (2) many Canons that were sound in substance were in need of editorial revision; (3) most of the Canons did not lend themselves to practical sanctions for violations; and (4) changed and changing conditions in our legal system and urbanized society required new statements of professional principles.

The original 32 Canons of Professional Ethics were adopted by the American Bar Association in 1908. They were based principally on the Code of Ethics adopted by the Alabama State Bar Association in 1887, which in turn has been borrowed largely from the lectures of Judge George Sharswood, published in 1854 under the title of *Professional Ethics*, and from the fifty resolutions included in David Hoffman's *A Course of Legal Study* (2d ed. 1836). Since then a limited number of amendments have been adopted on a piecemeal basis.

As far back as 1934 Mr. Justice (later Chief Justice) Harlan Fiske Stone, in his memorable address entitled *The Public Influence of the Bar*, made this observation:

> Before the Bar can function at all as a guardian of the public interests committed to its care, there must be appraisal and comprehension of the new conditions, and the chained relationship of the

lawyer to his clients, to his professional brethren and to the public. That appraisal must pass beyond the petty details of form and manners which have been so largely the subject of our Codes of Ethics, to more fundamental consideration of the way in which our professional activities affect the welfare of society as a whole. Our canons of ethics for the most part are generalizations designed for an earlier era.

Largely in that spirit, the committee appointed by President Powell in 1964 reached unanimous conclusion that further piecemeal amendment of the original Canons would not suffice. It proceeded to compose the Model Code of Professional Responsibility in response to the perceived need for change in the statement of professional principles for lawyers. . . .

PREAMBLE

The continued existence of a free and democratic society depends upon recognition of the concept that justice is based upon the rule of law grounded in respect for the dignity of the individual and his capacity through reason for enlightened self-government. Law so grounded makes justice possible, for only through such law does the dignity of the individual attain respect and protection. Without it, individual rights become subject to unrestrained power, respect for law is destroyed, and rational self-government is impossible.

Lawyers, as guardians of the law, play a vital role in the preservation of society. The fulfillment of this role requires an understanding by lawyers of their relationship with and function in our legal system. A consequent obligation of lawyers is to maintain the highest standards of ethical conduct.

In fulfilling his professional responsibilities, a lawyer necessarily assumes various roles that require the performance of many difficult tasks. Not every situation which he may encounter can be foreseen, but fundamental ethical principles are always present to guide him. Within the framework of these principles, a lawyer must with courage and foresight be able and ready to shape the body of the law to the ever-changing relationships of society.

The Model Code of Professional Responsibility points the way to the aspiring and provides standards by which to judge the transgressor. Each lawyer must find within his own conscience the touchstone against which to test the extent to which his actions should rise above minimum standards. But in the last analysis it is the desire for the respect and confidence of the members of his profession and of the society which he serves that should provide to a lawyer the incentive for the highest possible degree of ethical conduct. The possible loss of that respect and confidence is the ultimate sanction. So long as its practitioners are guided by these principles, the law will continue to be a noble profession. This is its greatness and its strength, which permit of no compromise.

PRELIMINARY STATEMENT

In furtherance of the principles stated in the Preamble, the American Bar Association has promulgated this Model Code of Professional Responsibility, consisting of three separate but interrelated parts: Canons, Ethical Considerations, and Disciplinary Rules. The Code is designed to be adopted by appropriate agencies both as an inspirational guide to the members of the profession and as a basis for disciplinary action when the conduct of a lawyer falls below the required minimum standards stated in the Disciplinary Rules.

Obviously the Canons, Ethical Considerations, and Disciplinary Rules cannot apply to non-lawyers; however, they do define the type of ethical conduct that the public has a right to expect not only of lawyers but also of their non-professional employees and associates in all matters pertaining to professional employment. A lawyer should ultimately be responsible for the conduct of his employees and associates in the course of the professional representation of the client.

The Canons are statements of axiomatic norms, expressing in general terms the standards of professional conduct expected of lawyers in their relationships with the public, with the legal system, and with the legal profession. They embody the general concepts from which the Ethical Considerations and the Disciplinary Rules are derived.

The Ethical Considerations are aspirational in character and represent the objectives toward which every member of the profession should strive. They constitute a body of principles upon which the lawyer can rely for guidance in many specific situations.

The Disciplinary Rules, unlike the Ethical Considerations, are mandatory in character. The Disciplinary Rules state the minimum level of conduct below which no lawyer can fall without being subject to disciplinary action. Within the framework of fair trial, the Disciplinary Rules should be uniformly applied to all lawyers, regardless of the nature of their professional activities. The Model Code makes no attempt to prescribe either disciplinary procedures or penalties for violation of a Disciplinary Rule, nor does it undertake to define standards for civil liability of lawyers for professional conduct. The severity of judgment against one found guilty of violating a Disciplinary Rule should be determined by the character of the offense and the attendant circumstances. An enforcing agency, in applying the Disciplinary Rules, may find interpretive guidance in the basic principles embodied in the Canons and in the objectives reflected in the Ethical Considerations.

CANON 1

A Lawyer Should Assist in Maintaining the Integrity and Competence of the Legal Profession

ETHICAL CONSIDERATIONS

EC 1-1   A basic tenet of the professional responsibility of lawyers is that every person in our society should have ready access to the independent professional services of a lawyer of integrity and competence. Maintaining the integrity and improving the competence of the bar to meet the highest standards is the ethical responsibility of every lawyer.

EC 1-2   The public should be protected from those who are not qualified to be lawyers by reason of a deficiency in education or moral standards or of other relevant factors but who nevertheless seek to practice law. To assure the maintenance of high moral and educational standards of the legal profession, lawyers should affirmatively assist courts and other appropriate bodies in promulgating, enforcing, and improving requirements for admission to the bar. In like manner, the bar has a positive obligation to aid in the continued improvement of all phases of pre-admission and post-admission legal education.

EC 1-3   Before recommending an applicant for admission, a lawyer should satisfy himself that the applicant is of good moral character. Although a lawyer should not become a self-appointed investigator or judge of applicants for admission, he should report to proper officials all unfavorable information he possesses relating to the character or other qualifications of an applicant.

EC 1-4   The integrity of the profession can be maintained only if conduct of lawyers in violation of the Disciplinary Rules is brought to the attention of the proper officials. A lawyer should reveal voluntarily to those officials all unprivileged knowledge of conduct of lawyers which he believes clearly to be in violation of the Disciplinary Rules. A lawyer should, upon request, serve on and assist committees and boards having responsibility for the administration of the Disciplinary Rules.

EC 1-5   A lawyer should maintain high standards of professional conduct and should encourage fellow lawyers to do likewise. He should be temperate and dignified, and he should refrain from all illegal and morally reprehensible conduct. Because of his position in society, even minor violations of law by a lawyer may tend to lessen public confidence in the legal profession. Obedience to law exemplifies respect for law. To lawyers especially, respect for the law should be more than a platitude.

EC 1-6   An applicant for admission to the bar or a lawyer may be unqualified, temporarily or permanently, for other than moral and educational reasons, such as mental or emotional instability. Lawyers should be diligent in taking steps to see that during a period of disqualification such person is not granted a license or, if licensed, is not permitted to practice. In like manner, when the disqualification has terminated, members of the bar should assist such person in being licensed, or, if licensed, in being restored to his full right to practice.

DISCIPLINARY RULES

DR 1-101 Maintaining Integrity and Competence of the Legal Profession.

(A) A lawyer is subject to discipline if he has made a materially false statement in, or if he has deliberately failed to disclose a material fact requested in connection with, his application for admission to the bar.

(B) A lawyer shall not further the application for admission to the bar of another person known by him to be unqualified in respect to character, education, or other relevant attribute.

DR 1-102 Misconduct.

(A) A lawyer shall not:
(1) Violate a Disciplinary Rule.
(2) Circumvent a Disciplinary Rule through actions of another.
(3) Engage in illegal conduct involving moral turpitude.
(4) Engage in conduct involving dishonesty, fraud, deceit, or misrepresentation.
(5) Engage in conduct that is prejudicial to the administration of justice.
(6) Engage in any other conduct that adversely reflects on his fitness to practice law.

DR 1-103 Disclosure of Information to Authorities.

(A) A lawyer possessing unprivileged knowledge of a violation of DR 1-102 shall report such knowledge to a tribunal or other authority empowered to investigate or act upon such violation.

(B) A lawyer possessing unprivileged knowledge or evidence concerning another lawyer or a judge shall reveal fully such knowledge or evidence upon proper request of a tribunal or other authority empowered to investigate or act upon the conduct of lawyers or judges.

CANON 2

A Lawyer Should Assist the Legal Profession in Fulfilling Its Duty to Make Legal Counsel Available

ETHICAL CONSIDERATIONS

EC 2-1   The need of members of the public for legal services is met only if they recognize their legal problems, appreciate the importance of seeking assistance, and are able to obtain the services of acceptable legal counsel. Hence, important functions of the legal profession are to educate laymen to recognize their problems, to facilitate the process of intelligent selection of lawyers, and to assist in making legal services fully available.

Recognition of Legal Problems

EC 2-2   The legal profession should assist laypersons to recognize legal problems because such problems may not be self-revealing and often are not timely noticed. Therefore, lawyers should encourage and participate in educational and public relations programs concerning our legal system with particular reference to legal problems that frequently arise. Preparation of advertisements and professional articles for lay publications and participation in seminars, lectures, and civic programs should be motivated by a desire to educate the public to an awareness of legal needs and to provide information relevant to the selection of the most appropriate counsel rather than to obtain publicity for particular lawyers. The problems of advertising on television require special consideration, due to the style, cost, and transitory nature of such media. If the interests of laypersons in receiving relevant lawyer advertising are not adequately served by print media and radio advertising, and if adequate safeguards to protect the public can reasonably be formulated, television advertising may serve a public interest.

EC 2-3   Whether a lawyer acts properly in volunteering in-person advice to a layperson to seek legal services depends upon the circumstances. The giving of advice that one should take legal action could well be in fulfillment of the duty of the legal profession to assist laypersons in recognizing legal problems. The advice is proper only if motivated by a desire to protect one who does not recognize that he may have legal problems or who is ignorant of his legal rights or obligations. It is improper if motivated by a desire to obtain personal benefit, secure personal publicity, or cause legal action to be taken merely to harass or injure another. A lawyer should not initiate an in-person contact with a non-client, personally or through a representative, for the purpose of being retained to represent him for compensation.

EC 2-4   Since motivation is subjective and often difficult to judge, the motives of a lawyer who volunteers in-person advice likely to produce legal controversy may well be suspect if he receives professional employment or other benefits as a result. A lawyer who volunteers in-person advice that one should obtain the services of a lawyer generally should not himself accept employment, compensation, or other benefit in connection with that matter. However, it is not improper for a lawyer to volunteer such advice and render resulting legal services to close friends, relatives, former clients (in regard to matters germane to former employment), and regular clients.

EC 2-5   A lawyer who writes or speaks for the purpose of educating members of the public to recognize their legal problems should carefully refrain from giving or appearing to give a general solution applicable to all apparently similar individual problems, since slight changes in fact situations may require a material variance in the applicable advice; otherwise, the public may be misled and misadvised. Talks and writings by lawyers for laymen should caution them not to attempt to solve individual problems upon the basis of the information contained therein.

Selection of a Lawyer

EC 2-6   Formerly a potential client usually knew the reputations of local lawyers for competency and integrity and therefore could select a practitioner in whom he had confidence. This traditional selection process worked well because it was initiated by the client and the choice was an informed one.

EC 2-7   Changed conditions, however, have seriously restricted the effectiveness of the traditional selection process. Often the reputations of lawyers are not sufficiently known to enable laymen to make intelligent choices. The law has become increasingly complex and specialized. Few lawyers are willing and competent to deal with every kind of legal matter, and many laymen have difficulty in determining the competence of lawyers to render different types of legal services. The selection of legal counsel is particularly difficult for transients, persons moving into new areas, persons of limited education or means, and others who have little or no contact with lawyers. Lack of information about the availability of lawyers, the qualifications of particular lawyers, and the expense of legal representation leads laypersons to avoid seeking legal advice.

EC 2-8   Selection of a lawyer by a layperson should be made on an informed basis. Advice and recommendation of third parties—relatives, friends, acquaintances, business associates, or other lawyers—and disclosure of relevant information about the lawyer and his practice may be helpful. A layperson is best served if the recommendation is disinterested and informed. In order that the recommendation be disinterested, a lawyer should not seek to influence another to recommend his employment. A lawyer should not compensate another person for recommending him, for influencing a prospective client to employ him, or to encourage future recommendations. Advertisements and public communications, whether in law lists, telephone directories, newspapers, other forms of print media, television or radio, should be formulated to convey only information that is necessary to make an appropriate selection. Such information includes: (1) office information, such as name, including name of law firm and names of professional associates; addresses; telephone numbers; credit card acceptability; fluency in foreign languages; and office hours; (2) relevant biographical information; (3) description of the practice, but only by using designations and definitions authorized by [the agency having jurisdiction of the subject under state law], for example, one or more fields of law in which the lawyer or law firm practices; a statement that practice is limited to one or more fields of law; and/or a statement that the lawyer or law firm specializes in a particular field of law practice, but only by using designations, definitions and standards authorized by [the agency having jurisdiction of the subject under state law]; and (4) permitted fee information. Self-laudation should be avoided.

Selection of a Lawyer: Lawyer Advertising

EC 2-9   The lack of sophistication on the part of many members of the public concerning legal services, the importance of the interests affected by the choice of a lawyer and prior experience with unrestricted lawyer advertising, require that special care be taken by lawyers to avoid misleading the public and to assure that the information set forth in any advertising is relevant to the selection of a lawyer. The lawyer must be mindful that the benefits of lawyer advertising depend upon its reliability and accuracy. Examples of information in lawyer advertising that would be deceptive include misstatements of fact, suggestions that the ingenuity or prior record of a lawyer rather than the justice of the claim are the principal factors likely to determine the result, inclusion of information irrelevant to selecting a lawyer, and representations concerning the quality of service, which cannot be measured or verified. Since lawyer advertising is calculated and not spontaneous, reasonable regulation of lawyer advertising designed to foster compliance with appropriate standards serves the public interest without impeding the flow of useful, meaningful, and relevant information to the public.

EC 2-10   A lawyer should ensure that the information contained in any advertising which the lawyer publishes, broadcasts or causes to be published or broadcast is relevant, is disseminated in an objective and understandable fashion, and would facilitate the prospective client's ability to compare the qualifications of the lawyers available to represent him. A lawyer should strive to communicate such information without undue emphasis upon style and advertising stratagems which serve to hinder rather than to facilitate intelligent selection of counsel. Because technological change is a recurrent feature of communications forms, and because perceptions of what is relevant in lawyer selection may change, lawyer advertising regulations should not be cast in rigid, unchangeable terms. Machinery is therefore available to advertisers and consumers for prompt consideration of proposals to change the rules governing lawyer advertising. The determination of any request for such change should depend upon whether the proposal is necessary in light of existing Code provisions, whether the proposal accords with standards of accuracy, reliability and truthfulness, and whether the proposal would facilitate informed selection of lawyers by potential consumers of legal services. Representatives of lawyers and consumers should be heard in addition to the applicant concerning any proposed change. Any change which is approved should be promulgated in the form of an amendment to the Code so that all lawyers practicing in the jurisdiction may avail themselves of its provisions.

EC 2-11   The name under which a lawyer conducts his practice may be a factor in the selection process. The use of a trade name or an assumed name could mislead laymen concerning the identity, responsibility, and status of those practicing thereunder. Accordingly, a lawyer in private practice should practice only under his own name, the name of a lawyer employing him, a designation containing the name of one or more of the lawyers practicing in a partnership, or, if permitted by law, the name of a professional legal corporation, which should be clearly designated as such. For many years some law firms have used a firm name retaining one or more names of deceased or retired partners and such practice is not improper if the firm is a bona fide successor of a firm in which the deceased or retired person was a member, if the use of the name is authorized by law or by contract, and if the public is not misled thereby. However, the name of a partner who withdraws from a firm but continues to practice law should be omitted from the firm name in order to avoid misleading the public.

EC 2-12   A lawyer occupying a judicial, legislative, or public executive or administrative position who has the right to practice law concurrently may allow his name to remain in the name of the firm if he actively continues to practice law as a member thereof. Otherwise, his name should be removed from the firm name, and he should not be identified as a past or present member of the firm; and he should not hold himself out as being a practicing lawyer.

EC 2-13   In order to avoid the possibility of misleading persons with whom he deals, a lawyer should be scrupulous in the representation of his professional status. He should not hold himself out as being a partner or associate of a law firm if he is not one in fact, and thus should not hold himself out as a partner or associate if he only shares offices with another lawyer.

EC 2-14   In some instances a lawyer confines his practice to a particular field of law. In the absence of state controls to insure the existence of special competence, a lawyer should not be permitted to hold himself out as a specialist or as having official recognition as a specialist, other than in the fields of admiralty, trademark, and patent law where a holding out as a specialist historically has been permitted. A lawyer may, however, indicate in permitted advertising, if it is factual, a limitation of his practice or one or more particular areas or fields of law in which he practices using designations and definitions authorized for that purpose by [the state agency having jurisdiction]. A lawyer practicing in a jurisdiction which certifies specialists must also be careful not to confuse laypersons as to his status. If a lawyer discloses areas of law in which he practices or to which he limits his practice, but is not certified in [the jurisdiction], he, and the designation authorized in [the jurisdiction], should avoid any implication that he is in fact certified.

EC 2-15   The legal profession has developed lawyer referral systems designed to aid individuals who are able to pay fees but need assistance in locating lawyers competent to handle their particular problems. Use of a lawyer referral system enables a layman to avoid an uninformed selection of a lawyer because such a system makes possible the employment of competent lawyers who have indicated an interest in the subject matter involved. Lawyers should support the principle of lawyer referral systems and should encourage the evolution of other ethical plans which aid in the selection of qualified counsel.

Financial Ability to Employ Counsel: Generally

EC 2-16   The legal profession cannot remain a viable force in fulfilling its role in our society unless its members receive adequate compensation for services rendered, and reasonable fees should be charged in appropriate cases to clients able to pay them. Nevertheless, persons unable to pay all or a portion of a reasonable fee should be able to obtain necessary legal services, and lawyers should support and participate in ethical activities designed to achieve that objective.

Financial Ability to Employ Counsel: Persons Able to Pay Reasonable Fees

EC 2-17   The determination of a proper fee requires consideration of the interests of both client and lawyer. A lawyer should not charge more than a reasonable fee, for excessive cost of legal service would deter laymen from utilizing the legal system in protection of their rights. Furthermore, an excessive charge abuses the professional relationship between lawyer and client. On the other hand, adequate compensation is necessary in order to enable the lawyer to serve his client effectively and to preserve the integrity and independence of the profession.

EC 2-18   The determination of the reasonableness of a fee requires consideration of all relevant circumstances, including those stated in the Disciplinary Rules. The fees of a lawyer will vary according to many factors, including the time required, his experience, ability, and reputation, the nature of the employment, the responsibility involved, and the results obtained. It is a commendable and long-standing tradition of the bar that special consideration is given in the fixing of any fee for services rendered a brother lawyer or a member of his immediate family.

EC 2-19   As soon as feasible after a lawyer has been employed, it is desirable that he reach a clear agreement with his client as to the basis of the fee charges to be made. Such a course will not only prevent later misunderstanding but will also work for good relations between the lawyer and the client. It is usually beneficial to reduce to writing the understanding of the parties regarding the fee, particularly when it is contingent. A lawyer should be mindful that many persons who desire to employ him may have had little or no experience with fee charges of lawyers, and for this reason he should explain fully to such persons the reasons for the particular fee arrangement he proposes.

EC 2-20   Contingent fee arrangements in civil cases have long been commonly accepted in the United States in proceedings to enforce claims. The historical bases of their acceptance are that (1) they often, and in a variety of circumstances, provide the only practical means by which one having a claim against another can economically afford, finance, and obtain the services of a competent lawyer to prosecute his claim, and (2) a successful prosecution of the claim produces a *res* out of which the fee can be paid. Although a lawyer generally should decline to accept employment on a contingent fee basis by one who is able to pay a reasonable fixed fee, it is not necessarily improper for a lawyer, where justified by the particular circumstances of a case, to enter into a contingent fee contract in a civil case with any client who, after being fully informed of all relevant factors, desires that arrangement. Because of the human relationships involved and the unique character of the proceedings, contingent fee arrangements in domestic relation cases are rarely justified. In administrative agency proceedings contingent fee contracts should be governed by the same consideration as in other civil cases. Public policy properly condemns contingent fee arrangements in criminal cases, largely on the ground that legal services in criminal cases do not produce a *res* with which to pay the fee.

EC 2-21   A lawyer should not accept compensation or any thing of value incident to his employment or services from one other than his client without the knowledge and consent of his client after full disclosure.

EC 2-22 Without the consent of his client, a lawyer should not associate in a particular matter another lawyer outside his firm. A fee may properly be divided between lawyers properly associated if the division is in proportion to the services performed and the responsibility assumed by each lawyer and if the total fee is reasonable.

EC 2-23 A lawyer should be zealous in his efforts to avoid controversies over fees with clients and should attempt to resolve amicably any differences on the subject. He should not sue a client for a fee unless necessary to prevent fraud or gross imposition by the client.

Financial Ability to Employ Counsel: Persons Unable to Pay Reasonable Fees

EC 2-24 A layman whose financial ability is not sufficient to permit payment of any fee cannot obtain legal services, other than in cases where a contingent fee is appropriate, unless the services are provided for him. Even a person of moderate means may be unable to pay a reasonable fee which is large because of the complexity, novelty, or difficulty of the problem or similar factors.

EC 2-25 Historically, the need for legal services of those unable to pay reasonable fees has been met in part by lawyers who donated their services or accepted court appointments on behalf of such individuals. The basic responsibility for providing legal services for those unable to pay ultimately rests upon the individual lawyer, and personal involvement in the problems of the disadvantaged can be one of the most rewarding experiences in the life of a lawyer. Every lawyer, regardless of professional prominence or professional workload, should find time to participate in serving the disadvantaged. The rendition of free legal services to those unable to pay reasonable fees continues to be an obligation of each lawyer, but the efforts of individual lawyers are often not enough to meet the need. Thus it has been necessary for the profession to institute additional programs to provide legal services. Accordingly, legal aid offices, lawyer referral services, and other related programs have been developed, and others will be developed, by the profession. Every lawyer should support all proper efforts to meet this need for legal services.

Acceptance and Retention of Employment

EC 2-26 A lawyer is under no obligation to act as adviser or advocate for every person who may wish to become his client; but in furtherance of the objective of the bar to make legal services fully available, a lawyer should not lightly decline proffered employment. The fulfillment of this objective requires acceptance by a lawyer of his share of tendered employment which may be unattractive both to him and the bar generally.

EC 2-27 History is replete with instances of distinguished and sacrificial services by lawyers who have represented unpopular clients and causes. Regardless of his personal feelings, a lawyer should not decline representation because a client or a cause is unpopular or community reaction is adverse.

EC 2-28 The personal preference of a lawyer to avoid adversary alignment against judges, other lawyers, public officials, or influential members of the community does not justify his rejection of tendered employment.

EC 2-29 When a lawyer is appointed by a court or requested by a bar association to undertake representation of a person unable to obtain counsel, whether for financial or other reasons, he should not seek to be excused from undertaking the representation except for compelling reasons. Compelling reasons do not include such factors as the repugnance of the subject matter of the proceeding, the identity or position of a person involved in the case, the belief of the lawyer that the defendant in a criminal proceeding is guilty, or the belief of the lawyer regarding the merits of the civil case.

EC 2-30 Employment should not be accepted by a lawyer when he is unable to render competent service or when he knows or it is obvious that the person seeking to employ him desires to institute or maintain an action merely for the purpose of harassing or maliciously injuring another. Likewise, a lawyer should decline employment if the intensity of his personal feeling, as distinguished from a community attitude, may impair his effective representation of a prospective client. If a lawyer knows a client has previously obtained counsel, he should not accept employment in the matter unless the other counsel approves or withdraws, or the client terminates the prior employment.

EC 2-31 Full availability of legal counsel requires both that persons be able to obtain counsel and that lawyers who undertake representation complete the work involved. Trial counsel for a convicted defendant should continue to represent his client by advising whether to take an appeal and, if the appeal is prosecuted, by representing him through the appeal unless new counsel is substituted or withdrawal is permitted by the appropriate court.

EC 2-32   A decision by a lawyer to withdraw should be made only on the basis of compelling circumstances, and in a matter pending before a tribunal he must comply with the rules of the tribunal regarding withdrawal. A lawyer should not withdraw without considering carefully and endeavoring to minimize the possible adverse effect on the rights of his client and the possibility of prejudice to his client as a result of his withdrawal. Even when he justifiably withdraws, a lawyer should protect the welfare of his client by giving due notice of his withdrawal, suggesting employment of other counsel, delivering to the client all papers and property to which the client is entitled, cooperating with counsel subsequently employed, and otherwise endeavoring to minimize the possibility of harm. Further, he should refund to the client any compensation not earned during the employment.

EC 2-33   As a part of the legal profession's commitment to the principle that high quality legal services should be available to all, attorneys are encouraged to cooperate with qualified legal assistance organizations providing prepaid legal services. Such participation should at all times be in accordance with the basic tenets of the profession: independence, integrity, competence and devotion to the interests of individual clients. An attorney so participating should make certain that his relationship with a qualified legal assistance organization in no way interferes with his independent, professional representation of the interests of the individual client. An attorney should avoid situations in which officials of the organization who are not lawyers attempt to direct attorneys concerning the manner in which legal services are performed for individual members, and should also avoid situations in which considerations of economy are given undue weight in determining the attorneys employed by an organization or the legal services to be performed for the member or beneficiary rather than competence and quality of service. An attorney interested in maintaining the historic traditions of the profession and preserving the function of a lawyer as a trusted and independent advisor to individual members of society should carefully assess such factors when accepting employment by, or otherwise participating in, a particular qualified legal assistance organization, and while so participating should adhere to the highest professional standards of effort and competence.

DISCIPLINARY RULES

DR 2-101   Publicity in General.

(A) A lawyer shall not, on behalf of himself, his partner, associate or any other lawyer affiliated with him or his firm, use or participate in the use of any form of public communication containing a false, fraudulent, misleading, deceptive, self-laudatory or unfair statement or claim.

(B) In order to facilitate the process of informed selection of a lawyer by potential consumers of legal services, a lawyer may publish or broadcast, subject to DR 2-103, the following information in print media distributed or over television or radio broadcast in the geographic area or areas in which the lawyer resides or maintains offices or in which a significant part of the lawyer's clientele resides, provided that the information disclosed by the lawyer in such publication or broadcast complies with DR 2-101(A), and is presented in a dignified manner.

(1) Name, including name of law firm and names of professional associates; addresses and telephone numbers;

(2) One or more fields of law in which the lawyer or law firm practices, a statement that practice is limited to one or more fields of law, or a statement that the lawyer or law firm specializes in a particular field of law practice, to the extent authorized under DR 2-105;

(3) Date and place of birth;

(4) Date and place of admission to the bar of state and federal courts;

(5) Schools attended, with dates of graduation, degrees and other scholastic distinctions;

(6) Public or quasi-public offices;

(7) Military service;

(8) Legal authorships;

(9) Legal teaching positions;

(10) Memberships, offices, and committee assignments, in bar associations;

(11) Membership and offices in legal fraternities and legal societies;

(12) Technical and professional licenses;

(13) Memberships in scientific, technical and professional associations and societies;

(14) Foreign language ability;

(15) Names and addresses of bank references;

(16) With their written consent, names of clients regularly represented;

(17) Prepaid or group legal services programs in which the lawyer participates;

(18) Whether credit cards or other credit arrangements are accepted;

(19) Office and telephone answering service hours;

(20) Fee for an initial consultation;

(21) Availability upon request of a written schedule of fees and/or estimate of the fee to be charged for specific services;

(22) Contingent fee rates subject to DR 2-106(C), provided that the statement discloses whether percentages are computed before or after deduction of costs;

(23) Range of fees for services, provided that the statement discloses that the specific fee within the range which will be charged will vary depending upon the particular matter to be handled for each client and the client is entitled without obligation to an estimate of the fee within the range likely to be charged, in print size equivalent to the largest print used in setting forth the fee information;

(24) Hourly rate, provided that the statement discloses that the total fee charged will depend upon the number of hours which must be devoted to the particular matter to be handled for each client and the client is entitled to without obligation an estimate of the fee likely to be charged, in print size at least equivalent to the largest print used in setting forth the fee information;

(25) Fixed fees for specific legal services, the description of which would not be misunderstood or be deceptive, provided that the statement discloses that the quoted fee will be available only to clients whose matters fall into the services described and that the client is entitled without obligation to a specific estimate of the fee likely to be charged in print size at least equivalent to the largest print used in setting forth the fee information.

(C) Any person desiring to expand the information authorized for disclosure in DR 2-101(B), or to provide for its dissemination through other forums may apply to [the agency having jurisdiction under state law]. Any such application shall be served upon [the agencies having jurisdiction under state law over the regulation of the legal profession and consumer matters] who shall be heard, together with the applicant, on the issue of whether the proposal is necessary in light of the existing provisions of the Code, accords with standards of accuracy, reliability and truthfulness, and would facilitate the process of informed selection of lawyers by potential consumers of legal services. The relief granted in response to any such application shall be promulgated as an amendment to DR 2-101(B), universally applicable to all lawyers.

(D) If the advertisement is communicated to the public over television or radio, it shall be pre-recorded, approved for broadcast by the lawyer, and a recording of the actual transmission shall be retained by the lawyer.

(E) If a lawyer advertises a fee for a service, the lawyer must render that service for no more than the fee advertised.

(F) Unless otherwise specified in the advertisement if a lawyer publishes any fee information authorized under DR 2-101(B) in a publication that is published more frequently than one time per month, the lawyer shall be bound by any representation made therein for a period of not less than 30 days after such publication. If a lawyer publishes any fee information authorized under DR 2-101(B) in a publication that is published once a month or less frequently, he shall be bound by any representation made therein until the publication of the succeeding issue. If a lawyer publishes any fee information authorized under DR 2-101(B) in a publication which has no fixed date for publication of a succeeding issue, the lawyer shall be bound by any representation made therein for a reasonable period of time after publication but in no event less than one year.

(G) Unless otherwise specified, if a lawyer broadcasts any fee information authorized under DR 2-101(B), the lawyer shall be bound by any representation made therein for a period of not less than 30 days after such broadcast.

(H) This rule does not prohibit limited and dignified identification of a lawyer as a lawyer as well as by name:

(1) In political advertisements when his professional status is germane to the political campaign or to a political issue.

(2) In public notices when the name and profession of a lawyer are required or authorized by law or are reasonably pertinent for a purpose other than the attraction of potential clients.

(3) In routine reports and announcements of a bona fide business, civic, professional, or political organization in which he serves as a director or officer.

(4) In and on legal documents prepared by him.

(5) In and on legal textbooks, treatises, and other legal publications, and in dignified advertisements thereof.

(I) A lawyer shall not compensate or give any thing of value to representatives of the press, radio, television, or other communication medium in anticipation of or in return for professional publicity in a news item.

DR 2-102 Professional Notices, Letterheads and Offices

(A) A lawyer or law firm shall not use or participate in the use of professional cards, professional announcement cards, office signs, letterheads, telephone directory listings, law lists, legal directory listings, or similar professional notices or devices, except that the following may be used if they are in dignified form:

(1) A professional card of a lawyer identifying him by name and as a lawyer, and giving his addresses, telephone numbers, the name of his law firm, and any information permitted under DR 2-105. A professional card of a law firm may also give the names of members and associates. Such cards may be used for identification.

(2) A brief professional announcement card stating new or changed associations or addresses, change of firm name, or similar matters pertaining to the professional office of a lawyer or law firm, which may be mailed to lawyers, clients, former clients, personal friends, and relatives. It shall not state biographical data except to the extent reasonably necessary to identify the lawyer or to explain the change in his association, but it may state the immediate past position of the lawyer. It may give the names and dates of predecessor firms in a continuing line of succession. It shall not state the nature of the practice except as permitted under DR 2-105.

(3) A sign on or near the door of the office and in the building directory identifying the law office. The sign shall not state the nature of the practice, except as permitted under DR 2-105.

(4) A letterhead of a lawyer identifying him by name and as a lawyer, and giving his addresses, telephone numbers, the name of his law firm, associates and any information permitted under DR 2-105. A letterhead of a law firm may also give the names of members and associates, and names and dates relating to deceased and retired members. A lawyer may be designated "Of Counsel" on a letterhead if he has a continuing relationship with a lawyer or law firm, other than as a partner or associate. A lawyer or law firm may be designated as "General Counsel" or by similar professional reference on stationery of a client if he or the firm devotes a substantial amount of professional time in the

representation of that client. The letterhead of a law firm may give the names and dates of predecessor firms in a continuing line of succession.

(B) A lawyer in private practice shall not practice under a trade name, a name that is misleading as to the identity of the lawyer or lawyers practicing under such name, or a firm name containing names other than those of one or more of the lawyers in the firm, except that the name of a professional corporation or professional association may contain "P.C." or "P.A." or similar symbols indicating the nature of the organization, and if otherwise lawful a firm may use as, or continue to include in, its name the name or names of one or more deceased or retired members of the firm or of a predecessor firm in a continuing line of succession. A lawyer who assumes a judicial, legislative, or public executive or administrative post or office shall not permit his name to remain in the name of a law firm or to be used in professional notices of the firm during any significant period in which he is not actively and regularly practicing law as a member of the firm, and during such period other members of the firm shall not use his name in the firm name or in professional notices of the firm.

(C) A lawyer shall not hold himself out as having a partnership with one or more other lawyers or professional corporations unless they are in fact partners.

(D) A partnership shall not be formed or continued between or among lawyers licensed in different jurisdictions unless all enumerations of the members and associates of the firm on its letterhead and in other permissible listings make clear the jurisdictional limitations on those members and associates of the firm not licensed to practice in all listed jurisdictions; however, the same firm name may be used in each jurisdiction.

(E) Nothing contained herein shall prohibit a lawyer from using or permitting the use of, in connection with his name, an earned degree or title derived therefrom indicating his training in the law.

DR 2-103   Recommendation of Professional Employment.

(A) A lawyer shall not, except as authorized in DR 2-101(B), recommend employment, as a private practitioner, of himself, his partner, or associate to a layperson who has not sought his advice regarding employment of a lawyer.

(B) A lawyer shall not compensate or give anything of value to a person or organization to recommend or secure his employment by a client, or as a reward for having made a recommendation resulting in his employment by a client, except that he may pay the usual and reasonable fees or dues charged by any of the organizations listed in DR 2-103(D).

(C) A lawyer shall not request a person or organization to recommend or promote the use of his services or those of his partner or associate, or any other lawyer affiliated with him or his firm, as a private practitioner, except as authorized in DR 2-101, and except that

(1) He may request referrals from a lawyer referral service operated, sponsored, or approved by a bar association and may pay its fees incident thereto.

(2) He may cooperate with the legal service activities of any of the offices or organizations enumerated in DR 2-103(D)(1) through (4) and may perform legal services for those to whom he was recommended by it to do such work if:

(a) The person to whom the recommendation is made is a member or beneficiary of such office or organizations; and

(b) The lawyer remains free to exercise his independent professional judgment on behalf of his client.

(D) A lawyer or his partner or associate or any other lawyer affiliated with him or his firm may be recommended, employed or paid by, or may cooperate with, one of the following offices or organizations that promote the use of his services or those of his partner or associate or any other lawyer affiliated with him or his firm if there is no interference with the exercise of independent professional judgment in behalf of his client:

(1) A legal aid office or public defender office:

(a) Operated or sponsored by a duly accredited law school.

(b) Operated or sponsored by a bona fide nonprofit community organization.

(c) Operated or sponsored by a governmental agency.

(d) Operated, sponsored, or approved by a bar association.

(2) A military legal assistance office.

(3) A lawyer referral service operated, sponsored, or approved by a bar association.

(4) Any bona fide organization that recommends, furnishes or pays for legal services to its members or beneficiaries provided the following conditions are satisfied:

(a) Such organization, including any affiliate, is so organized and operated that no profit is derived by it from the rendition of legal services by lawyers, and that, if the organization is organized for profit, the legal services are not rendered by lawyers employed, directed, supervised or selected by it except in connection with matters where such organization bears ultimate liability of its member or beneficiary.

(b) Neither the lawyer, nor his partner, nor associate, nor any other lawyer affiliated with him or his firm, nor any non-lawyer, shall have initiated or promoted such organization for the primary purpose of providing financial or other benefit to such lawyer, partner, associate or affiliated lawyer.

(c) Such organization is not operated for the purpose of procuring legal work or financial benefit for any lawyer as a private practitioner outside of the legal services program of the organization.

(d) The member or beneficiary to whom the legal services are furnished, and not such organization, is recognized as the client of the lawyer in the matter.

(e) Any member or beneficiary who is entitled to have legal services furnished or paid for by the organization may, if such member or beneficiary so desires, select counsel other than that furnished, selected or approved by the organization for the particular matter involved; and the legal service plan of such organization provides appropriate relief for any member or beneficiary who asserts a claim that representation by counsel furnished, selected or approved would be unethical, improper or inadequate under the circumstances of the matter involved and the plan provides an appropriate procedure for seeking such relief.

(f) The lawyer does not know or have cause to know that such organization is in violation of applicable laws, rules of court and other legal requirements that govern its legal service operations.

(g) Such organization has filed with the appropriate disciplinary authority at least annually a report with respect to its legal service plan, if any, showing its terms, its schedule of benefits, its subscription charges, agreements with counsel, and financial results of its legal service activities or, if it has failed to do so, the lawyer does not know or have cause to know of such failure.

(E) A lawyer shall not accept employment when he knows or it is obvious that the person who seeks his services does so as a result of conduct prohibited under this Disciplinary Rule.

DR 2-104   Suggestion of Need of Legal Services.

(A) A lawyer who has given unsolicited advice to a layman that he should obtain counsel or take legal action shall not accept employment resulting from that advice, except that:

(1) A lawyer may accept employment by a close friend, relative, former client (if the advice is germane to the former employment), or one whom the lawyer reasonably believes to be a client.

(2) A lawyer may accept employment that results from his participation in activities designed to educate laymen to recognize legal problems, to make intelligent selection of counsel, or to utilize available legal services if such activities are conducted or sponsored by a qualified legal assistance organization.

(3) A lawyer who is recommended, furnished or paid by any of the offices or organizations enumerated in DR 2-103(D)(1) through (4) may represent a member or beneficiary thereof, to the extent and under the conditions prescribed therein.

(4) Without affecting his right to accept employment, a lawyer may speak publicly or write for publication on legal topics so long as he does not emphasize his own professional experience or reputation and does not undertake to give individual advice.

(5) If success in asserting rights or defenses of his client in litigation in the nature of a class action is dependent upon the joinder of others, a lawyer may accept, but shall not seek, employment from those contacted for the purpose of obtaining their joinder.

DR 2-105   Limitation of Practice.

(A) A lawyer shall not hold himself out publicly as a specialist, as practicing in certain areas of law or as limiting his practice permitted under DR 2-101(B), except as follows:

(1) A lawyer admitted to practice before the United States Patent and Trademark Office may use the designation "Patents," "Patent Attorney," or "Patent Lawyer," or "Registered Patent Attorney" or any combination of those terms, on his letterhead and office sign.

(2) A lawyer who publicly discloses fields of law in which the lawyer or the law firm practices or states that his practice is limited to one or more fields of law shall do so by using designations and definitions authorized and approved by [the agency having jurisdiction of the subject under state law].

(3) A lawyer who is certified as a specialist in a particular field of law or law practice by [the authority having jurisdiction under state law over the subject of specialization by lawyers] may hold himself out as such, but only in accordance with the rules prescribed by that authority.

DR 2-106   Fees for Legal Services.

(A) A lawyer shall not enter into an agreement for, charge, or collect an illegal or clearly excessive fee.

(B) A fee is clearly excessive when, after a review of the facts, a lawyer of ordinary prudence would be left with a definite and firm conviction that the fee is in excess of a reasonable fee. Factors to be considered as guides in determining the reasonableness of a fee include the following:

(1) The time and labor required, the novelty and difficulty of the questions involved, and the skill requisite to perform the legal service properly.

(2) The likelihood, if apparent to the client, that the acceptance of the particular employment will preclude other employment by the lawyer.

(3) The fee customarily charged in the locality for similar legal services.

(4) The amount involved and the results obtained.

(5) The time limitations imposed by the client or by the circumstances.

(6) The nature and length of the professional relationship with the client.

(7) The experience, reputation, and ability of the lawyer or lawyers performing the services.

(8) Whether the fee is fixed or contingent.

(C) A lawyer shall not enter into an arrangement for, charge, or collect a contingent fee for representing a defendant in a criminal case.

DR 2-107   Division of Fees Among Lawyers.

(A) A lawyer shall not divide a fee for legal services with another lawyer who is not a partner in or associate of his law firm or law office, unless:

(1) The client consents to employment of the other lawyer after a full disclosure that a division of fees will be made.

(2) The division is made in proportion to the services performed and responsibility assumed by each.

(3) The total fee of the lawyers does not clearly exceed reasonable compensation for all legal services they rendered the client.

(B) This Disciplinary Rule does not prohibit payment to a former partner or associate pursuant to a separation or retirement agreement.

DR 2-108 Agreements Restricting the Practice of a Lawyer.

(A) A lawyer shall not be a party to or participate in a partnership or employment agreement with another lawyer that restricts the right of a lawyer to practice law after the termination of a relationship created by the agreement, except as a condition to payment of retirement benefits.

(B) In connection with the settlement of a controversy or suit, a lawyer shall not enter into an agreement that restricts his right to practice law.

DR 2-109 Acceptance of Employment.

(A) A lawyer shall not accept employment on behalf of a person if he knows or it is obvious that such person wishes to:

(1) Bring a legal action, conduct a defense, or assert a position in litigation, or otherwise have steps taken for him, merely for the purpose of harassing or maliciously injuring any person.

(2) Present a claim or defense in litigation that is not warranted under existing law, unless it can be supported by good faith argument for an extension, modification, or reversal of existing law.

DR 2-110 Withdrawal from Employment.

(A) In general.

(1) If permission for withdrawal from employment is required by the rules of a tribunal, a lawyer shall not withdraw from employment in a proceeding before that tribunal without its permission.

(2) In any event, a lawyer shall not withdraw from employment until he has taken reasonable steps to avoid foreseeable prejudice to the rights of his client, including giving due notice to his client, allowing time for employment of other counsel, delivering to the client all papers and property to which the client is entitled, and complying with applicable laws and rules.

(3) A lawyer who withdraws from employment shall refund promptly any part of a fee paid in advance that has not been earned.

(B) Mandatory withdrawal.

A lawyer representing a client before a tribunal, with its permission if required by its rules, shall withdraw from employment, and a lawyer representing a client in other matters shall withdraw from employment, if:

(1) He knows or it is obvious that his client is bringing the legal action, conducting the defense, or asserting a position in the litigation, or is otherwise having steps taken for him, merely for the purpose of harassing or maliciously injuring any person.

(2) He knows or it is obvious that his continued employment will result in violation of a Disciplinary Rule.

(3) His mental or physical condition renders it unreasonably difficult for him to carry out the employment effectively.

(4) He is discharged by his client.

(C) Permissive withdrawal.

If DR 2-110(B) is not applicable, a lawyer may not request permission to withdraw in matters pending before a tribunal, and may not withdraw in other matters, unless such request or such withdrawal is because:

(1) His client:

(a) Insists upon presenting a claim or defense that is not warranted under existing law and cannot be supported by good faith argument for an extension, modification, or reversal of existing law.

(b) Personally seeks to pursue an illegal course of conduct.

(c) Insists that the lawyer pursue a course of conduct that is illegal or that is prohibited under the Disciplinary Rules.

(d) By other conduct renders it unreasonably difficult for the lawyer to carry out his employment effectively.

(e) Insists, in a matter not pending before a tribunal, that the lawyer engage in conduct that is contrary to the judgment and advice of the lawyer but not prohibited under the Disciplinary Rules.

(f) Deliberately disregards an agreement or obligation to the lawyer as to expenses or fees.

(2) His continued employment is likely to result in a violation of a Disciplinary Rule.

(3) His inability to work with co-counsel indicates that the best interests of the client likely will be served by withdrawal.

(4) His mental or physical condition renders it difficult for him to carry out the employment effectively.

(5) His client knowingly and freely assents to termination of his employment.

(6) He believes in good faith, in a proceeding pending before a tribunal, that the tribunal will find the existence of other good cause for withdrawal.

CANON 3

A Lawyer Should Assist in Preventing the Unauthorized Practice of Law

ETHICAL CONSIDERATIONS

EC 3-1   The prohibition against the practice of law by a layman is grounded in the need of the public for integrity and competence of those who undertake to render legal services. Because of the fiduciary and personal character of the lawyer-client relationship and the inherently complex nature of our legal system, the public can better be assured of the requisite responsibility and competence if the practice of law is confined to those who are subject to the requirements and regulations imposed upon members of the legal profession.

EC 3-2   The sensitive variations in the considerations that bear on legal determinations often make it difficult even for a lawyer to exercise appropriate professional judgment, and it is therefore essential that the personal nature of the relationship of client and lawyer be preserved. Competent professional judgment is the product of a trained familiarity with law and legal processes, a disciplined, analytical approach to legal problems, and a firm ethical commitment.

EC 3-3   A non-lawyer who undertakes to handle legal matters is not governed as to integrity or legal competence by the same rules that govern the conduct of a lawyer. A lawyer is not only subject to that regulation but also is committed to high standards of ethical conduct. The public interest is best served in legal matters by a regulated profession committed to such standards. The Disciplinary Rules protect the public in that they prohibit a lawyer from seeking employment by improper overtures, from acting in cases of divided loyalties, and from submitting to the control of others in the exercise of his judgment. Moreover, a person who entrusts legal matters to a lawyer is protected by the attorney-client privilege and by the duty of the lawyer to hold inviolate the confidences and secrets of his client.

EC 3-4   A layman who seeks legal services often is not in a position to judge whether he will receive proper professional attention. The entrustment of a legal matter may well involve the confidences, the reputation, the property, the freedom, or even the life of the client. Proper protection of members of the public demands that no person be permitted to act in the confidential and demanding capacity of a lawyer unless he is subject to the regulations of the legal profession.

EC 3-5   It is neither necessary nor desirable to attempt the formulation of a single, specific definition of what constitutes the practice of law. Functionally, the practice of law relates to the rendition of services for others that call for the professional judgment of a lawyer. The essence of the professional judgment of the lawyer is his educated ability to relate the general body and philosophy of law to a specific legal problem of a client; and thus, the public interest will be better served if only lawyers are permitted to act in matters involving professional judgment. Where this professional judgment is not involved, non-lawyers, such as court clerks, police officers, abstracters, and many governmental employees, may engage in occupations that require a special knowledge of law in certain areas. But the services of a lawyer are essential in the public interest whenever the exercise of professional legal judgment is required.

EC 3-6   A lawyer often delegates tasks to clerks, secretaries, and other lay persons. Such delegation is proper if the lawyer maintains a direct relationship with his client, supervises the delegated work, and has complete professional responsibility for the work product. This delegation enables a lawyer to render legal service more economically and efficiently.

EC 3-7   The prohibition against a non-lawyer practicing law does not prevent a layman from representing himself, for then he is ordinarily exposing only himself to possible injury. The purpose of the legal profession is to make educated legal representation available to the public; but anyone who does not wish to avail himself of such representation is not required to do so. Even so, the legal profession should help members of the public to recognize legal problems and to understand why it may be unwise for them to act for themselves in matters having legal consequences.

EC 3-8   Since a lawyer should not aid or encourage a layman to practice law, he should not practice law in association with a layman or otherwise share legal fees with a layman. This does not mean, however, that the pecuniary value of the interest of a deceased lawyer in his firm or practice may not be paid to his estate or specified persons such as his widow or heirs. In like manner, profit-sharing retirement plans of a lawyer or law firm which include non-lawyer office employees are not improper. These limited exceptions to the rule against sharing legal fees with laymen are permissible since they do not aid or encourage laymen to practice law.

EC 3-9   Regulation of the practice of law is accomplished principally by the respective states. Authority to engage in the practice of law conferred in any jurisdiction is not per se a grant of the right to practice elsewhere, and it is improper for a lawyer to engage in practice where he is not permitted by law or by court order to do so. However, the demands of business and the mobility of our society pose distinct problems in the regulation of the practice of law by the states. In furtherance of the public interest, the legal profession should discourage regulation that unreasonably imposes territorial limitations upon the right of a lawyer to handle the legal affairs of his client or upon the opportunity of a client to obtain the services of a lawyer of his choice in all matters including the presentation of a contested matter in a tribunal before which the lawyer is not permanently admitted to practice.

DISCIPLINARY RULES

DR 3-101   Aiding Unauthorized Practice of Law.

   (A) A lawyer shall not aid a non-lawyer in the unauthorized practice of law.

   (B) A lawyer shall not practice law in a jurisdiction where to do so would be in violation of regulations of the profession in that jurisdiction.

DR 3-102   Dividing Legal Fees with a Non-Lawyer.

   (A) A lawyer or law firm shall not share legal fees with a non-lawyer, except that:

   (1) An agreement by a lawyer with his firm, partner, or associate may provide for the payment of money, over a reasonable period of time after his death, to his estate or to one or more specified persons.

(2) A lawyer who undertakes to complete unfinished legal business of a deceased lawyer may pay to the estate of the deceased lawyer that proportion of the total compensation which fairly represents the services rendered by the deceased lawyer.

(3) A lawyer or law firm may include non-lawyer employees in a retirement plan, even though the plan is based in whole or in part on a profit-sharing arrangement, providing such plan does not circumvent another Disciplinary Rule.

DR 3-103   Forming a Partnership with a Non-Lawyer.

(A) A lawyer shall not form a partnership with a non-lawyer if any of the activities of the partnership consist of the practice of law.

CANON 4

A Lawyer Should Preserve the Confidences and Secrets of a Client

ETHICAL CONSIDERATIONS

EC 4-1   Both the fiduciary relationship existing between lawyer and client and the proper functioning of the legal system require the preservation by the lawyer of confidences and secrets of one who has employed or sought to employ him. A client must feel free to discuss whatever he wishes with his lawyer and a lawyer must be equally free to obtain information beyond that volunteered by his client. A lawyer should be fully informed of all the facts of the matter he is handling in order for his client to obtain the full advantage of our legal system. It is for the lawyer in the exercise of his independent professional judgment to separate the relevant and important from the irrelevant and unimportant. The observance of the ethical obligation of a lawyer to hold inviolate the confidences and secrets of his client not only facilitates the full development of facts essential to proper representation of the client but also encourages laymen to seek early legal assistance.

EC 4-2   The obligation to protect confidences and secrets obviously does not preclude a lawyer from revealing information when his client consents after full disclosure, when necessary to perform his professional employment, when permitted by a Disciplinary Rule, or when required by law. Unless the client otherwise directs, a lawyer may disclose the affairs of his client to partners or associates of his firm. It is a matter of common knowledge that the normal operation of a law office exposes confidential professional information to non-lawyer employees of the office, particularly secretaries and those having access to the files; and this obligates a lawyer to exercise care in selecting and training his employees so that the sanctity of all confidences and secrets of his clients may be preserved. If the obligation extends to two or more clients as to the same information, a lawyer should obtain the permission of all before revealing the information. A lawyer must always be sensitive to the rights and wishes of his client and act scrupulously in the making of decisions which may involve the disclosure of information obtained in his professional relationship. Thus, in the absence of consent of his client after full disclosure, a lawyer should not associate another lawyer in the handling of a matter; nor should he, in the absence of consent, seek counsel from another lawyer if there is a reasonable possibility that the identity of the client or his confidences or secrets would be revealed to such lawyer. Both social amenities and professional duty should cause a lawyer to shun indiscreet conversations concerning his clients.

EC 4-3   Unless the client otherwise directs, it is not improper for a lawyer to give limited information from his files to an outside agency necessary for statistical, bookkeeping, accounting, data processing, banking, printing, or other legitimate purposes, provided he exercises due care in the selection of the agency and warns the agency that the information must be kept confidential.

EC 4-4   The attorney-client privilege is more limited than the ethical obligation of a lawyer to guard the confidences and secrets of his client. This ethical precept, unlike the evidentiary privilege, exists without regard to the nature or source of information or the fact that others share the knowledge. A lawyer should endeavor to act in a manner which preserves the evidentiary privilege; for example, he should avoid professional discussions in the presence of persons to whom the privilege does not extend. A lawyer owes an obligation to advise the client of the attorney-client privilege and timely to assert the privilege unless it is waived by the client.

EC 4-5 A lawyer should not use information acquired in the course of the representation of a client to the disadvantage of the client and a lawyer should not use, except with the consent of his client after full disclosure, such information for his own purposes. Likewise, a lawyer should be diligent in his efforts to prevent the misuse of such information by his employees and associates. Care should be exercised by a lawyer to prevent the disclosure of the confidences and secrets of one client to another, and no employment should be accepted that might require such disclosure.

EC 4-6 The obligation of a lawyer to preserve the confidences and secrets of his client continues after the termination of his employment. Thus a lawyer should not attempt to sell a law practice as a going business because, among other reasons, to do so would involve the disclosure of confidences and secrets. A lawyer should also provide for the protection of the confidences and secrets of his client following the termination of the practice of the lawyer, whether termination is due to death, disability, or retirement. For example, a lawyer might provide for the personal papers of the client to be returned to him and for the papers of the lawyer to be delivered to another lawyer or to be destroyed. In determining the method of disposition, the instructions and wishes of the client should be a dominant consideration.

DISCIPLINARY RULES

DR 4-101 Preservation of Confidences and Secrets of a Client.

(A) "Confidence" refers to information protected by the attorney-client privilege under applicable law, and "secret" refers to other information gained in the professional relationship that the client has requested be held inviolate or the disclosure of which would be embarrassing or would be likely to be detrimental to the client.

(B) Except when permitted under DR 4-101(C), a lawyer shall not knowingly:

(1) Reveal a confidence or secret of his client.

(2) Use a confidence or secret of his client to the disadvantage of the client.

(3) Use a confidence or secret of his client for the advantage of himself or of a third person, unless the client consents after full disclosure.

(C) A lawyer may reveal:

(1) Confidences or secrets with the consent of the client or clients affected, but only after a full disclosure to them.

(2) Confidences or secrets when permitted under Disciplinary Rules or required by law or court order.

(3) The intention of his client to commit a crime and the information necessary to prevent the crime.

(4) Confidences or secrets necessary to establish or collect his fee or to defend himself or his employees or associates against an accusation of wrongful conduct.

(D) A lawyer shall exercise reasonable care to prevent his employees, associates, and others whose services are utilized by him from disclosing or using confidences or secrets of a client, except that a lawyer may reveal the information allowed by DR 4-101(C) through an employee.

CANON 5

A Lawyer Should Exercise Independent Professional Judgment on Behalf of a Client

ETHICAL CONSIDERATIONS

EC 5-1 The professional judgment of a lawyer should be exercised, within the bounds of the law, solely for the benefit of his client and free of compromising influences and loyalties. Neither his personal interests, the interests of other clients, nor the desires of third persons should be permitted to dilute his loyalty to his client.

Interests of a Lawyer That May Affect His Judgment

EC 5-2   A lawyer should not accept proffered employment if his personal interests or desires will, or there is a reasonable probability that they will, affect adversely the advice to be given or services to be rendered the prospective client. After accepting employment, a lawyer carefully should refrain from acquiring a property right or assuming a position that would tend to make his judgment less protective of the interests of his client.

EC 5-3   The self-interest of a lawyer resulting from his ownership of property in which his client also has an interest or which may affect property of his client may interfere with the exercise of free judgment on behalf of his client. If such interference would occur with respect to a prospective client, a lawyer should decline employment proffered by him. After accepting employment, a lawyer should not acquire property rights that would adversely affect his professional judgment in the representation of his client. Even if the property interests of a lawyer do not presently interfere with the exercise of his independent judgment, but the likelihood of interference can reasonably be foreseen by him, a lawyer should explain the situation to his client and should decline employment or withdraw unless the client consents to the continuance of the relationship after full disclosure. A lawyer should not seek to persuade his client to permit him to invest in an undertaking of his client nor make improper use of his professional relationship to influence his client to invest in an enterprise in which the lawyer is interested.

EC 5-4   If, in the course of his representation of a client, a lawyer is permitted to receive from his client a beneficial ownership in publication rights relating to the subject matter of the employment, he may be tempted to subordinate the interests of his client to his own anticipated pecuniary gain. For example, a lawyer in a criminal case who obtains from his client television, radio, motion picture, newspaper, magazine, book, or other publication rights with respect to the case may be influenced, consciously or unconsciously, to a course of conduct that will enhance the value of his publication rights to the prejudice of his client. To prevent these potentially differing interests, such arrangements should be scrupulously avoided prior to the termination of all aspects of the matter giving rise to the employment, even though his employment has previously ended.

EC 5-5   A lawyer should not suggest to his client that a gift be made to himself or for his benefit. If a lawyer accepts a gift from his client, he is peculiarly susceptible to the charge that he unduly influenced or overreached the client. If a client voluntarily offers to make a gift to his lawyer, the lawyer may accept the gift, but before doing so, he should urge that his client secure disinterested advice from an independent, competent person who is cognizant of all the circumstances. Other than in exceptional circumstances, a lawyer should insist that an instrument in which his client desires to name him beneficially be prepared by another lawyer selected by the client.

EC 5-6   A lawyer should not consciously influence a client to name him as executor, trustee, or lawyer in an instrument. In those cases where a client wishes to name his lawyer as such, care should be taken by the lawyer to avoid even the appearance of impropriety.

EC 5-7   The possibility of an adverse effect upon the exercise of free judgment by a lawyer on behalf of his client during litigation generally makes it undesirable for the lawyer to acquire a proprietary interest in the cause of his client or otherwise to become financially interested in the outcome of the litigation. However, it is not improper for a lawyer to protect his right to collect a fee for his services by the assertion of legally permissible liens, even though by doing so he may acquire an interest in the outcome of litigation. Although a contingent fee arrangement gives a lawyer a financial interest in the outcome of litigation, a reasonable contingent fee is permissible in civil cases because it may be the only means by which a layman can obtain the services of a lawyer of his choice. But a lawyer, because he is in a better position to evaluate a cause of action, should enter into a contingent fee arrangement only in those instances where the arrangement will be beneficial to the client.

EC 5-8   A financial interest in the outcome of litigation also results if monetary advances are made by the lawyer to his client. Although this assistance generally is not encouraged, there are instances when it is not improper to make loans to a client. For example, the advancing or guaranteeing of payment of the costs and expenses of litigation by a lawyer may be the only way a client can enforce his cause of action, but the ultimate liability for such costs and expenses must be that of the client.

EC 5-9   Occasionally a lawyer is called upon to decide in a particular case whether he will be a witness or an advocate. If a lawyer is both counsel and witness, he becomes more easily impeachable for interest and thus may be a less effective witness. Conversely, the opposing counsel may be handicapped in challenging the credibility of the lawyer when the lawyer also appears as an advocate in the case. An advocate who becomes a witness is in the unseemly and ineffective position of arguing his own credibility. The roles of an advocate and of a witness are inconsistent; the function of an advocate is to advance or argue the cause of another, while that of a witness is to state facts objectively.

EC 5-10 Problems incident to the lawyer-witness relationship arise at different stages; they relate either to whether a lawyer should accept employment or should withdraw from employment. Regardless of when the problem arises, his decision is to be governed by the same basic considerations. It is not objectionable for a lawyer who is a potential witness to be an advocate if it is unlikely that he will be called as a witness because his testimony would be merely cumulative or if his testimony will relate only to an uncontested issue. In the exceptional situation where it will be manifestly unfair to the client for the lawyer to refuse employment or to withdraw when he will likely be a witness on a contested issue, he may serve as advocate even though he may be a witness. In making such decision, he should determine the personal or financial sacrifice of the client that may result from his refusal of employment or withdrawal therefrom, the materiality of his testimony, and the effectiveness of his representation in view of his personal involvement. In weighing these factors, it should be clear that refusal or withdrawal will impose an unreasonable hardship upon the client before the lawyer accepts or continues the employment. Where the question arises, doubts should be resolved in favor of the lawyer testifying and against his becoming or continuing as an advocate.

EC 5-11 A lawyer should not permit his personal interests to influence his advice relative to a suggestion by his client that additional counsel be employed. In like manner, his personal interests should not deter him from suggesting that additional counsel be employed; on the contrary, he should be alert to the desirability of recommending additional counsel when, in his judgment, the proper representation of his client requires it. However, a lawyer should advise his client not to employ additional counsel suggested by the client if the lawyer believes that such employment would be a disservice to the client, and he should disclose the reasons for his belief.

EC 5-12 Inability of co-counsel to agree on a matter vital to the representation of their client requires that their disagreement be submitted by them jointly to their client for his resolution, and the decision of the client shall control the action to be taken.

EC 5-13 A lawyer should not maintain membership in or be influenced by any organization of employees that undertakes to prescribe, direct, or suggest when or how he should fulfill his professional obligations to a person or organization that employs him as a lawyer. Although it is not necessarily improper for a lawyer employed by a corporation or similar entity to be a member of an organization of employees, he should be vigilant to safeguard his fidelity as a lawyer to his employer, free from outside influences.

Interests of Multiple Clients

EC 5-14 Maintaining the independence of professional judgment required of a lawyer precludes his acceptance or continuation of employment that will adversely affect his judgment on behalf of or dilute his loyalty to a client. This problem arises whenever a lawyer is asked to represent two or more clients who may have differing interests, whether such interests be conflicting, inconsistent, diverse, or otherwise discordant.

EC 5-15 If a lawyer is requested to undertake or to continue representation of multiple clients having potentially differing interests, he must weigh carefully the possibility that his judgment may be impaired or his loyalty divided if he accepts or continues the employment. He should resolve all doubts against the propriety of the representation. A lawyer should never represent in litigation multiple clients with differing interests; and there are few situations in which he would be justified in representing in litigation multiple clients with potentially differing interests. If a lawyer accepted such employment and the interests did become actually differing, he would have to withdraw from employment with likelihood of resulting hardship on the clients; and for this reason it is preferable that he refuse the employment initially. On the other hand, there are many instances in which a lawyer may properly serve multiple clients having potentially differing interests in matters not involving litigation. If the interests vary only slightly, it is generally likely that the lawyer will not be subjected to an adverse influence and that he can retain his independent judgment on behalf of each client; and if the interests become differing, withdrawal is less likely to have a disruptive effect upon the causes of his clients.

EC 5-16   In those instances in which a lawyer is justified in representing two or more clients having differing interests, it is nevertheless essential that each client be given the opportunity to evaluate his need for representation free of any potential conflict and to obtain other counsel if he so desires. Thus before a lawyer may represent multiple clients, he should explain fully to each client the implications of the common representation and should accept or continue employment only if the clients consent. If there are present other circumstances that might cause any of the multiple clients to question the undivided loyalty of the lawyer, he should also advise all of the clients of those circumstances.

EC 5-17   Typically recurring situations involving potentially differing interests are those in which a lawyer is asked to represent co-defendants in a criminal case, co-plaintiffs in a personal injury case, an insured and his insurer, and beneficiaries of the estate of a decedent. Whether a lawyer can fairly and adequately protect the interests of multiple clients in these and similar situations depends upon an analysis of each case. In certain circumstances, there may exist little chance of the judgment of the lawyer being adversely affected by the slight possibility that the interests will become actually differing; in other circumstances, the chance of adverse effect upon his judgment is not unlikely.

EC 5-18   A lawyer employed or retained by a corporation or similar entity owes his allegiance to the entity and not to a stockholder, director, officer, employee, representative, or other person connected with the entity. In advising the entity, a lawyer should keep paramount its interests and his professional judgment should not be influenced by the personal desires of any person or organization. Occasionally a lawyer for an entity is requested by a stockholder, director, officer, employee, representative, or other person connected with the entity to represent him in an individual capacity; in such case the lawyer may serve the individual only if the lawyer is convinced that differing interests are not present.

EC 5-19   A lawyer may represent several clients whose interests are not actually or potentially differing. Nevertheless, he should explain any circumstances that might cause a client to question his undivided loyalty. Regardless of the belief of a lawyer that he may properly represent multiple clients, he must defer to a client who holds the contrary belief and withdraw from representation of that client.

EC 5-20   A lawyer is often asked to serve as an impartial arbitrator or mediator in matters which involve present or former clients. He may serve in either capacity if he first discloses such present or former relationships. After a lawyer has undertaken to act as an impartial arbitrator or mediator, he should not thereafter represent in the dispute any of the parties involved.

Desires of Third Persons

EC 5-21   The obligation of a lawyer to exercise professional judgment solely on behalf of his client requires that he disregard the desires of others that might impair his free judgment. The desires of a third person will seldom adversely affect a lawyer unless that person is in a position to exert strong economic, political, or social pressures upon the lawyer. These influences are often subtle, and a lawyer must be alert to their existence. A lawyer subjected to outside pressures should make full disclosure of them to his client; and if he or his client believes that the effectiveness of his representation has been or will be impaired thereby, the lawyer should take proper steps to withdraw from representation of his client.

EC 5-22   Economic, political, or social pressures by third persons are less likely to impinge upon the independent judgment of a lawyer in a matter in which he is compensated directly by his client and his professional work is exclusively with his client. On the other hand, if a lawyer is compensated from a source other than his client, he may feel a sense of responsibility to someone other than his client.

EC 5-23   A person or organization that pays or furnishes lawyers to represent others possesses a potential power to exert strong pressures against the independent judgment of those lawyers. Some employers may be interested in furthering their own economic, political, or social goals without regard to the professional responsibility of the lawyer to his individual client. Others may be far more concerned with establishment or extension of legal principles than in the immediate protection of the rights of the lawyer's individual client. On some occasions, decisions on priority of work may be made by the employer rather than the lawyer with the result that prosecution of work already undertaken for clients is postponed to their detriment. Similarly, an employer may seek, consciously or unconsciously, to further its own economic interests through the action of the lawyers employed by it. Since a lawyer must always be free to exercise his professional judgment without regard to the interests or motives of a third person, the lawyer who is employed by one to represent another must constantly guard against erosion of his professional freedom.

EC 5-24   To assist a lawyer in preserving his professional independence, a number of courses are available to him. For example, a lawyer should not practice with or in the form of a professional legal corporation, even though the corporate form is permitted by law, if any director, officer, or stockholder of it is a non-lawyer. Although a lawyer may be employed by a business corporation with non-lawyers serving as directors or officers, and they necessarily have the right to make decisions of business policy, a lawyer must decline to accept direction of his professional judgment from any layman. Various types of legal aid offices are administered by boards of directors composed of lawyers and laymen. A lawyer should not accept employment from such an organization unless the board sets only broad policies and there is no interference in the relationship of the lawyer and the individual client he serves. Where a lawyer is employed by an organization, a written agreement that defines the relationship between him and the organization and provides for his independence is desirable since it may serve to prevent misunderstanding as to their respective roles. Although other innovations in the means of supplying legal counsel may develop, the responsibility of the lawyer to maintain his professional independence remains constant, and the legal profession must insure that changing circumstances do not result in loss of the professional independence of the lawyer.

DISCIPLINARY RULES

DR 5-101 Refusing Employment When the Interests of the Lawyer May Impair His Independent Professional Judgment.

(A) Except with the consent of his client after full disclosure, a lawyer shall not accept employment if the exercise of his professional judgment on behalf of his client will be or reasonably may be affected by his own financial, business, property, or personal interests.

(B) A lawyer shall not accept employment in contemplated or pending litigation if he knows or it is obvious that he or a lawyer in his firm ought to be called as a witness, except that he may undertake the employment and he or a lawyer in his firm may testify:

(1) If the testimony will relate solely to an uncontested matter.

(2) If the testimony will relate solely to a matter of formality and there is no reason to believe that substantial evidence will be offered in opposition to the testimony.

(3) If the testimony will relate solely to the nature and value of legal services rendered in the case by the lawyer or his firm to the client.

(4) As to any matter, if refusal would work a substantial hardship on the client because of the distinctive value of the lawyer or his firm as counsel in the particular case.

DR 5-102 Withdrawal as Counsel When the Lawyer Becomes a Witness.

(A) If, after undertaking employment in contemplated or pending litigation, a lawyer learns or it is obvious that he or a lawyer in his firm ought to be called as a witness on behalf of his client, he shall withdraw from the conduct of the trial and his firm, if any, shall not continue the representation in the trial, except that he may continue the representation and he or a lawyer in his firm may testify in the circumstances enumerated in DR 5-101(B)(1) through (4).

(B) If, after undertaking employment in contemplated or pending litigation, a lawyer learns or it is obvious that he or a lawyer in his firm may be called as a witness other than on behalf of his client, he may continue the representation until it is apparent that his testimony is or may be prejudicial to his client.

DR 5-103 Avoiding Acquisition of Interest in Litigation.

(A) A lawyer shall not acquire a proprietary interest in the cause of action or subject matter of litigation he is conducting for a client, except that he may:

(1) Acquire a lien granted by law to secure his fee or expenses.

(2) Contract with a client for a reasonable contingent fee in a civil case.

(B) While representing a client in connection with contemplated or pending litigation, a lawyer shall not advance or guarantee financial assistance to his client, except that a lawyer may advance or guarantee the expenses of litigation, including court costs, expenses of investigation, expenses of medical examination, and costs of obtaining and presenting evidence, provided the client remains ultimately liable for such expenses.

DR 5-104   Limiting Business Relations with a Client.

(A) A lawyer shall not enter into a business transaction with a client if they have differing interests therein and if the client expects the lawyer to exercise his professional judgment therein for the protection of the client, unless the client has consented after full disclosure.

(B) Prior to conclusion of all aspects of the matter giving rise to his employment, a lawyer shall not enter into any arrangement or understanding with a client or a prospective client by which he acquires an interest in publication rights with respect to the subject matter of his employment or proposed employment.

DR 5-105   Refusing to Accept or Continue Employment if the Interests of Another Client May Impair the Independent Professional Judgment of the Lawyer.

(A) A lawyer shall decline proffered employment if the exercise of his independent professional judgment in behalf of a client will be or is likely to be adversely affected by the acceptance of the proffered employment, or if it would be likely to involve him in representing differing interests, except to the extent permitted under DR 5-105(C).

(B) A lawyer shall not continue multiple employment if the exercise of his independent professional judgment in behalf of a client will be or is likely to be adversely affected by his representation of another client, or if it would be likely to involve him in representing differing interests, except to the extent permitted under DR 5-105(C).

(C) In the situations covered by DR 5-105(A) and (B), a lawyer may represent multiple clients if it is obvious that he can adequately represent the interest of each and if each consents to the representation after full disclosure of the possible effect of such representation on the exercise of his independent professional judgment on behalf of each.

(D) If a lawyer is required to decline employment or to withdraw from employment under a Disciplinary Rule, no partner, or associate, or any other lawyer affiliated with him or his firm, may accept or continue such employment.

DR 5-106   Settling Similar Claims of Clients.

(A) A lawyer who represents two or more clients shall not make or participate in the making of an aggregate settlement of the claims of or against his clients, unless each client has consented to the settlement after being advised of the existence and nature of all the claims involved in the proposed settlement, of the total amount of the settlement, and of the participation of each person in the settlement.

DR 5-107   Avoiding Influence by Others Than the Client.

(A) Except with the consent of his client after full disclosure, a lawyer shall not:

(1) Accept compensation for his legal services from one other than his client.

(2) Accept from one other than his client any thing of value related to his representation of or his employment by his client.

(B) A lawyer shall not permit a person who recommends, employs, or pays him to render legal services for another to direct or regulate his professional judgment in rendering such legal services.

(C) A lawyer shall not practice with or in the form of a professional corporation or association authorized to practice law for a profit, if:

(1) A non-lawyer owns any interest therein, except that a fiduciary representative of the estate of a lawyer may hold the stock or interest of the lawyer for a reasonable time during administration;

(2) A non-lawyer is a corporate director or officer thereof; or

(3) A non-lawyer has the right to direct or control the professional judgment of a lawyer.

CANON 6

A Lawyer Should Represent a Client Competently

ETHICAL CONSIDERATIONS

EC 6-1   Because of his vital role in the legal process, a lawyer should act with competence and proper care in representing clients. He should strive to become and remain proficient in his practice and should accept employment only in matters which he is or intends to become competent to handle.

EC 6-2   A lawyer is aided in attaining and maintaining his competence by keeping abreast of current legal literature and developments, participating in continuing legal education programs, concentrating in particular areas of the law, and by utilizing other available means. He has the additional ethical obligation to assist in improving the legal profession, and he may do so by participating in bar activities intended to advance the quality and standards of members of the profession. Of particular importance is the careful training of his younger associates and the giving of sound guidance to all lawyers who consult him. In short, a lawyer should strive at all levels to aid the legal profession in advancing the highest possible standards of integrity and competence and to meet those standards himself.

EC 6-3   While the licensing of a lawyer is evidence that he has met the standards then prevailing for admission to the bar, a lawyer generally should not accept employment in any area of the law in which he is not qualified. However, he may accept such employment if in good faith he expects to become qualified through study and investigation, as long as such preparation would not result in unreasonable delay or expense to his client. Proper preparation and representation may require the association by the lawyer of professionals in other disciplines. A lawyer offered employment in a matter in which he is not and does not expect to become so qualified should either decline the employment or, with the consent of his client, accept the employment and associate a lawyer who is competent in the matter.

EC 6-4   Having undertaken representation, a lawyer should use proper care to safeguard the interests of his client. If a lawyer has accepted employment in a matter beyond his competence but in which he expected to become competent, he should diligently undertake the work and study necessary to qualify himself. In addition to being qualified to handle a particular matter, his obligation to his client requires him to prepare adequately for and give appropriate attention to his legal work.

EC 6-5   A lawyer should have pride in his professional endeavors. His obligation to act competently calls for higher motivation than that arising from fear of civil liability or disciplinary penalty.

EC 6-6   A lawyer should not seek, by contract or other means, to limit his individual liability to his client for his malpractice. A lawyer who handles the affairs of his client properly has no need to attempt to limit his liability for his professional activities and one who does not handle the affairs of his client properly should not be permitted to do so. A lawyer who is a stockholder in or is associated with a professional legal corporation may, however, limit his liability for malpractice of his associates in the corporation, but only to the extent permitted by law.

DISCIPLINARY RULES

DR 6-101   Failing to Act Competently.

(A) A lawyer shall not:

(1) Handle a legal matter which he knows or should know that he is not competent to handle, without associating with him a lawyer who is competent to handle it.

(2) Handle a legal matter without preparation adequate in the circumstances.

(3) Neglect a legal matter entrusted to him.

DR 6-102   Limiting Liability to Client.

(A) A lawyer shall not attempt to exonerate himself from or limit his liability to his client for his personal malpractice.

CANON 7

A Lawyer Should Represent a Client Zealously Within the Bounds of the Law

ETHICAL CONSIDERATIONS

EC 7-1   The duty of a lawyer, both to his client and to the legal system, is to represent his client zealously within the bounds of the law, which includes Disciplinary Rules and enforceable professional regulations. The professional responsibility of a lawyer derives from his membership in a profession which has the duty of assisting members of the public to secure and protect available legal rights and benefits. In our government of laws and not of men, each member of our society is entitled to have his conduct judged and regulated in accordance with the law; to seek any lawful objective through legally permissible means; and to present for adjudication any lawful claim, issue, or defense.

EC 7-2   The bounds of the law in a given case are often difficult to ascertain. The language of legislative enactments and judicial opinions may be uncertain as applied to varying factual situations. The limits and specific meaning of apparently relevant law may be made doubtful by changing or developing constitutional interpretations, inadequately expressed statutes or judicial opinions, and changing public and judicial attitudes. Certainty of law ranges from well-settled rules through areas of conflicting authority to areas without precedent.

EC 7-3   Where the bounds of law are uncertain, the action of a lawyer may depend on whether he is serving as advocate or adviser. A lawyer may serve simultaneously as both advocate and adviser, but the two roles are essentially different. In asserting a position on behalf of his client, an advocate for the most part deals with past conduct and must take the facts as he finds them. By contrast, a lawyer serving as adviser primarily assists his client in determining the course of future conduct and relationships. While serving as advocate, a lawyer should resolve in favor of his client doubts as to the bounds of the law. In serving a client as adviser, a lawyer in appropriate circumstances should give his professional opinion as to what the ultimate decisions of the courts would likely be as to the applicable law.

Duty of the Lawyer to a Client

EC 7-4   The advocate may urge any permissible construction of the law favorable to his client, without regard to his professional opinion as to the likelihood that the construction will ultimately prevail. His conduct is within the bounds of the law, and therefore permissible, if the position taken is supported by the law or is supportable by a good faith argument for an extension, modification, or reversal of the law. However, a lawyer is not justified in asserting a position in litigation that is frivolous.

EC 7-5   A lawyer as adviser furthers the interest of his client by giving his professional opinion as to what he believes would likely be the ultimate decision of the courts on the matter at hand and by informing his client of the practical effect of such decision. He may continue in the representation of his client even though his client has elected to pursue a course of conduct contrary to the advice of the lawyer so long as he does not thereby knowingly assist the client to engage in illegal conduct or to take a frivolous legal position. A lawyer should never encourage or aid his client to commit criminal acts or counsel his client on how to violate the law and avoid punishment therefor.

EC 7-6   Whether the proposed action of a lawyer is within the bounds of the law may be a perplexing question when his client is contemplating a course of conduct having legal consequences that vary according to the client's intent, motive, or desires at the time of the action. Often a lawyer is asked to assist his client in developing evidence relevant to the state of mind of the client at a particular time. He may properly assist his client in the development and preservation of evidence of existing motive, intent, or desire; obviously, he may not do anything furthering the creation or preservation of false evidence. In many cases a lawyer may not be certain as to the state of mind of his client, and in those situations he should resolve reasonable doubts in favor of his client.

EC 7-7   In certain areas of legal representation not affecting the merits of the cause or substantially prejudicing the rights of a client, a lawyer is entitled to make decisions on his own. But otherwise the authority to make decisions is exclusively that of the client and, if made within the framework of the law, such decisions are binding on his lawyer. As typical examples in civil cases, it is for the client to decide whether he will accept a settlement offer or whether he will waive his right to plead an affirmative defense. A defense lawyer in a criminal case has the duty to advise his client fully on whether a particular plea to a charge appears to be desirable and as to the prospects of success on appeal, but it is for the client to decide what plea should be entered and whether an appeal should be taken.

EC 7-8   A lawyer should exert his best efforts to insure that decisions of his client are made only after the client has been informed of relevant considerations. A lawyer ought to initiate this decision-making process if the client does not do so. Advice of a lawyer to his client need not be confined to purely legal considerations. A lawyer should advise his client of the possible effect of each legal alternative. A lawyer should bring to bear upon this decision-making process the fullness of his experience as well as his objective viewpoint. In assisting his client to reach a proper decision, it is often desirable for a lawyer to point out those factors which may lead to a decision that is morally just as well as legally permissible. He may emphasize the possibility of harsh consequences that might result from assertion of legally permissible positions. In the final analysis, however, the lawyer should always remember that the decision whether to forego legally available objectives or methods because of non-legal factors is ultimately for the client and not for himself. In the event that the client in a non-adjudicatory matter insists upon a course of conduct that is contrary to the judgment and advice of the lawyer but not prohibited by Disciplinary Rules, the lawyer may withdraw from the employment.

EC 7-9   In the exercise of his professional judgment on those decisions which are for his determination in the handling of a legal matter, a lawyer should always act in a manner consistent with the best interests of his client. However, when an action in the best interest of his client seems to him to be unjust, he may ask his client for permission to forego such action.

EC 7-10   The duty of a lawyer to represent his client with zeal does not militate against his concurrent obligation to treat with consideration all persons involved in the legal process and to avoid the infliction of needless harm.

EC 7-11   The responsibilities of a lawyer may vary according to the intelligence, experience, mental condition or age of a client, the obligation of a public officer, or the nature of a particular proceeding. Examples include the representation of an illiterate or an incompetent, service as a public prosecutor or other government lawyer, and appearances before administrative and legislative bodies.

EC 7-12   Any mental or physical condition of a client that renders him incapable of making a considered judgment on his own behalf casts additional responsibilities upon his lawyer. Where an incompetent is acting through a guardian or other legal representative, a lawyer must look to such representative for those decisions which are normally the prerogative of the client to make. If a client under disability has no legal representative, his lawyer may be compelled in court proceedings to make decisions on behalf of the client. If the client is capable of understanding the matter in question or of contributing to the advancement of his interests, regardless of whether he is legally disqualified from performing certain acts, the lawyer should obtain from him all possible aid. If the disability of a client and the lack of a legal representative compel the lawyer to make decisions for his client, the lawyer should consider all circumstances then prevailing and act with care to safeguard and advance the interests of his client. But obviously a lawyer cannot perform any act or make any decision which the law requires his client to perform or make, either acting for himself if competent, or by a duly constituted representative if legally incompetent.

EC 7-13   The responsibility of a public prosecutor differs from that of the usual advocate; his duty is to seek justice, not merely to convict. This special duty exists because: (1) the prosecutor represents the sovereign and therefore should use restraint in the discretionary exercise of governmental powers, such as in the selection of cases to prosecute; (2) during trial the prosecutor is not only an advocate but he also may make decisions normally made by an individual client, and those affecting the public interest should be fair to all; and (3) in our system of criminal justice the accused is to be given the benefit of all reasonable doubts. With respect to evidence and witnesses, the prosecutor has responsibilities different from those of a lawyer in private practice: the prosecutor should make timely disclosure to the defense of available evidence, known to him, that tends to negate the guilt of the accused, mitigate the degree of the offense, or reduce the punishment. Further, a prosecutor should not intentionally avoid pursuit of evidence merely because he believes it will damage the prosecutor's case or aid the accused.

EC 7-14   A government lawyer who has discretionary power relative to litigation should refrain from instituting or continuing litigation that is obviously unfair. A government lawyer not having such discretionary power who believes there is lack of merit in a controversy submitted to him should so advise his superiors and recommend the avoidance of unfair litigation. A government lawyer in a civil action or administrative proceeding has the responsibility to seek justice and to develop a full and fair record, and he should not use his position or the economic power of the government to harass parties or to bring about unjust settlements or results.

EC 7-15   The nature and purpose of proceedings before administrative agencies vary widely. The proceedings may be legislative or quasi-judicial, or a combination of both. They may be *ex parte* in character, in which event they may originate either at the instance of the agency or upon motion of an interested party. The scope of an inquiry may be purely investigative or it may be truly adversary looking toward the adjudication of specific rights of a party or of classes of parties. The foregoing are but examples of some of the types of proceedings conducted by administrative agencies. A lawyer appearing before an administrative agency, regardless of the nature of the proceeding it is conducting, has the continuing duty to advance the cause of his client within the bounds of the law. Where the applicable rules of the agency impose specific obligations upon a lawyer, it is his duty to comply therewith, unless the lawyer has a legitimate basis for challenging the validity thereof. In all appearances before administrative agencies, a lawyer should identify himself, his client if identity of his client is not privileged and the representative nature of his appearance. It is not improper, however, for a lawyer to seek from an agency information available to the public without identifying his client.

EC 7-16   The primary business of a legislative body is to enact laws rather than to adjudicate controversies, although on occasion the activities of a legislative body may take on the characteristics of an adversary proceeding, particularly in investigative and impeachment matters. The role of a lawyer supporting or opposing proposed legislation normally is quite different from his role in representing a person under investigation or on trial by a legislative body. When a lawyer appears in connection with proposed legislation, he seeks to affect the lawmaking process, but when he appears on behalf of a client in investigatory or impeachment proceedings, he is concerned with the protection of the rights of his client. In either event, he should identify himself and his client, if identity of his client is not privileged, and should comply with applicable laws and legislative rules.

EC 7-17   The obligation of loyalty to his client applies only to a lawyer in the discharge of his professional duties and implies no obligation to adopt a personal viewpoint favorable to the interests or desires of his client. While a lawyer must act always with circumspection in order that his conduct will not adversely affect the rights of a client in a matter he is then handling, he may take positions on public issues and espouse legal reforms he favors without regard to the individual views of any client.

EC 7-18   The legal system in its broadest sense functions best when persons in need of legal advice or assistance are represented by their own counsel. For this reason a lawyer should not communicate on the subject matter of the representation of his client with a person he knows to be represented in the matter by a lawyer, unless pursuant to law or rule of court or unless he has the consent of the lawyer for that person. If one is not represented by counsel, a lawyer representing another may have to deal directly with the unrepresented person; in such an instance, a lawyer should not undertake to give advice to the person who is attempting to represent himself, except that he may advise him to obtain a lawyer.

Duty of the Lawyer to the Adversary System of Justice

EC 7-19   Our legal system provides for the adjudication of disputes governed by the rules of substantive, evidentiary, and procedural law. An adversary presentation counters the natural human tendency to judge too swiftly in terms of the familiar that which is not yet fully known; the advocate, by his zealous preparation and presentation of fact and law, enables the tribunal to come to the hearing with an open and neutral mind and to render impartial judgments. The duty of a lawyer to his client and his duty to the legal system are the same; to represent his client zealously within the bounds of the law.

EC 7-20   In order to function properly, our adjudicative process requires an informed, impartial tribunal capable of administering justice promptly and efficiently according to procedures that command public confidence and respect. Not only must there be competent, adverse presentation of evidence and issues, but a tribunal must be aided by rules appropriate to an effective and dignified process. The procedures under which tribunals operate in our adversary system have been prescribed largely by legislative enactments, court rules and decisions, and administrative rules. Through the years certain concepts of proper professional conduct have become rules of law applicable to the adversary adjudicative process. Many of these concepts are the bases for standards of professional conduct set forth in the Disciplinary Rules.

EC 7-21   The civil adjudicative process is primarily designed for the settlement of disputes between parties, while the criminal process is designed for the protection of society as a whole. Threatening to use, or using, the criminal process to coerce adjustment of private civil claims or controversies is a subversion of that process; further, the person against whom the criminal process is so misused may be deterred from asserting his legal rights and thus the usefulness of the civil process in settling private disputes is impaired. As in all cases of abuse of judicial process, the improper use of criminal process tends to diminish public confidence in our legal system.

EC 7-22 Respect for judicial rulings is essential to the proper administration of justice; however, a litigant or his lawyer may, in good faith and within the framework of the law, take steps to test the correctness of a ruling of a tribunal.

EC 7-23 The complexity of law often makes it difficult for a tribunal to be fully informed unless the pertinent law is presented by the lawyers in the cause. A tribunal that is fully informed on the applicable law is better able to make a fair and accurate determination of the matter before it. The adversary system contemplates that each lawyer will present and argue the existing law in the light most favorable to his client. Where a lawyer knows of legal authority in the controlling jurisdiction directly adverse to the position of his client, he should inform the tribunal of its existence unless his adversary has done so; but, having made such disclosure, he may challenge its soundness in whole or in part.

EC 7-24 In order to bring about just and informed decisions, evidentiary and procedural rules have been established by tribunals to permit the inclusion of relevant evidence and argument and the exclusion of all other considerations. The expression by a lawyer of his personal opinion as to the justness of a cause, as to the credibility of a witness, as to the culpability of a civil litigant, or as to the guilt or innocence of an accused is not a proper subject for argument to the trier of fact. It is improper as to factual matters because admissible evidence possessed by a lawyer should be presented only as sworn testimony. It is improper as to all other matters because, were the rule otherwise, the silence of a lawyer on a given occasion could be construed unfavorably to his client. However, a lawyer may argue, on his analysis of the evidence, for any position or conclusion with respect to any of the foregoing matters.

EC 7-25 Rules of evidence and procedure are designed to lead to just decisions and are part of the framework of the law. Thus while a lawyer may take steps in good faith and within the framework of the law to test the validity of rules, he is not justified in consciously violating such rules and he should be diligent in his efforts to guard against his unintentional violation of them. As examples, a lawyer should subscribe to or verify only those pleadings that he believes are in compliance with applicable law and rules; a lawyer should not make any prefatory statement before a tribunal in regard to the purported facts of the case on trial unless he believes that his statement will be supported by admissible evidence; a lawyer should not ask a witness a question solely for the purpose of harassing or embarrassing him; and a lawyer should not by subterfuge put before a jury matters which it cannot properly consider.

EC 7-26 The law and Disciplinary Rules prohibit the use of fraudulent, false, or perjured testimony or evidence. A lawyer who knowingly participates in introduction of such testimony or evidence is subject to discipline. A lawyer should, however, present any admissible evidence his client desires to have presented unless he knows, or from facts within his knowledge should know, that such testimony or evidence is false, fraudulent, or perjured.

EC 7-27 Because it interferes with the proper administration of justice, a lawyer should not suppress evidence that he or his client has a legal obligation to reveal or produce. In like manner, a lawyer should not advise or cause a person to secrete himself or to leave the jurisdiction of a tribunal for the purpose of making him unavailable as a witness therein.

EC 7-28 Witnesses should always testify truthfully and should be free from any financial inducements that might tempt them to do otherwise. A lawyer should not pay or agree to pay a non-expert witness an amount in excess of reimbursement for expenses and financial loss incident to his being a witness; however, a lawyer may pay or agree to pay an expert witness a reasonable fee for his services as an expert. But in no event should a lawyer pay or agree to pay a contingent fee to any witness. A lawyer should exercise reasonable diligence to see that his client and lay associates conform to these standards.

EC 7-29 To safeguard the impartiality that is essential to the judicial process, veniremen and jurors should be protected against extraneous influences. When impartiality is present, public confidence in the judicial system is enhanced. There should be no extrajudicial communication with veniremen prior to trial or with jurors during trial by or on behalf of a lawyer connected with the case. Furthermore, a lawyer who is not connected with the case should not communicate with or cause another to communicate with a venireman or a juror about the case. After the trial, communication by a lawyer with jurors is permitted so long as he refrains from asking questions or making comments that tend to harass or embarrass the juror or to influence actions of the juror in future cases. Were a lawyer to be prohibited from communicating after trial with a juror, he could not ascertain if the verdict might be subject to legal challenge, in which event the invalidity of a verdict might go undetected. When an extrajudicial communication by a lawyer with a juror is permitted by law, it should be made considerately and with deference to the personal feelings of the juror.

EC 7-30   Vexatious or harassing investigations of veniremen or jurors seriously impair the effectiveness of our jury system. For this reason, a lawyer or anyone on his behalf who conducts an investigation of veniremen or jurors should act with circumspection and restraint.

EC 7-31   Communications with or investigations of members of families of veniremen or jurors by a lawyer or by anyone on his behalf are subject to the restrictions imposed upon the lawyer with respect to his communications with or investigations of veniremen and jurors.

EC 7-32   Because of his duty to aid in preserving the integrity of the jury system, a lawyer who learns of improper conduct by or towards a venireman, a juror, or a member of the family of either should make a prompt report to the court regarding such conduct.

EC 7-33   A goal of our legal system is that each party shall have his case, criminal or civil, adjudicated by an impartial tribunal. The attainment of this goal may be defeated by dissemination of news or comments which tend to influence judge or jury. Such news or comments may prevent prospective jurors from being impartial at the outset of the trial and may also interfere with the obligation of jurors to base their verdict solely upon the evidence admitted in the trial. The release by a lawyer of out-of-court statements regarding an anticipated or pending trial may improperly affect the impartiality of the tribunal. For these reasons, standards for permissible and prohibited conduct of a lawyer with respect to trial publicity have been established.

EC 7-34   The impartiality of a public servant in our legal system may be impaired by the receipt of gifts or loans. A lawyer, therefore, is never justified in making a gift or a loan to a judge, a hearing officer, or an official or employee of a tribunal except as permitted by Section C(4) of Canon 5 of the Code of Judicial Conduct, but a lawyer may make a contribution to the campaign fund of a candidate for judicial office in conformity with Section B(2) under Canon 7 of the Code of Judicial Conduct.

EC 7-35   All litigants and lawyers should have access to tribunals on an equal basis. Generally, in adversary proceedings a lawyer should not communicate with a judge relative to a matter pending before, or which is to be brought before, a tribunal over which he presides in circumstances which might have the effect or give the appearance of granting undue advantage to one party. For example, a lawyer should not communicate with a tribunal by a writing unless a copy thereof is promptly delivered to opposing counsel or to the adverse party if he is not represented by a lawyer. Ordinarily an oral communication by a lawyer with a judge or hearing officer should be made only upon adequate notice to opposing counsel, or, if there is none, to the opposing party. A lawyer should not condone or lend himself to private importunities by another with a judge or hearing officer on behalf of himself or his client.

EC 7-36   Judicial hearings ought to be conducted through dignified and orderly procedures designed to protect the rights of all parties. Although a lawyer has the duty to represent his client zealously, he should not engage in any conduct that offends the dignity and decorum of proceedings. While maintaining his independence, a lawyer should be respectful, courteous, and above-board in his relations with a judge or hearing officer before whom he appears. He should avoid undue solicitude for the comfort or convenience of judge or jury and should avoid any other conduct calculated to gain special consideration.

EC 7-37   In adversary proceedings, clients are litigants and though ill feeling may exist between clients, such ill feeling should not influence a lawyer in his conduct, attitude, and demeanor towards opposing lawyers. A lawyer should not make unfair or derogatory personal reference to opposing counsel. Haranguing and offensive tactics by lawyers interfere with the orderly administration of justice and have no proper place in our legal system.

EC 7-38   A lawyer should be courteous to opposing counsel and should accede to reasonable requests regarding court proceedings, settings, continuances, waiver of procedural formalities, and similar matters which do not prejudice the rights of his client. He should follow local customs of courtesy or practice, unless he gives timely notice to opposing counsel of his intention not to do so. A lawyer should be punctual in fulfilling all professional commitments.

EC 7-39   In the final analysis, proper functioning of the adversary system depends upon cooperation between lawyers and tribunals in utilizing procedures which will preserve the impartiality of tribunals and make their decisional processes prompt and just, without impinging upon the obligation of lawyers to represent their clients zealously within the framework of the law.

DISCIPLINARY RULES

DR 7-101 Representing a Client Zealously.

(A) A lawyer shall not intentionally:

(1) Fail to seek the lawful objectives of his client through reasonably available means permitted by law and the Disciplinary Rules, except as provided by DR 7-101(B). A lawyer does not violate this Disciplinary Rule, however, by acceding to reasonable requests of opposing counsel which do not prejudice the rights of his client, by being punctual in fulfilling all professional commitments, by avoiding offensive tactics, or by treating with courtesy and consideration all persons involved in the legal process.

(2) Fail to carry out a contract of employment entered into with a client for professional services, but he may withdraw as permitted under DR 2-110, DR 5-102, and DR 5-105.

(3) Prejudice or damage his client during the course of the professional relationship, except as required under DR 7-102(B).

(B) In his representation of a client, a lawyer may:

(1) Where permissible, exercise his professional judgment to waive or fail to assert a right or position of his client.

(2) Refuse to aid or participate in conduct that he believes to be unlawful, even though there is some support for an argument that the conduct is legal.

DR 7-102 Representing a Client Within the Bounds of the Law.

(A) In his representation of a client, a lawyer shall not:

(1) File a suit, assert a position, conduct a defense, delay a trial, or take other action on behalf of his client when he knows or when it is obvious that such action would serve merely to harass or maliciously injure another.

(2) Knowingly advance a claim or defense that is unwarranted under existing law, except that he may advance such claim or defense if it can be supported by good faith argument for an extension, modification, or reversal of existing law.

(3) Conceal or knowingly fail to disclose that which he is required by law to reveal.

(4) Knowingly use perjured testimony or false evidence.

(5) Knowingly make a false statement of law or fact.

(6) Participate in the creation or preservation of evidence when he knows or it is obvious that the evidence is false.

(7) Counsel or assist his client in conduct that the lawyer knows to be illegal or fraudulent.

(8) Knowingly engage in other illegal conduct or conduct contrary to a Disciplinary Rule.

(B) A lawyer who receives information clearly establishing that:

(1) His client has, in the course of the representation, perpetrated a fraud upon a person or tribunal shall promptly call upon his client to rectify the same, and if his client refuses or is unable to do so, he shall reveal the fraud to the affected person or tribunal, except when the information is protected as a privileged communication.

(2) A person other than his client has perpetrated a fraud upon a tribunal shall promptly reveal the fraud to the tribunal.

DR 7-103 Performing the Duty of Public Prosecutor or Other Government Lawyer.

(A) A public prosecutor or other government lawyer shall not institute or cause to be instituted criminal charges when he knows or it is obvious that the charges are not supported by probable cause.

(B) A public prosecutor or other government lawyer in criminal litigation shall make timely disclosure to counsel for the defendant, or to the defendant if he has no counsel, of the existence of evidence, known to the prosecutor or other government lawyer, that tends to negate the guilt of the accused, mitigate the degree of the offense, or reduce the punishment.

DR 7-104 Communicating With One of Adverse Interest.

(A) During the course of his representation of a client a lawyer shall not:

(1) Communicate or cause another to communicate on the subject of the representation with a party he knows to be represented by a lawyer in that matter unless he has the prior consent of the lawyer representing such other party or is authorized by law to do so.

(2) Give advice to a person who is not represented by a lawyer, other than the advice to secure counsel, if the interests of such person are or have a reasonable possibility of being in conflict with the interests of his client.

DR 7-105 Threatening Criminal Prosecution.

(A) A lawyer shall not present, participate in presenting, or threaten to present criminal charges solely to obtain an advantage in a civil matter.

DR 7-106 Trial Conduct.

(A) A lawyer shall not disregard or advise his client to disregard a standing rule of a tribunal or a ruling of a tribunal made in the course of a proceeding, but he may take appropriate steps in good faith to test the validity of such rule or ruling.

(B) In presenting a matter to a tribunal, a lawyer shall disclose:

(1) Legal authority in the controlling jurisdiction known to him to be directly adverse to the position of his client and which is not disclosed by opposing counsel.

(2) Unless privileged or irrelevant, the identities of the clients he represents and of the persons who employed him.

(C) In appearing in his professional capacity before a tribunal, a lawyer shall not:

(1) State or allude to any matter that he has no reasonable basis to believe is relevant to the case or that will not be supported by admissible evidence.

(2) Ask any question that he has no reasonable basis to believe is relevant to the case and that is intended to degrade a witness or other person.

(3) Assert his personal knowledge of the facts in issue, except when testifying as a witness.

(4) Assert his personal opinion as to the justness of a cause, as to the credibility of a witness, as to the culpability of a civil litigant, or as to the guilt or innocence of an accused; but he may argue, on his analysis of the evidence, for any position or conclusion with respect to the matters stated herein.

(5) Fail to comply with known local customs of courtesy or practice of the bar or a particular tribunal without giving to opposing counsel timely notice of his intent not to comply.

(6) Engage in undignified or discourteous conduct which is degrading to a tribunal.

(7) Intentionally or habitually violate any established rule of procedure or of evidence.

DR 7-107 Trial Publicity.

(A) A lawyer participating in or associated with the investigation of a criminal matter shall not make or participate in making an extrajudicial statement that a reasonable person would expect to be disseminated by means of public communication and that does more than state without elaboration:

(1) Information contained in a public record.

(2) That the investigation is in progress.

(3) The general scope of the investigation including a description of the offense and, if permitted by law, the identity of the victim.

(4) A request for assistance in apprehending a suspect or assistance in other matters and the information necessary thereto.

(5) A warning to the public of any dangers.

(B) A lawyer or law firm associated with the prosecution or defense of a criminal matter shall not, from the time of the filing of a complaint, information, or indictment, the issuance of an arrest warrant, or arrest until the commencement of the trial or disposition without trial, make or participate in making an extrajudicial statement that a reasonable person would expect to be disseminated by means of public communication and that relates to:

(1) The character, reputation, or prior criminal record (including arrests, indictments, or other charges of crime) of the accused.

(2) The possibility of a plea of guilty to the offense charged or to a lesser offense.

(3) The existence or contents of any confession, admission, or statement given by the accused or his refusal or failure to make a statement.

(4) The performance or results of any examinations or tests or the refusal or failure of the accused to submit to examinations or tests.

(5) The identity, testimony, or credibility of a prospective witness.

(6) Any opinion as to the guilt or innocence of the accused, the evidence, or the merits of the case.

(C) DR 7-107(B) does not preclude a lawyer during such period from announcing:

(1) The name, age, residence, occupation, and family status of the accused.

(2) If the accused has not been apprehended, any information necessary to aid in his apprehension or to warn the public of any dangers he may present.

(3) A request for assistance in obtaining evidence.

(4) The identity of the victim of the crime.

(5) The fact, time, and place of arrest, resistance, pursuit, and use of weapons.

(6) The identity of investigating and arresting officers or agencies and the length of the investigation.

(7) At the time of seizure, a description of the physical evidence seized, other than a confession, admission, or statement.

(8) The nature, substance, or text of the charge.

(9) Quotations from or references to public records of the court in the case.

(10) The scheduling or result of any step in the judicial proceedings.

(11) That the accused denies the charges made against him.

(D) During the selection of a jury or the trial of a criminal matter, a lawyer or law firm associated with the prosecution or defense of a criminal matter shall not make or participate in making an extra-judicial statement that a reasonable person would expect to be disseminated by means of public communication and that relates to the trial, parties, or issues in the trial or other matters that are reasonably likely to interfere with a fair trial, except that he may quote from or refer without comment to public records of the court in the case.

(E) After the completion of a trial or disposition without trial of a criminal matter and prior to the imposition of sentence, a lawyer or law firm associated with the prosecution or defense shall not make or participate in making an extrajudicial statement that a reasonable person would expect to be disseminated by public communication and that is reasonably likely to affect the imposition of sentence.

(F) The foregoing provisions of DR 7-107 also apply to professional disciplinary proceedings and juvenile disciplinary proceedings when pertinent and consistent with other law applicable to such proceedings.

(G) A lawyer or law firm associated with a civil action shall not during its investigation or litigation make or participate in making an extrajudicial statement, other than a quotation from or reference to public records, that a reasonable person would expect to be disseminated by means of public communication and that relates to:

(1) Evidence regarding the occurrence or transaction involved.

(2) The character, credibility, or criminal record of a party, witness, or prospective witness.

(3) The performance or results of any examinations or tests or the refusal or failure of a party to submit to such.

(4) His opinion as to the merits of the claims or defenses of a party, except as required by law or administrative rule.

(5) Any other matter reasonably likely to interfere with a fair trial of the action.

(H) During the pendency of an administrative proceeding, a lawyer or law firm associated therewith shall not make or participate in making a statement, other than a quotation from or reference to public records, that a reasonable person would expect to be disseminated by means of public communication if it is made outside the official course of the proceeding and relates to:

(1) Evidence regarding the occurrence or transaction involved.

(2) The character, credibility, or criminal record of a party, witness, or prospective witness.

(3) Physical evidence or the performance or results of any examinations or tests or the refusal or failure of a party to submit to such.

(4) His opinion as to the merits of the claims, defenses, or positions of an interested person.

(5) Any other matter reasonably likely to interfere with a fair hearing.

(I) The foregoing provisions of DR 7-107 do not preclude a lawyer from replying to charges of misconduct publicly made against him or from participating in the proceedings of legislative, administrative, or other investigative bodies.

(J) A lawyer shall exercise reasonable care to prevent his employees and associates from making an extrajudicial statement that he would be prohibited from making under DR 7-107.

DR 7-108 Communicaton with or Investigation of Jurors.

(A) Before the trial of a case a lawyer connected therewith shall not communicate with or cause another to communicate with anyone he knows to be a member of the venire from which the jury will be selected for the trial of the case.

(B) During the trial of a case:

(1) A lawyer connected therewith shall not communicate with or cause another to communicate with any member of the jury.

(2) A lawyer who is not connected therewith shall not communicate with or cause another to communicate with a juror concerning the case.

(C) DR 7-108(A) and (B) do not prohibit a lawyer from communicating with veniremen or jurors in the course of official proceedings.

(D) After discharge of the jury from further consideration of a case with which the lawyer was connected, the lawyer shall not ask questions of or make comments to a member of that jury that are calculated merely to harass or embarrass the juror or to influence his actions in future jury service.

(E) A lawyer shall not conduct or cause, by financial support or otherwise, another to conduct a vexatious or harassing investigation of either a venireman or a juror.

(F) All restrictions imposed by DR 7-108 upon a lawyer also apply to communications with or investigations of members of a family of a venireman or a juror.

(G) A lawyer shall reveal promptly to the court improper conduct by a venireman or a juror, or by another toward a venireman or a juror or a member of his family, of which the lawyer has knowledge.

DR 7-109   Contact with Witesses.

(A) A lawyer shall not suppress any evidence that he or his client has a legal obligation to reveal or produce.

(B) A lawyer shall not advise or cause a person to secrete himself or to leave the jurisdiction of a tribunal for the purpose of making him unavailable as a witness therein.

(C) A lawyer shall not pay, offer to pay, or acquiesce in the payment of compensation to a witness contingent upon the content of his testimony or the outcome of the case. But a lawyer may advance, guarantee, or acquiesce in the payment of:

(1) Expenses reasonably incurred by a witness in attending or testifying.

(2) Reasonable compensation to a witness for his loss of time in attending or testifying.

(3) A reasonable fee for the professional services of an expert witness.

DR 7-110   Contact with Officils.

(A) A lawyer shall not give or lend any thing of value to a judge, official, or employee of a tribunal except as permitted by Section C(4) of Canon 5 of the Code of Judicial Conduct, but a lawyer may make a contribution to the campaign fund of a candidate for judicial office in conformity with Section B(2) under Canon 7 of the Code of Judicial Conduct.

(B) In an adversary proceeding, a lawyer shall not communicate, or cause another to communicate, as to the merits of the cause with a judge or an official before whom the proceeding is pending, except:

(1) In the course of official proceedings in the cause.

(2) In writing if he promptly delivers a copy of the writing to opposing counsel or to the adverse party if he is not represented by a lawyer.

(3) Orally upon adequate notice to opposing counsel or to the adverse party if he is not represented by a lawyer.

(4) As otherwise authorized by law, or by Section A(4) under Canon 3 of the Code of Judicial Conduct.

CANON 8

A Lawyer Should Assist in Improving the Legal System

ETHICAL CONSIDERATIONS

EC 8-1   Changes in human affairs and imperfections in human institutions make necessary constant efforts to maintain and improve our legal system. This system should function in a manner that commands public respect and fosters the use of legal remedies to achieve redress of grievances. By reason of education and experience, lawyers are especially qualified to recognize deficiencies in the legal system and to initiate corrective measures therein. Thus they should participate in proposing and supporting legislation and programs to improve the system, without regard to the general interests or desires of clients or former clients.

EC 8-2   Rules of law are deficient if they are not just, understandable, and responsive to the needs of society. If a lawyer believes that the existence or absence of a rule of law, substantive or procedural, causes or contributes to an unjust result, he should endeavor by lawful means to obtain appropriate changes in the law. He should encourage the simplification of laws and the repeal or amendment of laws that are outmoded. Likewise, legal procedures should be improved whenever experience indicates a change is needed.

EC 8-3   The fair administration of justice requires the availability of competent lawyers. Members of the public should be educated to recognize the existence of legal problems and the resultant need for legal services, and should be provided methods for intelligent selection of counsel. Those persons unable to pay for legal services should be provided needed services. Clients and lawyers should not be penalized by undue geographical restraints upon representation in legal matters, and the bar should address itself to improvements in licensing, reciprocity, and admission procedures consistent with the needs of modern commerce.

EC 8-4   Whenever a lawyer seeks legislative or administrative changes, he should identify the capacity in which he appears, whether on behalf of himself, a client, or the public. A lawyer may advocate such changes on behalf of a client even though he does not agree with them. But when a lawyer purports to act on behalf of the public, he should espouse only those changes which he conscientiously believes to be in the public interest.

EC 8-5   Fraudulent, deceptive, or otherwise illegal conduct by a participant in a proceeding before a tribunal or legislative body is inconsistent with fair administration of justice, and it should never be participated in or condoned by lawyers. Unless constrained by his obligation to preserve the confidences and secrets of his client, a lawyer should reveal to appropriate authorities any knowledge he may have of such improper conduct.

EC 8-6   Judges and administrative officials having adjudicatory powers ought to be persons of integrity, competence, and suitable temperament. Generally, lawyers are qualified, by personal observation or investigation, to evaluate the qualifications of persons seeking or being considered for such public offices, and for this reason they have a special responsibility to aid in the selection of only those who are qualified. It is the duty of lawyers to endeavor to prevent political considerations from outweighing judicial fitness in the selection of judges. Lawyers should protest earnestly against the appointment or election of those who are unsuited for the bench and should strive to have elected or appointed thereto only those who are willing to forego pursuits, whether of a business, political, or other nature, that may interfere with the free and fair consideration of questions presented for adjudication. Adjudicatory officials, not being wholly free to defend themselves, are entitled to receive the support of the bar against unjust criticism. While a lawyer as a citizen has a right to criticize such officials publicly, he should be certain of the merit of his complaint, use appropriate language, and avoid petty criticisms, for unrestrained and intemperate statements tend to lessen public confidence in our legal system. Criticisms motivated by reasons other than a desire to improve the legal system are not justified.

EC 8-7   Since lawyers are a vital part of the legal system, they should be persons of integrity, of professional skill, and of dedication to the improvement of the system. Thus a lawyer should aid in establishing, as well as enforcing, standards of conduct adequate to protect the public by insuring that those who practice law are qualified to do so.

EC 8-8   Lawyers often serve as legislators or as holders of other public offices. This is highly desirable, as lawyers are uniquely qualified to make significant contributions to the improvement of the legal system. A lawyer who is a public officer, whether full or part-time, should not engage in activities in which his personal or professional interests are or foreseeably may be in conflict with his official duties.

EC 8-9   The advancement of our legal system is of vital importance in maintaining the rule of law and in facilitating orderly changes; therefore, lawyers should encourage, and should aid in making, needed changes and improvements.

DISCIPLINARY RULES

DR 8-101   Action as a Public Official.

(A) A lawyer who holds public office shall not:

(1) Use his public position to obtain, or attempt to obtain, a special advantage in legislative matters for himself or for a client under circumstances where he knows or it is obvious that such action is not in the public interest.

(2) Use his public position to influence, or attempt to influence, a tribunal to act in favor of himself or of a client.

(3) Accept any thing of value from any person when the lawyer knows or it is obvious that the offer is for the purpose of influencing his action as a public official.

DR 8-102   Statements Concerning Judges and Other Adjudicatory Officers.

(A) A lawyer shall not knowingly make false statements of fact concerning the qualifications of a candidate for election or appointment to a judicial office.

(B) A lawyer shall not knowingly make false accusations against a judge or other adjudicatory officer.

DR 8-103 Lawyer Candidate for Judicial Office.

(A) A lawyer who is a candidate for judicial office shall comply with the applicable provisions of Canon 7 of the Code of Judicial Conduct.

CANON 9

A Lawyer Should Avoid Even the Appearance of Professional Impropriety

ETHICAL CONSIDERATIONS

EC 9-1   Continuation of the American concept that we are to be governed by rules of law requires that the people have faith that justice can be obtained through our legal system. A lawyer should promote public confidence in our system and in the legal profession.

EC 9-2   Public confidence in law and lawyers may be eroded by irresponsible or improper conduct of a lawyer. On occasion, ethical conduct of a lawyer may appear to laymen to be unethical. In order to avoid misunderstandings and hence to maintain confidence, a lawyer should fully and promptly inform his client of material developments in the matters being handled for the client. While a lawyer should guard against otherwise proper conduct that has a tendency to diminish public confidence in the legal system or in the legal profession, his duty to clients or to the public should never be subordinate merely because the full discharge of his obligation may be misunderstood or may tend to subject him or the legal profession to criticism. When explicit ethical guidance does not exist, a lawyer should determine his conduct by acting in a manner that promotes public confidence in the integrity and efficiency of the legal system and the legal profession.

EC 9-3   After a lawyer leaves judicial office or other public employment, he should not accept employment in connection with any matter in which he had substantial responsibility prior to his leaving, since to accept employment would give the appearance of impropriety even if none exists.

EC 9-4   Because the very essence of the legal system is to provide procedures by which matters can be presented in an impartial manner so that they may be decided solely upon the merits, any statement or suggestion by a lawyer that he can or would attempt to circumvent those procedures is detrimental to the legal system and tends to undermine public confidence in it.

EC 9-5   Separation of the funds of a client from those of his lawyer not only serves to protect the client but also avoids even the appearance of impropriety, and therefore commingling of such funds should be avoided.

EC 9-6   Every lawyer owes a solemn duty to uphold the integrity and honor of his profession; to encourage respect for the law and for the courts and the judges thereof; to observe the Code of Professional Responsibility; to act as a member of a learned profession, one dedicated to public service; to cooperate with his brother lawyers in supporting the organized bar through the devoting of his time, efforts, and financial support as his professional standing and ability reasonably permit; to conduct himself so as to reflect credit on the legal profession and to inspire the confidence, respect, and trust of his clients and of the public; and to strive to avoid not only professional impropriety but also the appearance of impropriety.

EC 9-7   A lawyer has an obligation to the public to participate in collective efforts of the bar to reimburse persons who have lost money or property as a result of the misappropriation or defalcation of another lawyer, and contribution to a client's security fund is an acceptable method of meeting this obligation.

DISCIPLINARY RULES

DR 9-101   Avoiding Even the Appearance of Impropriety.

(A) A lawyer shall not accept private employment in a matter upon the merits of which he has acted in a judicial capacity.

(B) A lawyer shall not accept private employment in a matter in which he had substantial responsibility while he was a public employee.

(C) A lawyer shall not state or imply that he is able to influence improperly or upon irrelevant grounds any tribunal, legislative body, or public official.

DR 9-102   Preserving Identity of Funds and Property of a Client.

(A) All funds of clients paid to a lawyer or law firm, other than advances for costs and expenses, shall be deposited in one or more identifiable bank accounts maintained in the state in which the law office is situated and no funds belonging to the lawyer or law firm shall be deposited therein except as follows:

(1) Funds reasonably sufficient to pay bank charges may be deposited therein.

(2) Funds belonging in part to a client and in part presently or potentially to the lawyer or law firm must be deposited therein, but the portion belonging to the lawyer or law firm may be withdrawn when due unless the right of the lawyer or law firm to receive it is disputed by the client, in which event the disputed portion shall not be withdrawn until the dispute is finally resolved.

(B) A lawyer shall:

(1) Promptly notify a client of the receipt of his funds, securities, or other properties.

(2) Identify and label securities and properties of a client promptly upon receipt and place them in a safe deposit box or other place of safekeeping as soon as practicable.

(3) Maintain complete records of all funds, securities, and other properties of a client coming into the possession of the lawyer and render appropriate accounts to his client regarding them.

(4) Promptly pay or deliver to the client as requested by a client the funds, securities, or other properties in the possession of the lawyer which the client is entitled to receive.

DEFINITIONS

As used in the Disciplinary Rules of the Model Code of Professional Responsibility:

(1) **"Differing interests"** include every interest that will adversely affect either the judgment or the loyalty of a lawyer to a client, whether it be a conflicting, inconsistent, diverse, or other interest.

(2) **"Law firm"** includes a professional legal corporation.

(3) **"Person"** includes a corporation, an association, a trust, a partnership, and any other organization or legal entity.

(4) **"Professional legal corporation"** means a corporation, or an association treated as a corporation, authorized by law to practice law for profit.

(5) **"State"** includes the District of Columbia, Puerto Rico, and other federal territories and possessions.

(6) **"Tribunal"** includes all courts and all other adjudicatory bodies.

(7) **"A Bar association"** includes a bar association of specialists as referred to in DR 2-105(A)(1) or (4).

(8) **"Qualified legal assistance organization"** means an office or organization of one of the four types listed in DR 2-103(D)(1)-(4), inclusive, that meets all the requirements thereof.

RESTATEMENT OF THE LAW (THIRD), THE LAW GOVERNING LAWYERS (2000)

CHAPTER 1. REGULATION OF THE LEGAL PROFESSION

CHAPTER 3. CLIENT AND LAWYER: THE FINANCIAL AND PROPERTY RELATIONSHIP

TOPIC 1. LEGAL CONTROLS ON ATTORNEY FEES

TOPIC 2. A LAWYER'S CLAIM TO COMPENSATION

TOPIC 3. FEE-COLLECTION PROCEDURES

TOPIC 4. PROPERTY AND DOCUMENTS OF CLIENTS AND OTHERS

TOPIC 5. FEE-SPLITTING WITH A LAWYER NOT IN THE SAME FIRM

CHAPTER 4. LAWYER CIVIL LIABILITY

TOPIC 1. LIABILITY FOR PROFESSIONAL NEGLIGENCE AND BREACH OF FIDUCIARY DUTY

TOPIC 2. OTHER CIVIL LIABILITY

TOPIC 3. VICARIOUS LIABILITY

CHAPTER 5. CONFIDENTIAL CLIENT INFORMATION

TOPIC 1. CONFIDENTIALITY RESPONSIBILITIES OF LAWYERS

CHAPTER 6. REPRESENTING CLIENTS—IN GENERAL

TOPIC 1. LAWYER FUNCTIONS IN REPRESENTING CLIENTS—IN GENERAL

TOPIC 2. REPRESENTING ORGANIZATIONAL CLIENTS

TOPIC 3. LAWYER DEALINGS WITH A NONCLIENT

CHAPTER 1. REGULATION OF THE LEGAL PROFESSION

TOPIC 1. REGULATION OF LAWYERS—IN GENERAL

§ 1. Regulation of Lawyers—In General

Upon admission to the bar of any jurisdiction, a person becomes a lawyer and is subject to applicable law governing such matters as professional discipline, procedure and evidence, civil remedies, and criminal sanctions.

Comment:

b. Lawyer codes and background law. Today, as for the last quarter-century, professional discipline of a lawyer in the United States is conducted pursuant to regulations contained in regulatory codes that have been approved in most states by the highest court in the jurisdiction in which the lawyer has been admitted. Such codes are referred to in this Restatement as lawyer codes. Those codes are more or less patterned on model codes published by the American Bar Association, but only the version of the code officially adopted and in force in a jurisdiction regulates the activities of lawyers subject to it. While in most jurisdictions the lawyer code is adopted and subject to revision only through action of the highest court in the state (see Comment *c* hereto), in all jurisdictions at least some legislation is applicable to lawyers and law practice. See, e.g., § 56, Comments *i* and *j* (federal legislation and state consumer-protection laws applicable to lawyers); § 58(3) and Comment *b* thereto (statutes authorizing lawyers to practice in the form of limited-liability partnerships and similar types of law firms); § 68 and following (attorney-client privilege). Federal district courts generally have adopted the lawyer code of the jurisdiction in which the court sits, and all federal courts exercise the power to regulate lawyers appearing before them. Some administrative agencies, primarily within the federal government, have also regulated lawyers practicing before the agency, sometimes through lawyer codes adopted by the agency and specifically applicable to those practitioners. Although uniformity is desirable for many purposes, lawyer codes in fact differ markedly in certain respects from one jurisdiction to another, and no state follows any nationally promulgated bar-association model in all respects. . . .

The lawyer codes and much general law remain complementary. The lawyer codes draw much of their moral force and, in many particulars, the detailed description of their rules from preexisting legal requirements and concepts found in the law of torts, contracts, agency, trusts, property, remedies, procedure, evidence, and crimes. Thus, lawyer codes particularize some general legal rules in the particular occupational situation of lawyers but are not exhaustive of those rules. By the same token, lawyer codes often establish the same rules as would apply in a comparable situation involving a nonlawyer professional providing a related service or a rule very like it. The lawyer codes presuppose the general legal background thus referred to and its applicability to lawyers and the rules that make up that background, and they do not preclude application of remedies prescribed by other law. Particular lawyer conduct may violate a lawyer code, tort law, and a criminal statute, or it may have less than all those legal effects. Lawyer codes sometimes differ from other legal provisions with respect to such factors as the following: the specified mental state of the lawyer-actor defined in the standard of conduct; the required presence and kind or degree of harm on the part of the claimant or injured victim of the lawyer's action or nonaction; the possible relevance of reliance by others; and the extent of imputed knowledge, duty, and liability (see Topic 3, Introductory Note).

c. The inherent powers of courts. The highest courts in most states have ruled as a matter of state constitutional law that their power to regulate lawyers is inherent in the judicial function. Thus, the grant of judicial power in a state constitution devolves upon the courts the concomitant regulatory power. The power is said to derive both from the historical role of courts in the United States in regulating lawyers through admission and disbarment and from the traditional practice of courts in England. Admitting lawyers to practice (see § 2), formulating and amending lawyer codes (see Comment *b*), and regulating the system of lawyer discipline (see § 5, Comment *b*) are functions reserved in most states to the highest court of the state. . . .

Beyond affirmative empowerment, some state courts have further held that their constitutional power to regulate lawyers is exclusive of other branches of state government with respect to some matters. On that basis, those courts have held that an attempt by another branch of state government to regulate lawyers is an interference with that judicial power and a violation of the state's constitutionally mandated separation of powers. Some decisions have given effect to an otherwise-invalid statute or regulation on a notion of comity, when the court is persuaded of the wisdom of the enactment and convinced that it does not pose a threat to the court's overall regulation of lawyers. . . .

d. The role of bar associations. Beginning in the early decades of the 20th century, bar associations have played an increasingly active role in regulating the conduct of lawyers. Together with lawyers who work on disciplinary and similar committees within state- and federal-court systems, bar associations have become the chief embodiment of the concept that lawyers are a self-regulated profession. Self-regulation provides protection of lawyers against political control by the state. However, self-regulation also carries its own risk of under-regulation of lawyers as a whole, regulation (however strict) that is in the interest of lawyers as a group and not the public, or regulation that focuses disproportionately on groups of lawyers disfavored within the controlling bar association or committee. . . .

In a number of states, membership in the state's bar association is compulsory, in the sense that a lawyer otherwise appropriately admitted to practice must maintain active membership in the bar association as a condition of retention of a valid license to practice law within the jurisdiction. (Such mandatory bars are sometimes called "integrated" bars.) Decisions of the United States Supreme Court have limited the extent to which a member of such a mandatory bar association can be required to pay any portion of dues that supports activities not germane to the organization's functions in providing self-regulation. Those generally include activities of a political or ideological nature not directly connected to the regulation of lawyers and maintenance of the system of justice. Under those decisions, the bar must maintain a system for allocating dues payments for permissible and noncovered purposes and a process to permit lawyers to regain the portion of dues collected for noncovered purposes.

TOPIC 2. PROCESS OF PROFESSIONAL REGULATION

§ 2. Admission to Practice Law

In order to become a lawyer and qualify to practice law in a jurisdiction of admission, a prospective lawyer must comply with requirements of the jurisdiction relating to such matters as education, other demonstration of competence such as success in a bar examination, and character.

§ 3. Jurisdictional Scope of the Practice of Law by a Lawyer

A lawyer currently admitted to practice in a jurisdiction may provide legal services to a client:

(1) at any place within the admitting jurisdiction;

(2) before a tribunal or administrative agency of another jurisdiction or the federal government in compliance with requirements for temporary or regular admission to practice before that tribunal or agency; and

(3) at a place within a jurisdiction in which the lawyer is not admitted to the extent that the lawyer's activities arise out of or are otherwise reasonably related to the lawyer's practice under Subsection (1) or (2).

Comment:

e. Extra-jurisdictional law practice by a lawyer. Admission in a state permits a lawyer to maintain an office and otherwise practice law anywhere within its borders. No state today continues the restrictions of former centuries that limited practice to a particular judicial district or county in which a lawyer was admitted.

The rules governing interstate practice by nonlocal lawyers were formed at a time when lawyers conducted very little practice of that nature. Thus, the limitation on legal services threatened by such rules imposed little actual inconvenience. However, as interstate and international commerce, transportation, and communications have expanded, clients have increasingly required a truly interstate and international range of practice by their lawyers. (To a limited extent, many states recognize such needs in the international realm by providing for limited practice in the state by foreign legal consultants. See § 2, Comment g.) Applied literally, the old restrictions on practice of law in a state by a lawyer admitted elsewhere could seriously inconvenience clients who have need of such services within the state. Retaining locally admitted counsel would often cause serious delay and expense and could require the client to deal with unfamiliar counsel. Modern communications, including ready electronic connection to much of the law of every state, makes concern about a competent analysis of a distant state's law unfounded. Accordingly, there is much to be said for a rule permitting a lawyer to practice in any state, except for litigation matters or for the purpose of establishing a permanent in-state branch office. Results approaching that rule may arguably be required under the federal interstate commerce clause and the privileges and immunities clause. The approach of the Section is more guarded. However, its primary focus is appropriately on the needs of clients.

The extent to which a lawyer may practice beyond the borders of the lawyer's home state depends on the circumstances in which the lawyer acts in both the lawyer's home state and the other state. At one extreme, it is clear that a lawyer's admission to practice in one jurisdiction does not authorize the lawyer to practice generally in another jurisdiction as if the lawyer were also fully admitted there. Thus, a lawyer admitted in State A may not open an office in State B for the general practice of law there or otherwise engage in the continuous, regular, or repeated representation of clients within the other state.

Certainty is provided in litigated matters by procedures for securing the right to practice elsewhere, although the arrangement is limited to appearances as counsel in individual litigated matters. Apparently all states provide such a procedure for temporary admission of an unadmitted lawyer, usually termed admission pro hac vice. (Compare admission on-motion to the right to practice generally within a jurisdiction as described in § 2, Comment *b*.) Although the decision is sometimes described as discretionary, a court will grant admission pro hac vice if the lawyer applying for admission is in good standing in the bar of another jurisdiction and has complied with applicable requirements (sometimes requiring the association of local counsel), and if no reason is shown why the lawyer cannot be relied upon to provide competent representation to the lawyer's client in conformance with the local lawyer code. Such temporary admission is recognized in Subsection (2). Courts are particularly apt to grant such applications in criminal-defense representations. Some jurisdictions impose limitations, such as a maximum number of such admissions in a specified period. Admission pro hac vice normally permits the lawyer to engage within the jurisdiction in all customary and appropriate activities in conducting the litigation, including appropriate office practice. Activities in contemplation of such admission are also authorized, such as investigating facts or consulting with the client within the jurisdiction prior to drafting a complaint and filing the action.

A lawyer who is properly admitted to practice in a state with respect to litigation pending there, either generally or pro hac vice, may need to conduct proceedings and activities ancillary to the litigation in other states, such as counseling clients, dealing with co-counsel or opposing counsel, conducting depositions, examining documents, interviewing witnesses, negotiating settlements, and the like. Such activities incidental to permissible practice are appropriate and permissible.

Transactional and similar out-of-court representation of clients may raise similar issues, yet there is no equivalent of temporary admission pro hac vice for such representation, as there is in litigation. Even activities that bear close resemblance to in-court litigation, such as representation of clients in arbitration or in administrative hearings, may not include measures for pro hac vice appearance. Some activities are clearly permissible. Thus, a lawyer conducting activities in the lawyer's home state may advise a client about the law of another state, a proceeding in another state, or a transaction there, including conducting research in the law of the other state, advising the client about the application of that law, and drafting legal documents intended to have legal effect there. There is no per se bar against such a lawyer giving a formal opinion based in whole or in part on the law of another jurisdiction, but a lawyer should do so only if the lawyer has adequate familiarity with the relevant law. It is also clearly permissible for a lawyer from a home-state office to direct communications to persons and organizations in other states (in which the lawyer is not separately admitted), by letter, telephone, telecopier, or other forms of electronic communication. On the other hand, as with litigation, it would be impermissible for a lawyer to set up an office for the general practice of nonlitigation law in a jurisdiction in which the lawyer is not admitted as described in § 2.

When other activities of a lawyer in a non-home state are challenged as impermissible for lack of admission to the state's bar, the context in which and purposes for which the lawyer acts should be carefully assessed. Beyond home-state activities, proper representation of clients often requires a lawyer to conduct activities while physically present in one or more other states. Such practice is customary in many areas of legal representation. As stated in Subsection (3), such activities should be recognized as permissible so long as they arise out of or otherwise reasonably relate to the lawyer's practice in a state of admission. In determining that issue, several factors are relevant, including the following: whether the lawyer's client is a regular client of the lawyer or, if a new client, is from the lawyer's home state, has extensive contacts with that state, or contacted the lawyer there; whether a multistate transaction has other significant connections with the lawyer's home state; whether significant aspects of the lawyer's activities are conducted in the lawyer's home state; whether a significant aspect of the matter involves the law of the lawyer's home state; and whether either the activities of the client involve multiple jurisdictions or the legal issues involved are primarily either multistate or federal in nature. Because lawyers in a firm often practice collectively, the activities of all lawyers in the representation of a client are relevant. The customary practices of lawyers who engage in interstate law practice is one appropriate measure of the reasonableness of a lawyer's activities out of state. Association with local counsel may permit a lawyer to conduct in-state activities not otherwise permissible, but such association is not required in most instances of in-state practice. Among other things, the additional expense for the lawyer's client of retaining additional counsel and educating that lawyer about the client's affairs would make such required retention unduly burdensome.

Particularly in the situation of a lawyer representing a multistate or multinational organization, the question of geographical connection may be difficult to assess or establish. Thus, a multinational corporation wishing to select a location in the United States to build a new facility may engage a lawyer to accompany officers of the corporation to survey possible sites in several states, perhaps holding discussions with local governmental officers about such topics as zoning, taxation, environmental requirements, and the like. Such occasional, temporary in-state services, when reasonable and appropriate in performing the lawyer's functions for the client, are a proper aspect of practice and do not constitute impermissible practice in the other state.

Illustrations:

1. Lawyer has an office and is duly licensed to practice law in State A. Lawyer's office is in a community near State B, where Lawyer is not admitted to practice. In the past, several of Lawyer's clients have been residents of State B, and their legal issues sometimes involve research into issues of State B law. In order to provide better service to those clients and to attract business of other clients there, Lawyer rents space, hires nonlawyer assistants, and otherwise prepares premises for the general practice of law at a branch-office location in State B. While representation of residents of State B in Lawyer's office in State A is permissible, Lawyer may not open an office for the general practice of law in State B without obtaining general admission to practice there (see § 2).

2. Same facts as in Illustration 1, except that Lawyer represents a regulated Utility, which operates a power plant in State A near the border with State B. Lawyer's work for Utility principally relates to environmental issues, such as providing advice, obtaining permits, and otherwise complying with federal law and the law of State A. Utility also has occasional issues relating to compliance with the environmental laws of State B because of those same activities. It is permissible for Lawyer to travel to State B to deal with governmental officials with respect to environmental issues arising out of Utility's activities.

3. Same facts as in Illustration 2, except that Lawyer's original work for Utility in State A related to rate-setting proceedings before a utility commission in that state and before the Federal Energy Regulatory Commission. Under recent legislation, Utility may now be able to make retail sales of electricity to consumers in many states. Because of Lawyer's extensive knowledge of Utility's rate-related financial information, Utility has asked Lawyer to take charge of new rate applications in 15 other states, all being states in which Lawyer is not admitted to practice. Lawyer's work in those matters would involve extensive presence and activities in each of the other states until the necessary rates have been established. Although local counsel would often be retained in such matters, Lawyer and other lawyers in Lawyer's firm may permissibly conduct those activities in the other states on behalf of Utility.

4. Lawyer, who practices with a law firm in California, is a nationally known expert in corporate mergers and acquisitions. Utility is a major electricity generator and distributor in the southeastern United States. Under the new legislation referred to in Illustration 3, Utility is considering a hostile takeover of Old Company, an established regional electricity generator and distributor in the northeastern United States. Legal work on the acquisition would require the physical presence of Utility's mergers-and-acquisitions counsel in a number of states in addition to the West Coast state in which Lawyer is admitted, in addition to representation before at least one federal agency in Washington, D.C. Given the multistate and federal nature of the legal work, Lawyer and other members of Lawyer's firm may represent Utility as requested.

5. Lawyer is admitted to practice and has an office in Illinois, where Lawyer practices in the area

of trusts and estates, an area involving, among other things, both the law of wills, property, taxation, and trusts of a particular state and federal income, estate, and gift tax law. Client A, whom Lawyer has represented in estate-planning matters, has recently moved to Florida and calls Lawyer from there with a request that leads to Lawyer's preparation of a codicil to A's will, which Lawyer takes to Florida to obtain the necessary signatures. While there, A introduces Lawyer to B, a friend of A, who, after learning of A's estate-planning arrangements from A, wishes Lawyer to prepare a similar estate arrangement for B. Lawyer prepares the necessary documents and conducts legal research in Lawyer's office in Illinois, frequently conferring by telephone and letter with B in Florida. Lawyer then takes the documents to Florida for execution by B and necessary witnesses. Lawyer's activities in Florida on behalf of both A and B were permissible.

§ 4. Unauthorized Practice by a Nonlawyer

A person not admitted to practice as a lawyer (see § 2) may not engage in the unauthorized practice of law, and a lawyer may not assist a person to do so.

Comment:

a. Scope and cross-references. . . .

A nonlawyer who impermissibly engages in the practice of law may be subject to several sanctions, including injunction, contempt, and conviction for crime.

b. Unauthorized practice by a nonlawyer—in general. Courts, typically as the result of lawsuits brought by bar associations, began in the early part of the 20th century to adapt common-law rules to permit bar associations and lawyer-competitors to seek injunctions against some forms of unauthorized practice by nonlawyers. The courts also played a large role in attempting to define and delineate such practice. The primary justification given for unauthorized practice limitations was that of consumer protection—to protect consumers of unauthorized practitioner services against the significant risk of harm believed to be threatened by the nonlawyer practitioner's incompetence or lack of ethical constraints. Delineating the respective areas of permissible and impermissible activities has often been controversial. Some consumer groups and governmental agencies have criticized some restrictions as over-protective, anti-competitive, and costly to consumers.

In the latter part of the 20th century, unauthorized practice restrictions have lessened, to a greater or lesser extent, in most jurisdictions. In some few jurisdictions traditional restraints are apparently still enforced through active programs. In other jurisdictions, enforcement has effectively ceased, and large numbers of lay practitioners perform many traditional legal services. Debate continues about the broad public-policy elements of unauthorized-practice restrictions, including the delineation of lawyer-only practice areas. On areas of nonlawyer practice officially permitted, see Comment *c* hereof.

c. Delineation of unauthorized practice. The definitions and tests employed by courts to delineate unauthorized practice by nonlawyers have been vague or conclusory, while jurisdictions have differed significantly in describing what constitutes unauthorized practice in particular areas.

Certain activities, such as the representation of another person in litigation, are generally proscribed. Even in that area, many jurisdictions recognize exceptions for such matters as small-claims and landlord-tenant tribunals and certain proceedings in administrative agencies. Moreover, many jurisdictions have authorized law students and others not admitted in the state to represent indigent persons or others as part of clinical legal-education programs.

Controversy has surrounded many out-of-court activities such as advising on estate planning by bank trust officers, advising on estate planning by insurance agents, stock brokers, or benefit-plan and similar consultants, filling out or providing guidance on forms for property transactions by real-estate agents, title companies, and closing-service companies, and selling books or individual forms containing instructions on self-help legal services or accompanied by personal, nonlawyer assistance on filling them out in connection with legal procedures such as obtaining a marriage dissolution. The position of bar associations has traditionally been that nonlawyer provision of such services denies the person served the benefit of such legal measures as the attorney-client privilege, the benefits of such extraordinary duties as that of confidentiality of client information and the protection against conflicts of interest, and the protection of such measures as those regulating lawyer trust accounts and requiring lawyers to supervise nonlawyer personnel. Several jurisdictions recognize that many such services can be provided by nonlawyers without significant risk of incompetent service, that actual experience in several states with extensive nonlawyer provision of traditional legal services indicates no significant risk of harm to consumers of such services, that persons in need of legal services may be significantly aided in obtaining assistance at a much lower price than would be entailed by segregating out a portion of a transaction to be handled by a lawyer for a fee, and that many persons can ill afford, and most persons are at least inconvenienced by, the typically higher cost of lawyer services. In addition, traditional common-law and statutory consumer-protection measures offer significant protection to consumers of such nonlawyer services.

d. Pro se appearance. Every jurisdiction recognizes the right of an individual to proceed "pro se" by providing his or her own representation in any matter, whether or not the person is a lawyer. Because the appearance is personal only, it does not involve an issue of unauthorized practice. The right extends to self-preparation of legal documents and other kinds of out-of-court legal work as well as to in-court representation. In some jurisdictions, tribunals have inaugurated programs to assist persons without counsel in filing necessary papers, with appropriate cautions that court personnel assisting the person do not thereby undertake to provide legal assistance. The United States Supreme Court has held that a person accused of crime in a federal or state prosecution has, as an aspect of the right to the assistance of counsel, the constitutional right to waive counsel and to proceed pro se. In general, however, a person appearing pro se cannot represent any other person or entity, no matter how close the degree of kinship, ownership, or other relationship.

e. Unauthorized practice for and by entities. A limitation on pro se representation (see Comment *d*) found in many jurisdictions is that a corporation cannot represent itself in litigation and must accordingly always be represented by counsel. The rule applies, apparently, only to appearances in litigated matters. Thus a nonlawyer officer of a corporation may permissibly draft legal documents, negotiate complex transactions, and perform other tasks for the employing organization, even if the task is typically performed by lawyers for organizations. With respect to litigation, several jurisdictions except representation in certain tribunals, such as landlord-tenant and small-claims courts and in certain administrative proceedings (see Comment *c* hereto), where incorporation (typically of a small owner-operated business) has little bearing on the prerogative of the person to provide self-representation.

Under traditional concepts of unauthorized practice, a lawyer employed by an organization may provide legal services only to the organization as an entity with respect to its own interests and not, for example, to customers of the entity with respect to their own legal matters. Included within the powers of a lawyer retained by an organization (see § 3, Comment *f*) should be the capacity to perform legal services for all entities within the same organizational family. It has proved controversial whether a lawyer employed full time by an insurance company (see § 134) may represent policyholders of the company in covered matters.

§ 5. Professional Discipline

(1) A lawyer is subject to professional discipline for violating any provision of an applicable lawyer code.

(2) A lawyer is also subject to professional discipline under Subsection (1) for attempting to commit a violation, knowingly assisting or inducing another to do so, or knowingly doing so through the acts of another.

(3) A lawyer who knows of another lawyer's violation of applicable rules of professional conduct raising a substantial question of the lawyer's honesty or trustworthiness or the lawyer's fitness as a lawyer in some other respect must report that information to appropriate disciplinary authorities.

TOPIC 3. CIVIL JUDICIAL REMEDIES IN GENERAL

§ 6. Judicial Remedies Available to a Client or Nonclient for Lawyer Wrongs

For a lawyer's breach of a duty owed to the lawyer's client or to a nonclient, judicial remedies may be available through judgment or order entered in accordance with the standards applicable to the remedy awarded, including standards concerning limitation of remedies. Judicial remedies include the following:

(1) awarding a sum of money as damages;

(2) providing injunctive relief, including requiring specific performance of a contract or

enjoining its nonperformance;

(3) requiring restoration of a specific thing or awarding a sum of money to prevent unjust enrichment;

(4) ordering cancellation or reformation of a contract, deed, or similar instrument;

(5) declaring the rights of the parties, such as determining that an obligation claimed by the lawyer to be owed to the lawyer is not enforceable;

(6) punishing the lawyer for contempt;

(7) enforcing an arbitration award;

(8) disqualifying a lawyer from a representation;

(9) forfeiting a lawyer's fee (see § 37);

(10) denying the admission of evidence wrongfully obtained;

(11) dismissing the claim or defense of a litigant represented by the lawyer;

(12) granting a new trial; and

(13) entering a procedural or other sanction.

Comment:

d. Preventing unjust enrichment. A court in a civil action may order a lawyer to return specific property, such as client property wrongfully retained by a lawyer (see § 45). See also § 60(2) (accounting for profits from improper use of confidential information). Disciplinary authorities are also sometimes empowered to order restitution as a disciplinary sanction (see § 5, Comment *j*). On forfeiture of a lawyer's fees, see § 37.

e. Rescission or reformation of a transaction. Cancellation of an instrument with otherwise legal effect would be appropriate when, for example, a lawyer obtains a deed to a client's property through undue influence in violation of limitations on business dealings with a client (see § 126) or on client gifts to lawyers (see § 127) or when the instrument was prepared by a lawyer representing clients with substantial conflicts of interests (see § 130). The remedy implements substantive standards applicable to lawyers as an expression of the strong public policy of the jurisdiction.

f. Declaratory relief. Under standards otherwise governing the availability of declaratory relief, it may be appropriate for a court to enter an order declaring the respective rights of lawyer and client with respect to a disputed issue or the responsibilities of a lawyer with respect to a nonclient.

g. Contempt. An order providing a sanction for civil or criminal contempt may be appropriate for a lawyer's violation of a court injunction or similar order. See Comment *c*; see also § 105. In addition, a lawyer functioning as advocate in a proceeding may be subject to remedies through contempt orders without issuance of a prior judicial order where necessary and appropriate to maintain order in the courtroom or otherwise to prevent significant impairment of the proceedings (see § 105, Comment *e*). Included in such relief may be an appropriate sanction directed toward repairing or punishing harm that the lawyer's contemptuous conduct caused to the lawyer's own client.

h. Enforcing an arbitration award. As indicated in § 42, Comment *b*, a lawyer and client may agree to submit a dispute to binding arbitration, and a jurisdiction may require a lawyer to submit to fee arbitration when a client so elects. See also § 54, Comment *b* (malpractice arbitration). As with arbitration awards generally, a court may in an appropriate case enter an order enforcing such an award or denying it enforcement on appropriate grounds. On arbitration awards in a lawyer's favor and against a client or former client, see § 7, Comment *c*.

i. Disqualification from a representation. Disqualification of a lawyer and those affiliated with the lawyer from further participation in a pending matter has become the most common remedy for conflicts of interest in litigation (see Chapter 8). Disqualification draws on the inherent power of courts to regulate the conduct of lawyers (see § 1, Comment *c*) as well as the related inherent power of judges to regulate the course of proceedings before them and to issue injunctive and similar directive orders (see Comment *c* hereto). Disqualification, where appropriate, ensures that the case is well presented in court, that confidential information of present or former clients is not misused, and that a client's substantial interest in a lawyer's loyalty is protected. In most instances, determining whether a lawyer should be disqualified involves a balancing of several interests and is appropriate only when less-intrusive remedies are not reasonably available. . . .

Concern that motions to disqualify might be used to delay proceedings and harass opposing parties also requires that the motion to disqualify be timely. If a present or former client with knowledge of the conflict fails to take reasonably prompt steps to object or to seek a remedy, disqualification may be precluded. Whether an objection is timely depends on such circumstances as the length of delay from the time when the conflict was reasonably apparent, whether the movant was represented by counsel at relevant times, why the delay occurred, and whether acting now would result in prejudice to the responding party.

A file of the work done on a matter before disqualification by a disqualified lawyer may be provided to a successor lawyer in circumstances in which doing so does not threaten confidential information (see generally § 59) of the successful moving client. The party seeking to justify such a transfer may be required to show both that no impermissible confidential client information is contained in the material transferred, and that the former and new lawyers exchange none in the process of transferring responsibilities for the matter. . . .

When a lawyer undertakes a representation that is later determined to involve a conflict of interest that could not reasonably have been and in fact was not identified at an earlier point (see § 121, Comment g), the lawyer is not liable for damages or subject to professional discipline. In such a situation, disqualification may or may not be appropriate (see § 49, Illustration 2).

j. Denying the admissibility of evidence. If the admission of evidence on behalf of a party would violate the obligation owed by a lawyer to a client or former client (see generally § 60) or was obtained by a lawyer in violation of the lawyer's obligation not to mislead a nonclient (see § 98), the tribunal may exercise discretion to exclude the evidence, even if the evidence is not otherwise subject to exclusion because of the attorney-client privilege (see § 68 and following) or the work-product immunity (see § 87 and following). Exclusion is proper where it would place the parties in the position they would have occupied if the lawyer had not obtained the confidential information in the first place.

k. Dismissing a claim or defense. When a litigant bases an essential element of a claim or defense entirely on confidential client information improperly disclosed by a lawyer (see generally § 60), the tribunal may exercise discretion to dismiss the claim or defense. Such extreme relief is appropriate when no less drastic relief would adequately remedy the disclosure. If, on the other hand, the tribunal finds that the claim or defense would have been made notwithstanding the disclosure, a more appropriate remedy may be disqualification of the revealing lawyer if the lawyer presently represents the responding party and suppression of only such evidence (see Comment *j*) as would not be properly discoverable.

l. New trial. Where the determination in a case was affected prejudicially and substantially by a conflict of interest, by a lawyer misuse of confidential information of an objecting client, by a breach of rules governing admissibility of evidence or conduct of the proceeding, or by similarly wrongful conduct of a lawyer, the determination may be reversed and the matter retried. Tribunals are properly reluctant to grant such a remedy. On the other hand, it may be the only effective remedy in a particular case, for example in a criminal case in which a lawyer representing the defendant labored under an impermissible conflict of interest (see § 129). When the complaining party is the client of the offending lawyer in a civil case, tribunals generally relegate the client to such remedies as the client may have directly against the lawyer, concluding that reversal of a determination in favor of an otherwise uninvolved opposing party would be inappropriate (see § 26, Comment *d*).

m. Procedural or other sanctions. Most tribunals possess the power to provide sanctions against participants in litigation, including lawyers, who engage in seriously harassing or other sanctionable activities. See generally § 1; see also § 110. Such sanctions include an award of attorney fees to a party injured by the lawyer's conduct, a fine, or a reprimand. In appropriate circumstances, the court may determine that the client was blameless and the lawyer fully blameworthy and accordingly direct that the full weight of a sanction entered against a party be borne only by the lawyer and not by the lawyer's client (see § 110, Comment *g*). Rarely will such relief entail an award from the offending lawyer to that lawyer's own client. However, such an order may be appropriate, for example, when, due to the lawyer's offensive activities, the lawyer's client has retained another lawyer and the court retains jurisdiction to award such a sanction against the predecessor lawyer.

§ 7. Judicial Remedies Available to a Lawyer for Client Wrongs

A lawyer may obtain a remedy based on a present or former client's breach of a duty to the lawyer if the remedy:
    (1) is appropriate under applicable law governing the remedy; and
    (2) does not put the lawyer in a position prohibited by an applicable lawyer code.

TOPIC 4. LAWYER CRIMINAL OFFENSES

§ 8. Lawyer Criminal Offenses

The traditional and appropriate activities of a lawyer in representing a client in accordance with the requirements of the applicable lawyer code are relevant factors for the tribunal in assessing the propriety of the lawyer's conduct under the criminal law. In other respects, a lawyer is guilty of an offense for an act committed in the course of representing a client to the same extent and on the same basis as would a nonlawyer acting similarly.

TOPIC 5. LAW-FIRM STRUCTURE AND OPERATION

§ 9. Law-Practice Organizations—In General

(1) A lawyer may practice as a solo practitioner, as an employee of another lawyer or law firm, or as a member of a law firm constituted as a partnership, professional corporation, or similar entity.

(2) A lawyer employed by an entity described in Subsection (1) is subject to applicable law governing the creation, operation, management, and dissolution of the entity.

(3) Absent an agreement with the firm providing a more permissive rule, a lawyer leaving a law firm may solicit firm clients:

(a) prior to leaving the firm:

(i) only with respect to firm clients on whose matters the lawyer is actively and substantially working; and

(ii) only after the lawyer has adequately and timely informed the firm of the lawyer's intent to contact firm clients for that purpose; and

(b) after ceasing employment in the firm, to the same extent as any other nonfirm lawyer.

§ 10. Limitations on Nonlawyer Involvement in a Law Firm

(1) A nonlawyer may not own any interest in a law firm, and a nonlawyer may not be empowered to or actually direct or control the professional activities of a lawyer in the firm.

(2) A lawyer may not form a partnership or other business enterprise with a nonlawyer if any of the activities of the enterprise consist of the practice of law.

(3) A lawyer or law firm may not share legal fees with a person not admitted to practice as a lawyer, except that:

(a) an agreement by a lawyer with the lawyer's firm or another lawyer in the firm may provide for payment, over a reasonable period of time after the lawyer's death, to the lawyer's estate or to one or more specified persons;

(b) a lawyer who undertakes to complete unfinished legal business of a deceased lawyer may pay to the estate of the deceased lawyer a portion of the total compensation that fairly represents services rendered by the deceased lawyer; and

(c) a lawyer or law firm may include nonlawyer employees in a compensation or retirement plan, even though the plan is based in whole or in part on a profit-sharing arrangement.

§ 11. A Lawyer's Duty of Supervision

(1) A lawyer who is a partner in a law-firm partnership or a principal in a law firm organized as a corporation or similar entity is subject to professional discipline for failing to make reasonable efforts to ensure that the firm has in effect measures giving reasonable assurance that all lawyers in the firm conform to applicable lawyer-code requirements.

(2) A lawyer who has direct supervisory authority over another lawyer is subject to

professional discipline for failing to make reasonable efforts to ensure that the other lawyer conforms to applicable lawyer-code requirements.

(3) A lawyer is subject to professional discipline for another lawyer's violation of the rules of professional conduct if:

(a) the lawyer orders or, with knowledge of the specific conduct, ratifies the conduct involved; or

(b) the lawyer is a partner or principal in the law firm, or has direct supervisory authority over the other lawyer, and knows of the conduct at a time when its consequences can be avoided or mitigated but fails to take reasonable remedial measures.

(4) With respect to a nonlawyer employee of a law firm, the lawyer is subject to professional discipline if either:

(a) the lawyer fails to make reasonable efforts to ensure:

(i) that the firm in which the lawyer practices has in effect measures giving reasonable assurance that the nonlawyer's conduct is compatible with the professional obligations of the lawyer; and

(ii) that conduct of a nonlawyer over whom the lawyer has direct supervisory authority is compatible with the professional obligations of the lawyer; or

(b) the nonlawyer's conduct would be a violation of the applicable lawyer code if engaged in by a lawyer, and

(i) the lawyer orders or, with knowledge of the specific conduct, ratifies the conduct; or

(ii) the lawyer is a partner or principal in the law firm, or has direct supervisory authority over the nonlawyer, and knows of the conduct at a time when its consequences can be avoided or mitigated but fails to take reasonable remedial measures.

§ 12. Duty of a Lawyer Subject to Supervision

(1) For purposes of professional discipline, a lawyer must conform to the requirements of an applicable lawyer code even if the lawyer acted at the direction of another lawyer or other person.

(2) For purposes of professional discipline, a lawyer under the direct supervisory authority of another lawyer does not violate an applicable lawyer code by acting in accordance with the supervisory lawyer's direction based on a reasonable resolution of an arguable question of professional duty.

§ 13. Restrictions on the Right to Practice Law

(1) A lawyer may not offer or enter into a law-firm agreement that restricts the right of the lawyer to practice law after terminating the relationship, except for a restriction incident to the lawyer's retirement from the practice of law.

(2) In settling a client claim, a lawyer may not offer or enter into an agreement that restricts the right of the lawyer to practice law, including the right to represent or take particular action on behalf of other clients.

CHAPTER 2. THE CLIENT-LAWYER RELATIONSHIP

Introductory Note

The subject of this Chapter is, from one point of view, derived from the law of agency. It concerns a voluntary arrangement in which an agent, a lawyer, agrees to work for the benefit of a principal, a client. A lawyer is an agent, to whom clients entrust matters, property, and information, which may be of great importance and sensitivity, and whose work is usually not subject to detailed client supervision because of its complexity. Because those characteristics of the client-lawyer relationship make clients vulnerable to harm, and because of the importance to the legal system of faithful representation, the law stated in this Chapter provides a number of safeguards for clients beyond those generally provided to principals. The client-lawyer relationship normally comes into existence only if the client consents, and the client may end it at any time. The lawyer is subject to duties of care, loyalty, confidentiality, and communication, duties enforceable by the client and through disciplinary sanctions. The client also retains considerable authority to control the lawyer, although practical considerations often inhibit the use of that authority. The law also limits client authority for the protection of third persons dealing with the lawyer and for the convenience of the judicial system.

TOPIC 1. CREATING A CLIENT-LAWYER RELATIONSHIP

§ 14. Formation of a Client-Lawyer Relationship

A relationship of client and lawyer arises when:

(1) a person manifests to a lawyer the person's intent that the lawyer provide legal services for the person; and either

(a) the lawyer manifests to the person consent to do so; or

(b) the lawyer fails to manifest lack of consent to do so, and the lawyer knows or reasonably should know that the person reasonably relies on the lawyer to provide the services; or

(2) a tribunal with power to do so appoints the lawyer to provide the services.

Comment:

e. The lawyer's consent or failure to object. Like a client, a lawyer may manifest consent to creating a client-lawyer relationship in many ways. The lawyer may explicitly agree to represent the client or may indicate consent by action, for example by performing services requested by the client. An agent for the lawyer may communicate consent, for example, a secretary or paralegal with express, implied, or apparent authority to act for the lawyer in undertaking a representation.

A lawyer's consent may be conditioned on the successful completion of a conflict-of-interest check or on the negotiation of a fee arrangement. The lawyer's consent may sometimes precede the client's manifestation of intent, for example when an insurer designates a lawyer to represent an insured (see § 134, Comment *f*) who then accepts the representation. Although this Section treats separately the required communications of the client and the lawyer, the acts of each often illuminate those of the other.

Illustrations:

1. Client telephones Lawyer, who has previously represented Client, stating that Client wishes Lawyer to handle a pending antitrust investigation and asking Lawyer to come to Client's headquarters to explore the appropriate strategy for Client to follow. Lawyer comes to the headquarters and spends a day discussing strategy, without stating then or promptly thereafter that Lawyer has not yet decided whether to represent Client. Lawyer has communicated willingness to represent Client by so doing. Had Client simply asked Lawyer to discuss the possibility of representing Client, no client-lawyer relationship would result.

2. As part of a bar-association peer-support program, lawyer A consults lawyer B in confidence about an issue relating to lawyer A's representation of a client. This does not create a client-lawyer relationship between A's client and B. Whether a client-lawyer relationship exists between A and B depends on the foregoing and additional circumstances, including the nature of the program, the subject matter of the consultation, and the nature of prior dealings, if any, between them.

Even when a lawyer has not communicated willingness to represent a person, a client-lawyer relationship arises when the person reasonably relies on the lawyer to provide services, and the lawyer, who reasonably should know of this reliance, does not inform the person that the lawyer will not do so (see § 14(1)(b); see also § 51(2)). In many such instances, the lawyer's conduct constitutes implied assent. In others, the lawyer's duty arises from the principle of promissory estoppel, under which promises inducing reasonable reliance may be enforced to avoid injustice (see Restatement Second, Contracts § 90). In appraising whether the person's reliance was reasonable, courts consider that lawyers ordinarily have superior knowledge of what representation entails and that lawyers often encourage clients and potential clients to rely on them. The rules governing when a lawyer may withdraw from a representation (see § 32) apply to representations arising from implied assent or promissory estoppel.

Illustrations:

3. Claimant writes to Lawyer, describing a medical-malpractice suit that Claimant wishes to bring and asking Lawyer to represent Claimant. Lawyer does not answer the letter. A year later, the statute of limitations applicable to the suit expires. Claimant then sues Lawyer for legal malpractice for not having filed the suit on time. Under this Section no client-lawyer relationship was created (see § 50, Comment c). Lawyer did not communicate willingness to represent Claimant, and Claimant could not reasonably have relied on Lawyer to do so. On a lawyer's duty to a prospective client, see § 15.

4. Defendant telephones Lawyer's office and tells Lawyer's Secretary that Defendant would like Lawyer to represent Defendant in an automobile-violation proceeding set for hearing in 10 days, this being a type of proceeding that Defendant knows Lawyer regularly handles. Secretary tells Defendant to send in the papers concerning the proceeding, not telling Defendant that Lawyer would then decide whether to take the case, and Defendant delivers the papers the next day. Lawyer does not communicate with Defendant until the day before the hearing, when Lawyer tells Defendant that Lawyer does not wish to take the case. A trier of fact could find that a client-lawyer relationship came into existence when Lawyer failed to communicate that Lawyer was not representing Defendant. Defendant relied on Lawyer by not seeking other counsel when that was still practicable. Defendant's reliance was reasonable because Lawyer regularly handled Defendant's type of case, because Lawyer's agent had responded to Defendant's request for help by asking Defendant to transfer papers needed for the proceeding, and because the imminence of the hearing made it appropriate for Lawyer to inform Defendant and return the papers promptly if Lawyer decided not to take the case. . . .

f. Organizational, fiduciary, and class-action clients. When the client is a corporation or other organization, the organization's structure and organic law determine whether a particular agent has authority to retain and direct the lawyer. Whether the lawyer is to represent the organization, a person or entity associated with it, or more than one such persons and entities is a question of fact to be determined based on reasonable expectations in the circumstances (see Subsection (1)). Where appropriate, due consideration should be given to the unreasonableness of a claimed expectation of entering into a co-client status when a significant and readily apparent conflict of interest exists between the organization or other client and the associated person or entity claimed to be a co-client (see § 131).

Under Subsection (1)(b), a lawyer's failure to clarify whom the lawyer represents in circumstances calling for such a result might lead a lawyer to have entered into client-lawyer representations not intended by the lawyer. Hence, the lawyer must clarify whom the lawyer intends to represent when the lawyer knows or reasonably should know that, contrary to the lawyer's own intention, a person, individually, or agents of an entity, on behalf of the entity, reasonably rely on the lawyer to provide legal services to that person or entity (see Subsection (1)(b); see also § 103, Comment b (extent of a lawyer's duty to warn an unrepresented person that the lawyer represents a client with conflicting interests)). Such clarification may be required, for example, with respect to an officer of an entity client such as a corporation, with respect to one or more partners in a client partnership or in the case of affiliated organizations such as a parent, subsidiary, or similar organization related to a client person or client entity. An implication that such a relationship exists is more likely to be found when the lawyer performs personal legal services for an individual as well or where the organization is small and characterized by extensive common ownership and management. But the lawyer does not enter into a client-lawyer relationship with a person associated with an organizational client solely because the person communicates with the lawyer on matters relevant to the organization that are also relevant to the personal situation of the person. In all events, the question is one of fact based on the reasonable and apparent expectations of the person or entity whose status as client is in question.

In trusts and estates practice a lawyer may have to clarify with those involved whether a trust, a trustee, its beneficiaries or groupings of some or all of them are clients and similarly whether the client is an executor, an estate, or its beneficiaries. In the absence of clarification the inference to be drawn may depend on the circumstances and on the law of the jurisdiction. Similar issues may arise when a lawyer represents other fiduciaries with respect to their fiduciary responsibilities, for example a pension-fund trustee or another lawyer.

Class actions may pose difficult questions of client identification. For many purposes, the named class representatives are the clients of the lawyer for the class. On conflict-of-interest issues, see § 125,

Comment *f.* Yet class members who are not named representatives also have some characteristics of clients. For example, their confidential communications directly to the class lawyer may be privileged (compare § 70, Comment *c),* and opposing counsel may not be free to communicate with them directly (see § 99, Comment *l).*

Lawyers in class actions must sometimes deal with disagreements within the class and breaches by the named parties of their duty to represent class members. Although class representatives must be approved by the court, they are often initially self-selected, selected by their lawyer, or even (when a plaintiff sues a class of defendants) selected by their adversary. Members of the class often lack the incentive or knowledge to monitor the performance of the class representatives. Although members may sometimes opt out of the class, they may have no practical alternative other than remaining in the class if they wish to enforce their rights. Lawyers in class actions thus have duties to the class as well as to the class representatives.

A class-action lawyer may therefore be privileged or obliged to oppose the views of the class representatives after having consulted with them. The lawyer may also propose that opposing positions within the class be separately represented, that sub-classes be created, or that other measures be taken to ensure broader class participation. Withdrawal may be an option (see § 32), but one that is often undesirable because it may leave the class without effective representation. The lawyer should act for the benefit of the class as its members would reasonably define that benefit.

§ 15. A Lawyer's Duties to a Prospective Client

(1) When a person discusses with a lawyer the possibility of their forming a client-lawyer relationship for a matter and no such relationship ensues, the lawyer must:

(a) not subsequently use or disclose confidential information learned in the consultation, except to the extent permitted with respect to confidential information of a client or former client as stated in § § 61-67;

(b) protect the person's property in the lawyer's custody as stated in § § 44- 46; and

(c) use reasonable care to the extent the lawyer provides the person legal services.

(2) A lawyer subject to Subsection (1) may not represent a client whose interests are materially adverse to those of a former prospective client in the same or a substantially related matter when the lawyer or another lawyer whose disqualification is imputed to the lawyer under § § 123 and 124 has received from the prospective client confidential information that could be significantly harmful to the prospective client in the matter, except that such a representation is permissible if:

(a) (i) any personally prohibited lawyer takes reasonable steps to avoid exposure to confidential information other than information appropriate to determine whether to represent the prospective client, and (ii) such lawyer is screened as stated in § 124(2)(b) and (c); or

(b) both the affected client and the prospective client give informed consent to the representation under the limitations and conditions provided in § 122.

TOPIC 2. SUMMARY OF THE DUTIES UNDER A CLIENT-LAWYER RELATIONSHIP

§ 16. A Lawyer's Duties to a Client—In General

To the extent consistent with the lawyer's other legal duties and subject to the other provisions of this Restatement, a lawyer must, in matters within the scope of the representation:

(1) proceed in a manner reasonably calculated to advance a client's lawful objectives, as defined by the client after consultation;

(2) act with reasonable competence and diligence;

(3) comply with obligations concerning the client's confidences and property, avoid impermissible conflicting interests, deal honestly with the client, and not employ advantages arising from the client-lawyer relationship in a manner adverse to the client; and

(4) fulfill valid contractual obligations to the client.

§ 17. A Client's Duties to a Lawyer

Subject to the other provisions of this Restatement, in matters covered by the representation a client must:

(1) compensate a lawyer for services and expenses as stated in Chapter 3;

(2) indemnify the lawyer for liability to which the client has exposed the lawyer without the lawyer's fault; and

(3) fulfill any valid contractual obligations to the lawyer.

§ 18. Client-Lawyer Contracts

(1) A contract between a lawyer and client concerning the client-lawyer relationship, including a contract modifying an existing contract, may be enforced by either party if the contract meets other applicable requirements, except that:

(a) if the contract or modification is made beyond a reasonable time after the lawyer has begun to represent the client in the matter (see § 38(1)), the client may avoid it unless the lawyer shows that the contract and the circumstances of its formation were fair and reasonable to the client; and

(b) if the contract is made after the lawyer has finished providing services, the client may avoid it if the client was not informed of facts needed to evaluate the appropriateness of the lawyer's compensation or other benefits conferred on the lawyer by the contract.

(2) A tribunal should construe a contract between client and lawyer as a reasonable person in the circumstances of the client would have construed it.

§ 19. Agreements Limiting Client or Lawyer Duties

(1) Subject to other requirements stated in this Restatement, a client and lawyer may agree to limit a duty that a lawyer would otherwise owe to the client if:

(a) the client is adequately informed and consents; and

(b) the terms of the limitation are reasonable in the circumstances.

(2) A lawyer may agree to waive a client's duty to pay or other duty owed to the lawyer.

Comment:

c. Limiting a representation. Clients and lawyers may define in reasonable ways the services a lawyer is to provide (see § 16), for example to handle a trial but not any appeal, counsel a client on the tax aspects of a transaction but not other aspects, or advise a client about a representation in which the primary role has been entrusted to another lawyer. Such arrangements are not waivers of a client's right to more extensive services but a definition of the services to be performed. They are therefore treated separately under many lawyer codes as contracts limiting the objectives of the representation. Clients ordinarily understand the implications and possible costs of such arrangements. The scope of many such representations requires no explanation or disclaimer of broader involvement.

Some contracts limiting the scope or objectives of a representation may harm the client, for example if a lawyer insists on agreement that a proposed suit will not include a substantial claim that reasonably should be joined. Section 19(1) hence qualifies the power of client and lawyer to limit the representation. Taken together with requirements stated in other Sections, five safeguards apply.

First, a client must be informed of any significant problems a limitation might entail, and the client must consent (see § 19(1)(a)). For example, if the lawyer is to provide only tax advice, the client must be aware that the transaction may pose non-tax issues as well as being informed of any disadvantages involved in dividing the representation among several lawyers (see also § § 15 & 20).

Second, any contract limiting the representation is construed from the standpoint of a reasonable client (see § 18(2)).

Third, the fee charged by the lawyer must remain reasonable in view of the limited representation (see § 34).

Fourth, any change made an unreasonably long time after the representation begins must meet the more stringent tests of § 18(1) for postinception contracts or modifications.

Fifth, the terms of the limitation must in all events be reasonable in the circumstances (§ 19(1)(b)). When the client is sophisticated in such waivers, informed consent ordinarily permits the inference that the waiver is reasonable. For other clients, the requirement is met if, in addition to informed consent, the benefits supposedly obtained by the waiver—typically, a reduced legal fee or the ability to retain a particularly able lawyer—could reasonably be considered to outweigh the potential risk posed by the limitation. It is also relevant whether there were special circumstances warranting the limitation and whether it was the client or the lawyer who sought it. Also relevant is the choice available to clients; for example, if most local lawyers, but not lawyers in other communities, insist on the same limitation, client acceptance of the limitation is subject to special scrutiny.

The extent to which alternatives are constrained by circumstances might bear on reasonableness. For example, a client who seeks assistance on a matter on which the statute of limitations is about to run would not reasonably expect extensive investigation and research before the case must be filed. A lawyer may be asked to assist a client concerning an unfamiliar area because other counsel are unavailable. If the lawyer knows or should know that the lawyer lacks competence necessary for the representation, the lawyer must limit assistance to that which the lawyer believes reasonably necessary to deal with the situation.

Reasonableness also requires that limits on a lawyer's work agreed to by client and lawyer not infringe on legal rights of third persons or legal institutions. Hence, a contract limiting a lawyer's role during trial may require the tribunal's approval.

Illustrations:

1. Corporation wishes to hire Law Firm to litigate a substantial suit, proposing a litigation budget. Law Firm explains to Corporation's inside legal counsel that it can litigate the case within that budget but only by conducting limited discovery, which could materially lessen the likelihood of success. Corporation may waive its right to more thorough representation. Corporation will benefit by gaining representation by counsel of its choice at limited expense and could readily have bargained for more thorough and expensive representation.

2. A legal clinic offers for a small fee to have one of its lawyers (a tax specialist) conduct a half-hour review of a client's income-tax return, telling the client of the dangers or opportunities that the review reveals. The tax lawyer makes clear at the outset that the review may fail to find important tax matters and that clients can have a more complete consideration of their returns only if they arrange for a second appointment and agree to pay more. The arrangement is reasonable and permissible. The clients' consent is free and adequately informed, and clients gain the benefit of an inexpensive but expert tax review of a matter that otherwise might well receive no expert review at all.

3. Lawyer offers to provide tax-law advice for an hourly fee lower than most tax lawyers charge. Lawyer has little knowledge of tax law and asks Lawyer's occasional tax clients to agree to waive the requirement of reasonable competence. Such a waiver is invalid, even if clients benefit to some extent from the low price and consent freely and on the basis of adequate information. Moreover, allowing such general waivers would seriously undermine competence requirements essential for protection of the public, with little compensating gain. On prohibitions against limitations of a lawyer's liability, see § 54.

TOPIC 3. AUTHORITY TO MAKE DECISIONS

Introductory Note

. . . Traditionally, some lawyers considered that a client put affairs in the lawyer's hands, who then managed them as the lawyer thought would best advance the client's interests. So conducting the relationship can subordinate the client to the lawyer. The lawyer might not fully understand the client's best interests or might consciously or unconsciously pursue the lawyer's own interests. An opposite view of the client-lawyer relationship treats the lawyer as a servant of the client, who must do whatever the client wants limited only by the requirements of law. That view ignores the interest of the lawyer and of society that a lawyer practice responsibly and independently.

A middle view is that the client defines the goals of the representation and the lawyer implements them, but that each consults with the other. Except for certain matters reserved for client or lawyer to decide, the scope of the lawyer's authority is itself one of the subjects for consultation, with room for the client's wishes and the parties' contracts to modify the traditionally broad delegation of authority to the lawyer. This approach, accepted in this Restatement, permits a variety of allocations of authority.

§ 20. A Lawyer's Duty to Inform and Consult with a Client

(1) A lawyer must keep a client reasonably informed about the matter and must consult with a client to a reasonable extent concerning decisions to be made by the lawyer under § § 21-23.

(2) A lawyer must promptly comply with a client's reasonable requests for information.

(3) A lawyer must notify a client of decisions to be made by the client under § § 21-23 and must explain a matter to the extent reasonably necessary to permit the client to make informed decisions regarding the representation.

§ 21. Allocating the Authority to Decide Between a Client and a Lawyer

As between client and lawyer:

(1) A client and lawyer may agree which of them will make specified decisions, subject to the requirements stated in § § 18, 19, 22, 23, and other provisions of this Restatement. The agreement may be superseded by another valid agreement.

(2) A client may instruct a lawyer during the representation, subject to the requirements stated in § § 22, 23, and other provisions of this Restatement.

(3) Subject to Subsections (1) and (2) a lawyer may take any lawful measure within the scope of representation that is reasonably calculated to advance a client's objectives as defined by the client, consulting with the client as required by § 20.

(4) A client may ratify an act of a lawyer that was not previously authorized.

Comment:

e. A lawyer's authority in the absence of an agreement or instruction. A lawyer has authority to take any lawful measure within the scope of representation (see § 19) that is reasonably calculated to advance a client's objectives as defined by the client (see § 16), unless there is a contrary agreement or instruction and unless a decision is reserved to the client (see § 22). A lawyer, for example, may decide whether to move to dismiss a complaint and what discovery to pursue or resist. Absent a contrary agreement, instruction, or legal obligation (see § 23(2)), a lawyer thus remains free to exercise restraint, to accommodate reasonable requests of opposing counsel, and generally to conduct the representation in the same manner that the lawyer would recommend to other professional colleagues.

Signing a client's name to endorse a settlement check, however, is normally unauthorized and indeed may be a crime. A lawyer's presumptive authority does not extend to retaining another lawyer outside the first lawyer's firm to represent the client (see Restatement Second, Agency § 18), although a lawyer may consult confidentially about a client's case with another lawyer.

Because a lawyer is required to consult with a client and report on the progress of the representation (see § 20(1)), a client ordinarily should be kept sufficiently aware of what is occurring to intervene in the representation with instructions as to important decisions.

A lawyer often must make a decision without sufficient time to consult with the client. During a hearing, for example, decision must be made whether to object to another party's question, probe further answers of a witness, or seek a curative instruction. Such matters often involve technical legal and strategic considerations difficult for a client to assess. Sometimes a lawyer cannot reach a client within the time during which a decision must be made. In the absence of a contrary agreement or instruction, lawyers have authority to make such decisions. Generally, in making such decisions, the lawyer properly takes into account moral considerations and appropriate courtroom and professional decorum.

f. Ratification by a client. A client may ratify a lawyer's unauthorized act by explicit consent, by knowingly accepting its benefits, or by other conduct manifesting knowing approval after the act. . . . Ratification does not bar disciplinary proceedings against a lawyer, although the fact that the client ratified the unauthorized decision may be relevant in appraising the lawyer's conduct. As between lawyer and client, ratification does not absolve the lawyer if the client was obliged to affirm the lawyer's act in order to protect the client's interests or was induced to ratify by the lawyer's misrepresentation or other misconduct. The law governing ratification of acts by lawyers is the same as that applicable to other agents (see Restatement Second, Agency, Chapter 4).

Illustration:

2. Acting against Client's instructions, Lawyer negotiates a plea bargain with Prosecutor under which Client will plead guilty to pending criminal charges and receive a 10-year sentence. Client, learning of the bargain, discharges Lawyer and communicates with Prosecutor who states that, although Prosecutor would have agreed to a more lenient bargain, Prosecutor, believing that Lawyer deceived Prosecutor by claiming to have Client's authorization, declines to renegotiate the plea bargain. Client's only choice is therefore to affirm the bargain or to go to trial, in which event it is probable that, should Client be convicted, the court will impose a substantially longer sentence. Client elects to accept the bargain and pleads guilty, receiving the 10-year sentence. Client's election does not prevent professional discipline or bar whatever malpractice claim Client may have against Lawyer for the unauthorized plea bargain.

§ 22. Authority Reserved to a Client

(1) As between client and lawyer, subject to Subsection (2) and § 23, the following and comparable decisions are reserved to the client except when the client has validly authorized the lawyer to make the particular decision: whether and on what terms to settle a claim; how a criminal defendant should plead; whether a criminal defendant should waive jury trial; whether a criminal defendant should testify; and whether to appeal in a civil proceeding or criminal prosecution.

(2) A client may not validly authorize a lawyer to make the decisions described in Subsection (1) when other law (such as criminal-procedure rules governing pleas, jury-trial waiver, and defendant testimony) requires the client's personal participation or approval.

(3) Regardless of any contrary contract with a lawyer, a client may revoke a lawyer's authority to make the decisions described in Subsection (1).

§ 23. Authority Reserved to a Lawyer

As between client and lawyer, a lawyer retains authority that may not be overridden by a contract with or an instruction from the client:

(1) to refuse to perform, counsel, or assist future or ongoing acts in the representation that the lawyer reasonably believes to be unlawful;

(2) to make decisions or take actions in the representation that the lawyer reasonably believes to be required by law or an order of a tribunal.

§ 24. A Client with Diminished Capacity

(1) When a client's capacity to make adequately considered decisions in connection with the representation is diminished, whether because of minority, physical illness, mental disability, or other cause, the lawyer must, as far as reasonably possible, maintain a normal client-lawyer relationship with the client and act in the best interests of the client as stated in Subsection (2).

(2) A lawyer representing a client with diminished capacity as described in Subsection (1) and for whom no guardian or other representative is available to act, must, with respect to a matter within the scope of the representation, pursue the lawyer's reasonable view of the client's objectives or interests as the client would define them if able to make adequately considered decisions on the matter, even if the client expresses no wishes or gives contrary instructions.

(3) If a client with diminished capacity as described in Subsection (1) has a guardian or other person legally entitled to act for the client, the client's lawyer must treat that person as entitled to act with respect to the client's interests in the matter, unless:

(a) the lawyer represents the client in a matter against the interests of that person; or

(b) that person instructs the lawyer to act in a manner that the lawyer knows will violate the person's legal duties toward the client.

(4) A lawyer representing a client with diminished capacity as described in Subsection (1) may seek the appointment of a guardian or take other protective action within the scope of the representation when doing so is practical and will advance the client's objectives or interests, determined as stated in Subsection (2).

Comment:

c. Maintaining a normal client-lawyer relationship so far as possible. Disabilities in making decisions vary from mild to totally incapacitating; they may impair a client's ability to decide matters generally or only with respect to some decisions at some times; and they may be caused by childhood, old age, physical illness, retardation, chemical dependency, mental illness, or other factors. Clients should not be unnecessarily deprived of their right to control their own affairs on account of such disabilities. Lawyers, moreover, should be careful not to construe as proof of disability a client's insistence on a view of the client's welfare that a lawyer considers unwise or otherwise at variance with the lawyer's own views.

When a client with diminished capacity is capable of understanding and communicating, the lawyer should maintain the flow of information and consultation as much as circumstances allow (see § 20). The lawyer should take reasonable steps to elicit the client's own views on decisions necessary to the representation. Sometimes the use of a relative, therapist, or other intermediary may facilitate communication (see § § 70 & 71). Even when the lawyer is empowered to make decisions for the client (see Comment *d*), the lawyer should, if practical, communicate the proposed decision to the client so that the client will have a chance to comment, remonstrate, or seek help elsewhere. A lawyer may properly withhold from a disabled client information that would harm the client, for example when showing a psychiatric report to a mentally-ill client would be likely to cause the client to attempt suicide, harm another person, or otherwise act unlawfully (see § 20, Comment *b*, & § 46, Comment *c*).

A lawyer for a client with diminished capacity may be retained by a parent, spouse, or other relative of the client. Even when that person is not also a co-client, the lawyer may provide confidential client information to the person to the extent appropriate in providing representation to the client (see § 61). If the disclosure is to be made to a nonclient and there is a significant risk that the information may be used adversely to the client, the lawyer should consult with the client concerning such disclosure.

A client with diminished capacity is entitled to make decisions normally made by clients to the extent that the client is able to do so. The lawyer should adhere, to the extent reasonably possible, to the lawyer's usual function as advocate and agent of the client, not judge or guardian, unless the lawyer's role in the situation is modified by other law. The lawyer should, for example, help the client oppose confinement as a juvenile delinquent even though the lawyer believes that confinement would be in the long-term interests of the client and has unsuccessfully urged the client to accept confinement. Advancing the latter position should be left to opposing counsel.

If a client with diminished capacity owes fiduciary duties to others, the lawyer should be careful to avoid assisting in a violation of those duties (cf. § 51(4)).

d. Deciding for a client with diminished capacity. When a client's disability prevents maintaining a normal client-lawyer relationship and there is no guardian or other legal representative to make decisions for the client, the lawyer may be justified in making decisions with respect to questions within the scope of the representation that would normally be made by the client. A lawyer should act only on a reasonable belief, based on appropriate investigation, that the client is unable to make an adequately considered decision rather than simply being confused or misguided. Because a disability might vary from time to time, the lawyer must reasonably believe that the client is unable to make an adequately considered decision without prejudicial delay.

A lawyer's reasonable belief depends on the circumstances known to the lawyer and discoverable by reasonable investigation. Where practicable and reasonably available, independent professional evaluation of the client's capacity may be sought. If a conflict of interest between client and lawyer is involved (see § 125), disinterested evaluation by another lawyer may be appropriate. Careful consideration is required of the client's circumstances, problems, needs, character, and values, including interests of the client beyond the matter in which the lawyer represents the client. If the client, when able to decide, had expressed views relevant to the decision, the lawyer should follow them unless there is reason to believe that changed circumstances would change those views. The lawyer should also give appropriate weight to the client's presently expressed views.

A lawyer may bring the client's diminished capacity before a tribunal when doing so is reasonably calculated to advance the client's objectives or interests as the client would define them if able to do so rationally. A proceeding seeking appointment of a guardian for the client is one example (see Comment *e*). A lawyer may also raise the issue of the client's incompetence to stand trial in a criminal prosecution or, when a client is incompetent to stand trial, interpose the insanity defense. In such situations, the court and the adversary process provide some check on the lawyer's decision.

In some jurisdictions, if a criminal defendant's competence to stand trial is reasonably arguable, the defendant's lawyer must bring the issue to the court's attention, whether or not the lawyer reasonably believes this to be for the client's benefit. That should not be considered a duty to the client flowing from the representation and is not provided for by this Section.

A lawyer must also make necessary decisions for an incompetent client when it is impractical or undesirable to have a guardian appointed or to take other similar protective measures. For example, when a court appoints a lawyer to represent a young child, it may consider the lawyer to be in effect the child's guardian ad litem. When a client already has a guardian but retains counsel to proceed against that guardian, a court often will not appoint a second guardian to make litigation decisions for the client. Other situations exist in which appointment of a guardian would be too expensive, traumatic, or otherwise undesirable or impractical in the circumstances.

It is often difficult to decide whether the conditions of this Section have been met. A lawyer who acts reasonably and in good faith in perplexing circumstances is not subject to professional discipline or malpractice or similar liability (see Chapter 4). In some situations (for example, when a lawyer discloses a client's diminished capacity to a tribunal against a client's wishes), the lawyer might be required to attempt to withdraw as counsel if the disclosure causes the client effectively to discharge the lawyer (see § 32(2)(c)).

e. Seeking appointment of a guardian. When a client's diminished capacity is severe and no other practical method of protecting the client's best interests is available, a lawyer may petition an appointment of a guardian or other representative to make decisions for the client. A general or limited power of attorney may sometimes be used to avoid the expense and possible embarrassment of a guardianship.

The client might instruct the lawyer to seek appointment of a guardian or take other protective measures. On the use of confidential client information in a guardianship proceeding, see § 61 and § 69, Comment *f.*

A lawyer is not required to seek a guardian for a client whenever the conditions of Subsection (4) are satisfied. For example, it may be clear that the courts will not appoint a guardian or that doing so is not in the client's best interests (see § 16 & Comment *d* hereto).

f. Representing a client for whom a guardian or similar person may act. When a guardian has been appointed, the guardian normally speaks for the client as to matters covered by the guardianship. (When under the law of the jurisdiction a client's power of attorney remains in effect during a disability, the appointee has such authority.) The lawyer therefore should normally follow the decisions of the guardian as if they were those of the client. That principle does not apply when the lawyer is representing the client in proceedings against the guardian, for example, in an attempt to have the guardianship terminated or its terms altered. The law sometimes authorizes the client to bypass a guardian—for example, when a mature minor seeks a court order authorizing her to have an abortion without having to disclose her pregnancy to her parents or guardians. The lawyer may also believe that the guardian is violating fiduciary duties owed to the client and may then seek relief setting aside the guardian's decision or replacing the guardian (see also § 51(4)). If the lawyer believes the guardian to be acting lawfully but inconsistently with the best interests of the client, the lawyer may remonstrate with the guardian or withdraw under § 32(3)(d) (see § 23, Comment *c*).

When a guardian retains a lawyer to represent the guardian, the guardian is the client.

TOPIC 4. A LAWYER'S AUTHORITY TO ACT FOR A CLIENT

§ 25. Appearance Before a Tribunal

A lawyer who enters an appearance before a tribunal on behalf of a person is presumed to represent that person as a client. The presumption may be rebutted.

§ 26. A Lawyer's Actual Authority

A lawyer's act is considered to be that of a client in proceedings before a tribunal or in dealings with third persons when:
(1) the client has expressly or impliedly authorized the act;
(2) authority concerning the act is reserved to the lawyer as stated in § 23; or
(3) the client ratifies the act.

Comment:

b. Rationale. Legal representation saves the client's time and effort and enables legal work to be delegated to an expert. Lawyers therefore are recognized as agents for their clients in litigation and other legal matters. Indeed, courts commonly will not allow a corporation to participate in litigation through an agent other than a lawyer.

Allowing clients to act through lawyers also subjects clients to obligations and disabilities. With respect to the rights of a third person, the client is bound when a case is lost or a negotiation handled disadvantageously by a lawyer. Attributing the acts of lawyers to their clients is warranted by the fact that, in an important sense, they really are acts authorized by the principal. Much serious activity in business and personal affairs is done through lawyers. The same considerations apply, with qualifications, in holding the client liable for certain wrongs committed by the lawyer (see Comment *d* hereto).

Binding clients to the acts of their lawyers can be unfair in some circumstances. A client might have authorized a lawyer's conduct only in general terms, without contemplating the particular acts that lead to liability. However, it has been regarded as more appropriate for costs flowing from a lawyer's misconduct generally to be borne by the client rather than by an innocent third person. Where the lawyer rather than the client is directly to blame, the client may be able to recover any losses by suing the lawyer, a right not generally accorded to nonclients (see Chapter 4). In practice, however, clients are sometimes unable to control their lawyer's conduct and accordingly may sometimes be excused from the consequences of their lawyer's behavior when that can be done without seriously harming others (see § 29).

d. Effects of attributing authorized acts to a client. When a lawyer's act is attributed to a client various legal consequences might follow for the client. If the act consisted of assenting to a contract, the client is bound by the contract (see Restatement Second, Agency, Chapter 6). If the lawyer was authorized to bring or defend a lawsuit, the client is bound by the result. Likewise, the client is bound by authorized lawyer action or inaction during litigation, for example when the lawyer asks a question that elicits an answer harmful to the client or files a frivolous motion.

When a lawyer's act is wrongful and causes injury to a third person, the client as principal is liable as provided by agency law (see Restatement Second, Agency, Chapter 7; see also § 27, Comment *e*).

§ 27. A Lawyer's Apparent Authority

A lawyer's act is considered to be that of the client in proceedings before a tribunal or in dealings with a third person if the tribunal or third person reasonably assumes that the lawyer is authorized to do the act on the basis of the client's (and not the lawyer's) manifestations of such authorization.

Comment:

b. Rationale. Under the law of agency, a client is bound by the lawyer's act or failure to act when the client has vested the lawyer with apparent authority—an appearance of authority arising from and in accordance with the client's manifestations to third persons (see Restatement Second, Agency § 8). Apparent authority can be identical to, greater, or less than a lawyer's actual authority (see id. Comment *a*). The concepts of actual and apparent authority often lead to similar results. The same acts or statements of a client that confer actual authority can serve to manifest authority to a third person and vice versa. Apparent authority extends beyond actual authority in a lawyer's transactions with third persons when the client has limited the lawyer's actual authority but the limitation has not been disclosed to that person and, instead, the client has manifested to the third person that the lawyer has authority to act in the matter.

Apparent authority exists when and to the extent a client causes a third person to form a reasonable belief that a lawyer is authorized to act for the client. Permitting disavowal would allow clients at their convenience to ratify or disavow their lawyer's acts despite the client's inconsistent manifestation of the lawyer's authority. It would also impose on the third person the burden of proving a fact better known to the client. A client usually can make clear to third persons the limited scope of a lawyer's authority or take care to act in ways that do not manifest authority that the client does not intend.

Recognizing a lawyer as agent creates a risk that a client will be bound by an act the client never intended to authorize. Several safeguards are therefore included in the apparent-authority principle. First, the client must in fact have retained the lawyer or given the third party reason to believe that the client has done so. Second, the client's own acts (including the act of retaining the lawyer) must have warranted a reasonable observer in believing that the client authorized the lawyer to act. Third, the third person must in fact have such a belief. The test thus includes both an objective and a subjective element (see Restatement Second, Agency § 27). In some circumstances courts will take into account the lawyer's lack of actual authority in deciding whether to vacate a default (see § 29). If the client suffers detriment from a lawyer's act performed with apparent but not actual authority, the client can recover from the lawyer for acting beyond the scope of the lawyer's authority (see Comment *f* hereto & § 30; Restatement Second, Agency § 383).

c. Apparent authority created by retention of a lawyer. By retaining a lawyer, a client implies that the lawyer is authorized to act for the client in matters relating to the representation and reasonably appropriate in the circumstances to carry it out. Circumstances known to the third person can narrow the scope of apparent authority thus conferred, for example statements by the client or lawyer that the lawyer is to handle only specified matters (see § 21(2) & Comment *d* thereto). The client can also enlarge the lawyer's apparent authority, for example by acquiescing, to the outsider's knowledge, in the lawyer's taking certain action. In the absence of such variations, a lawyer has apparent authority to do acts that reasonably appear to be calculated to advance the client's objectives in the representation, except for matters reserved to the client under § 22. (For apparent authority with respect to matters reserved to the client, see Comment *d* hereto.)

When a lawyer's apparent authority is in question, what reasonably appears calculated to advance the client's objectives must be determined from the third person's viewpoint.

The third person's belief in the lawyer's authority must be reasonable. The same standard applies in a proceeding before a tribunal. However, because of the lawyer's broad actual authority in litigation (see § § 21 & 23), it will often be unnecessary to conduct a factual inquiry into whether a lawyer had apparent authority in the eyes of either the opposing party or the tribunal.

Illustrations:

1. At Judge's suggestion, Lawyer agrees that both parties to a civil action will waive further discovery and that the trial will begin the next week. Judge does not know, but opposing counsel does, that Lawyer's Client (which has many similar cases) instructs its lawyers in writing not to bring cases to trial without specified discovery, some of which Lawyer has not yet accomplished. Although Lawyer lacked actual authority to waive discovery, Lawyer had apparent authority from Judge's reasonable point of view, and Judge may hold Client to the trial date. Client's remedies are to seek discretionary release from the waiver (see § 29) and to seek to recover any damages from Lawyer for acting beyond authority (see Comment *f* hereto & § 30).

2. At a pretrial conference in a medical-malpractice case, Lawyer agrees with opposing counsel that neither party will call more than one expert witness at the trial. Opposing counsel is not aware that Lawyer's client (which has many similar cases) instructs its lawyers to present expert testimony from at least two witnesses in every medical-malpractice case involving more than a certain amount in claimed damages. Judge knows of the client's practice but does not inform opposing counsel. The opposing party can hold Lawyer's client to the contract, which Lawyer had apparent authority to make, unless the court releases the parties from the contract (see § 29).

d. Lawyer's apparent authority to settle and perform other acts reserved to a client. Generally a client is not bound by a settlement that the client has not authorized a lawyer to make by express, implied, or apparent authority (and that is not validated by later ratification under § 26(3)). Merely retaining a lawyer does not create apparent authority in the lawyer to perform acts governed by § 22. When a lawyer purports to enter a settlement binding on the client but lacks authority to do so, the burden of inconvenience resulting if the client repudiates the settlement is properly left with the opposing party, who should know that settlements are normally subject to approval by the client and who has no manifested contrary indication from the client. The opposing party can protect itself by obtaining clarification of the lawyer's authority. Refusing to uphold a settlement reached without the client's authority means that the case remains open, while upholding such a settlement deprives the client of the right to have the claim resolved on other terms.

f. Recovery against a lawyer. When a client is bound by an act of a lawyer with apparent but not actual authority, a lawyer is subject to liability to the client for any resulting damages to the client, unless the lawyer reasonably believed that the act was authorized by the client (see Restatement Second, Agency § 383; § § 16, 21, & 22 hereto). The lawyer can also be subject to professional discipline (see § 5) or procedural sanctions (see § 110) for harming the interests of a client through action taken without the client's consent.

If a lawyer's act does not bind the client, the lawyer can be subject to liability to a third person who dealt with the lawyer in good faith. Liability can be based on implied warranty of actual authority or on misrepresentation of the lawyer's authority (see § 30; Restatement Second, Agency § § 329 & 330). The lawyer is also subject to liability for damages to the client, for example the client's expenses of having the act declared not to be binding (see § 53, Comment *f* (client's recovery of legal fees in such an instance)).

§ 28. A Lawyer's Knowledge; Notification to a Lawyer; and Statements of a Lawyer

(1) Information imparted to a lawyer during and relating to the representation of a client is attributed to the client for the purpose of determining the client's rights and liabilities in matters in which the lawyer represents the client, unless those rights or liabilities require proof of the client's personal knowledge or intentions or the lawyer's legal duties preclude disclosure of the information to the client.

(2) Unless applicable law otherwise provides, a third person may give notification to a client, in a matter in which the client is represented by a lawyer, by giving notification to the client's lawyer, unless the third person knows of circumstances reasonably indicating that the lawyer's authority to receive notification has been abrogated.

(3) A lawyer's unprivileged statement is admissible in evidence against a client as if it were the client's statement if either:

(a) the client authorized the lawyer to make a statement concerning the subject; or

(b) the statement concerns a matter within the scope of the representation and was made by the lawyer during it.

§ 29. A Lawyer's Act or Advice as Mitigating or Avoiding a Client's Responsibility

(1) When a client's intent or mental state is in issue, a tribunal may consider otherwise admissible evidence of a lawyer's advice to the client.

(2) In deciding whether to impose a sanction on a person or to relieve a person from a criminal or civil ruling, default, or judgment, a tribunal may consider otherwise admissible evidence to prove or disprove that the lawyer who represented the person did so inadequately or contrary to the client's instructions.

§ 30. A Lawyer's Liability to a Third Person for Conduct on Behalf of a Client

(1) For improper conduct while representing a client, a lawyer is subject to professional discipline as stated in § 5, to civil liability as stated in Chapter 4, and to prosecution as provided in the criminal law (see § 7).

(2) Unless at the time of contracting the lawyer or third person disclaimed such liability, a lawyer is subject to liability to third persons on contracts the lawyer entered into on behalf of a client if:

(a) the client's existence or identity was not disclosed to the third person; or

(b) the contract is between the lawyer and a third person who provides goods or services used by lawyers and who, as the lawyer knows or reasonably should know, relies on the lawyer's credit.

(3) A lawyer is subject to liability to a third person for damages for loss proximately caused by the lawyer's acting without authority from a client under § 26 if:

(a) the lawyer tortiously misrepresents to the third person that the lawyer has authority to make a contract, conveyance, or affirmation on behalf of the client and the

third person reasonably relies on the misrepresentation; or

(b) the lawyer purports to make a contract, conveyance, or affirmation on behalf of the client, unless the lawyer manifests that the lawyer does not warrant that the lawyer is authorized to act or the other party knows that the lawyer is not authorized to act.

TOPIC 5. ENDING A CLIENT-LAWYER RELATIONSHIP

§ 31. Termination of a Lawyer's Authority

(1) A lawyer must comply with applicable law requiring notice to or permission of a tribunal when terminating a representation and with an order of a tribunal requiring the representation to continue.

(2) Subject to Subsection (1) and § 33, a lawyer's actual authority to represent a client ends when:

(a) the client discharges the lawyer;

(b) the client dies or, in the case of a corporation or similar organization, loses its capacity to function as such;

(c) the lawyer withdraws;

(d) the lawyer dies or becomes physically or mentally incapable of providing representation, is disbarred or suspended from practicing law, or is ordered by a tribunal to cease representing a client; or

(e) the representation ends as provided by contract or because the lawyer has completed the contemplated services.

(3) A lawyer's apparent authority to act for a client with respect to another person ends when the other person knows or should know of facts from which it can be reasonably inferred that the lawyer lacks actual authority, including knowledge of any event described in Subsection (2).

§ 32. Discharge by a Client and Withdrawal by a Lawyer

(1) Subject to Subsection (5), a client may discharge a lawyer at any time.

(2) Subject to Subsection (5), a lawyer may not represent a client or, where representation has commenced, must withdraw from the representation of a client if:

(a) the representation will result in the lawyer's violating rules of professional conduct or other law;

(b) the lawyer's physical or mental condition materially impairs the lawyer's ability to represent the client; or

(c) the client discharges the lawyer.

(3) Subject to Subsections (4) and (5), a lawyer may withdraw from representing a client if:

(a) withdrawal can be accomplished without material adverse effect on the interests of the client;

(b) the lawyer reasonably believes withdrawal is required in circumstances stated in Subsection (2);

(c) the client gives informed consent;

(d) the client persists in a course of action involving the lawyer's services that the lawyer reasonably believes is criminal, fraudulent, or in breach of the client's fiduciary duty;

(e) the lawyer reasonably believes the client has used or threatens to use the lawyer's services to perpetrate a crime or fraud;

(f) the client insists on taking action that the lawyer considers repugnant or imprudent;

(g) the client fails to fulfill a substantial financial or other obligation to the lawyer regarding the lawyer's services and the lawyer has given the client reasonable warning that the lawyer will withdraw unless the client fulfills the obligation;

(h) the representation has been rendered unreasonably difficult by the client or by the irreparable breakdown of the client-lawyer relationship; or

(i) other good cause for withdrawal exists.

(4) In the case of permissive withdrawal under Subsections (3)(f)-(i), a lawyer may not withdraw if the harm that withdrawal would cause significantly exceeds the harm to the lawyer or others in not withdrawing.

(5) Notwithstanding Subsections (1)-(4), a lawyer must comply with applicable law requiring notice to or permission of a tribunal when terminating a representation and with a valid order of a tribunal requiring the representation to continue.

§ 33. A Lawyer's Duties When a Representation Terminates

(1) In terminating a representation, a lawyer must take steps to the extent reasonably practicable to protect the client's interests, such as giving notice to the client of the termination, allowing time for employment of other counsel, surrendering papers and property to which the client is entitled, and refunding any advance payment of fee the lawyer has not earned.

(2) Following termination of a representation, a lawyer must:

(a) observe obligations to a former client such as those dealing with client confidences (see Chapter 5), conflicts of interest (see Chapter 8), client property and documents (see § § 44-46), and fee collection (see § 41);

(b) take no action on behalf of a former client without new authorization and give reasonable notice, to those who might otherwise be misled, that the lawyer lacks authority to act for the client;

(c) take reasonable steps to convey to the former client any material communication the lawyer receives relating to the matter involved in the representation; and

(d) take no unfair advantage of a former client by abusing knowledge or trust acquired by means of the representation.

CHAPTER 3. CLIENT AND LAWYER: THE FINANCIAL AND PROPERTY RELATIONSHIP

TOPIC 1. LEGAL CONTROLS ON ATTORNEY FEES

§ 34. Reasonable and Lawful Fees

A lawyer may not charge a fee larger than is reasonable in the circumstances or that is prohibited by law.

§ 35. Contingent-Fee Arrangements

(1) A lawyer may contract with a client for a fee the size or payment of which is contingent on the outcome of a matter, unless the contract violates § 34 or another provision of this Restatement or the size or payment of the fee is:

(a) contingent on success in prosecuting or defending a criminal proceeding; or

(b) contingent on a specified result in a divorce proceeding or a proceeding concerning custody of a child.

(2) Unless the contract construed in the circumstances indicates otherwise, when a lawyer has contracted for a contingent fee, the lawyer is entitled to receive the specified fee only when and to the extent the client receives payment.

§ 36. Forbidden Client-Lawyer Financial Arrangements

(1) A lawyer may not acquire a proprietary interest in the cause of action or subject matter of litigation that the lawyer is conducting for a client, except that the lawyer may:

(a) acquire a lien as provided by § 43 to secure the lawyer's fee or expenses; and

(b) contract with a client for a contingent fee in a civil case except when prohibited as stated in § 35.

(2) A lawyer may not make or guarantee a loan to a client in connection with pending or contemplated litigation that the lawyer is conducting for the client, except that the lawyer may make or guarantee a loan covering court costs and expenses of litigation, the repayment of which to the lawyer may be contingent on the outcome of the matter.

(3) A lawyer may not, before the lawyer ceases to represent a client, make an agreement giving the lawyer literary or media rights to a portrayal or account based in substantial part on information relating to the representation.

§ 37. Partial or Complete Forfeiture of a Lawyer's Compensation

A lawyer engaging in clear and serious violation of duty to a client may be required to forfeit some or all of the lawyer's compensation for the matter. Considerations relevant to the question of forfeiture include the gravity and timing of the violation, its willfulness, its effect on the value of the lawyer's work for the client, any other threatened or actual harm to the client, and the adequacy of other remedies.

Comment:

a. Scope and cross-references; relation to other doctrines. Even if a fee is otherwise reasonable (see § 34) and complies with the other requirements of this Chapter, this Section can in some circumstances lead to forfeiture. See also § 41, on abusive fee-collection methods, and § 43, Comments *f* and *g,* discussing the discharge of attorney liens. A client who has already paid a fee subject to forfeiture can sue to recover it (see § § 33(1) & 42).

A lawyer's improper conduct can reduce or eliminate the fee that the lawyer may reasonably charge under § 34 (see Comment *c* thereof). A lawyer is not entitled to be paid for services rendered in violation of the lawyer's duty to a client or for services needed to alleviate the consequences of the lawyer's misconduct. See Restatement Second, Agency § 469 (agent entitled to no compensation for conduct which is disobedient or breach of duty of loyalty to principal). A tribunal will also consider misconduct more broadly, as evidence of the lawyer's lack of competence and loyalty, and hence of the value of the lawyer's services.

Illustration:

1. Lawyer has been retained at an hourly rate to negotiate a contract for Client. Lawyer assures the other parties that Client has consented to a given term, knowing this to be incorrect. Lawyer devotes five hours to working out the details of the term. When Client insists that the term be stricken (see § 22), Lawyer devotes four more hours to explaining to the other parties that Lawyer's lack of authority and Client's rejection of the term requires further negotiations. Lawyer is not entitled to compensation for any of those nine hours of time under either § 34 or § 39. The tribunal, moreover, may properly consider the incident if it bears on the value of such of Lawyer's other time as is otherwise reasonably compensable.

Second, under contract law a lawyer's conduct can render unenforceable the lawyer's fee contract with a client. Thus under contract law the misconduct could constitute a material breach of contract (see § 40) or vitiate the formation of the contract (as in the case of misrepresentations concerning the lawyer's credentials). Alternatively, the contract can be unenforceable because it contains an unlawful provision (see Restatement Second, Contracts § § 163, 164, 184, 237, 241, & 374; Restatement Second, Agency § 467). In some cases, although the contract is unenforceable on its own terms, the lawyer will still be able to recover the fair value of services rendered (see § 39, Comment *e*).

Third, a lawyer's misconduct can constitute malpractice rendering the lawyer liable for any resulting damage to the client under the common law or, in some jurisdictions, a consumer-protection statute (see § 41, Comment *b*). Malpractice damages can be greater or smaller than the forfeited fees. Conduct constituting malpractice is not always the same as conduct warranting fee forfeiture. A lawyer's negligent legal research, for example, might constitute malpractice, but will not necessarily lead to fee forfeiture. On malpractice liability and measures of damages generally, see § 53. On the duty of an agent to recompense a principal for loss caused by the agent's breach of duty, see Restatement Second, Agency § 401.

b. Rationale. The remedy of fee forfeiture presupposes that a lawyer's clear and serious violation of a duty to a client destroys or severely impairs the client-lawyer relationship and thereby the justification of the lawyer's claim to compensation. See Restatement Second, Trusts § 243 (court has discretion to deny or reduce compensation of trustee who commits breach of trust); cf. Restatement Second, Agency § 456(b) (willful and deliberate breach disentitles agent to recover in quantum meruit when agency contract does not apportion compensation). Forfeiture is also a deterrent. The damage that misconduct causes is often difficult to assess. In addition, a tribunal often can determine a forfeiture sanction more easily than a right to compensating damages.

Forfeiture of fees, however, is not justified in each instance in which a lawyer violates a legal duty, nor is total forfeiture always appropriate. Some violations are inadvertent or do not significantly harm the client. Some can be adequately dealt with by the remedies described in Comment *a* or by a partial forfeiture (see Comment *e*). Denying the lawyer all compensation would sometimes be an excessive sanction, giving a windfall to a client. The remedy of this Section should hence be applied with discretion.

c. Violation of a duty to a client. This Section provides for forfeiture when a lawyer engages in a clear and serious violation (see Comment *d* hereto) of a duty to the client. The source of the duty can be civil or criminal law, including, for example, the requirements of an applicable lawyer code or the law of malpractice. The misconduct might have occurred when the lawyer was retained, during the representation, or during attempts to collect a fee (see § 41). On improper withdrawal as a ground for forfeiture, see § 40, Comment *e.*

The Section refers only to duties that a lawyer owes to a client, not to those owed to other persons. That a lawyer, for example, harassed an opponent in litigation without harming the client does not warrant relieving the client of any duty to pay the lawyer. On other remedies in such situations, see § 110. But sometimes harassing a nonclient will also violate the lawyer's duty to the client, perhaps exposing the client to demands for sanctions or making the client's cause less likely to prevail. Forfeiture will then be appropriate unless the client is primarily responsible for the breach of duty to a nonclient.

d. A clear and serious violation—relevant factors. A lawyer's violation of duty to a client warrants fee forfeiture only if the lawyer's violation was clear. A violation is clear if a reasonable lawyer, knowing the relevant facts and law reasonably accessible to the lawyer, would have known that the conduct was wrongful. The sanction of fee forfeiture should not be applied to a lawyer who could not have been expected to know that conduct was forbidden, for example when the lawyer followed one reasonable interpretation of a client-lawyer contract and another interpretation was later held correct.

To warrant fee forfeiture a lawyer's violation must also be serious. Minor violations do not justify leaving the lawyer entirely unpaid for valuable services rendered to a client, although some such violations will reduce the size of the fee or render the lawyer liable to the client for any harm caused (see Comment *a* hereto).

In approaching the ultimate issue of whether violation of duty warrants fee forfeiture, several factors are relevant. The extent of the misconduct is one factor. Normally, forfeiture is more appropriate for repeated or continuing violations than for a single incident. Whether the breach involved knowing violation or conscious disloyalty to a client is also relevant. See Restatement Second, Agency § 469 (forfeiture for willful and deliberate breach). Forfeiture is generally inappropriate when the lawyer has not done anything willfully blameworthy, for example, when a conflict of interest arises during a representation because of the unexpected act of a client or third person.

Forfeiture should be proportionate to the seriousness of the offense. For example, a lawyer's failure to keep a client's funds segregated in a separate account (see § 44) should not result in forfeiture if the funds are preserved undiminished for the client. But forfeiture is justified for a flagrant violation even though no harm can be proved.

The adequacy of other remedies is also relevant. If, for example, a lawyer improperly withdraws from a representation and is consequently limited to a quantum meruit recovery significantly smaller than the fee contract provided (see § 40), it might be unnecessary to forfeit the quantum meruit recovery as well.

e. Extent of forfeiture. Ordinarily, forfeiture extends to all fees for the matter for which the lawyer was retained, such as defending a criminal prosecution or incorporating a corporation. (For a possibly more limited loss of fees under other rules, see Comment *a* hereto.) See § 42 (client's suit for refund of fees already paid). Forfeiture does not extend to a disbursement made by the lawyer to the extent it has conferred a benefit on the client (see § 40, Comment *d*).

Sometimes forfeiture for the entire matter is inappropriate, for example when a lawyer performed valuable services before the misconduct began, and the misconduct was not so grave as to require forfeiture of the fee for all services. Ultimately the question is one of fairness in view of the seriousness of the lawyer's violation and considering the special duties imposed on lawyers, the gravity, timing, and likely consequences to the client of the lawyer's misbehavior, and the connection between the various services performed by the lawyer.

When a lawyer-employee of a client is discharged for misconduct, except in an extreme instance this Section does not warrant forfeiture of all earned salary and pension entitlements otherwise due. The lawyer's loss of employment will itself often be a penalty graver than would be the loss of a fee for a single matter for a nonemployee lawyer. Employers, moreover, are often in a better position to protect themselves against misconduct of their lawyer-employees through supervision and other means. See Comment *a* hereto; Restatement Second, Agency § 401. For an employer's liability for unjust discharge of a lawyer employee, see § 32, Comment *b*.

TOPIC 2. A LAWYER'S CLAIM TO COMPENSATION

§ 38. Client-Lawyer Fee Contracts

(1) Before or within a reasonable time after beginning to represent a client in a matter, a lawyer must communicate to the client, in writing when applicable rules so provide, the basis or rate of the fee, unless the communication is unnecessary for the client because the lawyer has previously represented that client on the same basis or at the same rate.

(2) The validity and construction of a contract between a client and a lawyer concerning the lawyer's fees are governed by § 18.

(3) Unless a contract construed in the circumstances indicates otherwise:

(a) a lawyer may not charge separately for the lawyer's general office and overhead expenses;

(b) payments that the law requires an opposing party or that party's lawyer to pay as attorney-fee awards or sanctions are credited to the client, not the client's lawyer, absent a contrary statute or court order; and

(c) when a lawyer requests and receives a fee payment that is not for services already rendered, that payment is to be credited against whatever fee the lawyer is entitled to collect.

§ 39. A Lawyer's Fee in the Absence of a Contract

If a client and lawyer have not made a valid contract providing for another measure of compensation, a client owes a lawyer who has performed legal services for the client the fair value of the lawyer's services.

Comment:

c. Applying the fair-value standard. Assessing the fair value of a lawyer's services might require answers to three questions. What fees are customarily charged by comparable lawyers in the community for similar legal services? What would a fully informed and properly advised client in the client's situation agree to pay for such services? In light of those and other relevant circumstances, what is a fair fee (see Comment *b* hereto)?

In some cases, a standard market rate for a legal service might in fact exist. A lawyer who proves that a standard fee exists in the area should ordinarily be entitled to receive it, unless the client shows that a sophisticated, informed, and properly advised client in the client's situation would have refused to pay the standard fee—for example, because such a client would have decided not to proceed (see Comment *b(ii)* hereto). Similarly, a client should not be required to pay more than the standard fee unless the lawyer shows that, because of the circumstances of the case, a sophisticated, informed, and properly advised client would have agreed to pay a higher fee.

Calculation of an hourly fee might provide guidance. Except in certain areas such as criminal-defense or tort-plaintiff representation, hourly fees are a common contractual basis of payment for legal services. The hourly fee would be that charged by lawyers of similar experience and other credentials in comparable cases, but not more than the standard rate of the lawyer in question for that type of work. The lawyer must show, by records or otherwise, the hours actually and reasonably devoted to the case in view of the importance of the case to the client, the client's financial situation and instructions, and the time that a comparable lawyer would have needed.

The standard rate or hourly fee might be modified by other factors bearing on fairness, including success in the representation and whether the lawyer assumed part of the risk of the client's loss, as in a contingent-fee contract (see § 35). Reference can be made to the factors in § 34, Comment *c*. Concerning expenses and disbursements paid by the lawyer and attorney-fee awards and sanctions collected from an opposing party, the principles of § 38(3)(a) and (b) apply.

A conservative evaluation is usually appropriate in assessing fees under this Section. When a lawyer fails to agree with the client in advance on the fee to be charged, the client should not have to pay as much as some clients might have agreed to pay. A fair-value fee under this Section is thus less than the highest contractual fee that would be upheld as reasonable under § 34.

§ 40. Fees on Termination

If a client-lawyer relationship ends before the lawyer has completed the services due for a matter and the lawyer's fee has not been forfeited under § 37:

(1) a lawyer who has been discharged or withdraws may recover the lesser of the fair value of the lawyer's services as determined under § 39 and the ratable proportion of the compensation provided by any otherwise enforceable contract between lawyer and client for the services performed; except that

(2) the tribunal may allow such a lawyer to recover the ratable proportion of the compensation provided by such a contract if:

(a) the discharge or withdrawal is not attributable to misconduct of the lawyer;

(b) the lawyer has performed severable services; and

(c) allowing contractual compensation would not burden the client's choice of counsel or the client's ability to replace counsel.

TOPIC 3. FEE-COLLECTION PROCEDURES

§ 41. Fee-Collection Methods

In seeking compensation claimed from a client or former client, a lawyer may not employ collection methods forbidden by law, use confidential information (as defined in Chapter 5) when not permitted under § 65, or harass the client.

§ 42. Remedies and the Burden of Persuasion

(1) A fee dispute between a lawyer and a client may be adjudicated in any appropriate proceeding, including a suit by the lawyer to recover an unpaid fee, a suit for a refund by a client, an arbitration to which both parties consent unless applicable law renders the lawyer's consent unnecessary, or in the court's discretion a proceeding ancillary to a pending suit in which the lawyer performed the services in question.

(2) In any such proceeding the lawyer has the burden of persuading the trier of fact, when relevant, of the existence and terms of any fee contract, the making of any disclosures to the client required to render a contract enforceable, and the extent and value of the lawyer's services.

§ 43. Lawyer Liens

(1) Except as provided in Subsection (2) or by statute or rule, a lawyer does not acquire a lien entitling the lawyer to retain the client's property in the lawyer's possession in order

to secure payment of the lawyer's fees and disbursements. A lawyer may decline to deliver to a client or former client an original or copy of any document prepared by the lawyer or at the lawyer's expense if the client or former client has not paid all fees and disbursements due for the lawyer's work in preparing the document and nondelivery would not unreasonably harm the client or former client.

(2) Unless otherwise provided by statute or rule, client and lawyer may agree that the lawyer shall have a security interest in property of the client recovered for the client through the lawyer's efforts, as follows:

(a) the lawyer may contract in writing with the client for a lien on the proceeds of the representation to secure payment for the lawyer's services and disbursements in that matter;

(b) the lien becomes binding on a third party when the party has notice of the lien;

(c) the lien applies only to the amount of fees and disbursements claimed reasonably and in good faith for the lawyer's services performed in the representation; and

(d) the lawyer may not unreasonably impede the speedy and inexpensive resolution of any dispute concerning those fees and disbursements or the lien.

(3) A tribunal where an action is pending may in its discretion adjudicate any fee or other dispute concerning a lien asserted by a lawyer on property of a party to the action, provide for custody of the property, release all or part of the property to the client or lawyer, and grant such other relief as justice may require.

(4) With respect to property neither in the lawyer's possession nor recovered by the client through the lawyer's efforts, the lawyer may obtain a security interest on property of a client only as provided by other law and consistent with § § 18 and 126. Acquisition of such a security interest is a business or financial transaction with a client within the meaning of § 126.

TOPIC 4. PROPERTY AND DOCUMENTS OF CLIENTS AND OTHERS

§ 44. Safeguarding and Segregating Property

(1) A lawyer holding funds or other property of a client in connection with a representation, or such funds or other property in which a client claims an interest, must take reasonable steps to safeguard the funds or property. A similar obligation may be imposed by law on funds or other property so held and owned or claimed by a third person. In particular, the lawyer must hold such property separate from the lawyer's property, keep records of it, deposit funds in an account separate from the lawyer's own funds, identify tangible objects, and comply with related requirements imposed by regulatory authorities.

(2) Upon receiving funds or other property in a professional capacity and in which a client or third person owns or claims an interest, a lawyer must promptly notify the client or third person. The lawyer must promptly render a full accounting regarding such property upon request by the client or third person.

§ 45. Surrendering Possession of Property

(1) Except as provided in Subsection (2), a lawyer must promptly deliver, to the client or nonclient so entitled, funds or other property in the lawyer's possession belonging to a client or nonclient.

(2) A lawyer may retain possession of funds or other property of a client or nonclient if:

(a) the client or nonclient consents;

(b) the lawyer's client is entitled to the property, the lawyer appropriately possesses the property for purposes of the representation, and the client has not asked for delivery of the property;

(c) the lawyer has a valid lien on the property (see § 43);

(d) there are substantial grounds for dispute as to the person entitled to the property; or

(e) delivering the property to the client or nonclient would violate a court order or other legal obligation of the lawyer.

§ 46. Documents Relating to a Representation

(1) A lawyer must take reasonable steps to safeguard documents in the lawyer's possession relating to the representation of a client or former client.

(2) On request, a lawyer must allow a client or former client to inspect and copy any document possessed by the lawyer relating to the representation, unless substantial grounds exist to refuse.

(3) Unless a client or former client consents to nondelivery or substantial grounds exist for refusing to make delivery, a lawyer must deliver to the client or former client, at an appropriate time and in any event promptly after the representation ends, such originals and copies of other documents possessed by the lawyer relating to the representation as the client or former client reasonably needs.

(4) Notwithstanding Subsections (2) and (3), a lawyer may decline to deliver to a client or former client an original or copy of any document under circumstances permitted by § 43(1).

TOPIC 5. FEE-SPLITTING WITH A LAWYER NOT IN THE SAME FIRM

§ 47. Fee-Splitting Between Lawyers Not in the Same Firm

A division of fees between lawyers who are not in the same firm may be made only if:

(1) (a) the division is in proportion to the services performed by each lawyer or (b) by agreement with the client, the lawyers assume joint responsibility for the representation;

(2) the client is informed of and does not object to the fact of division, the terms of the division, and the participation of the lawyers involved; and

(3) the total fee is reasonable (see § 34).

CHAPTER 4. LAWYER CIVIL LIABILITY

TOPIC 1. LIABILITY FOR PROFESSIONAL NEGLIGENCE AND BREACH OF FIDUCIARY DUTY

§ 48. Professional Negligence—Elements and Defenses Generally

In addition to the other possible bases of civil liability described in § § 49, 55, and 56, a lawyer is civilly liable for professional negligence to a person to whom the lawyer owes a duty of care within the meaning of § 50 or § 51, if the lawyer fails to exercise care within the meaning of § 52 and if that failure is a legal cause of injury within the meaning of § 53, unless the lawyer has a defense within the meaning of § 54.

§ 49. Breach of Fiduciary Duty—Generally

In addition to the other possible bases of civil liability described in § § 48, 55, and 56, a lawyer is civilly liable to a client if the lawyer breaches a fiduciary duty to the client set forth in § 16(3) and if that failure is a legal cause of injury within the meaning of § 53, unless the lawyer has a defense within the meaning of § 54.

§ 50. Duty of Care to a Client

For purposes of liability under § 48, a lawyer owes a client the duty to exercise care within the meaning of § 52 in pursuing the client's lawful objectives in matters covered by the representation.

§ 51. Duty of Care to Certain Nonclients

For purposes of liability under § 48, a lawyer owes a duty to use care within the meaning of § 52 in each of the following circumstances:

(1) to a prospective client, as stated in § 15;

(2) to a nonclient when and to the extent that:

(a) the lawyer or (with the lawyer's acquiescence) the lawyer's client invites the nonclient to rely on the lawyer's opinion or provision of other legal services, and the nonclient so relies; and

(b) the nonclient is not, under applicable tort law, too remote from the lawyer to be entitled to protection;

(3) to a nonclient when and to the extent that:

(a) the lawyer knows that a client intends as one of the primary objectives of the representation that the lawyer's services benefit the nonclient;

(b) such a duty would not significantly impair the lawyer's performance of obligations to the client; and

(c) the absence of such a duty would make enforcement of those obligations to the client unlikely; and

(4) to a nonclient when and to the extent that:

(a) the lawyer's client is a trustee, guardian, executor, or fiduciary acting primarily to perform similar functions for the nonclient;

(b) the lawyer knows that appropriate action by the lawyer is necessary with respect to a matter within the scope of the representation to prevent or rectify the breach of a fiduciary duty owed by the client to the nonclient, where (i) the breach is a crime or fraud or (ii) the lawyer has assisted or is assisting the breach;

(c) the nonclient is not reasonably able to protect its rights; and

(d) such a duty would not significantly impair the performance of the lawyer's obligations to the client.

Comment:

a. Scope and cross-references. This Section sets forth the limited circumstances in which a lawyer owes a duty of care to a nonclient. . . .

As stated in § 54(1), a lawyer is not liable under this Section for any action or inaction the lawyer reasonably believed to be required by law, including a professional rule. As stated in § § 66(3) and 67(4), a lawyer who takes action or decides not to take action permitted under those Sections is not, solely by reason of such action or inaction, liable for damages.

In appropriate circumstances, a lawyer is also subject to liability to a nonclient on grounds other than negligence (see § § 48 & 56), for litigation sanctions (see § 110), and for acting without authority (see § 30). On indemnity and contribution, see § 53, Comment *i.* This Section does not consider those liabilities, such as liabilities arising under securities or similar legislation. Nor does the Section consider when a lawyer found liable to a nonclient may recover from a client under such theories as indemnity, contribution, or subrogation. On a client's liability to a nonclient arising out of a lawyer's conduct, see § 26, Comment *d.*

b. Rationale. Lawyers regularly act in disputes and transactions involving nonclients who will foreseeably be harmed by inappropriate acts of the lawyers. Holding lawyers liable for such harm is sometimes warranted. Yet it is often difficult to distinguish between harm resulting from inappropriate lawyer conduct on the one hand and, on the other hand, detriment to a nonclient resulting from a lawyer's fulfilling the proper function of helping a client through lawful means. Making lawyers liable to nonclients, moreover, could tend to discourage lawyers from vigorous representation. Hence, a duty of care to nonclients arises only in the limited circumstances described in the Section. Such a duty must be applied in light of those conflicting concerns.

c. Opposing parties. A lawyer representing a party in litigation has no duty of care to the opposing party under this Section, and hence no liability for lack of care, except in unusual situations such as when a litigant is provided an opinion letter from opposing counsel as part of a settlement (see Subsection (2) and Comment *e* hereto). Imposing such a duty could discourage vigorous representation of the lawyer's own client through fear of liability to the opponent. Moreover, the opposing party is protected by the rules and procedures of the adversary system and, usually, by counsel. In some circumstances, a lawyer's negligence will entitle an opposing party to relief other than damages, such as vacating a settlement induced by negligent misrepresentation. For a lawyer's liability to sanctions, which may include payments to an opposing party, based on certain litigation misconduct, see § 110. See also § 56, on liability for intentional torts.

Similarly, a lawyer representing a client in an arm's-length business transaction does not owe a duty of care to opposing nonclients, except in the exceptional circumstances described in this Section. On liability for aiding a client's unlawful conduct, see § 56.

Illustration:

1. Lawyer represents Plaintiff in a personal-injury action against Defendant. Because Lawyer fails to conduct an appropriate factual investigation, Lawyer includes a groundless claim in the complaint. Defendant incurs legal expenses in obtaining dismissal of this claim. Lawyer is not liable for negligence to Defendant. Lawyer may, however, be subject to litigation sanctions for having asserted a claim without proper investigation (see § 110). On claims against lawyers for wrongful use of civil proceedings and the like, see § 57(2) and Comment *d* thereto.

d. Prospective clients (Subsection (1)). When a person discusses with a lawyer the possibility of their forming a client-lawyer relationship, and even if no such relationship arises, the lawyer may be liable for failure to use reasonable care to the extent the lawyer advises or provides other legal services for the person (see § 15(2) and the Comments thereto). On duties to a former client, see § 50, Comment *c*.

e. Inviting reliance of a nonclient (Subsection (2)). When a lawyer or that lawyer's client (with the lawyer's acquiescence) invites a nonclient to rely on the lawyer's opinion or other legal services, and the nonclient reasonably does so, the lawyer owes a duty to the nonclient to use care (see § 52), unless the jurisdiction's general tort law excludes liability on the ground of remoteness. Accordingly, the nonclient has a claim against the lawyer if the lawyer's negligence with respect to the opinion or other legal services causes injury to the nonclient (see § 95). The lawyer's client typically benefits from the nonclient's reliance, for example, when providing the opinion was called for as a condition to closing under a loan agreement, and recognition of such a claim does not conflict with duties the lawyer properly owed to the client. Allowing the claim tends to benefit future clients in similar situations by giving nonclients reason to rely on similar invitations. See Restatement Second, Torts § 552. If a client is injured by a lawyer's negligence in providing opinions or services to a nonclient, for example because that renders the client liable to the nonclient as the lawyer's principal, the lawyer may have corresponding liability to the client (see § 50).

Clients or lawyers may invite nonclients to rely on a lawyer's legal opinion or services in various circumstances (see § 95). For example, a sales contract for personal property may provide that as a condition to closing the seller's lawyer will provide the buyer with an opinion letter regarding the absence of liens on the property being sold (see id., Illustrations 1 & 2; § 52, Illustration 2). A nonclient may require such an opinion letter as a condition for engaging in a transaction with a lawyer's client. A lawyer's opinion may state the results of a lawyer's investigation and analysis of facts as well as the lawyer's legal conclusions (see § 95). On when a lawyer may properly decline to provide an opinion and on a lawyer's duty when a client insists on nondisclosure, see § 95, Comment *d*. A lawyer's acquiescence in use of the lawyer's opinion may be manifested either before or after the lawyer renders it.

In some circumstances, reliance by unspecified persons may be expected, as when a lawyer for a borrower writes an opinion letter to the original lender in a bank credit transaction knowing that the letter will be used to solicit other lenders to become participants in syndication of the loan. Whether a subsequent syndication participant can recover for the lawyer's negligence in providing such an opinion letter depends on what, if anything, the letter says about reliance and whether the jurisdiction in question, as a matter of general tort law, adheres to the limitations on duty of Restatement Second, Torts § 552(2) or those of Ultramares Corp. v. Touche, 174 N.E. 441 (N.Y.1931), or has rejected such limitations. To account for such differences in general tort law, Subsection (2) refers to applicable law excluding liability to persons too remote from the lawyer.

When a lawyer owes a duty to a nonclient under this Section, whether the nonclient's cause of action may be asserted in contract or in tort should be determined by reference to the applicable law of professional liability generally. The cause of action ordinarily is in substance identical to a claim for negligent misrepresentation and is subject to rules such as those concerning proof of materiality and reliance (see Restatement Second, Torts § § 552-554). For liability under securities legislation, see § 56, Comment *i*. Whether the representations are actionable may be affected by the duties of disclosure, if any, that the client owes the nonclient (see § 98, Comment *e*). In the absence of such duties of disclosure, the duty of a lawyer providing an opinion is ordinarily limited to using care to avoid making or adopting misrepresentations. On a lawyer's obligations in furnishing an opinion, see § 95, Comment *c*. On intentionally making or assisting misrepresentations, see § 56, Comment *f*, and § 98.

A lawyer may avoid liability to nonclients under Subsection (2) by making clear that an opinion or representation is directed only to a client and should not be relied on by others. Likewise, a lawyer may limit or avoid liability under Subsection (2) by qualifying a representation, for example by making clear through limiting or disclaiming language in an opinion letter that the lawyer is relying on facts provided by the client without independent investigation by the lawyer (assuming that the lawyer does not know the facts provided by the client to be false, in which case the lawyer would be liable for misrepresentation). The effectiveness of a limitation or disclaimer depends on whether it was reasonable in the circumstances to conclude that those provided with the opinion would receive the limitation or disclaimer and understand its import. The relevant circumstances include customary practices known to the recipient concerning the construction of opinions and whether the recipient is represented by counsel or a similarly experienced agent.

When a nonclient is invited to rely on a lawyer's legal services, other than the lawyer's opinion, the analysis is similar. For example, if the seller's lawyer at a real-estate closing offers to record the deed for the buyer, the lawyer is subject to liability to the buyer for negligence in doing so, even if the buyer did not thereby become a client of the lawyer. When a nonclient is invited to rely on a lawyer's nonlegal services, the lawyer's duty of care is determined by the law applicable to providers of the services in question.

f. A nonclient enforcing a lawyer's duties to a client (Subsection (3)). When a lawyer knows (see Comment *h* hereto) that a client intends a lawyer's services to benefit a third person who is not a client, allowing the nonclient to recover from the lawyer for negligence in performing those services may promote the lawyer's loyal and effective pursuit of the client's objectives. The nonclient, moreover, may be the only person likely to enforce the lawyer's duty to the client, for example because the client has died.

A nonclient's claim under Subsection (3) is recognized only when doing so will both implement the client's intent and serve to fulfill the lawyer's obligations to the client without impairing performance of those obligations in the circumstances of the representation. A duty to a third person hence exists only when the client intends to benefit the third person as one of the primary objectives of the representation, as in the Illustrations below and in Comment *g* hereto. Without adequate evidence of such an intent, upholding a third person's claim could expose lawyers to liability for following a client's instructions in circumstances where it would be difficult to prove what those instructions had been. Threat of such liability would tend to discourage lawyers from following client instructions adversely affecting third persons. When the claim is that the lawyer failed to exercise care in preparing a document, such as a will, for which the law imposes formal or evidentiary requirements, the third person must prove the client's intent by evidence that would satisfy the burden of proof applicable to construction or reformation (as the case may be) of the document. See Restatement Third, Property (Donative Transfers) § § 11.2 and 12.1 (Tentative Draft No. 1, 1995) (preponderance of evidence to resolve ambiguity in donative instruments; clear and convincing evidence to reform such instruments).

Subsections (3) and (4), although related in their justifications, differ in application. In situations falling under Subsection (3), the client need not owe any preexisting duty to the intended beneficiary. The scope of the intended benefit depends on the client's intent and the lawyer's undertaking. On the other hand, the duty under Subsection (4) typically arises when a lawyer helps a client-fiduciary to carry out a duty of the fiduciary to a beneficiary recognized and defined by trust or other law.

Illustrations:

2. Client retains Lawyer to prepare and help in the drafting and execution of a will leaving Client's estate to Nonclient. Lawyer prepares the will naming Nonclient as the sole beneficiary, but negligently arranges for Client to sign it before an inadequate number of witnesses. Client's intent to benefit Nonclient thus appears on the face of the will executed by Client. After Client dies, the will is held

ineffective due to the lack of witnesses, and Nonclient is thereby harmed. Lawyer is subject to liability to Nonclient for negligence in drafting and supervising execution of the will.

3. Same facts as in Illustration 2, except that Lawyer arranges for Client to sign the will before the proper number of witnesses, but Nonclient later alleges that Lawyer negligently wrote the will to name someone other than Nonclient as the legatee. Client's intent to benefit Nonclient thus does not appear on the face of the will. Nonclient can establish the existence of a duty from Lawyer to Nonclient only by producing clear and convincing evidence that Client communicated to Lawyer Client's intent that Nonclient be the legatee. If Lawyer is held liable to Nonclient in situations such as this and the preceding Illustration, applicable principles of law may provide that Lawyer may recover from their unintended recipients the estate assets that should have gone to Nonclient.

4. Same facts as in Illustration 2, except that Lawyer arranges for Client to sign the will before the proper number of witnesses. After Client's death, Heir has the will set aside on the ground that Client was incompetent and then sues Lawyer for expenses imposed on Heir by the will, alleging that Lawyer negligently assisted Client to execute a will despite Client's incompetence. Lawyer is not subject to liability to Heir for negligence. Recognizing a duty by lawyers to heirs to use care in not assisting incompetent clients to execute wills would impair performance of lawyers' duty to assist clients even when the clients' competence might later be challenged. Whether Lawyer is liable to Client's estate or personal representative (due to privity with the lawyer) is beyond the scope of this Restatement. On a lawyer's obligations to a client with diminished capacity, see § 24.

g. A liability insurer's claim for professional negligence. Under Subsection (3), a lawyer designated by an insurer to defend an insured owes a duty of care to the insurer with respect to matters as to which the interests of the insurer and insured are not in conflict, whether or not the insurer is held to be a co-client of the lawyer (see § 134, Comment *f*). For example, if the lawyer negligently fails to oppose a motion for summary judgment against the insured and the insurer must pay the resulting adverse judgment, the insurer has a claim against the lawyer for any proximately caused loss. In such circumstances, the insured and insurer, under the insurance contract, both have a reasonable expectation that the lawyer's services will benefit both insured and insurer. Recognizing that the lawyer owes a duty to the insurer promotes enforcement of the lawyer's obligations to the insured. However, such a duty does not arise when it would significantly impair, in the circumstances of the representation, the lawyer's performance of obligations to the insured. For example, if the lawyer recommends acceptance of a settlement offer just below the policy limits and the insurer accepts the offer, the insurer may not later seek to recover from the lawyer on a claim that a competent lawyer in the circumstances would have advised that the offer be rejected. Allowing recovery in such circumstances would give the lawyer an interest in recommending rejection of a settlement offer beneficial to the insured in order to escape possible liability to the insurer.

h. Duty based on knowledge of a breach of fiduciary duty owed by a client (Subsection (4)). A lawyer representing a client in the client's capacity as a fiduciary (as opposed to the client's personal capacity) may in some circumstances be liable to a beneficiary for a failure to use care to protect the beneficiary. The duty should be recognized only when the requirements of Subsection (4) are met and when action by the lawyer would not violate applicable professional rules (see § 54(1)). The duty arises from the fact that a fiduciary has obligations to the beneficiary that go beyond fair dealing at arm's length. A lawyer is usually so situated as to have special opportunity to observe whether the fiduciary is complying with those obligations. Because fiduciaries are generally obliged to pursue the interests of their beneficiaries, the duty does not subject the lawyer to conflicting or inconsistent duties. A lawyer who knowingly assists a client to violate the client's fiduciary duties is civilly liable, as would be a nonlawyer (see Restatement Second, Trusts § 326). Moreover, to the extent that the lawyer has assisted in creating a risk of injury, it is appropriate to impose a preventive and corrective duty on the lawyer (cf. Restatement Second, Torts § 321).

The duty recognized by Subsection (4) is limited to lawyers representing only a limited category of the persons described as fiduciaries—trustees, executors, guardians, and other fiduciaries acting primarily to fulfill similar functions. Fiduciary responsibility, imposing strict duties to protect specific property for the benefit of specific, designated persons, is the chief end of such relationships. The lawyer is hence less likely to encounter conflicting considerations arising from other responsibilities of the fiduciary-client than are entailed in other relationships in which fiduciary duty is only a part of a broader role. Thus, Subsection (4) does not apply when the client is a partner in a business partnership, a corporate officer or director, or a controlling stockholder.

The scope of a client's fiduciary duties is delimited by the law governing the relationship in question (see, e.g., Restatement Second, Trusts § § 169-185). Whether and when such law allows a beneficiary to assert derivatively the claim of a trust or other entity against a lawyer is beyond the scope of this Restatement (see Restatement Second, Trusts § 282). Even when a relationship is fiduciary, not all the attendant duties are fiduciary. Thus, violations of duties of loyalty by a fiduciary are ordinarily considered breaches of fiduciary duty, while violations of duties of care are not.

Sometimes a lawyer represents both a fiduciary and the fiduciary's beneficiary and thus may be liable to the beneficiary as a client under § 50 and may incur obligations concerning conflict of interests (see § § 130-131). A lawyer who represents only the fiduciary may avoid such liability by making clear to the beneficiary that the lawyer represents the fiduciary rather than the beneficiary (compare § 103, Comment e).

The duty recognized by Subsection (4) arises only when the lawyer knows that appropriate action by the lawyer is necessary to prevent or mitigate a breach of the client's fiduciary duty. As used in this Subsection and Subsection (3) (see Comment f), "know" is the equivalent of the same term defined in ABA Model Rules of Professional Conduct, Terminology ¶ [5] (1983) ("... 'Knows' denotes actual knowledge of the fact in question. A person's knowledge may be inferred from circumstances."). The concept is functionally the same as the terminology "has reason to know" as defined in Restatement Second, Torts § 12(1) (actor has reason to know when actor "has information from which a person of reasonable intelligence or of the superior intelligence of the actor would infer that the fact in question exists, or that such person would govern his conduct upon the assumption that such facts exists."). The "know" terminology should not be confused with "should know" (see id. § 12(2)). As used in Subsection (3) and (4) "knows" neither assumes nor requires a duty of inquiry.

Generally, a lawyer must follow instruction of the client-fiduciary (see § 21(2) hereto) and may assume in the absence of contrary information that the fiduciary is complying with the law. The duty stated in Subsection (4) applies only to breaches constituting crime or fraud, as determined by applicable law and subject to the limitations set out in § 67, Comment d, and § 82, Comment d, or those in which the lawyer has assisted or is assisting the fiduciary. A lawyer assists fiduciary breaches, for example, by preparing documents needed to accomplish the fiduciary's wrongful conduct or assisting the fiduciary to conceal such conduct. On the other hand, a lawyer subsequently consulted by a fiduciary to deal with the consequences of a breach of fiduciary duty committed before the consultation began is under no duty to inform the beneficiary of the breach or otherwise to act to rectify it. Such a duty would prevent a person serving as fiduciary from obtaining the effective assistance of counsel with respect to such a past breach.

Liability under Subsection (4) exists only when the beneficiary of the client's fiduciary duty is not reasonably able to protect its rights. That would be so, for example, when the fiduciary client is a guardian for a beneficiary unable (for reasons of youth or incapacity) to manage his or her own affairs. By contrast, for example, a beneficiary of a family voting trust who is in business and has access to the relevant information has no similar need of protection by the trustee's lawyer. In any event, whether or not there is liability under this Section, a lawyer may be liable to a nonclient as stated in § 56.

A lawyer owes no duty to a beneficiary if recognizing such duty would create conflicting or inconsistent duties that might significantly impair the lawyer's performance of obligations to the lawyer's client in the circumstances of the representation. Such impairment might occur, for example, if the lawyer were subject to liability for assisting the fiduciary in an open dispute with a beneficiary or for assisting the fiduciary in exercise of its judgment that would benefit one beneficiary at the expense of another. For similar reasons, a lawyer is not subject to liability to a beneficiary under Subsection (4) for representing the fiduciary in a dispute or negotiation with the beneficiary with respect to a matter affecting the fiduciary's interests.

Under Subsection (4) a lawyer is not liable for failing to take action that the lawyer reasonably believes to be forbidden by professional rules (see § 54(1)). Thus, a lawyer is not liable for failing to disclose confidences when the lawyer reasonably believes that disclosure is forbidden. For example, a lawyer is under no duty to disclose a prospective breach in a jurisdiction that allows disclosure only regarding a crime or fraud threatening imminent death or substantial bodily harm. However, liability could result from failing to attempt to prevent the breach of fiduciary duty through means that do not entail disclosure. In any event, a lawyer's duty under this Section requires only the care set forth in § 52.

Illustrations:

5. Lawyer represents Client in Client's capacity as trustee of an express trust for the benefit of Beneficiary. Client tells Lawyer that Client proposes to transfer trust funds into Client's own account, in circumstances that would constitute embezzlement. Lawyer informs Client that the transfer would

be criminal, but Client nevertheless makes the transfer, as Lawyer then knows. Lawyer takes no steps to prevent or rectify the consequences, for example by warning Beneficiary or informing the court to which Client as trustee must make an annual accounting. The jurisdiction's professional rules do not forbid such disclosures (see § 67). Client likewise makes no disclosure. The funds are lost, to the harm of Beneficiary. Lawyer is subject to liability to Beneficiary under this Section.

6. Same facts as in Illustration 5, except that Client asserts to Lawyer that the account to which Client proposes to transfer trust funds is the trust's account. Even though lawyer could have exercised diligence and thereby discovered this to be false, Lawyer does not do so. Lawyer is not liable to the harmed Beneficiary. Lawyer did not owe Beneficiary a duty to use care because Lawyer did not know (although further investigation would have revealed) that appropriate action was necessary to prevent a breach of fiduciary duty by Client.

7. Same facts as in Illustration 5, except that Client proposes to invest trust funds in a way that would be unlawful, but would not constitute a crime or fraud under applicable law. Lawyer's services are not used in consummating the investment. Lawyer does nothing to discourage the investment. Lawyer is not subject to liability to Beneficiary under this Section.

§ 52. The Standard of Care

(1) **For purposes of liability under § § 48 and 49, a lawyer who owes a duty of care must exercise the competence and diligence normally exercised by lawyers in similar circumstances.**

(2) **Proof of a violation of a rule or statute regulating the conduct of lawyers:**

(a) **does not give rise to an implied cause of action for professional negligence or breach of fiduciary duty;**

(b) **does not preclude other proof concerning the duty of care in Subsection (1) or the fiduciary duty; and**

(c) **may be considered by a trier of fact as an aid in understanding and applying the standard of Subsection (1) or § 49 to the extent that (i) the rule or statute was designed for the protection of persons in the position of the claimant and (ii) proof of the content and construction of such a rule or statute is relevant to the claimant's claim.**

§ 53. Causation and Damages

A lawyer is liable under § 48 or § 49 only if the lawyer's breach of a duty of care or breach of fiduciary duty was a legal cause of injury, as determined under generally applicable principles of causation and damages.

Comment:

b. Action by a civil litigant: loss of a judgment. In a lawyer-negligence or fiduciary-breach action brought by one who was the plaintiff in a former and unsuccessful civil action, the plaintiff usually seeks to recover as damages the damages that would have been recovered in the previous action or the additional amount that would have been recovered but for the defendant's misconduct. To do so, the plaintiff must prove by a preponderance of the evidence that, but for the defendant lawyer's misconduct, the plaintiff would have obtained a more favorable judgment in the previous action. The plaintiff must thus prevail in a "trial within a trial." All the issues that would have been litigated in the previous action are litigated between the plaintiff and the plaintiff's former lawyer, with the latter taking the place and bearing the burdens that properly would have fallen on the defendant in the original action. Similarly, the plaintiff bears the burden the plaintiff would have borne in the original trial; in considering whether the plaintiff has carried that burden, however, the trier of fact may consider whether the defendant lawyer's misconduct has made it more difficult for the plaintiff to prove what would have been the result in the original trial. (On a lawyer's right to disclose client confidences when reasonably necessary in defending against a claim, see § § 64 and 80.) Similar principles apply when a former civil defendant contends that, but for the misconduct of the defendant's former lawyer, the defendant would have secured a better result at trial.

What would have been the result of a previous trial presenting issues of fact normally is an issue for the factfinder in the negligence or fiduciary-breach action. What would have been the result of an appeal in the previous action is, however, an issue of law to be decided by the judge in the negligence or fiduciary-breach action. The judges or jurors who heard or would have heard the original trial or appeal may not be called as witnesses to testify as to how they would have ruled. That would constitute an inappropriate burden on the judiciary and jurors and an unwise personalization of the issue of how a reasonable judge or jury would have ruled.

A plaintiff may show that the defendant's negligence or fiduciary breach caused injury other than the loss of a judgment. For example, a plaintiff may contend that, in a previous action, the plaintiff would have obtained a settlement but for the malpractice of the lawyer who then represented the plaintiff. A plaintiff might contend that the defendant in the previous action made a settlement offer, that the plaintiff's then lawyer negligently failed to inform plaintiff of the offer (see § 20(3)), and that, if informed, plaintiff would have accepted the offer. If the plaintiff can prove this, the plaintiff can recover the difference between what the claimant would have received under the settlement offer and the amount, if any, the claimant in fact received through later settlement or judgment. Similarly, in appropriate circumstances, a plaintiff who can establish that the negligence or fiduciary breach of the plaintiff's former lawyer deprived the plaintiff of a substantial chance of prevailing and that, due to that misconduct, the results of a previous trial cannot be reconstructed, may recover for the loss of that chance in jurisdictions recognizing such a theory of recovery in professional-malpractice cases generally.

The plaintiff in a previous civil action may recover without proving the results of a trial if the party claims damages other than loss of a judgment. For example, a lawyer who negligently discloses a client's trade secret during litigation might be liable for harm to the client's business caused by the disclosure.

Even when a plaintiff would have recovered through trial or settlement in a previous civil action, recovery in the negligence or fiduciary-breach action of what would have been the judgment or settlement in the previous action is precluded in some circumstances. Thus, the lawyer's misconduct will not be the legal cause of loss to the extent that the defendant lawyer can show that the judgment or settlement would have been uncollectible, for example because the previous defendant was insolvent and uninsured. The defendant lawyer bears the burden of coming forward with evidence that this was so. Placement of this burden on the defending lawyer is appropriate because most civil judgments are collectible and because the defendant lawyer was the one who undertook to seek the judgment that the lawyer now calls worthless. The burden of persuading the jury as to collectibility remains upon the plaintiff.

c. Action by a civil litigant: attorney fees that would have been due. When it is shown that a plaintiff would have prevailed in the former civil action but for the lawyer's legal fault, it might be thought that—applying strict causation principles—the damages to be recovered in the legal-malpractice action should be reduced by the fee due the lawyer in the former matter. That is, the plaintiff has lost the net amount recovered after paying that attorney fee. Yet if the net amount were all the plaintiff could recover in the malpractice action, the defendant lawyer would in effect be credited with a fee that the lawyer never earned, and the plaintiff would have to pay two lawyers (the defendant lawyer and the plaintiff's lawyer in the malpractice action) to recover one judgment.

Denial of a fee deduction hence may be an appropriate sanction for the defendant lawyer's misconduct: to the extent that the lawyer defendant did not earn a fee due to the lawyer's misconduct, no such fee may be deducted in calculating the recovery in the malpractice action. The same principles apply to a legal-malpractice plaintiff who was a defendant in a previous civil action. The appropriateness and extent of disallowing deduction of the fee are determined under the standards of § 37 governing fee forfeiture. In some circumstances, those standards allow the lawyer to be credited with fees for services that benefited the client. See § 37, Comment *e.*

d. Action by a criminal defendant. A convicted criminal defendant suing for malpractice must prove both that the lawyer failed to act properly and that, but for that failure, the result would have been different, for example because a double-jeopardy defense would have prevented conviction. Although most jurisdictions addressing the issue have stricter rules, under this Section it is not necessary to prove that the convicted defendant was in fact innocent. As required by most jurisdictions addressing the issue, a convicted defendant seeking damages for malpractice causing a conviction must have had that conviction set aside when process for that relief on the grounds asserted in the malpractice action is available.

A judgment in a postconviction proceeding is binding in the malpractice action to the extent provided by the law of judgments. That law prevents a convicted defendant from relitigating an issue decided in a postconviction proceeding after a full and fair opportunity to litigate, even though the lawyer sued was not a party to that proceeding and is hence not bound by any decision favorable to the defendant. See Restatement Second, Judgments § § 27-29. Some jurisdictions hold public defenders immune from malpractice suits.

g. Damages for emotional distress. General principles applicable to the recovery of damages for emotional distress apply to legal-malpractice actions. In general, such damages are inappropriate in types of cases in which emotional distress is unforeseeable. Thus, emotional-distress damages are ordinarily not recoverable when a lawyer's misconduct causes the client to lose profits from a commercial transaction, but are ordinarily recoverable when misconduct causes a client's imprisonment. The law in some jurisdictions permits recovery for emotional-distress damages only when the defendant lawyer's conduct was clearly culpable (see also § 56, Comment g).

h. Punitive damages. Whether punitive damages are recoverable in a legal-malpractice action depends on the jurisdiction's generally applicable law. Punitive damages are generally permitted only on a showing of intentional or reckless misconduct by a defendant.

A few decisions allow a plaintiff to recover from a lawyer punitive damages that would have been recovered from the defendant in an underlying action but for the lawyer's misconduct. However, such recovery is not required by the punitive and deterrent purposes of punitive damages. Collecting punitive damages from the lawyer will neither punish nor deter the original tortfeasor and calls for a speculative reconstruction of a hypothetical jury's reaction.

§ 54. Defenses; Prospective Liability Waiver; Settlement with a Client

(1) Except as otherwise provided in this Section, liability under § § 48 and 49 is subject to the defenses available under generally applicable principles of law governing respectively actions for professional negligence and breach of fiduciary duty. A lawyer is not liable under § 48 or § 49 for any action or inaction the lawyer reasonably believed to be required by law, including a professional rule.

(2) An agreement prospectively limiting a lawyer's liability to a client for malpractice is unenforceable.

(3) The client or former client may rescind an agreement settling a claim by the client or former client against the person's lawyer if:

(a) the client or former client was subjected to improper pressure by the lawyer in reaching the settlement; or

(b) (i) the client or former client was not independently represented in negotiating the settlement, and (ii) the settlement was not fair and reasonable to the client or former client.

(4) For purposes of professional discipline, a lawyer may not:

(a) make an agreement prospectively limiting the lawyer's liability to a client for malpractice; or

(b) settle a claim for such liability with an unrepresented client or former client without first advising that person in writing that independent representation is appropriate in connection therewith.

TOPIC 2. OTHER CIVIL LIABILITY

§ 55. Civil Remedies of a Client Other Than for Malpractice

(1) A lawyer is subject to liability to a client for injury caused by breach of contract in the circumstances and to the extent provided by contract law.

(2) A client is entitled to restitutionary, injunctive, or declaratory remedies against a lawyer in the circumstances and to the extent provided by generally applicable law governing such remedies.

§ 56. Liability to a Client or Nonclient Under General Law

Except as provided in § 57 and in addition to liability under § § 48-55, a lawyer is subject to liability to a client or nonclient when a nonlawyer would be in similar circumstances.

§ 57. Nonclient Claims—Certain Defenses and Exceptions to Liability

(1) In addition to other absolute or conditional privileges, a lawyer is absolutely privileged to publish matter concerning a nonclient if:

(a) the publication occurs in communications preliminary to a reasonably anticipated proceeding before a tribunal or in the institution or during the course and as a part of such a proceeding;

(b) the lawyer participates as counsel in that proceeding; and

(c) the matter is published to a person who may be involved in the proceeding, and the publication has some relation to the proceeding.

(2) A lawyer representing a client in a civil proceeding or procuring the institution of criminal proceedings by a client is not liable to a nonclient for wrongful use of civil proceedings or for malicious prosecution if the lawyer has probable cause for acting, or if the lawyer acts primarily to help the client obtain a proper adjudication of the client's claim in that proceeding.

(3) A lawyer who advises or assists a client to make or break a contract, to enter or dissolve a legal relationship, or to enter or not enter a contractual relation, is not liable to a nonclient for interference with contract or with prospective contractual relations or with a legal relationship, if the lawyer acts to advance the client's objectives without using wrongful means.

TOPIC 3. VICARIOUS LIABILITY

§ 58. Vicarious Liability

(1) A law firm is subject to civil liability for injury legally caused to a person by any wrongful act or omission of any principal or employee of the firm who was acting in the ordinary course of the firm's business or with actual or apparent authority.

(2) Each of the principals of a law firm organized as a general partnership without limited liability is liable jointly and severally with the firm.

(3) A principal of a law firm organized other than as a general partnership without limited liability as authorized by law is vicariously liable for the acts of another principal or employee of the firm to the extent provided by law.

CHAPTER 5. CONFIDENTIAL CLIENT INFORMATION

TOPIC 1. CONFIDENTIALITY RESPONSIBILITIES OF LAWYERS

§ 59. Definition of "Confidential Client Information"

Confidential client information consists of information relating to representation of a client, other than information that is generally known.

§ 60. A Lawyer's Duty to Safeguard Confidential Client Information

(1) Except as provided in § § 61-67, during and after representation of a client:

(a) the lawyer may not use or disclose confidential client information as defined in § 59 if there is a reasonable prospect that doing so will adversely affect a material interest of the client or if the client has instructed the lawyer not to use or disclose such information;

(b) the lawyer must take steps reasonable in the circumstances to protect confidential client information against impermissible use or disclosure by the lawyer's associates or agents that may adversely affect a material interest of the client or otherwise than as instructed by the client.

(2) Except as stated in § 62, a lawyer who uses confidential information of a client for

the lawyer's pecuniary gain other than in the practice of law must account to the client for any profits made.

Comment:

l. Use or disclosure of confidential information of co-clients. A lawyer may represent two or more clients in the same matter as co-clients either when there is no conflict of interest between them (see § 121) or when a conflict exists but the co-clients have adequately consented (see § 122). When a conflict of interest exists, as part of the process of obtaining consent, the lawyer is required to inform each co-client of the effect of joint representation upon disclosure of confidential information (see § 122, Comment *c(i)*), including both that all material information will be shared with each co-client during the course of the representation and that a communicating co-client will be unable to assert the attorney-client privilege against the other in the event of later adverse proceedings between them (see § 75).

Sharing of information among the co-clients with respect to the matter involved in the representation is normal and typically expected. As between the co-clients, in many such relationships each co-client is under a fiduciary duty to share all information material to the co-clients' joint enterprise. Such is the law, for example, with respect to members of a partnership. Limitation of the attorney-client privilege as applied to communications of co-clients is based on an assumption that each intends that his or her communications with the lawyer will be shared with the other co-clients but otherwise kept in confidence (see § 75, Comment *d*). Moreover, the common lawyer is required to keep each of the co-clients informed of all information reasonably necessary for the co-client to make decisions in connection with the matter (see § 20). The lawyer's duty extends to communicating information to other co-clients that is adverse to a co-client, whether learned from the lawyer's own investigation or learned in confidence from that co-client.

Co-clients may understand from the circumstances those obligations on the part of the lawyer and their own obligations, or they may explicitly agree to share information. Co-clients can also explicitly agree that the lawyer is not to share certain information, such as described categories of proprietary, financial, or similar information with one or more other co-clients (see § 75, Comment *d*). A lawyer must honor such agreements. If one co-client threatens physical harm or other types of crimes or fraud against the other, an exception to the lawyer's duty of confidentiality may apply (see § § 66-67).

There is little case authority on the responsibilities of a lawyer when, in the absence of an agreement among the co-clients to restrict sharing of information, one co-client provides to the lawyer material information with the direction that it not be communicated to another co-client. The communicating co-client's expectation that the information be withheld from the other co-client may be manifest from the circumstances, particularly when the communication is clearly antagonistic to the interests of the affected co-client. The lawyer thus confronts a dilemma. If the information is material to the other co-client, failure to communicate it would compromise the lawyer's duties of loyalty, diligence (see § 16(1) & (2)), and communication (see § 20) to that client. On the other hand, sharing the communication with the affected co-client would compromise the communicating client's hope of confidentiality and risks impairing that client's trust in the lawyer.

Such circumstances create a conflict of interest among the co-clients (see § 121 & § 122, Comment *h*). The lawyer cannot continue in the representation without compromising either the duty of communication to the affected co-client or the expectation of confidentiality on the part of the communicating co-client. Moreover, continuing the joint representation without making disclosure may mislead the affected client or otherwise involve the lawyer in assisting the communicating client in a breach of fiduciary duty or other misconduct. Accordingly, the lawyer is required to withdraw unless the communicating client can be persuaded to permit sharing of the communication (see § 32(2)(a)). Following withdrawal, the lawyer may not, without consent of both, represent either co-client adversely to the other with respect to the same or a substantially related matter (see § 121, Comment *e(i)*).

In the course of withdrawal, the lawyer has discretion to warn the affected co-client that a matter seriously and adversely affecting that person's interests has come to light, which the other co-client refuses to permit the lawyer to disclose. Beyond such a limited warning, the lawyer, after consideration of all relevant circumstances, has the further discretion to inform the affected co-client of the specific communication if, in the lawyer's reasonable judgment, the immediacy and magnitude of the risk to the affected co-client outweigh the interest of the communicating client in continued secrecy. In making such determinations, the lawyer may take into account superior legal interests of the lawyer or of affected third persons, such as an interest implicated by a threat of physical harm to the lawyer or another person. See also § 66.

Illustration:

2. Lawyer has been retained by Husband and Wife to prepare wills pursuant to an arrangement under which each spouse agrees to leave most of their property to the other (compare § 130, Comment c, Illustrations 1-3). Shortly after the wills are executed, Husband (unknown to Wife) asks Lawyer to prepare an inter vivos trust for an illegitimate child whose existence Husband has kept secret from Wife for many years and about whom Husband had not previously informed Lawyer. Husband states that Wife would be distraught at learning of Husband's infidelity and of Husband's years of silence and that disclosure of the information could destroy their marriage. Husband directs Lawyer not to inform Wife. The inter vivos trust that Husband proposes to create would not materially affect Wife's own estate plan or her expected receipt of property under Husband's will, because Husband proposes to use property designated in Husband's will for a personally favored charity. In view of the lack of material effect on Wife, Lawyer may assist Husband to establish and fund the inter vivos trust and refrain from disclosing Husband's information to Wife.

3. Same facts as Illustration 2, except that Husband's proposed inter vivos trust would significantly deplete Husband's estate, to Wife's material detriment and in frustration of the Spouses' intended testamentary arrangements. If Husband refuses to inform Wife or to permit Lawyer to do so, Lawyer must withdraw from representing both Husband and Wife. In the light of all relevant circumstances, Lawyer may exercise discretion whether to inform Wife either that circumstances, which Lawyer has been asked not to reveal, indicate that she should revoke her recent will or to inform Wife of some or all the details of the information that Husband has recently provided so that Wife may protect her interests. Alternatively, Lawyer may inform Wife only that Lawyer is withdrawing because Husband will not permit disclosure of relevant information.

4. Lawyer represents both A and B in forming a business. Before the business is completely formed, A discloses to Lawyer that he has been convicted of defrauding business associates on two recent occasions. The circumstances of the communication from A are such that Lawyer reasonably infers that A believes that B is unaware of that information and does not want it provided to B. Lawyer reasonably believes that B would call off the arrangement with A if B were made aware of the information. Lawyer must first attempt to persuade A either to inform B directly or to permit Lawyer to inform B of the information. Failing that, Lawyer must withdraw from representing both A and B. In doing so, Lawyer has discretion to warn B that Lawyer has learned in confidence information indicating that B is at significant risk in carrying through with the business arrangement, but that A will not permit Lawyer to disclose that information to B. On the other hand, even if the circumstances do not warrant invoking § 67, Lawyer has the further discretion to inform B of the specific nature of A's communication to B if Lawyer reasonably believes this necessary to protect B's interests in view of the immediacy and magnitude of the threat that Lawyer perceives posed to B.

Even if the co-clients have agreed that the lawyer will keep certain categories of information confidential from one or more other co-clients, in some circumstances it might be evident to the lawyer that the uninformed co-client would not have agreed to nondisclosure had that co-client been aware of the nature of the adverse information. For example, a lawyer's examination of confidential financial information, agreed not to be shown to another co-client to reduce antitrust concerns, could show in fact, contrary to all exterior indications, that the disclosing co-client is insolvent. In view of the co-client's agreement, the lawyer must honor the commitment of confidentiality and not inform the other client, subject to the exceptions described in § 67. The lawyer must, however, withdraw if failure to reveal would mislead the affected client, involve the lawyer in assisting the communicating client in a course of fraud, breach of fiduciary duty, or other unlawful activity, or, as would be true in most such instances, involve the lawyer in representing conflicting interests.

§ 61. Using or Disclosing Information to Advance Client Interests

A lawyer may use or disclose confidential client information when the lawyer reasonably believes that doing so will advance the interests of the client in the representation.

§ 62. Using or Disclosing Information with Client Consent

A lawyer may use or disclose confidential client information when the client consents

after being adequately informed concerning the use or disclosure.

§ 63. Using or Disclosing Information When Required by Law

A lawyer may use or disclose confidential client information when required by law, after the lawyer takes reasonably appropriate steps to assert that the information is privileged or otherwise protected against disclosure.

§ 64. Using or Disclosing Information in a Lawyer's Self-Defense

A lawyer may use or disclose confidential client information when and to the extent that the lawyer reasonably believes necessary to defend the lawyer or the lawyer's associate or agent against a charge or threatened charge by any person that the lawyer or such associate or agent acted wrongfully in the course of representing a client.

§ 65. Using or Disclosing Information in a Compensation Dispute

A lawyer may use or disclose confidential client information when and to the extent that the lawyer reasonably believes necessary to permit the lawyer to resolve a dispute with the client concerning compensation or reimbursement that the lawyer reasonably claims the client owes the lawyer.

§ 66. Using or Disclosing Information to Prevent Death or Serious Bodily Harm

(1) A lawyer may use or disclose confidential client information when the lawyer reasonably believes that its use or disclosure is necessary to prevent reasonably certain death or serious bodily harm to a person.

(2) Before using or disclosing information under this Section, the lawyer must, if feasible, make a good-faith effort to persuade the client not to act. If the client or another person has already acted, the lawyer must, if feasible, advise the client to warn the victim or to take other action to prevent the harm and advise the client of the lawyer's ability to use or disclose information as provided in this Section and the consequences thereof.

(3) A lawyer who takes action or decides not to take action permitted under this Section is not, solely by reason of such action or inaction, subject to professional discipline, liable for damages to the lawyer's client or any third person, or barred from recovery against a client or third person.

Comment:

b. Rationale. The exception recognized by this Section is based on the overriding value of life and physical integrity. Threats to life or body encompassed within this Section may be the product of an act of the client or a nonclient and may be created by wrongful acts, by accident, or by circumstances. See Comment *c.* In all such events, the ultimate threat is the same, and its existence suffices to warrant a lawyer's taking corrective steps to prevent the threatened death or serious bodily harm. . . .

c. Use or disclosure to prevent death or serious bodily harm. Subsection (1) applies whenever a lawyer has a reasonable basis for believing that use or disclosure of a client's confidential information is necessary to prevent reasonably certain death or serious bodily harm to a person. On what constitutes reasonable belief, see § 67, Comment *h.* A threat within Subsection (1) need not be the product of a client act; an act of a nonclient threatening life or personal safety is also included, as is a threat created through accident or natural causes. It follows that if such a threat is created by a person, whether a client or a nonclient, there is no requirement that the act be criminal or otherwise unlawful.

Illustration:

1. Lawyer is representing Defendant, a responding party in a suit by Plaintiff seeking damages for personal injuries arising out of a vehicle accident. Lawyer asks Doctor, as a consulting expert, to conduct an evaluation of medical evidence submitted by Plaintiff in support of a claim of personal injury. Following the examination, Doctor reports to Lawyer that Plaintiff has an undiagnosed aortal

aneurism, which is serious and life-threatening but which can readily be repaired through surgery. Lawyer knows from work on the case that Plaintiff, as well as Plaintiff's treating physician, lawyer, and medical experts, are unaware of the condition. Lawyer is also aware that, if notified of the condition, Plaintiff will likely claim significant additional damages following corrective surgery. Despite Lawyer's urging, Defendant refuses to permit revelation of the condition to Plaintiff. Under this Section, Lawyer has discretion under Subsection (1) to reveal the condition to Plaintiff.

So long as the predicate threat to life or body exists, discretion under Subsection (1) exists notwithstanding that the threat is created by the completed act of a person (including a client) or that the lawyer's information comes from otherwise privileged conversations.

Illustrations: . . .

3. As the result of confidential disclosures at a meeting with engineers employed by Client Corporation, Lawyer reasonably believes that one of the engineers released a toxic substance into a city's water-supply system. Lawyer reasonably believes that the discharge will cause reasonably certain death or serious bodily harm to elderly or ill persons within a short period and that Lawyer's disclosure of the discharge is necessary to permit authorities to remove that threat or lessen the number of its victims. Lawyer's efforts to persuade responsible Client Corporation personnel to take corrective action have been unavailing. Although the act creating the threat has already occurred, Lawyer has discretion to disclose under Subsection (1) for the purpose of preventing the consequences of the act.

In circumstances such as those in Illustration 3, the Section applies even if the act creating the threat of death or serious bodily harm was not a crime or fraud. In other situations, the likelihood that other actors know about and will eliminate the risk may be relevant. Most situations will be intensely fact-sensitive. For example, the character of a threatened act as a crime or fraud suggests a state of mind on the part of the perpetrator that is more threatening to the intended victim than an act that is merely negligent or not wrongful, and thus may more readily warrant the lawyer's conclusion that the risk of harm is great.

Serious bodily harm within the meaning of the Section includes life-threatening illness and injuries and the consequences of events such as imprisonment for a substantial period and child sexual abuse. It also includes a client's threat of suicide.

Illustration:

4. Lawyer advises Manufacturer on product-liability matters. Lawyer had previously advised Manufacturer that use of Component A in a consumer product did not create an unreasonable risk of harm and was in compliance with consumer-protection and other law. Lawyer has now learned that Supplier, unknown to Manufacturer, provided Component A in a form not in compliance with Manufacturer's specifications. Manufacturer promptly altered its production methods so as to avoid any significant risk of harm in products manufactured in the future. There is a slight statistical chance that a consumer using the prior version of the product containing the noncomplying version of Component A might suffer serious bodily harm, but only in a highly unlikely combination of circumstances. Manufacturer's responsible officers have decided not to issue a public notice of the slightly increased risk of harm. Lawyer does not have discretion under this Section to use or disclose Manufacturer's confidential information to make a public warning of the slightly increased risk of harm.

f. Appropriate action. A lawyer's use or disclosure under this Section is a last resort when no other available action is reasonably likely to prevent the threatened death or serious bodily harm. Use or disclosure, when made, should be no more extensive than the lawyer reasonably believes necessary to accomplish the relevant purpose.

Preventive steps that a lawyer may appropriately take include consulting with relatives or friends of the person likely to cause the death or serious bodily harm and with other advisers to that person. (The lawyer may also seek the assistance of such persons in efforts to persuade the person not to act or to warn the threatened victim (see Comment *e* hereto).) A lawyer may also consult with law-enforcement authorities or agencies with jurisdiction over the type of conduct involved in order to prevent it and warn a threatened victim. . . .

When a lawyer has taken action under the Section, in all but extraordinary cases the relationship between lawyer and client would have so far deteriorated as to make the lawyer's effective representation of the client impossible. Generally, therefore, the lawyer is required to withdraw from the representation (see § 32(2)(a) & Comment *f* thereto), unless the client gives informed consent to the lawyer's continued representation notwithstanding the lawyer's adverse use or disclosure of information. In any event, the lawyer generally must inform the client of the fact of the lawyer's use or disclosure (see § 20(1)), unless the lawyer has a superior interest in not informing the client, such as to protect the lawyer from wrongful retaliation by the client, to effectuate permissible measures that are not yet complete, or to prevent the client from inflicting further harms on third persons.

g. Effects of a lawyer taking or not taking discretionary remedial action. A lawyer's decision to take action to disclose or not to disclose under this Section is discretionary with the lawyer (compare § 63 (disclosure required by law)). Such action would inevitably conflict to a significant degree with the lawyer's customary role of protecting client interests. Critical facts may be unclear, emotions may be high, and little time may be available in which the lawyer must decide on an appropriate course of action. Subsequent re-examination of the reasonableness of a lawyer's action in the light of later developments would be unwarranted; reasonableness of the lawyer's belief at the time and in the circumstances in which the lawyer acts is alone controlling. . . .

Because the interests protected by the rule are those of the public and third persons, the discretion of a lawyer to take action consistent with the Section may not be contracted away by agreement between the lawyer and the client or the lawyer and a third person (compare § 23(1)).

§ 67. Using or Disclosing Information to Prevent, Rectify, or Mitigate Substantial Financial Loss

(1) A lawyer may use or disclose confidential client information when the lawyer reasonably believes that its use or disclosure is necessary to prevent a crime or fraud, and:

(a) the crime or fraud threatens substantial financial loss;

(b) the loss has not yet occurred;

(c) the lawyer's client intends to commit the crime or fraud either personally or through a third person; and

(d) the client has employed or is employing the lawyer's services in the matter in which the crime or fraud is committed.

(2) If a crime or fraud described in Subsection (1) has already occurred, a lawyer may use or disclose confidential client information when the lawyer reasonably believes its use or disclosure is necessary to prevent, rectify, or mitigate the loss.

(3) Before using or disclosing information under this Section, the lawyer must, if feasible, make a good-faith effort to persuade the client not to act. If the client or another person has already acted, the lawyer must, if feasible, advise the client to warn the victim or to take other action to prevent, rectify, or mitigate the loss. The lawyer must, if feasible, also advise the client of the lawyer's ability to use or disclose information as provided in this Section and the consequences thereof.

(4) A lawyer who takes action or decides not to take action permitted under this Section is not, solely by reason of such action or inaction, subject to professional discipline, liable for damages to the lawyer's client or any third person, or barred from recovery against a client or third person.

Comment:

b. Rationale. The exceptions recognized in this Section reflect a balance between the competing considerations of protecting interests in client confidentiality and lawyer loyalty to clients, on the one hand, and protecting the interests of society and third persons in avoiding substantial financial consequences of crimes or frauds, on the other. The integrity, professional reputation, and financial interests of the lawyer can also be implicated under Subsections (1) and (2) in view of the requirement that the lawyer's services have been employed in commission of the crime or fraud. The exceptions are also justified on the ground that the client is not entitled to the protection of confidentiality when the client knowingly causes substantial financial harm through a crime or fraud and when, as required under Subsections (1) and (2), the client has in effect misused the client-lawyer relationship for that purpose. In most instances of unlawful client acts that threaten such consequences to others, it may be hoped that the client's own sober reflection and the lawyer's counseling (see Comment *i* hereto) will lead the client to refrain from the act or to prevent or mitigate its consequences. . . .

The exceptions stated in this Section permit a lawyer to exercise discretion to prevent the described loss to third persons, even though adverse effects might befall the client as a result. The exceptions are extraordinary. The only acts covered under the Section are the described crimes or frauds that threaten substantial financial loss to others. Clients remain protected in consulting a lawyer concerning the legal consequences of any such act in which the lawyer's services were not employed, including acts constituting crimes or frauds.

The discretion recognized in this Section may to an unknowable extent lessen some clients' willingness to consult freely with their lawyers. In this respect, the Section has an effect similar to that of the crime-fraud exception to the attorney-client privilege (see § 82; see also Comment *d* hereto). The social benefits of allowing a lawyer to prevent, mitigate, or rectify substantial financial loss to intended victims of criminal or fraudulent client acts under the described circumstances warrant incurring that additional risk.

Not all crimes and frauds are covered by this Section, but only those that involve a risk of substantial financial loss. The Section applies when a client intends to commit a crime or fraud either personally or through a third person (see Subsection (1)(c)). What constitutes a crime or a fraud is determined under otherwise applicable law. The distinction between acts entailing risks of such loss and other acts that may also be criminal or fraudulent reflects a balance between client confidentiality (see § 60, Comment *b*) and protection of third persons. It could be argued that a lawyer's discretion should be constrained in another manner, for example through case-by-case balancing of those competing interests, perhaps including as a factor the extent to which exercise of the lawyer's discretion would harm the client. Lawyers can be expected to take into account that and other relevant considerations in determining whether to exercise the professional discretion that the Section recognizes. However, the Section does not require that the lawyer exercise discretion only after explicitly making such an evaluation or in any other particular manner.

c. Comparison with the crime-fraud exception to the attorney-client privilege. This Section generally corresponds to the crime-fraud exception to the attorney-client privilege (see § 82, Comment *d*). Somewhat different considerations underlie the two rules and they operate in different settings, testimonial and nontestimonial. This Section and § 82 both apply to client crimes or frauds. Both apply to acts that a client intends to commit and to acts by a third person whom the client intends to aid.

This Section applies only when the likelihood of financial loss is great and the lawyer reasonably believes that use or revelation is necessary to prevent the crime or fraud or to prevent, rectify, or mitigate the loss it causes (see Comment *f* hereto). In contrast, the crime-fraud exception to the attorney-client privilege stated in § 82 applies without regard to the consequences of the intended act so long as the act itself is a crime or fraud. That exception to the attorney-client privilege applies only when a client consults a lawyer with intention to obtain assistance to commit a crime or fraud or so uses the lawyer's services, whereas the Section applies regardless of the client's intention at the time of consultation (see Comment *g* hereto). The crime-fraud exception to the attorney-client privilege is administered by a tribunal and applies only when a lawyer or another person is called upon to give evidence, whereas the Section concerns action that a lawyer may take on the basis of a reasonable belief and outside of any proceeding and thus without direction from a judicial officer. Finally, this Section is limited to client acts in which a lawyer's services are employed; the crime-fraud exception applies whether or not the lawyer's services are so employed. Due to the several differences in the requirements for this Section and § 82, a finding that a lawyer permissibly used or disclosed confidential client information under this Section and a determination whether § 82 applies must be made independently.

Lawyer disclosure under this Section is taken in the lawyer's personal capacity and not as agent. Accordingly, such disclosure would not constitute disclosure by an agent of the client for purposes of subject-matter waiver of other confidential communications under § 79 (see § 79, Comment *c*).

e. Employment of the lawyer's services in the client's act. Use or disclosure under either Subsection (1) or (2) requires that the lawyer's services are being or were employed in commission of a criminal or fraudulent act. The lawyer's involvement need not be known to or discoverable by the victim or other person. Subsections (1) and (2) apply without regard either to the lawyer's prior knowledge of the client's intended use of the lawyer's services or to when the lawyer forms a reasonable basis for a belief concerning the nature of the client's act. Such employment may occur, for example, when a client has a document prepared by the lawyer for use in a criminal or fraudulent scheme, receives the lawyer's advice concerning the act to assist in carrying it out, asks the lawyer to appear before a court or administrative agency as part of a transaction, or obtains advice that will assist the client in avoiding detection or apprehension for the crime or fraud. It is not necessary that the lawyer's services have been critical to success of the client's act or that the services were specifically requested by the client. It suffices if the services were or are being employed in the commission of the act.

Illustrations:

   1. As part of a business transaction, Lawyer on behalf of Client prepares and sends to Victim an opinion letter helpful to Client in completing an aspect of the transaction. At the time of preparing and sending the opinion letter, Lawyer had no reason to believe that the transaction was other than proper, but Lawyer thereafter receives information giving reason to believe the transaction constitutes a crime or fraud by Client within this Section. If the other conditions of the Section are present, Lawyer's opinion letter will have been employed in commission of Client's act, and Lawyer accordingly has discretion to use or disclose confidential information of Client as provided in the Section.

   2. Client has put in place a scheme to defraud Victim of substantial funds. After doing so, but before Victim has actually lost any funds, Client seeks Lawyer's assistance in meeting regulatory action and a suit by Victim seeking restitution that might ensue. Despite Lawyer's counseling, Client refuses to warn Victim, return the funds, or take other corrective action. Because Lawyer's services have not been employed in the commission of Client's fraud, Lawyer may not use or disclose Client's confidential information under this Section.

Legal assistance provided only after the client's crime or fraud has already been committed is not within this Section, whether or not loss to the victim has already occurred, if the lawyer's services are not employed for the purposes of a further crime or fraud, such as the crime of obstruction of justice or other unlawful attempt to cover up the prior wrongful act. While applicable law may provide that a completed act is regarded for some purposes as a continuing offense, the limitation of Subsection (1)(d) applies with attention to the time at which the client's acts actually occurred.

Illustrations:

   3. Client has been charged by a regulatory agency with participation in a scheme to defraud Victim. Client seeks the assistance of Lawyer in defending against the charges. The loss to Victim has already occurred. During the initial interview and thereafter, Lawyer is provided with ample reason to believe that Client's acts were fraudulent and caused substantial financial loss to Victim. Because Lawyer's services were not employed by Client in committing the fraud, Lawyer does not have discretion under this Section to use or disclose Client's confidential information.

   4. The same facts as in Illustration 3, except that the law of the applicable jurisdiction provides that each day during which a wrongdoer in the position of Client fails to make restitution to Victim constitutes a separate offense of the same type as the original wrong. Notwithstanding the continuing-offense law, commission of the fraudulent act of Client has already occurred without use of Lawyer's services. As in Illustration 3, Lawyer does not have discretion under this Section to use or disclose Client's confidential information.

   f. Use or disclosure to prevent (Subsection (1)) or to rectify or mitigate (Subsection (2)) a client wrongful act. . . . Action by the lawyer to prevent, rectify, or mitigate loss under Subsection (2) is in addition to and goes beyond that permitted for preventive purposes under Subsection (1). Actions to prevent, rectify, or mitigate the loss caused by the client's act include correcting or preventing the effects of the client's criminal or fraudulent act, even if the client's crime or fraud has already occurred and regardless of whether its impact has been visited upon the victim. Thus, a lawyer who acquires information from which the lawyer reasonably believes that a client has already defrauded a victim in a scheme in which the lawyer's services were employed may disclose the fraud to the victim when necessary to permit the victim to take possible corrective action, such as to initiate proceedings promptly in order to seize or recover assets fraudulently obtained by the client.

Once use or disclosure of information has been made to prevent, rectify, or mitigate loss under Subsection (2), the lawyer is not further warranted in actively assisting the victim on an ongoing basis in pursuing a remedy against the lawyer's client or in any similar manner aiding the victim or harming the client. Thus, a lawyer is not warranted under this Section in serving as legal counsel for a victim (see also § 132), volunteering to serve as witness in a proceeding by the victim, or cooperating with an administrative agency in obtaining compensation for victims. The lawyer also may not use or disclose information for the purpose of voluntarily assisting a law-enforcement agency to apprehend and prosecute the client, unless the lawyer reasonably believes that such disclosure would be necessary to prevent, rectify, or mitigate the victim's loss. On the rule that disclosure of confidential client information does not constitute waiver of the client's privilege due to subsequent disclosure by an agent, see Comment *c* hereto.

Illustrations:

   5. Lawyer has assisted Client in preparing documents by means of which Client will obtain a

$5,000,000 loan from Bank. The loan closing occurred on Monday and Bank will make the funds available for Client's use on Wednesday. On Tuesday Client reveals to Lawyer for the first time that Client knowingly obtained the loan by means of a materially false statement of Client's assets. Assuming that the other conditions for application of Subsection (2) are present, while Client's fraudulent act of obtaining the loan has, in large part, already occurred, Lawyer has discretion under the Subsection to use or disclose Client's confidential information to prevent the consequences of the fraud (final release of the funds from Bank) from occurring.

6. The same facts as in Illustration 5, except that Lawyer learned of the fraud on Wednesday after Bank had already released the funds to Client. Under Subsection (2), Lawyer's use or disclosure would be permissible if necessary for the purpose, for example, of enabling Bank to seize assets of Client in its possession or control as an offset against the fraudulently obtained loan or to prevent Client from sending the funds overseas and thereby making it difficult or impossible to trace them.

TOPIC 2. THE ATTORNEY-CLIENT PRIVILEGE

§ 68. Attorney-Client Privilege

Except as otherwise provided in this Restatement, the attorney-client privilege may be invoked as provided in § 86 with respect to:

(1) a communication
(2) made between privileged persons
(3) in confidence
(4) for the purpose of obtaining or providing legal assistance for the client.

Comment:

c. *Rationale supporting the privilege.* The modern attorney-client privilege evolved from an earlier reluctance of English courts to require lawyers to breach the code of a gentleman by being compelled to reveal in court what they had been told by clients. The privilege, such as it was then, belonged to the lawyer. It was a rule congenial with the law, which prevailed in England until the mid-19th century, that made parties to litigation themselves incompetent to testify, whether called as witnesses in their own behalf or by their adversaries. The modern conception of the privilege, reflected in this Restatement, protects clients, not lawyers, and clients have primary authority to determine whether to assert the privilege (see § 86) or waive it (see §§ 78- 80).

The rationale for the privilege is that confidentiality enhances the value of client-lawyer communications and hence the efficacy of legal services. The rationale is founded on three related assumptions. First, vindicating rights and complying with obligations under the law and under modern legal processes are matters often too complex and uncertain for a person untrained in the law, so that clients need to consult lawyers. The second assumption is that a client who consults a lawyer needs to disclose all of the facts to the lawyer and must be able to receive in return communications from the lawyer reflecting those facts. It is assumed that, in the absence of such frank and full discussion between client and lawyer, adequate legal assistance cannot be realized. Many legal rules are complex and most are fact-specific in their application. Lawyers are much better situated than nonlawyers to appreciate the effect of legal rules and to identify facts that determine whether a legal rule is applicable. Full disclosure by clients facilitates efficient presentation at trials and other proceedings and in a lawyer's advising functions.

The third assumption supporting the privilege is controversial—that clients would be unwilling to disclose personal, embarrassing, or unpleasant facts unless they could be assured that neither they nor their lawyers could be called later to testify to the communication. Relatedly, it is assumed that lawyers would not feel free in probing client's stories and giving advice unless assured that they would not thereby expose the client to adverse evidentiary risk. Those assumptions cannot be tested but are widely believed by lawyers to be sound. The privilege implies an impairment of the search for truth in some instances. Recognition of the privilege reflects a judgment that this impairment is outweighed by the social and moral values of confidential consultations. The privilege provides a zone of privacy within which a client may more effectively exercise the full autonomy that the law and legal institutions allow.

The evidentiary consequences of the privilege are indeterminate. If the behavioral assumptions supporting the privilege are well-founded, perhaps the evidence excluded by the privilege would not have come into existence save for the privilege. In any event, testimony concerning out-of-court communications often would be excluded as hearsay, although some of it could come in under exceptions such as that for statements against interest. The privilege also precludes an abusive litigation practice of calling an opposing lawyer as a witness.

Some judicial fact findings undoubtedly have been erroneous because the privilege excluded relevant evidence. The privilege creates tension with the right to confront and cross-examine opposing witnesses. It excuses lawyers from giving relevant testimony and precludes full examination of clients. The privilege no doubt protects wrongdoing in some instances. To that extent the privilege may facilitate serious social harms. The crime-fraud exception to the privilege (see § 82) results in forced disclosure of some such confidential conversations, but certainly not all.

Suggestions have been made that the privilege be conditional, not absolute, and thus inapplicable in cases where extreme need can be shown for admitting evidence of attorney-client communications. The privilege, however, is not subject to ad hoc exceptions. The predictability of a definite rule encourages forthright discussions between client and lawyer. The law accepts the risks of factual error and injustice in individual cases in deference to the values that the privilege vindicates.

d. Source of the law concerning the privilege. In most of the states, the privilege is defined by statute or rule, typically in an evidence code; in a few states, the privilege is common law. In the federal system, the definition of the privilege is left to the common-law process with respect to issues on which federal law applies. Federal Rule of Evidence 501 provides generally that questions of privilege "shall be governed by the principles of the common law as they may be interpreted by the courts of the United States in the light of reason and experience." On elements of a claim or defense as to which state law supplies the rule of decision, however, Rule 501 provides that the federal courts are to apply the attorney-client privilege of the relevant state.

§ 69. Attorney-Client Privilege—"Communication"

A communication within the meaning of § 68 is any expression through which a privileged person, as defined in § 70, undertakes to convey information to another privileged person and any document or other record revealing such an expression.

Comment:

b. Communications qualifying for the privilege. A communication can be in any form. Most confidential client communications to a lawyer are written or spoken words, but the privilege applies to communication through technologically enhanced methods such as telephone and telegraph, audio or video tape recording, film, telecopier, and other electronic means. However, communications through a public mode may suggest the absence of a reasonable expectation of confidentiality (see § 71, Comment *e*).

c. Intercepted communications. The communication need not in fact succeed; for example, an intercepted communication is within this Section (see § 71, Comment *c* (eavesdroppers)).

Illustration:

1. Lawyer represents Client in a pending criminal investigation. Lawyer directs Client to make a tape recording detailing everything that Client knows about an unlawful enterprise for Lawyer's review. Client makes the tape recording in secret. A cell mate, after learning of the tape recording, informs the prosecutor who causes the tape to be seized under a subpoena. The attorney-client privilege covers the tape recording.

For the rule where a communication is disclosed to nonprivileged persons, see § 79.

d. Distinction between the content of a communication and knowledge of facts. The attorney-client privilege protects only the content of the communication between privileged persons, not the knowledge of privileged persons about the facts themselves. Although a client cannot be required to testify about communications with a lawyer about a subject, the client may be required to testify about what the client knows concerning the same subject. The client thus may invoke the privilege with respect to the question "Did you tell your lawyer the light was red?" but not with respect to the question "Did you see that the light was red?" Similarly, the privilege does not apply to preexisting documents or other tangible evidence (see Comment *j*), even if they concern the same subject as a privileged communication.

Illustration:

2. Client, a defendant in a breach-of-contract suit, confidentially informs Lawyer about Client's recollection of a course of dealings between Client and a subcontractor, Plaintiff in the pending contract suit. The attorney-client privilege does not prevent Plaintiff from requiring Client to testify at

a deposition or trial concerning Client's present recollection of the course of dealings between Client and Plaintiff. Plaintiff may not, however, require Lawyer or Client to testify concerning what Client told Lawyer about those same facts.

e. Communicative client acts. The privilege extends to nonverbal communicative acts intended to convey information. For example, a client may communicate with a lawyer through facial expressions or other communicative bodily motions or gestures (nodding or shaking the head or holding up a certain number of fingers to indicate number) or acting out a recalled incident. On the other hand, the privilege does not extend to a client act simply because the client performed the act in the lawyer's presence. The privilege applies when the purpose in performing the act is to convey information to the lawyer.

Illustrations:

3. Client, charged with a crime, retains Lawyer as defense counsel. Lawyer obtains a police report stating that the perpetrator of the crime had a tattooed right forearm. Lawyer asks Client whether Client's right arm is tattooed. In answer, Client rolls up his right sleeve revealing his forearm. The information that the lawyer thereby acquires derives from a protected communication.

4. The same facts as in Illustration 3, except that, shortly after the crime, Client appears at Lawyer's office wearing a short-sleeved shirt. The observation by Lawyer that Client had a tattoo on his arm is not a communication protected by the privilege.

5. Lawyer represents Client in a divorce and child-custody proceeding. While accompanying Client in a visit to the residence of Client's child, Lawyer observes Client physically break into the premises. Lawyer's knowledge is not protected as a communication from Client.

f. A lawyer's testimony on a client's mental state. A lawyer may have knowledge about a client's mental state based on the client's communications with the lawyer. That knowledge may be relevant, for example, in the context of determining whether an accused is competent to stand trial. The lawyer in such cases is uniquely competent to testify concerning the client's ability to assist in presenting a defense. Testimony may be elicited that concerns the client's mode of thought but not if it would disclose particulars that would tend to incriminate the client. On representing a client with diminished capacity, see § 24.

g. Client identity, the fact of consultation, fee payment, and similar matters. Courts have sometimes asserted that the attorney-client privilege categorically does not apply to such matters as the following: the identity of a client; the fact that the client consulted the lawyer and the general subject matter of the consultation; the identity of a nonclient who retained or paid the lawyer to represent the client; the details of any retainer agreement; the amount of the agreed-upon fee; and the client's whereabouts. Testimony about such matters normally does not reveal the content of communications from the client. However, admissibility of such testimony should be based on the extent to which it reveals the content of a privileged communication. The privilege applies if the testimony directly or by reasonable inference would reveal the content of a confidential communication. But the privilege does not protect clients or lawyers against revealing a lawyer's knowledge about a client solely on the ground that doing so would incriminate the client or otherwise prejudice the client's interests.

Illustration:

6. Client consults Lawyer about Client's taxes. In the consultation, Client communicates to Lawyer Client's name and information indicating that Client owes substantial amounts in back taxes. The fact that Client owes back taxes is not known to the taxing authorities. Lawyer sends a letter to the taxing authorities and encloses a bank draft to cover the back taxes of Client. Lawyer does so to gain an advantage for Client under the tax laws by providing a basis for arguing against the accrual of penalties for continued nonpayment of taxes. Neither Lawyer's letter nor the bank draft reveals the identity of Client. (For the purpose of the Illustration, it is assumed that the client-lawyer communication occurred for the purpose of obtaining legal assistance (see § 72)). In a grand-jury proceeding investigating Client's past failure to pay taxes, Lawyer cannot be required to testify concerning the identity of Client because, on the facts of the Illustration, that testimony would by reasonable inference reveal a confidential communication from Client, Client's communication concerning Client's nonpayment of taxes.

A client also enjoys the constitutional protection against self-incrimination. But this right does not provide a basis on which the client's lawyer can refuse to reveal incriminating information about the client that is not protected by the attorney-client privilege. The precise interaction of the attorney-client and self-incrimination privileges is beyond the scope of this Restatement. Protection may also be provided by the constitutional guarantee of the right to counsel. On the application of the attorney-client privilege to a lawyer's testimony about how the lawyer came into the possession of instrumentalities of crime or the fruits of crime, see § 119.

h. A record of a privileged communication. The privilege applies both to communications when made and to confidential records of such communications, such as a lawyer's note of the conversation. The privilege applies to a record when a communication embodied in the record can be traced to a privileged person as its expressive source (see § 70) and the record was created (see § 71) and preserved (see § 79) in a confidential state.

i. Lawyer communications to a client. Confidential communications by a lawyer to a client are also protected, including a record of a privileged communication such as a memorandum to a confidential file or to another lawyer or other person privileged to receive such a communication under § 71. Some decisions have protected a lawyer communication only if it contains or expressly refers to a client communication. That limitation is rejected here in favor of a broader rule more likely to assure full and frank communication (see § 68, Comment *c*). Moreover, the broader rule avoids difficult questions in determining whether a lawyer's communication itself discloses a client communication. A lawyer communication may also be protected by the work-product immunity (see Topic 3).

Illustration:

> 7. Lawyer writes a confidential letter to Client offering legal advice on a tax matter on which Client had sought Lawyer's professional assistance. Lawyer's letter is based in part on information that Client supplied to Lawyer, in part on information gathered by Lawyer from third persons, and in part on Lawyer's legal research. Even if each such portion of the letter could be separated from the others, the letter is a communication under this Section, and neither Lawyer nor Client can be made to disclose or testify about any of its contents.

A lawyer may serve as the conduit for information to be conveyed from third persons to the lawyer's client. For most purposes, notice to a lawyer constitutes notice to the lawyer's client (see § 28(1)). In any event, both lawyer and client can be required to testify to the message for which the lawyer served as conduit. Lawyers in such situations serve, not as confidants, but as a communicative link between their clients and opposing parties, courts, and other legal institutions. Were such communications privileged, an opposing party would be required to communicate directly with the client, in derogation of the rule that communications with represented parties must be conducted through their lawyers (see § 99).

j. Preexisting documents and records. A client may communicate information to a lawyer by sending writings or other kinds of documentary or electronic recordings that came into existence prior to the time that the client communicates with the lawyer. The privilege protects the information that the client so communicated but not the preexisting document or record itself. A client-authored document that is not a privileged document when originally composed does not become privileged simply because the client has placed it in the lawyer's hands. However, if a document was a privileged preexisting document and was delivered to the lawyer under circumstances that otherwise would make its communication privileged, it remains privileged in the hands of the lawyer.

Illustrations:

> 8. Client confidentially delivers Client's business records to Lawyer, who specializes in tax matters, in order to obtain Lawyer's legal advice about taxes. As business records, the documents were not themselves prepared for the purpose of obtaining legal advice and are not protected by another testimonial privilege. They gain no privileged status by the fact that Client delivers them to Lawyer in seeking legal advice.

> 9. Client possesses a memorandum prepared by Client to communicate with Lawyer A during an earlier representation by Lawyer A. Client takes the memorandum to Lawyer B in confidence to obtain legal services on a different matter. The memorandum qualified as a privileged communication in the earlier matter. While in the hands of Lawyer B, the memorandum remains protected by the attorney-client privilege due to its originally privileged nature.

§ 70. Attorney-Client Privilege—"Privileged Persons"

Privileged persons within the meaning of § 68 are the client (including a prospective client), the client's lawyer, agents of either who facilitate communications between them, and agents of the lawyer who facilitate the representation.

Comment:

e. Privileged agents for a client or lawyer: in general. The privilege normally applies to communications involving persons who on their own behalf seek legal assistance from a lawyer (see § 72). However, a client need not personally seek legal assistance, but may appoint a third person to do so as the client's agent (e.g., § 134, Comment *f*). Whether a third person is an agent of the client or lawyer or a nonprivileged "stranger" is critical in determining application of the attorney-client privilege. If the third person is an agent for the purpose of the privilege, communications through or in the presence of that person are privileged; if the third person is not an agent, then the communications are not in confidence (see § 71) and are not privileged. Accordingly, a lawyer should allow a nonclient to participate only upon clarifying that person's role and when it reasonably appears that the benefit of that person's presence offsets the risk of a later claim that the presence of a third person forfeited the privilege.

f. A client's agent for communication. A person is a confidential agent for communication if the person's participation is reasonably necessary to facilitate the client's communication with a lawyer or another privileged person and if the client reasonably believes that the person will hold the communication in confidence. Factors that may be relevant in determining whether a third person is an agent for communication include the customary relationship between the client and the asserted agent, the nature of the communication, and the client's need for the third person's presence to communicate effectively with the lawyer or to understand and act upon the lawyer's advice.

Illustrations:

1. The police arrest Client and do not permit Client to communicate directly with Client's regular legal counsel, Lawyer. Client asks Friend, a person whom Client trusts to keep information confidential, to convey to Lawyer the message that Lawyer should not permit the police to search Client's home. Friend is an agent for communication.

2. Client and Lawyer do not speak a language known by the other. Client uses Translator to communicate an otherwise privileged message to Lawyer. Translator is an acquaintance of Client. Translator is an agent for communication.

3. Client regularly employs Secretary to record and transcribe Client's important business letters, including confidential correspondence. Client uses the services of Secretary to prepare a letter to Lawyer. Secretary is an agent for communication.

An agent for communication need not take a direct part in client-lawyer communications, but may be present because of the Client's psychological or other need. A business person may be accompanied by a business associate or expert consultant who can assist the client in interpreting the legal situation.

Illustrations:

4. Client, 16 years old, is represented by Lawyer. Client's parents accompany Client at a meeting with Lawyer concerning a property interest of Client. Client's parents are appropriate agents for communication.

5. Client is advised by Accountant to consult a lawyer about a legal problem involving complex questions of tax accounting. Client, who does not fully understand the nature of the accounting questions, asks Accountant to accompany Client to a consultation with Lawyer so that Accountant can explain the nature of Client's legal matter to Lawyer. Accountant is Client's agent for communication. That would also be true if Accountant were to explain Lawyer's legal advice in business or accounting terms more understandable to Client.

The privilege applies to communications to and from the client disclosed to persons who hire the lawyer as an incident of the lawyer's engagement. Thus, the privilege covers communications by a client-insured to an insurance-company investigator who is to convey the facts to the client's lawyer designated by the insurer, as well as communications from the lawyer for the insured to the insurer in providing a progress report or discussing litigation strategy or settlement (see § 134, Comment *f*). Such situations must be distinguished from communications by an insured to an insurance investigator who will report to the company, to which the privilege does not apply.

g. A lawyer's agent. A lawyer may disclose privileged communications to other office lawyers and with appropriate nonlawyer staff—secretaries, file clerks, computer operators, investigators, office managers, paralegal assistants, telecommunications personnel, and similar law-office assistants. On the duty of a lawyer to protect client information being handled by nonlawyer personnel, see § 60(1)(b). The privilege also extends to communications to and from the client that are disclosed to independent contractors retained by a lawyer, such as an accountant or physician retained by the lawyer to assist in

217

providing legal services to the client and not for the purpose of testifying.

h. An incompetent person as a client. When a client is mentally or physically incapacitated from effectively consulting with a lawyer, a representative may communicate with the incompetent person's lawyer under the protection of the privilege. The privilege also extends to any communications between the incompetent person and the representative relating to the communication with the lawyer.

Illustration:

> 6. Client is mentally incapacitated, and a court has appointed Guardian as the guardian of the person and property of Client. A question has arisen concerning a right of Client in certain property, and Lawyer is retained to represent the interests of Client in the property. Guardian serves as the agent for communication of Client in discussing the matter with Lawyer.

§ 71. Attorney-Client Privilege—"In Confidence"

A communication is in confidence within the meaning of § 68 if, at the time and in the circumstances of the communication, the communicating person reasonably believes that no one will learn the contents of the communication except a privileged person as defined in § 70 or another person with whom communications are protected under a similar privilege.

§ 72. Attorney-Client Privilege—Legal Assistance as the Object of a Privileged Communication

A communication is made for the purpose of obtaining or providing legal assistance within the meaning of § 68 if it is made to or to assist a person:

(1) who is a lawyer or who the client or prospective client reasonably believes to be a lawyer; and

(2) whom the client or prospective client consults for the purpose of obtaining legal assistance.

§ 73. The Privilege for an Organizational Client

When a client is a corporation, unincorporated association, partnership, trust, estate, sole proprietorship, or other for-profit or not-for-profit organization, the attorney-client privilege extends to a communication that:

(1) otherwise qualifies as privileged under § § 68-72;

(2) is between an agent of the organization and a privileged person as defined in § 70;

(3) concerns a legal matter of interest to the organization; and

(4) is disclosed only to:

> **(a) privileged persons as defined in § 70; and**
>
> **(b) other agents of the organization who reasonably need to know of the communication in order to act for the organization.**

Comment:

a. Scope and cross-references. This Section states the conditions under which an organization can claim the attorney-client privilege. The requirements of § § 68-72 must be satisfied, except that this Section recognizes a special class of agents who communicate in behalf of the organizational client (see Comment *d*). The Section also requires that the communication relate to a matter of interest to the organization as such (see Subsection (3) & Comment *f* hereto) and that it be disclosed within the organization only to persons having a reasonable need to know of it (see Subsection (4)(b) & Comment *g* hereto).

Conflicts of interest between an organizational client and its officers and other agents are considered in § 131, Comment *e.* On the application of the privilege to governmental organizations and officers, see § 74.

b. Rationale. The attorney-client privilege encourages organizational clients to have their agents confide in lawyers in order to realize the organization's legal rights and to achieve compliance with law (Comment *d* hereto). Extending the privilege to corporations and other organizations was formerly a matter of doubt but is no longer questioned. However, two pivotal questions must be resolved.

The first is defining the group of persons who can make privileged communications on behalf of an organization. Balance is required. The privilege should cover a sufficiently broad number of organizational communications to realize the organization's policy objectives, but not insulate ordinary intraorganizational communications that may later have importance as evidence. Concern has been expressed, for example, that the privilege would afford organizations "zones of silence" that would be free of evidentiary scrutiny. A subsidiary problem is whether persons who would be nonprivileged occurrence witnesses with respect to communications to a lawyer representing a natural person can be conduits of privileged communications when the client is an organization. That problem has been addressed in terms of the "subject-matter" and "control-group" tests for the privilege (see Comment *d*).

Second is the problem of defining the types of organizations treated as clients for purposes of the privilege. It is now accepted that the privilege applies to corporations, but some decisions have questioned whether the privilege should apply to unincorporated associations, partnerships, or sole proprietorships. Neither logic nor principle supports limiting the organizational privilege to the corporate form (see Comment *c* hereto).

c. Application of the privilege to an organization. As stated in the Section, the privilege applies to all forms of organizations. A corporation with hundreds of employees could as well be a sole proprietorship if its assets were owned by a single person rather than its shares being owned by the same person. It would be anomalous to accord the privilege to a business in corporate form but not if it were organized as a sole proprietorship. In general, an organization under this Section is a group having a recognizable identity as such and some permanency. Thus, an organization under this Section ordinarily would include a law firm, however it may be structured (as a professional corporation, a partnership, a sole proprietorship, or otherwise). The organization need not necessarily be treated as a legal entity for any other legal purpose. The privilege extends as well to charitable, social, fraternal, and other nonprofit organizations such as labor unions and chambers of commerce.

d. An agent of an organizational client. As stated in Subsection (2), the communication must involve an agent of the organization, on one hand, and, on the other, a privileged person within the meaning of § 70, such as the lawyer for the organization. Persons described in Subsection (4)(b) may disclose the communication under a need-to-know limitation (see Comment *g* hereto). The existence of a relationship of principal and agent between the organizational client and the privileged agent is determined according to agency law (see generally Restatement Second, Agency § § 1-139).

Some decisions apply a "control group" test for determining the scope of the privilege for an organization. That test limits the privilege to communications from persons in the organization who have authority to mold organizational policy or to take action in accordance with the lawyer's advice. The control-group circle excludes many persons within an organization who normally would cooperate with an organization's lawyer. Such a limitation overlooks that the division of functions within an organization often separates decisionmakers from those knowing relevant facts. Such a limitation is unnecessary to prevent abuse of the privilege (see Comment *g*) and significantly frustrates its purpose.

Other decisions apply a "subject matter" test. That test extends the privilege to communications with any lower-echelon employee or agent so long as the communication relates to the subject matter of the representation. In substance, those decisions comport with the need-to-know formulation in this Section (see Comment *g*).

It is not necessary that the agent receive specific direction from the organization to make or receive the communication (see Comment *h*).

Agents of the organization who may make privileged communications under this Section include the organization's officers and employees. For example, a communication by any employee of a corporation to the corporation's lawyer concerning the matter as to which the lawyer was retained to represent the corporation would be privileged, if other conditions of the privilege are satisfied. The concept of agent also includes independent contractors with whom the corporation has a principal-agent relationship and extends to agents of such persons when acting as subagents of the organizational client. For example, a foreign-based corporation may retain a general agency (perhaps a separate corporation) in an American city for the purpose of retaining counsel to represent the interests of the foreign-based corporation. Communications by the general agency would be by an agent for the purpose of this Section.

For purpose of the privilege, when a parent corporation owns controlling interest in a corporate subsidiary, the parent corporation's agents who are responsible for legal matters of the subsidiary are considered agents of the subsidiary. The subsidiary corporation's agents who are responsible for affairs of the parent are also considered agents of the parent for the purpose of the privilege. Directors of a corporation are not its agents for many legal purposes, because they are not subject to the control of the corporation (see Restatement Second, Agency § 14C). However, in communications with the organization's counsel, a director who communicates in the interests and for the benefit of the corporation is its agent for the purposes of this Section. Depending on the circumstances, a director acts in that capacity both when participating in a meeting of directors and when communicating individually with a lawyer for the corporation about the corporation's affairs. Communications to and from nonagent constituents of a corporation, such as shareholders and creditors, are not privileged.

In the case of a partnership, general partners and employees and other agents and subagents of the partnership may serve as agents of the organization for the purpose of making privileged communications (see generally Restatement Second, Agency § 14A). Limited partners who have no other relationship (such as employee) with the limited partnership are analogous to shareholders of a corporation and are not such agents.

In the case of an unincorporated association, agents whose communications may be privileged under this Section include officers and employees and other contractual agents and subagents. Members of an unincorporated association, for example members of a labor union, are not, solely by reason of their status as members, agents of the association for the purposes of this Section. In some situations, for example, involving a small unincorporated association with very active members, the members might be considered agents for the purpose of this Section on the ground that the association functionally is a partnership whose members are like partners.

In the case of an enterprise operated as a sole proprietorship, agents who may make communications privileged under this Section with respect to the proprietorship include employees or contractual agents and subagents of the proprietor.

Communications of a nonagent constituent of the organization may be independently privileged under § 75 where the person is a co-client along with the organization. If the agent of the organization has a conflict of interest with the organization, the lawyer for the organization must not purport to represent both the organization and the agent without consent (see § 131, Comment c). The lawyer may not mislead the agent about the nature of the lawyer's loyalty to the organization (see § 103). If a lawyer fails to clarify the lawyer's role as representative solely of the organization and the organization's agent reasonably believes that the lawyer represents the agent, the agent may assert the privilege personally with respect to the agent's own communications (compare § 72(2), Comment f; see also § 131, Comment e).

The lawyer must also observe limitations on the extent to which a lawyer may communicate with a person of conflicting interests who is not represented by counsel (see § 103) and limitations on communications with persons who are so represented (see § 99 and following).

e. The temporal relationship of principal-agent. Under Subsection (2), a person making a privileged communication to a lawyer for an organization must then be acting as agent of the principal-organization. The objective of the organizational privilege is to encourage the organization to have its agents communicate with its lawyer (see Comment d hereto). Generally, that premise implies that persons be agents of the organization at the time of communicating. The privilege may also extend, however, to communications with a person with whom the organization has terminated, for most other purposes, an agency relationship. A former agent is a privileged person under Subsection (2) if, at the time of communicating, the former agent has a continuing legal obligation to the principal-organization to furnish the information to the organization's lawyer. The scope of such a continuing obligation is determined by the law of agency and the terms of the employment contract (see Restatement Second, Agency § 275, Comment e, & § 381, Comment f). The privilege covers communications with a lawyer for an organization by a retired officer of the organization concerning a matter within the officer's prior responsibilities that is of legal importance to the organization.

Subsection (2) does not include a person with whom the organization established a principal-agent relationship predominantly for the purpose of providing the protection of the privilege to the person's communications, if the person was not an agent at the time of learning the information. For example, communications between the lawyer for an organization and an eyewitness to an event whose communications would not otherwise be privileged cannot be made privileged simply through the organization hiring the person to consult with the organization's lawyer. (As to experts and similar persons employed by a lawyer, see § 70, Comment g).

Ordinarily, an agent communicating with an organization's lawyer within this Section will have acquired the information in the course of the agent's work for the organization. However, it is not necessary that the communicated information be so acquired. Thus, a person may communicate under this Section with respect to information learned prior to the relationship or learned outside the person's functions as an agent, so long as the person bears an agency relationship to the principal-organization at the time of the communication and the communication concerns a matter of interest to the organization (see Comment *f*). For example, a chemist for an organization who communicates to the organization's lawyer information about a process that the chemist learned prior to being employed by the organization makes a privileged communication if the other conditions of this Section are satisfied.

f. Limitation to communications relating to the interests of the organization. Subsection (3) requires that the communication relate to a legal matter of interest to the organization. The lawyer must be representing the organization as opposed to the agent who communicates with the lawyer, such as its individual officer or employee. A lawyer representing such an officer or employee, of course, can have privileged communications with that client. But the privilege will not be that of the organization. When a lawyer represents as co-clients both the organization and one of its officers or employees, the privileged nature of communications is determined under § 75. On the conflicts of interest involved in such representations, see § 131, Comment *e*.

g. The need-to-know limitation on disclosing privileged communications. Communications are privileged only if made for the purpose of obtaining legal services (see § 72), and they remain privileged only if neither the client nor an agent of the client subsequently discloses the communication to a nonprivileged person (see § 79; see also § 71, Comment *d*). Those limitations apply to organizational clients as provided in Subsection (4). Communications become, and remain, so protected by the privilege only if the organization does not permit their dissemination to persons other than to privileged persons. Agents of a client to whom confidential communications may be disclosed are generally defined in § 70, Comment *f*, and agents of a lawyer are defined in § 70, Comment *g*. Included among an organizational client's agents for communication are, for example, a secretary who prepares a letter to the organization's lawyer on behalf of a communicating employee.

The need-to-know limitation of Subsection (4)(b) permits disclosing privileged communications to other agents of the organization who reasonably need to know of the privileged communication in order to act for the organization in the matter. Those agents include persons who are responsible for accepting or rejecting a lawyer's advice on behalf of the organization or for acting on legal assistance, such as general legal advice, provided by the lawyer. Access of such persons to privileged communications is not limited to direct exchange with the lawyer. A lawyer may be required to take steps assuring that attorney-client communications will be disseminated only among privileged persons who have a need to know. Persons defined in Subsection (4)(b) may be apprised of privileged communications after they have been made, as by examining records of privileged communications previously made, in order to conduct the affairs of the organization in light of the legal services provided.

Illustration:

1. Lawyer for Organization makes a confidential report to President of Organization, describing Organization's contractual relationship with Supplier, and advising that Organization's contract with Supplier could be terminated without liability. President sends a confidential memorandum to Manager, Organization's purchasing manager, asking whether termination of the contract would nonetheless be inappropriate for business reasons. Because Manager's response would reasonably depend on several aspects of Lawyer's advice, Manager would have need to know the justifying reason for Lawyer's advice that the contract could be terminated. Lawyer's report to President remains privileged notwithstanding that President shared it with Manager.

The need-to-know concept properly extends to all agents of the organization who would be personally held financially or criminally liable for conduct in the matter in question or who would personally benefit from it, such as general partners of a partnership with respect to a claim for or against the partnership. It extends to persons, such as members of a board of directors and senior officers of an organization, whose general management and supervisory responsibilities include wide areas of organizational activities and to lower-echelon agents of the organization whose area of activity is relevant to the legal advice or service rendered.

Dissemination of a communication to persons outside those described in Subsection (4)(b) implies that the protection of confidentiality was not significant (see § 71, Comment *b*). An organization may not immunize documents and other communications generated or circulated for a business or other nonlegal purpose (see § 72).

h. Directed and volunteered agent communications. It is not necessary that a superior organizational authority specifically direct an agent to communicate with the organization's lawyer. Unless instructed to the contrary, an agent has authority to volunteer information to a lawyer when reasonably related to the interests of the organization. An agent has similar authority to respond to a request for information from a lawyer for the organization. And the lawyer for the organization ordinarily may seek relevant information directly from employees and other agents without prior direction from superior authorities in the organization.

i. Inside legal counsel and outside legal counsel. The privilege under this Section applies without distinction to lawyers who are inside legal counsel or outside legal counsel for an organization (see § 72, Comment *c*). Communications predominantly for a purpose other than obtaining or providing legal services for the organization are not within the privilege (see § 72, Comment *c*). On the credentials of a lawyer for the purposes of the privilege, see § 72(1), Comment *e*.

j. Invoking and waiving the privilege of an organizational client. The privilege for organizational clients can be asserted and waived only by a responsible person acting for the organization for this purpose. On waiver, see § § 78-80. Communications involving an organization's director, officer, or employee may qualify as privileged, but it is a separate question whether such a person has authority to invoke or waive the privilege on behalf of the organization. If the lawyer was representing both the organization and the individual as co-clients, the question of invoking and waiving the privilege is determined under the rule for co-clients (see § 75, Comment *e*). Whether a lawyer has formed a client-lawyer relationship with a person affiliated with the organization, as well as with the organization, is determined under § 14. Communications of such a person who approaches a lawyer for the organization as a prospective client are privileged as provided in § 72. Unless the person's contrary intent is reasonably manifest to a lawyer for the organization, the lawyer acts properly in assuming that a communication from any such person is on behalf and in the interest of the organization and, as such, is privileged in the interest of the organization and not of the individual making the communication. When the person manifests an intention to make a communication privileged against the organization, the lawyer must resist entering into such a client-lawyer relationship and receiving such a communication if doing so would constitute an impermissible conflict of interest (see § 131, Comment *e*).

An agent or former agent may have need for a communication as to which the organization has authority to waive the privilege, for example, when the agent is sued personally. A tribunal may exercise discretion to order production of such a communication for benefit of the agent if the agent establishes three conditions. First, the agent must show that the agent properly came to know the contents of the communication. Second, the agent must show substantial need of the communication. Third, the agent must show that production would create no material risk of prejudice or embarrassment to the organization beyond such evidentiary use as the agent may make of the communication. Such a risk may be controlled by protective orders, redaction, or other measures.

Illustration:

2. Lawyer, representing only Corporation, interviews Employee by electronic mail in connection with reported unlawful activities in Corporation's purchasing department in circumstances providing Corporation with a privilege with respect to their communications. Corporation later dismisses Employee, who sues Corporation, alleging wrongful discharge. Employee files a discovery request seeking all copies of communications between Employee and Lawyer. The tribunal has discretion to order discovery under the conditions stated in the preceding paragraph. In view of the apparent relationship of Employee's statements to possible illegal activities, it is doubtful that Employee could persuade the tribunal that access by Employee would create no material risk that third persons, such as a government agency, would thereby learn of the communication and thus gain a litigation or other advantage with respect to Corporation.

k. Succession in legal control of an organization. When ownership of a corporation or other organization as an entity passes to successors, the transaction carries with it authority concerning asserting or waiving the privilege. After legal control passes in such a transaction, communications from directors, officers, or employees of the acquired organization to lawyers who represent only the predecessor organization, if it maintains a separate existence from the acquiring organization, may no longer be covered by the privilege. When a corporation or other organization has ceased to have a legal existence such that no person can act in its behalf, ordinarily the attorney-client privilege terminates (see generally § 77, Comment *c*).

Illustration:

3. X, an officer of Ajax Corporation, communicates in confidence with Lawyer, who represents Ajax, concerning dealings between Ajax and one of its creditors, Vendor Corporation. Ajax later is declared bankrupt and a bankruptcy court appoints Trustee as the trustee in bankruptcy for Ajax.

Thereafter, Lawyer is called to the witness stand in litigation between Vendor Corporation and Trustee. Trustee has authority to determine whether the attorney-client privilege should be asserted or waived on behalf of the bankrupt Ajax Corporation with respect to testimony by Lawyer about statements by X. X cannot assert a privilege because X was not a client of Lawyer in the representation. Former officers and directors of Ajax cannot assert the privilege because control of the corporation has passed to Trustee.

A lawyer for an organization is ordinarily authorized to waive the privilege in advancing the interests of the client (see § 61 & § 79, Comment c). Otherwise, when called to testify, a lawyer is required to invoke the privilege on behalf of the client (see § 86(1)(b)). On waiver, see § § 78-80.

§ 74. The Privilege for a Governmental Client

Unless applicable law otherwise provides, the attorney-client privilege extends to a communication of a governmental organization as stated in § 73 and of an individual employee or other agent of a governmental organization as a client with respect to his or her personal interest as stated in § § 68-72.

Comment:

c. Application of the general attorney-client-privilege rules to a governmental client. The general requirements of the attorney-client privilege apply with respect to assertedly privileged communications of a governmental client. For example, the privilege extends only to communication for the purpose of obtaining or giving legal assistance (see § 72).

The privilege does not apply to a document that has an independent legal effect as an operative statement of governmental policy. For example, a memorandum by a government lawyer that directs, rather than advises, a governmental officer to act in a certain way is not protected by the privilege. Such a document is a necessarily public statement of public policy and as such is meant to be publicly disseminated (see § 71, Comment e).

Communications between a lawyer representing one governmental agency and an employee of another governmental agency are privileged only if the lawyer represents both agencies (see § 75) or if the communication is pursuant to a common-interest arrangement (see § 76).

d. Individual government employees and agents. Employees and agents of a governmental agency may have both official and personal interests in a matter. A police officer sued for damages for the alleged use of excessive force, for example, may be both officially and personally interested in the lawsuit. The officer has the right to consult counsel of the officer's choice with respect to the officer's personal interests. If the officer consults a lawyer retained by the officer's agency or department, the principles of § 73, Comment j, determine whether the officer is a co-client with the agency or department (see § 75) or is not a client of the lawyer. Government lawyers may be prohibited from the private practice of law or accepting a matter adverse to the government. Thus, the fact that the common employer of both lawyer and officer is a government agency may affect the reasonableness of the officer's claim of expectation that the lawyer could function as personal counsel for the officer. On the conflict-of-interest limitations on such joint representations, see § 131, Comment e. If a lawyer is retained by the agency as separate counsel to represent the personal interests of the employee, for purposes of the privilege the employee is the sole client. As with agents of nongovernmental organizations, the status of a governmental employee or agent as co-client (see § 75), individual client, or nonrepresented communicating agent of the agency sometimes may be difficult to determine. Inquiry in such cases should focus upon the employment relationship of the lawyer and the reasonable belief of the agent at the time of communicating.

e. Invoking and waiving the privilege of a governmental client. The privilege for governmental entities may be asserted or waived by the responsible public official or body. The identity of that responsible person or body is a question of local governmental law. In some states, for example, the state's attorney general decides matters of litigation policy for state agencies, including decisions about the privilege. In other states, such decisions are made by another executive officer or agency in suits in which the attorney general otherwise conducts the litigation. As a general proposition, the official or body that is empowered to assert or forego a claim or defense is entitled to assert or forego the privilege for communications relating to the claim or defense. Waiver of the privilege is determined according to the standards set forth in § 73, Comment j. See also Comment d hereto.

§ 75. The Privilege of Co-Clients

(1) If two or more persons are jointly represented by the same lawyer in a matter, a communication of either co-client that otherwise qualifies as privileged under § § 68-72 and relates to matters of common interest is privileged as against third persons, and any co-client may invoke the privilege, unless it has been waived by the client who made the communication.

(2) Unless the co-clients have agreed otherwise, a communication described in Subsection (1) is not privileged as between the co-clients in a subsequent adverse proceeding between them.

Comment:

b. The co-client privilege. Under Subsection (1), communications by co-clients with their common lawyer retain confidential characteristics as against third persons. The rule recognizes that it may be desirable to have multiple clients represented by the same lawyer.

c. Delimiting co-client situations. Whether a client-lawyer relationship exists between each client and the common lawyer is determined under § 14, specifically whether they have expressly or impliedly agreed to common representation in which confidential information will be shared. A co-client representation can begin with a joint approach to a lawyer or by agreement after separate representations had begun. However, clients of the same lawyer who share a common interest are not necessarily co-clients. Whether individuals have jointly consulted a lawyer or have merely entered concurrent but separate representations is determined by the understanding of the parties and the lawyer in light of the circumstances (see § 14).

Co-client representations must also be distinguished from situations in which a lawyer represents a single client, but another person with allied interests cooperates with the client and the client's lawyer (see § 76).

The scope of the co-client relationship is determined by the extent of the legal matter of common interest. For example, a lawyer might also represent one co-client on other matters separate from the common one. On whether, following the end of a co-client relationship, the lawyer may continue to represent one former co-client adversely to the interests of another, see § 121, Comment *e*. On the confidentiality of communications during a co-client representation, see Comment *d* hereto.

d. The subsequent-proceeding exception to the co-client privilege. As stated in Subsection (2), in a subsequent proceeding in which former co-clients are adverse, one of them may not invoke the attorney-client privilege against the other with respect to communications involving either of them during the co-client relationship. That rule applies whether or not the co-client's communication had been disclosed to the other during the co-client representation, unless they had otherwise agreed.

Rules governing the co-client privilege are premised on an assumption that co-clients usually understand that all information is to be disclosed to all of them. Courts sometimes refer to this as a presumed intent that there should be no confidentiality between co-clients. Fairness and candor between the co-clients and with the lawyer generally precludes the lawyer from keeping information secret from any one of them, unless they have agreed otherwise (see § 60, Comment *l*).

Illustration:

1. Client X and Client Y jointly consult Lawyer about establishing a business, without coming to any agreement about the confidentiality of their communications to Lawyer. X sends a confidential memorandum to Lawyer in which X outlines the proposed business arrangement as X understands it. The joint representation then terminates, and Y knows that X sent the memorandum but not its contents. Subsequently, Y files suit against X to recover damages arising out of the business venture. Although X's memorandum would be privileged against a third person, in the litigation between X and Y the memorandum is not privileged. That result follows although Y never knew the contents of the letter during the joint representation.

Whether communications between the lawyer and a client that occurred before formation of a joint representation are subject to examination depends on the understanding at the time that the new person was joined as a co-client.

Co-clients may agree that the lawyer will not disclose certain confidential communications of one co-client to other co-clients. If the co-clients have so agreed and the co-clients are subsequently involved in adverse proceedings, the communicating client can invoke the privilege with respect to such communications not in fact disclosed to the former co-client seeking to introduce it. In the absence of such an agreement, the lawyer ordinarily is required to convey communications to all interested co-clients (see § 60, Comment *l*). A co-client may also retain additional, separate counsel on the matter of the common representation; communications with such counsel are not subject to this Section.

e. Standing to assert the co-client privilege; waiver. If a third person attempts to gain access to or to introduce a co-client communication, each co-client has standing to assert the privilege. The objecting client need not have been the source of the communication or previously have known about it.

The normal rules of waiver (see § § 78-80) apply to a co-client's own communications to the common lawyer. Thus, in the absence of an agreement with co-clients to the contrary, each co-client may waive the privilege with respect to that co-client's own communications with the lawyer, so long as the communication relates only to the communicating and waiving client.

One co-client does not have authority to waive the privilege with respect to another co-client's communications to their common lawyer. If a document or other recording embodies communications from two or more co-clients, all those co-clients must join in a waiver, unless a nonwaiving co-client's communication can be redacted from the document.

Disclosure of a co-client communication in the course of subsequent adverse proceeding between co-clients operates as waiver by subsequent disclosure under § 79 with respect to third persons.

§ 76. The Privilege in Common-Interest Arrangements

(1) If two or more clients with a common interest in a litigated or nonlitigated matter are represented by separate lawyers and they agree to exchange information concerning the matter, a communication of any such client that otherwise qualifies as privileged under § § 68-72 that relates to the matter is privileged as against third persons. Any such client may invoke the privilege, unless it has been waived by the client who made the communication.

(2) Unless the clients have agreed otherwise, a communication described in Subsection (1) is not privileged as between clients described in Subsection (1) in a subsequent adverse proceeding between them.

Comment:

b. Rationale. The rule in this Section permits persons who have common interests to coordinate their positions without destroying the privileged status of their communications with their lawyers. For example, where conflict of interest disqualifies a lawyer from representing two co-defendants in a criminal case (see § 129), the separate lawyers representing them may exchange confidential communications to prepare their defense without loss of the privilege. Clients thus can elect separate representation while maintaining the privilege in cooperating on common elements of interest.

c. Confidentiality and common-interest rules. The common-interest privilege somewhat relaxes the requirement of confidentiality (see § 71) by defining a widened circle of persons to whom clients may disclose privileged communications. As a corollary, the rule also limits what would otherwise be instances of waiver by disclosing a communication (compare § 79). Communications of several commonly interested clients remain confidential against the rest of the world, no matter how many clients are involved. However, the known presence of a stranger negates the privilege for communications made in the stranger's presence.

Exchanging communications may be predicated on an express agreement, but formality is not required. It may pertain to litigation or to other matters. Separately represented clients do not, by the mere fact of cooperation under this Section, impliedly undertake to exchange all information concerning the matter of common interest.

d. The permissible extent of common-interest disclosures. Under the privilege, any member of a client set—a client, the client's agent for communication, the client's lawyer, and the lawyer's agent (see § 70)—can exchange communications with members of a similar client set. However, a communication directly among the clients is not privileged unless made for the purpose of communicating with a privileged person as defined in § 70. A person who is not represented by a lawyer and who is not himself or herself a lawyer cannot participate in a common-interest arrangement within this Section.

e. Extent of common interests. The communication must relate to the common interest, which may be either legal, factual, or strategic in character. The interests of the separately represented clients need not be entirely congruent.

Illustration:

1. Lawyer One separately represents Corporation A and Lawyer Two represents Corporation B in defending a products-liability action brought by a common adversary, Plaintiff X. The two lawyers agree to exchange otherwise privileged communications of their respective clients concerning settlement strategies. Plaintiff Y later sues Corporation A and Corporation B for damages for alleged defects involving the same products and attempts to obtain discovery of the communications between Lawyer One and Lawyer Two. The communications exchanged between the lawyers for Corporation A and Corporation B are privileged and cannot be discovered.

Unlike the relationship between co-clients, the common-interest relationship does not imply an undertaking to disclose all relevant information (compare § 75, Comment *d*). Confidential communications disclosed to only some members of the arrangement remain privileged against other members as well as against the rest of the world.

§ 77. Duration of the Privilege

Unless waived (see § § 78-80) or subject to exception (see § § 81-85), the attorney-client privilege may be invoked as provided in § 86 at any time during or after termination of the relationship between client or prospective client and lawyer.

Comment:

d. Situations of need and hardship. The law recognizes no exception to the rule of this Section. Set out below are considerations that may support such an exception, although no court or legislature has adopted it.

It would be desirable that a tribunal be empowered to withhold the privilege of a person then deceased as to a communication that bears on a litigated issue of pivotal significance. The tribunal could balance the interest in confidentiality against any exceptional need for the communication. The tribunal also could consider limiting the proof or sealing the record to limit disclosure. Permitting such disclosure would do little to inhibit clients from confiding in their lawyers. The fortuity of death prevents waiver of the privilege by the client. Appointing a personal representative to consider waiving the privilege simply transforms the issue into one before a probate court. It would be more direct to permit the judge in the proceeding in which the evidence is offered to make a determination based on the relevant factors.

§ 78. Agreement, Disclaimer, or Failure to Object

The attorney-client privilege is waived if the client, the client's lawyer, or another authorized agent of the client:
  (1) agrees to waive the privilege;
  (2) disclaims protection of the privilege and
    (a) another person reasonably relies on the disclaimer to that person's detriment; or
    (b) reasons of judicial administration require that the client not be permitted to revoke the disclaimer; or
  (3) in a proceeding before a tribunal, fails to object properly to an attempt by another person to give or exact testimony or other evidence of a privileged communication.

§ 79. Subsequent Disclosure

The attorney-client privilege is waived if the client, the client's lawyer, or another authorized agent of the client voluntarily discloses the communication in a nonprivileged communication.

Comment:

b. Subsequent disclosure. Voluntary disclosure of a privileged communication is inconsistent with a later claim that the communication is to be protected. When the disclosure has been made voluntarily, it is unnecessary that there have been detrimental reliance (compare § 78(2)).

c. Authorized disclosure by a lawyer or other agent. The privilege is waived if the client's lawyer or another authorized agent of the client discloses the communication acting under actual or apparent authority. A lawyer generally has implied authority to disclose confidential client communications in the course of representing a client (see § 27, Comment *c*; see also § 61). Ratification of the agent's authority has the same effect (see § 26, Comment *e*). Whether a subagent of the client or lawyer has authority to waive is governed by agency law. A file clerk in a law firm, for example, does not have implied authority.

Unauthorized disclosure by a lawyer not in pursuit of the client's interests does not constitute waiver under this Section. For example, disclosure of a client's confidential information to prevent a threat to the life or safety of another (§ 66) or to prevent a client crime or fraud (§ 67) does not constitute waiver within the meaning of this Section, although another basis for finding the privilege inapplicable may apply.

Because of the lawyer's apparent authority to act for the client, a lawyer's failure to consult the client about disclosing privileged information generally will not affect the rights of third persons. A third person may not, however, reasonably rely on acts of an opposing lawyer or other agent constituting manifest disregard of responsibility for the client's interests (see also § 60, Comment *l*, & § 71, Comment *c* (eavesdroppers)). Upon discovery of an agent's wrongful disclosure, the client must promptly take reasonable steps to suppress or recover the wrongfully disclosed communication in order to preserve the privilege.

Illustration:

1. Lawyer sends a confidential memorandum containing privileged communications to Client for Client's review. Lawyer sends it by a reputable document-courier service. An employee of the document-courier service opens the sealed envelope, makes copies, and gives the copies to a government agency. As soon as the existence of the copies is discovered, Lawyer takes reasonable steps to recover them and demands that the document-courier service and the government agency return all communications taken or information gained from them. Even if the document-courier service is considered an agent of Lawyer for some purposes, its employee's actions do not waive Client's privilege in the communications.

d. A privileged subsequent disclosure. A subsequent disclosure that is itself privileged does not result in waiver. Thus, a client who discloses a communication protected by the attorney-client privilege to a second lawyer does not waive the privilege if the attorney-client privilege or work-product immunity protects the second communication. So also, showing a confidential letter from the client's lawyer to the client's spouse under circumstances covered by the marital privilege preserves the attorney-client privilege.

e. Extent of disclosure. Waiver results only when a nonprivileged person learns the substance of a privileged communication. Knowledge by the nonprivileged person that the client consulted a lawyer does not result in waiver, nor does disclosure of nonprivileged portions of a communication or its general subject matter. Public disclosure of facts that were discussed in confidence with a lawyer does not waive the privilege if the disclosure does not also reveal that they were communicated to the lawyer. See § 69, Comment *d* (distinction between communications and facts).

Illustrations:

2. Client, a defendant in a personal-injury action, makes a privileged communication to Lawyer concerning the circumstances of the accident. In a later judicial proceeding, Client, under questioning by Lawyer, testifies about the occurrence but not about what Client told Lawyer about the same matter. On cross-examination, the lawyer for Plaintiff inquires whether the Client's testimony is consistent with the account Client gave to Lawyer in confidence. Client's testimony did not waive the privilege.

3. The same facts as in Illustration 2, except that Client states that "I've testified exactly as I told Lawyer just a week after the accident happened. I told Lawyer that the skid marks made by Plaintiff's car were 200 feet long. And I've said the same things here." Such testimony waives the privilege by subsequent disclosure. On the extent of waiver, see Comment *f* hereto.

In the circumstances of Illustration 3, if the client merely testifies that the subject of skid marks was discussed with the client's lawyer, the privilege is not waived.

f. Partial subsequent disclosure and "subject matter" waiver. An initial disclosure resulting in waiver under this Section may consist of disclosure of fewer than all communications between lawyer and client on the subject. The question then arises whether an inquiring party is entitled to access to other relevant communications beyond those actually disclosed. (Similar questions can arise with respect to waiver under § 78 (waiver by agreement, disclaimer, or failure to object) and § 80 (waiver by putting assistance or communication in issue).)

General waiver of all related communications is warranted when a party has selectively offered in evidence before a factfinder only part of a more extensive communication or one of several related communications, and the opposing party seeks to test whether the partial disclosure distorted the context or meaning of the part offered. All authorities agree that in such a situation waiver extends to all otherwise-privileged communications on the same subject matter that are reasonably necessary to make a complete and balanced presentation (compare Federal Rules of Evidence, Rule 106). That breadth of waiver is required by considerations of forensic fairness, to prevent a partial disclosure that would otherwise mislead the factfinder because selectively incomplete. Similar considerations generally apply when the privilege holder makes a partial disclosure in pretrial proceedings, as in support of a motion for summary judgment or during a pretrial hearing on a request for provisional relief.

If partial disclosure occurs in a nontestimonial setting or in the context of pretrial discovery, a clear majority of decisions indicates that a similar broad waiver will be found, even though the disclosure is not intended to obtain advantage as a possibly misleading half-truth in testimony. Although arguably different considerations might apply (because of the absence of opportunity to mislead a factfinder by partial disclosure), courts insist in effect that a party who wishes to assert the privilege take effective steps to protect against even partial disclosure, regardless of the nontestimonial setting. In an appropriate factual setting, waiver may also be supportable on the ground that the partial disclosure was designed to mislead an opposing party in negotiations or was inconsistent with a candid exchange of information in pretrial discovery.

Parties may agree that disclosure of one privileged communication will not be regarded as waiver as to others, and a tribunal may so order, for example in a discovery protective order. Such an agreement or order governs questions of waiver both in the proceeding involved and, with respect to the parties to the agreement, in other proceedings.

g. *Voluntary subsequent disclosure.* To constitute waiver, a disclosure must be voluntary. The disclosing person need not be aware that the communication was privileged, nor specifically intend to waive the privilege. A disclosure in obedience to legal compulsion or as the product of deception does not constitute waiver.

Illustrations:

4. A burglar ransacks Client's confidential files and carries away copies of communications from Client to Lawyer protected by the attorney-client privilege. The police apprehend the burglar, recover the copies, and examine them in order to identify their owner. Client's right to invoke the privilege is not lost.

5. At a hearing before a tribunal, the presiding officer erroneously overrules Lawyer's objection to a question put to Client that calls for a communication protected by the attorney-client privilege. Client then testifies. By testifying, Client has not waived objection to efforts to elicit additional privileged communications in the litigation nor to claim on appeal that the hearing officer incorrectly overruled Lawyer's objection. Client also can seek protection of the attorney-client privilege in subsequent litigation.

On resisting disclosure by legal compulsion, see § 86.

h. *Inadvertent disclosure.* A subsequent disclosure through a voluntary act constitutes a waiver even though not intended to have that effect. It is important to distinguish between inadvertent waiver and a change of heart after voluntary waiver. Waiver does not result if the client or other disclosing person took precautions reasonable in the circumstances to guard against such disclosure. What is reasonable depends on circumstances, including: the relative importance of the communication (the more sensitive the communication, the greater the necessary protective measures); the efficacy of precautions taken and of additional precautions that might have been taken; whether there were externally imposed pressures of time or in the volume of required disclosure; whether disclosure was by act of the client or lawyer or by a third person; and the degree of disclosure to nonprivileged persons.

Once the client knows or reasonably should know that the communication has been disclosed, the client must take prompt and reasonable steps to recover the communication, to reestablish its confidential nature, and to reassert the privilege. Otherwise, apparent acceptance of the disclosure may reflect indifference to confidentiality. Even if fully successful retrieval is impracticable, the client must nonetheless take feasible steps to prevent further distribution.

Illustration:

6. Plaintiff has threatened Client with suit unless Client is able to persuade Plaintiff's lawyers that Client is free from fault. Plaintiff imposes a stringent deadline for Client's showing. Client authorizes

Lawyer to produce a large mass of documents. Although reviewed by Lawyer, the documents include a confidential memorandum by Client to Lawyer. The standard procedure of lawyers in the circumstances would not have included reexamining the copies prior to submission. Lawyer's inadvertent disclosure did not waive the privilege. After discovering the mistake, Client must promptly reassert the privilege and demand return of the document.

i. Consequences of client waiver of the privilege. Waiver ordinarily extends to the litigation in or in anticipation of which a disclosure was made and future proceedings as well, whether or not related to the original proceeding. However, if no actual disclosure resulted from the waiver, a client might be in a position to reassert the privilege. For example, inadvertent disclosure of a privileged document in discovery should not preclude subsequent assertion of the privilege against a different opponent in different litigation if the disclosure does not result in the document becoming known to anyone other than the party who received it.

§ 80. Putting Assistance or a Communication in Issue

(1) The attorney-client privilege is waived for any relevant communication if the client asserts as to a material issue in a proceeding that:

(a) the client acted upon the advice of a lawyer or that the advice was otherwise relevant to the legal significance of the client's conduct; or

(b) a lawyer's assistance was ineffective, negligent, or otherwise wrongful.

(2) The attorney-client privilege is waived for a recorded communication if a witness:

(a) employs the communication to aid the witness while testifying; or

(b) employed the communication in preparing to testify, and the tribunal finds that disclosure is required in the interests of justice.

§ 81. A Dispute Concerning a Decedent's Disposition of Property

The attorney-client privilege does not apply to a communication from or to a decedent relevant to an issue between parties who claim an interest through the same deceased client, either by testate or intestate succession or by an inter vivos transaction.

§ 82. Client Crime or Fraud

The attorney-client privilege does not apply to a communication occurring when a client:

(a) consults a lawyer for the purpose, later accomplished, of obtaining assistance to engage in a crime or fraud or aiding a third person to do so, or

(b) regardless of the client's purpose at the time of consultation, uses the lawyer's advice or other services to engage in or assist a crime or fraud.

Comment:

a. Scope and cross-references. . . . . On a lawyer's responsibilities with respect to counseling a client concerning illegal acts, see § 94. On a lawyer's responsibilities with respect to perjurious or other false evidence, see § 120. A lawyer's duty to safeguard confidential client information (see § 60(1)(b)) is subject to § § 66-67, permitting a lawyer to use or disclose information as reasonably necessary to prevent (or in some instances to mitigate) certain illegal acts of a client.

b. Rationale. When a client consults a lawyer intending to violate elemental legal obligations, there is less social interest in protecting the communication. Correlatively, there is a public interest in preventing clients from attempting to misuse the client-lawyer relationship for seriously harmful ends. Denying protection of the privilege can be founded on the additional moral ground that the client's wrongful intent forfeits the protection. The client can choose whether or not to commit or aid the act after consulting the lawyer and thus is able to avoid exposing secret communications. The exception does not apply to communications about client crimes or frauds that occurred prior to the consultation. Whether a communication relates to past or ongoing or future acts can be a close question. See Comment *e* hereto.

c. Intent of the client and lawyer. The client need not specifically understand that the contemplated act is a crime or fraud. The client's purpose in consulting the lawyer or using the lawyer's services may be

229

inferred from the circumstances. It is irrelevant that the legal service sought by the client (such as drafting an instrument) was itself lawful.

Illustrations:

> 1. Client is a member of a group engaged in the ongoing enterprise of importing and distributing illegal drugs. Client has agreed with confederates, as part of the consideration for participating in the enterprise, that Client will provide legal representation for the confederates when necessary. Client and Lawyer agree that, for a substantial monthly retainer, Lawyer will stand ready to provide legal services in the event that Client or Client's associates encounter legal difficulties during the operation of the enterprise. In a communication that otherwise qualifies as privileged under § 68, Client informs Lawyer of the identities of confederates in the enterprise. Client continues to engage in the criminal enterprise following the communication. The crime-fraud exception renders nonprivileged the communications between Client and Lawyer, including identification of Client's confederates.

> 2. Client, who is in financial difficulty, consults Lawyer A concerning the sale of a parcel of real estate owned by Client. Lawyer A provides legal services in connection with the sale. Client then asks Lawyer A to represent Client in petitioning for bankruptcy. Lawyer A advises Client that the bankruptcy petition must list the sale of the real estate because it occurred within the year previous to the date of filing the petition. Client ends the representation. Client shortly thereafter hires Lawyer B. Omitting to tell Lawyer B about the land sale, Client directs Lawyer B to file a bankruptcy petition that does not disclose the proceeds of the sale. In a subsequent proceeding in which Client's fraud in filing the petition is in issue, a tribunal would be warranted in inferring that Client consulted Lawyer A with the purpose of obtaining assistance to defraud creditors in bankruptcy and thus that the communications between Client and Lawyer A concerning report of the land sale in the bankruptcy petition are not privileged. It would also suffice should the tribunal find that Client attempted to use Lawyer A's advice about the required contents of a bankruptcy petition to defraud creditors by withholding information about the land sale from Lawyer B.

A client could intend criminal or fraudulent conduct but not carry through the intended act. The exception should not apply in such circumstances, for it would penalize a client for doing what the privilege is designed to encourage—consulting a lawyer for the purpose of achieving law compliance. By the same token, lawyers might be discouraged from giving full and candid advice to clients about legally questionable courses of action. On the other hand, a client may consult a lawyer about a matter that constitutes a criminal conspiracy but that is later frustrated—and, in that sense, not later accomplished (cf. Subsection (a))—or, similarly, about a criminal attempt. Such a crime is within the exception stated in the Section if its elements are established.

The crime-fraud exception applies regardless of the fact that the client's lawyer is unaware of the client's intent. The exception also applies if the lawyer actively participates in the crime or fraud. However, if a client does not intend to commit a criminal or fraudulent act, the privilege protects the client's communication even if the client's lawyer acts with a criminal or fraudulent intent in giving advice.

Illustration:

> 3. Lawyer, in complicity with confederates who are not clients, is furthering a scheme to defraud purchasers in a public offering of shares of stock. Client, believing that the stock offering is legitimate and ignorant of facts indicating its wrongful nature, seeks to participate in the offering as an underwriter. In the course of obtaining legal advice from Lawyer, Client conveys communications to Lawyer that are privileged under § 68. The crime-fraud exception does not prevent Client from asserting the attorney-client privilege, despite Lawyer's complicity in the fraud. . . .

d. Kinds of illegal acts included within the exception. The authorities agree that the exception stated in this Section applies to client conduct defined as a crime or fraud. Fraud, for the purpose of the exception, requires a knowing or reckless misrepresentation (or nondisclosure when applicable law requires disclosure) likely to injure another (see Restatement Second, Torts § § 525-530 (defining elements of fraudulent misrepresentation)).

The evidence codes and judicial decisions are divided on the question of extending the exception to other wrongs such as intentional torts, which, although not criminal or fraudulent, have hallmarks of clear illegality and the threat of serious harm. Legislatures and courts classify illegal acts as crimes and frauds for purposes and policies different from those defining the scope of the privilege. Thus, limiting the exception to crimes and frauds produces an exception narrower than principle and policy would otherwise indicate. Nonetheless, the prevailing view limits the exception to crimes and frauds. The actual instances in which a broader exception might apply are probably few and isolated, and it would be difficult to formulate a broader exception that is not objectionably vague.

Consultation about some acts of civil disobedience is privileged under the Section, for example violations of a law based on a nonfrivolous claim that the law is unconstitutional. The same is true of a communication concerning a contempt sanction necessary to obtain immediate appellate review of an order whose validity is challenged in good faith. (See § 94, Comment e, & § 105, Comment e.) If, however, the client's position is that the law is valid but there is a superior moral justification for violating it, this Section applies if its conditions are otherwise satisfied.

e. Continuing crimes and frauds. The crime-fraud exception depends on a distinction between past client wrongs and acts that are continuing or will occur in the future. The exception does not apply to communications about client criminal or fraudulent acts that occurred in the past. Communications about past acts are necessary in defending against charges concerning such conduct and, for example, providing background for legal advice concerning a present transaction that is neither criminal nor fraudulent. The possible social costs of denying access to relevant evidence of past acts is accepted in order to realize the enhanced legality and fairness that confidentiality fosters (see § 68, Comment c).

The exception does apply to client crimes or frauds that are ongoing or continuing. With respect to past acts that have present consequences, such as the possession of stolen goods, consultation of lawyer and client is privileged if it addresses how the client can rectify the effects of the illegal act—such as by returning the goods to their rightful owner—or defending the client against criminal charges arising out of the offense.

Illustration:

4. Client consults Lawyer about Client's indictment for the crimes of theft and of unlawfully possessing stolen goods. Applicable law treats possession of stolen goods as a continuing offense. Client is hiding the goods in a secret place, knowing that they are stolen. Confidential communications between Client and Lawyer concerning the indictment for theft and possession and the facts underlying those offenses are privileged. Confidential communications concerning ways in which Client can continue to possess the stolen goods, including information supplied by Client about their present location, are not protected by the privilege because of the crime-fraud exception. Confidential communications about ways in which Client might lawfully return the stolen goods to their owner are privileged.

Strict limitation of the exception to ongoing or future crimes and frauds would prohibit a lawyer from testifying that a client confessed to a crime for which an innocent person is on trial. The law of the United Kingdom recognizes an exception in such cases. At least in capital cases, the argument for so extending the exception seems compelling. Compare also § 66 (disclosure to prevent loss of life or serious bodily injury, whether or not risk is created by wrongful client act).

f. Invoking the crime-fraud exception. The crime-fraud exception is relevant only after the attorney-client privilege is successfully invoked. The person seeking access to the communication then must present a prima facie case for the exception. A prima facie case need show only a reasonable basis for concluding that the elements of the exception (see Comment d) exist. The showing must be made by evidence other than the contested communication itself. Once a prima facie showing is made, the tribunal has discretion to examine the communication or hear testimony about it in camera, that is, without requiring that the communications be revealed to the party seeking to invoke the exception (see § 86, Comment f).

Unless the crime-fraud exception plainly applies to a client-lawyer communication, a lawyer has an obligation to assert the privilege (see § 63, Comment b).

g. Effects of the crime-fraud exception. A communication to which the crime-fraud exception applies is not privileged under § 68 for any purpose. Evidence of the communication is admissible in the proceeding in which that determination is made or in another proceeding. The privilege still applies, however, to communications that were not for a purpose included within this Section. For example, a client who consulted a lawyer about several different matters on several different occasions could invoke the privilege with respect to consultations concerning matters unrelated to the illegal acts (compare § 79, Comment e). With respect to a lawyer's duty not to use or disclose client information even if not privileged, see § 60; compare § § 66-67.

§ 83. Lawyer Self-Protection

The attorney-client privilege does not apply to a communication that is relevant and reasonably necessary for a lawyer to employ in a proceeding:

(1) to resolve a dispute with a client concerning compensation or reimbursement that the lawyer reasonably claims the client owes the lawyer; or

(2) to defend the lawyer or the lawyer's associate or agent against a charge by any person that the lawyer, associate, or agent acted wrongfully during the course of representing a client.

§ 84. Fiduciary-Lawyer Communications

In a proceeding in which a trustee of an express trust or similar fiduciary is charged with breach of fiduciary duties by a beneficiary, a communication otherwise within § 68 is nonetheless not privileged if the communication:

(a) is relevant to the claimed breach; and

(b) was between the trustee and a lawyer (or other privileged person within the meaning of § 70) who was retained to advise the trustee concerning the administration of the trust.

§ 85. Communications Involving a Fiduciary Within an Organization

In a proceeding involving a dispute between an organizational client and shareholders, members, or other constituents of the organization toward whom the directors, officers, or similar persons managing the organization bear fiduciary responsibilities, the attorney-client privilege of the organization may be withheld from a communication otherwise within § 68 if the tribunal finds that:

(a) those managing the organization are charged with breach of their obligations toward the shareholders, members, or other constituents or toward the organization itself;

(b) the communication occurred prior to the assertion of the charges and relates directly to those charges; and

(c) the need of the requesting party to discover or introduce the communication is sufficiently compelling and the threat to confidentiality sufficiently confined to justify setting the privilege aside.

§ 86. Invoking the Privilege and Its Exceptions

(1) When an attempt is made to introduce in evidence or obtain discovery of a communication privileged under § 68:

(a) A client, a personal representative of an incompetent or deceased client, or a person succeeding to the interest of a client may invoke or waive the privilege, either personally or through counsel or another authorized agent.

(b) A lawyer, an agent of the lawyer, or an agent of a client from whom a privileged communication is sought must invoke the privilege when doing so appears reasonably appropriate, unless the client:

(i) has waived the privilege; or

(ii) has authorized the lawyer or agent to waive it.

(c) Notwithstanding failure to invoke the privilege as specified in Subsections (1)(a) and (1)(b), the tribunal has discretion to invoke the privilege.

(2) A person invoking the privilege must ordinarily object contemporaneously to an attempt to disclose the communication and, if the objection is contested, demonstrate each element of the privilege under § 68.

(3) A person invoking a waiver of or exception to the privilege (§ § 78-85) must assert it and, if the assertion is contested, demonstrate each element of the waiver or exception.

TOPIC 3. THE LAWYER WORK-PRODUCT IMMUNITY

§ 87. Lawyer Work-Product Immunity

(1) Work product consists of tangible material or its intangible equivalent in unwritten or oral form, other than underlying facts, prepared by a lawyer for litigation then in progress or in reasonable anticipation of future litigation.

(2) Opinion work product consists of the opinions or mental impressions of a lawyer; all other work product is ordinary work product.

(3) Except for material which by applicable law is not so protected, work product is immune from discovery or other compelled disclosure to the extent stated in § § 88 (ordinary work product) and 89 (opinion work product) when the immunity is invoked as described in § 90.

Comment:

b. Rationale. The Federal Rules of Civil Procedure in 1938 provided for notice pleading supplemented by expanded discovery. The Rules sought to eliminate the "sporting" concept of litigation in favor of more accurate factfinding and open truth-seeking. However, the discovery rules presupposed that counsel should be able to work within an area of professional confidentiality, described by the work-product rule. A companion assumption has been that the truth emerges from the adversary presentation of information by opposing sides, in which opposing lawyers competitively develop their own sources of factual and legal information. The work-product doctrine also protects client interests in obtaining diligent assistance from lawyers. A lawyer whose work product would be open to the other side might forgo useful preparatory procedures, for example, note-taking. The immunity also reduces the possibility that a lawyer would have to testify concerning witness statements (compare § 108).

Nonetheless, the work-product immunity is in tension with the purposes of modern discovery by impeding the pretrial exchange of information. The immunity also entails duplication of investigative efforts, perhaps increasing litigation costs. Enforcement of the immunity causes satellite litigation and additional expense.

Protection of lawyer thought processes (see § 89) is at the core of work-product rationale; accordingly, those are accorded the broadest protection. A lawyer's analysis can readily be replicated by an opposing lawyer and, in any event, would usually be inadmissible in evidence. Factual information gathered by a lawyer usually relates directly to controverted issues and generally is discoverable in forms that do not reveal the lawyer's thought processes.

Beyond that, the work-product rules are a set of compromises between openness and secrecy. Thus, under Federal Rule 26(b), the identity of witnesses must be disclosed even if ascertaining their identity has been burdensome or involved confidential consultations with a client. Similarly, under Rule 26(b) statements given by a party to an opposing lawyer are subject to discovery, even though such a statement necessarily reflects the lawyer's thought process in some degree. So also are the opinions of an expert who is expected to testify at trial. A nonparty witness's statement must be produced upon demand by that witness. A party's documents and other records are generally discoverable even if they have been reviewed by counsel. On the other hand, the identity of an expert consulted but who will not testify is protected against discovery, even if that expert's opinion is highly material. So also, the classification systems employed by a lawyer in reviewing a client's documents are not subject to discovery.

c. Applications of the work-product immunity. The work-product immunity operates primarily as a limitation on pretrial discovery, but it can apply to evidence at a trial or hearing. Work-product immunity is also recognized in criminal and administrative proceedings and is incorporated as a limitation on other types of disclosure, for example in the federal Freedom of Information Act. The scope of those applications of the work-product rule is generally beyond the scope of this Restatement.

d. The relationship of the work-product immunity to the attorney-client privilege. The attorney-client privilege is limited to communications between a client and lawyer and certain of their agents (see § 70); in contrast, work product includes many other kinds of materials (see Comment *f*), even when obtained from sources other than the client. Application of the attorney-client privilege absolutely bars discovery or testimonial use; in contrast, the work-product immunity is a qualified protection that, in various circumstances, can be overcome on a proper showing (see § § 88 & 89). The attorney-client privilege protects communications between client and lawyer regarding all kinds of legal services (see § 72); in contrast, the work-product immunity is limited to materials prepared for or in anticipation of litigation (see Comments *h-j*).

Work-product immunity is also similar to the rule recognized in some jurisdictions that a self-evaluation study and report is immune from discovery. The self-evaluation immunity is not limited to work performed in anticipation of litigation. The scope of self-evaluation and similar immunities is beyond the scope of this Restatement.

e. The source of the law concerning work-product immunity. In the federal system, work-product immunity is recognized both under Rule 26(b)(3) of the Federal Rules of Civil Procedure and as a common-law rule following the decision in *Hickman v. Taylor.* In a few states work-product immunity is established by common law, but in most states it is defined by statute or court rule. Some state statutes mirror Federal Rule of Civil Procedure 26(b)(3); others codify the principles of *Hickman v. Taylor* more broadly; and others codify pre-*Hickman* rules that were not adopted for the federal courts. State courts, in construing their statutes, often look to federal case law in applying work-product immunity.

f. Types of work-product materials. Work product includes tangible materials and intangible equivalents prepared, collected, or assembled by a lawyer. Tangible materials include documents, photographs, diagrams, sketches, questionnaires and surveys, financial and economic analyses, hand-written notes, and material in electronic and other technologically advanced forms, such as stenographic, mechanical, or electronic recordings or transmissions, computer data bases, tapes, and printouts. Intangible work product is equivalent work product in unwritten, oral or remembered form. For example, intangible work product can come into question by a discovery request for a lawyer's recollections derived from oral communications.

A compilation or distillation of non-work-product materials can itself be work product. For example, a lawyer's memorandum analyzing publicly available information constitutes work product. The selection or arrangement of documents that are not themselves protected might reflect mental impressions and legal opinions inherent in making a selection or arrangement. Thus, a lawyer's index of a client's preexisting and discoverable business files will itself be work product if prepared in anticipation of litigation. So also, the manner in which a lawyer has selected certain client files, organized them in pretrial work, and plans to present them at trial is work product.

g. The distinction between protected materials and nonprotected underlying facts. Work-product immunity does not apply to underlying facts of the incident or transaction involved in the litigation, even if the same information is contained in work product. For a comparison to the nonprivileged status accorded to facts under the attorney-client privilege, see § 69, Comment *d.*

The distinction between discoverable underlying facts and nondiscoverable work product can be difficult to draw. Relevant are the form of the question or request, the identity of the person who is to respond, and the form of a responsive answer. Immunity does not attach merely because the underlying fact was discovered through a lawyer's effort or is recorded only in otherwise protected work product, for example, in a lawyer's file memorandum. Immunity does not apply to an interrogatory seeking names of witnesses to the occurrence in question or whether a witness recounts a particular version of events, for example that a traffic light was red or green. On the other hand, an interrogatory seeking the substantially verbatim contents of the witness's unrecorded statement would be objectionable.

h. Anticipation of litigation: kinds of proceedings. The limitation of the work-product immunity to litigation activities is best explained by the origin of the rule in the context of litigation. "Litigation" includes civil and criminal trial proceedings, as well as adversarial proceedings before an administrative agency, an arbitration panel or a claims commission, and alternative-dispute-resolution proceedings such as mediation or mini-trial. It also includes a proceeding such as a grand jury or a coroner's inquiry or an investigative legislative hearing. In general, a proceeding is adversarial when evidence or legal argument is presented by parties contending against each other with respect to legally significant factual issues. Thus, an adversarial rulemaking proceeding is litigation for purposes of the immunity.

i. Anticipation of litigation: the reasonableness standard. Work-product immunity attaches when litigation is then in progress or there is reasonable anticipation of litigation by the lawyer at the time the material was prepared. On what constitutes litigation, see Comment *h* hereto. The fact that litigation did not actually ensue does not affect the immunity.

In one sense, almost all of a lawyer's work anticipates litigation to some degree, because preparing documents or arranging transactions is aimed at avoiding future litigation or enhancing a client's position should litigation occur. However, the immunity covers only material produced when apprehension of litigation was reasonable in the circumstances. The reasonableness of anticipation is determined objectively by considering the factual context in which materials are prepared, the nature of the materials, and the expected role of the lawyer in ensuing litigation.

Illustrations:

1. Employer's Lawyer writes to Physician, setting out circumstances of an employee's death and asking for Physician's opinion as to the cause, stating that Lawyer is preparing for a "possible claim" by the employee's executor for worker-compensation benefits. Lawyer's letter is protected work product.

2. Informed that agents of the Justice Department are questioning Publisher's customers, Lawyer for Publisher prepared a memorandum analyzing the antitrust implications of Publisher's standard contract form with commercial purchasers. Publisher's employees testify before a grand jury investigating antitrust issues in the publishing industry. Lawyer, reasonably believing there is a risk that the grand jury will indict Publisher, interviews the employees and prepares a debriefing memorandum. Both Lawyer's memorandum analyzing the contract form and Lawyer's debriefing memorandum were prepared in anticipation of litigation. The grand-jury proceeding is itself litigation for this purpose (see Comment *h*).

j. Future litigation. If litigation was reasonably anticipated, the immunity is afforded even if litigation occurs in an unanticipated way. For example, work product prepared during or in anticipation of a lawsuit remains immune in a subsequent suit for indemnification, whether or not the indemnification claim could have been anticipated. Work product prepared in anticipation of litigation remains protected in all future litigation.

§ 88. Ordinary Work Product

When work product protection is invoked as described in § 90, ordinary work product (§ 87(2)) is immune from discovery or other compelled disclosure unless either an exception recognized in § § 91-93 applies or the inquiring party:

(1) has a substantial need for the material in order to prepare for trial; and

(2) is unable without undue hardship to obtain the substantial equivalent of the material by other means.

Comment:

b. The need-and-hardship exception—in general. . . .

Demonstrating the requisite need and hardship requires the inquiring party to show that the material is relevant to the party's claim or defense, and that the inquiring party will likely be prejudiced in the absence of discovery. As a corollary, it must be shown that substantially equivalent material is not available or, if available, only through cost and effort substantially disproportionate to the amount at stake in the litigation and the value of the information to the inquiring party. The necessary showing is more easily made after other discovery has been completed.

The most common situation involves a prior statement by a witness who is absent, seriously ill, or deceased and thus now unavailable. See Federal Rule of Evidence 804(a). Another common situation concerns statements made contemporaneously with an event. Such statements are often the most reliable recording of recollections of that event and in that sense unique. A third situation is where the passage of time has dulled the memory of the witness.

Illustration:

1. Several witnesses testify before a grand jury investigating the publishing industry. Shortly afterward, Lawyer for Publisher debriefs the witnesses and writes memoranda of those interviews in anticipation of the possible indictment of Publisher and later civil suits. Six years later, Plaintiffs, representing a class of consumers, file an antitrust class action against Publisher and seek discovery of the non-opinion work-product portions of Lawyer's debriefing memoranda. Plaintiffs have been diligent in preparing their case and gathering evidence through other means and demonstrate that the witnesses now are unable to recall the events to which they testified. The court may order the memorandum produced. If the memorandum contains both ordinary and opinion work product, see § 89, Comment *c*.

Substantial need also exists when the material consists of tests performed nearly contemporaneously with a litigated event and substantially equivalent testing is no longer possible.

c. Material for impeachment. Need is shown when a requesting party demonstrates that there is likely to be a material discrepancy between a prior statement of a witness reflected in a lawyer's notes and a statement of the same person made later during discovery, such as during a deposition. The discrepancy must be of an impeaching quality. A clear case exists when the witness admits to such a discrepancy. However, the inquiring party may demonstrate a reasonable basis by inference from circumstances. In camera inspection of the statement may be appropriate to determine whether the material should be produced.

d. Witness statements. A statement given to a lawyer by a witness is work product. Being ordinary work product, a witness statement may be obtained by an opposing party only upon an appropriate showing of need and hardship. Under the Federal Rules and the law of many states, the person who gives a substantially verbatim statement has the right to obtain a copy of it.

§ 89. Opinion Work Product

When work product protection is invoked as described in § 90, opinion work product (§ 87(2)) is immune from discovery or other compelled disclosure unless either the immunity is waived or an exception applies (§ § 91-93) or extraordinary circumstances justify disclosure.

§ 90. Invoking the Lawyer Work-Product Immunity and Its Exceptions

(1) Work-product immunity may be invoked by or for a person on whose behalf the work product was prepared.

(2) The person invoking work-product immunity must object and, if the objection is contested, demonstrate each element of the immunity.

(3) Once a claim of work product has been adequately supported, a person entitled to invoke a waiver or exception must assert it and, if the assertion is contested, demonstrate each element of the waiver or exception.

§ 91. Voluntary Acts

Work-product immunity is waived if the client, the client's lawyer, or another authorized agent of the client:

(1) agrees to waive the immunity;

(2) disclaims protection of the immunity and:

(a) another person reasonably relies on the disclaimer to that person's detriment; or

(b) reasons of judicial administration require that the client not be permitted to revoke the disclaimer; or

(3) in a proceeding before a tribunal, fails to object properly to an attempt by another person to give or exact testimony or other evidence of work product; or

(4) discloses the material to third persons in circumstances in which there is a significant likelihood that an adversary or potential adversary in anticipated litigation will obtain it.

§ 92. Use of Lawyer Work Product in Litigation

(1) Work-product immunity is waived for any relevant material if the client asserts as to a material issue in a proceeding that:

(a) the client acted upon the advice of a lawyer or that the advice was otherwise relevant to the legal significance of the client's conduct; or

(b) a lawyer's assistance was ineffective, negligent, or otherwise wrongful.

(2) The work-product immunity is waived for recorded material if a witness

(a) employs the material to aid the witness while testifying, or

(b) employed the material in preparing to testify, and the tribunal finds that disclosure is required in the interests of justice.

§ 93. Client Crime or Fraud

Work-product immunity does not apply to materials prepared when a client consults a lawyer for the purpose, later accomplished, of obtaining assistance to engage in a crime or fraud or to aid a third person to do so or uses the materials for such a purpose.

CHAPTER 6. REPRESENTING CLIENTS—IN GENERAL

TOPIC 1. LAWYER FUNCTIONS IN REPRESENTING CLIENTS—IN GENERAL

§ 94. Advising and Assisting a Client—In General

(1) A lawyer who counsels or assists a client to engage in conduct that violates the rights of a third person is subject to liability:

(a) to the third person to the extent stated in § § 51 and 56-57; and

(b) to the client to the extent stated in § § 50, 55, and 56.

(2) For purposes of professional discipline, a lawyer may not counsel or assist a client in conduct that the lawyer knows to be criminal or fraudulent or in violation of a court order with the intent of facilitating or encouraging the conduct, but the lawyer may counsel or assist a client in conduct when the lawyer reasonably believes:

(a) that the client's conduct constitutes a good-faith effort to determine the validity, scope, meaning, or application of a law or court order; or

(b) that the client can assert a nonfrivolous argument that the client's conduct will not constitute a crime or fraud or violate a court order.

(3) In counseling a client, a lawyer may address nonlegal aspects of a proposed course of conduct, including moral, reputational, economic, social, political, and business aspects.

Comment:

f. Advice about enforcement policy. A lawyer's advice to a client about the degree of risk that a law violation will be detected or prosecuted violates the rule of Subsection (2) when the circumstances indicate that the lawyer thereby intended to counsel or assist the client's crime, fraud, or violation of a court order. No bright-line rule immunizes the lawyer from adverse legal consequences. In many borderline situations, the lawyer's intent will be a disputable question of fact (see Comments *a* & *c*), as will be questions of the lawyer's knowledge (see Comment *g*). Such questions will be determined from all the circumstances. In general, a lawyer may advise a client about enforcement policy in areas of doubtful legality so long as the lawyer does not knowingly counsel or assist the client to engage in criminal or fraudulent activity or activity that violates a court order. Clearly, such advice is permissible when the lawyer knows that nonenforcement amounts to effective abandonment of the prohibition and not simply temporary dereliction on the part of enforcing authorities or ignorance on their part of sufficient facts to bring an enforcement proceeding.

Illustrations:

1. Client plays cards with friends in Client's home and asks Lawyer whether it would be illegal for the players to place small bets on the games. Lawyer knows that a criminal statute prohibiting gambling literally applies to such betting. Lawyer also knows that as a matter of long-standing policy and practice, persons who gamble on social games played in private homes for small stakes are not prosecuted. Lawyer may advise Client about the nonenforcement policy and practice.

2. Lawyer reasonably believes that Client has a nonfrivolous basis for asserting on state income-tax returns that Client's use of a personal automobile is for a business purpose and thus that related expenses are a proper deduction. Among other things, Lawyer has advised Client concerning the likelihood of an audit by tax authorities if Client takes the intended deduction. Lawyer bases the

237

assessment of audit likelihood on published figures showing the incidence of audits for automobile use for taxpayers at Client's income level. In the course of that discussion, Client also asks Lawyer what the average taxpayer at Client's income level deducts for charitable contributions in a year without incurring an audit. From prior dealings with Client, Lawyer knows that Client seldom makes charitable contributions and in past years has not made contributions of more than a few dollars. In the circumstances, Lawyer's advice about enforcement policy concerning the automobile use was appropriate within Subsection (2). While the facts stated above suggest that advice concerning enforcement policy for charitable deductions would not be permissible, whether under all the facts Lawyer may so advise Client depends on whether Lawyer reasonably believes that Client will likely use Lawyer's advice to claim false deductions.

§ 95. An Evaluation Undertaken for a Third Person

(1) In furtherance of the objectives of a client in a representation, a lawyer may provide to a nonclient the results of the lawyer's investigation and analysis of facts or the lawyer's professional evaluation or opinion on the matter.

(2) When providing the information, evaluation, or opinion under Subsection (1) is reasonably likely to affect the client's interests materially and adversely, the lawyer must first obtain the client's consent after the client is adequately informed concerning important possible effects on the client's interests.

(3) In providing the information, evaluation, or opinion under Subsection (1), the lawyer must exercise care with respect to the nonclient to the extent stated in § 51(2) and not make false statements prohibited under § 98.

TOPIC 2. REPRESENTING ORGANIZATIONAL CLIENTS

§ 96. Representing an Organization as Client

(1) When a lawyer is employed or retained to represent an organization:

(a) the lawyer represents the interests of the organization as defined by its responsible agents acting pursuant to the organization's decision-making procedures; and

(b) subject to Subsection (2), the lawyer must follow instructions in the representation, as stated in § 21(2), given by persons authorized so to act on behalf of the organization.

(2) If a lawyer representing an organization knows of circumstances indicating that a constituent of the organization has engaged in action or intends to act in a way that violates a legal obligation to the organization that will likely cause substantial injury to it, or that reasonably can be foreseen to be imputable to the organization and likely to result in substantial injury to it, the lawyer must proceed in what the lawyer reasonably believes to be the best interests of the organization.

(3) In the circumstances described in Subsection (2), the lawyer may, in circumstances warranting such steps, ask the constituent to reconsider the matter, recommend that a second legal opinion be sought, and seek review by appropriate supervisory authority within the organization, including referring the matter to the highest authority that can act in behalf of the organization.

Comment:

e. A constituent's breach of a legal obligation to the client organization. A lawyer representing an organization is required to act with reasonable competence and diligence in the representation (see § 16(2)) and to use care in representing the organizational client (see § 50). The lawyer thus must not knowingly or negligently assist any constituent to breach a legal duty to the organization. However, a lawyer's duty of care to the organization is not limited to avoidance of assisting acts that threaten injury to a client. A lawyer is also required to act diligently and to exercise care by taking steps to prevent reasonably foreseeable harm to a client. Thus, Subsection (2) requires a lawyer to take action to protect the interests of the client organization with respect to certain breaches of legal duty to the organization by a constituent.

The lawyer is not prevented by rules of confidentiality from acting to protect the interests of the organization by disclosing within the organization communications gained from constituents who are not themselves clients. That follows even if disclosure is against the interests of the communicating person, of another constituent whose breach of duty is in issue, or of other constituents (see § 131, Comment *e*). Such disclosure within the organization is subject to direction of a constituent who is authorized to act for the organization in the matter and who is not complicit in the breach (see Comment *d*). The lawyer may withdraw any support that the lawyer may earlier have provided the intended act, such as by withdrawing an opinion letter or draft transaction documents prepared by the lawyer.

Illustration:

1. Lawyer represents Charity, a not-for-profit corporation. Charity promotes medical research through tax-deductible contributions made to it. President as chief executive officer of Charity retained Lawyer to represent Charity as outside general counsel and has extensively communicated in confidence with Lawyer on a variety of matters concerning Charity. President asks Lawyer to draft documents by which Charity would make a gift of a new luxury automobile to a social friend of President. In that and all other work, Lawyer represents only Charity and not President as a client. Lawyer concludes that such a gift would cause financial harm to Charity in violation of President's legal duties to it. Lawyer may not draft the documents. If unable to dissuade President from effecting the gift, Lawyer must take action to protect the interests of Charity (see Subsection (2) & Comment *f*). Lawyer may, for example, communicate with members of Charity's board of directors in endeavoring to prevent the gift from being effectuated.

f. Proceeding in the best interests of the client organization. Within the meaning of Subsection (2), a wrongful act of a constituent threatening substantial injury to a client organization may be of two types. One is an act or failure to act that violates a legal obligation to the organization and that would directly harm the organization, such as by unlawfully converting its assets. The other is an act or failure to act by the constituent that, although perhaps intended to serve an interest of the organization, will foreseeably cause injury to the client, such as by exposing the organization to criminal or civil liability.

In either circumstance, as stated in Subsection (2), if the threatened injury is substantial the lawyer must proceed in what the lawyer reasonably believes to be the best interests of the organization. Those interests are normally defined by appropriate managers of the organization in the exercise of the business and managerial judgment that would be exercised by a person of ordinary prudence in a similar position. The lawyer's duty of care is that of an ordinarily prudent lawyer in such a position (see ALI Principles of Corporate Governance: Analysis and Recommendations § 4.01, at 148-149 (1994)). In the face of threats of substantial injury to the organization of the kind described in Subsection (2), the lawyer must assess the following: the degree and imminence of threatened financial, reputational, and other harms to the organization; the probable results of litigation that might ensue against the organization or for which it would be financially responsible; the costs of taking measures within the organization to prevent or correct the harm; the likely efficaciousness of measures that might be taken; and similar considerations.

The measures that a lawyer may take are those described in Subsection (3), among others. Whether a lawyer has proceeded in the best interests of the organization is determined objectively, on the basis of the circumstances reasonably apparent to the lawyer at the time. Not all lawyers would attempt to resolve a problem defined in Subsection (2) in the same manner. Not all threats to an organization are of the same degree of imminence or substantiality. In some instances the constituent may be acting solely for reasons of self-interest. In others, the constituent may act on the basis of a business judgment whose utility or prudence may be doubtful but that is within the authority of the constituent. The lawyer's assessment of those factors may depend on the constituent's credibility and intentions, based on prior dealings between them and other information available to the lawyer.

The appropriate measures to take are ordinarily a matter for the reasonable judgment of the lawyer, with due regard for the circumstances in which the lawyer must function. Those circumstances include such matters as time and budgetary limitations and limitations of access to additional information and to persons who may otherwise be able to act. If one measure fails, the lawyer must, if the nature of the threat warrants and circumstances permit, take other reasonably available measures. With respect to the lawyer's possible liability to the organizational client, failure to take a particular remedial step is tested under the general standard of § 50. When the lawyer reasonably concludes that any particular step would not likely advance the best interests of the client, the step need not be taken.

Several options are described in Subsection (3). The lawyer may be able to prevent the wrongful act or its harmful consequences by urging reconsideration by the constituent who intends to commit the act. The lawyer may also suggest that the organization obtain a second legal or other expert opinion concerning the questioned activity. It may be appropriate to refer the matter to someone within the organization having authority to prevent the prospective harm, such as an official in the organization senior in authority to the constituent threatening to act. In appropriate circumstances, the lawyer may request intervention by the highest executive authority in the organization or by its governing body, such as a board of directors or the independent directors on the board, or by an owner of a majority of the stock in the organization. In determining how to proceed, the lawyer may be guided by the organization's internal policies and lines of authority or channels of communication.

In a situation arising under Subsection (2), a lawyer does not fulfill the lawyer's duties to the organizational client by withdrawing from the representation without attempting to prevent the constituent's wrongful act. However, the lawyer's threat to withdraw unless corrective action is taken may constitute an effective step in such an attempt.

If a lawyer has attempted appropriately but unsuccessfully to protect the best interests of the organizational client, the lawyer may withdraw if permissible under § 32. Particularly when the lawyer has unsuccessfully sought to enlist assistance from the highest authority within the organization, the lawyer will be warranted in withdrawing either because the client persists in a course of action involving the lawyer's services that the lawyer reasonably believes is criminal or fraudulent (see § 32(3)(d)) or because the client insists on taking action that the lawyer considers repugnant or imprudent (see § 32(3)(f)). On proportionality between certain grounds for withdrawal and possible harm to the organizational client that would be caused by withdrawal, see § 32, Comment *h(i)*. On the circumstances in which a lawyer is required to withdraw, see § 32(2). Following withdrawal, if the lawyer had fulfilled applicable duties prior to withdrawal, the lawyer has no further duty to initiate action to protect the interests of the client organization with respect to the matter. The lawyer continues to be subject to the duties owed to any former client, such as the duty not to become involved in subsequent adverse representations (see § 132) or otherwise to use or disclose the former client's confidential information adversely to the former client (see § 60).

Whether the lawyer may disclose a constituent's breach of legal duty to persons outside the organization is determined primarily under § § 66-67 (see also § § 61-64). In limited circumstances, it may clearly appear that limited disclosure to prevent or limit harm would be in the interests of the organizational client and that constituents who purport to forbid disclosure are not authorized to act for the organization. Whether disclosure in such circumstances is warranted is a difficult and rarely encountered issue, on which this Restatement does not take a position.

g. A constituent's breach of fiduciary duty to another constituent. One constituent of an organization may owe fiduciary duties to another such constituent, for example in some instances a majority stockholder to a minority holder. A lawyer representing only the organization has no duty to protect one constituent from another, including from a breach by one constituent of such fiduciary duties, unless the interests of the lawyer's client organization are at risk. On communicating with a nonclient constituent, see § 103, Comment *e*. However, if the lawyer represents as a client either the entity or the constituent owing fiduciary duties, the lawyer may not counsel or assist a breach of any fiduciary obligation owed by the constituent to the organization.

Illustrations:

2. Lawyer represents Client, a closely held corporation, and not any constituent of Client. Under law applicable to the corporation, a majority shareholder owes a fiduciary duty of fair dealing to a minority shareholder in a transaction caused by action of a board of directors whose members have been designated by the majority stockholder. The law provides that the duty is breached if the action detrimentally and substantially affects the value of the minority shareholder's stock. Majority Shareholder has asked the board of directors of Client, consisting of Majority Shareholder's designees, to adopt a plan for buying back stock of the majority's shareholders in Client. A minority shareholder has protested the plan as unfair to the minority shareholder. Lawyer may advise the board about the position taken by the minority shareholder, but is not obliged to advise against or otherwise seek to prevent action that is consistent with the board's duty to Client.

3. The same facts as in Illustration 2, except that Lawyer has reason to know that the plan violates applicable corporate law and will likely be successfully challenged by minority shareholders in a suit against Client and that Client will likely incur substantial expense as a result. Lawyer owes a duty to

Client to take action to protect Client, such as by advising Client's board about the risks of adopting the plan.

On conflicts of interest in cases of intra-organization disagreement, see § 131, Comment *h*.

The foregoing discussion assumes an entity of substantial size and significant degree of organization. On the other hand, in the case of a closely held organization, some decisions have held that a lawyer may owe duties to a nonclient constituent, such as one who owns a minority interest.

h. Relationships with constituent and affiliated organization. Subject to conflict-of-interest considerations addressed in § 131, a lawyer representing a client organization may also represent one or more constituents of the organization, such as an officer or director of the organization (§ 131, Comment *e*) or an organization affiliated with the client (see § 131, Comment *d*). On whether a lawyer has entered into a client-lawyer relationship with a constituent person or an organization affiliated with a client organization, see § 14, Comment *f*. On avoiding misleading a corporate constituent about the role of a lawyer for the organization, see § 103, Comment *e*.

§ 97. Representing a Governmental Client

A lawyer representing a governmental client must proceed in the representation as stated in § 96, except that the lawyer:

(1) possesses such rights and responsibilities as may be defined by law to make decisions on behalf of the governmental client that are within the authority of a client under § § 22 and 21(2);

(2) except as otherwise provided by law, must proceed as stated in § § 96(2) and 96(3) with respect to an act of a constituent of the governmental client that violates a legal obligation that will likely cause substantial public or private injury or that reasonably can be foreseen to be imputable to and thus likely result in substantial injury to the client;

(3) if a prosecutor or similar lawyer determining whether to file criminal proceedings or take other steps in such proceedings, must do so only when based on probable cause and the lawyer's belief, formed after due investigation, that there are good factual and legal grounds to support the step taken; and

(4) must observe other applicable restrictions imposed by law on those similarly functioning for the governmental client.

Comment:

c. Identity of a governmental client. No universal definition of the client of a governmental lawyer is possible. For example, it has been asserted that government lawyers represent the public, or the public interest. However, determining what individual or individuals personify the government requires reference to the need to sustain political and organizational responsibility of governmental officials, as well as the organizational arrangements structured by law within which governmental lawyers work. Those who speak for the governmental client may differ from one representation to another. The identity of the client may also vary depending on the purpose for which the question of identity is posed. For example, when government lawyers negotiate a disputed question of departmental jurisdiction between two federal agencies, it is not helpful to refer to the client of each of the lawyers as "the federal government" or "the public" when considering who is empowered to direct the lawyers' activities. For many purposes, the preferable approach on the question presented is to regard the respective agencies as the clients and to regard the lawyers working for the agencies as subject to the direction of those officers authorized to act in the matter involved in the representation (see Subsection (3)).

Government agencies exist in various forms, ranging from departments or governmental corporations that may sue and be sued in their own names, to divisions of government without such separate legal status, to legislatures or committees of legislatures. If a question arises concerning which of several possible governmental entities a government lawyer represents, the identity of the lawyer's governmental client depends on the circumstances. Relevant are such factors as the terms of retention or other manifestations of the reasonable understanding of the lawyer and the hiring authority involved, the anticipated scope and nature of the lawyer's services, particular regulatory arrangements relevant to the lawyer's work, and the history and traditions of the office (see also § 96, Comment *h*).

A lawyer employed by a governmental agency to represent persons accused of offenses in military court-martial proceedings, in a state-operated public-defender office, or in similar arrangements is properly regarded as representing the individual and not any governmental entity. That would be true despite the fact that for other legal purposes the lawyer is an officer or employee of the government. On the requirement that a lawyer not permit his or her exercise of independent professional judgment to be directed by a nonclient source of the lawyer's fee, see § 134(2) and Comment *d*.

Some litigation involving governmental policy is brought by or against individual governmental officials in their capacity as such, such as is commonly done in mandamus proceedings, habeas corpus proceedings, and agency proceedings brought in the name of the head of the agency or other officer. Proceeding in that form remains the required method of much federal-court litigation against state governmental officials because of the Eleventh Amendment prohibition against suits against a state as such. A lawyer representing a governmental official in such a proceeding is subject to this Section.

When a lawyer is retained to represent a specific individual, either in that person's public (see Comment *b*) or private (nongovernmental) capacity, the person (in the appropriate capacity) is the client, unless the use of the individual's name is merely nominal and the government is the interested party. As described above with respect to multiple agencies, the identity and the specification of the capacity of the person represented by the lawyer is determined by the undertaking and reasonable expectations of both the lawyer and individual (see § 14). A lawyer who represents a governmental official in the person's public capacity must conduct the representation to advance public interests as determined by appropriate governmental officers and not, if different, the personal interests of the occupant of the office (see generally Comment *f*).

j. Wrongdoing by a constituent of a governmental client. When a constituent of a governmental client has acted, failed to act, or proposes to act as stated in Subsection (2), the lawyer must proceed as stated in § 96(2) and (3). In addition, legislation or regulations may prescribe different conditions for the lawyer's actions, conferring broader authority on a governmental lawyer to prevent or rectify constituent wrongdoing.

Wrongful acts of a constituent of a governmental client that require or permit a governmental lawyer to take remedial action under Subsection (2) include any act that would violate law applicable to the client and that would cause substantial private or public injury. Injury to the property interests of the client, for example by reason of the constituent's unlawful conversion of public funds, results in a violation of the government's legal rights. In addition, the public interest in the integrity of government may reasonably lead a lawyer to conclude, for example, that misappropriation of a small sum warrants remedial action for the government that might not be warranted for a nongovernmental client. Unlawful acts of a governmental official may also violate the nonproprietary rights of third persons—such as depriving them of the right to vote or of the right to be free of racial or gender discrimination. When a lawyer is required to act to protect the best interests of a governmental client (compare § 96, Comment *f*), those interests are defined with reference to applicable constitutional, statutory, and regulatory definitions of the objectives and responsibilities of the governmental client.

If a constituent's acts fall within Subsection (2), a lawyer representing a governmental client must proceed as stated in § 96(3) and (4) with respect to those acts. With respect to referral of a matter to a higher authority, such a referral can often be made to allied governmental agencies, such as the government's general legal office, such as a state's office of attorney general.

TOPIC 3. LAWYER DEALINGS WITH A NONCLIENT

§ 98. Statements to a Nonclient

A lawyer communicating on behalf of a client with a nonclient may not:
 (1) knowingly make a false statement of material fact or law to the nonclient;
 (2) make other statements prohibited by law; or
 (3) fail to make a disclosure of information required by law.

Comment:

d. Subsequently discovered falsity. A lawyer who has made a representation on behalf of a client reasonably believing it true when made may subsequently come to know of its falsity. An obligation to disclose before consummation of the transaction ordinarily arises, unless the lawyer takes other corrective action. See Restatement Second, Agency § 348, Comment *c*; Restatement Second, Contracts § 161(a) (nondisclosure as equivalent to assertion when person "knows that disclosure of the fact is necessary to prevent some previous assertion from being a misrepresentation or from being fraudulent or material"). Disclosure, being required by law (see § 63), is not prohibited by the general rule of confidentiality (see § 60). Disclosure should not exceed what is required to comply with the disclosure obligation, for example by indicating to recipients that they should not rely on the lawyer's statement. On permissive disclosure to prevent or rectify a client's wrongful act, see § § 66-67.

§ 99. A Represented Nonclient—The General Anti-Contact Rule

(1) A lawyer representing a client in a matter may not communicate about the subject of the representation with a nonclient whom the lawyer knows to be represented in the matter by another lawyer or with a representative of an organizational nonclient so represented as defined in § 100, unless:

(a) the communication is with a public officer or agency to the extent stated in § 101;

(b) the lawyer is a party and represents no other client in the matter;

(c) the communication is authorized by law;

(d) the communication reasonably responds to an emergency; or

(e) the other lawyer consents.

(2) Subsection (1) does not prohibit the lawyer from assisting the client in otherwise proper communication by the lawyer's client with a represented nonclient.

Comment:

f. Prohibited forms of communication. Under the anti-contact rule of this Section, a lawyer ordinarily is not authorized to communicate with a represented nonclient even by letter with a copy to the opposite lawyer or even if the opposite lawyer wrongfully fails to convey important information to that lawyer's client (see § 20), such as a settlement offer. The rule prohibits all forms of communication, such as sending a represented nonclient a copy of a letter to the nonclient's lawyer or causing communication through someone acting as the agent of the lawyer (see § 5(2) & Comment *f* thereto) (prohibition against violation of duties through agents). The anti-contact rule applies to any communication relating to the lawyer's representation in the matter, whoever initiates the contact and regardless of the content of the ensuing communication.

h. A represented nonclient accused or suspected of a crime. Controversy has surrounded the question whether prosecutors are fully subject to the rule of this Section with respect to contact, prior to indictment, with represented nonclients accused or suspected of crime. Certain considerations favor a relaxed anti-contact rule. Law-enforcement officials traditionally have resorted to undercover means of gathering important evidence. If retention of a lawyer alone precluded direct prosecutorial contact, a knowledgeable criminal suspect could obtain immunity from otherwise lawful forms of investigation by retaining a lawyer, while unsophisticated suspects would have no similar protection. Moreover, nonlawyer law-enforcement personnel such as the police are not subject to the rule of this Section. Rigidly extending the anti-contact rule to prosecutors would create unfortunate incentives to eliminate them from involvement in investigations.

On the other hand, certain considerations argue in favor of an anti-contact rule for prosecutors. They are in a position to overreach suspects or interfere in client-lawyer relationships in the same manner as lawyers in private practice and may be tempted to do so to solve a crime. Accordingly, at a minimum, a suspect or accused has constitutional protection of the following kind: against governmental intrusion, including prosecutorial intrusion, into essentials of the client-lawyer relationship, such as attempts to dissuade a nonclient from retaining counsel or from trusting or consulting counsel already retained or assigned; against taking statements from a suspect who is in custody and has not effectively waived the right to counsel; and against such measures as unlawful searches of a lawyer's office or similar threats to client-lawyer confidentiality. Elaboration of such limitations is beyond the scope of this Restatement.

It has been extensively debated whether, beyond such constitutional protections, the anti-contact rule independently imposes all constraints of this Section on prosecutors or, to the contrary, whether the authorized-by-law exception (see Comment *g*) entirely removes such limitations. Both polar positions seem unacceptable. Organizations of prosecutors and lawyers are elaborating rules governing specific situations. The scope of such rules and the law in default of such rules are subjects beyond the scope of this Restatement. Prosecutor contact in compliance with law is within the authorized-by-law exception stated in

Subsection (1)(c).

k. A communication by a client with a represented nonclient. No general rule prevents a lawyer's client, either personally or through a nonlawyer agent, from communicating directly with a represented nonclient. Thus, while neither a lawyer nor a lawyer's investigator or other agent (see Comment *b* hereto) may contact the represented nonclient, the same bar does not extend to the client of the lawyer or the client's investigator or other agent.

As stated in Subsection (2), the anti-contact rule does not prohibit a lawyer from advising the lawyer's own client concerning the client's communication with a represented nonclient, including communications that may occur without the prior consent (compare Comment *j*) or knowledge of the lawyer for the nonclient.

The lawyer for a client intending to make such a communication may advise the client regarding legal aspects of the communication, such as whether an intended communication is libelous or would otherwise create risk for the client. Prohibiting such advice would unduly restrict the client's autonomy, the client's interest in obtaining important legal advice, and the client's ability to communicate fully with the lawyer. The lawyer may suggest that the client make such a communication but must not assist the client inappropriately to seek confidential information, to invite the nonclient to take action without the advice of counsel, or otherwise to overreach the nonclient.

Illustration:

6. Lawyer represents Owner, who has a worsening business relationship with Contractor. From earlier meetings, Lawyer knows that Contractor is represented by a lawyer in the matter. Owner drafts a letter to send to Contractor stating Owner's position in the dispute, showing a copy of the draft to Lawyer. Viewing the draft as inappropriate, Lawyer redrafts the letter, recommending that Client send out the letter as redrafted. Client does so, as Lawyer knew would occur. Lawyer has not violated the rule of this Section.

m. Clarifying, protective, and remedial orders of a tribunal. In situations of doubt involving communication with a represented nonclient, a clarifying ruling may be sought from a tribunal. A party seeking to protect against impermissible contact by an opposing lawyer may seek a protective or remedial ruling. A ruling may impose conditions on access and may expand or contract the general rule of this Section as appropriate in light of circumstances. For example, a ruling permitting access may require the lawyer to inform each contacted nonclient of the identity and interests of the lawyer's client, the right of the nonclient to refuse to be interviewed, and the right of the nonclient to request the presence of a lawyer during an interview. The court may grant access on condition that no statement taken will be admissible in evidence. Contact pursuant to the terms of such a ruling is authorized by law within the meaning of this Section (see Comment *h*).

n. Disqualification, evidence suppression, and related remedies. When contact has been made in violation of this Section, a court may disqualify the offending lawyer when necessary to protect against a significant risk of future misuse of confidential information obtained through the contact, when the contact has substantially interfered with the client's relationship with the client's lawyer, or when disqualification is appropriate to deter flagrant or reckless violations. A lawyer violating or threatening to violate the rule may be enjoined from doing so. A lawyer who violates the rule of this Section is also subject to professional discipline. Fines and fee-shifting sanctions may be warranted under applicable procedural law.

A court may also suppress or otherwise exclude from evidence statements, documents, or other material obtained in violation of the rule. When a release or other document affecting the interests of a represented nonclient is obtained in violation of the rule, the law against fraud or overreaching may permit the nonclient to obtain a ruling voiding the document. A tribunal may compel production of any statement taken in violation of the rule despite its status otherwise as protected work product (see § 87(3)).

§ 100. Definition of a Represented Nonclient

Within the meaning of § 99, a represented nonclient includes:

(1) a natural person represented by a lawyer; and:

(2) a current employee or other agent of an organization represented by a lawyer:

(a) if the employee or other agent supervises, directs, or regularly consults with the lawyer concerning the matter or if the agent has power to compromise or settle the matter;

(b) if the acts or omissions of the employee or other agent may be imputed to the organization for purposes of civil or criminal liability in the matter; or

(c) if a statement of the employee or other agent, under applicable rules of evidence, would have the effect of binding the organization with respect to proof of the matter.

Comment:

e. An employee or agent whose statement binds an organization under applicable evidence law (Subsection (2)(c)). Under evidence law generally applied a century ago and still in force in some jurisdictions for certain purposes, some employees and agents have the power to make statements that bind the principal, in the sense that the principal may not introduce evidence contradicting the binding statement. When such a binding-admission rule applies, under Subsection (2)(c) an employee or agent with power to make such a statement is a represented nonclient within the anti-contact rule of § 99. Such a person is analogous to a person who possesses power to settle a dispute on behalf of the organization (see Comment *c*).

However, under modern evidence law, employees and agents who lack authority to enter into binding contractual settlements on behalf of the organization have no power to make such binding statements. Modern evidence rules make certain statements of an employee or agent admissible notwithstanding the hearsay rule, but allow the organization to impeach or contradict such statements. Employees or agents are not included within Subsection (2)(c) solely on the basis that their statements are admissible evidence. A contrary rule would essentially mean that most employees and agents with relevant information would be within the anti-contact rule, contrary to the policies described in Comment *b*.

f. Instructing an employee or agent not to communicate with an opposing lawyer. A principal or the principal's lawyer may inform employees or agents of their right not to speak with opposing counsel and may request them not to do so (see § 116(4) & Comment *e* thereto). In certain circumstances, a direction to do so could constitute an obstruction of justice or a violation of other law. However, even when lawful, such an instruction is a matter of intra-organizational policy and not a limitation against a lawyer for another party who is seeking evidence. Thus, even if an employer, by general policy or specific directive, lawfully instructs all employees not to cooperate with another party's lawyer, that does not enlarge the scope of the anti-contact rule applicable to that lawyer.

§ 101. A Represented Governmental Agency or Officer

(1) Unless otherwise provided by law (see § 99(1)(c)) and except as provided in Subsection (2), the prohibition stated in § 99 against contact with a represented nonclient does not apply to communications with employees of a represented governmental agency or with a governmental officer being represented in the officer's official capacity.

(2) In negotiation or litigation by a lawyer of a specific claim of a client against a governmental agency or against a governmental officer in the officer's official capacity, the prohibition stated in § 99 applies, except that the lawyer may contact any officer of the government if permitted by the agency or with respect to an issue of general policy.

§ 102. Information of a Nonclient Known to Be Legally Protected

A lawyer communicating with a nonclient in a situation permitted under § 99 may not seek to obtain information that the lawyer reasonably should know the nonclient may not reveal without violating a duty of confidentiality to another imposed by law.

§ 103. Dealings with an Unrepresented Nonclient

In the course of representing a client and dealing with a nonclient who is not represented by a lawyer:

(1) the lawyer may not mislead the nonclient, to the prejudice of the nonclient, concerning the identity and interests of the person the lawyer represents; and

(2) when the lawyer knows or reasonably should know that the unrepresented nonclient misunderstands the lawyer's role in the matter, the lawyer must make

reasonable efforts to correct the misunderstanding when failure to do so would materially prejudice the nonclient.

TOPIC 4. LEGISLATIVE AND ADMINISTRATIVE MATTERS

§ 104. Representing a Client in Legislative and Administrative Matters

A lawyer representing a client before a legislature or administrative agency:

(1) must disclose that the appearance is in a representative capacity and not misrepresent the capacity in which the lawyer appears;

(2) must comply with applicable law and regulations governing such representations; and

(3) except as applicable law otherwise provides:

(a) in an adjudicative proceeding before a government agency or involving such an agency as a participant, has the legal rights and responsibilities of an advocate in a proceeding before a judicial tribunal; and

(b) in other types of proceedings and matters, has the legal rights and responsibilities applicable in the lawyer's dealings with a private person.

CHAPTER 7. REPRESENTING CLIENTS IN LITIGATION

TOPIC 1. ADVOCACY IN GENERAL

§ 105. Complying with Law and Tribunal Rulings

In representing a client in a matter before a tribunal, a lawyer must comply with applicable law, including rules of procedure and evidence and specific tribunal rulings.

§ 106. Dealing with Other Participants in Proceedings

In representing a client in a matter before a tribunal, a lawyer may not use means that have no substantial purpose other than to embarrass, delay, or burden a third person or use methods of obtaining evidence that are prohibited by law.

Comment:

b. Investigating and tape recording witnesses. A lawyer may conduct an investigation of a witness to gather information from or about the witness. Such an investigation may legitimately address potentially relevant aspects of the finances, associations, and personal life of the witness. In conducting such investigations personally or through others, however, a lawyer must observe legal constraints on intrusion on privacy. The law of some jurisdictions, for example, prohibits recording conversations with another person without the latter's consent. When secret recording is not prohibited by law, doing so is permissible for lawyers conducting investigations on behalf of their clients, but should be done only when compelling need exists to obtain evidence otherwise unavailable in an equally reliable form. Such a need may exist more readily in a criminal-defense representation. In conducting such an investigation, a lawyer must comply with the limitations of § 99 prohibiting contact with represented person, of § 102 restricting communication with persons who owe certain duties of confidentiality to others, and of § 103 prohibiting misleading an unrepresented person.

§ 107. Prohibited Forensic Tactics

In representing a client in a matter before a tribunal, a lawyer may not, in the presence of the trier of fact:

(1) state a personal opinion about the justness of a cause, the credibility of a witness, the culpability of a civil litigant, or the guilt or innocence of an accused, but the lawyer may argue any position or conclusion adequately supported by the lawyer's analysis of the

evidence; or

(2) allude to any matter that the lawyer does not reasonably believe is relevant or that will not be supported by admissible evidence.

§ 108. An Advocate as a Witness

(1) Except as provided in Subsection (2), a lawyer may not represent a client in a contested hearing or trial of a matter in which:

 (a) the lawyer is expected to testify for the lawyer's client; or

 (b) the lawyer does not intend to testify but (i) the lawyer's testimony would be material to establishing a claim or defense of the client, and (ii) the client has not consented as stated in § 122 to the lawyer's intention not to testify.

(2) A lawyer may represent a client when the lawyer will testify as stated in Subsection (1)(a) if:

 (a) the lawyer's testimony relates to an issue that the lawyer reasonably believes will not be contested or to the nature and value of legal services rendered in the proceeding;

 (b) deprivation of the lawyer's services as advocate would work a substantial hardship on the client; or

 (c) consent has been given by (i) opposing parties who would be adversely affected by the lawyer's testimony and, (ii) if relevant, the lawyer's client, as stated in § 122 with respect to any conflict of interest between lawyer and client (see § 125) that the lawyer's testimony would create.

(3) A lawyer may not represent a client in a litigated matter pending before a tribunal when the lawyer or a lawyer in the lawyer's firm will give testimony materially adverse to the position of the lawyer's client or materially adverse to a former client of any such lawyer with respect to a matter substantially related to the earlier representation, unless the affected client has consented as stated in § 122 with respect to any conflict of interest between lawyer and client (see § 125) that the testimony would create.

(4) A tribunal should not permit a lawyer to call opposing trial counsel as a witness unless there is a compelling need for the lawyer's testimony.

Comment:

d. An advocate appearing pro se. A lawyer (or any other party) appearing pro se is entitled to testify as a witness, but the lawyer is subject to the Section with respect to representing other co-parties as clients. The tribunal may order separate trials where joinder of the pro se lawyer-litigant with other parties would substantially prejudice a co-party or adverse party. When a lawyer appears as the advocate for a class and claims to be the party representative of the class as well, a tribunal may refuse to permit the litigation to proceed in that form.

§ 109. An Advocate's Public Comment on Pending Litigation

(1) In representing a client in a matter before a tribunal, a lawyer may not make a statement outside the proceeding that a reasonable person would expect to be disseminated by means of public communication when the lawyer knows or reasonably should know that the statement will have a substantial likelihood of materially prejudicing a juror or influencing or intimidating a prospective witness in the proceeding. However, a lawyer may in any event make a statement that is reasonably necessary to mitigate the impact on the lawyer's client of substantial, undue, and prejudicial publicity recently initiated by one other than the lawyer or the lawyer's client.

(2) A prosecutor must, except for statements necessary to inform the public of the nature and extent of the prosecutor's action and that serve a legitimate law-enforcement purpose, refrain from making extrajudicial comments that have a substantial likelihood of heightening public condemnation of the accused.

TOPIC 2. LIMITS ON ADVOCACY

§ 110. Frivolous Advocacy

(1) A lawyer may not bring or defend a proceeding or assert or controvert an issue therein, unless there is a basis for doing so that is not frivolous, which includes a good-faith argument for an extension, modification, or reversal of existing law.

(2) Notwithstanding Subsection (1), a lawyer for the defendant in a criminal proceeding or the respondent in a proceeding that could result in incarceration may so defend the proceeding as to require that the prosecutor establish every necessary element.

(3) A lawyer may not make a frivolous discovery request, fail to make a reasonably diligent effort to comply with a proper discovery request of another party, or intentionally fail otherwise to comply with applicable procedural requirements concerning discovery.

§ 111. Disclosure of Legal Authority

In representing a client in a matter before a tribunal, a lawyer may not knowingly:

(1) make a false statement of a material proposition of law to the tribunal; or

(2) fail to disclose to the tribunal legal authority in the controlling jurisdiction known to the lawyer to be directly adverse to the position asserted by the client and not disclosed by opposing counsel.

§ 112. Advocacy in Ex Parte and Other Proceedings

In representing a client in a matter before a tribunal, a lawyer applying for ex parte relief or appearing in another proceeding in which similar special requirements of candor apply must comply with the requirements of § 110 and § § 118-120 and further:

(1) must not present evidence the lawyer reasonably believes is false;

(2) must disclose all material and relevant facts known to the lawyer that will enable the tribunal to reach an informed decision; and

(3) must comply with any other applicable special requirements of candor imposed by law.

TOPIC 3. ADVOCATES AND TRIBUNALS

§ 113. Improperly Influencing a Judicial Officer

(1) A lawyer may not knowingly communicate ex parte with a judicial officer before whom a proceeding is pending concerning the matter, except as authorized by law.

(2) A lawyer may not make a gift or loan prohibited by law to a judicial officer, attempt to influence the officer otherwise than by legally proper procedures, or state or imply an ability so to influence a judicial officer.

§ 114. A Lawyer's Statements Concerning a Judicial Officer

A lawyer may not knowingly or recklessly make publicly a false statement of fact concerning the qualifications or integrity of an incumbent of a judicial office or a candidate for election to such an office.

§ 115. Lawyer Contact with a Juror

A lawyer may not:

(1) except as allowed by law, communicate with or seek to influence a person known by the lawyer to be a member of a jury pool from which the jury will be drawn;

(2) except as allowed by law, communicate with or seek to influence a member of a jury; or

(3) communicate with a juror who has been excused from further service:

(a) when that would harass the juror or constitute an attempt to influence the juror's actions as a juror in future cases; or

(b) when otherwise prohibited by law.

TOPIC 4. ADVOCATES AND EVIDENCE

§ 116. Interviewing and Preparing a Prospective Witness

(1) A lawyer may interview a witness for the purpose of preparing the witness to testify.

(2) A lawyer may not unlawfully obstruct another party's access to a witness.

(3) A lawyer may not unlawfully induce or assist a prospective witness to evade or ignore process obliging the witness to appear to testify.

(4) A lawyer may not request a person to refrain from voluntarily giving relevant testimony or information to another party, unless:

(a) the person is the lawyer's client in the matter; or

(b) (i) the person is not the lawyer's client but is a relative or employee or other agent of the lawyer or the lawyer's client, and (ii) the lawyer reasonably believes compliance will not materially and adversely affect the person's interests.

Comment:

b. Preparing a witness to testify. Under litigation practice uniformly followed in the United States, a lawyer may interview prospective witnesses prior to their testifying. A prospective witness is generally under no obligation to submit to such an interview. As a practical matter, rules requiring inquiry to support factual allegations in a complaint or other document (see § 110, Comment *c*) may require a lawyer to interview witnesses to gain the necessary factual foundation. Competent preparation for trial (see generally § 52(1)) (general negligence standard might also require pre-testimonial interviews with witnesses).

The work-product immunity (see Chapter 5, Topic 3) and the obligation of confidentiality regarding trial-preparation material (see § 60(1)), result in the process of witness preparation normally being confidential. Compare § 80(2)(b) (loss of confidentiality of material otherwise protected by attorney-client privilege); § 92(1) (same for work-product immunity).

Attempting to induce a witness to testify falsely as to a material fact is a crime, either subornation of perjury or obstruction of justice, and is ground for professional discipline and other remedies (see § 120, Comment *l*). It may also constitute fraud, warranting denial of the attorney-client privilege to client-lawyer communications relating to preparation of the witness (see § 82).

In preparing a witness to testify, a lawyer may invite the witness to provide truthful testimony favorable to the lawyer's client. Preparation consistent with the rule of this Section may include the following: discussing the role of the witness and effective courtroom demeanor; discussing the witness's recollection and probable testimony; revealing to the witness other testimony or evidence that will be presented and asking the witness to reconsider the witness's recollection or recounting of events in that light; discussing the applicability of law to the events in issue; reviewing the factual context into which the witness's observations or opinions will fit; reviewing documents or other physical evidence that may be introduced; and discussing probable lines of hostile cross-examination that the witness should be prepared to meet. Witness preparation may include rehearsal of testimony. A lawyer may suggest choice of words that might be employed to make the witness's meaning clear. However, a lawyer may not assist the witness to testify falsely as to a material fact (see § 120(1)(a)).

§ 117. Compensating a Witness

A lawyer may not offer or pay to a witness any consideration:

(1) in excess of the reasonable expenses of the witness incurred and the reasonable value of the witness's time spent in providing evidence, except that an expert witness may be offered and paid a noncontingent fee;

(2) contingent on the content of the witness's testimony or the outcome of the litigation; or

(3) otherwise prohibited by law.

§ 118. Falsifying or Destroying Evidence

(1) A lawyer may not falsify documentary or other evidence.

(2) A lawyer may not destroy or obstruct another party's access to documentary or other evidence when doing so would violate a court order or other legal requirements, or counsel or assist a client to do so.

Comment:

b. Falsifying documentary and other evidence. Advocates in the adversary system are primarily responsible for assembling documentary and other evidence to be presented. A lawyer thereby may serve as custodian of evidentiary material, which ordinarily should reach the proceeding in its original condition. A lawyer may not alter such material in any way that impairs its evidentiary value for other parties. Rules of procedure may permit alteration of evidence in the course of reasonable scientific tests by experts.

A lawyer may not forge a document or alter a document with the purpose of misleading another, such as by back-dating the document, removing the document to another file to create a false impression of its provenance, deleting or adding language or other characters to the document so as to alter its effect, or materially changing its physical appearance.

A document, such as an affidavit or declaration, prepared by a lawyer for verification by another person must include only factual statements that the lawyer reasonably believes the person would make if testifying in person before the factfinder. On a submission to a tribunal based on the lawyer's personal knowledge, such as the lawyer's own affidavit or declaration, see § 120.

c. Destroying documentary or other physical evidence. Unlawful destruction or concealment of documents or other evidence during or in anticipation of litigation may subvert fair and full exposition of the facts. On the other hand, it would be intolerable to require retention of all documents and other evidence against the possibility that an adversary in future litigation would wish to examine them. Accordingly, it is presumptively lawful to act pursuant to an established document retention-destruction program that conforms to existing law and is consistently followed, absent a supervening obligation such as a subpoena or other lawful demand for or order relating to the material. On a lawyer's advice to a client on such matters as document retention or suppression, see generally § 94. If the client informs the lawyer that the client intends to destroy a document unlawfully or in violation of a court order, the lawyer must not advise or assist the client to do so (id.).

It may be difficult under applicable criminal law to define the point at which legitimate destruction becomes unlawful obstruction of justice. Under criminal law, a lawyer generally is subject to constraints no different from those imposed on others. Obstruction of justice and similar statutes generally apply only when an official proceeding is ongoing or imminent. For example, The American Law Institute Model Penal Code § 241.7 (1985) provides that the offense of tampering with or fabricating physical evidence occurs only if "an official proceeding or investigation is pending or about to be instituted...."

A lawyer may not destroy evidence or conceal or alter it when a discovery demand, subpoena, or court order has directed the lawyer or the lawyer's client to turn over the evidence. Difficult questions of interpretation can arise with respect to destruction of documents in anticipation of a subpoena or similar process that has not yet issued at the time of destruction. For example, a company manufacturing a product that may cause injuries in the future is not, in the absence of specific prohibition, prohibited from destroying all manufacturing records after a period of time; but difficult questions of interpretation of obstruction-of-justice statutes may arise concerning such practices as culling incriminating documents while leaving others in place. No general statement can accurately describe the legality of record destruction; statutes and decisions in the particular jurisdiction must be consulted. In many jurisdictions, there is no applicable precedent. Legality may turn on such factual questions as the state of mind of the client or a lawyer.

Particular statutes and regulations may impose special obligations to retain records and files and to make them accessible to governmental officials. Procedural law or a tribunal ruling may impose other or additional obligations. For example, a lawyer may not knowingly withhold a document that has been properly requested in discovery unless the lawyer does so in procedurally proper form (see § 110,

Comment *e*). Conversely, a lawyer responding to a request for discovery of documents may not mix responsive and nonresponsive documents together in a way designed to obstruct detection of responsive documents (see id.).

Some jurisdictions have recognized an action for damages by a litigant who suffers loss from "spoliation"—an opposing party's or lawyer's unwarranted and injurious suppression of evidence. In some jurisdictions, an unfavorable evidentiary inference may be drawn from failure to produce material that was at one time in the possession and under the control of a party to litigation. The inference may be invoked even in circumstances in which destruction is otherwise lawful. Section 51 does not provide for a lawyer's liability to a nonclient for negligence in such a situation. Falsification or unlawful destruction of evidence may also constitute contempt or may be subject to the tribunal's inherent power to impose a suitable sanction (see § 1, Comment *c*).

§ 119. Physical Evidence of a Client Crime

With respect to physical evidence of a client crime, a lawyer:

(1) may, when reasonably necessary for purposes of the representation, take possession of the evidence and retain it for the time reasonably necessary to examine it and subject it to tests that do not alter or destroy material characteristics of the evidence; but

(2) following possession under Subsection (1), the lawyer must notify prosecuting authorities of the lawyer's possession of the evidence or turn the evidence over to them.

Comment:

a. . . . This Section applies to evidence of a client crime, contraband, weapons, and similar implements used in an offense. It also includes such material as documents and material in electronically retrievable form used by the client to plan the offense, documents used in the course of a mail-fraud violation, or transaction documents evidencing a crime.

Witness statements, photographs of the scene of a crime, trial exhibits, and the like prepared by a lawyer or the lawyer's assistants constitute work product and thus are not subject to the Section, even if such material could constitute evidence of a client crime for some purposes, such as if waived. See § 87, Comment *f*, and § 92, Comment *e*; see also § 87, Comment *b*, on the distinction between work-product materials and preexisting documents, such as client files or financial records.

b. Physical evidence of a client crime; retention for reasonably necessary examination. As stated in Subsection (1), a lawyer may legitimately need to possess evidence relating to a crime for the purpose of examining it to prepare a defense. A lawyer has the same privilege as prosecutors to possess and examine such material for the lawful purpose of assisting in the trial of criminal cases. Such an examination may include scientific tests, so long as they do not alter or destroy the value of the evidence for possible use by the prosecution. So long as the lawyer's possession is for that purpose, criminal laws that generally prohibit possession of contraband or other evidence of crimes are inapplicable to the lawyer. Nonetheless, possession of such material otherwise than in strict compliance with the requirements stated in this Section may subject the lawyer to risk of prosecution as an accessory after the fact for accepting evidence that might otherwise be found. A lawyer's office may also thereby be subject to search. In dealing with such evidence, a lawyer may not unlawfully alter, destroy, or conceal it (see § 118). On the prohibition against advising or assisting another person, including the client, to do so, see § 94.

c. Disposition of evidence of a client crime. Once a lawyer's reasonable need for examination of evidence of a client crime has been satisfied, a lawyer's responsibilities with respect to further possession of the evidence are determined under the criminal law and the law affecting confidentiality of client information (see generally Chapter 5). Under the general criminal law, physical evidence of a client crime in possession of the lawyer may not be retained to a point at which its utility as evidence for the prosecution is significantly impaired, such as by waiting until after the trial.

Some decisions have alluded to an additional option—returning the evidence to the site from which it was taken, when that can be accomplished without destroying or altering material characteristics of the evidence. That will often be impossible. The option would also be unavailable when the lawyer reasonably should know that the client or another person will intentionally alter or destroy the evidence.

Evidence subject to this Section will come to the attention of the authorities either through being turned over by the lawyer to them or through notification by the lawyer or another. In the latter case, the authorities may obtain the evidence from the lawyer by proper process. The prosecution and defense should make appropriate arrangements for introduction and authentication of the evidence at trial. Because of the risk of prejudice to the client, that should be done without improperly revealing the source of the evidence to the finder of fact. The parties may also agree that the tribunal may instruct the jury, without revealing the lawyer's involvement, that an appropriate chain of possession links the evidence to the place where it was located before coming into the lawyer's possession. In the absence of agreement to such an instruction by the defense, the prosecutor may offer evidence of the lawyer's possession if necessary to establish the chain of possession.

§ 120. False Testimony or Evidence

(1) A lawyer may not:

(a) knowingly counsel or assist a witness to testify falsely or otherwise to offer false evidence;

(b) knowingly make a false statement of fact to the tribunal;

(c) offer testimony or other evidence as to an issue of fact known by the lawyer to be false.

(2) If a lawyer has offered testimony or other evidence as to a material issue of fact and comes to know of its falsity, the lawyer must take reasonable remedial measures and may disclose confidential client information when necessary to take such a measure.

(3) A lawyer may refuse to offer testimony or other evidence that the lawyer reasonably believes is false, even if the lawyer does not know it to be false.

Comment:

b. Rationale. An advocate seeks to achieve the client's objectives (see § 16(1)) but in doing so may not distort factfinding by the tribunal by knowingly offering false testimony or other evidence.

A lawyer's discovery that testimony or other evidence is false may occur in circumstances suggesting complicity by the client in preparing or offering it, thus presenting the risk that remedial action by the lawyer can lead to criminal investigation or other adverse consequences for the client. At the very least, remedial action will deprive the client of whatever evidentiary advantage the false evidence would otherwise provide. It has therefore been asserted that remedial action by the lawyer is inconsistent with the requirements of loyalty and confidentiality (see § 60 and following). However, preservation of the integrity of the forum is a superior interest, which would be disserved by a lawyer's knowing offer of false evidence. Moreover, a client has no right to the assistance of counsel in offering such evidence. As indicated in Subsection (2), taking remedial measures required to correct false evidence may necessitate the disclosure of confidential client information otherwise protected under Chapter 5 (see Comment *h* hereto).

The procedural rules concerning burden of proof allocate responsibility for bringing forward evidence. A lawyer might know of testimony or other evidence vital to the other party, but unknown to that party or their advocate. The advocate who knows of the evidence, and who has complied with applicable rules concerning pretrial discovery and other applicable disclosure requirements (see, e.g, § 118), has no legal obligation to reveal the evidence, even though the proceeding thereby may fail to ascertain the facts as the lawyer knows them.

c. A lawyer's knowledge. A lawyer's obligations under Subsection (2) depend on what the lawyer knows and, in the case of Subsection (3), on what the lawyer reasonably believes (see Comment *j*). A lawyer's knowledge may be inferred from the circumstances. Actual knowledge does not include unknown information, even if a reasonable lawyer would have discovered it through inquiry. However, a lawyer may not ignore what is plainly apparent, for example, by refusing to read a document (see § 94, Comment *g*). A lawyer should not conclude that testimony is or will be false unless there is a firm factual basis for doing so. Such a basis exists when facts known to the lawyer or the client's own statements indicate to the lawyer that the testimony or other evidence is false.

d. Offer of false testimony or other false evidence. False testimony includes testimony that a lawyer knows to be false and testimony from a witness who the lawyer knows is only guessing or reciting what the witness has been instructed to say. This Section employs the terms "false testimony" and "false evidence" rather than "perjury" because the latter term defines a crime, which may require elements not relevant for application of the requirements of the Section in other contexts. For example, although a witness who testifies in good faith but contrary to fact lacks the mental state necessary for the crime of perjury, the rule of the Section nevertheless applies to a lawyer who knows that such testimony is false. When a lawyer is charged with the criminal offense of suborning perjury, the more limited definition appropriate to the criminal offense applies.

A lawyer's responsibility for false evidence extends to testimony or other evidence in aid of the lawyer's client offered or similarly sponsored by the lawyer. The responsibility extends to any false testimony elicited by the lawyer, as well as such testimony elicited by another lawyer questioning the lawyer's own client, another witness favorable to the lawyer's client, or a witness whom the lawyer has substantially prepared to testify (see § 116(1)). A lawyer has no responsibility to correct false testimony or other evidence offered by an opposing party or witness. Thus, a plaintiff's lawyer, aware that an adverse witness being examined by the defendant's lawyer is giving false evidence favorable to the plaintiff, is not required to correct it (compare Comment e). However, the lawyer may not attempt to reinforce the false evidence, such as by arguing to the factfinder that the false evidence should be accepted as true or otherwise sponsoring or supporting the false evidence (see also Comment e).

Illustrations:

1. Lawyer, representing Defendant, knows that a contract between Plaintiff's decedent and Defendant had been superseded by a materially revised version that was executed and retained by Defendant. Plaintiff's Counsel is unaware of the revised contract and has failed to seek information about it in discovery. At trial, Lawyer elicits testimony from Defendant by inquiring about "the contract that you and Plaintiff's decedent signed" and presents Defendant with the original contract, asking, "Is this the contract that you and Plaintiff's decedent signed?" Defendant responds affirmatively. Lawyer has violated Subsection (1)(c).

2. Same facts as in Illustration 1, except that Lawyer does not elicit the testimony there described and Plaintiff's Counsel, mistakenly believing that the revised contract was not in writing, offers an accurate account of its contents through the testimony of a third-party witness. Lawyer successfully objects to the proposed testimony under the jurisdiction's statute of frauds, thereby removing the only evidence known to Plaintiff's Counsel on which the factfinder could find that the original contract was superseded. Defendant offers no additional evidence, and Lawyer does not produce the revised contract. As a result the tribunal enters a directed verdict for Defendant. Lawyer did not violate this Section in making the successful objection, which kept out evidence, or in failing to inform the lawyer for Defendant of the evidence in fact available.

e. Counseling or assisting a witness to offer false testimony or other false evidence. A lawyer may not knowingly counsel or assist a witness to testify falsely or otherwise to offer false evidence as to a material issue of fact (Subsection (1)(a)). With respect to the right of a criminal defendant to testify and application of the rule to criminal-defense counsel, see Comment i hereto. If a lawyer knows that a witness will provide truthful evidence as to some matters but false evidence as to others, the lawyer must not elicit the false evidence. On affirmative remedial steps that a lawyer must take when a lawyer knows that a witness has offered false evidence, see Comment h.

Illustration:

3. Lawyer, representing as Plaintiffs the officers of a closed financial institution, seeks a preliminary injunction requiring governmental regulators to reopen the institution. Plaintiffs have the burden of establishing that certain documents were executed prior to closure of the institution. Lawyer drafts an affidavit for the signature of the president of the institution, stating that attached as exhibits are such documents. As Lawyer knows, the exhibits are in fact drafts that were not executed when dated but which have been backdated. Lawyer's offer of the affidavit would violate the rule of Subsection (1)(c).

The prohibitions against false evidence address matters offered in aid of the lawyer's client (see Comment d). It is not a violation to elicit from an adversary witness evidence known by the lawyer to be false and apparently adverse to the lawyer's client. The lawyer may have sound tactical reasons for doing so, such as eliciting false testimony for the purpose of later demonstrating its falsity to discredit the witness. Requiring premature disclosure could, under some circumstances, aid the witness in explaining away false testimony or recasting it into a more plausible form.

Illustration:

4. Lawyer, representing Plaintiff, takes the deposition of Witness, who describes the occurrence in question in a way unfavorable to Plaintiff. From other evidence, Lawyer knows that Witness is testifying falsely. Subsequently, the case is settled, and Lawyer never discloses the false nature of Witness's deposition testimony. Lawyer's conduct does not violate this Section.

f. A lawyer's statement of fact to a tribunal. A lawyer may make a submission to a tribunal based on the lawyer's personal knowledge, such as the lawyer's own affidavit or declaration or a representation made on the lawyer's own knowledge. For example, the lawyer may state during a scheduling conference that a conflict exists in the lawyer's trial schedule or state on appeal that certain evidence appears of record. In such statements the lawyer purports to convey information based on personal knowledge. A tribunal or another party should be able to rely on such a statement. Such a statement must have a reasonable basis for belief.

Illustration:

5. Lawyer, representing Accused in defending against criminal charges, files a motion to suppress a purported confession. Lawyer attaches to the motion a copy of a document that appears to be the written confession of Accused. Lawyer states in the motion that Lawyer obtained the document from a police file, but Lawyer takes the position in the motion that other evidence accompanying the motion indicates that the document is a forgery. Because Lawyer purports to be asserting as a personally known fact that the document was obtained from the police file, Lawyer must know from Lawyer's own knowledge that the document is what Lawyer asserts it to be. On the other hand, Lawyer may characterize the document as a forgery based on other evidence so long as Lawyer has a nonfrivolous basis for that position (see § 110(1), Subsection (2) & Comment *d* hereto), even if Lawyer does not personally believe that the document is a forgery.

For the purpose of Subsection (1)(b) a knowing false statement of fact includes a statement on which the lawyer then has insufficient information from which reasonably to conclude that the statement is accurate. A lawyer may make conditional or suppositional statements so long as they are so identified and are neither known to be false nor made without a reasonable basis in fact for their conditional or suppositional character.

Illustration:

6. Lawyer represents A Corporation as defendant in an action seeking damages. Lawyer has filed A Corporation's motion to dismiss for lack of personal jurisdiction. In support of the motion, Lawyer's affidavit states that an attached certificate of a governmental agency of State X is genuine. The certificate states the jurisdiction in which A Corporation is incorporated, a material issue on the motion. Lawyer sought such a certificate from the relevant agency, but the certificate had not arrived by the time for filing the affidavit. Lawyer accordingly prepares what Lawyer reasonably believes is an accurate copy of the certificate and signs it in the name of a governmental official, having seen a telecopied facsimile of the certificate transmitted from the state agency. The certificate arrives the day following the filing of the motion and corresponds to the document attached to Lawyer's affidavit. Lawyer has violated this Section, as well as § 118. Lawyer would not have violated this Section if Lawyer had stated in the affidavit that the attached document was a copy of a document the original of which would be supplied by supplemental submission.

For purposes of professional discipline, the lawyer codes prohibit a lawyer from making only a false statement of "material" fact. A similar condition attaches to the crime of perjury (although often not to the related crime of false swearing or false statements.) However, other procedural or substantive rules may contain no such qualification.

g. Remonstrating with a client or witness. Before taking other steps, a lawyer ordinarily must confidentially remonstrate with the client or witness not to present false evidence or to correct false evidence already presented. Doing so protects against possibly harsher consequences. The form and content of such a remonstration is a matter of judgment. The lawyer must attempt to be persuasive while maintaining the client's trust in the lawyer's loyalty and diligence. If the client insists on offering false evidence, the lawyer must inform the client of the lawyer's duty not to offer false evidence and, if it is offered, to take appropriate remedial action (see Comment *h*).

h. Reasonable remedial measures. A lawyer who has taken appropriate steps to avoid offering false evidence (see Comment *g*) may be required to take additional measures. A lawyer may be surprised by unexpected false evidence given by a witness or may come to know of its falsity only after it has been offered.

If the lawyer's client or the witness refuses to correct the false testimony (see Comment *g*), the lawyer must take steps reasonably calculated to remove the false impression that the evidence may have made on the finder of fact (Subsection (2)). Alternatively, a lawyer could seek a recess and attempt to persuade the witness to correct the false evidence (see Comment *g*). If such steps are unsuccessful, the lawyer must take other steps, such as by moving or stipulating to have the evidence stricken or otherwise withdrawn, or recalling the witness if the witness had already left the stand when the lawyer comes to know of the falsity. Once the false evidence is before the finder of fact, it is not a reasonable remedial measure for the lawyer simply to withdraw from the representation, even if the presiding officer permits withdrawal (see Comment *k* hereto). If no other remedial measure corrects the falsity, the lawyer must inform the opposing party or tribunal of the falsity so that they may take corrective steps.

To the extent necessary in taking reasonable remedial measures under Subsection (2), a lawyer may use or reveal otherwise confidential client information (see § 63). However, the lawyer must proceed so that, consistent with carrying out the measures (including, if necessary, disclosure to the opposing party or tribunal), the lawyer causes the client minimal adverse effects. The lawyer has discretion as to which measures to adopt, so long as they are reasonably calculated to correct the false evidence. If the lawyer makes disclosure to the opposing party or tribunal, thereafter the lawyer must leave further steps to the opposing party or tribunal. Whether testimony concerning client-lawyer communications with respect to the false evidence can be elicited is determined under § 82 (crime-fraud exception to attorney-client privilege). The lawyer's disclosure may give rise to a conflict between the lawyer and client requiring the lawyer to withdraw from the representation (see Comment *k* hereto).

Responsibilities of a lawyer under this Section extend to the end of the proceeding in which the question of false evidence arises. Thus, a lawyer representing a client on appeal from a verdict in a trial continues to carry responsibilities with respect to false evidence offered at trial, particularly evidence discovered to be false after trial (see Comment *i*). If a lawyer is discharged by a client or withdraws, whether or not for reasons associated with the false evidence, the lawyer's obligations under this Section are not thereby terminated. In such an instance, a reasonable remedial measure may consist of disclosing the matter to successor counsel.

Even after the proceeding concludes, the rule stated in other Sections of this Restatement may permit corrective or self-protective action, such as through notification of others of the fact of withdrawal (see § § 66-67 & 64).

i. False evidence in a criminal-defense representation. The rules stated in the Section generally govern defense counsel in criminal cases. The requirement stated in Comment *g* with respect to remonstrating with a client may often be relevant. However, because of the right to the effective assistance of counsel, withdrawal (see Comment *k*) may be inappropriate in response to threatened client perjury in a criminal case. If defense counsel withdraws, normally it will be necessary for the accused to retain another lawyer or for the court to appoint one, unless the accused proceeds without counsel. Replacement counsel also may have to deal with the same client demand to take the stand to testify falsely. A tribunal may also be concerned that controversy over false evidence may be contrived to delay the proceeding. In criminal cases many courts thus are strongly inclined not to permit withdrawal of defense counsel, particularly if trial is underway or imminent. Withdrawal may be required, however, if the accused denies defense counsel's assertion that presentation of false evidence is threatened.

Some courts permit an accused in such circumstances to give "open narrative" testimony, without requiring defense counsel to take affirmative remedial action as required under Subsection (2). Defense counsel asks only a general question about the events, provides no guidance through additional questions, and does not refer to the false evidence in subsequent argument to the factfinder. Counsel does not otherwise indicate to the presiding officer or opposing counsel that the testimony or other evidence is false, although such indication may be necessary to deal with a prosecutor's objection to use of the open-narrative form of testimony. From the unusual format of examination, prosecutor and presiding officer are likely to understand that the accused is offering false testimony, but an unguided jury may be unaware of or confused about its significance. That solution is not consistent with the rule stated in Subsection (2) or with the requirements of the lawyer codes in most jurisdictions.

However, the defendant may still insist on giving false testimony despite defense counsel's efforts to persuade the defendant not to testify or to testify accurately (see Comment *g*). The accused has the constitutional rights to take the witness stand and to offer evidence in self-defense (see § 22). Unlike counsel in a civil case, who can refuse to call a witness (including a client) who will offer false evidence (see Comment *e*), defense counsel in a criminal case has no authority (beyond persuasion) to prevent a client-accused from taking the witness stand. (Defense counsel does possess that authority with respect to nonclient witnesses and must exercise it consistent with this Section (see § 23).) If the client nonetheless insists on the right to take the stand, defense counsel must accede to the demand of the accused to testify. Thereafter defense counsel may not ask the accused any question if counsel knows that the response would be false. Counsel must also be prepared to take remedial measures, including disclosure, in the event that the accused indeed testifies falsely (see Comment *h*).

In one situation, disclosure of client perjury to the tribunal may not be feasible. When a criminal case is being tried without a jury, informing the judge of perjury by an accused might be tantamount to informing the factfinder of the guilt of the accused. In such an instance, disclosure to the prosecutor might suffice as a remedial measure. The prosecutor may not refer in the judge's presence to the information provided by defense counsel under this Section.

j. An advocate's discretion to refuse to offer testimony or other evidence reasonably believed to be false. The rule of Subsection (3) protects a lawyer from forced complicity in violations of the law and protects the tribunal and third persons from erroneous decisions. It also protects the lawyer's reputation as an honest person and as an advocate capable of discriminating between reliable and unreliable evidence. A lawyer may not by agreement with a client surrender the discretion stated in Subsection (3) (see § 23(1)).

The rule of Subsection (3) consists of two elements. First, the lawyer's knowledge is assessed objectively according to a standard of reasonable belief. (In contrast, a firm factual basis is necessary before the mandatory rules stated in Subsections (1) and (2) are applicable (see Comment *c*).) Second, a lawyer who reasonably believes (but does not know) that evidence is false, has discretion to offer or to refuse to offer it.

k. False evidence and the client-lawyer relationship. A lawyer's actions in accordance with this Section may impair the trust and respect that otherwise would exist between lawyer and client. A lawyer may be discharged by the client or withdraw from the representation (see § 32).

If a difference between lawyer and client over falsity occurs just before or during trial, a tribunal may refuse to permit a lawyer to withdraw when withdrawal would require the client to proceed without counsel (see § 32(4)).

l. Remedies. Violation of Subsections (1) and (2) may be sanctioned through professional discipline. Certain violations may also be remedied through appropriate sanctions in the proceeding (see § 110, Comment *g*). Criminal liability exists for perjury or subornation of perjury. A court may have discretion to disqualify a lawyer who violates a rule of the Section from further representation in the proceeding. Knowing use of perjured testimony may be a basis for granting a new trial or for vacating a judgment or setting aside a settlement based on the false evidence. A litigant has no damage remedy against an opposing lawyer for an alleged perjurious client based solely on violation of this Section. Compare § 57, Comments *d* and *e* (lawyer liability for abuse of process and similar intentional torts).

CHAPTER 8. CONFLICTS OF INTEREST

TOPIC 1. CONFLICTS OF INTEREST—IN GENERAL

§ 121. The Basic Prohibition of Conflicts of Interest

Unless all affected clients and other necessary persons consent to the representation under the limitations and conditions provided in § 122, a lawyer may not represent a client if the representation would involve a conflict of interest. A conflict of interest is involved if there is a substantial risk that the lawyer's representation of the client would be materially and adversely affected by the lawyer's own interests or by the lawyer's duties to another current client, a former client, or a third person.

Comment:

b. Rationale. The prohibition against lawyer conflicts of interest reflects several competing concerns. First, the law seeks to assure clients that their lawyers will represent them with undivided loyalty. A client is entitled to be represented by a lawyer whom the client can trust. Instilling such confidence is an objective important in itself. For example, the principle underlying the prohibition against a lawyer's filing suit against a present client in an unrelated matter (see § 128, Comment *e*) may also extend to situations, not involving litigation, in which significant impairment of a client's expectation of the lawyer's loyalty would be similarly likely. Contentious dealings, for example involving charges of bad faith against the client whom the lawyer represents in another matter would raise such a concern. So also would negotiating on behalf of one client when a large proportion of the lawyer's other client's net worth is at risk.

Second, the prohibition against conflicts of interest seeks to enhance the effectiveness of legal representation. To the extent that a conflict of interest undermines the independence of the lawyer's professional judgment or inhibits a lawyer from working with appropriate vigor in the client's behalf, the client's expectation of effective representation (see § 16) could be compromised.

Third, a client has a legal right to have the lawyer safeguard the client's confidential information (see § 60). Preventing use of confidential client information against the interests of the client, either to benefit the lawyer's personal interest, in aid of some other client, or to foster an assumed public purpose is facilitated through conflicts rules that reduce the opportunity for such abuse.

Fourth, conflicts rules help ensure that lawyers will not exploit clients, such as by inducing a client to make a gift to the lawyer (see § 127).

Finally, some conflict-of-interest rules protect interests of the legal system in obtaining adequate presentations to tribunals. In the absence of such rules, for example, a lawyer might appear on both sides of the litigation, complicating the process of taking proof and compromising adversary argumentation (see § 128).

On the other hand, avoiding conflicts of interest can impose significant costs on lawyers and clients. Prohibition of conflicts of interest should therefore be no broader than necessary. First, conflict avoidance can make representation more expensive. To the extent that conflict-of-interest rules prevent multiple clients from being represented by a single lawyer, one or both clients will be required to find other lawyers. That might entail uncertainty concerning the successor lawyers' qualifications, usually additional cost, and the inconvenience of separate representation. In matters in which individual claims are small, representation of multiple claimants might be required if the claims are effectively to be considered at all. Second, limitations imposed by conflicts rules can interfere with client expectations. At the very least, one of the clients might be deprived of the services of a lawyer whom the client had a particular reason to retain, perhaps on the basis of a long-time association with the lawyer. In some communities or fields of practice there might be no lawyer who is perfectly conflict-free. Third, obtaining informed consent to conflicted representation itself might compromise important interests. As discussed in § 122, consent to a conflict of interest requires that each affected client give consent based on adequate information. The process of obtaining informed consent is not only potentially time-consuming; it might also be impractical because it would require the disclosure of information that the clients would prefer not to have disclosed, for example, the subject matter about which they have consulted the lawyer. Fourth, conflicts prohibitions interfere with lawyers' own freedom to practice according to their own best judgment of appropriate professional behavior. It is appropriate to give significant weight to the freedom and professionalism of lawyers in the formulation of legal rules governing conflicts.

c. The general conflict-of-interest standard. The standard adopted in this Chapter answers the four questions to which any conflicts-of-interest standard must respond. Those are (i) What kind of effect is prohibited? (ii) How significant must the effect be? (iii) What probability must there be that the effect will occur? (iv) From whose perspective are conflicts of interest to be determined? The standard adopted here incorporates elements common to all three of the major lawyer codes developed in this century. It casts the answer to each question in terms of factual predicates and practical consequences that are reasonably susceptible of objective assessment by lawyers subject to the rules, by clients whom the rules affect, and by tribunals. . . .

"Adverse" effect relates to the quality of the representation, not necessarily the quality of the result obtained in a given case. The standard refers to the incentives faced by the lawyer before or during the representation because it often cannot be foretold what the actual result would have been if the representation had been conflict-free.

Illustration:

1. Lawyer has been retained by A and B, each a competitor for a single broadcast license, to assist each of them in obtaining the license from Agency. Such work often requires advocacy by the lawyer for an applicant before Agency. Lawyer's representation will have an adverse effect on both A and B as that term is used in this Section. Even though either A or B might obtain the license and thus arguably not have been adversely affected by the joint representation, Lawyer will have duties to A that restrict Lawyer's ability to urge B's application and vice versa. In most instances, informed consent of both A and B would not suffice to allow the dual representation (see § 122). . . .

Illustration:

3. Clients A and B have come to Lawyer for help in organizing a new business. Lawyer is satisfied that both clients are committed to forming the enterprise and that an agreement can be prepared that will embody their common undertaking. Nonetheless, because a substantial risk of future conflict

exists in any such arrangement, Lawyer must explain to the clients that because of future economic uncertainties inherent in any such undertaking, the clients' interests could differ in material ways in the future. Lawyer must obtain informed consent pursuant to § 122 before undertaking the common representation. . . .

Whether there is adverseness, materiality, and substantiality in a given circumstance is often dependent on specific circumstances that are ambiguous and the subject of conflicting evidence. Accordingly, there are necessarily circumstances in which the lawyer's avoidance of a representation is permissible but not obligatory. A lawyer also would be justified in withdrawing from some representations in circumstances in which it would be improper to disqualify the lawyer or the lawyer's firm.

d. Representation of a client. The prohibition of conflicts of interest ordinarily restricts a lawyer's activities only where those activities materially and adversely affect the lawyer's ability to represent a client including such an effect on a client's reasonable expectation of the lawyer's loyalty. . . .

For purposes of identifying conflicts of interest, a lawyer's client is ordinarily the person or entity that consents to the formation of the client-lawyer relationship, see § 14. For example, when a lawyer is retained by Corporation A, Corporation A is ordinarily the lawyer's client; neither individual officers of Corporation A nor other corporations in which Corporation A has an ownership interest, that hold an ownership interest in Corporation A, or in which a major shareholder in Corporation A has an ownership interest, are thereby considered to be the lawyer's client.

In some situations, however, the financial or personal relationship between the lawyer's client and other persons or entities might be such that the lawyer's obligations to the client will extend to those other persons or entities as well. That will be true, for example, where financial loss or benefit to the nonclient person or entity will have a direct, adverse impact on the client.

Illustrations:

6. Lawyer represents Corporation A in local real-estate transactions. Lawyer has been asked to represent Plaintiff in a products-liability action against Corporation B claiming substantial damages. Corporation B is a wholly owned subsidiary of Corporation A; any judgment obtained against Corporation B will have a material adverse impact on the value of Corporation B's assets and on the value of the assets of Corporation A. Just as Lawyer could not file suit against Corporation A on behalf of another client, even in a matter unrelated to the subject of Lawyer's representation of Corporation A (see § 128, Comment *e*), Lawyer may not represent Plaintiff in the suit against Corporation B without the consent of both Plaintiff and Corporation A under the limitations and conditions provided in § 122.

7. The same facts as in Illustration 6, except that Corporation B is not a subsidiary of Corporation A. Instead, 51 percent of the stock of Corporation A and 60 percent of the stock of Corporation B are owned by X Corporation. The remainder of the stock in both Corporation A and Corporation B is held by the public. Lawyer does not represent X Corporation. The circumstances are such that an adverse judgment against Corporation B will have no material adverse impact on the financial position of Corporation A. No conflict of interest is presented; Lawyer may represent Plaintiff in the suit against Corporation B. . . .

In yet other situations, the conflict of interest arises because the circumstances indicate that the confidence that a client reasonably reposes in the loyalty of a lawyer would be compromised due to the lawyer's relationship with another client or person whose interests would be adversely affected by the representation.

Illustration:

8. The same facts as in Illustration 7, except that one-half of Lawyer's practice consists of work for Corporation A. Plaintiff could reasonably believe that Lawyer's concern about a possible adverse reaction by Corporation A to the suit against Corporation B will inhibit Lawyer's pursuit of Plaintiff's case against Corporation B (see §§ 125 & 128). Lawyer may not represent Plaintiff in the suit against Corporation B unless Plaintiff consents to the representation under the limitations and conditions provided in § 122. Because Lawyer's representation of Corporation A is assumed in Illustration 7 not to be adversely affected by the representation of Plaintiff, the consent of Corporation A to the representation is not required.

Significant control of the nonclient by the client also might suffice to require a lawyer to treat the nonclient as if it were a client in determining whether a conflict of interest exists in a lawyer's representation of another client with interests adverse to the nonclient.

Illustration:

9. The same facts as in Illustration 7, except that X Corporation has elected a majority of the Directors of Corporation B and has approved its key officers. Officers of X Corporation regularly supervise decisions made by Corporation B, and Lawyer has regularly advised X Corporation on products-liability issues affecting all of the corporations in which X Corporation owns an interest. X Corporation has used that advice to give direction about minimizing claims exposure to Corporation B. Although Lawyer does not represent Corporation B, Lawyer's earlier assistance to X Corporation on products-liability matters was substantially related to the suit that Plaintiff has asked Lawyer to file against Corporation B (see § 132). Lawyer may not represent Plaintiff in the suit against Corporation B unless Plaintiff, X Corporation, and Corporation B consent to the representation under the limitations and conditions provided in § 122. In the circumstances, informed consent on behalf of Corporation B may be provided by officers of X Corporation who direct the legal affairs of Corporation B pursuant to applicable corporate law.

A conflict of interest can also arise because of specific obligations, such as the obligation to hold information confidential, that the lawyer has assumed to a nonclient.

Illustration:

10. Lawyer represents Association, a trade association in which Corporation C is a member, in supporting legislation to protect Association's industry against foreign imports. Lawyer does not represent any individual members of Association, including Corporation C, but at the request of Association and Lawyer, Corporation C has given Lawyer confidential information about Corporation C's cost of production. Plaintiff has asked Lawyer to sue Corporation C for unfair competition based on Corporation C's alleged pricing below the cost of production. Although Corporation C is not Lawyer's client, unless both Plaintiff and Corporation C consent to the representation under the limitations and conditions provided in § 122, Lawyer may not represent Plaintiff against Corporation C in the matter because of the serious risk of material adverse use of Corporation C's confidential information against Corporation C.

e(i). Withdrawal or consent in typical cases of postrepresentation conflict. If a lawyer withdraws from representation of multiple clients because of a conflict of interest (or for any other reason), the rule stated in § 132 prohibits representation in the same or a substantially related matter of a remaining client whose interests in the matter are materially adverse to the interests of a now-former client. For example, two clients previously represented by lawyers in a firm in the same transaction pursuant to effective consent might thereafter have a falling out such that litigation is in prospect (see § § 130 & 128). The firm may not withdraw from representing one client and take an adversary position against that client in behalf of the other in the subsequent litigation (see § 132, Comment *c*). The firm must obtain informed consent from both clients (see § 122) or withdraw entirely. Consent in advance to such continued representation may also be provided as stated in § 122, Comment *d*. The fact that neither joint client could assert the attorney-client privilege in subsequent litigation between them (see § 75) does not by itself negate the lawyer's more extensive obligations of confidentiality under § 60 and loyalty under § 16(1).

f. Sanctions and remedies for conflicts of interest. In addition to the sanction of professional discipline, disqualifying a lawyer from further participation in a pending matter is a common remedy for conflicts of interest in litigation (§ 6, Comment *i*). For matters not before a tribunal where disqualification can be sought, an injunction against a lawyer's further participation in the matter is a comparable remedy (§ 6, Comment *c*).

When a conflict of interest has caused injury to a client, the remedy of legal malpractice is available (§ § 48 and following). Availability of the sanction of fee forfeiture is considered in § 37. If the result in a matter was affected prejudicially by conflicting loyalties or misuse of confidential information by the lawyer, the result will sometimes be reversed or set aside. Some conflicts of interest subject a lawyer to criminal sanctions.

§ 122. Client Consent to a Conflict of Interest

(1) A lawyer may represent a client notwithstanding a conflict of interest prohibited by § 121 if each affected client or former client gives informed consent to the lawyer's representation. Informed consent requires that the client or former client have reasonably adequate information about the material risks of such representation to that client or

former client.

(2) **Notwithstanding the informed consent of each affected client or former client, a lawyer may not represent a client if:**

(a) **the representation is prohibited by law;**

(b) **one client will assert a claim against the other in the same litigation; or**

(c) **in the circumstances, it is not reasonably likely that the lawyer will be able to provide adequate representation to one or more of the clients.**

Comment:

b. Rationale. The prohibition against lawyer conflicts of interest is intended to assure clients that a lawyer's work will be characterized by loyalty, vigor, and confidentiality (see § 121, Comment *b*). The conflict rules are subject to waiver through informed consent by a client who elects less than the full measure of protection that the law otherwise provides. For example, a client in a multiple representation might wish to avoid the added costs that separate representation often entails. Similarly, a client might consent to a conflict where that is necessary in order to obtain the services of a particular law firm.

Other considerations, however, limit the scope of a client's power to consent to a conflicted representation. A client's consent will not be effective if it is based on an inadequate understanding of the nature and severity of the lawyer's conflict (Comment *c* hereto), violates law (Comment *g(i)*), or if the client lacks capacity to consent (Comment *c*). Client consent must also, of course, be free of coercion. Consent will also be insufficient to permit conflicted representation if it is not reasonably likely that the lawyer will be able to provide adequate representation to the affected clients, or when a lawyer undertakes to represent clients who oppose each other in the same litigation (Comment *g(iii)*).

In effect, the consent requirement means that each affected client or former client has the power to preclude the representation by withholding consent. When a client withholds consent, a lawyer's power to withdraw from representation of that client and proceed with the representation of the other client is determined under § 121, Comment *e*.

While a lawyer may elect to proceed with a conflicted representation after effective client consent as stated in this Section, a lawyer is not required to do so (compare § 14, Comment *g* (required representation by order of court)). A lawyer might be unwilling to accept the risk that a consenting client will later become disappointed with the representation and contend that the consent was defective, or the lawyer might conclude for other reasons that the lawyer's own interests do not warrant proceeding. In such an instance, the lawyer also may elect to withdraw if grounds permitting withdrawal are present under § 32. After withdrawal, a lawyer's ability to represent other clients is as described in § 121, Comment *e*.

c(i). The requirement of informed consent—adequate information. Informed consent requires that each affected client be aware of the material respects in which the representation could have adverse effects on the interests of that client. The information required depends on the nature of the conflict and the nature of the risks of the conflicted representation. The client must be aware of information reasonably adequate to make an informed decision.

Information relevant to particular kinds of conflicts is considered in several of the Sections hereafter. In a multiple-client situation, the information normally should address the interests of the lawyer and other client giving rise to the conflict; contingent, optional, and tactical considerations and alternative courses of action that would be foreclosed or made less readily available by the conflict; the effect of the representation or the process of obtaining other clients' informed consent upon confidential information of the client; any material reservations that a disinterested lawyer might reasonably harbor about the arrangement if such a lawyer were representing only the client being advised; and the consequences and effects of a future withdrawal of consent by any client, including, if relevant, the fact that the lawyer would withdraw from representing all clients (see § 121, Comment *e*). Where the conflict arises solely because a proposed representation will be adverse to an existing client in an unrelated matter, knowledge of the general nature and scope of the work being performed for each client normally suffices to enable the clients to decide whether or not to consent.

When the consent relates to a former-client conflict (see § 132), it is necessary that the former client be aware that the consent will allow the former lawyer to proceed adversely to the former client. Beyond that, the former client must have adequate information about the implications (if not readily apparent) of the adverse representation, the fact that the lawyer possesses the former client's confidential information, the measures that the former lawyer might undertake to protect against unwarranted disclosures, and the right of the former client to refuse consent. The former client will often be independently represented by counsel.

If so, communication with the former client ordinarily must be through successor counsel (see § 99 and following).

The lawyer is responsible for assuring that each client has the necessary information. A lawyer who does not personally inform the client assumes the risk that the client is inadequately informed and that the consent is invalid. A lawyer's failure to inform the clients might also bear on the motives and good faith of the lawyer. On the other hand, clients differ as to their sophistication and experience, and situations differ in terms of their complexity and the subtlety of the conflicts presented. The requirements of this Section are satisfied if the client already knows the necessary information or learns it from other sources. A client independently represented—for example by inside legal counsel or by other outside counsel—will need less information about the consequences of a conflict but nevertheless may have need of information adequate to reveal its scope and severity. When several lawyers represent the same client, responsibility to make disclosure and obtain informed consent may be delegated to one or more of the lawyers who appears reasonably capable of providing adequate information.

Disclosing information about one client or prospective client to another is precluded if information necessary to be conveyed is confidential (see § 60). The affected clients may consent to disclosure (see § 62), but it also might be possible for the lawyer to explain the nature of undisclosed information in a manner that nonetheless provides an adequate basis for informed consent. If means of adequate disclosure are unavailable, consent to the conflict may not be obtained.

The requirement of consent generally requires an affirmative response by each client. Ambiguities in a client's purported expression of consent should be construed against the lawyer seeking the protection of the consent (cf. § 18). In general, a lawyer may not assume consent from a client's silent acquiescence. However, consent may be inferred from active participation in a representation by a client who has reasonably adequate information about the material risks of the representation after a lawyer's request for consent. Even in the absence of consent, a tribunal applying remedies such as disqualification (see § 121, Comment *f*) will apply concepts of estoppel and waiver when an objecting party has either induced reasonable reliance on the absence of objection or delayed an unreasonable period of time in making objection.

Effective client consent to one conflict is not necessarily effective with respect to other conflicts or other matters. A client's informed consent to simultaneous representation of another client in the same matter despite a conflict of interest (see Topic 3) does not constitute consent to the lawyer's later representation of the other client in a manner that would violate the former-client conflict rule (see § 132; see also § 121, Comment *e(i)*).

Illustration:

> 1. Client A and Client B give informed consent to a joint representation by Lawyer to prepare a commercial contract. Lawyer's bill for legal services is paid by both clients and the matter is terminated. Client B then retains Lawyer to file a lawsuit against former Client A on the asserted ground that A breached the contract. Lawyer may not represent Client B against Client A in the lawsuit without A's informed consent (see § 132). Client A's earlier consent to Lawyer's joint representation to draft the contract does not itself permit Lawyer's later adversarial representation.

c(ii). The requirement of informed consent—the capacity of the consenting person. Each client whose consent is required must have the legal capacity to give informed consent. Consent purportedly given by a client who lacks legal capacity to do so is ineffective. Consent of a person under a legal disability normally must be obtained from a guardian or conservator appointed for the person. Consent of a minor normally is effective when given by a parent or guardian of the minor. In class actions certification of the class, determination that the interests of its members are congruent, and assessment of the adequacy of representation are typically made by a tribunal.

In some jurisdictions, a governmental unit might lack legal authority under applicable law to give consent to some conflicts of interest (see Comment *g(ii)* below).

When the person who normally would make the decision whether or not to give consent—members of a corporate board of directors, for example—is another interested client of the lawyer, or is otherwise self-interested in the decision whether to consent, special requirements apply to consent (see § § 131 & 135, Comment *d*). Similarly, an officer of a government agency capable of consenting might be disabled from giving consent when that officer is a lawyer personally interested in consenting to the conflict.

d. Consent to future conflicts. Client consent to conflicts that might arise in the future is subject to special scrutiny, particularly if the consent is general. A client's open-ended agreement to consent to all conflicts normally should be ineffective unless the client possesses sophistication in the matter in question and has had the opportunity to receive independent legal advice about the consent. A client's informed consent to a gift to a lawyer (see § 127) ordinarily should be given contemporaneously with the gift.

On the other hand, particularly in a continuing client-lawyer relationship in which the lawyer is expected to act on behalf of the client without a new engagement for each matter, the gains to both lawyer and client from a system of advance consent to defined future conflicts might be substantial. A client might, for example, give informed consent in advance to types of conflicts that are familiar to the client. Such an agreement could effectively protect the client's interest while assuring that the lawyer did not undertake a potentially disqualifying representation.

Illustrations:

2. Law Firm has represented Client in collecting commercial claims through Law Firm's New York office for many years. Client is a long-established and sizable business corporation that is sophisticated in commercial matters generally and specifically in dealing with lawyers. Law Firm also has a Chicago office that gives tax advice to many companies with which Client has commercial dealings. Law Firm asks for advance consent from Client with respect to conflicts that otherwise would prevent Law Firm from filing commercial claims on behalf of Client against the tax clients of Law Firm's Chicago office (see § 128). If Client gives informed consent the consent should be held to be proper as to Client. Law Firm would also be required to obtain informed consent from any tax client of its Chicago office against whom Client wishes to file a commercial claim, should Law Firm decide to undertake such a representation.

3. The facts being otherwise as stated in Illustration 2, Law Firm seeks advance consent from each of its Chicago-office corporate-tax clients to its representation of any of its other clients in matters involving collection of commercial claims adverse to such tax clients if the matters do not involve information that Law Firm might have learned in the tax representation. To provide further assurance concerning the protection of confidential information, the consent provides that, should Law Firm represent any client in a collection matter adverse to a tax client, a procedure to protect confidential information of the tax client will be established (compare § 124, Comment *d*). Unless such a tax client is shown to be unsophisticated about legal matters and relationships with lawyers, informed consent to the arrangement should be held to be proper.

If a material change occurs in the reasonable expectations that formed the basis of a client's informed consent, the new conditions must be brought to the attention of the client and new informed consent obtained (see also Comment *f* hereto (client revocation of consent)). If the new conflict is not consentable (see Comment *g* hereto), the lawyer may not proceed.

e. Partial or conditional consent. A client's informed consent to a conflict can be qualified or conditional. A client might consent, for example, to joint representation with one co-party but not another. Similarly, the client might condition consent on particular action being taken by the lawyer or law firm. For example, a former client might consent that the conflict of one individually prohibited lawyer should not be imputed (see § 123) to the rest of the firm, but only if the firm takes steps to assure that the prohibited lawyer is not involved in the representation (see § 124; see also Illustration 3 hereto). Such a partial or conditional consent can be valid even if an unconditional consent in the same situation would be invalid. For example, a client might give informed consent to a lawyer serving only in the role of mediator between clients (see § 130, Comment *d*), but not to the lawyer representing those clients opposing each other in litigation if mediation is unavailing (see Comment *g(iii)* hereto).

f. Revocation of consent through client action or a material change of circumstances. A client who has given informed consent to an otherwise conflicted representation may at any time revoke the consent (see § 21(2)). Revoking consent to the client's own representation, however, does not necessarily prevent the lawyer from continuing to represent other clients who had been jointly represented along with the revoking client. Whether the lawyer may continue the other representation depends on whether the client was justified in revoking the consent (such as because of a material change in the factual basis on which the client originally gave informed consent) and whether material detriment to the other client or lawyer would result. In addition, if the client had reserved the prerogative of revoking consent, that agreement controls the lawyer's subsequent ability to continue representation of other clients.

A material change in the factual basis on which the client originally gave informed consent can justify a client in withdrawing consent. For example, in the absence of an agreement to the contrary, the consent of a client to be represented concurrently with another (see Topic 3) normally presupposes that the co-clients will not develop seriously antagonistic positions. If such antagonism develops, it might warrant revoking consent. If the conflict is subject to informed consent (see Comment *(g)(iii)* hereto), the lawyer must thereupon obtain renewed informed consent of the clients, now adequately informed of the change of circumstances. If the conflict is not consentable, or the lawyer cannot obtain informed consent from the other client or decides not to proceed with the representation, the lawyer must withdraw from representing all affected clients adverse to any former client in the matter (see § 121, Comment *e*).

A client who has given informed consent to be represented as a joint client with another would be justified in revoking the consent if the common lawyer failed to represent that client with reasonable loyalty (see Comment *h* hereto). The client would also be justified in revoking consent if a co-client materially violated the express or implied terms of the consent, such as by abusing the first client's confidential information through disclosing important information to third persons without justification. Improper behavior of the other client or the lawyer might indicate that one or both of them cannot be trusted to respect the legitimate interests of the consenting client.

Illustration:

4. Client A and Client B validly consent to be represented by Lawyer in operating a restaurant in a city. After a period of amicable and profitable collaboration, Client A reasonably concludes that Lawyer has begun to take positions against Client A and consistently favoring the interests of Client B in the business. Reasonably concerned that Lawyer is no longer properly serving the interests of both clients, Client A withdraws consent. Withdrawal of consent is effective and justified (see Comment *h* hereto). Lawyer may not thereafter continue representing either Client A or Client B in a matter adverse to the other and substantially related to Lawyer's former representation of the clients (see § 121, Comment *e(i)*).

In the absence of valid reasons for a client's revocation of consent, the ability of the lawyer to continue representing other clients depends on whether material detriment to the other client or lawyer would result and, accordingly, whether the reasonable expectations of those persons would be defeated. Once the client or former client has given informed consent to a lawyer's representing another client, that other client as well as the lawyer might have acted in reliance on the consent. For example, the other client and the lawyer might already have invested time, money, and effort in the representation. The other client might already have disclosed confidential information and developed a relationship of trust and confidence with the lawyer. Or, a client relying on the consent might reasonably have elected to forgo opportunities to take other action.

Illustrations:

5. On Monday, Client A and Client B validly consent to being represented by Lawyer in the same matter despite a conflict of interest. On Wednesday, before either Client B or Lawyer has taken or forgone any significant action in reliance, Client A withdraws consent. Lawyer is no longer justified in continuing with the joint representation. Lawyer also may not continue to represent Client B alone without A's renewed informed consent to Lawyer's representation of B if doing so would violate other Sections of this Chapter, for example because A's and B's interests in the matter would be antagonistic or because Lawyer had learned confidential information from A relevant in the matter (see § 132; see also § 15, Comment *c*, & § 121, Comment *e(i)*). Similarly, if Client A on Wednesday did not unequivocally withdraw consent but stated to Lawyer that on further reflection Client A now had serious doubts about the wisdom of the joint representation, Lawyer could not reasonably take material steps in reliance on the consent. Before proceeding, Lawyer must clarify with Client A whether A indeed gives informed consent and whether the joint representation may thereby continue.

6. Clients A and B validly consent to Lawyer representing them jointly as co-defendants in a breach-of-contract action. On the eve of trial and after months of pretrial discovery on the part of all parties, Client A withdraws consent to the joint representation for reasons not justified by the conduct of Lawyer or Client B and insists that Lawyer cease representing Client B. At this point it would be difficult and expensive for Client B to find separate representation for the impending trial. Client A's withdrawal of consent is ineffective to prevent the continuing representation of B in the absence of compelling considerations such as harmful disloyalty by Lawyer.

7. Client A, who consulted Lawyer about a tax question, gave informed advance consent to Lawyer's representing any of Lawyer's other clients against Client A in matters unrelated to Client A's tax question. Client B, who had not theretofore been a client of Lawyer, wishes to retain Lawyer to file suit against Client A for personal injuries suffered in an automobile accident. After Lawyer informs Client B of the nature of Lawyer's work for Client A, and the nature and risks presented by any conflict that might be produced, Client B consents to the conflict of interest. After Lawyer has

undertaken substantial work in preparation of Client B's case, Client A seeks to withdraw the advance consent for reasons not justified by the conduct of Lawyer or Client B. Even though Client A was Lawyer's client before Client B was a client, the material detriment to both Lawyer and Client B would render Client A's attempt to withdraw consent ineffective.

The terms of the consent itself can control the effects of revocation of consent. A client's consent could state that it is conditioned on the client's right to revoke consent at any time for any reason. If so conditioned, the consent would cease to be effective if the client exercised that right.

g. Nonconsentable conflicts. Some conflicts of interest preclude adverse representation even if informed consent is obtained.

g(i). Representations prohibited by law. As stated in Subsection (2)(a), informed consent is unavailing when prohibited by applicable law. In some states, for example, the law provides that the same lawyer may not represent more than one defendant in a capital case and that informed consent does not cure the conflict (see § 129, Comment *c*). Under federal criminal statutes, certain representations by a former government lawyer (cf. § 133) are prohibited, and informed consent by the former client is not recognized as a defense.

g(ii). Consent by governmental clients. Decisional law in a minority of states has limited the extent to which a governmental client may consent to a conflict of interest. Subject to local law on the powers of governmental bodies and the requirement that any consenting governmental officer must be disinterested in the issues giving rise to the question of conflict (see Comment *c(ii)* hereto), such questions should otherwise be decided under the customary rules governing conflicts of interest.

g(iii). Conflicts between adversaries in litigation. When clients are aligned directly against each other in the same litigation, the institutional interest in vigorous development of each client's position renders the conflict nonconsentable (see § 128, Comment *c,* & § 129). The rule applies even if the parties themselves believe that the common interests are more significant in the matter than the interests dividing them. While the parties might give informed consent to joint representation for purposes of negotiating their differences (see § 130, Comment *d*), the joint representation may not continue if the parties become opposed to each other in litigation.

Illustration:

8. A and B wish to obtain an amicable dissolution of their marriage. State law treats marriage dissolution as a contested judicial proceeding. Lawyer is asked to represent both A and B in negotiation of the property settlement to be submitted to the court in the proceeding. Informed consent can authorize Lawyer to represent both parties in the property-settlement negotiations (subject to exceptions in some jurisdictions, where interests of children are involved, for example), but consent does not authorize Lawyer to represent both A and B if litigation is necessary to obtain the final decree. The parties may agree that Lawyer will represent only one of them in the judicial proceeding. The other party would either be represented by another lawyer or appear pro se (see § § 128 & 130).

Whether clients are aligned directly against each other within the meaning of this Comment requires examination of the context of the litigation. In multi-party litigation, a single lawyer might, for example, represent members of a class in a class action, multiple creditors or debtors in a bankruptcy proceeding, or multiple interested parties in environmental clean-up litigation (see § 128). Joint representation is appropriate following effective client consent, together with compliance with applicable statutory or rule requirements, which may require court approval of the representation after disclosure of the conflict. Such joint representation is appropriate, notwithstanding that the co-clients may have conflicting claims against each other in other matters as to which the lawyer is not providing representation. The clients may also give informed consent to joint representation while they negotiate any differences they may have in the matter in litigation, perhaps employing the lawyer as appropriate in such negotiations (see § 130, Comments *c* & *d*), or prior agreement on such negotiated matters may be a condition of the clients' consent (see Comment *e* hereto).Where the alignment of parties, clients, and claims is such that the lawyer will not oppose another client with respect to the matters of dispute between them, as indicated in s 122(2)(b), there is no conflict. Thus, in complex litigation, the same lawyer may represent two defendants with largely congruent positions with respect to their defense, if other counsel are representing the two clients with respect to a dispute between them.

g(iv). Other circumstances rendering a lawyer incapable of providing adequate representation. Concern for client autonomy generally warrants respecting a client's informed consent. In some situations, however, joint representation would be objectively inadequate despite a client's voluntary and informed consent. In criminal cases, for example, joint representation of co-defendants with irreconcilable or unreconciled interests might render their representation constitutionally inadequate and thus require a court to prohibit the joint representation (see § 129, Comment *c*). Similarly, a conflict of interest among class members might render a lawyer's representation in a class action inadequate despite informed consent by the class representatives (see § 128, Comment *d*; see also, e.g., § 131, Comment *f,* Illustration 5).

The general standard stated in Subsection (2)(c) assesses the likelihood that the lawyer will, following consent, be able to provide adequate representation to the clients. The standard includes the requirements both that the consented-to conflict not adversely affect the lawyer's relationship with either client and that it not adversely affect the representation of either client. In general, if a reasonable and disinterested lawyer would conclude that one or more of the affected clients could not consent to the conflicted representation because the representation would likely fall short in either respect, the conflict is nonconsentable.

Decisions holding that a conflict is nonconsentable often involve facts suggesting that the client, who is often unsophisticated in retaining lawyers, was not adequately informed or was incapable of adequately appreciating the risks of the conflict (compare Comments *c(i)* & *c(ii)* hereto). Decisions involving clients sophisticated in the use of lawyers, particularly when advised by independent counsel, such as by inside legal counsel, rarely hold that a conflict is nonconsentable.

The nature of the conflict is also important. The professional rules and court decisions indicate that informed consent will always suffice with respect to a former-client conflict of interest (§ 132). With respect to simultaneous-representation conflicts (Topic 3), when the matters are unrelated it would only be in unusual circumstances that a lawyer could not provide adequate representation with consent of all affected clients. On the other hand, when the representation involves the same matter or the matters are significantly related, it may be more difficult for the lawyer to provide adequate legal assistance to multiple clients (see, e.g., § 131, Comment *e,* Illustration 4).

Illustrations:

9. Lawyer occasionally represents Bank in collection matters and is doing so currently in one lawsuit. Employee requests Lawyer to file an employment-discrimination charge against Bank. Bank, acting through its inside legal counsel, gives informed consent to Lawyer's representation of Employee against Bank with respect to the matter. Employee, following discussion with Lawyer concerning the nature of Lawyer's collection representations of Bank, freely gives informed consent as well. The circumstances indicate no basis for concluding that Lawyer would be unable to provide adequate representation to Bank in the collection matters and to Employee in the discrimination claim against Bank.

10. Lawyer has been asked by Buyer and Seller to represent both of them in negotiating and documenting a complex real-estate transaction. The parties are in sharp disagreement on several important terms of the transaction. Given such differences, Lawyer would be unable to provide adequate representation to both clients.

11. The facts being otherwise as stated in Illustration 10, the parties are both in agreement on terms and possess comparable knowledge and experience in such transactions, but, viewed objectively, the transaction is such that both parties should receive extensive counseling concerning their rights in the transaction and possible optional arrangements, including security interests, guarantees, and other rights against each other and in resisting the claims of the other party for such rights. Given the scope of legal representation that each prospective client should receive, Lawyer would be unable to provide adequate representation to both clients.

A conflict can be rendered nonconsentable because of personal circumstances affecting the lawyer's ability in fact to provide adequate representation. For example, if the lawyer has such strong feelings of friendship toward one of two prospective joint clients that the lawyer could not provide adequate representation to the other client (compare Comment *h* hereto), the lawyer may not proceed with the joint representation.

h. Duties of a lawyer representing a client subject to a conflict consent. When a lawyer undertakes representation despite a conflict and after required disclosure and informed consent, the lawyer must represent all affected clients diligently and competently (see § 16) and must not regard informed consent as a basis for limiting the scope of the representation or favoring the interests of one client over the interests of another, except as expressly agreed under the informed consent. The lawyer must protect the confidential information of all affected clients (see § 60), subject to whatever modifications are warranted pursuant to the informed consent. On communicating information with each client in the absence of a different agreement among co-clients, see § 60, Comment *l,* and § 75, Comment *d.*

§ 123. Imputation of a Conflict of Interest to an Affiliated Lawyer

Unless all affected clients consent to the representation under the limitations and conditions provided in § 122 or unless imputation hereunder is removed as provided in § 124, the restrictions upon a lawyer imposed by § § 125-135 also restrict other affiliated lawyers who:

(1) are associated with that lawyer in rendering legal services to others through a law partnership, professional corporation, sole proprietorship, or similar association;

(2) are employed with that lawyer by an organization to render legal services either to that organization or to others to advance the interests or objectives of the organization; or

(3) share office facilities without reasonably adequate measures to protect confidential client information so that it will not be available to other lawyers in the shared office.

§ 124. Removing Imputation

(1) Imputation specified in § 123 does not restrict an affiliated lawyer when the affiliation between the affiliated lawyer and the personally prohibited lawyer that required the imputation has been terminated, and no material confidential information of the client, relevant to the matter, has been communicated by the personally prohibited lawyer to the affiliated lawyer or that lawyer's firm.

(2) Imputation specified in § 123 does not restrict an affiliated lawyer with respect to a former-client conflict under § 132, when there is no substantial risk that confidential information of the former client will be used with material adverse effect on the former client because:

(a) any confidential client information communicated to the personally prohibited lawyer is unlikely to be significant in the subsequent matter;

(b) the personally prohibited lawyer is subject to screening measures adequate to eliminate participation by that lawyer in the representation; and

(c) timely and adequate notice of the screening has been provided to all affected clients.

(3) Imputation specified in § 123 does not restrict a lawyer affiliated with a former government lawyer with respect to a conflict under § 133 if:

(a) the personally prohibited lawyer is subject to screening measures adequate to eliminate involvement by that lawyer in the representation; and

(b) timely and adequate notice of the screening has been provided to the appropriate government agency and to affected clients.

Comment:

c. Imputation after the termination of an affiliation.

c(i). Personally prohibited lawyer terminates the affiliation. During the time that a personally prohibited lawyer is associated with another lawyer, law firm, or other organization to which prohibition is imputed under § 123, the lawyer could reveal confidential information to any other lawyer within the organization. Accordingly, imputed prohibition of all lawyers in the firm is appropriately required by § 123. However, after the personally prohibited lawyer has left the firm, an irrebuttable presumption of continued sharing of client confidences or continued disloyalty induced by the affiliation is no longer justified.

The lawyers remaining in the affiliation may rebut the presumption that confidential information was shared during the period of actual affiliation. They have the burden of persuasion concerning three facts: (1) that no material confidential client information relevant to the matter was revealed to any lawyer remaining in the firm; (2) that the firm does not now possess or have access to sources of client confidential information, particularly client documents or files; and (3) that the personally prohibited lawyer will not share fees in the matter so as to have an interest in the representation.

A personally prohibited lawyer who enters a new law firm or other affiliation causes imputed prohibition of all affiliated lawyers as stated in § 123. Such imputation is subject to removal under

Subsection (2) or (3).

c(ii). A non-personally-prohibited lawyer terminates the affiliation. When a lawyer leaves a firm or other organization whose lawyers were subject to imputed prohibition owing to presence in the firm of another lawyer, the departed lawyer becomes free of imputation so long as that lawyer obtained no material confidential client information relevant to the matter. Similarly, lawyers in the new affiliation are free of imputed prohibition if they can carry the burden of persuading the finder of fact that the arriving lawyer did not obtain confidential client information about a questioned representation by another lawyer in the former affiliation.

d(i). Screening—in general. . . . Lawyer codes generally recognize the screening remedy in cases involving former government lawyers who have returned to private practice (see Comment *e* hereto). Screening to prevent imputation from former private-client representations has similar justification, giving clients wider choice of counsel and making it easier for lawyers to change employers. The rule in Subsection (2) thus permits screening as a remedy in situations in which the information possessed by a personally prohibited lawyer is not likely to be significant. The lawyer or firm seeking to remove imputation has the burden of persuasion that there is no substantial risk that confidential information of the former client will be used with material adverse effect on the former client.

Significance of the information is determined by its probable utility in the later representation, including such factors as the following: (1) whether the value of the information as proof or for tactical purposes is peripheral or tenuous; (2) whether the information in most material respects is now publicly known; (3) whether the information was of only temporary significance; (4) the scope of the second representation; and (5) the duration and degree of responsibility of the personally prohibited lawyer in the earlier representation.

The lawyer codes in most states impose disciplinary responsibility in a wider range of circumstances of former private-client representations. Specifically, most codes do not recognize that screening can preclude disqualification of a law firm by imputation from a personally prohibited lawyer, even if the screening is timely and effective and the client information involved is innocuous. The issue typically arises under motions to disqualify, not in disciplinary proceedings. A tribunal has discretion whether or not to require disqualification. Subsection (2) states a rule to guide exercise of that discretion.

d(ii). Screening—adequacy of measures. Screening must assure that confidential client information will not pass from the personally prohibited lawyer to any other lawyer in the firm. The screened lawyer should be prohibited from talking to other persons in the firm about the matter as to which the lawyer is prohibited, and from sharing documents about the matter and the like. Further, the screened lawyer should receive no direct financial benefit from the firm's representation, based upon the outcome of the matter, such as a financial bonus or a larger share of firm income directly attributable to the matter. However, it is not impermissible that the lawyer receives compensation and benefits under standing arrangements established prior to the representation. An adequate showing of screening ordinarily requires affidavits by the personally prohibited lawyer and by a lawyer responsible for the screening measures. A tribunal can require that other appropriate steps be taken.

If a lawyer in a law firm assertedly observing screening measures in fact breaches the screen and shares confidential information with lawyers proceeding adversely to the former client, the tribunal should take appropriate corrective measures. The screen should no longer be considered adequate to prevent disqualification of affiliated lawyers. Contempt might be an appropriate remedy to the extent that breach of the screen was knowing and deliberate and in violation of direct undertakings to the tribunal. In circumstances involving lesser culpability, lesser sanctions within the court's inherent power may be appropriate.

d(iii). Screening—timely and adequate notice of screening to all affected clients. An affected client will usually have difficulty demonstrating whether screening measures have been honored. Timely and adequate notice of the screening must therefore be given to the affected clients, including description of the screening measures reasonably sufficient to inform the affected client of their adequacy. Notice will give opportunity to protest and to allow arrangements to be made for monitoring compliance.

Notice should ordinarily be given as soon as practical after the lawyer or firm realizes or should realize the need for screening. Obligations of confidentiality to a current client, however, might justify reasonable delay. A firm advising about a possible takeover of a former client of a lawyer now in the firm, for example, need not provide notice until the attempt becomes known to the target client.

TOPIC 2. CONFLICTS OF INTEREST BETWEEN A LAWYER AND A CLIENT

§ 125. A Lawyer's Personal Interest Affecting the Representation of a Client

Unless the affected client consents to the representation under the limitations and conditions provided in § 122, a lawyer may not represent a client if there is a substantial risk that the lawyer's representation of the client would be materially and adversely affected by the lawyer's financial or other personal interests.

Comment:

f. Initiation and settlement of class actions and other multiple-client representations. Class actions and similar proceedings can raise a number of personal-interest conflict-of-interest questions. A class action can transform a modest claim into a set of claims of large consequence and often has potential for magnifying attorney's fees. An individual plaintiff usually begins with a concern about an individual wrong, and prompt and complete redress of that wrong is often the client's goal. A class action might be the only practical means of vindicating the client interest. However, a class action can substitute a longer, more complex proceeding for one more beneficial for the client's individual interests. Where bringing a claim as a class action might materially and adversely affect the interests of the individual client, that possibility must be disclosed to that client. On the determination of client-lawyer relationships in class actions, see § 14, Comment *f.*

Settlement of a class action or similar suit can also create a conflict concerning the lawyer's fee. The defendant, for example, might offer to settle the matter for an amount or kind of relief that is relatively generous to the lawyer's client if the lawyer will agree to accept a low fee award. Conversely, the defendant might acquiesce in a generous award of attorney's fees in exchange for relatively modest relief for the client's substantive claim. The latter arrangement must be rejected by the class lawyer as subordinating the interests of the lawyer's client to the lawyer's own interest.

The lawyer should make reasonable effort to separate settlement of the substantive claim from determination of the amount of attorney's fees. Some decisions have attempted to effectuate that requirement by forbidding settlement discussions to address the fee that the lawyer is to receive. Some commentators have urged that a court refuse to approve a settlement unless award of reasonable attorney's fees is to be judicially determined rather than negotiated. Neither of those suggestions gives adequate effect to the interests of the client in all cases.

A more appropriate arrangement, where possible, is for the lawyer's fee to be negotiated initially by the client and lawyer at the outset of the relationship, it being understood and disclosed to the client that the ultimate award may be scrutinized by the opposing party and approved by the court (compare § 22, Comment *c*). On interpretation of agreements between client and lawyer concerning fee awards, see § 38, Comment *f.* On aggregate settlement of claims involving multiple clients who are not class members, see § 128, Comment *d(i)*.

§ 126. Business Transactions Between a Lawyer and a Client

A lawyer may not participate in a business or financial transaction with a client, except a standard commercial transaction in which the lawyer does not render legal services, unless:

> **(1) the client has adequate information about the terms of the transaction and the risks presented by the lawyer's involvement in it;**

> **(2) the terms and circumstances of the transaction are fair and reasonable to the client; and**

> **(3) the client consents to the lawyer's role in the transaction under the limitations and conditions provided in § 122 after being encouraged, and given a reasonable opportunity, to seek independent legal advice concerning the transaction.**

§ 127. A Client Gift to a Lawyer

(1) A lawyer may not prepare any instrument effecting any gift from a client to the lawyer, including a testamentary gift, unless the lawyer is a relative or other natural object

of the client's generosity and the gift is not significantly disproportionate to those given other donees similarly related to the donor.

(2) A lawyer may not accept a gift from a client, including a testamentary gift, unless:

(a) the lawyer is a relative or other natural object of the client's generosity;

(b) the value conferred by the client and the benefit to the lawyer are insubstantial in amount; or

(c) the client, before making the gift, has received independent advice or has been encouraged, and given a reasonable opportunity, to seek such advice.

Comment:

a. Scope and cross-references. . . . The law of undue influence treats client gifts as presumptively fraudulent, so that the lawyer-donee bears a heavy burden of persuasion that the gift is fair and not the product of overreaching or otherwise an imposition upon the client. See Restatement Second, Trusts § 343, Comments *l* and *m* (voidability of gifts from beneficiary to trustee); cf. Restatement Second, Contracts § 177 (contracts voidable on ground of undue influence). This Section assumes, but does not restate fully, the law of undue influence. The Section is stricter than the general law of undue influence in some jurisdictions. For example, the Section prohibits a lawyer from accepting a gift from a client (apart from the three stated exceptions) even if the lawyer has not engaged in undue influence.

TOPIC 3. CONFLICTS OF INTEREST AMONG CURRENT CLIENTS

§ 128. Representing Clients with Conflicting Interests in Civil Litigation

Unless all affected clients consent to the representation under the limitations and conditions provided in § 122, a lawyer in civil litigation may not:

(1) represent two or more clients in a matter if there is a substantial risk that the lawyer's representation of one client would be materially and adversely affected by the lawyer's duties to another client in the matter; or

(2) represent one client to assert or defend a claim against or brought by another client currently represented by the lawyer, even if the matters are not related.

Comment:

d. Clients nominally aligned on the same side in the litigation. Multiple representation is precluded when the clients, although nominally on the same side of a lawsuit, in fact have such different interests that representation of one will have a material and adverse effect on the lawyer's representation of the other. Such conflicts can occur whether the clients are aligned as co-plaintiffs or co-defendants, as well as in complex and multiparty litigation.

d(i). Clients aligned as co-plaintiffs. No conflict of interest is ordinarily presented when two or more of a lawyer's clients assert claims against a defendant. However, sometimes two parties aligned on the same side of a case as co-claimants might wish to characterize the facts differently. The client-claimants might also have a potential lawsuit against each other. For example, a passenger in an automobile damage action might be a co-plaintiff with the driver of the car in a suit alleging negligence of the driver of the other car, but also be able to contend that the driver of the passenger's car was negligent as well, a conclusion that the driver would be motivated to deny. Where there are such possible claims, the lawyer must warn clients about the possibilities of such differences and obtain the consent of each before agreeing to represent them as co-claimants (see § 122).

When multiple claimants assert claims against a defendant who lacks sufficient assets to meet all of the damage claims, a conflict of interest might also be presented. Indeed, whether or not the defendant has assets sufficient to pay all claims, a proposed settlement might create conflicts because the plaintiffs differ in their willingness to accept the settlement. Before any settlement is accepted on behalf of multiple clients, their lawyer must inform each of them about all of the terms of the settlement, including the amounts that each of the other claimants will receive if the settlement is accepted. A similar conflict of interest can arise for a lawyer representing multiple defending parties.

Illustrations:

1. Lawyer represents A and B, pedestrians struck by an automobile as they stood at a street corner.

Each has sued C, the owner-driver, for $150,000. C has $100,000 in liability insurance coverage and no other assets with which to satisfy a judgment. Neither A nor B can be paid the full amount of their claims and any sum recovered by one will reduce the assets available to pay the other's claim. Because of the conflict of interest, Lawyer can continue to represent both A and B only with the informed consent of each (see § 122).

2. The same facts as in Illustration 1, except that C offers to settle A's claim for $60,000 and B's claim for $40,000. Lawyer must inform both A and B of all of the terms of the proposed settlement, including the amounts offered to each client. If one client wishes to accept and the other wishes to reject the proposed settlement, Lawyer may continue to represent both A and B only after a renewal of informed consent by each.

d(ii). Clients aligned as co-defendants in civil case. Clients aligned as co-defendants also can have conflicting interests. Each would usually prefer to see the plaintiff defeated altogether, but if the plaintiff succeeds, each will often prefer to see liability deflected mainly or entirely upon other defendants. Indeed, a plaintiff often sues multiple defendants in the hope that each of the defendants will take the position that another of them is responsible, thus enhancing the likelihood of the plaintiff's recovering. Such conflicts preclude joint representation, absent each co-defendant's informed consent (see § 122).

A contract between the parties can eliminate the conflict. When an employee injures someone in an incident arising out of the employment, for example, an employer that is capable of paying the judgment might agree in advance to hold the employee harmless in the matter so that only the employer will bear any judgment ultimately entered. If only one of the parties will ultimately be liable to the plaintiff, there is little reason to incur the expense of separate counsel. However, the initial conflict must be understood by both defendants and each must consent, particularly if the clients must negotiate an agreement governing who will bear ultimate liability (see § 130).

d(iii). Complex and multiparty litigation. Not all possibly differing interests of co-clients in complex and multiparty litigation involve material interests creating conflict. Determination whether a conflict of material interests exists requires careful attention to the context and other circumstances of the representation and in general should be based on whether (1) issues common to the clients' interests predominate, (2) circumstances such as the size of each client's interest make separate representation impracticable, and (3) the extent of active judicial supervision of the representation. For example, a lawyer might represent several unsecured creditors in a bankruptcy proceeding. In addition to general conflict-of-interest rules that may apply, a lawyer representing such multiple clients must also comply with statutory regulations if more stringent.

Similar considerations apply in representing multiple co-parties in class-action proceedings, due to the possible existence of different objectives or other interests of class members (see also § 125 on creation and settlement of class actions). A plaintiff class might agree, for example, that the local school system discriminates against a racial or ethnic minority, but there might be important differences within the class over what remedy is appropriate (see § 14, Comment *f*). As one possible corrective, under procedural law a class may be subdivided. Through that process objecting members of the class may be heard. However, such differences within the class do not necessarily produce conflicts requiring that the lawyer for the class not represent some or all members of the class or necessitate creation of subclasses. The tasks of a lawyer for a class may include monitoring and mediating such differences. In instances of intractable difference, the lawyer may proceed in what the lawyer reasonably concludes to be the best interests of the class as a whole, for example urging the tribunal to accept an appropriate settlement even if it is not accepted by class representatives or members of the class. In such instances, of course, the lawyer must inform the tribunal of the differing views within the class or on the part of a class representative.

e. Suing a present client in an unrelated matter. A lawyer's representation of Client A might require the lawyer to file a lawsuit against Client B whom the lawyer represents in an unrelated matter. Because the matters are unrelated, no confidential information is likely to be used improperly, nor will the lawyer take both sides in a single proceeding. However, the lawyer has a duty of loyalty to the client being sued. Moreover, the client on whose behalf suit is filed might fear that the lawyer would pursue that client's case less effectively out of deference to the other client. Thus, a lawyer may not sue a current client on behalf of another client, even in an unrelated matter, unless consent is obtained under the conditions and limitations of § 122. On identifying who is a present client, see § 14 and § 121, Comment *d*. On the possibility of informed consent in advance to such suits in certain cases, see § 122, Comment *d*.

Illustrations:

3. Lawyer represents Client B in seeking a tax refund. Client A wishes to file suit against Client B

in a contract action unrelated to the tax claim. Lawyer may not represent Client A in the suit against Client B as long as Lawyer represents Client B in the tax case, unless both clients give informed consent. On withdrawal, see § 121, Comment *e*.

4. The same facts as in Illustration 3, except that Client A's contract action is against corporation C, which is not Lawyer's client. After A's suit has been filed, C is acquired by and merged into Lawyer's client B, thus creating the conflict. Unauthorized use of confidential information would not be an issue in such a case, and any remedy imposed by a tribunal should minimize adverse impact on the parties. Because the action of B created the conflict, Lawyer might be permitted to withdraw from pursuing the tax claim on behalf of B, for example, but continue to pursue the contract action. Compare the discussion at § 132, Comment *e*.

f. Concurrently taking adverse legal positions on behalf of different clients. A lawyer ordinarily may take inconsistent legal positions in different courts at different times. While each client is entitled to the lawyer's effective advocacy of that client's position, if the rule were otherwise law firms would have to specialize in a single side of legal issues.

However, a conflict is presented when there is a substantial risk that a lawyer's action in Case A will materially and adversely affect another of the lawyer's clients in Case B. Factors relevant in determining the risk of such an effect include whether the issue is before a trial court or an appellate court; whether the issue is substantive or procedural; the temporal relationship between the matters; the practical significance of the issue to the immediate and long-run interests of the clients involved; and the clients' reasonable expectations in retaining the lawyer. If a conflict of interest exists, absent informed consent of the affected clients under § 122, the lawyer must withdraw from one or both of the matters. Informed client consent is provided for in § 122. On circumstances in which informed client consent would not allow the lawyer to proceed with representation of both clients, see § 122(2)(c) and Comment *g(iv)* thereto.

Illustrations:

5. Lawyer represents two clients in damage actions pending in different United States District Courts. In one case, representing the plaintiff, Lawyer will attempt to introduce certain evidence at trial and argue there for its admissibility. In the other case, representing a defendant, Lawyer will object to an anticipated attempt by the plaintiff to introduce similar evidence. Even if there is some possibility that one court's ruling might be published and cited as authority in the other proceeding, Lawyer may proceed with both representations without obtaining the consent of the clients involved.

6. The same facts as in Illustration 5, except that the cases have proceeded to the point where certiorari has been granted in each by the United States Supreme Court to consider the common evidentiary question. Any position that Lawyer would assert on behalf of either client on the legal issue common to each case would have a material and adverse impact on the interests of the other client. Thus, a conflict of interest is presented. Even the informed consent of both Client A and Client B would be insufficient to permit Lawyer to represent each before the Supreme Court.

§ 129. Conflicts of Interest in Criminal Litigation

Unless all affected clients consent to the representation under the limitations and conditions provided in § 122, a lawyer in a criminal matter may not represent:

(1) two or more defendants or potential defendants in the same matter; or

(2) a single defendant, if the representation would involve a conflict of interest as defined in § 121.

Comment:

c. Multiple criminal-defense representations. Subsection (1) recognizes that the representation of co-defendants in criminal cases involves at least the potential for conflicts of interest. For example, if one defendant is offered favorable treatment in return for testimony against a co-defendant, a single lawyer could not give advice favorable to one defendant's interests while adhering to the duty of loyalty to the other. Similarly, individual defendants might have had different motives for and understandings of events, so that establishing a common position among them is difficult. Witnesses who would be favorable to one defendant might be subject to cross-examination that would be unfavorable to another defendant. In closing argument, counsel must choose which facts to stress. For example, stressing the minor role of one defendant might imply the major role of another.

Because of such potential conflicts and the constitutional significance of the issues they raise, joint

representation in criminal cases often has a material and adverse effect on the representation of each defendant and thus cannot be undertaken in the absence of client consent under the limitations and conditions stated in § 122.

Criminal defendants might nonetheless consider it in their interest to be represented by a single lawyer even when the financial cost of separate counsel is not a factor. A single lawyer can help assure a common position and increase the likelihood that none of the co-defendants will cooperate with the prosecution against the others. For such reasons, a criminal conviction involving joint representation ordinarily is not impeachable absent a showing of timely objection and actual prejudice. Were the rule otherwise, defendants could avoid raising a conflict issue before trial so as to create an issue for later appeal.

On the other hand, both the prosecutor and the trial judge have a responsibility to assure a fair trial for each defendant. When a defense lawyer would be required to assume an adverse position with respect to one or more of the clients, the conflict is nonconsentable (see § 122(2)(b) & Comment *g(iii)* thereto). Efficient operation of the judicial system requires that a verdict not be vulnerable to contentions that a defendant was disadvantaged by an undisclosed conflict of interest. A prosecutor might object to joint-representation arrangements to assure that a conflict possibility is resolved before trial. Even without objection by the prosecutor or defendant, the tribunal may raise the issue on its own initiative and refuse to permit joint representation where there is a significant threat to the interest in the finality of judgments.

Illustrations:

1. A and B are co-defendants charged with a felony offense of armed robbery. They are both represented by Lawyer. The prosecutor believes that A planned the crime and was the only one carrying a weapon. The prosecutor offers to accept B's plea of guilty to a misdemeanor if B will testify against A. Lawyer's loyalty to A causes Lawyer to persuade B that the prosecutor's proposal should be rejected. Following a trial, both A and B are convicted of the felony. When plea negotiations involving B's separate interests began, B should have received independent counsel. In the circumstances, Lawyer could not properly represent A and B even with the informed consent of both clients (see § 122, Comment *g(iii)*).

2. The same facts as in Illustration 1, except that the evidence at trial is highly damaging to Defendant A but less so to Defendant B. Both defendants were represented by Lawyer, who did not consult with A and B concerning their conflicting interests. Lawyer spent most of the closing argument explaining away A's guilt and did not mention the weak case against B, because doing so would invite the jury to consider the greater likelihood of A's guilt. Lawyer could represent B only with the informed consent of B (see § 122).

d. A criminal-defense lawyer with conflicting duties to other clients. As required in Subsection (2), a conflict exists when a defense lawyer in a criminal matter has duties to clients in other matters that might conflict. A conflict exists, for example, if the lawyer also represents either a prosecutor or a prosecution witness in an unrelated matter. The conflict could lead the lawyer to be less vigorous in defending the criminal case in order to avoid offending the other client, or the lawyer might be constrained in cross-examining the other client (see § 60(1)). A lawyer who represents a criminal defendant may not represent the state in unrelated civil matters when such representation would have a material and adverse effect on the lawyer's handling of the criminal case.

Ordinarily, these conflicts may be waived by client consent under the limitations and conditions in § 122. Because the defendant's constitutional rights are implicated, court procedures often require that consent be made part of the formal record in the criminal case (see Comment *c* hereto).

§ 130. Multiple Representation in a Nonlitigated Matter

Unless all affected clients consent to the representation under the limitations and conditions provided in § 122, a lawyer may not represent two or more clients in a matter not involving litigation if there is a substantial risk that the lawyer's representation of one or more of the clients would be materially and adversely affected by the lawyer's duties to one or more of the other clients.

Comment:

b. Rationale. . . . Whether a lawyer can function in a situation of conflict (see § 121) depends on whether the conflict is consentable (see § 122(2)), which in turn depends on whether it is "reasonably likely that the lawyer will be able to provide adequate representation" to all affected clients (see § 122(2)).

Conflicted but unconsented representation of multiple clients, for example of the buyer and seller of property, is sometimes defended with the argument that the lawyer was performing the role of mere "scrivener" or a similarly mechanical role. The characterization is usually inappropriate. A lawyer must accept responsibility to give customary advice and customary range of legal services, unless the clients have given their informed consent to a narrower range of the lawyer's responsibilities. On limitations of a lawyer's responsibilities, see § 19(1).

c. Assisting multiple clients with common objectives, but conflicting interests. When multiple clients have generally common interests, the role of the lawyer is to advise on relevant legal considerations, suggest alternative ways of meeting common objectives, and draft instruments necessary to accomplish the desired results. Multiple representations do not always present a conflict of interest requiring client consent (see § 121). For example, in representing spouses jointly in the purchase of property as co-owners, the lawyer would reasonably assume that such a representation does not involve a conflict of interest. A conflict could be involved, however, if the lawyer knew that one spouse's objectives in the acquisition were materially at variance with those of the other spouse.

Illustrations:

1. Husband and Wife consult Lawyer for estate-planning advice about a will for each of them. Lawyer has had professional dealings with the spouses, both separately and together, on several prior occasions. Lawyer knows them to be knowledgeable about their respective rights and interests, competent to make independent decisions if called for, and in accord on their common and individual objectives. Lawyer may represent both clients in the matter without obtaining consent (see § 121). While each spouse theoretically could make a distribution different from the other's, including a less generous bequest to each other, those possibilities do not create a conflict of interest, and none reasonably appears to exist in the circumstances.

2. The same facts as in Illustration 1, except that Lawyer has not previously met the spouses. Spouse A does most of the talking in the initial discussions with Lawyer. Spouse B, who owns significantly more property than Spouse A, appears to disagree with important positions of Spouse A but to be uncomfortable in expressing that disagreement and does not pursue them when Spouse A appears impatient and peremptory. Representation of both spouses would involve a conflict of interest. Lawyer may proceed to provide the requested legal assistance only with consent given under the limitations and conditions provided in § 122.

3. The same facts as in Illustration 1, except that Lawyer has not previously met the spouses. But in this instance, unlike in Illustration 2, in discussions with the spouses, Lawyer asks questions and suggests options that reveal both Spouse A and Spouse B to be knowledgeable about their respective rights and interests, competent to make independent decisions if called for, and in accord on their common and individual objectives. Lawyer has adequately verified the absence of a conflict of interest and thus may represent both clients in the matter without obtaining consent (see § 122).

Clients might not fully understand the potential for conflict in their interests as the result of ignorance about their legal rights, about possible alternatives to those that the clients have considered prior to retaining the lawyer, or about the uncommunicated plans or objectives of another client. In other situations, prospective clients might agree on objectives when they first approach the common lawyer, but it should be reasonably apparent that a conflict is likely to develop as the representation proceeds. A client's right to communicate in confidence with the attorney should not be constrained by concern that discord might result (cf. § 75). A lawyer is not required to suggest or assume discord where none exists, but when a conflict is reasonably apparent or foreseeable, the lawyer may proceed with multiple representation only after all affected clients have consented as provided in § 122.

Illustration:

4. A, B, and C are interested in forming a partnership in which A is to provide the capital, B the basic patent, and C the management skill. Only C will spend significant amounts of time operating the business. A, B, and C jointly request Lawyer to represent them in creating the partnership. The different contributions to be made to the partnership alone indicate that the prospective partners have conflicts of interest with respect to the structure and governance of the partnership (see § 121). With the informed consent of each (see § 122), Lawyer may represent all three clients in forming the business. Lawyer may assist the clients in valuing their respective contributions and suggest arrangements to protect their respective interests. With respect to conflicts and informed consent in representing the partnership as well as the partners once the business is established, see § 131,

Comment *e*.

d. Clients with known differences to be resolved. Multiple prospective clients might already be aware that their interests and objectives are antagonistic to some degree. The lawyer must ascertain at the outset what kind of assistance the clients require. Service by the lawyer or another person as an arbitrator or mediator (and not as a lawyer representing clients), for example, might well serve the clients' interests.

When circumstances reasonably indicate that the prospective clients might be able to reach a reasonable reconciliation of their differences by agreement and with the lawyer's assistance, the lawyer may represent them after obtaining informed consent (see § 122). In particular, the lawyer should explain the effect of joint representation on the lawyer's ability to protect each client's confidential information (see § 75). If the joint representation is undertaken, the lawyer should help the clients reach agreement on outstanding issues but should not advance the interests of one of the clients to the detriment of another (see § 122, Comment *h*).

Relations among multiple clients can develop into adversarial, even litigated, matters. Even if the possibility of litigation is substantial and even though the consent does not permit the lawyer to represent one client against the other if litigation does ensue (see § 122(2)(b) & § 128), with informed consent a lawyer could accept multiple representation in an effort to reconcile the differences of the clients short of litigation. The lawyer should inform the clients that the effort to overcome differences might ultimately fail and require the lawyer's complete withdrawal from the matter, unless the clients agreed that the lawyer thereafter could continue to represent less than all clients (see § 121, Comment *e(i)*). The lawyer is not required to encourage each client to obtain independent advice about being jointly represented, but the lawyer should honor any client request for such an opportunity.

Illustrations:

5. The same facts as in Illustration 4, except that the partnership of A, B, and C is formed and commences business. The business encounters difficulty in securing customers and controlling costs, and it shortly appears that the business will fail unless additional funding is obtained. No outside funds are available, and A announces unwillingness to provide additional capital unless B and C agree to increase A's interest in the business. B and C believe that A is requesting an unreasonably large additional share. A, B, and C seek Lawyer's assistance in resolving their disagreements. A conflict clearly exists between the clients (§ 121). Lawyer may agree to represent the three clients in seeking to arrive at a mutually satisfactory resolution, but only after Lawyer obtains the informed consent of each client and there is a clear definition of the services that Lawyer will provide. In representing the clients, Lawyer may not favor the position of any client over the others (see § 122, Comment *h*).

6. Husband and Wife have agreed to obtain an uncontested dissolution of their marriage. They have consulted Lawyer to help them reach an agreement on disposition of their property. A conflict of interest clearly exists between the prospective clients (§ 121). If reasonable prospects of an agreement exist, Lawyer may accept the joint representation with the effective consent of both (see § 122). However, in the later dissolution proceeding, Lawyer may represent only one of the parties (see § 128, Comment *c*), and Lawyer must withdraw from representing both clients if their efforts to reach an agreement fail (see § 121, Comment *e(i)*).

§ 131. Conflicts of Interest in Representing an Organization

Unless all affected clients consent to the representation under the limitations and conditions provided in § 122, a lawyer may not represent both an organization and a director, officer, employee, shareholder, owner, partner, member, or other individual or organization associated with the organization if there is a substantial risk that the lawyer's representation of either would be materially and adversely affected by the lawyer's duties to the other.

Comment:

c. A challenge to the policy of a client organization. Individuals having responsible roles in an organization can disagree about the definition of its interests. However, that does not by itself indicate that a lawyer representing the organization has a conflict of interest within the meaning of § 121. If conduct of the organization is challenged as unlawful, the lawyer for the organization generally may defend at least until it is ruled upon by the tribunal or changed pursuant to the procedures of the organization. Such a change can occur, for example, because the lawyer is directed to settle the controversy as instructed by the agent (see § 21). . . .

On the lawyer's duty if the responsible agent is acting in violation of a duty to the organization, see § 96(2). On the lawyer's duty if the organization engages in a crime or fraud, see § 67. On the lawyer's right to withdraw from representation because of disagreement with the organizational policy, see § 32. On the lawyer's right to take public positions inconsistent with those of the lawyer's client, see § 125, Comment *e*. . . .

d. Conflicting interests of affiliated organizations. Whether a lawyer represents affiliated organizations as clients is a question of fact determined under § 14 (see Comment *f* thereto). When a lawyer represents two or more organizations with some common ownership or membership, whether a conflict exists is determined primarily on the basis of formal organizational distinctions. If a single business corporation has established two divisions within the corporate structure, for example, conflicting interests or objectives of those divisions do not create a conflict of interest for a lawyer representing the corporation. Differences within the organization are to be resolved through the organization's decisionmaking procedures. . . .

Illustration:

2. A Corporation owns 60 percent of the stock of B Corporation. All of the stock of A Corporation is publicly owned, as is the remainder of the stock in B Corporation. Lawyer has been asked by the President of A Corporation to act as attorney for B in causing B to make a proposed transfer of certain real property to A at a price whose fairness cannot readily be determined by reference to the general real-estate market. Lawyer may do so only with effective informed consent of the management of B (as well as that of A). The ownership of A and B is not identical and their interests materially differ in the proposed transaction.

e. Representation of an organization and an individual constituent. Representation of a client organization often is facilitated by a close working relationship between the lawyer and the organization's officers, directors, and employees. However, unless the lawyer and such an individual person enter into a client-lawyer relationship (see § 14, Comment *f*), the individual is not a client of the lawyer (see § 121, Comment *d*). With respect to the attorney-client privilege attaching to communications with a person affiliated with an organization, see § 73, Comment *j*.

When a lawyer proposes to represent both an organization and a person associated with it, such as an officer, director, or employee, whether a conflict exists is determined by an analysis of the interests of the organization as an entity and those of the individuals involved. That is true whether the multiple representation involves civil (see § 128) or criminal (see § 129) litigation or a nonlitigated matter (see § 130). The interests of the organization are those defined by its agents authorized to act in the matter (see § 96, Comment *d*). For example, when an organization is accused of wrongdoing, an individual such as a director, officer, or other agent will sometimes be charged as well, and the lawyer representing the organization might be asked also to represent the individual. Such representation would constitute a conflict of interest when the individual's interests are materially adverse to the interests of the organization (see § 121). When there is no material adversity of interest, such as when the individual owns all of the equity in the organization or played a routine role in the underlying transaction, no conflict exists. In instances of adversity, concurrent representation would be permissible with the consent of all affected clients under the limitations and conditions stated in § 122.

Consent by an organization can be given in any manner consistent with the organization's lawful decisionmaking procedures. Applicable corporate law may provide that an officer who is personally interested in the matter may not provide consent in the matter. In deciding whether to consent to multiple representation by outside counsel, the organization might rely upon the advice of inside legal counsel. Issues concerning informed consent by public organizations to otherwise conflicted representations are discussed in § 122, Comment *c*.

Illustrations:

3. President, the chief executive officer of Corporation, has been charged with discussing prices with the president of a competing firm. If found guilty, both President and Corporation will be subject to civil and criminal penalties. Lawyer, who is representing Corporation, has concluded after a thorough investigation that no such pricing discussions occurred. Both Corporation and President plan to defend on that ground. President has asked Lawyer to represent President as well as Corporation in the proceedings. Although the factual and legal defenses of President and Corporation appear to be consistent at the outset, the likelihood of conflicting positions in such matters as plea bargaining requires Lawyer to obtain the informed consent of both clients before proceeding with the

representation (see § 129, Comment *c*).

4. The same facts as in Illustration 3, except that after further factual investigation both President and Corporation now concede that the pricing discussions took place. One of President's defenses will be that the former general counsel of Corporation told President that discussion of general pricing practices with a competitor was not illegal. Corporation denies that such was the advice given and asserts that President acted without authority. The conflict between President and Corporation is so great that the same lawyer could not provide adequate legal services to both in the matter. Thus, continued representation of both is not subject to consent (see § 122, Comment *g(iii)*, & § § 128 & 129).

If a person affiliated with an organization makes an unsolicited disclosure of information to a lawyer who represents only the organization, indicating the person's erroneous expectation that the lawyer will keep the information confidential from the organization, the lawyer must inform the person that the lawyer does not represent the person (see § 103, Comment *e*). The lawyer generally is not prohibited from sharing the communication with the organization. However, the requirements stated in § 15, Comment *c*, with respect to safeguarding confidential information of a prospective client may apply. That would occur when the person reasonably appeared to be consulting the lawyer as present or prospective client with respect to the person's individual interests, and the lawyer failed to warn the associated person that the lawyer represents only the organization and could act against the person's interests as a result (see § 103, Comment *e*). With respect to a lawyer's duties when a person associated with the organization expressed an intent to act wrongfully and thereby threatens harm to the organization client, see § 96(2) and Comment *f* thereto.

Issues considered in this Comment may be particularly acute in the case of close corporations, small partnerships, and similar organizations in which, for example, one person with substantial ownership interests also manages. Such a manager may have a corresponding tendency to treat corporate and similar entity distinctions as mere formalities. In such instances, when ownership is so concentrated that no nonmanaging owner exists and in the absence of material impact on the interests of other nonclients (such as creditors in the case of an insolvent corporation), a lawyer acts reasonably in accepting in good faith a controlling manager's position that the interests of all controlling persons and the entity should be treated as if they were the same. Similar considerations apply when a close corporation or similar organization is owned and managed by a small number of owner-managers whose interests are not materially in conflict.

f. A challenge by a client organization to the action of an associated person. Both Subsections of this Section can be applicable when the organization challenges the action of one or more of its associated persons, such as an officer, director, or employee. The policy of the organization in the matter will be that established according to the organization's decisionmaking procedures (see § 96(1)(a)). Because the interests of the organization and the associated person are necessarily adverse, the conflict of interest ordinarily will not be subject to consent (see § 122(2)(c)). On the lawyer's dealing with threatened wrongdoing by a person associated with an organizational client, see § 96(2); see also § § 66-67.

Illustration:

5. Treasurer, the chief financial officer of Club, a private investment trust, has been accused of converting $25,000 of Club's assets for personal use. Responsible other officers of Club, acting on Club's behalf, retain Lawyer to recover the money from Treasurer. They direct Lawyer not to reveal the loss or file suit until other collection efforts have been exhausted. Lawyer may properly represent Club and in doing so must proceed in the manner directed. Further, although the matter is not yet in litigation, the interests of Club and Treasurer are so adverse that even informed consent of both would not permit their common representation by Lawyer in the matter (see § 122, Comment *g*).

g. Derivative action. When an organization such as a business corporation is sued in a derivative action, the organization is ordinarily aligned as an involuntary plaintiff. Persons associated with the organization who are accused of breaching a duty to the organization, typically officers and directors of the organization, are ordinarily named as defendants. The theory of a derivative action is that relief is sought from the individuals for the benefit of the organization. Even with informed consent of all affected clients, the lawyer for the organization ordinarily may not represent an individual defendant as well (see § 128, Comment *c*). If, however, the disinterested directors conclude that no basis exists for the claim that the defending officers and directors have acted against the interests of the organization, the lawyer may, with the effective consent of all clients, represent both the organization and the officers and directors in defending the suit (see § 122).

In a derivative action, if the advice of the lawyer acting for the organization was an important factor in the action of the officers and directors that gave rise to the suit, it is appropriate for the lawyer to represent, if anyone, the officers and directors and for the organization to obtain new counsel. Because the lawyer would be representing clients with interests adverse to the corporation, consent of the corporation would be required. That would be true even if the lawyer withdrew from representing the corporation in order to represent the individuals (see § 132, Comment *c*). Whom the lawyer should represent in the matter, if anyone, should be determined by responsible agents of the organization. Ordinarily, those will be persons who are not named and are not likely to be named parties in the case.

If an action challenging an act of an organization is not a derivative action, whether a conflict exists is determined under § 128, Comment *d(ii)*.

h. Proxy fights and takeover attempts. Outsiders or insiders might challenge incumbent management for control of organizations. Incumbent management, shareholders, creditors, and employees will all be affected by such a contest in various ways. When the challenge to incumbent management comes from outside the management group, the role of the lawyer representing the organization must be to follow policies adopted by the organization, in accordance with the organization's decisionmaking procedures. Persons authorized to act on behalf of the organization determine the organization's interest in responding to the challenge (see § 96(1)).

When all or part of incumbent management seeks to obtain control of the organization, typically by restructuring ownership of and authority in the organization, a conflict of interest is presented between the individual interests of those members of management and the holders of ownership and authority. Because of their personal interests, those members of management ordinarily would not be appropriate agents to direct the work of a lawyer for the organization with respect to the takeover attempt. Whether a lawyer's personal interests, for example, those based on longtime association with incumbent management, preclude the lawyer from representing the organization or the managers seeking control depends on whether the lawyer's personal interests create a substantial risk of material and adverse effect on the representation (see § 125).

Similar considerations apply when a contest over ownership or control arises within a closely held corporation or similar small organization such as a two-person partnership. If the lawyer also represents a principal in such an enterprise personally, the possibility of conflict is increased if the lawyer undertakes to represent that person in such a contest. When it reasonably appears that the lawyer can serve effectively in the role of conciliator between contending factions, the lawyer may undertake to do so with effective consent of all affected clients (see § 130, Comment *d*). In other cases, however, the lawyer will be required to withdraw from representing all of the individual interests (see § 132).

TOPIC 4. CONFLICTS OF INTEREST WITH A FORMER CLIENT

§ 132. A Representation Adverse to the Interests of a Former Client

Unless both the affected present and former clients consent to the representation under the limitations and conditions provided in § 122, a lawyer who has represented a client in a matter may not thereafter represent another client in the same or a substantially related matter in which the interests of the former client are materially adverse. The current matter is substantially related to the earlier matter if:

(1) the current matter involves the work the lawyer performed for the former client; or

(2) there is a substantial risk that representation of the present client will involve the use of information acquired in the course of representing the former client, unless that information has become generally known.

Comment:

b. Rationale. The rule described in this Section accommodates four policies. First, absent the rule, a lawyer's incentive to serve a present client might cause the lawyer to compromise the lawyer's continuing duties to the former client (see § 33). Specifically, the lawyer might use confidential information of the former client contrary to that client's interest and in violation of § 60. The second policy consideration is the converse of the first. The lawyer's obligations to the former client might constrain the lawyer in representing the present client effectively, for example, by limiting the questions the lawyer could ask the former client in testimony. Third, at the time the lawyer represented the former client, the lawyer should have no incentive to lay the basis for subsequent representation against that client, such as by drafting provisions in a contract that could later be construed against the former client. Fourth, and pointing the other way, because much law practice is transactional, clients often retain lawyers for service only on specific cases or issues. A rule that would transform each engagement into a lifetime commitment would make lawyers reluctant to take new, relatively modest matters.

c. The relationship between current-client and former-client conflicts rules. The difference between a former-client conflict under this Section and a present-client conflict considered in Topic 3 (§ § 128-130) is that this Section applies only to representation in the same or a substantially related matter. The present-client conflict rules prohibit adverse representation regardless of the lack of any other relationship between them. If the two representations overlap in time, the rules of § § 128-130 apply.

Withdrawal is effective to render a representation "former" for the purposes of this Section if it occurs at a point that the client and lawyer had contemplated as the end of the representation (see § 32, Comment *c*). The representation will also be at an end for purposes of this Section if the existing client discharges the lawyer (other than for cause arising from the improper representation) or if other grounds for mandatory or permissive withdrawal by the lawyer exist (see § 32), and the lawyer is not motivated primarily by a desire to represent the new client.

If a lawyer is approached by a prospective client seeking representation in a matter adverse to an existing client, the present-client conflict may not be transformed into a former-client conflict by the lawyer's withdrawal from the representation of the existing client. A premature withdrawal violates the lawyer's obligation of loyalty to the existing client and can constitute a breach of the client-lawyer contract of employment (see § 32, Comment *c*). On withdrawal when a dispute arises between two or more of the lawyer's clients, see § 121, Comment *e(i)*. On advance consent, see id. and § 122, especially Comment *d*.

d. The same or a substantially related matter. As indicated in the Section, three types of former-client conflicts are prohibited.

d(i). Switching sides in the same matter. Representing one side and then switching to represent the other in the same matter clearly implicates loyalty to the first client and protection of that client's confidences. Similar considerations apply in nonlitigated matters. For example, a lawyer negotiating a complex agreement on behalf of Seller could not withdraw and represent Buyer against the interests of Seller in the same transaction. Switching sides in a litigated matter can also risk confusing the trier of fact. Just as a lawyer may not represent both sides concurrently in the same case (see § § 128-130), the lawyer also may not represent them consecutively.

d(ii). Attacking a lawyer's own former work. Beyond switching sides in the same matter, the concept of substantial relationship applies to later developments out of the original matter. A matter is substantially related if it involves the work the lawyer performed for the former client. For example, a lawyer may not on behalf of a later client attack the validity of a document that the lawyer drafted if doing so would materially and adversely affect the former client. Similarly, a lawyer may not represent a debtor in bankruptcy in seeking to set aside a security interest of a creditor that is embodied in a document that the lawyer previously drafted for the creditor.

Illustration:

1. Lawyer has represented Husband in a successful effort to have Wife removed as beneficiary of his life insurance policy. After Husband's death, Wife seeks to retain Lawyer to negotiate with the insurance company to set aside the change of beneficiary and obtain the proceeds of the policy for Wife. The subsequent representation would require that Lawyer attack the work Lawyer performed for Husband. Accordingly, Lawyer may not accept Wife as a client in the matter.

d(iii). The substantial-relationship test and the protection of confidential information of a former client. The substantial-relationship standard is employed most frequently to protect the confidential information of the former client obtained in the course of the representation. A subsequent matter is substantially related to an earlier matter within the meaning of Subsection (2) if there is a substantial risk that the subsequent representation will involve the use of confidential information of the former client obtained in the course of the representation in violation of § 60. "Confidential information" is defined in § 59. Substantial risk exists where it is reasonable to conclude that it would materially advance the client's position in the subsequent matter to use confidential information obtained in the prior representation.

A concern to protect a former client's confidential information would be self-defeating if, in order to obtain its protection, the former client were required to reveal in a public proceeding the particular communication or other confidential information that could be used in the subsequent representation. The interests of subsequent clients also militate against extensive inquiry into the precise nature of the lawyer's representation of the subsequent client and the nature of exchanges between them.

The substantial-relationship test avoids requiring disclosure of confidential information by focusing upon the general features of the matters involved and inferences as to the likelihood that confidences were imparted by the former client that could be used to adverse effect in the subsequent representation. The inquiry into the issues involved in the prior representation should be as specific as possible without thereby revealing the confidential client information itself or confidential information concerning the second client. When the prior matter involved litigation, it will be conclusively presumed that the lawyer obtained confidential information about the issues involved in the litigation. When the prior matter did not involve litigation, its scope is assessed by reference to the work that the lawyer undertook and the array of information that a lawyer ordinarily would have obtained to carry out that work. The information obtained by the lawyer might also be proved by inferences from redacted documents, for example. On the use of in camera procedures to disclose confidential material to the tribunal but not to an opposing party, see § 86, Comment f.

Illustrations:

2. Lawyer represented Client A for a period of five years lobbying on environmental issues relating to uranium production. In the course of the representation in one matter, Lawyer learned the basis for Client A's uranium-production decisions. Lawyer now has been asked to represent Client B, a purchaser of uranium, in an antitrust action against A and others alleging a conspiracy to impose limits on production. It is likely that Client B's claims against A would include addressing the same production decisions about which Lawyer earlier learned. Use of confidential information concerning A's production decisions learned in the earlier representation would materially advance the position of Client B in the antitrust matter. The matters are substantially related, and Lawyer may not represent Client B without effective consent of both A and B (see § 122).

3. Lawyer was general inside legal counsel to Company A for many years, dealing with all aspects of corporate affairs and management. Lawyer was dismissed from that position when Company A hired a new president. Company B has asked Lawyer to represent it in an antitrust suit against Company A based on facts arising after Lawyer left Company A's employ but involving broad charges of anti-competitive practices of Company A that, if true, were occurring at the time that Lawyer represented Company A. Lawyer may not represent Company B in the antitrust action. Because of the breadth of confidential client information of Company A to which Lawyer is likely to have had access during the earlier representation and the breadth of issues open in the antitrust claim of Company B, a substantial risk exists that use of that information would materially advance Company B's position in the later representation.

4. Lawyer represented Client A, a home builder, at the closings of the sales of several homes Client A had built in Tract X. Lawyers performing such work normally might encounter issues relating to marketability of title. A is now represented by other counsel. Client B has asked Lawyer to represent him in a suit against A in connection with B's sale to A of Tract Y, a parcel of land owned by Client B on which A plans to build homes. The present suit involves the marketability of the title to Tract Y. Although both representations involve marketability of title, it is unlikely that Lawyer's knowledge of marketability of Tract X would be relevant to the litigation involving the marketability of title to Tract Y. Accordingly, the matters are not substantially related. Lawyer may represent Client B against A without informed consent of A.

As used in this Section, the term "matter" includes not only representation in a litigated case, but also any representation involving a contract, claim, charge, or other subject of legal advice (compare § 133, Comment e). The term "matter" ordinarily does not include a legal position taken on behalf of a former client unless the underlying facts are also related. For example, a lawyer who successfully argued that a statute is constitutional on behalf of a former client may later argue that the statute is unconstitutional on behalf of a present client in a case not involving the former client, even though the lawyer's success on behalf of the present client might adversely affect the former client (compare § 128, Comment f).

Information that is confidential for some purposes under § 59 (so that, for example, a lawyer would not be free to discuss it publicly (see § 60)) might nonetheless be so general, readily observable, or of little value in the subsequent representation that it should not by itself result in a substantial relationship. Thus, a lawyer may master a particular substantive area of the law while representing a client, but that does not preclude the lawyer from later representing another client adversely to the first in a matter involving the same legal issues, if the matters factually are not substantially related. A lawyer might also have learned a former client's preferred approach to bargaining in settlement discussions or negotiating business points in a transaction, willingness or unwillingness to be deposed by an adversary, and financial ability to withstand extended litigation or contract negotiations. Only when such information will be directly in issue or of unusual value in the subsequent matter will it be independently relevant in assessing a substantial relationship.

e. A subsequent client with interests "materially adverse" to the interests of a former client. A later representation is prohibited if the second client's interests are materially adverse to those of the former client (see § 121, Comments *c(i)* (adverseness) & *c(ii)* (materiality)). The scope of a client's interests is normally determined by the scope of work that the lawyer undertook in the former representation. Thus, a lawyer who undertakes to represent a corporation with respect to the defense of a personal-injury claim involving only issues of causation and damages does not represent the corporation with respect to other interests. The lawyer may limit the scope of representation specifically for the purpose of avoiding a future conflict (see § 16). Similarly, the lawyer may limit the scope of representation of a later client so as to avoid representation substantially related to that undertaken for a previous client.

Illustration:

5. Lawyer formerly represented Client A in obtaining FDA approval to market prescription drug X for treating diseases of the eye. Client B has now asked Lawyer for legal assistance to obtain FDA approval for sale of prescription drug Y for treating diseases of the skin. Client B is also interested in possibly later application for FDA approval to market a different form of drug Y to treat diseases of the eye, thus significantly reducing the profitability of Client A's drug X. Confidential information that Lawyer gained in representing Client A in the earlier matter would be substantially related to work that Lawyer would do with respect to any future application by Client B for use of drug Y for eye diseases (although the information would not relate to the use of drug Y for treating diseases of the skin). Client B and Lawyer agree that Lawyer's work will relate only to FDA approval for use of drug Y to treat diseases of the skin. Thus limited, Lawyer's work for Client B does not involve representation adverse to former Client A on a substantially related matter.

f. A lawyer's subsequent use of confidential information. Even if a subsequent representation does not involve the same or a substantially related matter, a lawyer may not disclose or use confidential information of a former client in violation of § 60.

Illustration:

6. Lawyer, now a prosecutor, had formerly represented Client in defending against a felony charge. During the course of a confidential interview, Client related to Lawyer a willingness to commit perjury. Lawyer is now prosecuting another person, Defendant, for a matter not substantially related to the former prosecution. In the jurisdiction, a defendant is not required to serve notice of defense witnesses that will be called. During the defense case, Defendant's lawyer calls Client as an alibi witness. Lawyer could not reasonably have known previously that Client would be called. Because of the lack of substantial relationship between the matters, Lawyer was not prohibited from undertaking the prosecution. Because Lawyer's knowledge of Client's statement about willingness to lie is confidential client information under § 59, Lawyer may not use that information in cross-examining Client, but otherwise Lawyer may cross-examine Client vigorously.

g. A lawyer's duties of confidentiality other than to a former client. The principles in this Section presuppose that the lawyer in question has previously represented the person adversely affected by the present representation. Whether a client-lawyer relationship exists is considered in § 14 and § 121, Comment *d*. Two situations present analogous problems—communications with a prospective client and confidential information about a nonclient learned in representing a former client.

g(i). Duties to a prospective client. A lawyer's obligation of confidentiality with respect to information revealed during an initial consultation prior to the decision about formation of a lawyer-client relationship is considered in § 15, Comment *c*.

g(ii). Duties to a person about whom a lawyer learned confidential information while representing a former client. A lawyer might have obligations to persons who were not the lawyer's clients but about whom information was revealed to the lawyer under circumstances obligating the lawyer not to use or disclose the information. Those obligations arise under other law, particularly under the law of agency. For example, a lawyer might incur obligations of confidentiality as the subagent of a principal whom the lawyer's client serves as an agent (see Restatement Second, Agency § § 5, 241, & 396). An important difference between general agency law and the law governing lawyers is that general agency law does not normally impute a restriction to other persons. Thus, when a lawyer's relationship to a nonclient is not that of lawyer-client but that, for example, of subagent-principal, imputation might not be required under the law governing subagents.

Illustrations:

7. Lawyer has represented Hospital in several medical-malpractice cases. In the course of preparing to defend one such case, Lawyer reviewed the confidential medical file of Patient who was not a party in the action. From the file, Lawyer learned that Patient had been convicted of a narcotics offense in another jurisdiction. Patient is now a material witness for the defense in an unrelated case that Lawyer has filed on behalf of Plaintiff. Adequate representation of Plaintiff would require Lawyer to cross-examine Patient about the narcotics conviction in an effort to undermine Patient's credibility. Lawyer may not reveal information about Patient that Hospital has an obligation to keep confidential. That limitation in turn may preclude effective representation of Plaintiff in the pending case. However if, without violating the obligation to Patient, Lawyer can adequately reveal to Plaintiff the nature of the conflict of interest and the likely effect of restricted cross-examination, Lawyer may represent Plaintiff with Plaintiff's informed consent (see § 122, Comment c).

8. Lawyer represents Underwriter in preparing to sell an issue of Company's bonds; Lawyer does not represent Company. Several questions concerning facts have arisen in drafting disclosure documents pertaining to the issue. Under applicable law, Underwriter must be satisfied that the facts are not material. Lawyer obtains confidential information from Company in the course of preparing Lawyer's opinion for Underwriter. Among the information learned is that Company might be liable to A for breach of contract. Unless the information has become generally known (see § 59), Lawyer may not represent A in a breach of contract action against Company because the information was learned from Company in confidence.

In the circumstances described in Illustration 8, standards of agency law or other law might permit the underwriter to provide services to another customer in a subsequent transaction so long as the underwriter takes appropriate steps to screen its employees. A lawyer affiliated with the disqualified lawyer could represent the underwriter in the second transaction after appropriate screening of the disqualified lawyer (compare § 124).

A lawyer's duties as fiduciary to nonclient third persons might create a conflict of interest with clients of the lawyer (see § 135).

A lawyer who learns confidential information from a person represented by another lawyer pursuant to a common-interest sharing arrangement (see § 76) is precluded from a later representation adverse to the former sharing person when information actually shared by that person with the lawyer or the lawyer's client is material and relevant to the later matter (see Illustration 8, above). Such a threatened use of shared information is inconsistent with the undertaking of confidentiality that is part of such an arrangement.

h. A lawyer with only a minor role in a prior representation. The specific tasks in which a lawyer was engaged might make the access to confidential client information insignificant. The lawyer bears the burden of persuasion as to that issue and as to the absence of opportunity to acquire confidential information. When such a burden has been met, the lawyer is not precluded from proceeding adversely to the former client (see § 124, Comment d, Illustration 3).

i. Withdrawal from representing an "accommodation" client. With the informed consent of each client as provided in § 122, a lawyer might undertake representation of another client as an accommodation to the lawyer's regular client, typically for a limited purpose in order to avoid duplication of services and consequent higher fees. If adverse interests later develop between the clients, even if the adversity relates to the matter involved in the common representation, circumstances might warrant the inference that the "accommodation" client understood and impliedly consented to the lawyer's continuing to represent the regular client in the matter. Circumstances most likely to evidence such an understanding are that the lawyer has represented the regular client for a long period of time before undertaking representation of the other client, that the representation was to be of limited scope and duration, and that the lawyer was not expected to keep confidential from the regular client any information provided to the lawyer by the other client. On obtaining express consent in advance to later representation of the regular client in such circumstances, see § 122, Comment d. The lawyer bears the burden of showing that circumstances exist to warrant an inference of understanding and implied consent. On other situations of withdrawal, see § 121, Comment e.

j. Cure of conflicts created by transactions of a client. A lawyer may withdraw in order to continue an adverse representation against a theretofore existing client when the matter giving rise to the conflict and requiring withdrawal comes about through initiative of the clients. An example is a client's acquisition of an interest in an enterprise against which the lawyer is proceeding on behalf of another client. However, if the client's acquisition of the other enterprise was reasonably foreseeable by the lawyer when the lawyer undertook representation of the client, withdrawal will not cure the conflict. In any event, continuing the representation must be otherwise consistent with the former-client conflict rules.

§ 133. A Former Government Lawyer or Officer

(1) A lawyer may not act on behalf of a client with respect to a matter in which the lawyer participated personally and substantially while acting as a government lawyer or officer unless both the government and the client consent to the representation under the limitations and conditions provided in § 122.

(2) A lawyer who acquires confidential information while acting as a government lawyer or officer may not:

(a) if the information concerns a person, represent a client whose interests are materially adverse to that person in a matter in which the information could be used to the material disadvantage of that person; or

(b) if the information concerns the governmental client or employer, represent another public or private client in circumstances described in § 132(2).

Comment:

b. Rationale. Prohibitions on the activities of former government lawyers are based on concerns similar to those protecting former private clients. Because those concerns apply somewhat differently to government clients, however, the rule of this Section is both broader and narrower than that of § 132.

First, the protection accorded government confidential information is parallel to that for confidential information of private clients. As discussed in § 74, however, statutes requiring openness in government operations might limit the government information that is given protection. Second, since government agencies have special powers to allocate public benefits and burdens, it is reasonable to prohibit a lawyer while in government from taking action designed to improve the lawyer's opportunities upon leaving government service.

On the other hand, government agencies must be able to recruit able lawyers. If the experience gained could not be used after lawyers left government service, recruiting lawyers would be more difficult. There is also a public interest in having lawyers in private practice who have served in government and understand both the substance and rationale of government policy. The experience of such lawyers might sometimes enable clients to achieve higher levels of compliance with law. Thus, this Section protects three government functions, those of client, recruiter of able employees, and law enforcer.

c. Personal and substantial involvement. This Section forbids former government lawyers or officers from taking on matters on which they worked personally and substantially while in government. Former government lawyers are not forbidden to work on matters solely because the matters were pending in the agency during the period of their employment.

The standard of "substantiality" is both formal and functional. A lawyer who signed a complaint on behalf of the government is substantially involved in the matter even if the lawyer knew few of the underlying facts. An action undertaken by a lawyer in the name of a superior is also within the rule.

e. Definition of a "matter." The term "matter," as applied to former government employees, is often defined as a judicial or other proceeding, application, request for a ruling or other determination, contract, claim, controversy, investigation, charge, accusation, arrest, or other particular matter involving a specific party or parties. Drafting of a statute or regulation of general applicability is not included under that definition, nor is work on a case of the same type (but not the same parties) as the one in which the lawyer seeks to be involved. The definition is narrower than that governing former-client conflicts of interest under § 132 (see id., Comment *d(iii)*).

Illustrations:

4. While serving in the general counsel's office of the state revenue department, Lawyer was involved in the drafting of regulations to implement new amendments to the state tax law. The regulations affected a large number of taxpayers. When Lawyer returns to private practice, Lawyer may advise taxpayers seeking to determine how the regulations apply, suing to have the regulations construed or challenging the constitutionality of the statute or regulations.

5. In the capacity of city corporation counsel, Lawyer participated in drafting and negotiating the terms of an ordinance to rezone a specific tract of land of a major developer. Now that Lawyer has returned to private practice, the developer has sought to retain Lawyer in a lawsuit to construe the ordinance to permit more housing density than the city asserts the ordinance permits. Lawyer may not accept the case. The work by Lawyer on behalf of city was not of general application and was analogous to representation of the city in a case involving a particular party and parcel of land.

TOPIC 5. CONFLICTS OF INTEREST DUE TO A LAWYER'S OBLIGATION TO A THIRD PERSON

§ 134. Compensation or Direction of a Lawyer by a Third Person

(1) A lawyer may not represent a client if someone other than the client will wholly or partly compensate the lawyer for the representation, unless the client consents under the limitations and conditions provided in § 122 and knows of the circumstances and conditions of the payment.

(2) A lawyer's professional conduct on behalf of a client may be directed by someone other than the client if:

(a) the direction does not interfere with the lawyer's independence of professional judgment;

(b) the direction is reasonable in scope and character, such as by reflecting obligations borne by the person directing the lawyer; and

(c) the client consents to the direction under the limitations and conditions provided in § 122.

Comment:

c. Third-person fee payment. This Section accommodates two values implicated by third-person payment of legal fees. First, it requires that a lawyer's loyalty to the client not be compromised by the third-person source of payment. The lawyer's duty of loyalty is to the client alone, although it may also extend to any co-client when that relationship is either consistent with the duty owing to each co-client or is consented to in accordance with § 122. Second, however, the Section acknowledges that it is often in the client's interest to have legal representation paid for by another. Most liability-insurance contracts, for example, provide that the insurer will provide legal representation for an insured who is charged with responsibility for harm to another (see also Comment *f* hereto). Lawyers paid by civil-rights organizations have helped citizens pursue their individual rights and establish legal principles of general importance. Similarly, lawyers in private practice or in a legal-services organization may be appointed or otherwise come to represent indigent persons pursuant to arrangements under which their fees will be paid by a governmental body (see Comment *g*).

d. Third-person direction of a representation. The principle that a lawyer must exercise independent professional judgment on behalf of the client (Subsection (2)(a)) is reflected in the requirement of the lawyer codes that no third person control or direct a lawyer's professional judgment on behalf of a client. Consistent with that requirement, a third person may, with the client's consent and otherwise in the circumstances and to the extent stated in Subsection (2), direct the lawyer's representation of the client. When the conditions of the Subsection are satisfied, the client has, in effect, transferred to the designated third person the client's prerogatives of directing the lawyer's activities (see § 21(2)). The third person's directions must allow for effective representation of the client, and the client must give informed consent to the exercise of the power of direction by the third person. The direction must be reasonable in scope and character, such as by reflecting obligations borne by the person directing the lawyer. Such directions are reasonable in scope and character if, for example, the third party will pay any judgment rendered against the client and makes a decision that defense costs beyond those designated by the third party would not significantly change the likely outcome. Informed client consent may be effective with respect to many forms of direction, ranging from informed consent to particular instances of direction, such as in a representation in which the client otherwise directs the lawyer, to informed consent to general direction of the lawyer by another, such as an insurer or indemnitor on whom the client has contractually conferred the power of direction (see Comment *f*).

Illustration:

> 1. Resettle, a nonprofit organization, works to secure better living conditions for refugees. Resettle's board of directors believes that a case should be filed to test whether a federal policy of detaining certain refugees is legally justified. Client is a refugee who has recently been detained under the federal policy, and Resettle has offered to pay Lawyer to seek Client's release from detention. With the informed consent of Client, Lawyer may accept payment by Resettle and may agree to make contentions that Resettle wishes to have tested by the litigation.

Just as there are limits to client consent in § 122, there are limits to the restrictions on scope of the representation permitted under this Section. See § 122, Comment *g* (nonconsentable conflicts).

Illustrations:

> 2. Client is charged with the crime of illegally selling securities. Client's employer, Brokerage, has offered to pay Lawyer to defend Client on the condition that Client agree not to implicate Brokerage or any of its other employees in the crimes charged against Client. Lawyer may not accept the representation on those terms. Whether to accept a plea bargain, for example, and whether to implicate others in the wrongdoing are matters about which the client, not the person paying for the defense, must have the authority to make decisions (see § 22).

> 3. Same facts as stated in Illustration 2, except that there is no substantial factual or legal basis for implicating Brokerage or any of its other employees and Client consents to accept Lawyer's representation on the condition stated by Brokerage under the limitations and conditions provided in § 122, including knowledge that Brokerage has stated the condition. Under such circumstances, Client's consent authorizes Lawyer to accept payment from Brokerage and adhere to the described conditions.

e. Preserving confidential client information. Although a legal fee may be paid or direction given by a third person, a lawyer must protect the confidential information of the client. Informed client consent to the third-person payment or direction does not by itself constitute informed consent to the lawyer's revealing such information to that person. Consent to reveal confidential client information must meet the separate requirements of § 62.

Illustration:

> 4. Employer has agreed to pay for representation of Employee in defending a claim involving facts arguably arising out of pursuit of Employer's business. Employer asks Lawyer what Employee intends to testify about the circumstances of Employee's actions. Without consent of Employee as provided in § 62, Lawyer may not give Employer that information.

On a lawyer's discretion to disclose confidential information of a client to a co-client in the representation, see § 60, Comment *l*.

f. Representing an insured. A lawyer might be designated by an insurer to represent the insured under a liability-insurance policy in which the insurer undertakes to indemnify the insured and to provide a defense. The law governing the relationship between the insured and the insurer is, as stated in Comment *a*, beyond the scope of the Restatement. Certain practices of designated insurance-defense counsel have become customary and, in any event, involve primarily standardized protection afforded by a regulated entity in recurring situations. Thus a particular practice permissible for counsel representing an insured may not be permissible under this Section for a lawyer in noninsurance arrangements with significantly different characteristics.

It is clear in an insurance situation that a lawyer designated to defend the insured has a client-lawyer relationship with the insured. The insurer is not, simply by the fact that it designates the lawyer, a client of the lawyer. Whether a client-lawyer relationship also exists between the lawyer and the insurer is determined under § 14. Whether or not such a relationship exists, communications between the lawyer and representatives of the insurer concerning such matters as progress reports, case evaluations, and settlement should be regarded as privileged and otherwise immune from discovery by the claimant or another party to the proceeding. Similarly, communications between counsel retained by an insurer to coordinate the efforts of multiple counsel for insureds in multiple suits and such coordinating counsel are subject to the privilege. Because and to the extent that the insurer is directly concerned in the matter financially, the insurer should be accorded standing to assert a claim for appropriate relief from the lawyer for financial loss proximately caused by professional negligence or other wrongful act of the lawyer. Compare § 51, Comment *g*.

The lawyer's acceptance of direction from the insurer is considered in Subsection (2) and Comment *d* hereto. With respect to client consent (see Comment *b* hereto) in insurance representations, when there appears to be no substantial risk that a claim against a client-insured will not be fully covered by an insurance policy pursuant to which the lawyer is appointed and is to be paid, consent in the form of the acquiescence of the client-insured to an informative letter to the client-insured at the outset of the representation should be all that is required. The lawyer should either withdraw or consult with the client-insured (see § 122) when a substantial risk that the client-insured will not be fully covered becomes apparent (see § 121, Comment *c(iii)*).

Illustration:

5. Insurer, a liability-insurance company, has issued a policy to Policyholder under which Insurer is to provide a defense and otherwise insure Policyholder against claims covered under the insurance policy. A suit filed against Policyholder alleges that Policyholder is liable for a covered act and for an amount within the policy's monetary limits. Pursuant to the policy's terms, Insurer designates Lawyer to defend Policyholder. Lawyer believes that doubling the number of depositions taken, at a cost of $5,000, would somewhat increase Policyholder's chances of prevailing and Lawyer so informs Insurer and Policyholder. If the insurance contract confers authority on Insurer to make such decisions about expense of defense, and Lawyer reasonably believes that the additional depositions can be forgone without violating the duty of competent representation owed by Lawyer to Policyholder (see § 52), Lawyer may comply with Insurer's direction that taking depositions would not be worth the cost.

Material divergence of interest might exist between a liability insurer and an insured, for example, when a claim substantially in excess of policy limits is asserted against an insured. If the lawyer knows or should be aware of such an excess claim, the lawyer may not follow directions of the insurer if doing so would put the insured at significantly increased risk of liability in excess of the policy coverage. Such occasions for conflict may exist at the outset of the representation or may be created by events that occur thereafter. The lawyer must address a conflict whenever presented. To the extent that such a conflict is subject to client consent (see § 122(2)(c)), the lawyer may proceed after obtaining client consent under the limitations and conditions stated in § 122.

When there is a question whether a claim against the insured is within the coverage of the policy, a lawyer designated to defend the insured may not reveal adverse confidential client information of the insured to the insurer concerning that question (see § 60) without explicit informed consent of the insured (see § 62). That follows whether or not the lawyer also represents the insurer as co-client and whether or not the insurer has asserted a "reservation of rights" with respect to its defense of the insured (compare § 60, Comment *l* (confidentiality in representation of co-clients in general)).

With respect to events or information that create a conflict of interest between insured and insurer, the lawyer must proceed in the best interests of the insured, consistent with the lawyer's duty not to assist client fraud (see § 94) and, if applicable, consistent with the lawyer's duties to the insurer as co-client (see § 60, Comment *l*). If the designated lawyer finds it impossible so to proceed, the lawyer must withdraw from representation of both clients as provided in § 32 (see also § 60, Comment *l*). The designated lawyer may be precluded by duties to the insurer from providing advice and other legal services to the insured concerning such matters as coverage under the policy, claims against other persons insured by the same insurer, and the advisability of asserting other claims against the insurer. In such instances, the lawyer must inform the insured in an adequate and timely manner of the limitation on the scope of the lawyer's services and the importance of obtaining assistance of other counsel with respect to such matters. Liability of the insurer with respect to such matters is regulated under statutory and common-law rules such as those governing liability for bad-faith refusal to defend or settle. Those rules are beyond the scope of this Restatement (see Comment *a* hereto).

g. Legal service and similarly funded representations. Lawyers who provide representation to indigent persons may do so pursuant to various arrangements under which their fees or other compensation will be paid by a governmental agency or similar funding organization. For example, a lawyer may represent clients as a staff attorney of a legal aid, military legal assistance, or similar organization, with compensation in the form of a salary paid by the organization. Lawyers in private practice may be appointed by a court, defender or legal-service organization, or bar association to represent a person accused of crime or a person involved in a civil matter (see § 14, Comment *g*), with the lawyer's fee to be paid by the government or organization, often pursuant to a schedule of fees. Certain for-profit legal-service arrangements have also been approved, under which individual private practitioners provide assistance to participants who pay a flat charge to the legal-service organization for limited legal services. Regardless of the method of appointment, the form of compensation, or the nature of the paying organization (for example, whether governmental or private or whether nonprofit or for-profit), the lawyer's representation of and relationship with the individual client must proceed as provided for in this Section.

§ 135. A Lawyer with a Fiduciary or Other Legal Obligation to a Nonclient

Unless the affected client consents to the representation under the limitations and conditions provided in § 122, a lawyer may not represent a client in any matter with respect to which the lawyer has a fiduciary or other legal obligation to another if there is a substantial risk that the lawyer's representation of the client would be materially and adversely affected by the lawyer's obligation.

Conversion Table: Final Restatement Sections and Drafts*

Draft = tentative and proposed final drafts (1988-1998)
FINAL = final restatement sections (2000)

Draft #	Final #	Draft #	Final #	Draft #	Final #	Draft #	Final #
1-8	**1-8**	53	**41**	124	**74**	167	**107**
10	**9**	54	**42**	125	**75**	168	**108**
11	**10**	55	**43**	126	**76**	169	**109**
12	**11**	56	**44**	127	**77**	170	**110**
13	**12**	57	**45**	128	**78**	171	**111**
14	**13**	58	**46**	129	**79**	172	**112**
26	**14**	59	**47**	130	**80**	173	**113**
27	**15**	70 (71)	**48**	131	**81**	174	**114**
28	**16**	71	**49**	132	**82**	175	**115**
29	**17**	72	**50**	133	**83**	176	**116**
29A	**18**	73	**51**	134A	**84**	177	**117**
30	**19**	74	**52**	134B	**85**	178	**118**
31	**20**	75	**53**	135	**86**	179	**119**
32	**21**	76	**54**	136	**87**	180	**120**
33	**22**	76A	**55**	137	**88**	201	**121**
34	**23**	77	**56**	138	**89**	202	**122**
35	**24**	78	**57**	139	**90**	203	**123**
37	**25**	79	**58**	140	**91**	204	**124**
38	**26**	111	**59**	141	**92**	206	**125**
39	**27**	112	**60**	142	**93**	207	**126**
40	**28**	113	**61**	151	**94**	208	**127**
41	**29**	114	**62**	152	**95**	209	**128**
42	**30**	115	**63**	155	**96**	210	**129**
43	**31**	116	**64**	156	**97**	211	**130**
44	**32**	117	**65**	157	**98**	212	**131**
45	**33**	117A	**66**	158	**99**	213	**132**
46	**34**	117B	**67**	159	**100**	214	**133**
47	**35**	118	**68**	161	**101**	215	**134**
48	**36**	119	**69**	162	**102**	216	**135**
49	**37**	120	**70**	163	**103**		
50	**38**	121	**71**	164	**104**		
51	**39**	122	**72**	165	**105**		
52	**40**	123	**73**	166	**106**		

---

* Restatement of the Law (Third), The Law Governing Lawyers, was developed in the course of eight Tentative Drafts (1988-1994; 1997) and two Proposed Final Drafts (1996 and 1998), all of which were considered at Annual Meetings of The American Law Institute. Section numbers in the final text were renumbered to make them consecutive. Because many sections of the tentative and proposed drafts have been discussed in cases, articles, and texts under their original or draft numbers, the following table is provided to facilitate conversion.

SELECTED FEDERAL STATUTES, REGULATIONS, AND RULES

FEDERAL STATUTES AND REGULATIONS

15 U.S.C.

CHAPTER 98: PUBLIC COMPANY ACCOUNTING REFORM AND CORPORATE RESPONSIBILITY

§ 7245   Rules of professional responsibility for attorneys (Sarbanes-Oxley Act)

SEC FINAL RULE, 69 FR 70342, 17 CFR PART 205 (SARBANES-OXLEY REGULATIONS)

§ 205.1 Purpose and scope
§ 205.2 Definitions
§ 205.3 Issuer as client
§ 205.4 Responsibilities of supervisory attorneys
§ 205.5 Responsibilities of a subordinate attorney
§ 205.6 Sanctions and discipline
§ 205.7 No private right of action

18 U.S.C.

CHAPTER 11: BRIBERY, GRAFT, AND CONFLICTS OF INTEREST

§ 201. Bribery of public officials and witnesses
§ 202. Definitions
§ 207. Restrictions on former officers, employees, and elected officials of the executive and legislative branches
§ 216. Penalties and injunctions

CHAPTER 73: OBSTRUCTION OF JUSTICE

§ 1503. Influencing or injuring officer or juror generally
§ 1505. Obstruction of proceedings before departments, agencies, and committees
§ 1509. Obstruction of court orders
§ 1510. Obstruction of criminal investigations
§ 1519. Destruction, alteration, or falsification of records in Federal investigations and bankruptcy

CHAPTER 79: PERJURY

§ 1621. Perjury generally
§ 1622. Subornation of perjury

28 U.S.C.

CHAPTER 5: DISTRICT COURTS

§ 144. Bias or prejudice of judge

CHAPTER 31: THE ATTORNEY GENERAL

§ 530B. Ethical standards for attorneys for the Government

FEDERAL RULES OF CIVIL PROCEDURE

Rule 11. Signing of Pleadings, Motions, and Other Papers; Representations to Court; Sanctions
Rule 23. Class Actions
Rule 26. General Provisions Governing Discovery; Duty of Disclosure
Rule 37. Failure to Make Disclosure or Cooperate in Discovery; Sanctions
Rule 60. Relief from Judgment or Order

FEDERAL RULES OF APPELLATE PROCEDURE

Rule 38. Frivolous Appeal—Damages and Costs

SARBANES-OXLEY ACT & REGULATIONS

15 U.S.C.
CHAPTER 98: PUBLIC COMPANY ACCOUNTING REFORM AND CORPORATE RESPONSIBILITY

§ 7245. Rules of professional responsibility for attorneys.

Not later than 180 days after July 30, 2002, the Commission shall issue rules, in the public interest and for the protection of investors, setting forth minimum standards of professional conduct for attorneys appearing and practicing before the Commission in any way in the representation of issuers, including a rule—

(1) requiring an attorney to report evidence of a material violation of securities law or breach of fiduciary duty or similar violation by the company or any agent thereof, to the chief legal counsel or the chief executive officer of the company (or the equivalent thereof); and

(2) if the counsel or officer does not appropriately respond to the evidence (adopting, as necessary, appropriate remedial measures or sanctions with respect to the violation), requiring the attorney to report the evidence to the audit committee of the board of directors of the issuer or to another committee of the board of directors comprised solely of directors not employed directly or indirectly by the issuer, or to the board of directors.

SEC FINAL RULE, 69 FR 70342, 17 CFR PART 205

STANDARDS OF PROFESSIONAL CONDUCT FOR ATTORNEYS APPEARING AND PRACTICING BEFORE THE COMMISSION IN THE REPRESENTATION OF AN ISSUER

§ 205.1 Purpose and scope.

This part sets forth minimum standards of professional conduct for attorneys appearing and practicing before the Commission in the representation of an issuer. These standards supplement applicable standards of any jurisdiction where an attorney is admitted or practices and are not intended to limit the ability of any jurisdiction to impose additional obligations on an attorney not inconsistent with the application of this part. Where the standards of a state or other United States jurisdiction where an attorney is admitted or practices conflict with this part, this part shall govern.

§ 205.2 Definitions.

For purposes of this part, the following definitions apply:

(a) Appearing and practicing before the Commission:

(1) Means:

(i) Transacting any business with the Commission, including communications in any form;

(ii) Representing an issuer in a Commission administrative proceeding or in connection with any Commission investigation, inquiry, information request, or subpoena;

(iii) Providing advice in respect of the United States securities laws or the Commission's rules or regulations thereunder regarding any document that the attorney has notice will be filed with or submitted to, or incorporated into any document that will be filed with or submitted to, the Commission, including the provision of such advice in the context of preparing, or participating in the preparation of, any such document; or

(iv) Advising an issuer as to whether information or a statement, opinion, or other writing is required under the United States securities laws or the Commission's rules or regulations thereunder to be filed with or submitted to, or incorporated into any document that will be filed with or submitted to, the Commission; but

(2) Does not include an attorney who:

(i) Conducts the activities in paragraphs (a)(1)(i) through (a)(1)(iv) of this section other than in the context of providing legal services to an issuer with whom the attorney has an attorney-client relationship; or

(ii) Is a non-appearing foreign attorney.

(b) Appropriate response means a response to an attorney regarding reported evidence of a material violation as a result of which the attorney reasonably believes:

(1) That no material violation, as defined in paragraph (i) of this section, has occurred, is ongoing, or is about to occur;

(2) That the issuer has, as necessary, adopted appropriate remedial measures, including appropriate steps or sanctions to stop any material violations that are ongoing, to prevent any material violation that has yet to occur, and to remedy or otherwise appropriately address any material violation that has already occurred and to minimize the likelihood of its recurrence; or

(3) That the issuer, with the consent of the issuer's board of directors, a committee thereof to whom a report could be made pursuant to § 205.3(b)(3), or a qualified legal compliance committee, has retained or directed an attorney to review the reported evidence of a material violation and either:

(i) Has substantially implemented any remedial recommendations made by such attorney after a reasonable investigation and evaluation of the reported evidence; or

(ii) Has been advised that such attorney may, consistent with his or her professional obligations, assert a colorable defense on behalf of the issuer (or the issuer's officer, director, employee, or agent, as the case may be) in any investigation or judicial or administrative proceeding relating to the reported evidence of a material violation.

(c) Attorney means any person who is admitted, licensed, or otherwise qualified to practice law in any jurisdiction, domestic or foreign, or who holds himself or herself out as admitted, licensed, or otherwise qualified to practice law.

(d) Breach of fiduciary duty refers to any breach of fiduciary or similar duty to the issuer recognized under an applicable Federal or State statute or at common law, including but not limited to misfeasance, nonfeasance, abdication of duty, abuse of trust, and approval of unlawful transactions.

(e) Evidence of a material violation means credible evidence, based upon which it would be unreasonable, under the circumstances, for a prudent and competent attorney not to conclude that it is reasonably likely that a material violation has occurred, is ongoing, or is about to occur.

(f) Foreign government issuer means a foreign issuer as defined in 17 CFR 230.405 eligible to register securities on Schedule B of the Securities Act of 1933 (15 U.S.C. 77a et seq., Schedule B).

(g) In the representation of an issuer means providing legal services as an attorney for an issuer, regardless of whether the attorney is employed or retained by the issuer.

(h) Issuer means an issuer (as defined in section 3 of the Securities Exchange Act of 1934 (15 U.S.C. 78c)), the securities of which are registered under section 12 of that Act (15 U.S.C. 78l), or that is required to file reports under section 15(d) of that Act (15 U.S.C. 78o(d)), or that files or has filed a registration statement that has not yet become effective under the Securities Act of 1933 (15 U.S.C. 77a et seq.), and that it has not withdrawn, but does not include a foreign government issuer. For purposes of paragraphs (a) and (g) of this section, the term "issuer" includes any person controlled by an issuer, where an attorney provides legal services to such person on behalf of, or at the behest, or for the benefit of the issuer, regardless of whether the attorney is employed or retained by the issuer.

(i) Material violation means a material violation of an applicable United States federal or state securities law, a material breach of fiduciary duty arising under United States federal or state law, or a similar material violation of any United States federal or state law.

(j) Non-appearing foreign attorney means an attorney:

(1) Who is admitted to practice law in a jurisdiction outside the United States;

(2) Who does not hold himself or herself out as practicing, and does not give legal advice regarding, United States federal or state securities or other laws (except as provided in paragraph (j)(3)(ii) of this section); and

(3) Who:

(i) Conducts activities that would constitute appearing and practicing before the Commission only incidentally to, and in the ordinary course of, the practice of law in a jurisdiction outside the United States; or

(ii) Is appearing and practicing before the Commission only in consultation with counsel, other than a non-appearing foreign attorney, admitted or licensed to practice in a state or other United States jurisdiction.

(k) Qualified legal compliance committee means a committee of an issuer (which also may be an audit or other committee of the issuer) that:

(1) Consists of at least one member of the issuer's audit committee (or, if the issuer has no audit committee, one member from an equivalent committee of independent directors) and two or more members of the issuer's board of directors who are not employed, directly or indirectly, by the issuer and who are not, in the case of a registered investment company, "interested persons" as defined in section 2(a)(19) of the Investment Company Act of 1940 (15 U.S.C. 80a-2(a)(19));

(2) Has adopted written procedures for the confidential receipt, retention, and consideration of any report of evidence of a material violation under § 205.3;

(3) Has been duly established by the issuer's board of directors, with the authority and responsibility:

(i) To inform the issuer's chief legal officer and chief executive officer (or the equivalents thereof) of any report of evidence of a material violation (except in the circumstances described in § 205.3(b)(4));

(ii) To determine whether an investigation is necessary regarding any report of evidence of a material violation by the issuer, its officers, directors, employees or agents and, if it determines an investigation is necessary or appropriate, to:

(A) Notify the audit committee or the full board of directors;

(B) Initiate an investigation, which may be conducted either by the chief legal officer (or the equivalent thereof) or by outside attorneys; and

(C) Retain such additional expert personnel as the committee deems necessary; and

(iii) At the conclusion of any such investigation, to:

(A) Recommend, by majority vote, that the issuer implement an appropriate response to evidence of a material violation; and

(B) Inform the chief legal officer and the chief executive officer (or the equivalents thereof) and the board of directors of the results of any such investigation under this section and the appropriate remedial measures to be adopted; and

(4) Has the authority and responsibility, acting by majority vote, to take all other appropriate action, including the authority to notify the Commission in the event that the issuer fails in any material respect to implement an appropriate response that the qualified legal compliance committee has recommended the issuer to take.

(l) Reasonable or reasonably denotes, with respect to the actions of an attorney, conduct that would not be unreasonable for a prudent and competent attorney.

(m) Reasonably believes means that an attorney believes the matter in question and that the circumstances are such that the belief is not unreasonable.

(n) Report means to make known to directly, either in person, by telephone, by e-mail, electronically, or in writing.

§ 205.3 Issuer as client.

(a) Representing an issuer. An attorney appearing and practicing before the Commission in the representation of an issuer owes his or her professional and ethical duties to the issuer as an organization. That the attorney may work with and advise the issuer's officers, directors, or employees in the course of representing the issuer does not make such individuals the attorney's clients.

(b) Duty to report evidence of a material violation.

(1) If an attorney, appearing and practicing before the Commission in the representation of an issuer, becomes aware of evidence of a material violation by the issuer or by any officer, director, employee, or agent of the issuer, the attorney shall report such evidence to the issuer's chief legal officer (or the equivalent thereof) or to both the issuer's chief legal officer and its chief executive officer (or the equivalents thereof) forthwith. By communicating such information to the issuer's officers or directors, an attorney does not reveal client confidences or secrets or privileged or otherwise protected information related to the attorney's representation of an issuer.

(2) The chief legal officer (or the equivalent thereof) shall cause such inquiry into the evidence of a material violation as he or she reasonably believes is appropriate to determine whether the material violation described in the report has occurred, is ongoing, or is about to occur. If the chief legal officer (or the equivalent thereof) determines no material violation has occurred, is ongoing, or is about to occur, he or she shall notify the reporting attorney and advise the reporting attorney of the basis for such determination. Unless the chief legal officer (or the equivalent thereof) reasonably believes that no material violation has occurred, is ongoing, or is about to occur, he or she shall take all reasonable steps to cause the issuer to adopt an appropriate response, and shall advise the reporting attorney thereof. In lieu of causing an inquiry under this paragraph (b), a chief legal officer (or the equivalent thereof) may refer a report of evidence of a material violation to a qualified legal compliance committee under paragraph (c)(2) of this section if the issuer has duly established a qualified legal compliance committee prior to the report of evidence of a material violation.

(3) Unless an attorney who has made a report under paragraph (b)(1) of this section reasonably believes that the chief legal officer or the chief executive officer of the issuer (or the equivalent thereof) has provided an appropriate response within a reasonable time, the attorney shall report the evidence of a material violation to:

(i) The audit committee of the issuer's board of directors;

(ii) Another committee of the issuer's board of directors consisting solely of directors who are not employed, directly or indirectly, by the issuer and are not, in the case of a registered investment company, "interested persons" as defined in section 2(a)(19) of the Investment Company Act of 1940 (15 U.S.C. 80a-2(a)(19)) (if the issuer's board of directors has no audit committee); or

(iii) The issuer's board of directors (if the issuer's board of directors has no committee consisting solely of directors who are not employed, directly or indirectly, by the issuer and are not, in the case of a registered investment company, "interested persons" as defined in section 2(a)(19) of the Investment Company Act of 1940 (15 U.S.C. 80a-2(a)(19))).

(4) If an attorney reasonably believes that it would be futile to report evidence of a material violation to the issuer's chief legal officer and chief executive officer (or the equivalents thereof) under paragraph (b)(1) of this section, the attorney may report such evidence as provided under paragraph (b)(3) of this section.

(5) An attorney retained or directed by an issuer to investigate evidence of a material violation reported under paragraph (b)(1), (b)(3), or (b)(4) of this section shall be deemed to be appearing and practicing before the Commission. Directing or retaining an attorney to investigate reported evidence of a material violation does not relieve an officer or director of the issuer to whom such evidence has been reported under paragraph (b)(1), (b)(3), or (b)(4) of this section from a duty to respond to the reporting attorney.

(6) An attorney shall not have any obligation to report evidence of a material violation under this paragraph (b) if:

(i) The attorney was retained or directed by the issuer's chief legal officer (or the equivalent thereof) to investigate such evidence of a material violation and:

(A) The attorney reports the results of such investigation to the chief legal officer (or the equivalent thereof); and

(B) Except where the attorney and the chief legal officer (or the equivalent thereof) each reasonably believes that no material violation has occurred, is ongoing, or is about to occur, the chief legal officer (or the equivalent thereof) reports the results of the investigation to the issuer's board of directors, a committee thereof to whom a report could be made pursuant to paragraph (b)(3) of this section, or a qualified legal compliance committee; or

(ii) The attorney was retained or directed by the chief legal officer (or the equivalent thereof) to assert, consistent with his or her professional obligations, a colorable defense on behalf of the issuer (or the issuer's officer, director, employee, or agent, as the case may be) in any investigation or judicial or administrative proceeding relating to such evidence of a material violation, and the chief legal officer (or the equivalent thereof) provides reasonable and timely reports on the progress and outcome of such proceeding to the issuer's board of directors, a committee thereof to whom a report could be made pursuant to paragraph (b)(3) of this section, or a qualified legal compliance committee.

(7) An attorney shall not have any obligation to report evidence of a material violation under this paragraph (b) if such attorney was retained or directed by a qualified legal compliance committee:

(i) To investigate such evidence of a material violation; or

(ii) To assert, consistent with his or her professional obligations, a colorable defense on behalf of the issuer (or the issuer's officer, director, employee, or agent, as the case may be) in any investigation or judicial or administrative proceeding relating to such evidence of a material violation.

(8) An attorney who receives what he or she reasonably believes is an appropriate and timely response to a report he or she has made pursuant to paragraph (b)(1), (b)(3), or (b)(4) of this section need do nothing more under this section with respect to his or her report.

(9) An attorney who does not reasonably believe that the issuer has made an appropriate response within a reasonable time to the report or reports made pursuant to paragraph (b)(1), (b)(3), or (b)(4) of this section shall explain his or her reasons therefor to the chief legal officer (or the equivalent thereof), the chief executive officer (or the equivalent thereof), and directors to whom the attorney reported the evidence of a material violation pursuant to paragraph (b)(1), (b)(3), or (b)(4) of this section.

(10) An attorney formerly employed or retained by an issuer who has reported evidence of a material violation under this part and reasonably believes that he or she has been discharged for so doing may notify the issuer's board of directors or any committee thereof that he or she believes that he or she has been discharged for reporting evidence of a material violation under this section.

(c) Alternative reporting procedures for attorneys retained or employed by an issuer that has established a qualified legal compliance committee.

(1) If an attorney, appearing and practicing before the Commission in the representation of an issuer, becomes aware of evidence of a material violation by the issuer or by any officer, director, employee, or agent of the issuer, the attorney may, as an alternative to the reporting requirements of paragraph (b) of this section, report such evidence to a qualified legal compliance committee, if the issuer has previously formed such a committee. An attorney who reports evidence of a material violation to such a qualified legal compliance committee has satisfied his or her obligation to report such evidence and is not required to assess the issuer's response to the reported evidence of a material violation.

(2) A chief legal officer (or the equivalent thereof) may refer a report of evidence of a material violation to a previously established qualified legal compliance committee in lieu of causing an inquiry to be conducted under paragraph (b)(2) of this section. The chief legal officer (or the equivalent thereof) shall inform the reporting attorney that the report has been referred to a qualified legal compliance committee. Thereafter, pursuant to the requirements under § 205.2(k), the qualified legal compliance committee shall be responsible for responding to the evidence of a material violation reported to it under this paragraph (c).

(d) Issuer confidences.

(1) Any report under this section (or the contemporaneous record thereof) or any response thereto (or the contemporaneous record thereof) may be used by an attorney in connection with any investigation, proceeding, or litigation in which the attorney's compliance with this part is in issue.

(2) An attorney appearing and practicing before the Commission in the representation of an issuer may reveal to the Commission, without the issuer's consent, confidential information related to the representation to the extent the attorney reasonably believes necessary:

(i) To prevent the issuer from committing a material violation that is likely to cause substantial injury to the financial interest or property of the issuer or investors;

(ii) To prevent the issuer, in a Commission investigation or administrative proceeding from committing perjury, proscribed in 18 U.S.C. 1621; suborning perjury, proscribed in 18 U.S.C. 1622; or committing any act proscribed in 18 U.S.C. 1001 that is likely to perpetrate a fraud upon the Commission; or

(iii) To rectify the consequences of a material violation by the issuer that caused, or may cause, substantial injury to the financial interest or property of the issuer or investors in the furtherance of which the attorney's services were used.

§ 205.4 Responsibilities of supervisory attorneys.

(a) An attorney supervising or directing another attorney who is appearing and practicing before the Commission in the representation of an issuer is a supervisory attorney. An issuer's chief legal officer (or the equivalent thereof) is a supervisory attorney under this section.

(b) A supervisory attorney shall make reasonable efforts to ensure that a subordinate attorney, as defined in § 205.5(a), that he or she supervises or directs conforms to this part. To the extent a subordinate attorney appears and practices before the Commission in the representation of an issuer, that subordinate attorney's supervisory attorneys also appear and practice before the Commission.

(c) A supervisory attorney is responsible for complying with the reporting requirements in § 205.3 when a subordinate attorney has reported to the supervisory attorney evidence of a material violation.

(d) A supervisory attorney who has received a report of evidence of a material violation from a subordinate attorney under § 205.3 may report such evidence to the issuer's qualified legal compliance committee if the issuer has duly formed such a committee.

§ 205.5 Responsibilities of a subordinate attorney.

(a) An attorney who appears and practices before the Commission in the representation of an issuer on a matter under the supervision or direction of another attorney (other than under the direct supervision or direction of the issuer's chief legal officer (or the equivalent thereof)) is a subordinate attorney.

(b) A subordinate attorney shall comply with this part notwithstanding that the subordinate attorney acted at the direction of or under the supervision of another person.

(c) A subordinate attorney complies with § 205.3 if the subordinate attorney reports to his or her supervising attorney under § 205.3(b) evidence of a material violation of which the subordinate attorney has become aware in appearing and practicing before the Commission.

(d) A subordinate attorney may take the steps permitted or required by § 205.3(b) or (c) if the subordinate attorney reasonably believes that a supervisory attorney to whom he or she has reported evidence of a material violation under § 205.3(b) has failed to comply with § 205.3.

§ 205.6 Sanctions and discipline.

(a) A violation of this part by any attorney appearing and practicing before the Commission in the representation of an issuer shall subject such attorney to the civil penalties and remedies for a violation of the federal securities laws available to the Commission in an action brought by the Commission thereunder.

(b) An attorney appearing and practicing before the Commission who violates any provision of this part is subject to the disciplinary authority of the Commission, regardless of whether the attorney may also be subject to discipline for the same conduct in a jurisdiction where the attorney is admitted or practices. An administrative disciplinary proceeding initiated by the Commission for violation of this part may result in an attorney being censured, or being temporarily or permanently denied the privilege of appearing or practicing before the Commission.

(c) An attorney who complies in good faith with the provisions of this part shall not be subject to discipline or otherwise liable under inconsistent standards imposed by any state or other United States jurisdiction where the attorney is admitted or practices.

(d) An attorney practicing outside the United States shall not be required to comply with the requirements of this part to the extent that such compliance is prohibited by applicable foreign law.

§ 205.7 No private right of action.

(a) Nothing in this part is intended to, or does, create a private right of action against any attorney, law firm, or issuer based upon compliance or noncompliance with its provisions.

(b) Authority to enforce compliance with this part is vested exclusively in the Commission.

18 U.S.C.
CHAPTER 11: BRIBERY, GRAFT, AND CONFLICTS OF INTEREST

§ 201. Bribery of public officials and witnesses

(a) For the purpose of this section—

(1) the term "public official" means Member of Congress, Delegate, or Resident Commissioner, either before or after such official has qualified, or an officer or employee or person acting for or on behalf of the United States, or any department, agency or branch of Government thereof, including the District of Columbia, in any official function, under or by authority of any such department, agency, or branch of Government, or a juror;

(2) the term "person who has been selected to be a public official" means any person who has been nominated or appointed to be a public official, or has been officially informed that such person will be so nominated or appointed; and

(3) the term "official act" means any decision or action on any question, matter, cause, suit, proceeding or controversy, which may at any time be pending, or which may by law be brought before any public official, in such official's official capacity, or in such official's place of trust or profit.

(b) Whoever—

(1) directly or indirectly, corruptly gives, offers or promises anything of value to any public official or person who has been selected to be a public official, or offers or promises any public official or any person who has been selected to be a public official to give anything of value to any other person or entity, with intent—

(A) to influence any official act; or

(B) to influence such public official or person who has been selected to be a public official to commit or aid in committing, or collude in, or allow, any fraud, or make opportunity for the commission of any fraud, on the United States; or

(C) to induce such public official or such person who has been selected to be a public official to do or omit to do any act in violation of the lawful duty of such official or person;

(2) being a public official or person selected to be a public official, directly or indirectly, corruptly demands, seeks, receives, accepts, or agrees to receive or accept anything of value personally or for any other person or entity, in return for:

(A) being influenced in the performance of any official act;

(B) being influenced to commit or aid in committing, or to collude in, or allow, any fraud, or make opportunity for the commission of any fraud, on the United States; or

(C) being induced to do or omit to do any act in violation of the official duty of such official or person;

(3) directly or indirectly, corruptly gives, offers, or promises anything of value to any person, or offers or promises such person to give anything of value to any other person or entity, with intent to influence the testimony under oath or affirmation of such first-mentioned person as a witness upon a trial, hearing, or other proceeding, before any court, any committee of either House or both Houses of Congress, or any agency, commission, or officer authorized by the laws of the United States to hear evidence or take testimony, or with intent to influence such person to absent himself therefrom;

(4) directly or indirectly, corruptly demands, seeks, receives, accepts, or agrees to receive or accept anything of value personally or for any other person or entity in return for being influenced in testimony under oath or affirmation as a witness upon any such trial, hearing, or other proceeding, or in return for absenting himself therefrom;

shall be fined under this title or not more than three times the monetary equivalent of the thing of value, whichever is greater, or imprisoned for not more than fifteen years, or both, and may be disqualified from holding any office of honor, trust, or profit under the United States.

(c) Whoever—

(1) otherwise than as provided by law for the proper discharge of official duty—

(A) directly or indirectly gives, offers, or promises anything of value to any public official, former public official, or person selected to be a public official, for or because of any official act performed or to be performed by such public official, former public official, or person selected to be a public official; or

(B) being a public official, former public official, or person selected to be a public official, otherwise than as provided by law for the proper discharge of official duty, directly or indirectly demands, seeks, receives, accepts, or agrees to receive or accept anything of value personally for or because of any official act performed or to be performed by such official or person;

(2) directly or indirectly, gives, offers, or promises anything of value to any person, for or because of the testimony under oath or affirmation given or to be given by such person as a witness upon a trial, hearing, or other proceeding, before any court, any committee of either House or both Houses of Congress, or any agency, commission, or officer authorized by the laws of the United States to hear evidence or take testimony, or for or because of such person's absence therefrom;

(3) directly or indirectly, demands, seeks, receives, accepts, or agrees to receive or accept anything of value personally for or because of the testimony under oath or affirmation given or to be given by such person as a witness upon any such trial, hearing, or other proceeding, or for or because of such person's absence therefrom;

shall be fined under this title or imprisoned for not more than two years, or both.

(d) Paragraphs (3) and (4) of subsection (b) and paragraphs (2) and (3) of subsection (c) shall not be construed to prohibit the payment or receipt of witness fees provided by law, or the payment, by the party upon whose behalf a witness is called and receipt by a witness, of the reasonable cost of travel and subsistence incurred and the reasonable value of time lost in attendance at any such trial, hearing, or proceeding, or in the case of expert witnesses, a reasonable fee for time spent in the preparation of such opinion, and in appearing and testifying.

(e) The offenses and penalties prescribed in this section are separate from and in addition to those prescribed in sections 1503, 1504, and 1505 of this title.

§ 202. Definitions

(a) For the purpose of sections 203, 205, 207, 208, and 209 of this title the term "special Government employee" shall mean an officer or employee of the executive or legislative branch of the United States Government, of any independent agency of the United States or of the District of Columbia, who is retained, designated, appointed, or employed to perform, with or without compensation, for not to exceed one hundred and thirty days during any period of three hundred and sixty-five consecutive days, temporary duties either on a full-time or intermittent basis, a part-time United States commissioner, a part-time United States magistrate judge, or, regardless of the number of days of appointment, an independent counsel appointed under chapter 40 of title 28 and any person appointed by that independent counsel under section 594(c) of title 28. Notwithstanding the next preceding sentence, every person serving as a part-time local representative of a Member of Congress in the Member's home district or State shall be classified as a special Government employee. . . .

(b) For the purposes of sections 205 and 207 of this title, the term "official responsibility" means the direct administrative or operating authority, whether intermediate or final, and either exercisable alone or with others, and either personally or through subordinates, to approve, disapprove, or otherwise direct Government action.

(c) Except as otherwise provided in such sections, the terms "officer" and "employee" in sections 203, 205, 207 through 209, and 218 of this title shall not include the President, the Vice President, a Member of Congress, or a Federal judge. . . .

§ 207. Restrictions on former officers, employees, and elected officials of the executive and legislative branches

(a) Restrictions on all officers and employees of the executive branch and certain other agencies. —

(1) Permanent restrictions on representation on particular matters.—Any person who is an officer or employee (including any special Government employee) of the executive branch of the United States (including any independent agency of the United States), or of the District of Columbia, and who, after the termination of his or her service or employment with the United States or the District of Columbia, knowingly makes, with the intent to influence, any communication to or appearance before any officer or employee of any department, agency,

court, or court-martial of the United States or the District of Columbia, on behalf of any other person (except the United States or the District of Columbia) in connection with a particular matter—

(A) in which the United States or the District of Columbia is a party or has a direct and substantial interest,

(B) in which the person participated personally and substantially as such officer or employee, and

(C) which involved a specific party or specific parties at the time of such participation,

shall be punished as provided in section 216 of this title.

(2) Two-year restrictions concerning particular matters under official responsibility.—Any person subject to the restrictions contained in paragraph (1) who, within 2 years after the termination of his or her service or employment with the United States or the District of Columbia, knowingly makes, with the intent to influence, any communication to or appearance before any officer or employee of any department, agency, court, or court-martial of the United States or the District of Columbia, on behalf of any other person (except the United States or the District of Columbia), in connection with a particular matter—

(A) in which the United States or the District of Columbia is a party or has a direct and substantial interest,

(B) which such person knows or reasonably should know was actually pending under his or her official responsibility as such officer or employee within a period of 1 year before the termination of his or her service or employment with the United States or the District of Columbia, and

(C) which involved a specific party or specific parties at the time it was so pending, shall be punished as provided in section 216 of this title.

(3) Clarification of restrictions. —The restrictions contained in paragraphs (1) and (2) shall apply—

(A) in the case of an officer or employee of the executive branch of the United States (including any independent agency), only with respect to communications to or appearances before any officer or employee of any department, agency, court, or court-martial of the United States on behalf of any other person (except the United States), and only with respect to a matter in which the United States is a party or has a direct and substantial interest; and

(B) in the case of an officer or employee of the District of Columbia, only with respect to communications to or appearances before any officer or employee of any department, agency, or court of the District of Columbia on behalf of any other person (except the District of Columbia), and only with respect to a matter in which the District of Columbia is a party or has a direct and substantial interest.

(b) One-year restrictions on aiding or advising. —

(1) In general.—Any person who is a former officer or employee of the executive branch of the United States (including any independent agency) and is subject to the restrictions contained in subsection (a)(1), or any person who is a former officer or employee of the legislative branch or a former Member of Congress, who personally and substantially participated in any ongoing trade or treaty negotiation on behalf of the United States within the 1-year period preceding the date on which his or her service or employment with the United States terminated, and who had access to information concerning such trade or treaty negotiation which is exempt from disclosure under section 552 of title 5, which is so designated by the appropriate department or agency, and which the person knew or should have known was so designated, shall not, on the basis of that information, knowingly represent, aid, or advise any other person (except the United States) concerning such ongoing trade or treaty negotiation for a period of 1 year after

his or her service or employment with the United States terminates. Any person who violates this subsection shall be punished as provided in section 216 of this title.

(2) Definition.—For purposes of this paragraph—

(A) the term "trade negotiation" means negotiations which the President determines to undertake to enter into a trade agreement pursuant to section 1102 of the Omnibus Trade and Competitiveness Act of 1988, and does not include any action taken before that determination is made; and

(B) the term "treaty" means an international agreement made by the President that requires the advice and consent of the Senate.

(c) One-year restrictions on certain senior personnel of the executive branch and independent agencies. —

(1) Restrictions.—In addition to the restrictions set forth in subsections (a) and (b), any person who is an officer or employee (including any special Government employee) of the executive branch of the United States (including an independent agency), who is referred to in paragraph (2), and who, within 1 year after the termination of his or her service or employment as such officer or employee, knowingly makes, with the intent to influence, any communication to or appearance before any officer or employee of the department or agency in which such person served within 1 year before such termination, on behalf of any other person (except the United States), in connection with any matter on which such person seeks official action by any officer or employee of such department or agency, shall be punished as provided in section 216 of this title.

(2) Persons to whom restrictions apply.—

(A) Paragraph (1) shall apply to a person (other than a person subject to the restrictions of subsection (d))—

(i) employed at a rate of pay specified in or fixed according to subchapter II of chapter 53 of title 5,

(ii) employed in a position which is not referred to in clause (i) and for which that person is paid at a rate of basic pay which is equal to or greater than 86.5 percent of the rate of basic pay for level II of the Executive Schedule, or, for a period of 2 years following the enactment of the National Defense Authorization Act for Fiscal Year 2004, a person who, on the day prior to the enactment of that Act, was employed in a position which is not referred to in clause (i) and for which the rate of basic pay, exclusive of any locality-based pay adjustment under section 5304 or section 5304a of title 5, was equal to or greater than the rate of basic pay payable for level 5 of the Senior Executive Service on the day prior to the enactment of that Act,

(iii) appointed by the President to a position under section 105(a)(2)(B) of title 3 or by the Vice President to a position under section 106(a)(1)(B) of title 3,

(iv) employed in a position which is held by an active duty commissioned officer of the uniformed services who is serving in a grade or rank for which the pay grade (as specified in section 201 of title 37) is pay grade O-7 or above; or

(v) assigned from a private sector organization to an agency under chapter 37 of title 5.

(B) Paragraph (1) shall not apply to a special Government employee who serves less than 60 days in the 1-year period before his or her service or employment as such employee terminates.

(C) At the request of a department or agency, the Director of the Office of Government Ethics may waive the restrictions contained in paragraph (1) with respect to any position, or category of positions, referred to in clause (ii) or (iv) of subparagraph (A), in such department or agency if the Director determines that—

(i) the imposition of the restrictions with respect to such position or positions would create an undue hardship on the department or agency in obtaining qualified personnel to fill such position or positions, and

(ii) granting the waiver would not create the potential for use of undue influence or unfair advantage. . . .

§ 216. Penalties and injunctions

(a) The punishment for an offense under section 203, 204, 205, 207, 208, or 209 of this title is the following:

(1) Whoever engages in the conduct constituting the offense shall be imprisoned for not more than one year or fined in the amount set forth in this title, or both.

(2) Whoever willfully engages in the conduct constituting the offense shall be imprisoned for not more than five years or fined in the amount set forth in this title, or both.

(b) The Attorney General may bring a civil action in the appropriate United States district court against any person who engages in conduct constituting an offense under section 203, 204, 205, 207, 208, or 209 of this title and, upon proof of such conduct by a preponderance of the evidence, such person shall be subject to a civil penalty of not more than $50,000 for each violation or the amount of compensation which the person received or offered for the prohibited conduct, whichever amount is greater. The imposition of a civil penalty under this subsection does not preclude any other criminal or civil statutory, common law, or administrative remedy, which is available by law to the United States or any other person.

(c) If the Attorney General has reason to believe that a person is engaging in conduct constituting an offense under section 203, 204, 205, 207, 208, or 209 of this title, the Attorney General may petition an appropriate United States district court for an order prohibiting that person from engaging in such conduct. The court may issue an order prohibiting that person from engaging in such conduct if the court finds that the conduct constitutes such an offense. The filing of a petition under this section does not preclude any other remedy which is available by law to the United States or any other person.

CHAPTER 73: OBSTRUCTION OF JUSTICE

§ 1503. Influencing or injuring officer or juror generally

(a) Whoever corruptly, or by threats or force, or by any threatening letter or communication, endeavors to influence, intimidate, or impede any grand or petit juror, or officer in or of any court of the United States, or officer who may be serving at any examination or other proceeding before any United States magistrate judge or other committing magistrate, in the discharge of his duty, or injures any such grand or petit juror in his person or property on account of any verdict or indictment assented to by him, or on account of his being or having been such juror, or injures any such officer, magistrate judge, or other committing magistrate in his person or property on account of the performance of his official duties, or corruptly or by threats or force, or by any threatening letter or communication, influences, obstructs, or impedes, or endeavors to influence, obstruct, or impede, the due administration of justice, shall be punished as provided in subsection (b). If the offense under this section occurs in connection with a trial of a criminal case, and the act in violation of this section involves the threat of physical force or physical force, the maximum term of imprisonment which may be imposed for the offense shall be the higher of that otherwise provided by law or the maximum term that could have been imposed for any offense charged in such case.

(b) The punishment for an offense under this section is—

(1) in the case of a killing, the punishment provided in sections 1111 and 1112;

(2) in the case of an attempted killing, or a case in which the offense was committed against a petit juror and in which a class A or B felony was charged, imprisonment for not more than 20 years, a fine under this title, or both; and

(3) in any other case, imprisonment for not more than 10 years, a fine under this title, or both.

§ 1505. Obstruction of proceedings before departments, agencies, and committees

Whoever, with intent to avoid, evade, prevent, or obstruct compliance, in whole or in part, with any civil investigative demand duly and properly made under the Antitrust Civil Process Act, willfully withholds, misrepresents, removes from any place, conceals, covers up, destroys, mutilates, alters, or by other means falsifies any documentary material, answers to written interrogatories, or oral testimony, which is the subject of such demand; or attempts to do so or solicits another to do so; or

Whoever corruptly, or by threats or force, or by any threatening letter or communication influences, obstructs, or impedes or endeavors to influence, obstruct, or impede the due and proper administration of the law under which any pending proceeding is being had before any department or agency of the United States, or the due and proper exercise of the power of inquiry under which any inquiry or investigation is being had by either House, or any committee of either House or any joint committee of the Congress—

Shall be fined under this title or imprisoned not more than five years, or both.

§ 1509. Obstruction of court orders

Whoever, by threats or force, willfully prevents, obstructs, impedes, or interferes with, or willfully attempts to prevent, obstruct, impede, or interfere with, the due exercise of rights or the performance of duties under any order, judgment, or decree of a court of the United States, shall be fined under this title or imprisoned not more than one year, or both.

No injunctive or other civil relief against the conduct made criminal by this section shall be denied on the ground that such conduct is a crime.

§ 1510. Obstruction of criminal investigations

(a) Whoever willfully endeavors by means of bribery to obstruct, delay, or prevent the communication of information relating to a violation of any criminal statute of the United States by any person to a criminal investigator shall be fined under this title, or imprisoned not more than five years, or both.

(b)(1) Whoever, being an officer of a financial institution, with the intent to obstruct a judicial proceeding, directly or indirectly notifies any other person about the existence or contents of a subpoena for records of that financial institution, or information that has been furnished to the grand jury in response to that subpoena, shall be fined under this title or imprisoned not more than 5 years, or both.

(2) Whoever, being an officer of a financial institution, directly or indirectly notifies—

(A) a customer of that financial institution whose records are sought by a grand jury subpoena; or

(B) any other person named in that subpoena;

about the existence or contents of that subpoena or information that has been furnished to the grand jury in response to that subpoena, shall be fined under this title or imprisoned not more than one year, or both.

(3) As used in this subsection—

(A) the term "an officer of a financial institution" means an officer, director, partner, employee, agent, or attorney of or for a financial institution; and

(B) the term "subpoena for records" means a Federal grand jury subpoena or a Department of Justice subpoena (issued under section 3486 of title 18), for customer records that has been served relating to a violation of, or a conspiracy to violate—

(i) section 215, 656, 657, 1005, 1006, 1007, 1014, 1344, 1956, 1957, or chapter 53 of title 31; or

(ii) section 1341 or 1343 affecting a financial institution.

(c) As used in this section, the term "criminal investigator" means any individual duly authorized by a department, agency, or armed force of the United States to conduct or engage in investigations of or prosecutions for violations of the criminal laws of the United States.

§ 1519. Destruction, alteration, or falsification of records in Federal investigations and bankruptcy

Whoever knowingly alters, destroys, mutilates, conceals, covers up, falsifies, or makes a false entry in any record, document, or tangible object with the intent to impede, obstruct, or influence the investigation or proper administration of any matter within the jurisdiction of any department or agency of the United States or any case filed under title 11, or in relation to or contemplation of any such matter or case, shall be fined under this title, imprisoned not more than 20 years, or both.

CHAPTER 79: PERJURY

§ 1621. Perjury generally

Whoever—

(1) having taken an oath before a competent tribunal, officer, or person, in any case in which a law of the United States authorizes an oath to be administered, that he will testify, declare, depose, or certify truly, or that any written testimony, declaration, deposition, or certificate by him subscribed, is true, willfully and contrary to such oath states or subscribes any material matter which he does not believe to be true; or

(2) in any declaration, certificate, verification, or statement under penalty of perjury as permitted under section 1746 of title 28, United States Code, willfully subscribes as true any material matter which he does not believe to be true;

is guilty of perjury and shall, except as otherwise expressly provided by law, be fined under this title or imprisoned not more than five years, or both. This section is applicable whether the statement or subscription is made within or without the United States.

§ 1622. Subornation of perjury

Whoever procures another to commit any perjury is guilty of subornation of perjury, and shall be fined under this title or imprisoned not more than five years, or both.

28 U.S.C.
CHAPTER 5: DISTRICT COURTS

§ 144. Bias or prejudice of judge

Whenever a party to any proceeding in a district court makes and files a timely and sufficient affidavit that the judge before whom the matter is pending has a personal bias or prejudice either against him or in favor of any adverse party, such judge shall proceed no further therein, but another judge shall be assigned to hear such proceeding.

The affidavit shall state the facts and the reasons for the belief that bias or prejudice exists, and shall be filed not less than ten days before the beginning of the term at which the proceeding is to be heard, or good cause shall be shown for failure to file it within such time. A party may file only one such affidavit in any case. It shall be accompanied by a certificate of counsel of record stating that it is made in good faith.

CHAPTER 31: THE ATTORNEY GENERAL

§ 530B. Ethical standards for attorneys for the Government

(a) An attorney for the Government shall be subject to State laws and rules, and local Federal court rules, governing attorneys in each State where such attorney engages in that attorney's duties, to the same extent and in the same manner as other attorneys in that State.

(b) The Attorney General shall make and amend rules of the Department of Justice to assure compliance with this section.

(c) As used in this section, the term "attorney for the Government" includes any attorney described in section 77.2(a) of part 77 of title 28 of the Code of Federal Regulations and also includes any independent counsel, or employee of such a counsel, appointed under chapter 40.

FEDERAL RULES OF CIVIL PROCEDURE

Rule 11. Signing of Pleadings, Motions, and Other Papers; Representations to Court; Sanctions

(a) Signature. Every pleading, written motion, and other paper shall be signed by at least one attorney of record in the attorney's individual name, or, if the party is not represented by an attorney, shall be signed by the party. Each paper shall state the signer's address and telephone number, if any. Except when otherwise specifically provided by rule or statute, pleadings need not be verified or accompanied by affidavit. An unsigned paper shall be stricken unless omission of the signature is corrected promptly after being called to the attention of the attorney or party.

(b) Representations to Court. By presenting to the court (whether by signing, filing, submitting, or later advocating) a pleading, written motion, or other paper, an attorney or unrepresented party is certifying that to the best of the person's knowledge, information, and belief, formed after an inquiry reasonable under the circumstances,—

(1) it is not being presented for any improper purpose, such as to harass or to cause unnecessary delay or needless increase in the cost of litigation;

(2) the claims, defenses, and other legal contentions therein are warranted by existing law or by a nonfrivolous argument for the extension, modification, or reversal of existing law or the establishment of new law;

(3) the allegations and other factual contentions have evidentiary support or, if specifically so identified, are likely to have evidentiary support after a reasonable opportunity for further investigation or discovery; and

(4) the denials of factual contentions are warranted on the evidence or, if specifically so identified, are reasonably based on a lack of information or belief.

(c) Sanctions. If, after notice and a reasonable opportunity to respond, the court determines that subdivision (b) has been violated, the court may, subject to the conditions stated below, impose an appropriate sanction upon the attorneys, law firms, or parties that have violated subdivision (b) or are responsible for the violation.

(1) How Initiated.

(A) By Motion. A motion for sanctions under this rule shall be made separately from other motions or requests and shall describe the specific conduct alleged to violate subdivision (b). It shall be served as provided in Rule 5, but shall not be filed with or presented to the court unless, within 21 days after service of the motion (or such other period as the court may prescribe), the challenged paper, claim, defense, contention, allegation, or denial is not withdrawn or appropriately corrected. If warranted, the court may award to the party prevailing on the motion the reasonable expenses and attorney's fees incurred in presenting or opposing the motion. Absent exceptional circumstances, a law firm shall be held jointly responsible for violations committed by its partners, associates, and employees.

(B) On Court's Initiative. On its own initiative, the court may enter an order describing the specific conduct that appears to violate subdivision (b) and directing an attorney, law firm, or party to show cause why it has not violated subdivision (b) with respect thereto.

(2) Nature of Sanction; Limitations. A sanction imposed for violation of this rule shall be limited to what is sufficient to deter repetition of such conduct or comparable conduct by others similarly situated. Subject to the limitations in subparagraphs (A) and (B), the sanction may consist of, or include, directives of a nonmonetary nature, an order to pay a penalty into court, or, if imposed on motion and warranted for effective deterrence, an order directing payment to the movant of some or all of the reasonable attorneys' fees and other expenses incurred as a direct result of the violation.

(A) Monetary sanctions may not be awarded against a represented party for a violation of subdivision (b)(2).

(B) Monetary sanctions may not be awarded on the court's initiative unless the court issues its order to show cause before a voluntary dismissal or settlement of the claims made by or against the party which is, or whose attorneys are, to be sanctioned.

(3) Order. When imposing sanctions, the court shall describe the conduct determined to constitute a violation of this rule and explain the basis for the sanction imposed.

(d) Inapplicability to Discovery. Subdivisions (a) through (c) of this rule do not apply to disclosures and discovery requests, responses, objections, and motions that are subject to the provisions of Rules 26 through 37.

Rule 23.   Class Actions

(a) Prerequisites to a Class Action. One or more members of a class may sue or be sued as representative parties on behalf of all only if (1) the class is so numerous that joinder of all members is impracticable, (2) there are questions of law or fact common to the class, (3) the claims or defenses of the representative parties are typical of the claims or defenses of the class, and (4) the representative parties will fairly and adequately protect the interests of the class.

(b) Class Actions Maintainable. An action may be maintained as a class action if the prerequisites of subdivision (a) are satisfied, and in addition:

(1) the prosecution of separate actions by or against individual members of the class would create a risk of

(A) inconsistent or varying adjudications with respect to individual members of the class which would establish incompatible standards of conduct for the party opposing the class, or

(B) adjudications with respect to individual members of the class which would as a practical matter be dispositive of the interests of the other members not parties to the adjudications or substantially impair or impede their ability to protect their interests; or

(2) the party opposing the class has acted or refused to act on grounds generally applicable to the class, thereby making appropriate final injunctive relief or corresponding declaratory relief with respect to the class as a whole; or

(3) the court finds that the questions of law or fact common to the members of the class predominate over any questions affecting only individual members, and that a class action is superior to other available methods for the fair and efficient adjudication of the controversy. The matters pertinent to the findings include: (A) the interest of members of the class in individually controlling the prosecution or defense of separate actions; (B) the extent and nature of any litigation concerning the controversy already commenced by or against members of the class; (C) the desirability or undesirability of concentrating the litigation of the claims in

the particular forum; (D) the difficulties likely to be encountered in the management of a class action.

(c) Determining by Order Whether to Certify a Class Action; Appointing Class Counsel; Notice and Membership in Class; Judgment; Multiple Classes and Subclasses.

(1)(A) When a person sues or is sued as a representative of a class, the court must—at an early practicable time—determine by order whether to certify the action as a class action.

(B) An order certifying a class action must define the class and the class claims, issues, or defenses, and must appoint class counsel under Rule 23(g).

(C) An order under Rule 23(c)(1) may be altered or amended before final judgment.

(2)(A) For any class certified under Rule 23(b)(1) or (2), the court may direct appropriate notice to the class.

(B) For any class certified under Rule 23(b)(3), the court must direct to class members the best notice practicable under the circumstances, including individual notice to all members who can be identified through reasonable effort. The notice must concisely and clearly state in plain, easily understood language:

• the nature of the action,

• the definition of the class certified,

• the class claims, issues, or defenses,

• that a class member may enter an appearance through counsel if the member so desires,

• that the court will exclude from the class any member who requests exclusion, stating when and how members may elect to be excluded, and

• the binding effect of a class judgment on class members under Rule 23(c)(3).

(3) The judgment in an action maintained as a class action under subdivision (b)(1) or (b)(2), whether or not favorable to the class, shall include and describe those whom the court finds to be members of the class. The judgment in an action maintained as a class action under subdivision (b)(3), whether or not favorable to the class, shall include and specify or describe those to whom the notice provided in subdivision (c)(2) was directed, and who have not requested exclusion, and whom the court finds to be members of the class.

(4) When appropriate (A) an action may be brought or maintained as a class action with respect to particular issues, or (B) a class may be divided into subclasses and each subclass treated as a class, and the provisions of this rule shall then be construed and applied accordingly.

(d) Orders in Conduct of Actions. In the conduct of actions to which this rule applies, the court may make appropriate orders: (1) determining the course of proceedings or prescribing measures to prevent undue repetition or complication in the presentation of evidence or argument; (2) requiring, for the protection of the members of the class or otherwise for the fair conduct of the action, that notice be given in such manner as the court may direct to some or all of the members of any step in the action, or of the proposed extent of the judgment, or of the opportunity of members to signify whether they consider the representation fair and adequate, to intervene and present claims or defenses, or otherwise to come into the action; (3) imposing conditions on the representative parties or on intervenors; (4) requiring that the pleadings be amended to eliminate therefrom allegations as to representation of absent persons, and that the action proceed accordingly; (5) dealing with similar procedural matters. The orders may be combined with an order under Rule 16, and may be altered or amended as may be desirable from time to time.

(e) Settlement, Voluntary Dismissal, or Compromise.

(1)(A) The court must approve any settlement, voluntary dismissal, or compromise of the claims, issues, or defenses of a certified class.

(B) The court must direct notice in a reasonable manner to all class members who would be bound by a proposed settlement, voluntary dismissal, or compromise.

(C) The court may approve a settlement, voluntary dismissal, or compromise that would bind class members only after a hearing and on finding that the settlement, voluntary dismissal, or compromise is fair, reasonable, and adequate.

(2) The parties seeking approval of a settlement, voluntary dismissal, or compromise under Rule 23(e)(1) must file a statement identifying any agreement made in connection with the proposed settlement, voluntary dismissal, or compromise.

(3) In an action previously certified as a class action under Rule 23(b)(3), the court may refuse to approve a settlement unless it affords a new opportunity to request exclusion to individual class members who had an earlier opportunity to request exclusion but did not do so.

(4)(A) Any class member may object to a proposed settlement, voluntary dismissal, or compromise that requires court approval under Rule 23(e)(1)(A).

(B) An objection made under Rule 23(e)(4)(A) may be withdrawn only with the court's approval.

(f) Appeals. A court of appeals may in its discretion permit an appeal from an order of a district court granting or denying class action certification under this rule if application is made to it within ten days after entry of the order. An appeal does not stay proceedings in the district court unless the district judge or the court of appeals so orders.

(g) Class Counsel.

(1) Appointing Class Counsel.

(A) Unless a statute provides otherwise, a court that certifies a class must appoint class counsel.

(B) An attorney appointed to serve as class counsel must fairly and adequately represent the interests of the class.

(C) In appointing class counsel, the court

(i) must consider:

• the work counsel has done in identifying or investigating potential claims in the action,

• counsel's experience in handling class actions, other complex litigation, and claims of the type asserted in the action,

• counsel's knowledge of the applicable law, and

• the resources counsel will commit to representing the class;

(ii) may consider any other matter pertinent to counsel's ability to fairly and adequately represent the interests of the class;

(iii) may direct potential class counsel to provide information on any subject pertinent to the appointment and to propose terms for attorney fees and nontaxable costs; and

(iv) may make further orders in connection with the appointment.

(2) Appointment Procedure.

(A) The court may designate interim counsel to act on behalf of the putative class before determining whether to certify the action as a class action.

(B) When there is one applicant for appointment as class counsel, the court may appoint that applicant only if the applicant is adequate under Rule 23(g)(1)(B) and (C). If more than one adequate applicant seeks appointment as class counsel, the court must appoint the applicant best able to represent the interests of the class.

(C) The order appointing class counsel may include provisions about the award of attorney fees or nontaxable costs under Rule 23(h).

(h) Attorney Fees Award. In an action certified as a class action, the court may award reasonable attorney fees and nontaxable costs authorized by law or by agreement of the parties as follows:

(1) Motion for Award of Attorney Fees. A claim for an award of attorney fees and nontaxable costs must be made by motion under Rule 54(d)(2), subject to the provisions of this

subdivision, at a time set by the court. Notice of the motion must be served on all parties and, for motions by class counsel, directed to class members in a reasonable manner.

(2) Objections to Motion. A class member, or a party from whom payment is sought, may object to the motion.

(3) Hearing and Findings. The court may hold a hearing and must find the facts and state its conclusions of law on the motion under Rule 52(a).

(4) Reference to Special Master or Magistrate Judge. The court may refer issues related to the amount of the award to a special master or to a magistrate judge as provided in Rule 54(d)(2)(D).

Rule 26.   General Provisions Governing Discovery; Duty of Disclosure

(a) Required Disclosures; Methods to Discover Additional Matter.

(1) Initial Disclosures. Except in categories of proceedings specified in Rule 26(a)(1)(E), or to the extent otherwise stipulated or directed by order, a party must, without awaiting a discovery request, provide to other parties:

(A) the name and, if known, the address and telephone number of each individual likely to have discoverable information that the disclosing party may use to support its claims or defenses, unless solely for impeachment, identifying the subjects of the information;

(B) a copy of, or a description by category and location of, all documents, data compilations, and tangible things that are in the possession, custody, or control of the party and that the disclosing party may use to support its claims or defenses, unless solely for impeachment;

(C) a computation of any category of damages claimed by the disclosing party, making available for inspection and copying as under Rule 34 the documents or other evidentiary material, not privileged or protected from disclosure, on which such computation is based, including materials bearing on the nature and extent of injuries suffered; and

(D) for inspection and copying as under Rule 34 any insurance agreement under which any person carrying on an insurance business may be liable to satisfy part or all of a judgment which may be entered in the action or to indemnify or reimburse for payments made to satisfy the judgment.

(E) The following categories of proceedings are exempt from initial disclosure under Rule 26(a)(1):

(i) an action for review on an administrative record;

(ii) a petition for habeas corpus or other proceeding to challenge a criminal conviction or sentence;

(iii) an action brought without counsel by a person in custody of the United States, a state, or a state subdivision;

(iv) an action to enforce or quash an administrative summons or subpoena;

(v) an action by the United States to recover benefit payments;

(vi) an action by the United States to collect on a student loan guaranteed by the United States;

(vii) a proceeding ancillary to proceedings in other courts; and

(viii) an action to enforce an arbitration award.

These disclosures must be made at or within 14 days after the Rule 26(f) conference unless a different time is set by stipulation or court order, or unless a party objects during the conference that initial disclosures are not appropriate in the circumstances of the action and states the objection in the Rule 26(f) discovery plan. In ruling on the objection, the court must determine what disclosures—if any—are to be made, and set the time for disclosure. Any party first served or otherwise joined after the Rule 26(f) conference must make these disclosures within 30 days after being served or joined unless a different time is set by stipulation or court order. A party must make its initial disclosures based on the information then reasonably available to it and is not excused from making its disclosures because it has not fully completed its investigation of the case or because it challenges the sufficiency of another party's disclosures or because another party has not made its disclosures.

(2) Disclosure of Expert Testimony.

(A) In addition to the disclosures required by paragraph (1), a party shall disclose to other parties the identity of any person who may be used at trial to present evidence under Rules 702, 703, or 705 of the Federal Rules of Evidence.

(B) Except as otherwise stipulated or directed by the court, this disclosure shall, with respect to a witness who is retained or specially employed to provide expert testimony in the case or whose duties as an employee of the party regularly involve giving expert testimony, be accompanied by a written report prepared and signed by the witness. The report shall contain a complete statement of all opinions to be expressed and the basis and reasons therefor; the data or other information considered by the witness in forming the opinions; any exhibits to be used as a summary of or support for the opinions; the qualifications of the witness, including a list of all publications authored by the witness within the preceding ten years; the compensation to be paid for the study and testimony; and a listing of any other cases in which the witness has testified as an expert at trial or by deposition within the preceding four years.

(C) These disclosures shall be made at the times and in the sequence directed by the court. In the absence of other directions from the court or stipulation by the parties, the disclosures shall be made at least 90 days before the trial date or the date the case is to be ready for trial or, if the evidence is intended solely to contradict or rebut evidence on the same subject matter identified by another party under paragraph (2)(B), within 30 days after the disclosure made by the other party. The parties shall supplement these disclosures when required under subdivision (e)(1).

(3) Pretrial Disclosures. In addition to the disclosures required by Rule 26(a)(1) and (2), a party must provide to other parties and promptly file with the court the following information regarding the evidence that it may present at trial other than solely for impeachment:

(A) the name and, if not previously provided, the address and telephone number of each witness, separately identifying those whom the party expects to present and those whom the party may call if the need arises;

(B) the designation of those witnesses whose testimony is expected to be presented by means of a deposition and, if not taken stenographically, a transcript of the pertinent portions of the deposition testimony; and

(C) an appropriate identification of each document or other exhibit, including summaries of other evidence, separately identifying those which the party expects to offer and those which the party may offer if the need arises.

Unless otherwise directed by the court, these disclosures must be made at least 30 days before trial. Within 14 days thereafter, unless a different time is specified by the court, a party may serve and promptly file a list disclosing (i) any objections to the use under Rule 32(a) of a deposition designated by another party under Rule 26(a)(3)(B), and (ii) any objection, together with the grounds therefor, that may be made to the admissibility of materials identified under Rule 26(a)(3)(C). Objections not so disclosed, other than objections under Rules 402 and 403 of the Federal Rules of Evidence, are waived unless excused by the court for good cause.

(4) Form of Disclosures. Unless the court orders otherwise, all disclosures under Rules 26(a)(1) through (3) must be made in writing, signed, and served.

(5) Methods to Discover Additional Matter. Parties may obtain discovery by one or more of the following methods: depositions upon oral examination or written questions; written

interrogatories; production of documents or things or permission to enter upon land or other property under Rule 34 or 45(a)(1)(C), for inspection and other purposes; physical and mental examinations; and requests for admission.

(b) Discovery Scope and Limits. Unless otherwise limited by order of the court in accordance with these rules, the scope of discovery is as follows:

(1) In General. Parties may obtain discovery regarding any matter, not privileged, that is relevant to the claim or defense of any party, including the existence, description, nature, custody, condition, and location of any books, documents, or other tangible things and the identity and location of persons having knowledge of any discoverable matter. For good cause, the court may order discovery of any matter relevant to the subject matter involved in the action. Relevant information need not be admissible at the trial if the discovery appears reasonably calculated to lead to the discovery of admissible evidence. All discovery is subject to the limitations imposed by Rule 26(b)(2)(i), (ii), and (iii).

(2) Limitations. By order, the court may alter the limits in these rules on the number of depositions and interrogatories or the length of depositions under Rule 30. By order or local rule, the court may also limit the number of requests under Rule 36. The frequency or extent of use of the discovery methods otherwise permitted under these rules and by any local rule shall be limited by the court if it determines that: (i) the discovery sought is unreasonably cumulative or duplicative, or is obtainable from some other source that is more convenient, less burdensome, or less expensive; (ii) the party seeking discovery has had ample opportunity by discovery in the action to obtain the information sought; or (iii) the burden or expense of the proposed discovery outweighs its likely benefit, taking into account the needs of the case, the amount in controversy, the parties' resources, the importance of the issues at stake in the litigation, and the importance of the proposed discovery in resolving the issues. The court may act upon its own initiative after reasonable notice or pursuant to a motion under Rule 26(c).

(3) Trial Preparation: Materials. Subject to the provisions of subdivision (b)(4) of this rule, a party may obtain discovery of documents and tangible things otherwise discoverable under subdivision (b)(1) of this rule and prepared in anticipation of litigation or for trial by or for another party or by or for that other party's representative (including the other party's attorney, consultant, surety, indemnitor, insurer, or agent) only upon a showing that the party seeking discovery has substantial need of the materials in the preparation of the party's case and that the party is unable without undue hardship to obtain the substantial equivalent of the materials by other means. In ordering discovery of such materials when the required showing has been made, the court shall protect against disclosure of the mental impressions, conclusions, opinions, or legal theories of an attorney or other representative of a party concerning the litigation.

A party may obtain without the required showing a statement concerning the action or its subject matter previously made by that party. Upon request, a person not a party may obtain without the required showing a statement concerning the action or its subject matter previously made by that person. If the request is refused, the person may move for a court order. The provisions of Rule 37(a)(4) apply to the award of expenses incurred in relation to the motion. For purposes of this paragraph, a statement previously made is (A) a written statement signed or otherwise adopted or approved by the person making it, or (B) a stenographic, mechanical, electrical, or other recording, or a transcription thereof, which is a substantially verbatim recital of an oral statement by the person making it and contemporaneously recorded.

(4) Trial Preparation: Experts.

(A) A party may depose any person who has been identified as an expert whose opinions may be presented at trial. If a report from the expert is required under subdivision (a)(2)(B), the deposition shall not be conducted until after the report is provided.

(B) A party may, through interrogatories or by deposition, discover facts known or opinions held by an expert who has been retained or specially employed by another party in anticipation of litigation or preparation for trial and who is not expected to be called as a witness at trial, only as provided in Rule 35(b) or upon a showing of exceptional circumstances under which it is impracticable for the party seeking discovery to obtain facts or opinions on the same subject by other means.

(C) Unless manifest injustice would result, (i) the court shall require that the party seeking discovery pay the expert a reasonable fee for time spent in responding to discovery under this subdivision; and (ii) with respect to discovery obtained under subdivision (b)(4)(B) of this rule the court shall require the party seeking discovery to pay the other party a fair portion of the fees and expenses reasonably incurred by the latter party in obtaining facts and opinions from the expert.

(5) Claims of Privilege or Protection of Trial Preparation Materials. When a party withholds information otherwise discoverable under these rules by claiming that it is privileged or subject to protection as trial preparation material, the party shall make the claim expressly and shall describe the nature of the documents, communications, or things not produced or disclosed in a manner that, without revealing information itself privileged or protected, will enable other parties to assess the applicability of the privilege or protection.

(c) Protective Orders. Upon motion by a party or by the person from whom discovery is sought, accompanied by a certification that the movant has in good faith conferred or attempted to confer with other affected parties in an effort to resolve the dispute without court action, and for good cause shown, the court in which the action is pending or alternatively, on matters relating to a deposition, the court in the district where the deposition is to be taken may make any order which justice requires to protect a party or person from annoyance, embarrassment, oppression, or undue burden or expense, including one or more of the following:

(1) that the disclosure or discovery not be had;

(2) that the disclosure or discovery may be had only on specified terms and conditions, including a designation of the time or place;

(3) that the discovery may be had only by a method of discovery other than that selected by the party seeking discovery;

(4) that certain matters not be inquired into, or that the scope of the disclosure or discovery be limited to certain matters;

(5) that discovery be conducted with no one present except persons designated by the court;

(6) that a deposition, after being sealed, be opened only by order of the court;

(7) that a trade secret or other confidential research, development, or commercial information not be revealed or be revealed only in a designated way; and

(8) that the parties simultaneously file specified documents or information enclosed in sealed envelopes to be opened as directed by the court.

If the motion for a protective order is denied in whole or in part, the court may, on such terms and conditions as are just, order that any party or other person provide or permit discovery. The provisions of Rule 37(a)(4) apply to the award of expenses incurred in relation to the motion.

(d) Timing and Sequence of Discovery. Except in categories of proceedings exempted from initial disclosure under Rule 26(a)(1)(E), or when authorized under these rules or by order or agreement of the parties, a party may not seek discovery from any source before the parties have conferred as required by Rule 26(f). Unless the court upon motion, for the convenience of parties and witnesses and in the interests of justice, orders otherwise, methods of discovery may be used in any sequence, and the fact that a party is conducting discovery, whether by deposition or otherwise, does not operate to delay any other party's discovery.

(e) Supplementation of Disclosures and Responses. A party who has made a disclosure under subdivision (a) or responded to a request for discovery with a disclosure or response is under a duty to supplement or correct the disclosure or response to include information thereafter acquired if ordered by the court or in the following circumstances:

(1) A party is under a duty to supplement at appropriate intervals its disclosures under subdivision (a) if the party learns that in some material respect the information disclosed is incomplete or incorrect and if the additional or corrective information has not otherwise been made known to the other parties during the discovery process or in writing. With respect to testimony of an expert from whom a report is required under subdivision (a)(2)(B) the duty extends both to information contained in the report and to information provided through a deposition of the expert, and any additions or other changes to this information shall be disclosed by the time the party's disclosures under Rule 26(a)(3) are due.

(2) A party is under a duty seasonably to amend a prior response to an interrogatory, request for production, or request for admission if the party learns that the response is in some material respect incomplete or incorrect and if the additional or corrective information has not otherwise been made known to the other parties during the discovery process or in writing.

(f) Conference of Parties; Planning for Discovery. Except in categories of proceedings exempted from initial disclosure under Rule 26(a)(1)(E) or when otherwise ordered, the parties must, as soon as practicable and in any event at least 21 days before a scheduling conference is held or a scheduling order is due under Rule 16(b), confer to consider the nature and basis of their claims and defenses and the possibilities for a prompt settlement or resolution of the case, to make or arrange for the disclosures required by Rule 26(a)(1), and to develop a proposed discovery plan that indicates the parties' views and proposals concerning:

(1) what changes should be made in the timing, form, or requirement for disclosures under Rule 26(a), including a statement as to when disclosures under Rule 26(a)(1) were made or will be made:

(2) the subjects on which discovery may be needed, when discovery should be completed, and whether discovery should be conducted in phases or be limited to or focused upon particular issues;

(3) what changes should be made in the limitations on discovery imposed under these rules or by local rule, and what other limitations should be imposed; and

(4) any other orders that should be entered by the court under Rule 26(c) or under Rule 16(b) and (c).

The attorneys of record and all unrepresented parties that have appeared in the case are jointly responsible for arranging the conference, for attempting in good faith to agree on the proposed discovery plan, and for submitting to the court within 14 days after the conference a written report outlining the plan. A court may order that the parties or attorneys attend the conference in person. If necessary to comply with its expedited schedule for Rule 16(b) conferences, a court may by local rule (i) require that the conference between the parties occur fewer than 21 days before the scheduling conference is held or a scheduling order is due under Rule 16(b), and (ii) require that the written report outlining the discovery plan be filed fewer than 14 days after the conference between the parties, or excuse the parties from submitting a written report and permit them to report orally on their discovery plan at the Rule 16(b) conference.

(g) Signing of Disclosures, Discovery Requests, Responses, and Objections.

(1) Every disclosure made pursuant to subdivision (a)(1) or subdivision (a)(3) shall be signed by at least one attorney of record in the attorney's individual name, whose address shall be stated. An unrepresented party shall sign the disclosure and state the party's address. The signature of the attorney or party constitutes a certification that to the best of the signer's knowledge, information, and belief, formed after a reasonable inquiry, the disclosure is complete and correct as of the time it is made.

(2) Every discovery request, response, or objection made by a party represented by an attorney shall be signed by at least one attorney of record in the attorney's individual name, whose address shall be stated. An unrepresented party shall sign the request, response, or objection and state the party's address. The signature of the attorney or party constitutes a certification that to the best of the signer's knowledge, information, and belief, formed after a reasonable inquiry, the request, response, or objection is:

(A) consistent with these rules and warranted by existing law or a good faith argument for the extension, modification, or reversal of existing law;

(B) not interposed for any improper purpose, such as to harass or to cause unnecessary delay or needless increase in the cost of litigation; and

(C) not unreasonable or unduly burdensome or expensive, given the needs of the case, the discovery already had in the case, the amount in controversy, and the importance of the issues at stake in the litigation.

If a request, response, or objection is not signed, it shall be stricken unless it is signed promptly after the omission is called to the attention of the party making the request, response, or objection, and a party shall not be obligated to take any action with respect to it until it is signed.

(3) If without substantial justification a certification is made in violation of the rule, the court, upon motion or upon its own initiative, shall impose upon the person who made the certification, the party on whose behalf the disclosure, request, response, or objection is made, or both, an appropriate sanction, which may include an order to pay the amount of the reasonable expenses incurred because of the violation, including a reasonable attorney's fee.

Rule 37.   Failure to Make Disclosure or Cooperate in Discovery; Sanctions

(a) Motion for Order Compelling Disclosure or Discovery. A party, upon reasonable notice to other parties and all persons affected thereby, may apply for an order compelling disclosure or discovery as follows:

(1) Appropriate Court. An application for an order to a party shall be made to the court in which the action is pending. An application for an order to a person who is not a party shall be made to the court in the district where the discovery is being, or is to be, taken.

(2) Motion.

(A) If a party fails to make a disclosure required by Rule 26(a), any other party may move to compel disclosure and for appropriate sanctions. The motion must include a certification that the movant has in good faith conferred or attempted to confer with the party not making the disclosure in an effort to secure the disclosure without court action.

(B) If a deponent fails to answer a question propounded or submitted under Rules 30 or 31, or a corporation or other entity fails to make a designation under Rule 30(b)(6) or 31(a), or a party fails to answer an interrogatory submitted under Rule 33, or if a party, in response to a request for inspection submitted under Rule 34, fails to respond that inspection will be permitted as requested or fails to permit inspection as requested, the discovering party may move for an order compelling an answer, or a designation, or an order compelling inspection in accordance with the request. The motion must include a certification that the movant has in good faith conferred or attempted to confer with the person or party failing to make the discovery in an effort to secure the information or material without court action. When taking a deposition on oral examination, the proponent of the question may complete or adjourn the examination before applying for an order.

(3) Evasive or Incomplete Disclosure, Answer, or Response. For purposes of this subdivision an evasive or incomplete disclosure, answer, or response is to be treated as a failure to disclose, answer, or respond.

(4) Expenses and Sanctions.

(A) If the motion is granted or if the disclosure or requested discovery is provided after the motion was filed, the court shall, after affording an opportunity to be heard, require the party or deponent whose conduct necessitated the motion or the party or attorney advising such conduct or both of them to pay to the moving party the reasonable expenses incurred in making the motion, including attorney's fees, unless the court finds that the motion was filed without the movant's first making a good faith effort to obtain the disclosure or discovery without court action, or that the opposing party's nondisclosure, response, or objection was substantially justified, or that other circumstances make an award of expenses unjust.

(B) If the motion is denied, the court may enter any protective order authorized under Rule 26(c) and shall, after affording an opportunity to be heard, require the moving party or the attorney filing the motion or both of them to pay to the party or deponent who opposed the motion the reasonable expenses incurred in opposing the motion, including attorney's fees, unless the court finds that the making of the motion was substantially justified or that other circumstances make an award of expenses unjust.

(C) If the motion is granted in part and denied in part, the court may enter any protective order authorized under Rule 26(c) and may, after affording an opportunity to be heard, apportion the reasonable expenses incurred in relation to the motion among the parties and persons in a just manner.

(b) Failure to Comply with Order.

(1) Sanctions by Court in District Where Deposition is Taken. If a deponent fails to be sworn or to answer a question after being directed to do so by the court in the district in which the deposition is being taken, the failure may be considered a contempt of that court.

(2) Sanctions by Court in Which Action is Pending. If a party or an officer, director, or managing agent of a party or a person designated under Rule 30(b)(6) or 31(a) to testify on behalf of a party fails to obey an order to provide or permit discovery, including an order made under subdivision (a) of this rule or Rule 35, or if a party fails to obey an order entered under Rule 26(f), the court in which the action is pending may make such orders in regard to the failure as are just, and among others the following:

(A) An order that the matters regarding which the order was made or any other designated facts shall be taken to be established for the purposes of the action in accordance with the claim of the party obtaining the order;

(B) An order refusing to allow the disobedient party to support or oppose designated claims or defenses, or prohibiting that party from introducing designated matters in evidence;

(C) An order striking out pleadings or parts thereof, or staying further proceedings until the order is obeyed, or dismissing the action or proceeding or any part thereof, or rendering a judgment by default against the disobedient party;

(D) In lieu of any of the foregoing orders or in addition thereto, an order treating as a contempt of court the failure to obey any orders except an order to submit to a physical or mental examination;

(E) Where a party has failed to comply with an order under Rule 35(a) requiring that party to produce another for examination, such orders as are listed in paragraphs (A), (B), and (C) of this subdivision, unless the party failing to comply shows that that party is unable to produce such person for examination.

In lieu of any of the foregoing orders or in addition thereto, the court shall require the party failing to obey the order or the attorney advising that party or both to pay the reasonable expenses, including attorney's fees, caused by the failure, unless the court finds that the failure was substantially justified or that other circumstances make an award of expenses unjust.

(c) Failure to Disclose; False or Misleading Disclosure; Refusal to Admit.

(1) A party that without substantial justification fails to disclose information required by Rule 26(a) or 26(e)(1), or to amend a prior response to discovery as required by Rule 26(e)(2), is not, unless such failure is harmless, permitted to use as evidence at a trial, at a hearing, or on a motion any witness or information not so disclosed. In addition to or in lieu of this sanction, the court, on motion and after affording an opportunity to be heard, may impose other appropriate sanctions. In addition to requiring payment of reasonable expenses, including attorney's fees, caused by the failure, these sanctions may include any of the actions authorized under Rule 37(b)(2)(A), (B), and (C) and may include informing the jury of the failure to make the disclosure.

(2) If a party fails to admit the genuineness of any document or the truth of any matter as requested under Rule 36, and if the party requesting the admissions thereafter proves the genuineness of the document or the truth of the matter, the requesting party may apply to the court for an order requiring the other party to pay the reasonable expenses incurred in making that proof, including reasonable attorney's fees. The court shall make the order unless it finds that (A) the request was held objectionable pursuant to Rule 36(a), or (B) the admission sought was of no substantial importance, or (C) the party failing to admit had reasonable ground to believe that the party might prevail on the matter, or (D) there was other good reason for the failure to admit.

(d) Failure of Party to Attend at Own Deposition or Serve Answers to Interrogatories or Respond to Request for Inspection. If a party or an officer, director, or managing agent of a party or a person designated under Rule 30(b)(6) or 31(a) to testify on behalf of a party fails (1) to appear before the officer who is to take the deposition, after being served with a proper notice, or (2) to serve answers or objections to interrogatories submitted under Rule 33, after proper service of the interrogatories, or (3) to serve a written response to a request for inspection submitted under Rule 34, after proper service of the request, the court in which the action is pending on motion may make such orders in regard to the failure as are just, and among others it may take any action authorized under subparagraphs (A), (B), and (C) of subdivision (b)(2) of this rule. Any motion specifying a failure under clause (2) or (3) of this subdivision shall include a certification that the movant has in good faith conferred or attempted to confer with the party failing to answer or respond in an effort to obtain such answer or response without court action. In lieu of any order or in addition thereto, the court shall require the party failing to act or the attorney advising that party or both to pay the reasonable expenses, including attorney's fees, caused by the failure unless the court finds that the failure was substantially justified or that other circumstances make an award of expenses unjust.

The failure to act described in this subdivision may not be excused on the ground that the discovery sought is objectionable unless the party failing to act has a pending motion for a protective order as provided by Rule 26(c).

(e) [Abrogated]

(f) [Repealed]

(g) Failure to Participate in the Framing of a Discovery Plan. If a party or a party's attorney fails to participate in good faith in the development and submission of a proposed discovery plan as required by Rule 26(f), the court may, after opportunity for hearing, require such party or attorney to pay to any other party the reasonable expenses, including attorney's fees, caused by the failure.

Rule 60. Relief from Judgment or Order

(a) Clerical Mistakes. Clerical mistakes in judgments, orders or other parts of the record and errors therein arising from oversight or omission may be corrected by the court at any time of its own initiative or on the motion of any party and after such notice, if any, as the court orders.

During the pendency of an appeal, such mistakes may be so corrected before the appeal is docketed in the appellate court, and thereafter while the appeal is pending may be so corrected with leave of the appellate court.

(b) Mistakes; Inadvertence; Excusable Neglect; Newly Discovered Evidence; Fraud, Etc. On motion and upon such terms as are just, the court may relieve a party or a party's legal representative from a final judgment, order, or proceeding for the following reasons: (1) mistake, inadvertence, surprise, or excusable neglect; (2) newly discovered evidence which by due diligence could not have been discovered in time to move for a new trial under Rule 59(b); (3) fraud (whether heretofore denominated intrinsic or extrinsic), misrepresentation, or other misconduct of an adverse party; (4) the judgment is void; (5) the judgment has been satisfied, released, or discharged, or a prior judgment upon which it is based has been reversed or otherwise vacated, or it is no longer equitable that the judgment should have prospective application; or (6) any other reason justifying relief from the operation of the judgment. The motion shall be made within a reasonable time, and for reasons (1), (2), and (3) not more than one year after the judgment, order, or proceeding was entered or taken. A motion under this subdivision (b) does not affect the finality of a judgment or suspend its operation. This rule does not limit the power of a court to entertain an independent action to relieve a party from a judgment, order, or proceeding, or to grant relief to a defendant not actually personally notified as provided in Title 28, U.S.C., § 1655, or to set aside a judgment for fraud upon the court. Writs of coram nobis, coram vobis, audita querela, and bills of review and bills in the nature of a bill of review, are abolished, and the procedure for obtaining any relief from a judgment shall be by motion as prescribed in these rules or by an independent action.

FEDERAL RULES OF APPELLATE PROCEDURE

Rule 38.   Frivolous Appeal—Damages and Costs

If a court of appeals determines that an appeal is frivolous, it may, after a separately filed motion or notice from the court and reasonable opportunity to respond, award just damages and single or double costs to the appellee.

ABA MODEL CODE OF JUDICIAL CONDUCT (2004)

The Model Code of Judicial Conduct was adopted by the House of Delegates of the American Bar Association on August 7, 1990 and amended on August 6, 1997, August 10, 1999, and August 12, 2003.

CONTENTS

PREAMBLE

TERMINOLOGY

CANON 1: A judge shall uphold the integrity and independence of the judiciary.

CANON 2: A judge shall avoid impropriety and the appearance of impropriety in all of the judge's activities.

CANON 3: A judge shall perform the duties of judicial office impartially and diligently.

CANON 4: A judge shall so conduct the judge's extra-judicial activities as to minimize the risk of conflict with judicial obligations.

CANON 5: A judge or judicial candidate shall refrain from inappropriate political activity.

PREAMBLE

Our legal system is based on the principle that an independent, fair and competent judiciary will interpret and apply the laws that govern us. The role of the judiciary is central to American concepts of justice and the rule of law. Intrinsic to all sections of this Code are the precepts that judges, individually and collectively, must respect and honor the judicial office as a public trust and strive to enhance and maintain confidence in our legal system. The judge is an arbiter of facts and law for the resolution of disputes and a highly visible symbol of government under the rule of law.

The Code of Judicial Conduct is intended to establish standards for ethical conduct of judges. It consists of broad statements called Canons, specific rules set forth in Sections under each Canon, a Terminology Section, an Application Section and Commentary. The text of the Canons and the Sections, including the Terminology and Application Sections, is authoritative. The Commentary, by explanation and example, provides guidance with respect to the purpose and meaning of the Canons and Sections. The Commentary is not intended as a statement of additional rules. When the text uses "shall" or "shall not," it is intended to impose binding obligations the violation of which can result in disciplinary action. When "should" or "should not" is used, the text is intended as hortatory and as a statement of what is or is not appropriate conduct but not as a binding rule under which a judge may be disciplined. When "may" is used, it denotes permissible discretion or, depending on the context, it refers to action that is not covered by specific proscriptions.

The Canons and Sections are rules of reason. They should be applied consistent with constitutional requirements, statutes, other court rules and decisional law and in the context of all relevant circumstances. The Code is to be construed so as not to impinge on the essential independence of judges in making judicial decisions.

The Code is designed to provide guidance to judges and candidates for judicial office and to provide a structure for regulating conduct through disciplinary agencies. It is not designed or intended as a basis for civil liability or criminal prosecution. Furthermore, the purpose of the Code would be subverted if the Code were invoked by lawyers for mere tactical advantage in a proceeding.

The text of the Canons and Sections is intended to govern conduct of judges and to be binding upon them. It is not intended, however, that every transgression will result in disciplinary action. Whether disciplinary action is appropriate, and the degree of discipline to be imposed, should be determined through a reasonable and reasoned application of the text and should depend on such factors as the seriousness of the transgression, whether there is a pattern of improper activity and the effect of the improper activity on others or on the judicial system. See ABA Standards Relating to Judicial Discipline and Disability Retirement.

The Code of Judicial Conduct is not intended as an exhaustive guide for the conduct of judges. They should also be governed in their judicial and personal conduct by general ethical standards. The Code is intended, however, to state basic standards which should govern the conduct of all judges and to provide guidance to assist judges in establishing and maintaining high standards of judicial and personal conduct.

TERMINOLOGY

Terms explained below are noted with an asterisk (*) in the Sections where they appear. In addition, the Sections where terms appear are referred to after the explanation of each term below.

"**Aggregate**" in relation to contributions for a candidate under Sections 3E(1)(e) and 5C(3) and (4) denotes not only contributions in cash or in kind made directly to a candidate's committee or treasurer, but also, except in retention elections, all contributions made indirectly with the understanding that they will be used to support the election of the candidate or to oppose the election of the candidate's opponent. See Sections 3 E(1)(e), 5C(3) and 5C(4).

"**Appropriate authority**" denotes the authority with responsibility for initiation of disciplinary process with respect to the violation to be reported. See Sections 3D(1) and 3D(2).

"**Candidate.**" A candidate is a person seeking selection for or retention in judicial office by election or appointment. A person becomes a candidate for judicial office as soon as he or she makes a public announcement of candidacy, declares or files as a candidate with the election or appointment authority, or authorizes solicitation or acceptance of contributions or support. The term "candidate" has the same meaning when applied to a judge seeking election or appointment to non-judicial office. See Preamble and Sections 5A, 5B, 5C and 5E.

"**Continuing part-time judge.**" A continuing part-time judge is a judge who serves repeatedly on a part-time basis by election or under a continuing appointment, including a retired judge subject to recall who is permitted to practice law. See Application Section C.

"**Court personnel**" does not include the lawyers in a proceeding before a judge. See Sections 3B(7)(c) and 3B(9).

"**De minimis**" denotes an insignificant interest that could not raise reasonable question as to a judge's impartiality. See Sections 3E(1)(c) and 3E(1)(d).

"**Economic interest**" denotes ownership of a more than de minimis legal or equitable interest, or a relationship as officer, director, advisor or other active participant in the affairs of a party, except that:

(i) ownership of an interest in a mutual or common investment fund that holds securities is not an economic interest in such securities unless the judge participates in the management of the fund or a proceeding pending or impending before the judge could substantially affect the value of the interest;

(ii) service by a judge as an officer, director, advisor or other active participant in an educational, religious, charitable, fraternal or civic organization, or service by a judge's spouse, parent or child as an officer, director, advisor or other active participant in any organization does not create an economic interest in securities held by that organization;

(iii) a deposit in a financial institution, the proprietary interest of a policy holder in a mutual insurance company, of a depositor in a mutual savings association or of a member in a credit union, or a similar proprietary interest, is not an economic interest in the organization unless a proceeding pending or impending before the judge could substantially affect the value of the interest;

(iv) ownership of government securities is not an economic interest in the issuer unless a proceeding pending or impending before the judge could substantially affect the value of the securities.

See Sections 3E(1)(c) and 3E(2).

"**Fiduciary**" includes such relationships as executor, administrator, trustee, and guardian. See Sections 3E(2) and 4E.

"**Impartiality**" or "**impartial**" denotes absence of bias or prejudice in favor of, or against, particular parties or classes of parties, as well as maintaining an open mind in considering issues that may come before the judge. See Sections 2A, 3B(10), 3E(1), 5A(3)(a) and 5A(3)(d)(i).

"**Knowingly,**" "**knowledge,**" "**known**" or "**knows**" denotes actual knowledge of the fact in question. A person's knowledge may be inferred from circumstances. See Sections 3D, 3E(1), and 5A(3).

"**Law**" denotes court rules as well as statutes, constitutional provisions and decisional law. See Sections 2A, 3A, 3B(2), 3B(6), 4B, 4C, 4D(5), 4F, 4I, 5A(2), 5A(3), 5B(2), 5C(1), 5C(3) and 5D.

"Member of the candidate's family" denotes a spouse, child, grandchild, parent, grandparent or other relative or person with whom the candidate maintains a close familial relationship. See Section 5A(3)(a).

"Member of the judge's family" denotes a spouse, child, grandchild, parent, grandparent, or other relative or person with whom the judge maintains a close familial relationship. See Sections 4D(3), 4E and 4G.

"Member of the judge's family residing in the judge's household" denotes any relative of a judge by blood or marriage, or a person treated by a judge as a member of the judge's family, who resides in the judge's household. See Sections 3E(1) and 4D(5).

"Nonpublic information" denotes information that, by law, is not available to the public. Nonpublic information may include but is not limited to: information that is sealed by statute or court order, impounded or communicated in camera; and information offered in grand jury proceedings, presentencing reports, dependency cases or psychiatric reports. See Section 3B(11).

"Periodic part-time judge." A periodic part-time judge is a judge who serves or expects to serve repeatedly on a part-time basis but under a separate appointment for each limited period of service or for each matter. See Application Section D.

"Political organization" denotes a political party or other group, the principal purpose of which is to further the election or appointment of candidates to political office. See Sections 5A(1), 5B(2) and 5C(1).

"Pro tempore part-time judge." A pro tempore part-time judge is a judge who serves or expects to serve once or only sporadically on a part-time basis under a separate appointment for each period of service or for each case heard. See Application Section E.

"Public election." This term includes primary and general elections; it includes partisan elections, nonpartisan elections and retention elections. See Section 5C.

"Require." The rules prescribing that a judge "require" certain conduct of others are, like all of the rules in this Code, rules of reason. The use of the term "require" in that context means a judge is to exercise reasonable direction and control over the conduct of those persons subject to the judge's direction and control. See Sections 3B(3), 3B(4), 3B(5), 3B(6), 3B(9) and 3C(2).

"Third degree of relationship." The following persons are relatives within the third degree of relationship: great-grandparent, grandparent, parent, uncle, aunt, brother, sister, child, grandchild, great-grandchild, nephew or niece. See Section 3E(1)(d).

CANON 1

A JUDGE SHALL UPHOLD THE INTEGRITY AND INDEPENDENCE OF THE JUDICIARY

A. An independent and honorable judiciary is indispensable to justice in our society. A judge should participate in establishing, maintaining and enforcing high standards of conduct, and shall personally observe those standards so that the integrity and independence of the judiciary will be preserved. The provisions of this Code are to be construed and applied to further that objective.

Commentary:

Deference to the judgments and rulings of courts depends upon public confidence in the integrity and independence of judges. The integrity and independence of judges depends in turn upon their acting without fear or favor. A judiciary of integrity is one in which judges are known for their probity, fairness, honesty, uprightness, and soundness of character. An independent judiciary is one free of inappropriate outside influences. Although judges should be independent, they must comply with the law, including the provisions of this Code. Public confidence in the impartiality of the judiciary is maintained by the adherence of each judge to this responsibility. Conversely, violation of this Code diminishes public confidence in the judiciary and thereby does injury to the system of government under law.

CANON 2

A JUDGE SHALL AVOID IMPROPRIETY AND THE APPEARANCE OF IMPROPRIETY IN ALL OF THE JUDGE'S ACTIVITIES

A. A judge shall respect and comply with the law* and shall act at all times in a manner that promotes public confidence in the integrity and impartiality* of the judiciary.

Commentary:

Public confidence in the judiciary is eroded by irresponsible or improper conduct by judges. A judge must avoid all impropriety and appearance of impropriety. A judge must expect to be the subject of constant public scrutiny. A judge must therefore accept restrictions on the judge's conduct that might be viewed as burdensome by the ordinary citizen and should do so freely and willingly. Examples are the restrictions on judicial speech imposed by Sections 3(B)(9) and (10) that are indispensable to the maintenance of the integrity, impartiality, and independence of the judiciary.

The prohibition against behaving with impropriety or the appearance of impropriety applies to both the professional and personal conduct of a judge. Because it is not practicable to list all prohibited acts, the proscription is necessarily cast in general terms that extend to conduct by judges that is harmful although not specifically mentioned in the Code. Actual improprieties under this standard include violations of law, court rules or other specific provisions of this Code. The test for appearance of impropriety is whether the conduct would create in reasonable minds a perception that the judge's ability to carry out judicial responsibilities with integrity, impartiality and competence is impaired.

See also Commentary under Section 2C.

B. A judge shall not allow family, social, political or other relationships to influence the judge's judicial conduct or judgment. A judge shall not lend the prestige of judicial office to advance the private interests of the judge or others; nor shall a judge convey or permit others to convey the impression that they are in a special position to influence the judge. A judge shall not testify voluntarily as a character witness.

Commentary:

Maintaining the prestige of judicial office is essential to a system of government in which the judiciary functions independently of the executive and legislative branches. Respect for the judicial office facilitates the orderly conduct of legitimate judicial functions. Judges should distinguish between proper and improper use of the prestige of office in all of their activities. For example, it would be improper for a judge to allude to his or her judgeship to gain a personal advantage such as deferential treatment when stopped by a police officer for a traffic offense. Similarly, judicial letterhead must not be used for conducting a judge's personal business.

A judge must avoid lending the prestige of judicial office for the advancement of the private interests of others. For example, a judge must not use the judge's judicial position to gain advantage in a civil suit involving a member of the judge's family. In contracts for publication of a judge's writings, a judge should retain control over the advertising to avoid exploitation of the judge's office. As to the acceptance of awards, see Section 4D(5)(a) and Commentary.

Although a judge should be sensitive to possible abuse of the prestige of office, a judge may, based on the judge's personal knowledge, serve as a reference or provide a letter of recommendation. However, a judge must not initiate the communication of information to a sentencing judge or a probation or corrections officer but may provide to such persons information for the record in response to a formal request.

Judges may participate in the process of judicial selection by cooperating with appointing authorities and screening committees seeking names for consideration, and by responding to official inquiries concerning a person being considered for a judgeship. See also Canon 5 regarding use of a judge's name in political activities.

A judge must not testify voluntarily as a character witness because to do so may lend the prestige of the judicial office in support of the party for whom the judge testifies. Moreover, when a judge testifies as a witness, a lawyer who regularly appears before the judge may be placed in the awkward position of cross-examining the judge. A judge may, however, testify when properly summoned. Except in unusual circumstances where the demands of justice require, a judge should discourage a party from requiring the judge to testify as a character witness.

C. A judge shall not hold membership in any organization that practices invidious discrimination on the basis of race, sex, religion or national origin.

Commentary:

Membership of a judge in an organization that practices invidious discrimination gives rise to perceptions that the judge's impartiality is impaired. Section 2C refers to the current practices of the organization. Whether an organization practices invidious discrimination is often a complex question to which judges should be sensitive. The answer cannot be determined from a mere examination of an organization's current membership rolls but rather depends on how the organization selects members and other relevant factors, such as that the organization is dedicated to the preservation of religious, ethnic or cultural values of legitimate common interest to its members, or that it is in fact and effect an intimate, purely private organization whose membership limitations could not be constitutionally prohibited. Absent such factors, an organization is generally said to discriminate invidiously if it arbitrarily excludes from membership on the basis of race, religion, sex or national origin persons who would otherwise be admitted to membership. *See New York State Club Assn. Inc. v. City of New York*, 487 U.S. 1 (1988); *Board of Directors of Rotary International v. Rotary Club of Duarte*, 481 U.S. 537 (1987); *Roberts v. United States Jaycees*, 468 U.S. 609 (1984).

Although Section 2C relates only to membership in organizations that invidiously discriminate on the basis of race, sex, religion or national origin, a judge's membership in an organization that engages in any discriminatory membership practices prohibited by the law of the jurisdiction also violates Canon 2 and Section 2A and gives the appearance of impropriety. In addition, it would be a violation of Canon 2 and Section 2A for a judge to arrange a meeting at a club that the judge knows practices invidious discrimination on the basis of race, sex, religion or national origin in its membership or other policies, or for the judge to regularly use such a club. Moreover, public manifestation by a judge of the judge's knowing approval of invidious discrimination on any basis gives the appearance of impropriety under Canon 2 and diminishes public confidence in the integrity and impartiality of the judiciary, in violation of Section 2A.

When a person who is a judge in the date this Code becomes effective [in the jurisdiction in which the person is a judge][2] learns that an organization to which the judge belongs engages in invidious discrimination that would preclude membership under Section 2C or under Canon 2 and Section 2A, the judge is permitted, in lieu of resigning, to make immediate efforts to have the organization discontinue its invidiously discriminatory practices, but is required to suspend participation in any other activities of the organization. If the organization fails to discontinue its invidiously discriminatory practices as promptly as possible (and in all events within a year of the judge's first learning of the practices), the judge is required to resign immediately from the organization.

CANON 3

A JUDGE SHALL PERFORM THE DUTIES OF JUDICIAL OFFICE IMPARTIALLY AND DILIGENTLY

A. Judicial Duties in General. The judicial duties of a judge take precedence over all the judge's other activities. The judge's judicial duties include all the duties of the judge's office prescribed by law*. In the performance of these duties, the following standards apply.
B. Adjudicative Responsibilities.
(1) A judge shall hear and decide matters assigned to the judge except those in which disqualification is required.

---

[2] The language within the brackets should be deleted when the jurisdiction adopts this provision.

(2) A judge shall be faithful to the law* and maintain professional competence in it. A judge shall not be swayed by partisan interests, public clamor or fear of criticism.

(3) A judge shall require* order and decorum in proceedings before the judge.

(4) A judge shall be patient, dignified and courteous to litigants, jurors, witnesses, lawyers and others with whom the judge deals in an official capacity, and shall require* similar conduct of lawyers, and of staff, court officials and others subject to the judge's direction and control.

Commentary:

The duty to hear all proceedings fairly and with patience is not inconsistent with the duty to dispose promptly of the business of the court. Judges can be efficient and businesslike while being patient and deliberate.

(5) A judge shall perform judicial duties without bias or prejudice. A judge shall not, in the performance of judicial duties, by words or conduct manifest bias or prejudice, including but not limited to bias or prejudice based upon race, sex, religion, national origin, disability, age, sexual orientation or socioeconomic status, and shall not permit staff, court officials and others subject to the judge's direction and control to do so.

Commentary:

A judge must refrain from speech, gestures or other conduct that could reasonably be perceived as sexual harassment and must require the same standard of conduct of others subject to the judge's direction and control.

A judge must perform judicial duties impartially and fairly. A judge who manifests bias on any basis in a proceeding impairs the fairness of the proceeding and brings the judiciary into disrepute. Facial expression and body language, in addition to oral communication, can give to parties or lawyers in the proceeding, jurors, the media and others an appearance of judicial bias. A judge must be alert to avoid behavior that may be perceived as prejudicial.

(6) A judge shall require* lawyers in proceedings before the judge to refrain from manifesting, by words or conduct, bias or prejudice based upon race, sex, religion, national origin, disability, age, sexual orientation or socioeconomic status, against parties, witnesses, counsel or others. This Section 3B(6) does not preclude legitimate advocacy when race, sex, religion, national origin, disability, age, sexual orientation or socioeconomic status, or other similar factors, are issues in the proceeding.

(7) A judge shall accord to every person who has a legal interest in a proceeding, or that person's lawyer, the right to be heard according to law*. A judge shall not initiate, permit, or consider ex parte communications, or consider other communications made to the judge outside the presence of the parties concerning a pending or impending proceeding except that:

(a) Where circumstances require, ex parte communications for scheduling, administrative purposes or emergencies that do not deal with substantive matters or issues on the merits are authorized; provided:

(i) the judge reasonably believes that no party will gain a procedural or tactical advantage as a result of the ex parte communication, and

(ii) the judge makes provision promptly to notify all other parties of the substance of the ex parte communication and allows an opportunity to respond.

(b) A judge may obtain the advice of a disinterested expert on the law* applicable to a proceeding before the judge if the judge gives notice to the parties of the person consulted and the substance of the advice, and affords the parties reasonable opportunity to respond.

(c) A judge may consult with court personnel* whose function is to aid the judge in carrying out the judge's adjudicative responsibilities or with other judges.

(d) A judge may, with the consent of the parties, confer separately with the parties and their lawyers in an effort to mediate or settle matters pending before the judge.

(e) A judge may initiate or consider any ex parte communications when expressly authorized by law* to do so.

Commentary:

The proscription against communications concerning a proceeding includes communications from lawyers, law teachers, and other persons who are not participants in the proceeding, except to the limited extent permitted.

To the extent reasonably possible, all parties or their lawyers shall be included in communications with a judge.

Whenever presence of a party or notice to a party is required by Section 3B(7), it is the party's lawyer, or if the party is unrepresented the party, who is to be present or to whom notice is to be given.

An appropriate and often desirable procedure for a court to obtain the advice of a disinterested expert on legal issues is to invite the expert to file a brief *amicus curiae*.

Certain ex parte communication is approved by Section 3B(7) to facilitate scheduling and other administrative purposes and to accommodate emergencies. In general, however, a judge must discourage ex parte communication and allow it only if all the criteria stated in Section 3B(7) are clearly met. A judge must disclose to all parties all ex parte communications described in Sections 3B(7)(a) and 3B(7)(b) regarding a proceeding pending or impending before the judge.

A judge must not independently investigate facts in a case and must consider only the evidence presented.

A judge may request a party to submit proposed findings of fact and conclusions of law, so long as the other parties are apprised of the request and are given an opportunity to respond to the proposed findings and conclusions.

A judge must make reasonable efforts, including the provision of appropriate supervision, to ensure that Section 3B(7) is not violated through law clerks or other personnel on the judge's staff.

If communication between the trial judge and the appellate court with respect to a proceeding is permitted, a copy of any written communication or the substance of any oral communication should be provided to all parties.

(8) A judge shall dispose of all judicial matters promptly, efficiently and fairly.

Commentary:

In disposing of matters promptly, efficiently and fairly, a judge must demonstrate due regard for the rights of the parties to be heard and to have issues resolved without unnecessary cost or delay. Containing costs while preserving fundamental rights of parties also protects the interests of witnesses and the general public. A judge should monitor and supervise cases so as to reduce or eliminate dilatory practices, avoidable delays and unnecessary costs. A judge should encourage and seek to facilitate settlement, but parties should not feel coerced into surrendering the right to have their controversy resolved by the courts.

Prompt disposition of the court's business requires a judge to devote adequate time to judicial duties, to be punctual in attending court and expeditious in determining matters under submission, and to insist that court officials, litigants and their lawyers cooperate with the judge to that end.

(9) A judge shall not, while a proceeding is pending or impending in any court, make any public comment that might reasonably be expected to affect its outcome or impair its fairness or make any nonpublic comment that might substantially interfere with a fair trial or hearing. The judge shall require* similar abstention on the part of court personnel* subject to the judge's direction and control. This Section does not prohibit judges from making public statements in the course of their official duties or from explaining for public information the procedures of the court. This Section does not apply to proceedings in which the judge is a litigant in a personal capacity.

(10) A judge shall not, with respect to cases, controversies or issues that are likely to come before the court, make pledges, promises or commitments that are inconsistent with the impartial* performance of the adjudicative duties of the office.

Commentary:

Sections 3B(9) and (10) restrictions on judicial speech are essential to the maintenance of the integrity, impartiality, and independence of the judiciary. A pending proceeding is one that has begun but not yet reached final disposition. An impending proceeding is one that is anticipated but not yet begun. The requirement that judges abstain from public comment regarding a pending or impending proceeding continues during any appellate process and until final disposition. Sections 3B(9) and (10) do not prohibit a judge from commenting on proceedings in which the judge is a litigant in a personal capacity, but in cases such as a writ of mandamus where the judge is a litigant in an official capacity, the judge must not comment publicly. The conduct of lawyers relating to trial publicity is governed by [Rule 3.6 of the ABA Model Rules of Professional Conduct]. (Each jurisdiction should substitute an appropriate reference to its rule.)

(11) A judge shall not commend or criticize jurors for their verdict other than in a court order or opinion in a proceeding, but may express appreciation to jurors for their service to the judicial system and the community.

Commentary:

Commending or criticizing jurors for their verdict may imply a judicial expectation in future cases and may impair a juror's ability to be fair and impartial in a subsequent case.

(12) A judge shall not disclose or use, for any purpose unrelated to judicial duties, nonpublic information* acquired in a judicial capacity.

C. Administrative Responsibilities.

(1) A judge shall diligently discharge the judge's administrative responsibilities without bias or prejudice and maintain professional competence in judicial administration, and should cooperate with other judges and court officials in the administration of court business.

(2) A judge shall require* staff, court officials and others subject to the judge's direction and control to observe the standards of fidelity and diligence that apply to the judge and to refrain from manifesting bias or prejudice in the performance of their official duties.

(3) A judge with supervisory authority for the judicial performance of other judges shall take reasonable measures to assure the prompt disposition of matters before them and the proper performance of their other judicial responsibilities.

(4) A judge shall not make unnecessary appointments. A judge shall exercise the power of appointment impartially and on the basis of merit. A judge shall avoid

nepotism and favoritism. **A judge shall not approve compensation of appointees beyond the fair value of services rendered.**

(5) A judge shall not appoint a lawyer to a position if the judge either knows that the lawyer has contributed more then [$] within the prior [   ] years to the judge's election campaign,[3] or learns of such a contribution by means of a timely motion by a party or other person properly interested in the matter, unless

(a) **the position is substantially uncompensated;**

(b) **the lawyer has been selected in rotation from a list of qualified and available lawyers compiled without regard to their having made political contributions; or**

(c) **the judge or another presiding or administrative judge affirmatively finds that no other lawyer is willing, competent and able to accept the position.**

Commentary:

Appointees of a judge include assigned counsel, officials such as referees, commissioners, special masters, receivers and guardians and personnel such as clerks, secretaries and bailiffs. Consent by the parties to an appointment or an award of compensation does not relieve the judge of the obligation prescribed by Section 3C(4).

D. Disciplinary Responsibilities.

(1) A judge who receives information indicating a substantial likelihood that another judge has committed a violation of this Code should take appropriate action. A judge having knowledge* that another judge has committed a violation of this Code that raises a substantial question as to the other judge's fitness for office shall inform the appropriate authority*.

(2) A judge who receives information indicating a substantial likelihood that a lawyer has committed a violation of the Rules of Professional Conduct [substitute correct title if the applicable rules of lawyer conduct have a different title] should take appropriate action. A judge having knowledge* that a lawyer has committed a violation of the Rules of Professional Conduct [substitute correct title if the applicable rules of lawyer conduct have a different title] that raises a substantial question as to the lawyer's honesty, trustworthiness or fitness as a lawyer in other respects shall inform the appropriate authority*.

(3) Acts of a judge, in the discharge of disciplinary responsibilities, required or permitted by Sections 3D(1) and 3D(2) are part of a judge's judicial duties and shall be absolutely privileged, and no civil action predicated thereon may be instituted against the judge.

Commentary:

Appropriate action may include direct communication with the judge or lawyer who has committed the violation, other direct action if available, and reporting the violation to the appropriate authority or other agency or body.

E. Disqualification.

(1) A judge shall disqualify himself or herself in a proceeding in which the judge's impartiality might reasonably be questioned, including but not limited to instances where:

---

[3] This provision is meant to be applicable wherever judges are subject to public election; specific amount and time limitations, to be determined based on circumstances within the jurisdiction, should be inserted in the brackets.

Commentary:

Under this rule, a judge is disqualified whenever the judge's impartiality might reasonably be questioned, regardless whether any of the specific rules in Section 3E(1) apply. For example, if a judge were in the process of negotiating for employment with a law firm, the judge would be disqualified from any matters in which that law firm appeared, unless the disqualification was waived by the parties after disclosure by the judge.

A judge should disclose on the record information that the judge believes the parties or their lawyers might consider relevant to the question of disqualification, even if the judge believes there is no real basis for disqualification.

By decisional law, the rule of necessity may override the rule of disqualification. For example, a judge might be required to participate in judicial review of a judicial salary statute, or might be the only judge available in a matter requiring immediate judicial action, such as a hearing on probable cause or a temporary restraining order. In the latter case, the judge must disclose on the record the basis for possible disqualification and use reasonable efforts to transfer the matter to another judge as soon as practicable.

> **(a)** the judge has a personal bias or prejudice concerning a party or a party's lawyer, or personal knowledge* of disputed evidentiary facts concerning the proceeding;
>
> **(b)** the judge served as a lawyer in the matter in controversy, or a lawyer with whom the judge previously practiced law served during such association as a lawyer concerning the matter, or the judge has been a material witness concerning it;

Commentary:

A lawyer in a government agency does not ordinarily have an association with other lawyers employed by that agency within the meaning of Section 3E(1)(b); a judge formerly employed by a government agency, however, should disqualify himself or herself in a proceeding if the judge's impartiality might reasonably be questioned because of such association.

> **(c)** the judge knows* that he or she, individually or as a fiduciary, or the judge's spouse, parent or child wherever residing, or any other member of the judge's family residing in the judge's household*, has an economic interest* in the subject matter in controversy or in a party to the proceeding or has any other more than de minimis* interest that could be substantially affected by the proceeding;
>
> **(d)** the judge or the judge's spouse, or a person within the third degree of relationship* to either of them, or the spouse of such a person:
>
> > **(i)** is a party to the proceeding, or an officer, director or trustee of a party;
> >
> > **(ii)** is acting as a lawyer in the proceeding;
> >
> > **(iii)** is known* by the judge to have a more than de minimis* interest that could be substantially affected by the proceeding;
> >
> > **(iv)** is to the judge's knowledge* likely to be a material witness in the proceeding.
>
> **(e)** the judge knows or learns by means of a timely motion that a party or a party's lawyer has within the previous [ ] year[s] made aggregate* contributions to the judge's campaign in an amount that is greater than

[[[$] for an individual or [$] for an entity]]] [[is reasonable and appropriate for an individual or an entity]]. [4]

         (f) the judge, while a judge or a candidate* for judicial office, has made a public statement that commits, or appears to commit, the judge with respect to

                (i) an issue in the proceeding; or
                (ii) the controversy in the proceeding.

Commentary:

The fact that a lawyer in a proceeding is affiliated with a law firm with which a relative of the judge is affiliated does not of itself disqualify the judge. Under appropriate circumstances, the fact that "the judge's impartiality might reasonably be questioned" under Section 3E(1), or that the relative is known by the judge to have an interest in the law firm that could be "substantially affected by the outcome of the proceeding" under Section 3E(1)(d)(iii) may require the judge's disqualification.

         (2) A judge shall keep informed about the judge's personal and fiduciary* economic interests*, and make a reasonable effort to keep informed about the personal economic interests of the judge's spouse and minor children residing in the judge's household.

         F. Remittal of Disqualification. A judge disqualified by the terms of Section 3E may disclose on the record the basis of the judge's disqualification and may ask the parties and their lawyers to consider, out of the presence of the judge, whether to waive disqualification. If following disclosure of any basis for disqualification other than personal bias or prejudice concerning a party, the parties and lawyers, without participation by the judge, all agree that the judge should not be disqualified, and the judge is then willing to participate, the judge may participate in the proceeding. The agreement shall be incorporated in the record of the proceeding.
Commentary:

A remittal procedure provides the parties an opportunity to proceed without delay if they wish to waive the disqualification. To assure that consideration of the question of remittal is made independently of the judge, a judge must not solicit, seek or hear comment on possible remittal or waiver of the disqualification unless the lawyers jointly propose remittal after consultation as provided in the rule. A party may act through counsel if counsel represents on the record that the party has been consulted and consents. As a practical matter, a judge may wish to have all parties and their lawyers sign the remittal agreement.

CANON 4

A JUDGE SHALL SO CONDUCT THE JUDGE'S EXTRA-JUDICIAL ACTIVITIES AS TO MINIMIZE THE RISK OF CONFLICT WITH JUDICIAL OBLIGATIONS

         A. Extra-judicial Activities in General. A judge shall conduct all of the judge's extra-judicial activities so that they do not:

         (1) cast reasonable doubt on the judge's capacity to act impartially as a judge;
         (2) demean the judicial office; or
         (3) interfere with the proper performance of judicial duties.

---

[4] This provision is meant to be applicable wherever judges are subject to public election. Jurisdictions that adopt specific dollar limits on contributions in section 5(C)(3) should adopt the same limits in section 3(E)(1)(e). Where specific dollar amounts determined by local circumstances are not used, the "reasonable and appropriate" language should be used.

Commentary:

Complete separation of a judge from extra-judicial activities is neither possible nor wise; a judge should not become isolated from the community in which the judge lives.

Expressions of bias or prejudice by a judge, even outside the judge's judicial activities, may cast reasonable doubt on the judge's capacity to act impartially as a judge. Expressions which may do so include jokes or other remarks demeaning individuals on the basis of their race, sex, religion, national origin, disability, age, sexual orientation or socioeconomic status. See Section 2C and accompanying Commentary.

B. Avocational Activities. A judge may speak, write, lecture, teach and participate in other extra-judicial activities concerning the law*, the legal system, the administration of justice and non-legal subjects, subject to the requirements of this Code.

Commentary:

As a judicial officer and person specially learned in the law, a judge is in a unique position to contribute to the improvement of the law, the legal system, and the administration of justice, including revision of substantive and procedural law and improvement of criminal and juvenile justice. To the extent that time permits, a judge is encouraged to do so, either independently or through a bar association, judicial conference or other organization dedicated to the improvement of the law. Judges may participate in efforts to promote the fair administration of justice, the independence of the judiciary and the integrity of the legal profession and may express opposition to the persecution of lawyers and judges in other countries because of their professional activities.

In this and other Sections of Canon 4, the phrase "subject to the requirements of this Code" is used, notably in connection with a judge's governmental, civic or charitable activities. This phrase is included to remind judges that the use of permissive language in various Sections of the Code does not relieve a judge from the other requirements of the Code that apply to the specific conduct.

C. Governmental, Civic or Charitable Activities.
(1) A judge shall not appear at a public hearing before, or otherwise consult with, an executive or legislative body or official except on matters concerning the law*, the legal system or the administration of justice or except when acting pro se in a matter involving the judge or the judge's interests.
Commentary:

See Section 2B regarding the obligation to avoid improper influence.

(2) A judge shall not accept appointment to a governmental committee or commission or other governmental position that is concerned with issues of fact or policy on matters other than the improvement of the law*, the legal system or the administration of justice. A judge may, however, represent a country, state or locality on ceremonial occasions or in connection with historical, educational or cultural activities.

Commentary:

Section 4C(2) prohibits a judge from accepting any governmental position except one relating to the law, legal system or administration of justice as authorized by Section 4C(3). The appropriateness of accepting extra-judicial assignments must be assessed in light of the demands on judicial resources created by crowded dockets and the need to protect the courts from involvement in extra-judicial matters that may prove to be controversial. Judges should not accept governmental appointments that are likely to interfere with the effectiveness and independence of the judiciary.

Section 4C(2) does not govern a judge's service in a nongovernmental position. See Section 4C(3) permitting service by a judge with organizations devoted to the improvement of the law, the legal system or the administration of justice and with educational, religious, charitable, fraternal or civic organizations not conducted for profit. For example, service on the board of a public educational institution, unless it were a law school, would be prohibited under Section 4C(2), but service on the board of a public law school or any private educational institution would generally be permitted under Section 4C(3).

(3) A judge may serve as an officer, director, trustee or non-legal advisor of an organization or governmental agency devoted to the improvement of the law*, the legal system or the administration of justice or of an educational, religious, charitable, fraternal or civic organization not conducted for profit, subject to the following limitations and the other requirements of this Code.

Commentary:

Section 4C(3) does not apply to a judge's service in a governmental position unconnected with the improvement of the law, the legal system or the administration of justice; see Section 4C(2).

See Commentary to Section 4B regarding use of the phrase "subject to the following limitations and the other requirements of this Code." As an example of the meaning of the phrase, a judge permitted by Section 4C(3) to serve on the board of a fraternal institution may be prohibited from such service by Sections 2C or 4A if the institution practices invidious discrimination or if service on the board otherwise casts reasonable doubt on the judge's capacity to act impartially as a judge.

Service by a judge on behalf of a civic or charitable organization may be governed by other provisions of Canon 4 in addition to Section 4C. For example, a judge is prohibited by Section 4G from serving as a legal advisor to a civic or charitable organization.

(a) A judge shall not serve as an officer, director, trustee or non-legal advisor if it is likely that the organization

(i) will be engaged in proceedings that would ordinarily come before the judge, or

(ii) will be engaged frequently in adversary proceedings in the court of which the judge is a member or in any court subject to the appellate jurisdiction of the court of which the judge is a member.

Commentary:

The changing nature of some organizations and of their relationship to the law makes it necessary for a judge regularly to reexamine the activities of each organization with which the judge is affiliated to determine if it is proper for the judge to continue the affiliation. For example, in many jurisdictions charitable hospitals are now more frequently in court than in the past. Similarly, the boards of some legal aid organizations now make policy decisions that may have political significance or imply commitment to causes that may come before the courts for adjudication.

(b) A judge as an officer, director, trustee or non-legal advisor, or as a member or otherwise:

(i) may assist such an organization in planning fund-raising and may participate in the management and investment of the organization's funds, but shall not personally participate in the solicitation of funds or other fund-raising activities, except that a judge may solicit funds from other judges over whom the judge does not exercise supervisory or appellate authority;

(ii) may make recommendations to public and private fund-granting organizations on projects and programs concerning the law*, the legal system or the administration of justice;

(iii) shall not personally participate in membership solicitation if the solicitation might reasonably be perceived as coercive or, except as permitted in Section 4C(3)(b)(i), if the membership solicitation is essentially a fund-raising mechanism;

(iv) shall not use or permit the use of the prestige of judicial office for fund-raising or membership solicitation.

Commentary:

A judge may solicit membership or endorse or encourage membership efforts for an organization devoted to the improvement of the law, the legal system or the administration of justice or a nonprofit educational, religious, charitable, fraternal or civic organization as long as the solicitation cannot reasonably be perceived as coercive and is not essentially a fund-raising mechanism. Solicitation of funds for an organization and solicitation of memberships similarly involve the danger that the person solicited will feel obligated to respond favorably to the solicitor if the solicitor is in a position of influence or control. A judge must not engage in direct, individual solicitation of funds or memberships in person, in writing or by telephone except in the following cases: 1) a judge may solicit for funds or memberships other judges over whom the judge does not exercise supervisory or appellate authority, 2) a judge may solicit other persons for membership in the organizations described above if neither those persons nor persons with whom they are affiliated are likely ever to appear before the court on which the judge serves and 3) a judge who is an officer of such an organization may send a general membership solicitation mailing over the judge's signature.

Use of an organization letterhead for fund-raising or membership solicitation does not violate Section 4C(3)(b) provided the letterhead lists only the judge's name and office or other position in the organization, and, if comparable designations are listed for other persons, the judge's judicial designation. In addition, a judge must also make reasonable efforts to ensure that the judge's staff, court officials and others subject to the judge's direction and control do not solicit funds on the judge's behalf for any purpose, charitable or otherwise.

A judge must not be a speaker or guest of honor at an organization's fund-raising event, but mere attendance at such an event is permissible if otherwise consistent with this Code.

D. Financial Activities.

(1) A judge shall not engage in financial and business dealings that:

(a) may reasonably be perceived to exploit the judge's judicial position, or

(b) involve the judge in frequent transactions or continuing business relationships with those lawyers or other persons likely to come before the court on which the judge serves.

Commentary:

The Time for Compliance provision of this Code (Application, Section F) postpones the time for compliance with certain provisions of this Section in some cases.

When a judge acquires in a judicial capacity information, such as material contained in filings with the court, that is not yet generally known, the judge must not use the information for private gain. See Section 2B; see also Section 3B(11).

A judge must avoid financial and business dealings that involve the judge in frequent transactions or continuing business relationships with persons likely to come either before the judge personally or before other judges on the judge's court. In addition, a judge should discourage members of the judge's family from engaging in dealings that would reasonably appear to exploit the judge's judicial position. This rule is necessary to avoid creating an appearance of exploitation of office or favoritism and to minimize the potential for disqualification. With respect to affiliation of relatives of a judge with law firms appearing before the judge, see Commentary to Section 3E(1) relating to disqualification.

Participation by a judge in financial and business dealings is subject to the general prohibitions in Section 4A against activities that tend to reflect adversely on impartiality, demean the judicial office, or interfere with the proper performance of judicial duties. Such participation is also subject to the general prohibition in Canon 2 against activities involving impropriety or the appearance of impropriety and the prohibition in Section 2B against the misuse of the prestige of judicial office. In addition, a judge must maintain high standards of conduct in all of the judge's activities, as set forth in Canon 1. See Commentary for Section 4B regarding use of the phrase "subject to the requirements of this Code."

(2) A judge may, subject to the requirements of this Code, hold and manage investments of the judge and members of the judge's family*, including real estate, and engage in other remunerative activity.

Commentary:

This Section provides that, subject to the requirements of this Code, a judge may hold and manage investments owned solely by the judge, investments owned solely by a member or members of the judge's family, and investments owned jointly by the judge and members of the judge's family.

(3) A judge shall not serve as an officer, director, manager, general partner, advisor or employee of any business entity except that a judge may, subject to the requirements of this Code, manage and participate in:

(a) a business closely held by the judge or members of the judge's family*, or

(b) a business entity primarily engaged in investment of the financial resources of the judge or members of the judge's family.

Commentary:

Subject to the requirements of this Code, a judge may participate in a business that is closely held either by the judge alone, by members of the judge's family, or by the judge and members of the judge's family.

Although participation by a judge in a closely-held family business might otherwise be permitted by Section 4D(3), a judge may be prohibited from participation by other provisions of this Code when, for example, the business entity frequently appears before the judge's court or the participation requires significant time away from judicial duties. Similarly, a judge must avoid participating in a closely-held family business if the judge's participation would involve misuse of the prestige of judicial office.

(4) A judge shall manage the judge's investments and other financial interests to minimize the number of cases in which the judge is disqualified. As soon as the judge can do so without serious financial detriment, the judge shall divest himself or herself of investments and other financial interests that might require frequent disqualification.

(5) A judge shall not accept, and shall urge members of the judge's family residing in the judge's household* not to accept, a gift, bequest, favor or loan from anyone except for:

Commentary:

Section 4D(5) does not apply to contributions to a judge's campaign for judicial office, a matter governed by Canon 5.

Because a gift, bequest, favor or loan to a member of the judge's family residing in the judge's household might be viewed as intended to influence the judge, a judge must inform those family members of the relevant ethical constraints upon the judge in this regard and discourage those family members from violating them. A judge cannot, however, reasonably be expected to know or control all of the financial or business activities of all family members residing in the judge's household.

(a) a gift incident to a public testimonial, books, tapes and other resource materials supplied by publishers on a complimentary basis for official use, or an invitation to the judge and the judge's spouse or guest to attend a bar-related function or an activity devoted to the improvement of the law*, the legal system or the administration of justice;

Commentary:

Acceptance of an invitation to a law-related function is governed by Section 4D(5)(a); acceptance of an invitation paid for by an individual lawyer or group of lawyers is governed by Section 4D(5)(h).

A judge may accept a public testimonial or a gift incident thereto only if the donor organization is not an organization whose members comprise or frequently represent the same side in litigation, and the testimonial and gift are otherwise in compliance with other provisions of this Code. See Sections 4A(1) and 2B.

> **(b) a gift, award or benefit incident to the business, profession or other separate activity of a spouse or other family member of a judge residing in the judge's household, including gifts, awards and benefits for the use of both the spouse or other family member and the judge (as spouse or family member), provided the gift, award or benefit could not reasonably be perceived as intended to influence the judge in the performance of judicial duties;**
>
> **(c) ordinary social hospitality;**
>
> **(d) a gift from a relative or friend, for a special occasion, such as a wedding, anniversary or birthday, if the gift is fairly commensurate with the occasion and the relationship;**

Commentary:

A gift to a judge, or to a member of the judge's family living in the judge's household, that is excessive in value raises questions about the judge's impartiality and the integrity of the judicial office and might require disqualification of the judge where disqualification would not otherwise be required. See, however, Section 4D(5)(e).

> **(e) a gift, bequest, favor or loan from a relative or close personal friend whose appearance or interest in a case would in any event require disqualification under Section 3E;**
>
> **(f) a loan from a lending institution in its regular course of business on the same terms generally available to persons who are not judges;**
>
> **(g) a scholarship or fellowship awarded on the same terms and based on the same criteria applied to other applicants; or**
>
> **(h) any other gift, bequest, favor or loan, only if: the donor is not a party or other person who has come or is likely to come or whose interests have come or are likely to come before the judge; and, if its value exceeds $150.00, the judge reports it in the same manner as the judge reports compensation in Section 4H.**

Commentary:

Section 4D(5)(h) prohibits judges from accepting gifts, favors, bequests or loans from lawyers or their firms if they have come or are likely to come before the judge; it also prohibits gifts, favors, bequests or loans from clients of lawyers or their firms when the clients' interests have come or are likely to come before the judge.

E. Fiduciary Activities.

> **(1) A judge shall not serve as executor, administrator or other personal representative, trustee, guardian, attorney in fact or other fiduciary*, except for the estate, trust or person of a member of the judge's family*, and then only if such service will not interfere with the proper performance of judicial duties.**

(2) A judge shall not serve as a fiduciary* if it is likely that the judge as a fiduciary will be engaged in proceedings that would ordinarily come before the judge, or if the estate, trust or ward becomes involved in adversary proceedings in the court on which the judge serves or one under its appellate jurisdiction.

(3) The same restrictions on financial activities that apply to a judge personally also apply to the judge while acting in a fiduciary* capacity.

Commentary:

The Time for Compliance provision of this Code (Application, Section F) postpones the time for compliance with certain provisions of this Section in some cases.

The restrictions imposed by this Canon may conflict with the judge's obligation as a fiduciary. For example, a judge should resign as trustee if detriment to the trust would result from divestiture of holdings the retention of which would place the judge in violation of Section 4D(4).

F. Service as Arbitrator or Mediator. A judge shall not act as an arbitrator or mediator or otherwise perform judicial functions in a private capacity unless expressly authorized by law*.

Commentary:

Section 4F does not prohibit a judge from participating in arbitration, mediation or settlement conferences performed as part of judicial duties.

G. Practice of Law. A judge shall not practice law. Notwithstanding this prohibition, a judge may act pro se and may, without compensation, give legal advice to and draft or review documents for a member of the judge's family*.

Commentary:

This prohibition refers to the practice of law in a representative capacity and not in a pro se capacity. A judge may act for himself or herself in all legal matters, including matters involving litigation and matters involving appearances before or other dealings with legislative and other governmental bodies. However, in so doing, a judge must not abuse the prestige of office to advance the interests of the judge or the judge's family. See Section 2(B).

The Code allows a judge to give legal advice to and draft legal documents for members of the judge's family, so long as the judge receives no compensation. A judge must not, however, act as an advocate or negotiator for a member of the judge's family in a legal matter.

*****

Canon 6, new in the 1972 Code, reflected concerns about conflicts of interest and appearances of impropriety arising from compensation for off-the-bench activities. Since 1972, however, reporting requirements that are much more comprehensive with respect to what must be reported and with whom reports must be filed have been adopted by many jurisdictions. The Committee believes that although reports of compensation for extra-judicial activities should be required, reporting requirements preferably should be developed to suit the respective jurisdictions, not simply adopted as set forth in a national model code of judicial conduct. Because of the Committee's concern that deletion of this Canon might lead to the misconception that reporting compensation for extra-judicial activities is no longer important, the substance of Canon 6 is carried forward as Section 4H in this Code for adoption in those jurisdictions that do not have other reporting requirements. In jurisdictions that have separately established reporting requirements, Section 4H(2) (Public Reporting) may be deleted and the caption for Section 4H modified appropriately.

*****

H. Compensation, Reimbursement and Reporting.

(1) Compensation and Reimbursement. A judge may receive compensation and reimbursement of expenses for the extra-judicial activities permitted by this Code, if the source of such payments does not give the appearance of influencing the

judge's performance of judicial duties or otherwise give the appearance of impropriety.

> **(a) Compensation shall not exceed a reasonable amount nor shall it exceed what a person who is not a judge would receive for the same activity.**

> **(b) Expense reimbursement shall be limited to the actual cost of travel, food and lodging reasonably incurred by the judge and, where appropriate to the occasion, by the judge's spouse or guest. Any payment in excess of such an amount is compensation.**

(2) Public Reports. A judge shall report the date, place and nature of any activity for which the judge received compensation, and the name of the payor and the amount of compensation so received. Compensation or income of a spouse attributed to the judge by operation of a community property law is not extra-judicial compensation to the judge. The judge's report shall be made at least annually and shall be filed as a public document in the office of the clerk of the court on which the judge serves or other office designated by law*.

Commentary:

See Section 4D(5) regarding reporting of gifts, bequests and loans.

The Code does not prohibit a judge from accepting honoraria or speaking fees provided that the compensation is reasonable and commensurate with the task performed. A judge should ensure, however, that no conflicts are created by the arrangement. A judge must not appear to trade on the judicial position for personal advantage. Nor should a judge spend significant time away from court duties to meet speaking or writing commitments for compensation. In addition, the source of the payment must not raise any question of undue influence or the judge's ability or willingness to be impartial.

I. Disclosure of a judge's income, debts, investments or other assets is required only to the extent provided in this Canon and in Sections 3E and 3F, or as otherwise required by law*.

Section 3E requires a judge to disqualify himself or herself in any proceeding in which the judge has an economic interest. See "economic interest" as explained in the Terminology Section. Section 4D requires a judge to refrain from engaging in business and from financial activities that might interfere with the impartial performance of judicial duties; Section 4H requires a judge to report all compensation the judge received for activities outside judicial office. A judge has the rights of any other citizen, including the right to privacy of the judge's financial affairs, except to the extent that limitations established by law are required to safeguard the proper performance of the judge's duties.

CANON 5[5]

---

[5] Introductory Note to Canon 5: There is wide variation in the methods of judicial selection used, both among jurisdictions and within the jurisdictions themselves. In a given state, judges may be selected by one method initially, retained by a different method, and selected by still another method to fill interim vacancies.

According to figures compiled in 1987 by the National Center for State Courts, 32 states and the District of Columbia use a merit selection method (in which an executive such as a governor appoints a judge from a group of nominees selected by a judicial nominating commission) to select judges in the state either initially or to fill an interim vacancy. Of those 33 jurisdictions, a merit selection method is used in 18 jurisdictions to choose judges of courts of last resort, in 13 jurisdictions to choose judges of intermediate appellate courts, in 12 jurisdictions to choose judges of general jurisdiction courts and in 5 jurisdictions to choose judges of limited jurisdiction courts.

Methods of judicial selection other than merit selection include nonpartisan election (10 states use it for initial selection at all court levels, another 10 states use it for initial selection for at least one court level) and partisan election (8 states use it for initial selection at all court levels, another 7 states use it for initial selection for at least one level). In a small minority of the states, judicial selection methods include executive or legislative appointment (without nomination of a group of potential appointees by a judicial nominating commission) and court selection. In addition, the federal judicial system utilizes an executive appointment method. See State Court Organization 1987 (National Center for State Courts, 1988).

A JUDGE OR JUDICIAL CANDIDATE SHALL REFRAIN FROM INAPPROPRIATE POLITICAL ACTIVITY

A. ALL JUDGES AND CANDIDATES

(1) Except as authorized in Sections 5B(2), 5C(1) and 5C(3), a judge or a candidate* for election or appointment to judicial office shall not:

(a) act as a leader or hold an office in a political organization*;

(b) publicly endorse or publicly oppose another candidate for public office;

(c) make speeches on behalf of a political organization;

(d) attend political gatherings; or

(e) solicit funds for, pay an assessment to or make a contribution to a political organization or candidate, or purchase tickets for political party dinners or other functions.

Commentary:

A judge or candidate for judicial office retains the right to participate in the political process as a voter.

Where false information concerning a judicial candidate is made public, a judge or another judicial candidate having knowledge of the facts is not prohibited by Section 5A(1) from making the facts public.

Section 5A(1)(a) does not prohibit a candidate for elective judicial office from retaining during candidacy a public office such as county prosecutor, which is not "an office in a political organization."

Section 5A(1)(b) does not prohibit a judge or judicial candidate from privately expressing his or her views on judicial candidates or other candidates for public office.

A candidate does not publicly endorse another candidate for public office by having that candidate's name on the same ticket.

(2) A judge shall resign from judicial office upon becoming a candidate* for a non-judicial office either in a primary or in a general election, except that the judge may continue to hold judicial office while being a candidate for election to or serving as a delegate in a state constitutional convention if the judge is otherwise permitted by law* to do so.

(3) A candidate* for a judicial office:

(a) shall maintain the dignity appropriate to judicial office and act in a manner consistent with the impartiality,* integrity and independence of the judiciary, and shall encourage members of the candidate's family* to adhere to the same standards of political conduct in support of the candidate as apply to the candidate;

Commentary:

Although a judicial candidate must encourage members of his or her family to adhere to the same standards of political conduct in support of the candidate that apply to the candidate, family members are free to participate in other political activity.

(b) shall prohibit employees and officials who serve at the pleasure of the candidate*, and shall discourage other employees and officials subject to the candidate's direction and control from doing on the candidate's behalf what the candidate is prohibited from doing under the Sections of this Canon;

(c) except to the extent permitted by Section 5C(2), shall not authorize or knowingly* permit any other person to do for the candidate* what the candidate is prohibited from doing under the Sections of this Canon;

(d) shall not:

(i) with respect to cases, controversies, or issues that are likely to come before the court, make pledges, promises, or commitments that are inconsistent with the impartial* performance of the adjudicative duties of the office; or

(ii) knowingly* misrepresent the identity, qualifications, present position or other fact concerning the candidate or an opponent;

Commentary:

Section 5A(3)(d) prohibits a candidate for judicial office from making statements that commit the candidate regarding cases, controversies or issues likely to come before the court. As a corollary, a candidate should emphasize in any public statement the candidate's duty to uphold the law regardless of his or her personal views. See also Sections 3B(9) and (10), the general rules on public comment by judges. Section 5A(3)(d) does not prohibit a candidate from making pledges or promises respecting improvements in court administration. Nor does this Section prohibit an incumbent judge from making private statements to other judges or court personnel in the performance of judicial duties. This Section applies to any statement made in the process of securing judicial office, such as statements to commissions charged with judicial selection and tenure and legislative bodies confirming appointment. See also Rule 8.2 of the ABA Model Rules of Professional Conduct.

(e) may respond to personal attacks or attacks on the candidate's record as long as the response does not violate Section 5A(3)(d).

Commentary:

Section 5B(2) provides a limited exception to the restrictions imposed by Sections 5A(1) and 5D. Under Section 5B(2), candidates seeking reappointment to the same judicial office or appointment to another judicial office or other governmental office may apply for the appointment and seek appropriate support.

Although under Section 5B(2) non-judge candidates seeking appointment to judicial office are permitted during candidacy to retain office in a political organization, attend political gatherings and pay ordinary dues and assessments, they remain subject to other provisions of this Code during candidacy. See Sections 5B(1), 5B(2)(a), 5E and Application Section.

C. Judges and Candidates Subject to Public Election.

(1) A judge or a candidate* subject to public election* may, except as prohibited by law*:

(a) at any time

(i) purchase tickets for and attend political gatherings;

(ii) identify himself or herself as a member of a political party; and

(iii) contribute to a political organization*;

(b) when a candidate for election

(i) speak to gatherings on his or her own behalf;

(ii) appear in newspaper, television and other media advertisements supporting his or her candidacy;

(iii) distribute pamphlets and other promotional campaign literature supporting his or her candidacy; and

(iv) publicly endorse or publicly oppose other candidates for the same judicial office in a public election in which the judge or judicial candidate is running.

Commentary:

Section 5C(1) permits judges subject to election at any time to be involved in limited political activity. Section 5D, applicable solely to incumbent judges, would otherwise bar this activity.

> **(2) A candidate* shall not personally solicit or accept campaign contributions or personally solicit publicly stated support. A candidate may, however, establish committees of responsible persons to conduct campaigns for the candidate through media advertisements, brochures, mailings, candidate forums and other means not prohibited by law. Such committees may solicit and accept reasonable campaign contributions, manage the expenditure of funds for the candidate's campaign and obtain public statements of support for his or her candidacy. Such committees are not prohibited from soliciting and accepting reasonable campaign contributions and public support from lawyers. A candidate's committees may solicit contributions and public support for the candidate's campaign no earlier than [one year] before an election and no later than [90] days after the last election in which the candidate participates during the election year. A candidate shall not use or permit the use of campaign contributions for the private benefit of the candidate or others.**

Commentary:

There is legitimate concern about a judge's impartiality when parties whose interests may come before a judge, or the lawyers who represent such parties, are known to have made contributions to the election campaigns of judicial candidates. This is among the reasons that merit selection of judges is a preferable manner in which to select the judiciary. Notwithstanding that preference, Section 5C(2) recognizes that in many jurisdictions judicial candidates must raise funds to support their candidacies for election to judicial office. It therefore permits a candidate, other than a candidate for appointment, to establish campaign committees to solicit and accept public support and reasonable financial contributions. In order to guard against the possibility that conflicts of interest will arise, the candidate must instruct his or her campaign committees at the start of the campaign to solicit or accept only contributions that are reasonable and appropriate under the circumstances. Though not prohibited, campaign contributions of which a judge has knowledge, made by lawyers or others who appear before the judge may, by virtue of their size or source, raise questions about a judge's impartiality and be cause for disqualification as provided under Section 3E.

Campaign committees established under Section 5C(2) should manage campaign finances responsibly, avoiding deficits that might necessitate post-election fund-raising, to the extent possible. Such committees must at all times comply with applicable statutory provisions governing their conduct.

Section 5C(2) does not prohibit a candidate from initiating an evaluation by a judicial selection commission or bar association, or subject to the requirements of this Code, from responding to a request for information from any organization.

> **(3) A candidate shall instruct his or her campaign committee(s) at the start of the campaign not to accept campaign contributions for any election that exceed, in the aggregate*, [$] from an individual or [$] from an entity. This limitation is in addition to the limitations provided in Section 5C(2). [6]**
>
> **(4) In addition to complying with all applicable statutory requirements for disclosure of campaign contributions, campaign committees established by a candidate shall file with [ ][7] a report stating the name, address, occupation and**

---

[6] Jurisdictions wishing to adopt campaign contribution limits that are lower than generally applicable campaign finance regulations provide should adopt this provision, inserting appropriate dollar amounts where brackets appear.

[7] Each jurisdiction should identify an appropriate depository for the information required under this provision, giving consideration to the public's need for convenient and timely access to the information. Electronic filing is to be preferred.

employer of each person who has made campaign contributions to the committee whose value in the aggregate* exceed [$] [8.] The report must be filed within [ ] [9] days following the election.

(5) Except as prohibited by law*, a candidate* for judicial office in a public election* may permit the candidate's name: (a) to be listed on election materials along with the names of other candidates for elective public office, and (b) to appear in promotions of the ticket.

Commentary:

Section 5C(5) provides a limited exception to the restrictions imposed by Section 5A(1).

D. Incumbent Judges. A judge shall not engage in any political activity except (i) as authorized under any other Section of this Code, (ii) on behalf of measures to improve the law*, the legal system or the administration of justice, or (iii) as expressly authorized by law.

Commentary:

Neither Section 5D nor any other section of the Code prohibits a judge in the exercise of administrative functions from engaging in planning and other official activities with members of the executive and legislative branches of government. With respect to a judge's activity on behalf of measures to improve the law, the legal system and the administration of justice, see Commentary to Section 4B and Section 4C(1) and its Commentary.

E. Applicability. Canon 5 generally applies to all incumbent judges and judicial candidates*. A successful candidate, whether or not an incumbent, is subject to judicial discipline for his or her campaign conduct; an unsuccessful candidate who is a lawyer is subject to lawyer discipline for his or her campaign conduct. A lawyer who is a candidate for judicial office is subject to [Rule 8.2(b) of the ABA Model Rules of Professional Conduct]. (An adopting jurisdiction should substitute a reference to its applicable rule.)

APPLICATION OF THE CODE OF JUDICIAL CONDUCT

A. Anyone, whether or not a lawyer, who is an officer of a judicial system[10] and who performs judicial functions, including an officer such as a magistrate, court commissioner, special master or referee, is a judge within the meaning of this Code. All judges shall comply with this Code except as provided below.

Commentary:

The four categories of judicial service in other than a full-time capacity are necessarily defined in general terms because of the widely varying forms of judicial service. For the purposes of this Section, as long as a retired judge is subject to recall the judge is considered to "perform judicial functions." The determination of which category and, accordingly, which specific Code provisions apply to an individual judicial officer, depend upon the facts of the particular judicial service.

---

[8] Jurisdictions wishing to adopt campaign contribution disclosure levels lower than those set in generally applicable campaign finance regulations should adopt this provision, inserting appropriate dollar amounts where brackets appear.

[9] A time period chosen by the adopting jurisdiction should appear in the bracketed space.

[10] Applicability of this Code to administrative law judges should be determined by each adopting jurisdiction. Administrative law judges generally are affiliated with the executive branch of government rather than the judicial branch and each adopting jurisdiction should consider the unique characteristics of particular administrative law judge positions in adopting and adapting the Code for administrative law judges. *See, e.g.*, Model Code of Judicial Conduct for Federal Administrative Law Judges, endorsed by the National Conference of Administrative Law Judges in February 1989.

B. Retired Judge Subject to Recall. A retired judge subject to recall who by law is not permitted to practice law is not required to comply:

(1) except while serving as a judge, with Section 4F; and

(2) at any time with Section 4E.

C. Continuing Part-time Judge. A continuing part-time judge*:

(1) is not required to comply

(a) except while serving as a judge, with Section 3B(9); and

(b) at any time with Sections 4C(2), 4D(3), 4E(1), 4F, 4G, 4H, 5A(1), 5B(2) and 5D.

(2) shall not practice law in the court on which the judge serves or in any court subject to the appellate jurisdiction of the court on which the judge serves, and shall not act as a lawyer in a proceeding in which the judge has served as a judge or in any other proceeding related thereto.

Commentary:

When a person who has been a continuing part-time judge is no longer a continuing part-time judge, including a retired judge no longer subject to recall, that person may act as a lawyer in a proceeding in which he or she has served as a judge or in any other proceeding related thereto only with the express consent of all parties pursuant to [Rule 1.12(a) of the ABA Model Rules of Professional Conduct]. (An adopting jurisdiction should substitute a reference to its applicable rule).

D. Periodic Part-time Judge. A periodic part-time judge*:

(1) is not required to comply

(a) except while serving as a judge, with Section 3B(9);

(b) at any time, with Sections 4C(2), 4C(3)(a), 4D(1)(b), 4D(3), 4D(4), 4D(5), 4E, 4F, 4G, 4H, 5A(1), 5B(2) and 5D.

(2) shall not practice law in the court on which the judge serves or in any court subject to the appellate jurisdiction of the court on which the judge serves, and shall not act as a lawyer in a proceeding in which the judge has served as a judge or in any other proceeding related thereto.

Commentary:

When a person who has been a periodic part-time judge is no longer a periodic part-time judge (no longer accepts appointments), that person may act as a lawyer in a proceeding in which he or she has served as a judge or in any other proceeding related thereto only with the express consent of all parties pursuant to [Rule 1.12(a) of the ABA Model Rules of Professional Conduct]. (An adopting jurisdiction should substitute a reference to its applicable rule).

E. Pro Tempore Part-time Judge. A pro tempore part-time judge*:

(1) is not required to comply

(a) except while serving as a judge, with Sections 2A, 2B, 3B(9) and 4C(1);

(b) at any time with Sections 2C, 4C(2), 4C(3)(a), 4C(3)(b), 4D(1)(b), 4D(3), 4D(4), 4D(5), 4E, 4F, 4G, 4H, 5A(1), 5A(2), 5B(2) and 5D.

(2) A person who has been a pro tempore part-time judge* shall not act as a lawyer in a proceeding in which the judge has served as a judge or in any other proceeding related thereto except as otherwise permitted by [Rule 1.12(a) of the ABA Model Rules of Professional Conduct]. (An adopting jurisdiction should substitute a reference to its applicable rule.)

F. Time for Compliance. A person to whom this Code becomes applicable shall comply immediately with all provisions of this Code except Sections 4D(2), 4D(3) and 4E

and shall comply with these Sections as soon as reasonably possible and shall do so in any event within the period of one year.

Commentary:

If serving as a fiduciary when selected as judge, a new judge may, notwithstanding the prohibitions in Section 4E, continue to serve as fiduciary but only for that period of time necessary to avoid serious adverse consequences to the beneficiary of the fiduciary relationship and in no event longer than one year. Similarly, if engaged at the time of judicial selection in a business activity, a new judge may, notwithstanding the prohibitions in Section 4D(3), continue in that activity for a reasonable period but in no event longer than one year.